The Complete Life Encyclopedia

The Complete Life Encyclopedia

A MINIRTH MEIER NEW LIFE FAMILY RESOURCE

Frank Minirth, M.D.

Paul Meier, M.D.

Stephen Arterburn, M.Ed.

A
JANET
THOMA
BOOK

THOMAS NELSON PUBLISHERS
Nashville • Atlanta • London • Vancouver

Acknowledgment

Many thanks to Jim Denney, who skillfully compiled and edited the manuscript.

Published in Nashville, Tennessee, by Thomas Nelson, Inc., Publishers, and distributed in Canada by Word Communications, Ltd., Richmond, British Columbia.

The Bible version used in this publication is THE NEW KING JAMES VERSION. Copyright © 1979, 1980, 1982, 1990, Thomas Nelson, Inc., Publishers.

Library of Congress Cataloging-in-Publication Data

Minirth, Frank B.
    The complete life encyclopedia : a Minirth Meier New Life family resource / Frank Minirth, Paul Meier, Stephen Arterburn.
        p.   cm.
    Includes bibliographical references and index.
    ISBN 0-8407-7590-3
    1. Mental health—Religious aspects—Christianity—Encyclopedias. I. Meier, Paul D.   II. Arterburn, Stephen, 1953–   .   III. Title.
BT732.4.M55   1995
613—dc20   94–45070
                                                                      CIP

Printed in the United States of America.
2 3 4 5 6 — 00 99 98 97 96 95

CONTENTS

INTRODUCTION

For years, it has been our dream to write a comprehensive, popular-level reference book—a single source people could turn to for biblically based, medically sound information on problems affecting the human body, mind, and spirit. Now that dream is a reality.

We call this book *The Complete Life Encyclopedia,* and we have designed it to be interesting to read, easy to use, and practical to apply to every aspect of your life and your family members' lives. Here are some of the features you'll find in this book:

- Alphabetical arrangement. We wanted you to have fast, easy access to information on every topic.
- Complete cross-referencing. By turning to one article, you can find references to other related topics.
- Lay language. We wanted this book to be practical and user-friendly, so we have been careful to keep technical terms to a minimum. Any "doctor talk" in this book is carefully defined and clearly explained.
- Self-tests. This is an interactive book, designed to help you gain useful insight into your unique emotional and spiritual issues.
- Stories of real people and real situations. We wanted this book to be not a dry textbook but a lively, interesting, involving book to read. The stories in this book bring the concepts alive.

Over the past two decades, the doctors of our Minirth Meier New Life Clinics nationwide have written scores of books on dozens of subjects. Our goal has been to share as widely as possible our experience in caring for people with medical, emotional, and spiritual problems. In many ways, this book is the capstone of all the other books our clinics have produced.

It is important to recognize that some psychological and psychiatric problems can only be treated by trained, experienced professional therapists. Yet there are many problems that could be greatly alleviated if the individuals themselves—or the people who love them—could better understand the principles of the Bible and good emotional health. By making this information available in nontechnical language, we hope to give you a better understanding of, and greater charge over, your emotional well-being.

Understandably, some Christians wonder whether it is really possible to mix psychology with the Christian faith. "Why do I need psychology or psychiatry?" they ask. "Doesn't the Bible give me all the information I need to solve my problems?"

At the Minirth Meier New Life Clinics, we uphold the Bible as the inerrant Word of God. It is God's revelation of Himself and His principles for healthy, successful, effective living. There is no other book that comes close to approaching the level of insight and practical application that we can find in the Book of Books.

And yet, though the Bible is all true, it does not contain all information. The Bible does not tell us, for example, how to repair a carburetor or how to build a space shuttle or how to make a polio vaccine. Nowhere in the sixty-six books of the Bible do we learn how to perform a triple-bypass operation or how to shrink tumors with chemotherapy and radiation. A great deal of useful, and even vital, information can be found in sources outside the Bible.

The same is true in matters of emotional health. The Bible gives us a firm foundation for understanding how humans "tick" and why humans "malfunction." Through the Bible, we understand the devastating effects of sin and the healing power of God's love, grace, and forgiveness. By combining our biblical understanding of human nature and human behavior with the psychological and medical knowledge that has been amassed over the past century, we can further understand the details of how people function and why they become dysfunctional.

The Bible teaches that we are whole human beings made up of three dimensions: the body, the soul (consisting of mind, emotion, and will), and the spirit (see Genesis 2:7 and 1 Thessalonians 5:23). Whenever we treat a client at the Minirth Meier New Life Clinics, we always look at the entire person in all three dimensions. We consider, first, his or her spiritual condition and spiritual needs. Then we consider his or her psychological (soul) needs. Then we consider any medical problems that may exist.

The person who has come to the clinic because of an emotional problem such as depression may have a spiritual problem—an ongoing pattern of sin or a need to trust God at a deeper level. Or this person may have a soul problem, such as having been abused during childhood; this person may need to resolve some painful memories and emotions. Or this person may have biochemical depression and could be significantly helped by carefully monitored dosages of Prozac or Wellbutrin. Or there could be some combination of all three dimensions involved.

We have seen literally thousands of people helped and healed by this carefully balanced, biblically based, three-dimensional approach to emotional health. The principles and insights of psychology and psychiatry are tools that both Christian therapists and Christian laypeople can put to good use to make life more satisfying and healthy and to make Christians more effective and functional. We continually study to deepen our understanding of Scripture and to broaden our knowledge of psychological and psychiatric science, always keeping before us the attitude of servanthood expressed in Isaiah 50:4:

> The Lord GOD has given Me
> The tongue of the learned,
> That I should know how to speak
> A word in season to him who is weary.

Throughout the history of the Minirth Meier New Life Clinics, we have focused on maintaining a balanced approach to emotional well-being—a balance between biblical truth and scientific knowledge, between feelings and behavior, between past hurts and present responsibility, and between theory and practice. The number of our clinics continues to grow, and each of these facilities is staffed with people trained in psychiatry and other areas of medical specialization, psychology, addiction recovery, marriage and family counseling, child counseling, pastoral counseling, and theology. We have sought to distill the rich insights of these many disciplines into this book. The medical and psychological advice in this book is tested and is as sound as we can make it.

We want you to be aware, however, that no book can substitute for individual medical or psychological care and counseling. If you are experiencing severe emotional problems, then we hope you will use this book as a support and a guide to enable you to seek the most appropriate professional care for your problems. If you are already under the care of a doctor or counselor (particularly if that professional is a Christian practitioner), and if you encounter any advice in this book that is contrary to what your doctor tells you, then please follow your doctor's advice. He or she is the person who has actually examined you and who has the best perspective on your individual needs and issues. You may use this book as a background source so that you can ask your doctor more informed questions, but always be guided by your doctor's advice.

Our prayer for this book is that God will use it in your life to bring you closer to wholeness, completeness, and wellness, and that Jesus Christ will be glorified. In the words of Paul (1 Thess. 5:23), "May your whole spirit, soul, and body be preserved blameless at the coming of our Lord Jesus Christ."

Frank Minirth, M.D.
Paul Meier, M.D.
Stephen Arterburn, M.Ed.

The Complete Life Encyclopedia

Abnormal Psychology

What is "abnormal"? What is "normal"?

The term *abnormal psychology* once referred to psychological behavior that was "deviant"—that is, significantly different from the norm. Today, we hear very little about what is "deviant." Instead, abnormal psychology usually involves a disorder in which there is emotional distress (a painful symptom) plus dysfunction (impaired behavioral or psychological functioning). By *emotional distress,* we mean internal conflicts that produce intense and prolonged feelings of anxiety, insecurity, fear, or unhappiness. There are many categories of emotional distress that are not considered abnormal. For example, it is not abnormal for a person to be depressed after the death of a loved one. Grief, though painful, is functional and enables a person to recover from the shock of loss. Grieving is what a person is *supposed* to do after a major loss.

Most psychologists and psychiatrists believe a person should not be considered abnormal simply because he or she exhibits behavior or thinking that is not "normal." The individual may be unusual and behaviorally different from the norm without exhibiting dysfunctional behavior or thinking. Deviance means not meeting the expectations of society. But what is normal in one society can be deviant in another—a fact that Christians should understand very well. As we look at the Scriptures, we see many people who clearly deviated from the norms of their society, yet they were the most emotionally and mentally healthy people in their society: the Old Testament prophets, the apostle Paul, and Jesus Himself! They differed from the norm, but their thinking was functional—far more functional than the dysfunctional society in which they lived.

The same principle is true today. As Christians, we are called in many ways to be "deviant," to live in contrast to our society. "And do not be conformed to this world," says Paul in Romans 12:2, "but be transformed by the renewing of your mind, that you may prove what is that good and acceptable and perfect will of God." In other words, Paul is saying, "Be deviant from the world around you, but be functional and renewed in your thinking."

So if deviance from the norms of society does not automatically define abnormal psychology, what does?

In addition to dysfunctionality, there are several other ways of approaching and understanding abnormality. For example, we view those who have severe emotional problems as *being disordered* or *having a disorder.* Note the semantic distinction between these two terms. The prevalent approach among psychologists today is to separate the disorder from the person, to say that the disorder is something the person *has.* For example, an individual is not an alcoholic; that individual *has* an alcohol dependency. As Christians, we must question this approach, because it implies a lack of personal responsibility.

> ■
>
> *In truth, since we live in such a dysfunctional world, the more Christlike we become, the more abnormal we will be (in certain respects), the more functional our thinking will be, and the more effective our behavior will be in achieving God's purpose.*
>
> ■

1

At the Minirth Meier New Life Clinics, we believe that *individual choices* and *individual responsibility* are key components of emotional healing and that it does no service to the disordered person to suggest that his or her abnormality is a "disease" that has invaded from the outside. It is a cluster of symptoms that affect a person's innermost being but that are also *affected by* that person's innermost being—the spirit, the mind, the will, and the emotions. We believe that it is only valid to separate the individual from his or her disorder when there is a physical problem—brain damage or hormonal problems, for example—at the base of that disorder.

Perhaps one of the best ways to understand what is abnormal and unhealthy is to draw a contrast and to look at what good mental and emotional health is. A healthy person is able to function well—intellectually, emotionally, physically, and spiritually. Healthy individuals can adapt to new situations, tolerate stress, and exercise self-control. Healthy individuals are in touch with reality. They face life with a general attitude of confidence. They relate well to others, form friendships, give and accept love, and are able to cooperate with legitimate authority. We believe that the healthiest individuals of all are those who demonstrate these qualities along with a strong faith in God, since living for God gives meaning and a sense of purpose and direction to life.

CAUSES OF EMOTIONAL PROBLEMS

Mental illness is usually caused by a number of factors, not just one. One or more of the following may be the cause:

- disease and other organic causes (perhaps the most obvious organic disorder with a mental/emotional component is Alzheimer's disease)
- genetic background (heredity)
- environmental background (childhood issues)
- spiritual problems (such as sin, religious addiction, and legalism)
- precipitating stress (recent or current issues)

Environmental influences that can lead to emotional disorders include such childhood hurts as:

- nutritional deprivation
- emotional trauma
- parental rejection and neglect
- physical or sexual abuse
- lack of discipline or overindulgence
- religious abuse (having been reared under the teaching and example that suggest that God's love is conditional and His judgment is harsh)
- an excessively passive father and excessively dominant mother
- parents who were excessively demanding and perfectionistic
- parents who were excessively protective
- having been raised in an atmosphere of continual conflict

THE COMPLETE LIFE ENCYCLOPEDIA

These environmental factors indicate trends and statistical tendencies. That is, when we examine the background of emotionally troubled people, we tend to find a number of these factors. This is not to say that people who have such factors in their background are automatically fated to have emotional problems. Nor does this suggest that people with such factors in their background are excused for irresponsible or maladaptive behavior. Through therapy, with the help of Christ and the support of caring family members and fellow Christians, individuals *can* learn to cope with these factors and *can* experience mental and emotional healing.

A precipitating stress is an event or situation in a person's current life that contributes to a psychological problem. Examples of precipitating stress include marital difficulties, job stress, or financial problems. When people go to a counselor or therapist for help, it is usually because of a precipitating stress that they feel is unmanageable. During counseling, they often uncover other issues besides the precipitating stress—issues that may be even more fundamental to the emotional problem but that were hidden from their conscious awareness.

■

Genetic and environmental backgrounds are important factors in emotional problems, but it is crucial to remember that they do not excuse present conduct. Regardless of the past, we are still responsible for making healthy choices today, and the words of the apostle Paul in Galatians 6:7 still hold true: "Whatever a man sows, that he will also reap."

■

Many people who think they are in control of their lives are actually being dominated by hidden emotions, conflicts, drives, and motives. They emphasize precipitating stresses as the sole source of their pain in life. "If only my spouse would change, my life would be great," or "If only I had enough money, all my problems would be solved." It is the job of a psychologist or psychiatrist to look beyond those precipitating stresses and to help individuals discover issues that are hidden inside and that combine with precipitating stresses to create unhappiness and dysfunction.

VARIETIES OF EMOTIONAL DISORDERS

Following are seven broad categories of emotional disorders. There are other categories besides these seven, but the ones we will discuss here are the most commonly observed forms:

- anxiety disorders
- mood disorders
- psychotic disorders
- stress and adjustment disorders
- dissociative disorders
- somatoform disorders
- personality disorders

Anxiety Disorders

The National Institute of Mental Health has estimated that 8 to 15 percent of the population has some form of anxiety disorder. Anxiety disorders include:

3

Imagining Illnesses

As we conduct a brief survey of psychological problems, a word of caution is in order. Many people, as they hear the symptoms of various disorders being described, begin to doubt their own mental health and believe that they observe some of these same symptoms in themselves. This is very common. Carried to an extreme, it becomes what we call an iatrogenic illness, that is, an imagined illness induced in a person by the power of suggestion. Iatrogenic illness is a well-known phenomenon in medical schools, with students sometimes developing the symptoms of each disease they study. As you read, try to maintain a reasoned perspective and remember three principles:

1. Normal people often manifest abnormal behavior from time to time, and there is usually no cause for alarm.

2. To be considered abnormal and unhealthy, the behavior must interfere with an individual's functioning in relationships or at work, or must cause considerable and prolonged emotional distress to that person.

3. If you are prone to iatrogenic illness, you may read about a disorder and only note the symptoms you think you have, while ignoring other listed symptoms that you don't have. Be objective as you read. Note the full range of symptoms that are listed, and you may be able to set your mind at ease.

If you feel strongly concerned about a particular disorder, consult a counselor or therapist and be frank about your symptoms and suspicions. With a "second opinion" from a genuinely qualified professional, you will be able either to resolve your worries or to begin treatment of any actual problems you may have.

- *Phobias.* Anxiety from past or present stress is focused on a specific object or situation. Phobic individuals avoid these specific objects or situations because of irrational fears.
- *Panic disorder.* Anxiety is left unfocused and free-floating, so that a person feels panic without knowing why.
- *Obsessive-compulsive disorder.* Anxiety is displaced onto obsessive thinking, worry, and compulsive behavior.
- *Generalized anxiety disorder.* The anxious individual demonstrates excessive talking, irritability, overdependence, poor concentration, and lack of sleep.

Mood Disorders

Also called affective disorders, mood disorders are characterized by the emotional extremes of either depression or elation. Examples of mood disorders include:

- *Manic-depression.* Also called bipolar disorder, because it involves swings from one emotional pole to the other, from depression to euphoria. In the manic or euphoric mode, the individual appears happy, energetic, nervous, talkative, enthusiastic, ambitious, and optimistic. He has a grandiose, inflated view of his own abilities

4

and self-worth. In the depressed mode, he is sad, filled with painful thoughts, anxious, and delusional, and he feels little or no self-worth. He is full of guilt and despondency. The most dangerous aspect of manic-depression is increased possibility of suicide, although the impaired judgment of manic-depression can also lead an individual to make serious mistakes in social settings, relationships, and financial commitments. (See MANIC-DEPRESSION.)

- *Cyclothymia.* This disorder is similar to manic-depression but is less severe. Whereas an individual with manic-depression may oscillate fairly frequently between depressed and euphoric phases, the cyclothymic individual experiences much slower, longer cycles, perhaps remaining either euphoric or depressed for a period of months or years.

- *Major depression.* This disorder affects more women than men and is most common among people in their forties and fifties. Symptoms include moodiness, frequent crying or moping, unkempt personal appearance, painful thinking, guilt, self-blame, anxiety, and physical symptoms such as sleep and appetite disturbances, decreased sexual interest, headaches, and interrupted menstrual cycles in women. An extended form of major depression is called dysthymia. (See DEPRESSION.)

Psychotic Disorders

In a psychotic disorder, the individual is in some way out of touch with reality. Examples of psychotic disorders include:

- *Schizophrenia.* The four distinguishing features of schizophrenia are (1) flat, dull, or inappropriate mood, indicated by a blank stare (flat affect) or by laughing or smiling while relating a sad story; (2) a tendency to ramble from topic to topic without logical association; (3) detachment, preoccupation, and absorption in a world of private fantasies (autism); and (4) severely reduced motivation and reduced ability to make choices (ambivalence). Schizophrenia may also be accompanied by delusions and hallucinations. (See SCHIZOPHRENIA.)

- *Delusional disorder.* This disorder is similar to schizophrenia in that the individual is out of touch with reality, may have a flat or inappropriate mood, and may be detached and self-absorbed. The delusional individual, unlike the schizophrenic, tends to have orderly ways of thinking. The thinking is unrealistic and may even be paranoid ("The CIA is bugging my bedroom; my landlord is poisoning my drinking water"), but one can carry on and follow a conversation with a delusional individual.

Stress and Adjustment Disorders

Stress and adjustment disorders are related to specific precipitating stresses. A post-traumatic stress disorder is related to the intense stress of a traumatic event (such as war, a natural disaster, rape, a car accident, or an airplane crash). It is characterized by anxiety, recurrent nightmares, disturbed concentration, disturbed sleep, guilt, and depression.

Adjustment disorders result when a person's functioning is impaired because of an inability to cope with stress and change. Symptoms may include a depressed or anxious mood, withdrawal, hostile conduct, lack of motivation, and physical symptoms such as sleep and appetite disturbances, decreased sexual interest, and headaches.

Dissociative Disorders

Dissociative disorders are recognized by changes in an individual's consciousness or identity. Symptoms and forms of dissociative disorders include memory loss (amnesia), sleepwalking (somnambulism), fugue (a type of amnesia), multiple personality disorder, and depersonalization. Dissociative disorders are related to and triggered by events or situations that an individual is unable to recall. They are so called because a person with such a disorder becomes dissociated from his or her identity.

An individual may become unable to recall a specific period of his or her life—say, a period of a few hours or days (localized amnesia). Or he or she may have no recollection of an entire lifetime (general amnesia). A person with continuous amnesia seems to be unable to store memories on an ongoing basis.

An individual experiencing fugue may wander away from home and even establish a new identity as a totally different person—and will not even realize that he or she has forgotten anything. When the individual returns to the normal state, he or she remembers the prefugue past but forgets everything that happened during the fugue state.

An individual with multiple personality disorder is dominated by a number of personalities, and he or she may change dramatically and suddenly from one personality to the next. Sometimes one personality will have no knowledge of the others. In such cases, it is common for the primary personality to be very proper and moralistic; one of the secondary personalities is likely to be quite the opposite.

A person experiencing depersonalization disorder experiences feelings of unreality and separation from self.

Dissociative disorders are generally the result of disturbances in early emotional growth and development. The individual may repress sad or anxious feelings and memories in order to avoid painful emotions or difficult situations.

Somatoform Disorders

Somatoform disorders are physical disorders for which no medical cause can be found. Somatoform symptoms arise from displacement of emotional conflicts onto the body. Somatoform disorders include:

- *Somatization disorder* (Briquet's syndrome). This involves dramatic, vague, multiple complaints, often in various parts of the body, without any medical explanation. Sexual difficulties are often involved. This disorder is more common among women than men.
- *Conversion disorder.* Emotional conflicts are represented as sensory or muscle control problems, such as loss of feeling, deafness, blindness, disturbances in skin sensation, pain, paralysis of limbs, paralysis of vocal cords, involuntary tics or twitches, or recurring peculiar movements. Symptoms may come and go in response to precipitating stress.
- *Somatoform pain disorder.* Pain, without medical cause, is unconsciously used by the individual to avoid activity that is upsetting.

- *Hypochondriasis.* The individual is preoccupied with bodily function or a fear of disease.
- *Body dysmorphic disorder.* The individual is obsessively preoccupied with some imagined physical deformity.

Somatoform disorders should not be confused with fake disorders in which people—for whatever reason—consciously make up symptoms of illness.

Personality Disorders

Personality disorders are deeply ingrained patterns of negative, self-defeating behavior. In a truly disordered personality, these patterns are so firmly entrenched that the affected individual is extremely resistant to treatment, and the personality disorder tends to be present throughout the individual's life. (For a more comprehensive discussion of this subject, see PERSONALITY TYPES AND DISORDERS.)

The variety of emotional problems that human beings are prone to is nothing short of astounding. If, after reading this concise survey of abnormal psychology, you feel

MAJOR PERSONALITY DISORDERS	
Disorder	**Characteristics**
Antisocial	Violation of the rights of others
Avoidant	Hypersensitivity to rejection
Borderline	Instability in a variety of areas
Dependent	Failure to assume responsibility for one's own life
Histrionic	Overly emotional/expressive, egocentric, having poor sexual adjustment
Narcissistic	Grandiose sense of self-importance
Obsessive-compulsive	Preoccupation with rules, order, and details
Paranoid	Suspicion, mistrust of people, hypersensitivity
Passive-aggressive	Passive resistance to demands for adequate performance
Schizoid	Withdrawn, reserved, seclusive
Schizotypal	Oddity of thinking and behavior (sometimes called "simple schizophrenia")

that you or someone close to you is experiencing one of these disorders, we recommend you contact a Christian counselor or therapist for insight and treatment.
See also MENTAL HEALTH; PERSONALITY TYPES AND DISORDERS

Abortion

The year was 1983, just ten years after the U.S. Supreme Court legalized a surgical procedure called *induced abortion* in all fifty states. Lynette was unmarried and pregnant—and she was scared. Just nineteen years old, she was too afraid and ashamed to turn to her parents or her pastor for counsel. Instead, she talked to her friends at school, and they convinced her that the only thing to do was have an abortion. After all, society and the Supreme Court said it was okay. Her friends said it was okay. So she went to a clinic near her college campus, and there (to use the polite euphemism) her pregnancy was "terminated."

In the years following her abortion, Lynette experienced intense feelings of guilt and shame, coupled with serious bouts of depression. Her guilt feelings were rooted in the fact that she had violated her own moral standards by engaging in premarital sex, by covering up and hiding the resulting pregnancy from her parents, and by taking the life of her unborn child. Though her friends told her that having an abortion was "no big deal—just like having your tonsils out," something inside Lynette told her that what she had done was wrong.

"CHOICE" OR "LIFE": IS ABORTION ALWAYS WRONG?

A fetus is a unique and irreplaceable human being.

Induced abortion is a procedure performed on a pregnant woman that causes the fetus (unborn child) to be killed so that the pregnancy is ended. The fetus may be killed within the uterus and later expelled, or an "unviable" fetus (too small and underdeveloped to live outside the uterus) may be removed from the uterus and allowed to die. *Induced abortion* should not be confused with *spontaneous abortion,* more commonly called a miscarriage, in which a fetus dies as the involuntary result of disease, accident, genetic factors, or biochemical incompatibility of the mother and the fetus. Induced abortions are called *therapeutic abortions* when they are performed in order to:

- preserve the life of the mother;
- end a pregnancy that has resulted from rape or incest; or
- prevent the birth of a deformed or genetically abnormal child.

8

Some Christians believe that abortion is never justified for any reason. But many Christian theologians, physicians, and ethicists believe that abortion may be justified in order to save the life of the mother or to spare an innocent victim of rape or incest the additional trauma of bearing the child of a criminal perpetrator.

The abortion of an abnormal or impaired child (such as a child with Down's syndrome or spina bifida) is very difficult to justify from a Christian point of view. Though it is tragic that a person must grow up physically or mentally handicapped, this is no justification for killing that person in the womb. Individuals with deformities and impairments can often lead lives that are quite happy and productive. At the Minirth Meier New Life Clinics, we encourage people who face the choice of aborting an abnormal fetus to consider giving that child a chance to live.

It is important to understand, however, that all of these therapeutic abortions amount to *less than 2 percent* of the 1.6 million abortions performed every year in the United States. The fact is that the vast majority of abortions are performed for the purpose of *birth control*. About 40 percent of abortions are performed on repeat clients, and roughly half of abortion clients and their partners were not using any form of contraceptive at the time of conception. We firmly believe that abortion for the purpose of birth control cannot be justified from a Christian point of view because abortion kills a human being.

Advocates of "abortion choice" or "abortion rights" take the position that a fetus is not a human being. They depersonalize the unborn child as "an unviable tissue mass." Or they say it is part of the woman's body and assert that a woman has a total and unrestrained "right to choose" what she does with her own body—even though seat belt laws, drug laws, and suicide laws clearly limit our "right to choose" what we do with our own bodies in other areas of life. Moreover, from a scientific point of view, we know that an unborn fetus is not just an "unviable tissue mass," nor is the unborn fetus part of the woman's body. It is enclosed by the woman's body, but it is a fully distinct human being.

From the moment of conception, an unborn child is a genetically unique individual. Its chromosomal makeup is different from the mother's. Its heartbeat is detectable within about twenty days of conception. Its brainwaves are apparent at seven weeks. It can swallow, make a fist, and even change its facial expression at nine weeks. Though the unborn child receives life-giving oxygen and nutrients via the placenta and umbilical cord, mother and child have their own separate and distinct circulatory systems; the blood of the mother and the fetus never mingle. And in roughly half of all pregnancies, this "tissue mass" that is "part of a woman's body" is physically, chromosomally, and hormonally *male*. From a purely scientific point of view, then, the idea that a fetus is "part of a woman's body" is absurd.

THE SPIRITUAL AND EMOTIONAL EFFECTS OF ABORTION

Like Lynette, many women experience extreme depression in the aftermath of an abortion. Feelings of guilt, bitterness, anger, and despair are quite common in women

■

Some women appear to feel little or no remorse after an abortion, mainly because they have denied the guilt and buried it inside or because they have been indoctrinated by proabortion arguments. If we hear over and over again that an unborn baby is really just "placental material," we may become desensitized to the truth that abortion destroys a human being.

■

9

who have had abortions, and these feelings often occur or recur many years after the abortion.

Several emotions are associated with the decision to have an abortion. The first is *denial:* the woman tries to convince herself that nothing is ethically wrong with her decision. *Blame* may be passed on to others, followed by *anger* turned outward, possibly toward the man who impregnated her. Finally, she may feel *guilt* and *self-hatred.* If the woman remains in this state, with her emotional conflict unresolved, the inner turmoil may result in severe depression.

Jennifer was a patient who came to a Minirth Meier New Life Clinic because of a long struggle with depression. In therapy, it emerged that she had undergone two abortions some years earlier. The abortion clinic had used misleading terms and rationalizations to cover up the fact that she was taking the life of her unborn child. When asked about these abortions, Jennifer simply parroted the euphemisms and arguments that the abortion clinic counselor had told her. As a result, she had repressed her guilt for years. Finally, she developed a depression that was so severe that she became psychotic and completely lost touch with reality.

When Jennifer was admitted to the hospital, we gave her medication that stabilized her perception of reality to the point where we could counsel her. We then learned that her depression and other negative feelings started a few months after her second abortion, although she denied feeling guilty about what she had done. In further counseling, we repeatedly returned to the subject. Each time abortion was mentioned, tears welled up in her eyes, and she tensed up and silently folded her arms or looked away and wept uncontrollably—yet she persistently denied feeling any remorse. It took Jennifer many months of counseling to gain the strength to squarely face what she had done. After she admitted the true nature of the abortion to herself and asked God to forgive her, she was finally able to forgive herself—and her depression lifted.

For a complete discussion of the moral, spiritual, and emotional dimensions of the abortion issue, we suggest you read *The Mourning After: Help for the Postabortion Syndrome* by Terry L. Selby (Baker Book House, 1990).

> **Many women who have had abortions feel as if neither God nor other people can ever love them again. But abortion is not an unforgivable sin. There is hope, healing, and recovery—and there is forgiveness. The Bible tells us (Ps. 103:12), "As far as the east is from the west, so far has He removed our transgressions from us."**

Abuse

Richie, age eight, is in the hospital with broken bones, a dislocated shoulder, and severe facial contusions. He was beaten then kicked down a flight of stairs by his rageaholic father, who is now in police custody. It is quite obvious, just to look at him, that Richie is a victim of abuse.

Tanya, age thirteen, has taken on the role of mother to Linda, her divorced mother, age thirty-four. Tanya prepares the meals, washes the clothes, and even "counsels" her mother about her problems. Linda has shared with Tanya every sordid detail of the recent divorce—including intimate details of the sexual problems between her and her ex-husband. Tanya has no bruises or broken bones, and Linda does not deliberately intend to cause her daughter any harm, yet Tanya is also a victim of abuse—in this case, a form of emotional abuse called emotional incest.

Lou and Martha are in their late seventies and in failing health. Their daughter, Joyce, has moved into their home to "take care" of them. She keeps them imprisoned in their home, forbids them any contact with friends, and feeds them food that is as unpalatable as any meal in a Russian gulag. She verbally berates her frail, aged parents, and, when she grows tired of verbally abusing them, she sometimes slaps them or beats them with her fists. Lou and Martha are the victims of an underreported and growing problem in our society: *parent abuse*.

These are three very different stories, but they have a single common denominator: *abuse*.

WHAT CONSTITUTES ABUSE?

One truth clearly emerges from these varied and dissimilar stories of abuse: the problem of abuse wears many faces and takes many forms. These forms include:

- child abuse
- incest
- emotional incest
- emotional abuse
- spouse abuse
- parent abuse
- physical abuse (violence)
- authority abuse
- sexual abuse

From the stories we have just seen, it is clear that some forms of abuse are so clearly destructive that they are classified by law as criminal acts, whereas other forms of abuse are so subtle that they can rarely be dealt with in a court of law. What all forms of abuse have in common is that they cause psychological and emotional damage to the victim. They cause the victim to be impaired in his or her sense of security, of being loved, of being capable, of being worthy, of being whole.

Obviously, some of these categories of abuse overlap and may be found in clusters in the life of one individual. An abused child, for example, often grows up and gravitates toward abusive personalities when selecting a mate and ends up experiencing spouse abuse. Often, during counseling sessions in the clinics or on our Minirth Meier New Life Clinics' radio call-in program, we will enumerate these various forms of abuse, and the patient or caller will respond, "Yes! I had five of those forms of abuse in my home while I was growing up!" One form of abuse often breeds another, and another.

Let's take a closer look at the various specific categories of abuse.

ABUSE OF ADULTS

There are a number of different categories of abuse toward adults. Among the most common and emotionally damaging forms are:

- spouse abuse
- parent abuse or abuse of the elderly
- authority abuse

Spouse Abuse

Spouse abuse is the act of physically assaulting and battering one's mate. This form of abuse used to be called "wife beating," under the assumption that women were the only victims. The gender-neutral term is actually more correct, since there are cases, however rare, in which the husband is the victim. All forms of domestic assault are criminal acts, and if you are a victim of spouse abuse, you should not expose yourself to attack for one more minute. *Get out now and report this crime to the police.* Don't take chances with domestic violence. Some of the most violent, brutal crimes of all are domestic crimes because they involve extremely intense emotions. Victims of spouse abuse have been battered beyond recognition, and many have died. If you have children, take them with you and get out of the house immediately. Go to a women's shelter or the house of a friend—someplace where your violent mate will not be able to find you. We also strongly urge you to press charges against your mate and prosecute the crime, not for the sake of getting even but for the sake of confronting the abuser with the consequences of his actions.

If you are assaulted by your mate, you will likely experience feelings of terror ("He's going to kill me!"), and you may experience a feeling of separation from your body, a feeling that "this is like a dream, this isn't real, this isn't happening to me." Afterwards, you may seem amazingly controlled and even emotionless—or you may cry uncontrollably. You may become hostile and defensive, or you may go into a trancelike state. It is common to feel numbness, shock, and guilt ("I brought this on myself") after a traumatic episode of abuse.

The guilt issue is extremely important to understand. In some cases, abusive individuals behave abusively without any provocation whatsoever. In other cases, abused individuals may play a role in triggering the abuse through some sort of provocative behavior. In a small number of cases, abuse victims repeatedly provoke their mates, because of either bitterness against their mates or an unconscious masochistic desire to be punished. However, you must always remember that *you are not to blame for your mate's attack upon you.* Your mate is 100 percent responsible for remaining self-controlled. Domestic violence is never justified, regardless of any provocation. Avoid beating yourself down for getting beaten up.

If you feel you *did* engage in behavior that provoked the attack, and particularly if you have a pattern of doing so, then this is an issue you need to work on in counseling. One reason for resolving this psychological issue is to make sure you don't repeat the mistake in this relationship, or in a future relationship. People who marry abusers once often do so again and again. Through counseling, you can discover why you are attracted to abusive personalities, and what you can do to avoid placing yourself in danger in the future.

Some religious extremists teach that women are to be submissive to their husbands even to the point of allowing themselves to be abused. This is dangerous advice, and it is unbiblical. In Ephesians 5:22, we read "Wives, submit to your own husbands, as to the Lord," but we also read (verse 25), "Husbands, love your wives, just as Christ also loved the church and gave Himself for her." This instruction from the Lord was intended to teach mutual love and respect in normal husband-wife relationships. It is not a universal teaching intended to cover such extreme situations as a husband who repeatedly commits a felony against his wife!

In situations involving abuse, those who are victimized must step out of the victim role. By removing yourself from the house and from the victim role, you confront your mate's abusive behavior and put your mate on notice that you are no longer accepting that behavior. If there is to be any chance of restoring the marriage, you must convey to your mate (preferably through a third party, such as a counselor) that the marriage hinges on your mate's willingness to undergo intensive counseling for his violent tendencies. It should be a long time (if ever) before any attempt at reconciliation should be made; there should be considerable evidence that the abuser has gotten his behavior under control. The abuser should be in an ongoing accountability group (such as a Twelve Step group for rageaholics) for many years to come.

Don't make excuses for staying in a destructive relationship: "I can't afford to leave. I'll never make it on my own. I have no place to go." A women's shelter will take care of your short-term needs and the needs of your children and will put you in touch with services that will enable you to get on your feet and rebuild your life away from the harmful influence of an abusive mate.

Parent Abuse or Abuse of the Elderly

Elderly people often become ill, infirm, and dependent—and their weakness at this time in their lives makes them especially vulnerable to abuse. They may be abused by their adult children, who may be motivated by revenge or bitterness over some past slight or abuse, either real or imagined. Or they may be abused by irresponsible health care providers in a hospital or nursing home. Though this form of abuse is rare, those who love and care for the elderly should be on the alert for any signs of abuse: bruises, lacerations, broken bones, or other injuries that cannot be plausibly accounted for. Of special concern are injuries that are part of a pattern or that appear to be deliberately inflicted by another person (bruises, welts, red marks, gouges that appear to be caused by hands, fingernails, belts, or other objects). Check the background of anyone you suspect, looking particularly for any prior suspicions, allegations, reprimands, or convictions—but do not make careless allegations that would subject you to legal liability. If you strongly suspect or become convinced that a senior adult has been abused, consult an attorney to find out the best way to handle the situation in your state.

But above all else, take immediate steps to remove the elderly individual from danger.

Authority Abuse

People have become increasingly concerned in recent years about clergy, doctors, therapists, and attorneys who sexually exploit their parishioners or clients. Such incidences fall under a category called *authority abuse,* and in most states such acts of abuse are considered felonies. Although this is a very real ethical issue, it is one that has been sensationalized in recent years, and actual cases are probably rare. Even if the sexual relationship involves consent on the part of the client or parishioner, and even if the client or parishioner initiated the relationship, the sexual activity is properly understood to be a form of abuse perpetrated by the professional against the client or parishioner.

ABUSE OF CHILDREN

Child abuse, whether sexual, physical, or emotional, is probably the most damaging and traumatic experience a child can be subjected to because so many critical boundaries are violated in the process. A child enters the world trusting and dependent upon his or her adult caregivers for guidance and survival. The child views these adults as godlike figures, incapable of doing wrong. So if the child is beaten or sexually abused by these infallible godlike beings, the child reasons that they must have been right in doing so and the child must have done something very bad or must be a very bad person to deserve such treatment. As a result, the child grows into adulthood with a set of intensely negative messages implanted in his or her conscious and unconscious mind:

- I'm a very bad person.
- I'm dirty. No good person would ever want to have anything to do with me.
- My sexuality is bad (in the case of sexual abuse).
- God hates me.
- God must think I'm bad because He didn't protect me from abuse.

It is easy to see, then, why so many abused children grow up to be people with broken self-esteem, damaged sexuality, and major difficulties in experiencing healthy relationships with God.

Whether the abuse is active (physically violent, verbally destructive, or sexualized) or passive (neglectful, judgmental, unloving, and emotionally distant), the child tends to grow up thinking that the abusive pattern is "normal." The child's home environment is his or her world, and children have no external standards of normalcy to judge their own families against. Whatever they grew up with is "normal." Many people do not realize how severely *abnormal* their own families of origin were until they become adults and either marry or spend significant time in other homes, observing other families' patterns of behavior.

Active child abuse involves all illegal forms of behavior toward a child: violent beating and battering of a child or sexual molestation of any degree, up to and including intercourse. *If you are aware of a situation where a child is being violently abused or sexually molested, you should report it to the local police or child protective agency immediately.* Active abuse also includes such destructive—but not necessarily illegal—manifestations as extreme rage or verbal abuse. Whenever a child is shrieked at, told he or she is worthless, or beaten down with shame or blame, that child is being actively abused.

There are other ways of abusing a child that are subtle and silent but equally pervasive and damaging. We call this behavior toward a child passive abuse. Tragically, many instances of passive abuse are never identified as such. A parent who neglects a child because he or she has a problem with alcoholism or drug abuse is passively abusing that child, and society is quick to condemn such passive abusers. But the parent who neglects a child's emotional needs because he or she devotes all time and energy to a thriving business, a political career, or a Christian ministry may actually be *applauded* and *awarded* for behavior that is destructive to that child. Whenever a parent becomes so preoccupied—with work or with substance abuse or with some other pastime—that he or she is emotionally or physically unavailable to the child, abuse is taking place.

Parent Figures and Child Abuse

We tend to think of child abuse as something perpetrated by parents on their biological children. But any adult with a parentlike authority role in the life of a child can have the power to abuse: stepparents, adoptive parents, foster parents, grandparents, aunts or uncles, and even powerful mentors such as extended-family members, coaches, teachers, or church leaders. In our counseling experience at the clinics, we sometimes encounter clients who deal with five or six parent figures in their lives. All of these parent figures have the power to shape a child's life for better or worse.

Passive abuse occurs when a parent constantly brushes the child aside and ignores and belittles that child's need for affection, affirmation, and security. Clearly, a parent can't be available to a child all the time; sometimes work, an emergency, or fatigue requires that a child be told, "Not now, I'll talk to you later." But a child becomes passively abused when fed a constant diet of unfeeling brush-offs:

"Can't you see I'm busy?"

"I said, 'Later!' Now get lost, will you?"

"Go play outside or something!"

"Get out of my way!"

"No, you can't help me! You'll just make a mess."

"You're too little to do it right!"

Another form of passive abuse occurs when a child is deprived of normal, appropriate affection and affirmation. There may be no active abuse, such as screaming or condemnation, but neither is there praise, encouragement, support, or love. Elaine's father, for example, was never harsh toward her, yet in all the years she was growing up, she never once heard her father call her by name or tell her he loved her. Many other people come to the clinic for counseling with issues stemming from never having been touched, held, or embraced as children. All children need to experience affectionate, nonsexual touching from their parents—a hug, an arm around the shoulder, some gentle roughhousing or wrestling on the living room floor. When that affirming touch is withheld, passive abuse is taking place.

Passive abuse can rob a child of his or her childhood, leaving only a blank space where fond memories should be. Amanda, now in her twenties, knows that her father was preoccupied with a major legal battle when she was ten—but she cannot remember being ten. Her father certainly didn't intend to abuse her, but his problems were so great and consumed so much of his time that he was simply not available to her during a crucial time of her childhood.

Passive abuse may be the result of factors a parent is not able to control, such as chronic depression. Or the parent's belief system—such as an excessive tendency toward legalism—may send an abusive message to the child. As a result, the child who is hungry for grace, love, and acceptance may experience only judgment, condemnation, estrangement, and rejection.

Child abuse can be further categorized according to the *kind* of abuse involved: physical abuse (violence), sexual abuse (including incest), verbal abuse, emotional incest, and emotional abuse.

Physical Abuse

No parent is perfect. Even the best parent will make mistakes in parenting out of either ignorance or frustration. Humans make mistakes. The difference between an occasional misstep and truly damaging abuse is one of *degree* and *consistency*. Occasional mistakes can be repented of and apologized for, and the effects of those mistakes can be healed. But a severe and consistent pattern of abusive behavior creates long-term damage in the mind and soul of a child.

Sexual Abuse

By strict definition, *incest* involves sexual relations between two people who are so closely related that they are forbidden by law to marry. But the term is now commonly applied to the sexual abuse of a child by a parent or stepparent, aunt, uncle, grandparent, or older sibling. If sex acts are committed against a child by a nonrelative, the offense is called *child sexual abuse* or *sexual molestation.*

Acts that constitute sexual abuse of a child are not limited merely to sexual penetration. Children can be sexually abused without even being touched. Abusive sexual acts that can be very harmful to a child include encouraging a child to masturbate; exposing oneself to a child; committing sexual acts in the presence of a child; talking to the child about one's own sexual behavior; exposing a child to pornographic material; photographing or videotaping a child nude or in sexually suggestive ways; touching a child for the sake of one's own sexual arousal; invading a child's privacy in the bathroom or while the child is dressing; making sexually suggestive remarks or jokes to a child; and anal, oral, or vaginal intercourse with a child.

Although the crime of incest is considered almost unspeakable in our society, therapists see thousands of such cases, including incest between mothers and their sons and between fathers and their daughters. Incest occurs even in Christian homes. We once counseled a missionary who was committing incest with his daughter—and then twisting Scripture out of context in order to justify it.

■

One recent poll revealed that about 5 percent of adult women and 2 percent of adult men had sexual experiences with a parent or stepparent of the opposite sex while growing up. Those percentages may seem low, but for behavior as damaging as incest, the numbers are much too high.

■

It is extremely important that cases of incest be reported to the proper authorities, so the perpetrator can be stopped before others are victimized and the healing process can begin for the victim. Though the effects of incest are devastating, incest survivors can usually be helped to lead normal lives.

Incest victims often experience intense guilt feelings, even though they are innocent of wrongdoing. Children crave the love and affection of their parents. If a child does not receive the appropriate kind of affection and has not experienced a healthy family relationship, he or she may eventually succumb to incestuous advances as a means of filling that emptiness inside where love and attention belong. If the incest begins at an early age, the child does not even understand what is happening, much less that the incest is wrong.

A father may begin abusing his daughter when she reaches early adolescence and begins taking on the appearance of a woman. A common line used by incestuous fathers is "This is my way of showing that I love you." Children may believe such lines because it is natural for children to form their impressions about life from their parents. Because of childlike trust, fear of the parent's wrath or rejection, or the normal childlike tendency to submit to a parent's authority, the child may engage in the incestuous behavior without resistance or complaint. But a child has not experienced sufficient maturity and formation of his or her own self truly to give consent.

When an incestuous relationship is exposed, the adult perpetrator will sometimes claim that the *child* was the seducer! But it is always the adult's responsibility to maintain appropriate boundaries with a child, and the child in an incestuous relationship must always be viewed as the innocent victim. The child may even experience sexual gratification in the relationship (which will in turn lead to intense feelings of confusion, guilt, and self-hate in that child), but that does not mean the child is guilty. Rather, it means that the adult was able to manipulate that child's feelings and sexuality for his or her own gratification.

An incestuous parent typically uses blackmail to keep the abuse secret: "Don't tell anyone, or the police might take me to jail and our whole family will be destroyed—and it will be all your fault." Or he or she plays on the sympathies of the child: "I'm so unhappy. Your mother (or father) never gives me any affection. You're the only person who really understands me, who knows how to give me what I need." Or the parent preys on the child's basic vulnerability and defenselessness: "If you tell, nobody will believe you. They'll say you made it all up." The incestuous parent enlists or bullies the victim into a conspiracy of silence.

Ironically, the other parent usually suspects what is going on but does not risk intervening. Why? The mother may be a passive participant in this abusive pattern because she wishes to ignore her husband's sexual needs, perhaps because of abuse in her own background. If her husband can get his needs met through their daughter, then she doesn't have to be bothered with sex. So she looks the other way and pretends not to notice. Though much less common, it still nevertheless happens that a husband who is weak-willed and ineffectual will allow his wife to abuse a child because he lacks the strength to confront the behavior. When confronted with the fact of incest under his or her roof, the passive parent almost always denies it and lashes out at the accuser—even if that accuser is the abused child. Yet it is extremely rare for children to fabricate a story of incestuous abuse. A parent who passively allows the other parent to abuse a

■

In an incestuous relationship, the child is never to blame.

■

child is just as guilty as the active abuser, since he or she has a responsibility to protect and nurture that child.

Anger is a common result of incest. When a daughter realizes that her father has been using and exploiting her and that he never really loved her, she usually experiences tremendous bitterness toward him. Daughters of incestuous fathers commonly seek out and develop crushes on exploitative, abusive men, repeating the struggles and unhealthy behavior patterns of childhood.

■

Incest survivors often find it difficult to set appropriate boundaries and are easily exploited and abused as adults. They tend to ignore their own needs in order to meet the needs and demands of others. They believe other people are important and that they themselves are unimportant. They commonly express the belief, "I don't deserve to be happy."

■

In adulthood, incest victims often have great difficulty enjoying a sexual relationship in marriage because of psychological blocks from their early years. Painful memories and distorted concepts of sexuality actually prevent the chemical and neurological releases that enable a person to enjoy a healthy sex life.

Incest survivors often accept the blame for their own victimization and describe themselves as feeling "dirty." Some incest victims falsely blame themselves. This false guilt leads to low self-esteem, self-hate, and even suicidal depression. Incest victims often repress their anger at their abusive parent, feeling it is sinful to display anger, particularly toward a parent whom (according to the Bible) they are supposed to show "honor."

Part of the healing process for incest survivors is to learn that it is okay to be angry, that it is the abusive parent who is the guilty party, and that it is possible to forgive and get on with the business of living. With Christian inpatient or outpatient counseling, incest victims become aware of the rage they have stored up and learn to express it in a healthy way. Prayer guidance helps victims overcome the anger and forgive the people who have violated them (see FORGIVENESS). As incest survivors turn their desire for vengeance over to God, the healing of the soul begins.

Emotional Incest

The term *emotional incest* is misleading in some ways, since it raises connotations of overt sexual abuse. In emotional incest, there is usually no sexual behavior at all (although it can lead to sexual incest in some extreme cases). Emotional incest is extreme role reversal between a parent and a child. The difference between sexual incest and emotional incest is this: in sexual incest, the abusive parent treats the child as a substitute for an adult sex partner; in emotional incest, the parent assumes the child's role and treats the child as a substitute parent.

This role reversal is subtle and elusive, and is much harder to identify and isolate than passive abuse. Denial is much more intense here, too. In fact, one reason we use the powerfully loaded term *emotional incest* is to get the attention of the adult abuser. People who engage in emotional incest tend to downplay and deny the damage that they are doing to their children, so therapists need to give this behavior a very serious, startling label in order to help the abuser understand the seriousness of the abuse. Emotional incest is not as obvious as sexual incest, but it does involve a damaging distortion of family roles—and it does cause long-term emotional harm to the child.

Emotional incest often occurs in families where there is little love between the parents. On an unconscious level, the abusive parent thinks, "I don't care much for my spouse, but I have this child, whom I love more than life itself. Since I get no affection from my spouse, I'll just get the affection I crave from my child." It is a case of an emotionally incomplete person trying to find completion in a littler person.

The story of Ginny and her mother, Ann, is a prime example of emotional incest. Ann was chronically depressed and had nearly ceased functioning as a wife and mother. She slept in till noon, stayed in her bathrobe all day, and took pills to dull her emotional pain. By age nine, Ginny was making breakfast for herself, her brother, and her mother. Her first stop when she got home from school was to go upstairs to her parents' bedroom and see if Ann needed any help. Then she would take care of any household chores that needed to be done. By the time her dad got home, Ginny would start dinner—something simple or instant. For all practical purposes, Ginny had become the mommy, and Ginny's mother had become a dependent child.

Ginny's dad was also involved in this distorted system. Without even being aware of what was happening, he had come to depend on Ginny, not only for the work she did around the house but for emotional support as well. He shared with her his concerns about work, finances, and the emotional problems of Ginny's mother. A nine-year-old child was being forced to shoulder a set of burdens that would bend the back of a mature adult. Her childhood and all the emotional nurturing and security that are supposed to be a natural part of childhood were being slowly bled out of her life.

Children who are forced into this kind of role reversal with their parents usually carry tragic emotional consequences into adulthood, including intense feelings of guilt and inadequacy. As adults, they feel an obsessive, driven sense of responsibility to meet other people's needs. No matter how much they do for others, they feel they haven't done enough. Emotional incest is a perfect setup for producing defeated, depressed adults who are easily manipulated by guilt and who are caught in a vicious cycle of failure, self-blame, and shame.

Emotional Abuse

Emotional abuse is the control of a child by means of manipulating that child's fear, guilt, shame, or other negative emotions. Compared with more overt forms of abuse, such as physical or sexual abuse, emotional abuse is subtle and can take many forms. Some examples:

Controlling. The controlling parent is one who has never cut the emotional umbilical cord and who wants his or her children to remain so dependent that they cannot make independent decisions or take independent action. Such parents often use guilt as a manipulative tool. They send such messages as, "If you really loved me, you'd meet my needs." Or, "If you don't do what I want, I will suffer." Or, "How can you do this to me after all the pain and heartache I've gone through for you?"

Other controlling parents use terror to get their way. Either subtly or directly, they send the message, "Do as I say or else. Or else I won't love you. Or else I might have a heart attack and die. Or else I may never speak to you again." Controlling parents manipulate the emotions of children, using shame, blame, and fear as weapons of control.

Emotional abandonment. Weak, unavailable fathers and cold, unavailable mothers are a major source of emotional abuse, which often leads to emotional problems when the children become adults. Parents are supposed to offer support, physical and emotional closeness, and leadership to their children, and children expect their parents to blaze a trail for them into the world. When parents neglect and abandon their children emotionally, the children are left without models, without mentors, without a sense of security, without parents they can honor and respect.

People who are emotionally abandoned as children often grow into adulthood looking for mates who are just as weak or unavailable or unloving as their parents. They yoke themselves with substance abusers, unloving narcissists, failure-prone ne'er-do-wells, or unavailable workaholics—and the same miserable struggles that began in childhood are repeated and continued in their marriages. While consciously seeking someone strong and loving, they unconsciously gravitate toward someone who is weak and self-centered—and then experience disappointment after disappointment.

Authoritarianism. An autocratic or rigidly authoritarian parenting style can be a form of emotional abuse. When the parent's way of thinking is the only permissible way of thinking, when the parent's view is the only acceptable view, when the child has no avenue for questioning or independent analysis and opinion, abuse results. When the authoritarian parent uses God and the Bible as a justification for his or her domineering and dictatorial behavior, when the parent imposes legalism and excessive moralism on the child—along with a heavy dose of judgment, guilt, and shame—the result is *religious abuse.*

There is often a fine line between sound, healthy parental authority and the emotional abuse of rigid authoritarianism. But true biblical parental authority is always tempered with love and grace. If a child grows up feeling intensely fearful of God's judgment, unaware of God's love and mercy, and shameful and worthless rather than forgiven and valued by God, then there is a good chance that he or she has been subjected to religious abuse and a rigidly authoritarian parental style.

UNDOING THE DAMAGE TO YOUR OWN CHILDREN

Parents sometimes come to the clinic with a burden of fear and guilt. Perhaps they were abused as children and now see evidence that the generational cycle of abuse is being carried on in their behavior toward their own children. They want to stop hurting their children and, if at all possible, undo the damage they have already done. If you feel you have hurt your children through either active or passive abuse of any kind, there are steps you can take to promote healing in your relationship with your child.

Step 1: Honestly admit what you have done. Admit it to yourself and confess it to God. Ask God to heal you of the issues and emotions that cause you to hurt your child. Ask Him to transform you into the kind of loving, patient parent He wants you to be, and ask Him to heal the emotional scars of your child. Pray for opportunities to minister love to your child and for moment-by-moment wisdom to love and guide your children toward a healthy self-image and a trusting faith in God.

Step 2: Get immediate professional help so that your child will be protected and so that you can begin to recover. Call a child abuse hotline. Talk to a Christian counselor or pastor. If you are feeling that you lack control and you may be endangering your child, have a trusted friend or family member care for your child for a few days so that you can get help in getting your feelings and behavior under control.

If you really love your child, you will do that work and endure that pain in order to become whole and healed. It's difficult to nurture a child if you've never been nurtured and loved yourself.

Step 3: Ask your child's forgiveness. Let your child know that you regret your actions and that you, not your child, were responsible for that behavior. Affirm your love to your child. You may say, "I love you, but grownups make mistakes sometimes. The way I acted toward you was wrong. I'm very sorry. Please forgive me." Be specific about what you did wrong. Tell your child that God is helping you to understand why you sometimes behave inappropriately and that with God's help you are trying to be a better parent.

Step 4: Spend time with your child. Every day is an opportunity to strengthen your relationship with your child, to affirm and encourage your child, to help your child feel secure in your own love and the love of God the Father. Look your child in the eye and say, "I love you, I thank God that He made you, and I think you're great." Do special, memorable activities with your child that demonstrate that you enjoy spending time with him or her.

Step 5: Commit yourself to a long-term process of healing and recovery. The best thing you can do for your child is become a whole person—and that takes work, commitment, and even pain. If you have significant unresolved issues from your own childhood, seek professional counseling. Your own recovery is the most important key to your child's recovery and growth toward emotionally healthy adulthood.

Was I Abused as a Child?

Part 1: Examining Your Childhood

Check the statements that apply to you.

_____ 1. Do you recall being sexually abused or molested as a child?

_____ 2. Did a parent, older sibling, or other adult ever do anything to you, then tell you it had to be kept secret?

_____ 3. Did your parents inflict severe physical pain on you? Did they ever discipline you in such a way that you were left with scars, welts, bruises, broken bones, or other injuries?

_____ 4. Were you frequently or continually scared of your parents?

_____ 5. Did your parents frequently call you bad names or tell you that you were bad or that they hated you?

_____ 6. Did your parents drink to excess or use drugs?

_____ 7. Did your parents' behavior often make you feel angry, embarrassed, or ashamed?

_____ 8. Did you sometimes have to "clean up" after your parents or make excuses for them?

_____ 9. As a child, did you often find yourself taking care of your parents' emotional and physical needs?

      _____ Did a parent frequently confide major problems to you or rely on you for emotional support?

      _____ Did you sometimes find yourself cooking and doing other chores because your parent was emotionally incapacitated?

21

A B U S E

_____ 10. Are there periods in your childhood—say, an entire year or several years—that you cannot recall? Are there "blank spots" in your childhood memories?

Part 2: Examining Your Adult Life

Check those that apply.

_____ 1. Do your parents still treat you like a child?

_____ 2. Do your parents try to control you with guilt, threats, or manipulative behavior (fake illnesses, acting like a martyr, and so forth)?

_____ 3. Do you feel responsible for your parents' happiness or unhappiness? When they are unhappy, do you feel it's your job to make them feel better?

_____ 4. Do you feel that, no matter how hard you try, you will never be able to please your parents or be accepted by them?

_____ 5. Do you become anxious, agitated, angry, or fearful before or after a visit with your parents?

_____ 6. Do you frequently have physical problems (such as digestive disorders, headaches, or nausea) before or after a visit with your parents?

_____ 7. Do you continually think wishful thoughts like the following?
_____ "Someday, my parents will change."
_____ "Someday, my parents will like me."
_____ "Someday, my parents will give up drinking."
_____ "Someday, my parents will quit interfering in my life."

_____ 8. Do you sometimes experience intense negative emotions—rage, bitterness, sadness—for no apparent reason?

_____ 9. Do you expect the worst from life? Do you expect people to betray you, abuse you, exploit you, or abandon you? Do you have difficulty trusting people?

_____ 10. Do you have a tendency to become involved in abusive or destructive relationships?

Scoring the test: Even one or two checks to the above questions indicates that you have serious childhood issues to work through. If you haven't already, you should seek out a support group for survivors of childhood abuse, or you should seek counseling from a Christian therapist. Four or more "yes" answers indicates that you should definitely seek professional help in dealing with the toxic emotional residue of abuse.

RECOVERY FROM ABUSE

The damaging effects of childhood abuse *can* be reversed, and the painful memories and emotions of abuse *can* be healed. But recovery requires work—and it involves pain. At first, the recovery process seems to increase the pain we are seeking to heal, the pain of broken memories and tormented emotions. In the early stages of emotional recovery, most people think, "I'm not getting better! I'm getting worse! My pain is increasing!" But the pain of the recovery process is a surgical pain, the pain that tells us that healing has finally begun.

Recovery from abuse is a ten-stage process. Let's take a look at each of the stages:

Stage 1: Exploration and Discovery

In the first stage of recovery, you explore your life, your past, your feelings. You seek to uncover those hidden issues of your lost childhood that have created the pain of the present. You also seek to discover how those past issues have created emotional and behavioral problems in your present life—problems such as:

- addictions, compulsions, and obsessive behavior in your present lifestyle
- toxic emotional residue, such as depression, bitterness, rage, sadness, anxiety, and so forth
- abusive behavior toward others around you, especially toward your own children (the continuation of the cycle of abuse)

As you rummage through your past and present life, making discoveries that are often painful and unpleasant, you need to have someone who can listen to your pain and absorb your angry emotions. We recommend that, during this process, you use four resources to help you process these discoveries about your life:

1. A competent Christian therapist, psychologist, or psychiatrist.
2. A support group comprised of people who have experienced your issues and who understand your pain.
3. God. The more you bring Him into the process, the easier and swifter your recovery will advance. Ask God to strengthen you and reveal to you the truth of your abuse issues. Ask Him to penetrate your denial and illuminate your blind spots. Ask Him to open your eyes so that you can see yourself clearly and without distortion. The truth—God's truth about yourself and the abuse in your past—will set you free.
4. A private recovery journal or diary. Write down your insights and discoveries. In fact, it may be helpful to address your journal entries to God, like a series of personal letters to Him, telling Him about your progress in the exploration

---

The Ten Stages of the Recovery Process

1. **Exploration and Discovery:** You explore your past and present life to discover the truth about yourself and your feelings.
2. **Relationship History/Inventory:** You examine your past and present relationships, discover recurring patterns, and possibly reset your personal boundaries.
3. **Addiction Control:** You face your addictions and compulsions, and take the first steps toward mastering them.
4. **Leaving Home and Saying Goodbye:** You say the goodbyes that are appropriate to your healing. You may think you did that years ago, but you probably didn't.
5. **Grieving Your Losses:** Grieving is painful, part of the process of "hitting bottom." But this is as low as you go. You are about to begin moving out of the valley. From here on, you ascend the mountain of healing.
6. **New Self-Perceptions:** You begin to gain fresh, exciting perceptions about yourself. You make new decisions and positive changes in your life. This is the "eye-opener" stage—and it feels *great*.
7. **New Experiences:** You build a foundation of new experiences to bolster the decisions you've just made.
8. **Reparenting:** You rebuild your past, your present, and your future. The abuse of the past begins to fall away as you allow nurturing friends and a loving Heavenly Father to reparent you in a healthy way.
9. **Relationship Accountability:** You establish lines of accountability in your new and healthy set of relationships.
10. **Maintenance:** You embark on a maintenance program to keep you relationally and emotionally on track for the rest of your life.

process. Journaling is healing in several ways: if you address God in your journal, it becomes a form of prayer. Journaling forces you to think clearly about your issues, and often brings clarity and solutions that silent thinking does not bring. Finally, journaling gives you a record of your progress that you can reread and review. Someday, you will be able to look back over your journal and see how far you have come.

Stage 2: *Relationship History and Inventory*

At the clinic, we have our abuse-survivor clients write out in-depth relationship inventories. In such an inventory, you identify all the persons, past and present, who either left a mark or exercised influence on your life, beginning with family members. This includes the nuclear family, of course, but also extends to third-cousins or uncles-once-removed who have impacted your life for good or ill.

Family relationships create patterns and systems that affect every member of the family. It is rarely effective to look at one family relationship in isolation; the entire skein of family relationships must be explored in order for the abusive behavior to be understood and disarmed. It may well be, in a given family system, that Dad is the active abuser, but Mom may well be a passive participant as well, and Brother and Sister may have equally important roles as enablers, excusers, or additional victims of Dad's abusive behavior.

People often enter counseling saying, "I only want to work on this one relationship. If things were just better with this one person in my family, if he or she would just change, everything would be fine." Unfortunately, it rarely works that way. The behavior of one family member has ramifications that ripple out to all other members of that family system. The entire system must be examined for complete healing to take place.

In the relationship inventory, you call to mind the persons both living and dead who have affected your life, and you make peace with each one in an appropriate way. The more people who impacted your life, the more people you must make peace with. For example, people who were adopted or raised in foster care must come to terms with both their adoptive parents and their biological parents, whether they know them or not. And there are others, people outside your family, who have had a strong influence on who you are and the feelings you experience today: mentors, pastors, coaches, teachers, neighbors, boyfriends or girlfriends, partners of previous marriages—the list goes on.

"I don't have to include my first marriage, do I?" one client asked while writing out her relationship inventory. "It was awful, it only lasted six weeks, and we had it annulled. It's behind me now, and I don't even like to think about it. There's nothing significant about that relationship. Can't we just forget it?"

That was a red flag. We stopped her and talked through her feelings about her first marriage. It turned out that her feelings of failure, resentment, and guilt about that relationship were a major factor in her depression and her inability to get on with her life.

The purpose of the relationship inventory is to bring your relationships into clear focus. Don't dismiss any memory as being irrelevant or too embarrassing to write down. Of course, this kind of inventory has the best chance of helping you if you are being guided through it by a trained Christian therapist. The interaction of a therapist serves to jog your memory, force you to be honest with yourself, and keep you moving through the pain and into the healing. But even if you have no therapist right now to provide this kind of interaction, a relationship inventory can lead you toward greater self-awareness.

Prepare your list and examine it carefully, deliberately looking for patterns. For example, do you see resonances between the behavior of your abusive parent and the behavior of some of the people you've been romantically involved with as an adult? If possible, share the process with a trusted friend, pastoral counselor, support group, or similar confidant. Most important, share it in private conversation with God. He remembers those people better than you do, and He can lead you to the insight you need to find healing and recovery.

As the abusive patterns of your past and present life emerge in the relationship inventory, you will be better equipped to draw healthy boundaries (see BOUNDARIES) in your relationships so that you can move toward emotional and relational health.

Stage 3: Addiction Control

Abuse is a major factor in most addictions, and addiction is in turn a major factor in perpetuating the pain of abuse (see ADDICTION). The throbbing emotional hurt of the lost childhood experience continually sends a message to the unconscious mind of the abused individual, and that message keeps that individual locked in a vicious cycle of addiction. To the alcoholic or drug abuser, that message is, "You know you're worthless, you're empty! Want to forget what a nothing you are? Anesthetize yourself. Take another drink or another hit of cocaine." To the anorexic, that message is, "You're still too fat! No one will love you until you are thin enough. Starve yourself!" To the workaholic, that message is, "Still not good enough! Still not successful enough! Work harder, harder, harder!"

These destructive messages are like a hypnotic spell, holding the individual in their clutches. Somehow, the person has to break that grip, to snap out of that spell. It all starts with a single decision: "I will abstain from the thing I am addicted to. I don't know if I can do without my addiction tomorrow or next week or a year from now, but right now, during this hour, I will be sober." A decision to become sober must be made one day at a time—and even moment by moment.

Healing cannot take place while the individual is anesthetized by the addictive substance or behavior. When a patient comes to a Minirth Meier New Life Clinic for treatment of emotional problems such as alcoholism, we cannot say, "We understand you'll be in an alcoholic haze through counseling; we'll just try to get through to you as best we can until you gain enough insight to stop drinking." No, the drinking has to stop first, or the healing will never begin. So we start, if need be, with hospital-supervised medical detoxification. Once the addict is abstaining, progress on the issues underlying the addiction can begin.

Stage 4: Leaving Home and Saying Goodbye

Because abuse robs people of their childhood, it tends to keep them emotionally stunted and immature. That is one reason many abused people remain connected in dependent relationships with the very people who abused them. So a key step in recovery from the toxic after-effects of abuse is *leaving home*. That sounds so simple. But it can be very hard to do in practice.

There are two steps individuals must take to leave home and achieve true maturity, independence, and adulthood: (1) they have to genuinely leave their family of origin and say goodbye to Mom and Dad, and (2) they must say goodbye to false symbols of security. Neither step is easy.

We are, after all, born into families so that we might eventually leave them. The drive for independence begins as early as infancy, continues through the process of learning to walk, learning to explore, embarking upon "the terrible twos," entering kindergarten, getting that driver's license, going off to college, and on and on. The problem is that abuse short-circuits that process so that the abused individual never seems to make that final break. That person may have physically moved out of the house, may have a fine career and a family of his or her own, but at some hidden emotional level, the final break was never made. Goodbyes have been left unsaid. Childhood struggles and issues continue to rage on, and the abused person still feels like an abused child inside.

■

If you are involved in an addiction to alcohol or any other drug, prescription or otherwise, you should immediately seek medical help. Your addictive behavior must be interrupted as soon as possible, and it is dangerous to attempt to withdraw from a chemical dependency without medical supervision.

■

Saying goodbye to an abusive parent does not necessarily mean a severing of all ties but rather a declaration of independence. Sometimes, however—particularly if the pattern of abuse is still going on—it really is necessary to sever all connection with the abuser, but we are talking here about achieving emotional independence. In most cases, saying goodbye to your family of origin means saying, "I am still your child, but I'm on my own now. Emotionally, I will be a visitor here from time to time, but I am no longer a resident. You don't control me, you can no longer hurt me, and I no longer need to justify or explain myself to you. I no longer derive my sense of self-worth, my okayness, from you. I am an independent adult."

You can say goodbye to your parent in this way even if your parent is dead. Many people find release from the toxic emotions and the controlling power of an abusive past by going to the gravesites of their abusers and verbally, literally saying goodbye. This emotionally charged technique can bring about a great catharsis of the soul.

Another technique for saying goodbye to parents who are either living or dead is to write a letter. People who find it hard to speak their feelings aloud often find it much easier to put them in a letter. Such a letter doesn't have to be mailed or read by another person to be effective as a means of saying goodbye and beginning the healing process. The letter may be tucked away, torn up, or burned. The real healing power is in the catharsis, the emotional release that takes place when pent-up feelings are finally expressed and a painful chapter is finally closed.

The second step in leaving home is to *say goodbye to false security symbols.* A false security symbol is anything in your life to which you are inappropriately devoted. If you have an eating disorder, then that false security symbol in your life is food. It controls your thoughts and behavior. It has a stranglehold on your life and health. Or your false security symbol may be wealth, success, and power. Or a chemical dependency. Or sex. Or materialism. Or television. Whatever false symbol you use to feel secure and protected from the painful realities of life must be dealt with. Say goodbye to it—forever.

Stage 5: *Grieving Your Losses*

Grief is the part of death played by the living. In this sense, "death" does not just mean physical death. When you grieve your losses, you may be grieving the death of a dream, of a belief, of a goal, of an idea, or even of a part of yourself. The grief process was first mapped by Elisabeth Kübler-Ross, who broke that process down into a series of stages. (See also GRIEF AND LOSS.) We have adapted the Kübler-Ross model to include six stages of grief:

1. Shock and denial. The abused person who has not worked through the stages of grief is often like a person in shock. He or she seems to have no feelings and appears to sleepwalk through life. Ask this person about feelings of pain or anger about the abuse of the past and you'll likely hear, "What are you talking about? That was a long time ago. I'm fine. I don't have any problems." That is denial talking.

2. Anger. A common feature of abuse is that abusers usually forbid their victims to express anger. So abuse survivors often grow up feeling they have no right or permission to get angry. The anger is *there,* but it is unacknowledged and repressed. In our clinic, we often encourage people to get in touch with their submerged anger by attacking a punching bag or some other soft, energy-absorbent, inanimate object. We don't try to *make* people angry. We try to *liberate* the anger that was there all along. Anger is a natural, healthy, God-given mechanism for dealing with pain and loss. Paul told the Ephesians, "Be angry, and do not sin: do not let the sun go down on your wrath" (4:26). In other words, be aware of your anger: acknowledge it, release it, deal with it, and expunge it. Do not let your anger fester into bitterness, which is toxic and sinful.

3. Depression. Depression is anger turned inward—so it is not surprising that the depression stage usually follows the anger stage in the grief process. When anger goes underground, it creates an emotional numbness that can last a lifetime. Another emotion that frequently leads to depression is guilt—particularly false guilt (see GUILT). False guilt is usually a form of anger that has been turned against the self. When a person has become stuck in depression for a long period of time, particularly for several years, emotional healing becomes very difficult. That is why it is important, as you work through the grief process, to continue uncovering and releasing feelings of anger and guilt, so that you can avoid getting stuck in a state of depression.

4. Bargaining (and magical thinking). Bargaining with God is one of the most common of all human responses to painful situations: "God, if You'll just take me out of this mess, I'll do whatever You want!" It sounds childish, but it is a very common trait in adults. It seems we never quite outgrow our capacity for bargaining.

Closely allied to bargaining is magical thinking—the idea that if you just follow the right prescription, say the right magical formula, pray the right words and with enough faith, then everything's going to turn out all right. Maturity comes when you let go of your bargaining and say, "Not my will, God, but Yours." Wholeness comes when you let go of your magical thinking and say, "There is no magic formula, no magic power. I will face the reality of what is—and I will accept it."

5. Sadness. Sadness is a normal consequence of letting go of bargaining and magical thinking. Your unrealistic hope of magically or supernaturally changing your circumstances has evaporated, and you are left with an unpleasant truth. You have accepted a sad reality, and to respond by feeling sad is normal. Sadness is the appropriate response to sad events. People deal with sadness by shedding tears. But eventually sadness ends. Unlike chronic depression, sadness comes, you recognize it, live through it—and it goes away.

6. Forgiveness, resolution, and acceptance. Once the stage of sadness has passed, you reach the final, culminating step in the grief process, your goal from the beginning: *forgiveness, resolution, and acceptance.* This is what the Bible calls "the peace that passes understanding."

Forgiveness doesn't necessarily mean reconciliation with the abuser; it simply means that you release that person from your own judgment, anger, and bitterness, so that you can get on with your life (see FORGIVENESS).

How to Forgive Your Abuser

There are proven techniques you can use to accelerate your progress toward the forgiveness, resolution, and acceptance stage of the grief process. For example, imagine a meeting between yourself and your abuser in which you take that person by the hand and lead that person to a meadow where you encounter Jesus—then place that person's hand in Jesus' hand and turn that person over to Jesus. That abuser is no longer your concern; he or she is now in Jesus' hands, and He will deal with that abuser as only He can.

Another technique: write a story in which you take the abuser out of your life and give that person over to God. Or simply give that person over to God through prayer.

When it is hardest for us to forgive, we desperately need the power of God.

Once you have experienced forgiveness, you will naturally move on to acceptance and resolution. You accept the fact that the abuse happened, that the past cannot be changed, that what's done is done. This results in a major step—not a final step by any means, but a big first step—toward the full and healthy resolution of your abuse issues.

Another facet of acceptance is that you give up the struggle to change people who refuse to change. Perhaps you have been trying for years or decades to make your parents love you, respect you, and treat you well. But the fact is that they may never change. You will have to accept them as they are and get on with your life. Even if the people who abused you choose not to change or grow, you will continue to change and grow and reach for total emotional wholeness, because that is what's best for *you*.

These, then, are the six stages of grief as they apply to the recovery process in the life of an abuse survivor. In a normal grief process—say, the loss of a parent or a spouse—people can usually progress through these stages without the help of a therapist. The abuse survivor, however, tends to get stuck in one of these stages. This person may need to back up through the stages and repeat them until the emotional blockage shakes loose and grief proceeds.

What are the losses that the abuse survivor must grieve? The loss of a normal childhood, filled with love, affirmation, and a sense of security. The loss of emotional wholeness. The losses that come as a result of addictions or compulsions (the common by-products of abuse): lost relationships, a lost marriage, a lost career, a lost reputation, lost opportunities, lost self-respect and self-esteem.

If you are an abuse survivor, it is even appropriate for you to grieve the loss of your addictions, compulsions, denials, and excuses. Yes, these crutches and defense mechanisms must go, but it is painful to shed them. You have taken comfort and refuge in them and have used them to dull your pain and hide from some very ugly truths. But it's time to leave your old, inadequate, unhealthy coping mechanisms behind. It's time to push on toward wholeness and adulthood. So grieve the loss of your defense mechanisms—then move on.

People who have gone through more than one major form of abuse may have to grieve each one as a distinct experience. Physical abuses, sexual abuses, and abandonment each cut a unique kind of wound into one's psyche. Give yourself plenty of time to grieve your wounds. Move through the entire cycle of grief. Don't rush or skip a stage. If you work through your grief and flush out all the toxins of regret, guilt, and anger, you will be ready to move on to the next step and receive God's healing truth about yourself.

Stage 6: New Self-Perceptions

The next stage in the recovery process for abuse survivors is an exciting one, for it is here that you gain fresh new insights into the special person that you are. In this "eye-opener" stage, you replace the negative, distorted messages you received in your abusive past with new, true messages from your loving Heavenly Parent. Out go the bad messages: "I am unlovable. I am unworthy. I don't deserve to be happy." In come the truths of God: "God loves me. He makes me worthy by His grace. He wants me to experience His joy and peace."

This stage begins with an inventory of your self-perception. Write down your beliefs about yourself. Begin with, "I am . . ." Free-associate. Write down thoughts and feelings as quickly and furiously as they come to you. Do this for five minutes, then stop and take a break to clear your mind. Then take another five minutes to quickly, freely write down your thoughts and feelings about God. Begin with, "God is . . ."

If the first words you think of concerning God are words such as "critical," "mean," or "untrustworthy," then you will have learned something about the "I" messages within you. It will become clear that you feel that God is judging you, condemning you, hurting you, tricking you, and in short, *abusing* you, just as you were treated as a child. In other words, you are projecting an image of your abusive parents onto God. You think He views you and treats you as your abusive parents did—*and that's not a true message*. God does not want to condemn you or hurt you. He loves you and wants you to experience His joy.

In his book *Please Let Me Know You, God* (Thomas Nelson, 1993), Dr. Larry Stephens of the Minirth Meier New Life Clinics includes a list of affirmations—God's *true* messages to you and about you—taken from the Bible. An important part of gaining new, more accurate self-perceptions is to meditate these Bible-based statements every day:

"I am loved with an everlasting love" (Jer. 31:3).
"I am set free" (John 8:31–33).

■

Acceptance means you no longer base your own happiness, self-esteem, and security on their opinion of you and their treatment of you. Acceptance means you take charge of your own life and become your own person.

■

"I have abundant life" (John 10:10).

"I am a saint" (Rom. 1:7).

"I am free of shame and condemnation" (Rom. 8:1).

"I am a joint heir with Christ" (Rom. 8:17).

"I am being changed and conformed to the image of Christ" (Rom. 8:28–29; Phil. 1:6).

"I am a temple of the Holy Spirit" (1 Cor. 6:19).

"I am a new creation" (2 Cor. 5:17).

"I am holy and without blame before God" (Eph. 1:4).

"I am accepted in Christ" (Eph. 1:6).

"I am forgiven; all my sins are washed away" (Eph. 1:7).

"I am sealed by the Holy Spirit" (Eph. 1:13).

"I am God's workmanship" (Eph. 2:10).

"I am strong in the Lord" (Eph. 6:10).

"I have the peace of God, which surpasses understanding" (Phil. 4:7).

"I can do all things through Christ" (Phil. 4:13).

"I am complete in Christ" (Col. 2:10).

"I am beloved and chosen by God" (Col. 3:12; 1 Thess. 1:4).

"I am healed by the wounds of Christ" (1 Peter 2:24).

"I am victorious" (Rev. 21:7).

Write these statements on cards, post them on your dashboard, your bathroom mirror, your refrigerator. Pray over them and meditate them. Build God's truth about yourself into your heart and mind. In time, you'll find that these truths will gradually erase and overwrite the lies that were drummed into you during an abusive childhood. And these truths will set you free.

Stage 7: New Experiences

Now it's time to live out the new messages you received about yourself in Stage 6. New inner messages require new experiences to affirm them, if the heart is to accept them. And the best place to have those new messages affirmed and reaffirmed is in a support group or recovery group. There you will find willing ears and hearts to help you put your new "I" messages to work. The people in the group will empathize (they've all been there), they will listen, they will hold you accountable for your growth, and they will accept you right where you are. Talk about the pain of abuse, and they will understand. Talk about the changes you want to make, and they will tell you how they were able to make changes. You can take off your armor and drop your defenses, and no one will shoot you down.

Another new experience you need in order to affirm the new messages you have received about yourself is that of *setting new, healthy boundaries*. Boundaries provide an emotional safety zone between you and anyone who might try to abuse or exploit you. Boundaries provide rules and guidelines to keep your recovery on track—and *you* set the rules. Boundaries enable you to meet your own needs so that you can be healthy, whole, happy, productive, and in control of your own life and feelings. (For more information, see BOUNDARIES.)

Stage 8: Reparenting

People who have lost their childhoods becuase of abuse need to be reparented in a healthy way in order to reclaim the emotional nurturing that was denied them as children. True reparenting comes to us from God, our loving Heavenly Father, who is represented to us by His human agents: healthy family members, a support or recovery group, a therapy group, a therapist, or a healthy church community. Through these individuals and groups, God is able to give you the kind of parenting you were supposed to have the first time around but that was denied you because of human sin and abuse. These "surrogate parents" can now come alongside you and do what healthy, loving parents are supposed to do: nurture, affirm, and guide.

It is important in the reparenting process to have a person you can turn to as a mentor, a trailblazer, a guide. In recovery groups (such as Alcoholics Anonymous) that mentor is called a sponsor. The sponsor is an experienced, empathetic person who is available to oversee you and hold you accountable. He or she serves as:

- a sounding board and nonprofessional counselor, a listener;
- a friend;
- a daily contact;
- a source of unconditional, nonjudgmental support;
- a gentle but firm confronter, someone who cares enough to tell you the truth; and
- a helper and confidant who knows how to keep a secret.

■

It is very important that your mentor/ sponsor be of the same sex so that romantic issues don't arise that could complicate or derail your recovery.

■

We also experience the reparenting of God through prayer and meditation in His Word. God's unconditional love makes Him the best friend and counselor we can have. One way we learn to see Him more clearly as our Father is by seeking out in Scripture the advice a loving parent would give a child. We suggest you read Deuteronomy 5 and Ephesians 5—6. Insert your name as appropriate, and listen as if God is speaking directly to you. Focus on a problem or need and discuss it with God in prayer. Don't worry about formalities and speaking in "thees" and "thous." Just open your heart to Him as you would to a close friend or a loving, attentive, nurturing parent.

We also recommend you read *Healing the Child Within* by Charles L. Whitfield (Health Comm., 1987), *Becoming Your Own Parent* by Dennis Wholey (Doubleday, 1988), and *Reclaiming Your Inner Child: A Self-Discovery Workbook* by Ken Parker (Thomas Nelson, 1993). These books contain many healing concepts you can apply to your relationship with God.

Stage 9: Relationship Accountability

As you continue your recovery, it is important to monitor your relationships so that you can spot trouble early and make course corrections before trouble develops. To do that, you maintain an ongoing inventory of present relationships. This is a written inventory of all your present friends and acquaintances and how you relate to them.

This relationship inventory accomplishes two purposes: (1) it reveals any unhealthy patterns as they emerge, and (2) it helps you avoid hurtful relationships at a time when you are quite vulnerable. It is good to do this inventory on a regular basis (say, twice a year) and show it to a trusted confidant—a therapist, sponsor, or mentor. This confidant will help you to spot issues in your relationships that you may not be able to see and will help you penetrate your denial and other defense mechanisms.

The relationship inventory serves as a set of guardrails to keep you on the fast track to recovery. In this inventory, you assess your family relationships, friendships, and dating relationships, looking for signs of trouble: people who are emotionally unavailable; people who (in the dating realm) are morally off-limits (married or committed to someone else); people who are recently divorced; people who are addicted, compulsive, controlling, needy, dependent, or seductive; people who are abusive in any way.

As you complete this relationship inventory, you should ask yourself, "In any of these relationships, am I rescuing? Am I being taken advantage of? Is my self-esteem being enhanced or diminished by this relationship?" The answers to these questions will tell you whether you need to restructure your relationships and redraw your boundaries.

Stage 10: Maintenance

Maintenance is a day-to-day, year-to-year process you continue for the rest of your life. We recommend three categories of maintenance: (1) daily routine, (2) support and recovery groups, and (3) recycling. Let's look at each category in turn:

1. Daily routine. Daily maintenance should include a regular, special time for prayer in addition to the various pauses for prayer as needed during the day. As you talk to God, be sure to take time to listen to Him as well. You listen by being still for a few moments during your prayer time and by being sensitive to any thoughts that God brings to your mind as you pray. It's helpful to keep a notebook nearby as you pray so that you can jot down anything God tells you during your listening time—an insight, a task that needs to be done, a call you should make, a letter you should write, a relationship you should work on.

Scripture study and meditation is another indispensable part of your daily recovery routine. It is another form of listening to God, for the Bible is His love letter to us. It is there that we discover His heart and His will for our lives.

If you have struggled with an overpowering addiction or compulsion in your life, take a daily inventory of your lifestyle and habits. Are any old ways creeping back in? If you feel yourself slipping back into old problems and issues, immediately contact a therapist, support group, or sponsor who can help you get your recovery back on track.

Every three months or so, take inventory of your relationships. Do you see improvement? Regression? Are any new or disturbing patterns emerging? Talk this inventory over with a trusted friend or counselor. Make sure that you keep your boundaries intact and your relationships healthy.

2. Support and recovery groups. We've already stressed the importance of support and recovery groups in previous recovery stages: they can be helpful in your process of discovering abuse issues, sorting through relationship inventories, and so forth. But these groups can also be invaluable resources in helping you *keep* your recovery.

These groups are truly anonymous—no last names are ever used, just first names. You can introduce yourself if you wish, or just sit quietly and listen. The atmosphere is warm and friendly but never pushy or intrusive. Most of the people in the group have been where you are. In the meeting, people will talk about their pain and their

As you read the Bible, watch for His promises of parental love.

progress. One of the biggest boosts you'll receive from a support group is the sense that you are not alone with your issues. Many churches now offer Christ-centered support and recovery groups for a wide variety of issues, including various forms of abuse. Long-term involvement in a support group can be an invaluable resource in helping you maintain your recovery.

3. *Recycling.* Never be afraid to go back to the beginning and start over. As your maintenance proceeds, you may discover more issues, feelings, and memories that have not yet been dealt with. You may find yourself becoming angry all over again for abuses you thought were forgiven and released. Cycle back through the stages of recovery; explore and discover more of your past. Inventory your relationships. Face your addictions. Say your goodbyes again. Grieve your losses. Gain new insights and perspectives on yourself. Build new experiences. Reparent yourself. Reinstate lines of accountability. Keep moving forward as you maintain your recovery.

Throughout your journey toward wholeness, keep your eyes on your loving Heavenly Father. Whatever happened in the past, you can be assured that He is building something lasting, valuable, and beautiful in your life.

Addiction

The traditional image of an addicted person is that of a skid-row drunk or the stereotypical "dope fiend" who must have his periodic "fix" in order to fend off withdrawal. But in recent years, as we have gained greater understanding of the issue, we have learned that addictions come in all shapes and sizes and afflict people from all walks of life.

Clark had a great job as the manager of a shopping center, pulling down almost $200,000 a year. The center was sold to a large corporation, which fired Clark and installed its own management team. Even though Clark had been in the top 1 percent of American wage-earners and even though he had a daughter who was about to start college, he didn't have a dime of savings when his job ran out. In fact, he and his wife were thousands of dollars in debt to credit cards. For years, they had spent Clark's considerable income like it was water. Clark and his wife have an addiction: they are "spendaholics."

Sandy was raised in a dysfunctional family where she received little affection, attention, or affirmation. She views herself as unlovable, and her life is empty and friendless. She stuffs her emptiness with ice cream and chocolates, and now weighs more than three hundred pounds. Sandy has a food addiction.

Norm is a church elder and a pillar of his community. His wife dragged him into counseling after a discovery she made while cleaning out some file drawers in his den office: a huge stash of explicit hard-core pornography. Norm has an addiction to pornography.

Mike runs for his life. He is lean, hard-muscled, and fit from running as much as twenty miles a day. He has few friends, no outside activities or interests, and he's been divorced three times. Even though his last wife was also a fitness enthusiast, even she thought his devotion to running was obsessive. "I feel great when I run," Mike says defensively, "and when I'm not running, all I think about is getting back on the track. I'm a health nut. What's wrong with that?" The problem is that Mike is an addict. He is chemically dependent on endorphins, natural opiatelike chemicals that are released in the brain during extended exercise.

Sharon is in her thirties, the daughter of a rigid, legalistic church deacon. She married a man who is a virtual carbon copy of her father: stern, moralistic, condemning. Sharon's whole world revolves around her church, and she is continually involved in religious activities, trying to expunge a gnawing sense of guilt and shame within her. She has a long list of rituals she follows whenever the guilt feelings start to oppress her and fill her with a fear of eternal punishment: She prays repetitive phrases. She fasts for days, until she is almost too weak and dizzy to move. She sleeps with a Bible under her pillow. Is it possible to get too much religion? Absolutely! A genuine relationship with God produces peace and joy, not fear and guilt. Sharon's problem: she is addicted to religion.

Clearly, addictions come in all varieties.

WHAT IS ADDICTION?

Addiction is a compulsive or physical dependence upon a substance or person or behavior that provides a temporary sense of well-being—with the emphasis on *temporary*. The gratification that comes from indulging an addiction never lasts long, but the destructive effects, the damage to relationships, the feelings of shame and failure that addiction brings are long-lasting and far-reaching.

The focus of an addiction—the substance, person, or behavior upon which a person may form an excessive dependency—is called an addictive agent. The list of addictive agents includes (but is not limited to):

- drugs and alcohol
- food (compulsive overeating, bulimia)
- sex
- work and success
- control
- money (overspending, hoarding, gambling)
- approval (the need to please people)
- rescuing behavior
- dependency on toxic relationships
- physical illness (hypochondria)
- exercise, diet, and physical conditioning
- perfectionism
- cleanliness and avoidance of contamination

- obsession with being organized and structured
- materialism (obsession with acquiring things)
- preoccupation with entertainment (video, computers, movies, music)
- obsession with physical beauty (cosmetics, suntanning, clothes, style, cosmetic surgery)
- academic pursuits and excessive intellectualizing
- religiosity or religious legalism

Most of us can find ourselves and our own addictions in this list.

The Warning Signs and Treatment of Substance Abuse

All addictions are harmful, but the most deadly and dangerous forms of addiction involve substance abuse, such as addiction to alcohol or to drugs. You should be aware of the symptoms and warning signs of substance abuse, particularly if you have adolescents in your household. The warning signs of alcoholism or drug abuse in young people and adults are:

1. deterioration in family relationships; withdrawal from family activities, responsibilities, and chores
2. deterioration in school or work performance
3. negative personality changes, including listlessness, depression, nervousness, talkativeness, lying
4. lifestyle changes—hair length, dress, and choice of music that reflect identification with the drug culture
5. changes in sleep patterns—insomnia, sleeping in late, sleeping at odd times, reclusiveness
6. legal and moral problems—thefts from home, shoplifting, vandalism

If you observe any of these warning signs of substance abuse, you should be aware of the treatment options that exist. The cure for substance abuse (alcoholism or drug addiction) must take place in four phases:

1. The addiction must be identified, and the substance abuser must recognize and admit his or her problem. This may require an "intervention," in which friends and family members—with the help of a professional therapist—surround and confront the substance abuser and force this person to recognize the pain and destruction caused by the addiction.

2. Detoxification ("detox"), a medically supervised withdrawal from the drugs or alcohol. Detox must occur in a hospital environment. (Substance abusers who attempt to detox themselves without medical supervision run the risk of convulsions and death.)

3. Rehabilitation ("rehab"), a process of counseling and restructuring the life of the patient to be drug- or alcohol-free. Rehab can be performed on an inpatient or outpatient basis through:

- treatment programs (in the workplace, in the community, or through self-help organizations such as Alcoholics Anonymous or Narcotics Anonymous);
- hospitals and mental health clinics;

- individual psychotherapy; or
- family or group therapy.

4. Follow-up and maintenance, preferably with a Twelve Step recovery group. Daily meetings are recommended for the first few months to a year, becoming less frequent as a new sober lifestyle becomes reinforced.

The Addiction Cycle

At the Minirth Meier New Life Clinics, we believe that we are all, to some extent, codependent (see CODEPENDENCY). That is, we all engage, to one degree or another, in attempts to control our feelings and gratify our emotional needs by manipulating people, substances, or events outside of us. This codependent neediness compels us to seek some sort of addictive behavior to meet that need. For some of us, that emotional, codependent neediness arises because our parents or primary caretakers in childhood treated us with:

- neglect
- abuse
- lack of love and nurturing
- smothering overprotectiveness

For others, the emotional void may be the result of a disastrous love affair, a severe career disappointment, a family trauma, a major health problem. This emotional emptiness is the perfect setup for codependency and addiction.

Stage 1 in the addiction cycle is emotional emptiness. In this cycle, one factor leads to another, around and around, driving the addicted person deeper and deeper into addiction and robbing that person of any measure of control over his or her life and behavior. Another name for this first stage in the addictive cycle is *love hunger*—a gnawing emptiness and a craving for love, affirmation, and a sense of value.

Stage 2 is low self-esteem, a sensation of emotional pain, and this stage flows directly from Stage 1. Whenever we feel pain, we immediately reach for an anesthetic. So it is only natural that when people feel the emotional pain of low self-esteem, they will reach for something to dull that pain—a chemical substance, a pint of ice cream, a burst of endorphins from a heavy workout, immersion in a work addiction, a new and expensive purchase, or whatever it takes to feel temporarily "okay."

Thus, Stage 2 leads directly to *Stage 3,* the addictive agent. Alcohol, drugs, food, sex, rage, spending, and even religion—these are just anesthetics for the pain of low self-esteem.

Addictive agents always bring harm to the addicted person. Which brings us to *Stage 4,* consequences. The consequences of an alcohol addiction may include broken relationships, a lost job, a lost reputation, a deadly traffic accident, a driving-under-the-influence citation, and liver disease. The consequences of a food addiction may include obesity and heart disease. The consequences of a money addiction may include loss of a credit reputation and bankruptcy.

(It is at this stage, when the consequences often mount up so high and the addicted individual has sunk so low, that healing can begin, because it is here that the addicted individual "hits bottom," and the pain is so intense that he or she is willing to do *anything* to be healed of the addiction. Usually, the individual will have to go around the cycle many times, encountering consequence after consequence, before a true "bottom" is "hit.")

After experiencing the consequences of the addiction, the individual naturally moves to *Stage 5:* guilt and shame. He or she begins to think, *I don't deserve to be happy. I don't deserve to be healthy. I don't deserve to be sexual. I don't deserve financial security.* Most experts in the field of addiction and recovery agree that, at some level, all addictions are shame-based.

As shame worms its way into the individual's soul, it festers into *Stage 6:* self-hatred. Self-hatred takes the person down to an even deeper level of emptiness and love hunger—and he or she is back at Stage 1, ready to go around again, spiraling deeper and deeper into self-destructive addiction.

RECOVERY FROM ADDICTION

Once you understand the cyclical nature of addiction, it becomes clear what you must do in order to recover from addictions: find a way to *interrupt* the cycle and escape this terrible emotional merry-go-round. You must find a way to satisfy—in a true and lasting way—the love hunger. You must raise your self-esteem and heal your emotional pain so that an emotional anesthetic (the addictive agent) is no longer needed. By intercepting and halting the use of the addictive agent, you turn off the consequences, you end the guilt and shame, you reverse the process of self-hatred . . .

And the addiction is halted.

That is why the healing of addiction requires a multidimensional approach. Addiction can never be cured by simply removing the addictive agent. The addiction is a symptom of much deeper problems at work in various dimensions of your inner makeup. To be truly healed of addiction, you must first find healing in the various dimensions of your personality, including your relationships, your feelings, your childhood memories, and your relationship with God. To experience this multidimensional form of healing, you must:

1. work through the painful memories of dysfunctional family of origin;
2. repair your present relationships (in some cases, that may mean reconciling and growing closer in relationships; but in distorted or abusive relationships, it may mean redrawing boundaries and increasing the space or safety zone in the relationship);
3. choose an affirming, supportive recovery family where you can be reparented, encouraged, and held accountable—a support group, a Twelve Step recovery group, or a healthy church community; and
4. rebuild your relationship with God.

To recover from a problem as powerful and controlling as addiction, you need a strength beyond your own. In the case of severe physical addictions, such as alcoholism, drug addiction, or food addiction, your own body is fighting you. Your body chemistry has been altered, and not for the better. Obsessions and compulsions are stronger than the human will—so you need a *supernatural* will at your side, empowering you every step of the way.

The founders of Alcoholics Anonymous—the pioneers of addiction recovery—recognized early that the spiritual dimension was crucial to recovery. They noticed that addicts demonstrated an almost universal bitterness toward God—yet God was the only hope for these people! How could these addicted men and women be drawn to call upon a God they wanted nothing to do with?

They answered this dilemma by setting down the Twelve Steps of Alcoholics Anonymous. They talked about "a Power greater than ourselves" and "God as we understood Him." Such phrases stop short of meeting our core spiritual needs, since He is not "God as we understood Him" but God as He has revealed Himself. Yet the principle God has always employed is that people who need Him can reach out to Him from wherever they are and they will be heard.

The Twelve Steps—A Spiritual Road to Recovery

The spiritual lineage of the modern recovery movement goes back even beyond the founding of Alcoholics Anonymous in the mid-1930s. Alcoholics Anonymous was actually built on the foundation of a Christian revival movement called the Oxford Group. And the Oxford Group—which was originally called "A First Century Christian Fellowship"—had its roots in the intensely committed community, fellowship, and discipleship practiced in the New Testament church. The church of Acts, the Oxford Group, and Alcoholics Anonymous all have one core objective in common: they are all earnestly committed to taking a healing message of liberation to people who are trapped in hopelessness and despair.

One of the most formative influences on Alcoholics Anonymous was Dr. Frank Buchman, a Lutheran minister and founder of the Oxford Group. During the 1908 Keswick Convention in England, Buchman had a spiritual experience in which he felt God melting away his feelings of resentment toward some people who had seriously offended him and damaged his reputation. In that experience, he realized that his resentful feelings had distanced him from God and His unconditional love. Spiritually transformed, he committed himself to a life of surrender to God, building accountable relationships with other believers and making amends for sins and wrongs against others. These principles of Buchman's life became the core principles of the Oxford Group and were later adapted and codified into the Twelve Steps of AA.

Bill W., the founder of Alcoholics Anonymous, was strongly influenced by the principles of the Oxford Group. In 1934, while hospitalized for alcoholism, Bill was confronted by his old drinking buddy, Ebby Thatcher, who had found his sobriety in the Oxford Group. "I got religion," Ebby explained, and then he proceeded to describe the spiritual principles that had pulled him out of the gutter and back onto his feet. Bill—a hardened atheist—wanted nothing to do with Ebby's God.

But a short time later, Bill's addiction brought him to the place where, in desperation more than in faith, he reached out to a God he could hardly believe in. He described his conversion experience in these words:

■

Without spiritual growth, recovery is stunted. But with God, all things are possible—even freedom from addiction.

■

My depression deepened unbearably and finally it seemed to me as though I were at the very bottom of the pit. I still gagged badly at the notion of a Power greater than myself, but finally, just for the moment, the last vestige of my proud obstinacy was crushed. All at once I found myself crying out, "If there is a God, let Him show Himself! I am ready to do anything, anything!"

Suddenly, the room lit up with a great white light. I was caught up into an ecstasy which there are no words to describe. It seemed to me, in the mind's eye, that I was on a mountain and that a wind not of air but of spirit was blowing. And then it burst upon me that I was a free man. Slowly the ecstasy subsided. I lay on the bed, but now for a time I was in another world, a new world of consciousness. All about me and through me there was a wonderful feeling of Presence, and I thought to myself, "So this is the God of the preachers!" (From *Alcoholics Anonymous Comes of Age: A Brief History of A.A.* [AAWS, 1957].)

For the next three years, Bill W. pursued his recovery through the Oxford Group. In 1935, during a business trip to Akron, he experienced a strong urge to drink. Fearing a relapse, he called church after church, asking for an alcoholic he could talk to. He knew he could only keep his own recovery by giving it away to someone else. Finally, he was put in touch with Dr. Bob Smith, a surgeon—and an alcoholic. Bill shared his story and the two of them talked long into the night. Eventually, on June 10 of 1935, Dr. Bob had his last drink—and AA historians mark that date as the founding of Alcoholics Anonymous.

In 1937, Bill W. left the Oxford Group to form his own group. He saw that some alcoholics had trouble with the Oxford Group's strong doctrines and aggressive evangelism. But though he left the Oxford Group, he kept its core principles and refashioned them into the Twelve Steps of AA.

These same Twelve Steps are the basis of our modern recovery movement today and are used as a pathway to recovery for addictions ranging from cocaine addiction to compulsive overeating to compulsive shopping to sex addiction. Approximately a million Americans are now actively involved in some 500,000 recovery groups. They are finding hope and liberation from their addictions through a series of steps that have as their basis a real, available, unlimited power:

The healing power of God.

The Twelve Steps of Alcoholics Anonymous

1. We admitted we were powerless over alcohol—that our lives had become unmanageable.
2. Came to believe that a Power greater than ourselves could restore us to sanity.
3. Made a decision to turn our will and our lives over to the care of God *as we understood Him*.
4. Made a searching and fearless moral inventory of ourselves.
5. Admitted to God, to ourselves, and to another human being the exact nature of our wrongs.
6. Were entirely ready to have God remove all these defects of character.
7. Humbly asked Him to remove our shortcomings.
8. Made a list of all persons we had harmed, and became willing to make amends to them all.
9. Made direct amends to such people wherever possible, except when to do so would injure them or others.
10. Continued to take personal inventory and when we were wrong promptly admitted it.
11. Sought through prayer and meditation to improve our conscious contact with God *as we understood Him,* praying only for knowledge of His will for us and the power to carry that out.
12. Having had a spiritual awakening as the result of these stages, we tried to carry this message to alcoholics, and to practice these principles in all our affairs.

(The Twelve Steps are reprinted with permission of Alcoholics Anonymous World Services, Inc. Permission to reprint and adapt the Twelve Steps does not mean that AA has reviewed or approved the contents of this publication, nor that AA agrees with the views expressed herein. AA is a program of recovery from alcoholism. Use of the Twelve Steps in connection with programs which are patterned after AA but which address other problems does not imply otherwise.)

How to Start a Christian Recovery Group

A Twelve Step recovery group is a fellowship of people who have come together for one purpose: to find healing from their addictions. Recovery groups come in all shapes and sizes, and they exist for a wide variety of purposes. Some recovery groups average two or three people per meeting. Some average over a hundred. Some are for men only or women only. Some are focused on a single issue, such as alcoholism, codependency, or compulsive overeating. Some gather people with various problems into a single fellowship, all focused on healing their individual addictions by working the same Twelve Steps together.

Whatever its shape, size, or focus, a recovery group should provide eight things:

1. mutual support
2. the opportunity to listen to the stories of others and learn from their experience
3. the opportunity to confront those who are in denial or otherwise hurting their own recovery
4. the opportunity to learn about addiction and its causes
5. the opportunity to gain insight into one's own issues and motivations
6. the opportunity to work through one's own resistances and penetrate one's own denial
7. the opportunity to express and ventilate emotion
8. the opportunity to become involved in helping others

Note that a *Christian* recovery group has all of these eight dynamics, plus one more: it is a fellowship with Jesus Christ at the center.

The basis of a recovery group is the support we gain in relationships. This concept is as old as the book of Genesis, where God said, "It is not good that man should be alone" (Gen. 2:18). It is not surprising, then, that the process of healing from addiction should occur within a network of relationships. Recovery is a group experience. It cannot take place in isolation.

A recovery group is a fellowship of healing, not a treatment center. An alcoholic, for example, does not go to a recovery group to get sober. He must first go to a treatment center for medically supervised detoxification. After "detox," the alcoholic joins a recovery program such as AA or a Christian Twelve Step group in order to maintain his sobriety.

How do you begin a Christian recovery group? The process begins when you, as a pastor or layperson in your church, feel a burden for people who struggle with addictions. Perhaps you are in recovery yourself. Or you may have close friends or family members in recovery.

So you pray. And you read books and literature about recovery, including the AA classics such as *Alcoholics Anonymous* ([the Big Book] 1991) and *Twelve Steps and Twelve Traditions* (1953). You study the biblical basis of the Twelve Steps. You learn the traditions that have kept AA and other recovery groups functioning for more than half a century. If you are not intimately familiar with recovery issues, seek out several recovery "old-timers" to help design the program. Next, approach the leadership of your church and ask the pastors and the church board to lend their support to a recovery group in your church.

Some of the issues that need to be settled as you design a Christian recovery group include:

Group focus. Is the group concerned with recovery from addictive behavior such as substance abuse, overeating, or workaholism, or an adult/child issue such as abuse, neglect, or incest? If so, the group is a *recovery group.* Is the group intended as a mutual support system for a stress issue such as divorce, chronic illness, or parenting? Then it is a *support group.*

Group size, structure, and membership. Effective Twelve Step groups can range in size from three or four people to more than a hundred. In a group of about twenty, everyone can have a chance to share. In recovery groups, there is no such thing as "one size fits all." Some groups are structured and include lectures, workbooks, or scheduled themes for discussion. Others (along the lines of Alcoholics Anonymous) are unstructured and spontaneous. Seating is arranged in a circle—a "room without corners." An average meeting lasts an hour to an hour and a half. Some groups have an open membership, in which people are free to come and go, but groups that demand an especially high degree of trust and confidentiality (such as incest or rape) are best structured as closed groups.

Ground rules. In order to have a safe place in which members may share their issues vulnerably and honestly, the boundaries of the group need to be settled in advance. The ground rules governing participation in the group should be spelled out in literature and referenced occasionally by group leaders.

Atmosphere of acceptance. The key to an effective recovery group is unconditional acceptance. No one is ever judged or criticized for what he or she shares in the group or for what he or she believes. Atheists and agnostics are received just as warmly as Christians. There is no condemnation, no Bible pounding in a true Christian recovery group.

In every effective recovery group, there is accountability and sometimes even confrontation (especially when a group member is clearly in denial). But the accountability is surrounded by what we call "the warm fuzzies," an atmosphere of total support and caring. By "warm fuzzies," we mean there is a bond of empathy and unconditional love—what psychologist Norm Wright calls "a perfect commitment to an imperfect person." We forgive and accept others regardless of their shortcomings—but we do not self-destruct in the process. So, for example, if there is a person in our group who is an abusive and destructive personality, who tries to control the meeting, and who is harming others in their own recovery process, we don't simply say, "Well, we must accept him and love him where he is." Without bitterness or hatred, and with as much understanding as we can muster, we firmly confront his destructive behavior.

Affiliation. A Christian recovery group is not a Bible study, nor is it an Alcoholics Anonymous meeting. It is modeled on AA, but it is not affiliated with it. A Christian Twelve Step group is a fellowship of brothers and sisters in the Lord who come together to learn how to gain control of the areas of their lives that are out of control. It is not intended to take the place of either the church or secular programs such as AA. It is, in fact, a violation of AA traditions for an AA group to be affiliated with a church (AA and similar "anonymous" groups can rent meeting space in churches but are not sponsored by churches). That is why, if we want to have recovery groups where Jesus can truly be named as the Higher Power of the Twelve Steps, we must design such groups ourselves—modeled on the AA framework and traditions but unaffiliated with Alcoholics Anonymous. As Richard Peace of Gordon-Conwell Theological Seminary says, "A church starting a Twelve Step program has to be up-front right from the beginning about the Christian roots of the Twelve Steps, and that there is going to be a focus on Christ as the spiritual dimension of recovery."

For comprehensive guidance in designing a Christian Twelve Step recovery program, contact Overcomers Outreach, 2290 W. Whittier Blvd., Suite D, La Habra, CA 90631; 213-697-3994; and read *Steps to a New Beginning* by Sam Shoemaker, Dr. Frank Minirth, Dr. Richard Fowler, Dr. Brian Newman, and Dave Carder (Thomas Nelson, 1993).

See also ALCOHOLISM; CODEPENDENCY

Aggression

In human behavior, aggression is action that is motivated by angry emotions or hostile intentions and that inflicts pain, intimidation, anxiety, or emotional suffering on another person. Acts of aggression are *not* acts that *unintentionally* cause pain or harm to others.

Some examples of aggression:

Harry was driving home from work, feeling angry and frustrated about problems at work, about the bumper-to-bumper traffic on the freeway, and about the car's air conditioner, which had decided to quit working in the heat of a muggy mid-August day in central Texas. Just as traffic was starting to move a little faster past a stretch of construction work, a battered, black Camaro cut in front of him, forcing him to hit the brakes and swerve to the right. So Harry acted instinctively and aggressively. He tromped the accelerator and sped up, pulling alongside the Camaro, honking, gesturing obscenely, and swearing—in short, acting out his aggressions.

The driver of the Camaro was prepared to escalate the level of aggression. He took a pistol from the seat beside him, pointed it out the window of his car, and fired three times. Harry wasn't hit, but the sight of those muzzle flashes, the loud popping sounds, and the shattering of his own windshield had the effect of wilting all of his aggression in a big hurry. As the Camaro sped on, Harry quickly pulled his car over to the shoulder and, for the next half hour, tried to get his pulse and respiration rate under control while he reconsidered his own aggressive behavior.

Angie continually nags her husband Rob about his appearance. "Why do you always slouch that way?" she says. "Why do you have to dress like a bum? Go put on something decent! How come you never get your hair cut until the fifth or sixth time I say you need one? Sometimes I wonder why I married such a fat slob!" Rob never answers her nagging. Sometimes, just to turn off the noise, he will change his shirt or go to the barber, but usually he will either ignore her nagging (perhaps with a sneer or a sarcastic remark behind her back or under his breath) or he will actually *increase* his sloppy behavior. Sometimes, when choosing between a clean shirt in his closet or a dirty, wrinkled shirt in the hamper, Rob will dress from the hamper—just to aggravate Angie.

When she tells him he needs to lose weight, he often goes straight to the pantry and grabs a bag of cookies or potato chips and munches them in front of her. His behavior isn't overtly hostile, violent, or raging, but it is (in a subtle, passive way) designed to offend and infuriate his wife—and it is a form of aggression.

When it comes to disciplining her daughters, ages four and seven, Cindy claims to be from the "spare the rod and spoil the child" school. But if she could see a videotape of her "discipline" style throughout a typical day, Cindy would see that she does very little true disciplining of her children. She lets them run loose, without any structure or limits—until they do something that makes her mad. When the milk spills or the lamp shatters or the miniblinds are pulled off the wall, *then* Cindy decides it's time to apply the "rod"! She screams, berates, hits, and shakes her children—and she actually believes that she is practicing biblical discipline. The truth is, she is demonstrating aggression toward her children, and she is teaching them aggressive behavior patterns.

Aggressive punishment of children can be a powerful short-term way to suppress their behavior, but psychological research shows that it tends to produce aggressive children, who in turn act out their aggressions against smaller children and seek to resolve their hostilities by screaming and hitting. Moreover, Cindy's "discipline" style is clearly unbiblical, for the Scriptures teach that parents should not provoke their children to wrath (aggressive hostility) but should bring their children up in the training and admonition of the Lord (see Ephesians 6:4).

ACTIVE AGGRESSION VERSUS PASSIVE AGGRESSION

Aggression can be acted out in a variety of ways, but these forms of aggression generally fall into one of two categories: active aggression and passive aggression. Both forms are hostile and are ways of attacking the people we see as deserving of our hostility. Active aggression is easy to spot, because it is out in the open and frequently quite loud: explosiveness, shouting, screaming, accusing, raging, intimidation, blaming, sarcasm, griping, threatening, and (in extreme cases) violence. Active aggression is the attempt to preserve one's self (that is, one's personal sense of worth, one's needs, one's convictions, one's possessions) at the expense of someone else. Even very mild-mannered people, when they feel sufficiently threatened and frustrated, can become openly, actively aggressive.

People who are actively aggressive tend to have loud, obvious struggles with people in their families, workplaces, churches, and neighborhoods. They frequently expend a lot of hostile emotional energy on petty issues and nonessentials. They feel they cannot afford to lose even the little fights, so molehills are often defended with a ferocity that is better reserved for mountains. The aggressive tendencies of actively aggressive people are often rooted in a deep sense of insecurity, which causes them to shout louder and pound the table harder in order to be sure of being heard. Whatever the issue being contested, the *real* message conveyed by the shouting is, "Notice me! Respect me! I have legitimate needs! I can't stand to be ignored!"

Active aggression is one option for expressing needs and emotions, but it is a very unhealthy and destructive option. Another option that many people choose, however, is no more healthy and constructive than active aggression. This option is called passive aggression.

People who are passive-aggressive often don't think they are being aggressive at all. They deny their anger to themselves and to others because they believe that the expression of anger is sinful or disgraceful or because they do not want to face the active aggression of other people. They may rightly recognize that active aggression creates an atmosphere of mutual hurt and disrespect, but instead of dealing with their anger openly and honestly, they take their hostilities underground. Avoiding open warfare, they choose instead a cold war of hidden agendas and sabotage. Some examples of passive-aggressive behavior:

- The silent treatment—sulking, pouting, acting hurt.
- Procrastination, laziness, chronic tardiness.
- Lying about feelings: "What do you mean? I'm not mad! I'm fine, couldn't be better!" (Often, this behavior includes contradictory messages, such as hostile body language and a verbal message that nothing is wrong.)
- Ignoring people, staring straight ahead when spoken to.
- Back-stabbing, rumor-spreading, complaining, sabotaging people, but refusing to confront them face to face.
- Engaging in behavior that one knows is irritating and aggravating, but being careful not to cross the line that would invite open conflict.

Passive aggression is an attempt to control, wound, annoy, or undermine another person without risking open conflict or confrontation. Whereas healthy relationships do not keep score regarding right and wrong, the passive-aggressive individual continually keeps score—and plays to win in the battle for superiority. Passive aggression can be as destructive as active aggression—and is often even *more* destructive. Because it is harder to confront and pin down the passive aggressor than the active aggressor, it is harder for the conflict to be positively resolved. It can be extremely difficult to penetrate the denial and evasions of a passive aggressor and bring him or her to the negotiation table for peace talks.

> ## The Characteristics of Aggressive Behavior
>
> - Seeking to punish, intimidate, or destroy anyone who offends or opposes you
> - Not caring about other people's feelings or viewpoints
> - Being stubborn, unyielding, and demanding
> - Being critical and judgmental
> - Being self-centered and self-seeking
> - Taking no notice of your own faults and weaknesses
> - Being bitter and holding grudges

AGGRESSION AND ANGER

People often confuse anger and aggressive behavior. Mr. Grady, an elder in his church, had a reputation for being bullying and intimidating when he didn't get his way. During one church meeting, when it became clear that a vote would be taken and that his was a minority position, he stood up, pointed his finger at another elder, Mr.

Stone, and shouted, "I've had enough of your hidden agendas and sneaky manipulation, Stone! You come in here and try to control everything! You lie and cheat! How dare you call yourself a Christian!" Then Mr. Grady turned and stormed out of the meeting, slamming the door so hard the windows of the building rattled.

Later, the pastor tried to confront Mr. Grady about his aggressive behavior, but the man refused to admit any wrongdoing. "Hey, when a person gets angry," said Mr. Grady, "it's unhealthy to keep it in! I was just expressing how I felt, and that's therapeutic! I'm not going to apologize for doing something that is perfectly normal and natural. If Stone or anyone else can't handle that, well, that's their problem."

Anger is normal, and there is a healthy way to express anger, but Mr. Grady was wrong about the way he "expressed" his anger. He behaved aggressively, without concern for Mr. Stone's welfare or anyone else's. In doing what he considered to be "normal" and "therapeutic" for himself, he created enormous distress for everyone else at that church meeting.

Mr. Grady had confused being *aggressive* with being *assertive*. It is possible and desirable to be assertive without being aggressive. That is what the Bible means when it says, "Be angry, and do not sin: do not let the sun go down on your wrath. . . . Let all bitterness, wrath, anger, clamor, and evil speaking be put away from you, with all malice" (Eph. 4:26, 31). Behavior that is associated with wrath, bitterness, evil speaking, and malice is aggressive behavior, and it is sin. Assertive behavior, however, is healing and restoring.

Aggressive behavior is a reflection of our human sin nature. All of us, including Christians, have a battle raging within—a battle between our will to sin and our will to obey God, between hostile aggression and love. By understanding the true nature of aggression, we can be better prepared to deal with our anger in a way that is healthy for ourselves and others. We can learn how to be angry and not sin.
See also ANGER

> ### The Characteristics of Assertive Behavior
>
> - Seeking to help others, even in an angry or confrontational situation
> - Seeking to understand the feelings and intentions of others
> - Being flexible and seeking solutions and alternatives
> - Being willing to examine your own faults
> - Being forgiving and allowing for the fact that people make mistakes
> - Caring about the needs of others
> - Continually seeking self-improvement, not just victories in fights and arguments

Aging

We call them "the golden years," those years beyond age sixty (or thereabouts). For some people, those years truly are "golden." It is a time when the "rat race" of career and competition are over, and they can relax and enjoy the accumulated rewards of a lifetime. There is wisdom and peace that comes from years of experience. There is a perspective that only time can bring. Many senior adults can look back over their lives and say, "It's been a great life, but *these* are truly the *best* years of my life! I still have a lot to look forward to." The Bible makes it clear that God cares for people in their "golden years." "Even to your old age," says Isaiah 46:4, "I am He, and even to gray hairs I will carry you! . . . I will carry, and will deliver you."

PROBLEMS OF AGING

For many people, however, these years are not so "golden." As people grow older, they often experience problems such as:

- emotional losses
- depression
- hearing loss
- illness
- memory loss
- personality changes
- increased dependency

In the following sections, we will examine each of these issues of aging and how senior adults—and the people who love them—can respond to these issues to make these years as "golden" as possible.

Emotional Losses

When Daniel lost his wife of fifty-four years, he grieved, he cried, and he worked through his grief. He was just at a point where he was getting involved with his old activities and friends again, when suddenly he went into a deep depression. He wouldn't eat, he slept most of the day, his weight began to drop, and when he talked at all, he usually talked about dying. His son and daughter became alarmed about his condition and came to a Minirth Meier New Life Clinic for advice on how to help their father pull out of his life-threatening depression.

"What has been going on in your father's life lately?" the therapist asked. "Have there been any serious losses since your mother's death?"

"No, none," the grown children replied.

"None at all?"

"Well," said the daughter, "nothing major. There were only two things that happened around the time he went into his depression, but neither was anywhere near as serious as losing Mom."

"Well, what two things happened in Daniel's life?" asked the therapist.

"The motor vehicle department refused to renew his license, but that's no big deal," said Daniel's son. "After all, Dad hardly drove at all anymore—just to the grocery store and to church, and the HandyRide service can get him anyplace he needs to go. And the other thing was the dog."

"What dog?"

"I bought him a puppy after Mom died," said Daniel's daughter. "The puppy got out and was run over by a car—but he couldn't have been too attached to it. He only

46

had the dog a few months. After all, something like losing your driver's license and losing your dog wouldn't make you more depressed than losing your wife after fifty-four years, would it?"

The fact is, it could. Losses can affect senior adults in different and unexpected ways. Some of the losses experienced by senior adults include:

- loss of spouse
- loss of friends and family members
- loss of health
- loss of freedom and physical mobility
- financial losses
- loss of dreams, ambitions, and goals

It is easy to see how some of these losses—such as the loss of a mate—can create an enormous emotional hole in the life of a senior adult. Other losses, such as the loss of a driver's license or the realization that a cherished dream will never be fulfilled, are less tangible but often quite painful. All of these losses, whether tangible or intangible, must be fully and successfully grieved in order for the senior adult to get on with a healthy, satisfied life.

Sometimes, as in Daniel's case, the senior adult's response to loss will seem confusing and disproportionate. A minor loss may appear to be grieved more intensely than a major loss, such as the loss of a spouse.

> ## How Can You Help a Grieving Senior Adult?
>
> Here are some ways you can help a senior adult to continue making progress toward grief recovery after a major loss:
>
> 1. Encourage the grieving person to talk about the loss. Invite that person to share memories, whether happy or sad.
> 2. Listen nonjudgmentally. Help this person reexperience events and emotions that have been in the background for years.
> 3. Help the individual to remain connected with a support system (church, Bible study, grief support groups or classes).
> 4. Encourage the senior adult to maintain healthy routines and functioning: friendships, activities, personal hygiene, spiritual pursuits.

Many factors go into a person's reaction to a loss and help to determine whether or not that person's response to the loss will be healthy or unhealthy. Those factors include:

The timing of the loss. When losses come bunched together, they can overload a person's ability to respond to them. As in Daniel's case, a couple of minor losses following a major loss may be just enough additional stress to tip a person into a deep, dangerous depression. A person might respond to one loss by saying, "That was a terrible loss, but I'll get through this. I still have a life to lead." But that same person, by the third or fourth loss, may say, "Life is just too painful. I can't deal with this anymore." When Daniel lost his driver's license and his pet just a few months after the death of his wife, this cluster of losses became more than he could handle.

The meaning of the loss. The loss of a driver's license may not seem like a major loss, especially in the life of someone who rarely drives anymore. But the loss of that driver's license had cataclysmic emotional implications for Daniel. It was a major life transition to discover he could no longer just get in a car and go wherever he wanted. His freedom was limited. His competence was called into question. The loss—though minor in terms of its practical significance—had enormous emotional and symbolic significance. It said to Daniel, "Your life is over."

The upsetting of life's equilibrium. If a major loss occurs during a time of relative calm and stability in life, it will be painful but probably endurable. But if a major loss occurs at a time when a person is already emotionally off-balance because of financial problems, emotional stresses, family conflicts, and the like, then that loss could well be the shattering event that finally topples that person off the tightrope.

The circumstances surrounding the loss. If a senior adult loses a mate suddenly and unexpectedly at a time when the individual seems to have a great deal more living to do, that loss will probably seem more shocking, senseless, and painful than if the loss comes as a "release" after that mate has undergone a long battle against cancer, Alzheimer's disease, or some other chronic or debilitating condition. Also, if the senior adult experiences self-blame over the loss (whether or not that blame is valid), the grieving experience will be much more painful and intense.

Some Cautionary Words About the Grieving Process

Grief is a highly individualized process. No two people experience it at the same rate or in the same way. The stages of grief are only an approximation of the way people generally process grief. The actual progression of those stages will vary from person to person.

If someone close to you is going through the grief process, you may experience anxiety and emotional discomfort, coupled with a desire to hurry your loved one through the process. But a grieving person needs time to work through those feelings. Avoid the temptation to make yourself feel better by telling the grieving person to shut off his or her emotions.

If you suspect that your loved one is experiencing depression and despair that go beyond the usual depths of the grief experience, it is important to have that person assessed by a geriatric psychiatrist.

The grief process—the famous stages of grief popularized by Swiss psychiatrist Elisabeth Kübler-Ross—can progress in some unexpected ways in the life of a senior adult. (For more discussion, see DEPRESSION and GRIEF AND LOSS.) It is important to remember that this process normally occurs in response to any major loss in life—the death of a loved one, the loss of one's health or of one's life savings, or the impending loss of one's own life. For a younger or middle-aged adult, this process may take months or years to work through. In our geriatric experience, however, we often see this process follow a much shorter course in the life of a grieving senior adult. In many cases, an individual will suffer a loss and move (like an emotional express elevator!) right from denial all the way down to despair in a single plunge. If that person cannot move beyond the despair level, he or she is likely to settle into a severe and possibly life-threatening depression.

Depression

The principal warning sign of clinical depression after a loss is *a lack of progress in dealing with the loss (being "stuck")*. A long grieving period—several months to even two or three years—is not unusual or unhealthy in and of itself. During that period, however, you should see *some* progress in that person's emotional state on a consistent basis. You should see a gradual resumption of relationships with friends, involvement in activities and hobbies, and improvement in mood. If that person remains emotionally paralyzed, withdrawn, and nonfunctional, then he or she may be sliding into a deep clinical depression.

Other warning signs of clinical depression include sleeping disorders (frequently interrupted sleep, too much sleep, too little sleep, an inability to get to sleep); a long-term loss of appetite; evidence of sadness or anger feelings that last longer than three or four months; frequent crying; loss of interest in favorite activities (friendships, hobbies, recreational pursuits, affiliations, church); sitting alone and staring; and chronic lack of attention to grooming and personal hygiene. If you are dealing with a senior adult who shows signs of clinical depression, here are some actions you should take:

- Encourage the individual to undergo a full medical evaluation. A physician will look for physical problems that contribute to depression, such as depletion or imbalances of brain chemicals, nutrient deficiencies, medication problems, or glandular malfunction. There are many organic problems that can affect one's emotional state, and a geriatric specialist or psychiatrist can help identify and treat those problems.
- Be alert to any distorted thinking by the senior adult, as evidenced by such statements as, "Everyone would be better off without me," or "I'm just in the way." It is important that senior adults be assured of their continuing meaning and importance in the family.
- Be alert to any expressions of suicidal feelings. If a senior adult says, "I wish I could die," don't hesitate to discuss those feelings with that person, calmly and honestly. Avoid expressions of shock or judgment; be empathetic and understanding. If the individual appears to have a suicide plan, take positive action. Remove any means of suicide from the individual's reach and don't leave him or her alone. Immediately contact a therapist or suicide prevention agency.

Hearing Loss

Hearing loss is a significant communication problem for one-third of all women over sixty-five and half of all men over sixty-five. Though most age-related hearing problems can be alleviated by a hearing aid, roughly two-thirds of those who need hearing aids neglect or refuse to wear one, in large part because they consider hearing aids to be an embarrassing symbol of "getting old."

Aging often brings about a condition called *presbycusis,* a degeneration of the inner ear mechanism. This condition causes decreased sensitivity to high frequencies and a loss of ability to discriminate among the distinct sounds of speech. People with this condition can hear sounds, but the sounds they hear are muffled, indistinct, and difficult to understand. Every senior adult should have a periodic hearing evaluation, and a person who is experiencing problems understanding conversations should be tested by a physician. If a hearing problem is discovered that can be helped by a hearing aid, the doctor will write a prescription for the hearing device that is required for that particular form of hearing loss.

When senior adults experience hearing loss, there are simple steps that can be taken, by the senior adult and by those around him or her, that can make communication easier and more pleasant. These steps can be beneficial to the family relationships and communication and to the emotional health of the senior adult.

If you have a hearing impairment: When having conversations, avoid places where there is a lot of background noise—crowds, TVs, open windows with street noise. Avoid places where noise and echoes interfere with conversations, such as room corners with a lot of tile, plaster, or glass. Find a place to sit that is surrounded by upholstery, drapery, carpet, acoustical tile—places where background noise is absorbed instead of bounced around. If you don't understand what someone says, ask him or her to repeat it or to speak more distinctly and slowly.

If you are talking to someone with a hearing impairment: Don't shout, just speak a little louder, a little more clearly and carefully, and in briefer sentences. Even if the hearing-impaired person is not a lip-reader, it helps if that person can see your lips as you speak, so look him or her squarely in the face. Show that you are interested in the senior adult's feelings and thoughts; include that person in your conversation with a slightly elevated voice level and eye contact.

Illness

As the body ages, various systems in the body tend to operate at reduced efficiency. Bones become brittle through loss of calcium. The body becomes more susceptible to viral infection, so it becomes very important to ensure proper nutrition and have annual flu vaccinations. For obvious reasons, senior adults are more likely than any other age group to require medical attention and hospitalization. The fear of illness, debilitation, and hospitalization is great among senior adults. If you have a senior adult loved one, here are some suggestions for reducing that person's anxiety over potential illness and for making sure he or she gets the best possible care:

- Help the senior adult choose a doctor and a hospital that will be understanding of the special medical and emotional needs of geriatric patients. Check with friends, your pastor, and health care professionals to find doctors and hospitals that are known for dealing effectively and caringly for the medical and emotional needs of senior adults.
- Many senior adults tend to be submissive and intimidated in dealing with health care providers. They may need you to be assertive on their behalf. Be assertive, but *do not be abrasive*. With courtesy and respect, communicate to the hospital staff about the needs of the senior adult.
- Go with that person on doctor visits. Listen to the doctor's explanations, ask questions (particularly questions the senior adult might not think to ask), take notes, explain and interpret information, and help the individual sort through the medical options and decisions.
- Be aware of the senior adult's spiritual needs during an illness or hospitalization. Contact his or her church so that needs can be shared with prayer partners and so that Christian friends and a pastoral staff member can arrange to make a hospital visit. Pray with the senior adult and read Scripture or Christian books to him or her.

To a senior adult, physical illness is a tangible reminder of physical mortality. For some, life is a trial of illness, hospital confinement, invasive medical procedures, chronic pain, or living in a wheelchair. Those who are able to deal most effectively with chronic or terminal illness are those who can trust in God to ease their pain and to exchange their aging bodies for new, purified bodies in eternity.

Dr. Robert Hemfelt of the Minirth Meier New Life Clinics told us about his mother, who suffered from hip pain in her mid-seventies. She demonstrated the attitude that aging people need to have in order to face the issue of chronic or terminal pain. "I'm getting ready to lay down this body," she said. "After all, it's got a lot of mileage on it." Later, Mrs. Hemfelt suffered a heart attack and experienced kidney failure. Though the doctors told her they could keep her alive indefinitely on dialysis, she opted to forego heroic measures and to let nature have its way. "My body is a vehicle I picked up at birth, and I'll lay it down at death," she said, and two weeks later she peacefully went home to be with her Lord.

Memory Loss

Upon reaching age sixty-five, the average person has lost about 25 percent of his or her original 10 billion brain cells. That is one reason that, in older people, we usually see some deterioration in remembering, memorizing, focusing, and thinking. Normally, this loss of mental acuity is minor—after all, the average senior adult still has about 7.5 billion fully functioning brain cells!

But with aging come additional factors, beyond mere cell loss, that may accentuate memory loss. For example, the experiences of aging—such as loss, grief, or depression—can alter the balance of important brain chemicals called *neurotransmitters*. If there is a drop in the level of a neurotransmitter called *serotonin,* the individual can experience a decreased ability to focus and remember and may also display symptoms of moodiness, depression, and irritability.

Paradoxically, a person's memory processing capacity begins to slow down at just the time that he or she has the most knowledge to process—in fact, an entire lifetime of memories, experience, and learning. Many older people seem to forget facts or grope for words or information, but this doesn't mean they are becoming "senile." In the average senior adult, the memories are, in fact, still properly stored in the brain, but it takes a little longer for the "central processing unit" of the brain to access those memories.

There are essentially three broad categories of memory loss common to senior adults:

1. The normal mild slowdown of memory access that most aging adults experience.
2. Treatable, reversible memory impairments that result from drug reactions, illnesses, nutritional imbalances, injuries, or emotional issues. (Depression, loneliness, and even the fear of forgetfulness can aggravate memory loss.)
3. Alzheimer's disease, in which memory loss is irreversible.

Just the words "Alzheimer's disease" are enough to strike dread in the hearts of most people. It is common for people, when they or their loved ones experience one of the first two categories of memory loss above, to assume the worst and believe they are witnessing the first stages of Alzheimer's. It is important at such times to reassure ourselves and others that it is perfectly common and normal for a senior adult to forget details, to "draw a blank" on a friend's name, or to miss an appointment. Only a small percentage of the population (about 7 percent of those over age sixty-five) will ever develop Alzheimer's disease or a similar mentally degenerative condition. A little forgetfulness—though it can be *one* of the signs of early Alzheimer's—is also just a fact of life as we get older. (See ALZHEIMER'S DISEASE.)

But though a little forgetfulness may be normal in a senior adult, signs of significant forgetfulness or confusion should not be ignored or simply dismissed as part of "old age." Many times, these symptoms are the effects of temporary, treatable disorders, so a person who has such symptoms should always be seen by a physician. Often, one's ability to remember, concentrate, communicate, and enjoy life can be substantially improved with treatment.

Personality Changes

One of the most disturbing features of aging is how it often causes people we love to experience changes in personality. People we have looked up to for years as models of generosity, cordiality, kindness, courage, and faith may suddenly become self-centered, withdrawn, irritable, fearful, or bitter. Like memory loss, personality changes are often the result of lost brain cells. As mental functions change, reasoning, concentration, and judgment may be impaired. Behavior may become more extreme, unsociable, and even childish as the inhibitory centers of the brain—those centers that manage our emotions, our behavior, and our desires—begin to function less effectively.

Aging and the stress of emotional losses can contribute to chemical imbalances in the brain that affect the personality. For example, when a neurotransmitter called *dopamine* becomes too active in the brain, a person can experience hallucinations, delusions (irrational beliefs), and paranoia (the belief that one is being spied on, attacked, or conspired against). Another factor that can contribute to personality changes is a degenerative neurological disease such as Alzheimer's disease. Symptoms such as slurred speech, confusion, memory loss, and personality changes are indications that a person needs medical evaluation.

Increased Dependency

Chad and his wife have a decision to make. Chad's mother has been living independently in her own home ever since Chad's father died nine years ago. But lately it is becoming clear that Chad's mother is not as capable of living alone as she once was. Not long ago, she accidentally started a fire in the kitchen while preparing her dinner. A neighbor helped put out the fire before it could do much damage—but Chad shudders to think what *could* have happened. And two months earlier, she fell and, according to the doctor, could have easily broken her hip.

Chad is convinced that his mother can no longer live alone at home. So the decision Chad now faces is this: Should Chad place his mother in a nursing home or bring her home to live with him and his family?

This is a decision many people face regarding their senior adult parents. Some of the questions that need to be considered before inviting an aging parent to move in are:

- Does my parent need more care and attention than I can provide?
- Would it disrupt my family to have Mom or Dad move in with us?
- Is my parent manipulative or controlling?
- What are my real reasons for wanting to invite Mom or Dad to live with us? Am I really concerned about what's best for my parent? Or am I feeling guilty?

52

Our experience at the clinic suggests that it is rarely wise for senior adult parents to move in with their children. It becomes difficult for the family to maintain good boundaries. Husband and wife find it difficult to exercise discipline or deal with conflict in the presence of their senior adult parents. Family systems become disrupted. And a significantly dependent senior adult needs more intensive attention and caring than most people can supply.

Once your parent has come to live with you, it is very awkward to turn around and say, "Oops, we made a mistake! We've decided you need to live someplace else." Don't enter into this commitment without a lot of thought and counsel. Taking care of a dependent adult is a big and often stressful full-time job. Research shows that people who take care of elderly parents are more likely than the average person to experience depression, high blood pressure, ulcers, and other stress-related disorders. Don't take on this job unless you are sure you are up to it. If you do decide to care for an aging parent at home, we suggest you join a support group for caregivers of senior adults to help you deal with the issues and stresses of the job.

In most cases, we suggest that individuals who are concerned about the welfare of their senior adult parents consider some of the following options:

> ### Making a Nursing Home into a Home
>
> **If you make a decision to place your senior adult parent in a nursing or convalescent home, there are ways to improve the transition process and the quality of life for your parent:**
>
> 1. Involve your parent in all decisions.
> 2. Communicate to your parent that he or she is not losing a home, just moving to a new address. Reaffirm your love and continued involvement in his or her life in the years to come.
> 3. When your parent moves to the new home, throw a "housewarming" party, with gifts and streamers and balloons.
> 4. Help your parent select photos and keepsakes that will make the nursing home environment seem more like home.
> 5. Make a point of taking your parent out of the nursing home every so often for a visit with old friends and relatives, lunch at a restaurant, shopping, or some other enjoyable outing.

- a private duty nurse or companion in the parents' home;
- an "assisted-living" residential facility that provides apartment-style independence and privacy along with part-time nursing care;
- a nursing home or convalescent home; or
- at-home care combined with regular "extended weekend care" or "respite care," giving you and your family a brief weekend break from caring for Mom or Dad.

FACING—AND GRIEVING— YOUR MORTALITY

Arthur is in his early seventies and has just been diagnosed with terminal cancer. He is bitter and depressed. "My life is over," he moans. "This is the end."

Bernice is in her late sixties. She, too, has just been diagnosed with inoperable cancer. Ted, her husband, is already grieving—but amazingly, Bernice is smiling. "Don't be sad for me, Ted. I'd like to stay with you a few more years, but I'm going home instead. I know this will be very hard on you, Ted, but please, let's try to celebrate.

When I die, I don't want a funeral. I'd really be pleased if you would give me a 'going home party' instead."

These are two very different reactions to a universal human experience: death and dying. One of the inevitable aspects of aging is that it is a stage of preparation for the inevitable outcome of life—death. The so-called "golden years" are in fact a time of preparation for the final transition, a time in which to face our mortality. Certainly, we will grieve for our mortal life, which—as we approach the close of life—seems all too short. We will experience the stages of grief: a period of denial, of anger, perhaps some attempt to bargain with God, followed by depression and sadness. But if we work through our grief, we will come to a place of acceptance and, in many cases, celebration. *Celebration?* Yes, because, from a Christian perspective, both death and birth mark the beginning of a new life.

There was a time, not long ago, when people had a clearer sense that death was a gateway to a new beginning. Decades ago, when most people died at home with their families around them rather than in a hospital, entire families could witness death and see with their own eyes how a dying person felt and responded at the very brink of death. They could see how death so often came—not as a "last gasp" struggle, but as a release, as a voluntary letting go of life. Some people, as they slip in and out of consciousness in the last hours of their life, have been known to question whether they are still on earth or in heaven. They are so eager to make the transition from this life to the next that they become annoyed that they haven't died yet!

Have you truly come to a place where nothing matters to you next to the joy of knowing Jesus? Have you said good-bye to all the false idols you have clung to throughout your life? Have you made your peace and placed your trust completely in Jesus to save you and carry you through that gateway called death, and to bring you safely into your new life in Him?

Not everyone lets go of life so easily and gently, of course. Some, as they die, grip the sheets or latch on to the people around them, struggling to stay in this life to the last moment. What makes the difference between those who are ready and even eager to go and those who seemingly have to be pried out of their mortal bodies at the moment of their death? The difference lies in how people view life and death. Those who view death as an end of everything good and meaningful will fight until their last breath. Those who view death as a beginning will welcome death. Those who view death as something that invalidates life will view death with dread. Those who view death as that which completes this life will have no fear of death's finality.

If you are in advanced years, this is the time to prepare yourself for that final transition—not in a morbid or depressed way, but with a goal of successfully, joyfully completing your life. Whether your health is declining or holding strong, now is the time to make the positive decisions that will transform the close of your life into a celebration of a life well lived. Now is the time to:

Put your legal affairs in order. Over a third of all Americans die intestate (without a will). If you love the ones you leave behind, you should be sure to have an up-to-date will, prepared by an attorney. If you are leaving real property (such as a house), do not leave it to a number of heirs with undivided interests—for example, four children each with 25 percent ownership. Such arrangements could create family squabbles down the road when one heir wants to sell the property and the others do not. Arrange in your will to have the property sold and the proceeds divided.

Put your emotional affairs in order. If you are afraid of death, you need to ask yourself why. In our experience as therapists, we frequently find that people who are haunted by a strong apprehension about death have an underlying fear about life and living. Perhaps you are afraid of not having enough money to carry you through your retirement years. Perhaps you are anxious about an unhealed relationship. Or you may have unresolved emotions about some traumatic event in your past. We would encourage you to work through your emotional issues, preferably with a Christian counselor or therapist. In many cases, people who resolve their emotional misgivings about life are able at the same time to resolve their apprehension about death.

Put your relational affairs in order. Finish unfinished business. Where possible, mend broken relationships. Where necessary, seek and offer forgiveness.

Put your funeral affairs in order. Discuss with your spouse (or whoever will be responsible for carrying out your wishes) what you would like your funeral to be. Listen to your spouse's feelings on the subject. Put the plans in writing and keep them in a safe place where they can easily be located in the event of your death. (Do not put this or any other important document related to your death in a bank safe deposit box, since these boxes are often sealed upon the box-renter's demise. Leave it in the care of an attorney, trusted friend, or family member.)

Facing the fact that a funeral will, indeed, be held in your honor is a healthy step toward grieving and releasing your mortality. Some people may say, "How morbid!" But there is nothing morbid about facing the inevitable. Successfully grieving your mortality frees you to accept God's ultimate plan for you and enables you to live the years ahead fully, joyfully, and with a new freedom.

Put your spiritual affairs in order. What is the ultimate end of life? What are we here for? What was it all about, once it is all over? The non-Christian possesses no good hope at all. The Christian? All through his or her Christian experience, this person has been talking about faith in Christ. Now that faith is put to the test. The time for spiritual surrender has arrived. There are no more props or distractions in life. All the things that obscure the reality of eternity from our view have been stripped away. The core reality of life and death have been laid bare. There is no earthly person—no parent, no spouse, no pastor, no spiritual guide—who can shield you from the inevitability of death. At last you can turn your heart completely toward God.

If you have faced your own pending death honestly and squarely, then death becomes not only the last goodbye. It is truly the ultimate hello.

Alcoholism

Though illegal drugs such as cocaine and methamphetamines get most of the attention from the press and the public, the greatest drug problem in our society comes not from illegal drugs but from that perfectly legal, freely available drug called alcohol.

Nearly three-fourths of all Americans drink to some extent, and almost 10 percent of all Americans are heavy drinkers, consuming two or more drinks a day. Roughly 10 percent of all Americans—nearly twenty million people—will eventually become addicted to alcohol. This legal drug is the number three leading cause of death in our society, and a major factor in crimes of violence, suicides, and automobile deaths. Alcoholism also produces suffering and death by destroying the healthy functioning of the body. Cirrhosis of the liver, hepatitis, and delirium tremens are a few of the effects that long-term exposure to alcohol can have on the body and the mind.

SYMPTOMS OF ALCOHOLISM

There is an invisible line between alcohol abuse and alcohol addiction; not every person who gets drunk is an alcoholic. How, then, can you know if you or someone you care about has crossed that invisible line from abuse to addiction? Here are some of the warning signs:

1. *Withdrawal symptoms when alcohol intake is interrupted.* Withdrawal symptoms include intense anxiety, pronounced trembling ("the shakes") during the first twelve hours after withdrawal, irritability and anger, stomach or intestinal upset, and generalized discomfort. Withdrawal from alcohol should only be attempted under medical supervision in a hospital because (1) there is a greater chance that the withdrawal will be completed if it is supervised, and (2) in some cases, the withdrawal symptoms can be extreme and life-threatening, such as grand mal seizures, hallucinations, and delirium tremens.
2. *An inability to function appropriately in social, school, or work situations.* Alcoholism often leads to missed work, violence, drunk driving, lost jobs, and conflicts with friends and family.
3. *Telltale bodily symptoms.* Alcohol odor on the breath, tremors, flushed face, unexplained injuries (which may have occurred while intoxicated).
4. *Increased tolerance to the effects of alcohol.* Increased tolerance requires increased consumption in order to produce the "high" or the "buzz"—which means spiraling consumption and deepening dependency.
5. *Daily alcohol use in order to function.* Inability to curtail or stop drinking in spite of repeated attempts, habitual inability to sleep without a "nightcap" or two, drinking early in the morning.
6. *Alcohol-related illnesses.* Cirrhosis of the liver, hepatitis, gastritis, cerebellar brain degeneration, blood coagulation disorders, neuropathy, chronic brain syndrome (which affects thinking), and (in infants of alcohol-abusing women) fetal alcohol syndrome—birth defects, low birth weight, and/or mental retardation. Alcoholism is particularly acute in cases where the patient continues drinking despite such medical complications.

WHAT CAUSES ALCOHOLISM?

Many people drink alcohol for years and never develop an addiction. Others seem to become alcoholics quite soon after they begin drinking. There is currently no way to tell which person is going to become addicted and which will never be vulnerable to addiction. There are, however, several theories as to the underlying causes of alcoholism.

One theory holds that there is a link between genetics and alcoholism, and researchers have identified a specific gene that they believe predisposes some people to alcohol addiction. This would partially explain why alcoholism often seems to run in families (although environment—the fact that children learn about alcohol abuse from their parents—is an equally valid explanation). It is important to note that not everyone with this gene becomes an alcoholic. What is distressing about this theory is that some alcoholics, upon learning about this theory, misinterpret it as meaning they are *doomed* to alcoholism—and so they surrender to it. No one is doomed to die an alcoholic. A genetic disposition to alcoholism is just one factor of many, and all of these factors can be overcome.

Another theory holds that alcoholism is a learned response to problems and stress. Alcohol is a sedative that temporarily assuages the anxiety and emotional pain of present problems and past memories. People learn (often by watching alcohol-abusing friends or family members) that intoxication enables a person to avoid unpleasant feelings and situations. They also learn to use alcohol as an excuse for socially unacceptable behavior, such as fighting or flirting: "Don't blame him. He didn't know what he was doing. He had a few drinks in him."

The personality theory provides another explanation for alcoholism, suggesting that people with certain types of personality disorders are most likely to become addicts. Most addiction researchers agree that acute alcoholics usually display traits of a passive-dependent or passive-aggressive disorder. A passive-dependent personality is characterized by a failure to assume responsibility for his or her own life; he or she behaves indecisively, acts helpless, has a negative and self-defeating attitude, is inconsiderate and immature, and is easily depressed. A passive-aggressive personality is secretly hostile and resentful, tends to passively rebel against demands that he or she perform according to certain standards, and uses subtle means to sabotage his or her own performance for the purpose of aggravating others: being chronically late; making chronic mistakes; habitually forgetting important responsibilities; and drinking to impair performance.

Other personality disorders that can predispose people to alcoholism include the obsessive-compulsive disorder (perfectionists who feel conditionally accepted, and who drink to anesthetize the pain and resentment that accompanies imperfection and failure) and the sociopathic disorder (people-users who cheat and exploit others without conscience).

Whatever the causes of alcoholism, the treatments are roughly the same. The cure must take place in four phases (see "The Warning Signs and Treatment of Substance Abuse" under ADDICTION).

THE CHRISTIAN AND ALCOHOL

It comes as a surprise to most Christians that the statistics regarding alcoholism are virtually identical for Christians and non-Christians and that problem drinking is a hidden but very real issue in the Protestant church. Social drinking has become much more accepted in Christian circles than in previous years, so that nearly two-thirds of all Protestants—including large numbers of conservative evangelicals—now acknowledge having at least an occasional drink.

To be an evangelical is no longer automatically the equivalent of being a teetotaler. Previous generations of Christians were often warned from the pulpit about the "evils of alcohol" (though they were perhaps inadequately warned about the relational, emotional, and medical dangers of alcohol). Today, however, pastors rarely mention the subject—except, perhaps, to criticize those "narrow" and "rigid" Christians who still do oppose the use of alcohol.

At the clinic, we have seen an enormous number of lives and families—including many *Christian* lives and families—that have been ruined by alcohol. So we have a passionate desire to see Christians take this issue very seriously, become informed of the issue of chemical addiction (including addiction to alcohol), and become educated about the symptoms, prevention, addiction, and recovery aspects of this enormous social tragedy. To any Christian who drinks or who is considering taking up drinking, we would pose one question:

What benefits of drinking alcohol can you point to that would outweigh the obvious costs, risks, and tragedies that result from this legal but dangerous drug?

Alzheimer's Disease

Alzheimer's disease is an incurable degenerative disease of the brain, specifically affecting the nerve cells of the frontal and temporal lobes of the cerebrum. The disease was first described in 1906 by the German neuropathologist Alois Alzheimer, who discovered the condition during an autopsy of a fifty-five-year-old patient who had died with severe *dementia* (literally, "loss of mind"). During the autopsy, Alzheimer discovered abnormalities in the brain that we now know to be associated with the disease.

Because it used to be thought normal that people would lose their mental faculties with advanced age, the diagnosis of Alzheimer's disease was once applied only in cases where there was a loss of mental faculties at an early age—say, in one's thirties through sixties. Alzheimer's cases that occurred in people seventy or over were chalked up to "senile dementia." We now know, however, that Alzheimer's disease is the largest single cause of dementia regardless of age.

The symptoms of Alzheimer's disease include memory loss, language impairment, impaired reasoning capacity, problems with visual spatial abilities, personality changes (ranging from apathy to irritability), depression, delusions, and hallucinations. There may be alternating periods of increase and decline of the severity of the symptoms, but the symptoms inevitably worsen, and there is no known cure. In September 1993, the U.S. Food and Drug Administration approved a drug called tacrine that, though not a cure, may relieve some symptoms in certain patients.

Anyone who shows signs of confusion, forgetfulness, or other unusual behavior should be medically evaluated without delay. There are many conditions that occur during the aging process that, at first glance, give the mistaken appearance of early Alzheimer's. Many of these conditions are temporary and reversible if properly treated.

The risk of developing Alzheimer's disease is less than one in one hundred before age fifty but increases sharply thereafter, to one in fourteen at age sixty-five, one in four at age eighty, and almost one in three at age ninety. People with immediate family members with Alzheimer's are considered to have an increased risk of getting the disease. Researchers believe that both genetic and environmental factors may have a major contributory role in the disease.

Alzheimer's affects some two million Americans. The cause of the disease is still unknown, but we do know that the disease is accompanied by such abnormalities as:

- neurofibrillary tangles—fibrous structures within the nerve cells
- neuritic plaques, composed of degenerating nerve-cell elements and amyloid protein
- accumulation of aluminum in neuritic plaques and tangled neurons
- decreases in brain chemicals called *neurotransmitters*—substances such as acetylcholine, serotonin, norepinephrine, and somatostatin

What we don't yet know is whether these abnormalities cause Alzheimer's disease or whether the disease causes these abnormalities. The answer to this "chicken-and-egg" question may one day yield clues that would point us toward a cure for this tragic disease.

Anger

When most people think of anger, they imagine a person in a rage. They picture red faces, slamming doors, shouting, and intimidation. Certainly this is one aspect of anger, but anger is not a one-dimensional emotion. It is multifaceted and complex and should not be stereotyped. Anger is a universal human experience that can be found in any personality and temperament—shy or extroverted, perfectionistic or laid-back—and it can be expressed in many ways. We use the term *anger* to describe a number of feelings and behaviors: frustration, irritability, annoyance, blowing off steam, fretting. In order to manage anger effectively, productively, and in a way that is honoring to God, it is important to realize how each of these reactions is tied to the emotion we call anger.

SEVEN STEPS TOWARD EFFECTIVE ANGER MANAGEMENT

Step 1: Learn to recognize the many faces of anger. Richard was an easygoing man in his late twenties. He was raised in a Christian home where the biblical proverb, "A soft answer turns away wrath," was quoted more frequently than John 3:16. He couldn't recall a time when his mother and father ever had an argument, and none of Richard's friends could recall a time when he ever raised his voice in anger.

Richard's wife, Ellen, is another story. Raised in a large family, coming from what she calls "a hot-blooded ethnic background where screaming is just our way of saying, 'I love you,'" Ellen was never shy about expressing her anger. Freely. Exuberantly. Loudly. At the drop of a hat.

These contrasting styles of dealing with anger (or, in Richard's case, *not* dealing with it) were a major source of conflict in their marriage. Richard always felt threatened by Ellen's anger—and he also felt smugly self-righteous. "You really need to deal with your problem, Ellen," he would tell her. "As Christians, we're not supposed to blow up like this. Remember Proverbs 15:1: 'A soft answer turns away wrath, but a harsh word stirs up anger.'"

After being lectured by her husband on the evils of anger for the umpteenth time, Ellen decided it was time to provoke a showdown. After he quoted his favorite verse of Scripture, she responded, "Are you telling me you *never* get angry, Richard?"

"I give my anger to the Lord," he said softly.

"Ah," said Ellen, taking a handful of CDs from the rack atop the stereo. "Well, I'm glad you can be so spiritual and mature about your feelings."

"What are you doing?" asked Richard, a quizzical expression on his face.

"I'm going to see if you are really as saintly as you profess," she said, placing the stack of CDs on the floor at her feet. "Do you know what these are?"

"Oh, no. You wouldn't—"

Is anger good or bad? The answer: It all depends. There are times when anger is incorrectly associated with trivial matters. And there are times when anger may be associated with legitimate concerns but is managed irresponsibly. For example, it is legitimate to become angry if you see someone mistreating an animal. But it would be an irresponsible use of your anger to take up a gun and shoot the person who is mistreating the animal.

"These are your favorite CDs in the whole world."

"No," begged Richard, advancing toward Ellen but knowing he was too late, "not my Bela Fleck and the Flecktones collection!"

"Bingo," said Ellen—then she leaped up into the air and came down with both feet on the CDs. Shards of plastic flew in a hundred directions.

Richard's jaw dropped and he stared in dismay at the ruins of his favorite banjo jazz music.

"You still say you aren't angry, Richard?"

Richard turned without a word. In fact, he didn't say a word to Ellen for the next two weeks. When he finally spoke to her again, it was to deny that he ever felt any anger.

Though we don't endorse Ellen's destructive act, it is clear that Richard is the one in this relationship who had a greater problem dealing with anger. What Richard failed to understand is that *everybody* feels anger from time to time. It's normal. In fact, anger is a *God-given* emotion. True, the way people usually deal with this emotion is destructive and unhealthy. But Richard needed to learn that suppressing and denying anger is no more healthy than exploding in anger. Richard's anger was real, no matter how he tried to mask it. He needed to learn how to recognize the different faces of anger.

Anger Awareness

Whether you identify more with Richard or with Ellen, you too may have difficulty recognizing anger's many faces. The following inventory can help you become more aware of the operation of anger in your life and your relationships. Check the statements that apply to you.

_____ Impatience comes over me more frequently than I would like.

__✓__ I nurture critical thoughts quite easily.

__✓__ When I am displeased with someone, I sometimes shut down communication or withdraw.

__✓__ I feel inwardly annoyed when family and friends do not comprehend my needs.

_____ Tension mounts within me as I tackle a demanding task.

_____ I feel frustrated when I see someone else having fewer struggles than I do.

_____ When facing an important event, I may obsessively ponder how I must manage it.

__✓__ Sometimes I walk in another direction to avoid seeing someone I do not like.

_____ When discussing a controversial topic, my tone of voice is likely to become passionate and strong.

_____ I can accept a person who admits his or her mistakes, but I have a hard time accepting someone who refuses to admit his or her own weaknesses.

_____ When I talk about my irritations, I don't really want to hear an opposite point of view.

__✓__ It's hard for me to forget when someone does me wrong.

_____ When someone confronts me from a misinformed position, I am thinking of my rebuttal as he or she speaks.

__✓__ Sometimes my discouragement makes me want to quit.

_____ I can be quite aggressive in my business pursuits or even when playing a game just for fun.

__✓__ I struggle emotionally with the things in life that are not fair.

_____ Although I know it may not be right, I sometimes blame others for my problems.

_____ When someone openly speaks ill of me, my natural response is to think of how I can defend myself.

_____ Sometimes I speak slanderously about a person, not really caring how it may harm his or her reputation.

_____ I may act kindly on the outside while feeling frustrated on the inside.

_____ Sarcasm is a trait I use in expressing humor.

_____ When someone is clearly annoyed with me, I too easily jump into the conflict.

__✓__ At times I struggle with moods of depression or discouragement.

__✓__ I have been known to take an "I-don't-care" attitude toward the needs of others.

__✓__ When I am in an authority role, I sometimes speak too sternly or insensitively.

Now go back through the inventory and count the number of statements you checked. Everyone will recognize some of these characteristics, so don't worry about marking them.

If you checked ten items, your anger level is probably more constant than you might like.

If you checked fifteen or more, you can probably recount many disappointments and irritations. This indicates you are vulnerable to the extreme ill effects of open anger and rage, or to repressed anger in the form of guilt, bitterness, and resentment. But don't give up! Now that you have become more aware of the many faces of anger, you have taken a giant step toward managing your anger.

If you are interested in gaining a broader perspective of yourself, ask a close friend or trusted family member to complete the inventory, answering the questions as he or she thinks you would respond. It is often helpful and instructive to have other people mirror our character and personality traits back to us, so that we can see ourselves more clearly. Try to set aside any defensiveness (and anger!) as you do this part of the anger awareness inventory.

You will notice from the items in the inventory that anger can be expressed through a wide array of behaviors. Write down the expressions that seem to be the most common forms of your anger. (For example, "I resort to the silent treatment when someone offends me," or "I am often critical and sarcastic.")

1.

2.

3.

4.

You may show your anger in ways other than those mentioned in the inventory. As you become more self-aware, you will probably discover a number of such hidden expressions of anger.

Anger that is managed in a healthy and responsible way is (1) linked to a reasonable issue and (2) communicated in a caring and rational manner. Whenever you become angry, you have options as to how you will express that anger, and those options constitute your second step in healthy anger management.

Step 2: Admit that all angry expressions, good or bad, are the result of choices. "As a child," said Nancy, "I was trained to think anger was totally bad. Now I'm realizing there are moments when anger has its place, but I'm still learning to keep my anger from crossing the line into an inappropriate expression."

"Out of curiosity," asked Dr. Minirth, "how did you learn that anger is bad?"

"When I was a girl, my father had a tendency to explode in rages. Sometimes he was easy to relate to, but sometimes he would sink into a dark mood and go into tirades over minor problems. My mother and I were afraid of him. I vowed I would never be angry like that."

"You saw, even at an early age, that a raging anger has no place in a healthy personality," Dr. Minirth reflected. "But I'm hearing you imply you went too far in your good intentions. You learned to hide your anger because you believed it was always wrong."

"I really did believe that," Nancy replied. "I know now that anger can have some positive functions. But it's not easy erasing the old programming from my mind."

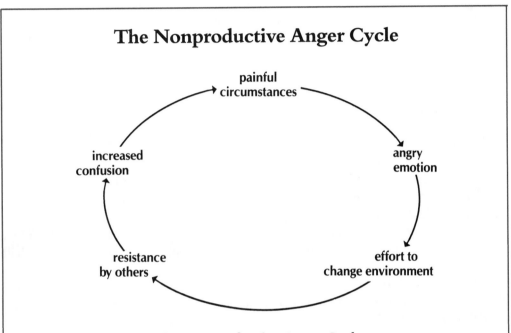

The Nonproductive Anger Cycle

This diagram illustrates how people keep themselves in a nonproductive anger cycle. First, there is a painful circumstance. A situation occurs in which the individual feels that he or she has been devalued, that his or her worth as a person has been insulted; or some need in that person's life has been ignored or unmet; or someone has shown disregard or contempt for values or convictions that are extremely important to him or her. This painful circumstance triggers the angry emotion.

At this point, most people will respond to their anger by attempting to change the environment (for example, convincing others of their errors, moving to a different part of the house, or plunging into a project to let off some steam). This is not always wrong, but it can be risky because it does not guarantee anger relief. Instead, it can lead to increased friction in personal relationships, which increases the angry person's emotional confusion. This moves the angry person back to the beginning of the cycle by creating an ongoing tendency toward painful intrusions.

How do you break the cycle of anger? By *making a choice* to manage your anger.

Nancy is hardly alone in her confusion. We have all seen that strong, corrosive kind of anger, either in ourselves or in others. It is painful and destructive. So it is understandable that many people conclude, *If this is what anger does, I want nothing to do with it.*

Once you have learned to identify anger and understand its meaning, you can learn to distinguish right and wrong ways of managing it. Although you may not always like the presence of your anger, you can make choices about how you handle it.

No two people are exactly alike in managing their anger. Temperaments and circumstances vary widely. But there are five general choices you can make when painful circumstances trigger an angry response within you. You can choose to respond by:

1. suppressing anger
2. open aggression
3. passive aggression
4. assertive anger
5. dropping anger

The first three choices are unhealthy and tend to perpetuate the anger cycle. Choices 4 and 5 interrupt the anger cycle and lead to effective, healthy management of anger. Let's examine each choice in turn:

1. Suppressing anger. For some, suppressing anger takes the form of denial: "Who, me? Angry? What makes you think I'm angry?" they ask as they snap pencils in half and grind the enamel off their molars. Others suppress their anger out of fear of what they might do and who they might hurt if they really "let go." And others suppress their anger because they want to maintain a front, an image of a person who never gets rattled or appears weak.

SELF-TEST — Anger Suppression

How about you? Do you ever hold your anger inside in an unhealthy way? To find out, check the items that apply to you:

____ I am very image-conscious.

____ I don't like to let others know my problems.

__X_ Even when I feel very flustered I portray myself publicly as having it all together.

____ I am rather reserved about sharing my problems or frustrations.

__X_ If a family member or friend upsets me I can let days pass without even mentioning it.

__X_ I have a tendency to be depressed and moody.

__X_ Resentful thinking is common for me, although many people would never suspect it.

____ I have suffered with physical complaints (for example, headaches, stomach ailments, sleep irregularity).

___X___ There are times when I wonder if my opinions or preferences are really valid.
_____ Sometimes I feel paralyzed when confronted by an unwanted situation.
_____ I'm not inclined to initiate conversations about sensitive or troublesome topics.

If you checked five or more of these statements, you probably have a solid pattern of repressing your anger.

People who habitually suppress their anger have usually been trained in early life to think that anger and other emotions are not normal or acceptable. They frequently have a history of having their feelings, ideas, and perceptions invalidated. They grow up fearing powerful retaliation if they register disagreement or even if they only demonstrate uniqueness. And they are so convinced their feelings will be rejected or disparaged that they decide, "What's the use?" Their suppression of anger represents a feeling of personal defeat. They are saying, in effect, "I don't matter. My feelings don't matter enough to be expressed."

Another explanation for suppressing anger is a smug, superior mind-set, as demonstrated by Richard toward his wife Ellen: "I'm not showing anger. You are. Obviously, you are the person with a problem." Usually these people tend toward rigidity of belief, including religious beliefs. Such people also tend to need the approval of the "right" people. They suppress their anger in the belief that it is dangerous to display human imperfection that might cause them to be lowered in the estimation of others.

Suppressing anger does not eliminate it. It only drives anger underground where it festers into a toxic emotion called bitterness. Suppression is unhealthy for the people who do it, and it creates unhealthy, dishonest relationships. Suppression of anger is a choice, but it is not a desirable choice.

2. *Open aggression.* This is the kind of expression most people think of when they hear the word *anger:* explosive rage, shouting, intimidation, blame, criticism, sarcasm. Open aggression is the expression of anger at the expense of someone else. Open aggression is a self-centered choice in dealing with anger: the focus of the openly aggressive individual is so much on his or her own needs and feelings that there is little or no sensitivity to the needs and feelings of others. Openly aggressive anger can be easily identified because it does not hide as suppressed anger does. The openly aggressive person says, in effect, "You don't matter. Your feelings don't matter. I don't care who I hurt. I only care that I get to express my anger."

Open Aggression

This self-test is designed to help you measure your own tendency toward open aggression in response to anger. Check the items that apply to you:

_____ I can be blunt and forceful when someone does something to frustrate me.
_____ As I speak my convictions my voice becomes increasingly louder.

_____ When someone confronts me about a problem, I am likely to offer a ready rebuttal.

_____ No one has to guess my opinion; I'm known for having unwavering viewpoints.

_____ When something goes wrong, I focus so sharply on fixing the problem that I overlook others' feelings.

_____ I have a history of getting caught in bickering matches with family members.

_____ During verbal disagreements with someone, I tend to repeat myself several times.

_____ I find it hard to keep my thoughts to myself when it is obvious that someone else is wrong.

_____ I have a reputation for being strong-willed.

_____ I tend to give advice, even when others have not asked for it.

If you checked five or more of these statements, you probably have a pattern of open aggressive anger. Predictably, you will have ongoing struggles with relatives and close associates.

Two major explanations can be given for open aggression. First, some people have a tendency to take a rigid stand and expend emotional energy on nonessentials. Intellectually, we all know that problems are an inevitable part of our sinful, imperfect world. But emotionally, we have a hard time keeping this truth in view. Your child leaves his clothes on the bedroom floor, even though you have repeatedly told him to put them away. Your employee repeatedly ignores directions, doing the job her own way, believing her way is better than your way. Your friend is chronically late to social engagements. Emotionally balanced people accept these aggravating imperfections and acknowledge their limited ability to force other people into a mold. But the openly aggressive person simply will not rest until these problems are solved once and for all. The result is ever-increasing tension, punctuated by frequent explosions.

Second, deep insecurity causes some people to try to "make themselves larger"— louder, more vehement, more violent—in an effort to make themselves heard. It is normal and healthy to want to be noticed and respected and to want to have basic emotional needs met. But openly aggressive people take this normal desire too far. They are so needy and desirous of respect that they communicate in unbending demands. Their emotional stability hangs by a thread. They are dependent upon others' cooperation. If they feel their feelings are not being received and understood by others, they express them more loudly. If they still do not feel understood, they try harder to be noticed—stamping their feet or pounding on a table. If they still do not feel understood, they may start pounding on the other person.

Open aggression is another option for expressing anger—but again, it is a poor option. People who continue in this mode will continue to hurt and offend other people, damage relationships and possibly their reputations, and carry out a series of power plays in their personal, business, and church relationships.

3. Passive aggression. Like open aggression, passive aggression is the expression of anger in order to preserve personal worth, draw attention to unmet needs, or preserve convictions at the expense of another person. But passive aggression operates secretly instead of openly, in large part because passive-aggressive people do not consider themselves competent to bring their anger out in the open. Passive-aggressive people feel that if they express their anger openly, it may expose them to counterattack or put them in a negative light. People who are passive-aggressive may deny being angry, because they believe that the expression of anger is sinful or disgraceful. (See ANGER for examples of passive-aggressive behavior.)

Passive-aggressive people say, in effect, "I don't matter, but you don't matter, either. I'm angry, but I don't feel capable of effectively expressing my anger. I want to strike back and hurt you—but I don't want to get caught!"

Passive Aggression

The following checklist provides some examples of passive-aggressive anger. Check the items that apply to you.

- _X_ When I am frustrated, I become silent, knowing it bothers other people.
- _X_ I am prone to sulk and pout.
- ____ When I don't want to do a project I will procrastinate. I can be lazy.
- ____ When someone asks if I am frustrated, I will lie and say, "No, everything is fine."
- _X_ There are times when I am deliberately evasive so others won't bother me.
- ____ I sometimes approach work projects halfheartedly.
- ____ When someone talks to me about my problems I stare straight ahead, deliberately obstinate.
- ____ I complain about people behind their backs but resist the opportunity to be open with them face to face.
- ____ Sometimes I become involved in behind-the-scenes misbehavior.
- ____ I sometimes refuse to do someone a favor, knowing this will irritate him or her.

If you checked five or more items, you show a strong inclination toward using passive aggression to express your anger. You may think you are succeeding in putting limits on your anger, but in fact you are only communicating the anger in a way that will perpetuate tensions.

Passive aggression is caused by a need to have control with the least amount of vulnerability. Because the passive-aggressive person assumes it is too risky to be open, he or she frustrates others by subtle sabotage. The need for control is evidence of a strong competitive spirit. Whereas healthy relationships do not keep score regarding right and wrong, the passive-aggressive person is out to win. Like the openly aggressive person, the passive-aggressive person is engaged in a battle for superiority. But this person has cleverly realized that too much honesty about personal differences lessens his or her ability to maintain an upper hand. Passive-aggressive anger is ultimately sly and dishonest.

■

Passive-aggressive expression of anger is a choice we make for dealing with our angry feelings, but it is no more healthy a choice than suppression or open aggression. Because it does not resolve problems, it is a poor choice for managing anger.

■

67

4. Assertive anger. When we express our anger assertively, we preserve our sense of self-worth, our needs, and our convictions while at the same time considering the needs and feelings of others. When we express our anger assertively rather than aggressively, we actually enable our relationships to grow stronger. Assertive anger is a mark of personal maturity and stability.

For some people, the word *assertive* suggests being "pushy" or "abrasive," but that's not what we mean here. True assertiveness is not abrasive, nor is it meant to harm. It is simply the quality of being willing to state one's views, feelings, needs, and convictions, firmly and fairly but with consideration and respect for the other person's views, feelings, needs, and convictions. Assertiveness is affirmed in Ephesians 4:26, which tells us, "Be angry, and do not sin." Some examples of godly, assertive expressions of anger:

- an overworked church member who politely but firmly says no to a request to do even more projects
- a parent who states guidelines for discipline without resorting to shouting, shaming, or berating the child
- a husband and wife who talk about their differences constructively, without sarcasm, blaming, or bringing up old offenses

Two key reminders will help you learn to communicate your anger constructively and assertively: (1) make sure the issues you raise are worth raising; don't exhaust your emotional energy on trivialities; and (2) be aware that your tone of voice can help create an atmosphere of respect for others. This is consistent with the Ephesians 4:15 instruction to speak the truth in love.

Assertiveness is not always easy. It requires self-discipline and respect for the dignity of others. It requires that we not just push selfish agendas on others. And it requires us to put our communications into the context of "the big picture," anticipating how they will affect future interactions. James 1:19 describes the assertive approach this way: "Let every man be swift to hear, slow to speak, slow to wrath."

The assertive approach to managing anger says, "I matter, and you matter too. I have a right to tell you I am angry, and you have a right to tell me your feelings. But we don't have a right to hurt each other." Assertive anger is a choice we can all make, and it is a choice that is caring, healthy, productive, and effective. But there is still one more approach to be explored.

5. Dropping anger. Of all the choices you have for dealing with your anger, the most difficult one is the choice to let it go. There are times when you can have appropriate convictions to communicate, yet assertiveness may not work. At this point one of your options is to choose to drop your anger. Dropping your anger means you accept your inability to control circumstances and you recognize your personal limits. This option includes tolerating differences as well as choosing to forgive. Here are some examples of dropping anger:

- A wife recognizes that, despite her discussions with her husband, he will always be perfectionistic. As a result, she draws her boundaries so that she will not always have to comply with his finicky preferences, but she also learns to accept him as he is.

- An adult son admits that his father has chosen not to love him. Rather than carry a grudge, he decides to forgive his father while also charting a new style of fathering with his own children.
- Rather than griping about company policy, an employee decides that no job is perfect, so he will do his best work in spite of his differences in preference.

Choosing to drop your anger is far different from suppressing it. Suppression represents phoniness or denial, whereas <u>dropping anger represents a commitment to godliness</u>. The person who chooses to let go of the anger is fully aware that grudges are an option, but he or she opts instead for a cleaner life, uncluttered by bitterness and dissension.

Here are some practical suggestions to help you make the choice to manage your anger by dropping it:

- Make yourself accountable to a trusted friend. Let that person know when you are struggling with feelings of anger.
- Live in the now. Forgive today. Don't worry about forgiving tomorrow. You don't have the ability to decide your emotions for tomorrow or ten years from now. You can only choose your emotional response today.
- Write out your feelings. Journal them or write a letter. Then read over them with the attitude that you will turn them loose.

✗ The idea that you can choose your attitude and your response to anger may be a new one to you. You may have never realized before that you can make choices in your management of anger. But you will find, as you gain more insight and your emotions become less mysterious to you, that your anger will gradually lose its control over you. Instead, you will be in control of your anger.

Step 3: Let go of excessive dependencies so your anger management is inwardly directed rather than externally determined. Anger does not arise in a vacuum. Anger thrives on unmet needs. Each of us has basic psychological needs that have to be adequately met if we are to enjoy emotional balance. When these needs are not met, we experience the emotions of distress, including anger. Persistent problems with anger imply unresolved psychological needs.

One warning: A common problem that arises when people attempt to drop their anger is that the anger returns at a later date. For example, a woman who chooses to forgive her rebellious adult son may live in peace until she learns new information about his misdeeds. Then old frustrations well up within her again, making her intensely angry. Did she somehow fail to drop her anger the first time? No. Dropping anger is a form of forgiveness, and it is often difficult for us to forgive once and for all. Frequently, we must continually forgive the same offense over and over, whenever it comes to mind, until it eventually fades away.

Of all the common human needs, the most obvious and important is the need for love. When people feel consistently loved, their emotions show it through their stability. But when they lack love, they respond to their rejected feelings with anger. Through anger they cry the unspoken question, *Why can't you just love me?*

People become angry when they feel rejected, left out, ignored, or misunderstood by the significant people in their lives—parents, siblings, spouse, friends, fellow Christians. The longer they go without feeling accepted and affirmed, the more anger they store. This stored anger can quickly sour into resentment and depression. The more a person struggles with anger, the more it indicates that some of his or her need for love has gone unmet, either in childhood or adulthood. Some examples:

- Shelly, a single woman in her thirties, is envious of her high school and college friends who are now married with children. She struggles with anger because of her own history of broken dating relationships.
- Tom, who has felt rejected by a group of his peers, feels angry because he had tried hard to be friendly, but to no avail.
- Wendy, a woman in her forties, recalls how demeaning her brother was to her during their childhood. She is insecure at family gatherings and resentful that no one ever stood up to him.

Step 4: Make a choice to trade your craving for emotional freedom. Melanie had come to our Minirth Meier New Life Clinic because of a long history of anxiety attacks. "Sometimes I feel so stressed," she said, "that I get short of breath and my chest feels tight. It's so traumatic I think I'm suffocating."

Dr. Minirth asked Melanie several questions about her overall health, then, making an educated guess, he asked, "Would you tell me what makes you angry?"

"Angry?" she asked, as if her secret had just been exposed. "Well, uh, yes, you might say I feel angry sometimes. But I haven't really put much thought into what makes me angry."

Actually, Melanie was hedging. She had a long laundry list of problems that fed her anger. But she had grown up in a very restrictive environment that discouraged open admission of imperfections. "We all feel frustration from time to time," Dr. Minirth prodded, "so anger is nothing to be afraid to admit. What frustrates you?"

Melanie spoke sheepishly at first, but she became more forceful as the words flowed. "We have a twenty-four-year-old son living at home who refuses to grow up. I've pleaded with my husband, Gary, to do something to get him out from under our roof. But honestly, Gary is the most stubborn man I know! I couldn't get through to him if I shouted through a megaphone. Our son knows he can get away with being lazy because Gary won't lift a finger to make him work!" As she spoke, red blotches broke out on her neck.

Dr. Minirth quietly replied, "And you've tried throughout your marriage to communicate your feelings to Gary but with little luck, right?" For the next twenty minutes, Dr. Minirth probed the areas of Melanie's life that made her angry: problems with extended family, with friends, with out-of-control debt. She summed up her feelings by saying, "Nothing in my world fits my preferences. Everywhere I turn, I feel controlled by things I can do absolutely nothing about!"

I feel controlled. Those three words cut to the heart of Melanie's anger. Seemingly deprived of the God-given privilege to choose for herself, Melanie felt controlled—imprisoned—by people and circumstances. The feeling of being controlled is a major factor in the anger of many people.

No human was created to be controlled by another. We've all grown up cherishing our liberty. With some justification, most of us resent the demands of people or institutions that take away our freedom to choose.

Do You Feel Controlled?

The following self-test will help you determine the level to which you feel controlled by outside forces and individuals. Check the statements that apply to you.

____	When I grew up I was expected to obey the rules with no questions asked.
_X_	I would like to speak more freely about personal matters, but to do so would only lead to arguments or disappointments.
____	When I share a unique opinion or preference, it is often met with a put-down or an invalidation.
_X_	The people I'd like to be most open with are too unavailable to me.
_X_	I feel as if I live in the midst of critics.
_X_	Peacefulness only seems to come when I can get away by myself.
____	I often calculate in advance the way I will use my words.
_X_	Some of my closest relationships have been soured by long stretches of silence and no communication.
____	I often feel that my performances are all that matters to others.
____	I have close relationships that could best be described as stressful.

If you checked five or more items, you probably are susceptible to easy anger, and your environment may have a rigidness that makes emotional composure difficult. ■

Control is not always bad. After all, we do need organization and structure to maintain peace in our lives. But excessive control creates more negatives than positives.

Why do we resent being controlled by others? Because we sense a message behind the control: "You can't be trusted." Controlling people believe that if they eliminate our choices, then they erase any chance that we will make a mistake or act irresponsibly.

Dr. Minirth and Melanie discussed how she had felt controlled by her husband, Gary. "He expects so much of me that I feel I'm just a machine to him. He doesn't care about *me*."

"You interpret his control as a lack of caring, and that interpretation sparks the anger," Dr. Minirth reflected. "When the anger arises, how do you handle it?"

"Sometimes I just suppress it," she replied, "sometimes I explode. A lot of times, I try to make him stop controlling me."

"In other words, he controls you, so you respond by attempting to countercontrol him."

At first Melanie tried to protest that she wasn't trying to control him at all, but the more she thought back over recent events in their relationship, the more she had to admit that Dr. Minirth's assessment was correct. In fact, it is very common for a person

People who feel controlled often allow others to control them. Perhaps they have been raised to believe that life is made up of obligations rather than choices. They can invariably recall instructions about how they were to speak and act as children, yet they draw a blank when asked how they were trained to make choices affecting the structure of their lives.

■

71

who feels controlled by someone else to try to break that person's oppressive grip by countercontrolling him or her. We practice countercontrol whenever we:

- feel we must correct the other person whenever he or she is being unfair
- get drawn into arguments with family members or associates who are stubborn
- feel compelled to point it out when others are illogical
- act uncooperatively with people who treat us unfavorably
- respond to confrontation with silence and defiant resistance
- determine that no one is going to get away with telling us what to do
- respond to other people's control with the question, "Why do you always have to . . . ?"

You do not have to subject yourself to the abusive or controlling behavior of others. Nor do you have to return evil for evil, controlling behavior for controlling behavior. You can choose a different response when others try to control you. You can choose to assert your feelings and your needs. If the other person does not respond, then you can step back from the situation and go on about your business. You are not obligated to lock yourself in mortal combat with this person, correct his or her illogic, or continue trying to move the person to your point of view when it is clear that his or her feet are set in stubborn cement. You can make a choice. You can state your position, then get on with your life.

Step 5: Ground yourself in truth by setting aside idealistic myths. Sometimes people set themselves up for anger by talking themselves into believing things that are not true. For example, a woman might conclude, after three or four bad experiences, that "all men are jerks." Or after a week of unusually frequent fights with his wife, a husband might conclude, "Our marriage has always been rotten. All we ever do is fight." This is called mythical thinking. Mythical thoughts usually contain an element of truth. But when myths are stretched to the extreme, they keep you from making healthy anger management choices. To manage your anger successfully, you must eliminate the false notions that perpetuate your pain and replace them with positive truths that will enable you to live a life that is rooted in healthy, godly realism. Some examples:

- I dislike the wrongs I've suffered, but I choose to thrive in spite of them.
- Others do not have to act correctly before I choose the proper direction for my anger.
- Choosing to drop my resentment is not the same as condoning wrong.
- I accept the freedom of others to live in unhealthy ways.
- I accept responsibility for my own emotions; others cannot force me to remain angry.
- Forgiveness and letting go of anger have nothing to do with winning or losing.
- It is not my duty to correct another person who chooses to gloat over his or her problems.

The more you are able to agree with these statements and incorporate them into your everyday life, the better you will be able to purge harmful anger from your life.

Step 6: Live in humility rather than self-preoccupied pride. From the beginning of life we are preoccupied with ourselves. One of the purposes of the process of maturation from childhood to adulthood is to burn the self-centered pride out of us, so that we can have a healthy view of ourselves. Many people, however, reach adulthood with a strong, unhealthy streak of pride still active in their personalities. A prideful, self-centered person is likely to become very angry if his will is thwarted or if her whims and wishes are not catered to. The only answer to this kind of anger, which is rooted in pride, is to seek to build humility into one's character. Humility means being willing to acknowledge your personal limits and recognizing that you are not the center of the universe and that no one is obligated to cater to your whims.

"If I set aside my pride in favor of humility," you may wonder, "doesn't that mean I lose a large portion of myself? Wouldn't I have to repress a lot of my real feelings?"

Some people believe it is a sign of strength to be prideful and demanding. Yet if we look at the example of Christ, we see that He modeled strength through humility, and He opposed pride wherever He found it. He could speak forcefully, but humility was the hallmark of His character.

If you practice humility only as an act of duty, it will indeed cause repressed emotions. But then, it wouldn't *really* be humility. You'd be living in legalism—which, paradoxically, is a subtle form of pride! True humility does not require any false manipulation of the emotions. Humility is not an obligation or a duty. It is a choice. You can choose to respond to your angry feelings by exploding in an openly aggressive rage or by slyly resorting to passive-aggressive sabotage—or you can choose humility. No one can take that choice away from you. By accepting your limits and setting aside your prideful self-preoccupations, you are not repressing your emotions. You are choosing to place a higher priority on a healthy, appropriate way of life.

Step 7: Verbalize your anger. Unfortunately, human beings are very human. They violate each other's God-given rights in many ways. What do you do with your anger when you feel your rights and your personhood have been violated? The emotionally healthy and biblically correct answer: you verbalize your angry feelings—and you "speak the truth in love."

In Ephesians 4:13–15, the apostle Paul urges believers toward unity and deeper knowledge of Christ, "speaking the truth in love" in order that they might become perfect (mature) and achieve the stature and fullness of Christ Himself. Though it's true that Paul has right doctrine primarily in mind in this passage, the phrase "speaking the truth in love" is excellent advice to follow when seeking the best way to deal with someone when you are angry. How then do you "speak the truth in love"?

For one thing, when you are angry, you can verbalize your anger gently, respectfully, and tactfully. To speak the truth in love means using the "I" message rather than the "you" message. Examples of "you" messages would include:

- "You should have called."
- "You shouldn't have said that!"
- "You are such a slob!"

How can you turn these "you" messages into "I" messages? Try:

- "I was upset when I didn't hear from you. I got worried."
- "I don't think what you said was fair, and I didn't appreciate it."
- "I get very irritated when the kitchen is left messy."

"I" messages are a simple device, but it's not easy to learn to use them consistently. The normal tendency is to use the same kind of "you" messages we have heard all our lives. Work on using "I" messages, particularly when you're feeling angry. When phrasing your "I" message, think through the situation carefully and avoid exaggerating. The key to using "I" messages is to put the responsibility for your own feelings on yourself. Do not accuse, demean, or attack the other person.

Anger is a powerful emotion. Handled carelessly, it creates divisions, it wounds souls, it devastates relationships. Handled with deliberate thought and Christlike love, anger can become a constructive force for relational growth and understanding.
See also AGGRESSION; CONFLICT AND CONFRONTATION; FORGIVENESS

Anorexia Nervosa and Bulimia

One of the most highly publicized tragedies involving an eating disorder was the story of singer Karen Carpenter. In 1983, at the age of thirty-two, she collapsed at her home and went into cardiac arrest. Despite frantic efforts to revive her, she was pronounced dead at the hospital. Cause of death: malnutrition, due to anorexia nervosa.

A related affliction, bulimia, has also taken its toll of lives. Dr. Frank Minirth recalls his days as a young resident physician, when he was working with a teenager named Mary. Although bulimia was not well known in those days, it was clear that Mary had a severe bulimic disorder—so severe that she had been hospitalized for treatment. Dr. Minirth made a number of suggestions for treating Mary by both medical and psychological means, but Mary and her mother resisted his diagnosis and his advice. Eventually, Mary seemed to recover, and she convinced the hospital staff to discharge her. Less than a week later, Dr. Minirth saw Mary return to the hospital—wheeled into the emergency room on a gurney. It was too late; she was already dead. Apparently, she had vomited extensively during that day, and her vomiting had triggered an irregular heartbeat and cardiac arrest. At that moment, Dr. Minirth made a decision to find out all he could about this tragic—and sometimes deadly—psychological and medical disorder.

RECOGNIZING THE BODY'S WARNING SIGNALS

Anorexia nervosa and bulimia are two closely related eating disorders. Both anorexia nervosa and bulimia are characterized by the compulsive drive to control weight by unhealthy means. *Anorexia nervosa* is defined as self-induced starvation resulting in extreme, often life-threatening weight loss. *Bulimia* is defined as a pattern of overindulging in food (bingeing), followed by self-induced vomiting or abuse of laxatives in order to produce weight loss.

Authorities estimate that about 1 percent of women between ages twelve and twenty-five suffer from anorexia, and about 1.5 percent in that age group suffer from bulimia. These disorders are commonly seen as women's disorders, although about 10 percent of anorexics or bulimics are men. Although eating disorders sometimes begin in later adulthood, most affected individuals develop the disorder in adolescence or young adulthood. Some young women "learn" anorexic or bulimic behavior from their school friends. Others seem to stumble on the "technique" of purging on their own.

Many of the physical effects of anorexia are similar to the effects of bulimia. It is important to understand these physical consequences of anorexic and bulimic behavior because they are the body's warning signals. Ignoring these warning signals could be harmful or even fatal. These effects include:

- A menstrual cycle that stops temporarily (amenorrhea) or becomes irregular (dysmenorrhea). Both the physical stress of bulimic purging and the malnutrition effects of anorexia can produce irregular periods. Bulimics tend to have periods with irregular intervals, whereas anorexics often miss three or more menstrual periods in a row.
- Digestive impairment resulting from the abuse of laxatives—deficiency of digestive enzymes, laxative-dependent bowel (a literal physical addiction to laxatives), and inflammatory bowel disorders.
- Imbalance of electrolytes (such as potassium, magnesium, or calcium) in the body, thereby bringing on irregular heartbeat (cardiac arrhythmia) and—in extreme cases—heart failure and death.
- Low white blood cell count (anemia) resulting from poor nutrition or an impaired immune system.
- Inflammation of the esophagus (esophagitis) resulting from self-induced vomiting.
- Erosion of tooth enamel, owing to gastric acids from self-induced vomiting.
- Brain and central nervous system disorders (including seizures) resulting from malnutrition.
- Glandular dysfunctions, including thyroid abnormalities, resulting in fatigue.
- Kidney problems, including kidney failure in extreme anorexics.
- Accumulation of abdominal fluids, resulting in "potbelly."
- Hiatal hernias.
- Low blood sugar (hypoglycemia), resulting in headaches and dizziness.
- Musculoskeletal problems owing to potassium deficiency, resulting in muscle spasms, pain, and muscle atrophy.
- Dry skin and thinning hair.

The effects of anorexia and bulimia are devastating to the medical, emotional, and even spiritual well-being of thousands of people. These disorders are responsible for an unimaginable toll of suffering and, in extreme cases, even death.

Assessing Eating Disorder Tendencies

To get a clearer sense of how healthy your eating habits are, answer the questions in the inventory below. Place the number of your answer in the space at the left of each question.

> 1 = Never
> 2 = Sometimes
> 3 = Often

A scoring key follows the inventory. (You may also take this quiz "by proxy" for someone you are concerned about. Just answer the questions on that person's behalf.)

____ I worry throughout the day about what I will or will not eat.
____ I get angry when people ask questions about what or how I eat.
____ I get angry when people push food on me and try to get me to eat.
____ I panic when I miss my exercise routine, afraid of gaining weight.
____ My friends tell me I am thin, but I feel fat.
____ I wish I was slimmer than all my friends.
____ I feel terrible about myself if I gain two or three pounds.
____ The most overwhelming fear I experience is the fear of being too fat.
____ I feel depressed and irritable, and spend increasing amounts of time alone.
____ I have eating habits that are different from those of my friends and family.
____ I am concerned about my eating habits, but I feel I can't tell anyone because no one would understand.
____ I enjoy cooking for others, as long as I don't have to eat what I cook.
____ I spend hours and hours absorbing books and magazine articles about weight loss.
____ I do my "enjoyable" eating alone, then eat less when I'm around other people.
____ I consume large amounts of food to the point where I feel sick and make myself vomit.
____ I find laxatives to be helpful in controlling my weight.
____ I fast (go without eating for a day or longer) in order to control my weight.
____ It is ____ that I do things perfectly.

> 1 = Not important
> 2 = Important
> 3 = Extremely important

____ My menstrual period has stopped or become irregular, but my doctor can find no medical cause.

> 1 = False
> 3 = True

Bear in mind that this inventory is not a scientific test. It is designed to help you spot possible problem areas in your attitudes and behavior toward food.

If you scored from 19 to 21, you probably do not have a significant emotional or behavioral issue with regard to your weight and eating habits. A score of 21 to 35 indicates that you are weight-conscious but not necessarily tending toward anorexia or bulimia. If you scored 35 to 56, then you show a strong tendency toward anorexia nervosa or bulimia and should consider getting help in dealing with your compulsive behavior issues. A psychologist or physician can help you determine what kind of evaluation and assistance would be appropriate.

CHARACTERISTICS OF ANOREXIA NERVOSA

The characteristics of anorexia nervosa are:

- compulsive, voluntary self-starvation (as the disorder progresses, individuals move far below their ideal weight)
- distorted body image; thinking, "I'm too fat!" even when dangerously thin
- occasional bingeing followed by strict dieting, fasting, or laxative abuse
- an obsession with food, dining, and recipes
- obsessive perfectionism
- an obsession with control
- low self-esteem
- obsessive and excessive exercise
- ritualized behavior involving food and exercise
- introverted and withdrawn behavior
- depression, irritability, lying and sneaking, self-hatred, guilt

Why do anorexics starve themselves? There are many emotional impulses that drive this behavior:

- "I have to starve myself today because I ate too much yesterday."
- "I deserve to be punished for last night's binge."
- "Food is my source of control; even if I can't control all areas of my life, I have the say about what goes in my mouth."
- "I'll show them! I'll punish them! If my husband/my parents/my boyfriend treats me like that, then fine, I won't eat!"

These reasons are all self-defeating—but then, compulsive behavior is not driven by logic. It is driven by emotion.

CHARACTERISTICS OF BULIMIA

The characteristics of bulimia are:

- a compulsive cycle of secretive bingeing (extreme overeating) and purging (self-induced vomiting or laxative abuse)

- extreme guilt following binges (this guilt drives the obsessive self-denial and self-punishment of purging)
- being within five to fifteen pounds of ideal body weight
- an inability to control eating once it has begun
- use of food as a friend, an anesthetic for emotional pain, and a tranquilizer—much as an alcoholic uses the bottle
- caloric intake per binge as high as 20,000 calories
- bingeing and purging sometimes accompanied by a practice of chewing food, then spitting it out without swallowing
- weight fluctuation that follows an alternating pattern of out-of-control bingeing and rigidly controlled self-denial and even fasting
- obsessive perfectionism
- ritualized behavior involving food and exercise
- an emotional longing for relationships and approval

Why do bulimics purge? For many of us, who see vomiting as one of the most disagreeable experiences imaginable, it is almost inconceivable that anyone would willingly put herself through the agony of gagging, retching, and throwing up several times a week, or even several times a day. But the bulimic doesn't live to purge. The bulimic looks forward to the binge. Purging is merely the act of atonement for the indulgence of bingeing. To the bulimic, food is a friend, assuaging her loneliness because she won't let people get close to her. Food is a tranquilizer, providing escape from pressures and stress. Food is a reward, gobbled down with the attitude, "I've had a hard day. I deserve these goodies."

Bulimics are very hard on themselves for their failures, and many (on either a conscious or an unconscious level) see their purging behavior as acts of atonement for the sin of bingeing. They tend not to accept grace and forgiveness very well, so they punish themselves by abusing their bodies. At the Minirth Meier New Life Clinics we have treated many sufferers of anorexia and bulimia who were active, sincere Christians. Many of them understood the theology of forgiveness and grace on an intellectual level, but they could not emotionally internalize it and believe that God could forgive them and affirm them by His grace. So they pursued their own attempts at self-destructive atonement. That is why we say that eating disorders have not only a medical and emotional component but a spiritual component as well.

ANOREXIA AND BULIMIA: COMPARISONS AND CONTRASTS

Anorexics and bulimics have much in common. Both develop rituals regarding food, exercise, and other aspects of their lives. Rituals are behaviors that people engage in, usually on a habitual basis, that have symbolic meaning. For example, whenever Judy, an anorexic, goes out to dinner with friends and eats a normal dinner, she invariably fasts for two days afterwards, a symbolic act of cleansing and self-denial to atone for her "indulgence" in a normal meal. And Helen, a bulimic, maintains a ritual of coffee for breakfast, a small plate of veggies for lunch, and a lonely junk-food binge (doughnuts, potato chips, candy, ice cream, cheesecake) for dinner, followed by purging and a desperate prayer for forgiveness before bed.

Bulimics and anorexics are both typically perfectionists when it comes to grades, clothes, and personal appearance. Like most perfectionists, they are subject to depression. They have low self-esteem. Some anorexics and bulimics, particularly when it becomes clear that their lives are out of control, are candidates for suicide. When an individual makes a statement such as, "I can't take this pain anymore" or "I just wish I could die," that person is sending a warning signal that should be taken seriously. Such individuals should immediately be hospitalized for their own safety.

There are also striking contrasts between bulimics and anorexics. To the bulimic, food is a friend and a sedative. To the anorexic, food is an enemy. Whereas anorexics starve themselves far below their ideal body weight, bulimics usually hover within five to ten pounds of their ideal weight. Bulimics tend to seek out relationships and peer approval, whereas anorexics are usually withdrawn and private; both, however, feel lonely and isolated inside, because of a secret they cannot share with anyone. Anorexics have superhuman control over their appetites. Bulimics have little or no control; once started, they cannot stop.

THE BULIMAREXIC

We sometimes see people at the clinic who alternate between the traits of anorexia and of bulimia. We call these people "bulimarexics." They may alternate between anorexia and bulimia from month to month or year to year. Sometimes an adolescent begins as an anorexic and graduates to bulimia later in life. This condition was first identified by Dr. Marlene Boskind-White and Dr. William C. White, Jr., in their book *Bulimarexia* (Norton, 1991). The condition is still not widely recognized, however, and it does not appear in the standard psychiatric reference, DSM-III-R (the *Diagnostic and Statistical Manual of Mental Disorders III-Revised,* American Psychiatric Press, 1987).

Even though this occurrence is rare, it is important to mention it because bulimarexics tend to have an unusual capacity for denial. They look at the list of symptoms and say, "I can't be anorexic, because I purge, and I can't be bulimic, because I starve myself. I'm not in that kind of danger." Bulimarexics must understand that they are in considerable danger, even though they don't fit neatly into one category or the other.

TREATMENT AND HEALING

Anorexia and bulimia are addictive disorders, and the behavior of these disorders is driven by the cycle of addiction. The addiction cycle has six major components: (1) an emotional emptiness (which we call "love hunger"), which in turn leads to (2) the emotional pain of low self-esteem, which leads the individual to reach for (3) an addictive agent to anesthetize the pain (starvation for the anorexic, bingeing for the bulimic), which then produces (4) consequences (medical problems and, in the bulimic, the need to purge), followed by (5) guilt and shame, which produces (6) self-hate, which returns the person to (1) love hunger, and the cycle begins all over again. The cycle is not just a circle, but a descending spiral, so that each time around the cycle, the addicted individual sinks deeper and deeper into the addiction and into despair. (See ADDIC-TION.)

Food is not the real issue in anorexia and bulimia. The real issue is *emotional pain*. That is why, at the Minirth Meier New Life Clinics, we do not focus solely on behavior treatment. The behavior is only the symptom; the cause lies much deeper. Although we usually start by treating the symptoms (which are often life-threatening), we always concentrate on the emotional issues that drive the behavior and produce the symptoms. Otherwise, the patient is likely to climb back aboard the addictive cycle as soon as the supervision is removed.

The first step in the treatment and healing of anorexia and bulimia is to deal with any medical complications posed by the disorder. We start with a comprehensive medical exam, including a complete physical, lab work, and a gynecological exam. If the medical complications are severe, the patient may be hospitalized in order to stabilize body functions and monitor nutrition. A body that has been starved cannot handle being fed all at once, so refeeding must take place in a carefully measured and controlled way. In some cases, antidepressants are administered, since the abuse of food is often a result, in part, of depression. Concentrated inpatient treatment may last for four to six weeks, followed by at least a year of outpatient treatment.

Less severe cases are often treated solely on an outpatient basis. Outpatient treatment usually consists of weekly individual and group counseling sessions. We have found that a combination of individual and group counseling is usually the most effective approach to treating anorexia and bulimia. This may seem like a long and arduous process, but unfortunately there is no magical cure for deep-rooted emotional and medical problems. Habits that take significant time to establish also take significant time and effort to extinguish.

A key issue to be resolved in the recovery process for anorexia and bulimia is the issue of body image. Most anorexics and bulimics hate what they see when they look in the mirror. This condition, which we call body hate, is quite common, particularly among women, whether a person has an eating disorder or not. People with body hate dwell on their flaws and have little or no awareness of their positive features. Body hate is exacerbated by a culture that emphasizes standards of beauty that equate being attractive with being thin. In people with eating disorders, body hate takes on excessive proportions, compelling them to reach for an impossible ideal.

Through individual and group therapy, we try to help the anorexic or bulimic understand that her body image is a distortion of her true physical self. We have seen people who literally looked like concentration camp victims, weighing only sixty-five or seventy pounds, on the verge of starving themselves to death, who would look at themselves in the mirror and continue to insist that they were *too fat!* The number on the scales is not the issue. The person's appearance is not the issue. Particularly in anorexia, but in bulimia as well, the real issue is emotional pain and an intense, irrational fear that cannot be dislodged by mere evidence of the scales or the mirror—the fear of getting fat.

We work with patients to help them learn to love the bodies God has provided as gifts to be enjoyed. Through individual therapy, we help anorexics and bulimics learn to appreciate pleasures of the five senses—taste, touch, sight, hearing, and smell. We encourage a healthy appreciation for God's special gift of sexuality and sexual pleasure for married couples and romantic pleasure (holding hands, kissing) for girlfriend-boyfriend relationships. We help people get in touch with the sensory messages the body is sending—messages that say, "I'm tense," "I'm anxious," "I'm tired," "I need exercise," "I need rest."

The key is to repattern the thinking of the anorexic or bulimic so that her life will be richer and more fulfilling and so that distorted ideas and emotional pain cannot have an opportunity to retrigger self-destructive behavior.

HOW TO BE A FRIEND TO AN ANOREXIC OR BULIMIC

What should you do if a close friend or loved one shows signs of anorexia or bulimia? Here are several steps you should take:

1. Lovingly confront the individual about her symptoms. An untreated eating disorder is addictive, damaging, and sometimes fatal. Some anorexics and bulimics actually *want* someone to notice their behavior. It is a cry for help. Even though she may protest or deny at first, some part of her may actually be relieved when you care enough to intervene.

2. Seek professional medical help for family members under legal age of majority. You are morally and legally responsible for the welfare of your minor children. There is a limit to how far you can intrude into the life of an adult, but if the individual is your own child, particularly a minor child, then you have a responsibility to act assertively and quickly to safeguard her health and her life. If that individual resists medical treatment, and you are not capable of getting that person to a doctor or hospital, seek the help and advice of someone you trust—a pastor, physician, therapist, or trusted friend. Don't drop the matter just because of resistance. A life is at stake.

3. Seek professional therapy and emotional support for the individual. Do everything within your power to get that person into individual therapy and a support group. The support of people who have been through the pain of a major eating disorder is of invaluable aid to recovery for those who are still caught in the addiction.

4. Be candid with the individual about her appearance. If she looks malnourished and emaciated, tell her so. Don't say she looks "thin" (which she might interpret as "good"); use words such as "gaunt" and "unhealthy." When she gains weight, tell her she is looking more beautiful. Make sure your honesty is coated with love.

5. Listen and empathize. Listening communicates caring and builds trust. Anorexics and bulimics need to sense our love and understanding more than they need to hear our advice. One of the most healing gifts you can give her is a safe place to share her deepest reality without being judged or criticized.

6. Show love and unconditional acceptance. An eating disorder is not pretty, and anorexics and bulimics can be very difficult to live with. They become depressed. They get angry. They sometimes lie and cover up. They accuse and blame. This is all part of the disorder, and you may be tempted to lose patience with her. We encourage you to persevere in love, and seek always to demonstrate affection and unconditional acceptance, even when it is not easy to do so.

7. *Seek God's strength.* God is the source of all strength, wisdom, and healing. As you seek to be a friend to the anorexia or bulimia sufferer, ask God for power to persevere beyond your depleted energy reserves. He has promised to "supply all your need according to His riches in glory by Christ Jesus" (Phil. 4:19).

For a detailed discussion of anorexia nervosa and bulimia, read *The Thin Disguise: Understanding and Overcoming Anorexia and Bulimia* by Pam Vredevelt, Dr. Deborah Newman, Harry Beverly, and Dr. Frank Minirth (Thomas Nelson, 1992).

Anxiety

Doctors call it *anxiety.* To nondoctors, the everyday term *worry* is a good approximation of what *anxiety* means. At the Minirth Meier New Life Clinics, we treat more cases of anxiety than any other type of mental disorder. In fact, we deal with various forms of anxiety every day.

When people think of anxiety, they usually think of various symptoms, such as sleeplessness, restlessness, an inability to concentrate, or a physical pain or tension (such as in the back or neck). These are all potential symptoms of anxiety, but they are not anxiety, in and of themselves. Carefully defined, anxiety is an emotion that a person experiences in the face of a perceived threat or a danger, characterized by an unpleasant anticipation of misfortune or doom. The word *perceived* is very important, because danger can be real or imagined. When the danger is real, anxiety can serve as a healthy warning. When the danger is imagined, however, anxiety is negative baggage that saps emotional and physical energy, robs people of happiness and peace, and keeps them from functioning effectively. In its severe forms, anxiety can emotionally paralyze a person.

Whether the danger is real or imagined, anxiety and all of its symptoms are real. But anxiety is treatable and curable, and its recurrence is often preventable. Recognized early and treated quickly, anxiety is one of the most curable of all emotional disorders. In fact, with insight and understanding of the nature of anxiety, many everyday forms of anxiety can be resolved by the individual himself or herself, without professional help.

THE SYMPTOMS AND WARNING SIGNS OF ANXIETY

Properly understood, anxiety can actually serve us and lead us toward greater mental and emotional health. It can serve the same function as a smoke alarm, alerting us to potential danger. When the alarm sounds, we look for the fire, extinguish it, and remove the danger. As you learn to read and interpret the warning signs of anxiety, you will be better equipped not only to improve your own mental health but to enhance the mental health of people around you.

The symptoms of anxiety are varied and sometimes difficult to recognize. The most obvious symptoms are problems with everyday functioning (insomnia, lack of concentration, pain, headaches, impaired judgment, problems in relationships) and negative feelings or moods (uneasiness, apprehension, dread, concern, tension, restlessness, worry).

Sometimes a person with anxiety senses pending misfortune or disaster, and as a result he or she will undergo the double pain of anxiety coupled with depression.

The symptoms of anxiety can be divided into several categories. These symptoms can, of course, also indicate other disorders, both physical and emotional, besides anxiety.

Physical Symptoms

- Cardiovascular symptoms: tension headaches, chest pain, increased blood pressure, rapid heartbeat, pounding heart
- Respiratory symptoms: sighing respirations, dizziness, light-headedness, labored breathing, hyperventilation, sense of choking or smothering, shortness of breath, "lump" in throat
- Musculoskeletal symptoms: eyelid twitching, fidgeting, muscle aches, muscle tension, tightness in chest, chest pain, tremors, quivering voice
- Gastrointestinal symptoms: anorexia, dry mouth, diarrhea, nausea, vomiting, stomach pain, painful swallowing, nervous stomach ("butterflies")
- Genitourinary symptoms: painful or frequent urination
- Dermatologic symptoms: clammy hands, flushed face, pallor, sweating, cold hands or feet, tingling
- Sensory and mental symptoms: blurred vision, ears ringing, numbness, foul taste in the mouth, impaired coordination, impaired judgment, impaired mental functioning, intense dreams

Behavioral Symptoms

Behavioral and physiological symptoms of anxiety include hyperalertness, irritability, uncertainty, tense posture, overdependence, apprehension, impaired concentration, poor memory, distraction, jumpiness or edginess, impatience, inability to sleep or fall asleep, startled reactions, talking too much, impaired sexual interest and functioning, and intense dreams. Behavioral symptoms may also include an immediate need to escape from the current situation and development of avoidance behavior.

Cognitive and Psychological Symptoms

Cognitive symptoms involve the way people think. These symptoms include fear of dying, fear of losing one's mind, fear of losing control, fear of fainting, and fear of public embarrassment.

In addition to the many symptoms described above, anxiety is a component of almost all psychiatric disorders, such as neuroses and psychoses. When anxiety is generalized and nonspecific (that is, there is a vague sense of doom without any specific threat or danger in mind), the condition is called a *generalized anxiety disorder*.

If the anxiety is focused on a neutral object (a sense of anxiety about dogs or elevators or flying on airplanes or being in open places), the condition is called a *phobia*. Phobias are illogical fears; the person consciously fears the dog or elevator or other object, but the real cause of the sense of dread or anxiety is hidden and subconscious (see FEARS AND PHOBIAS).

If the anxiety is displaced or refocused onto some form of compulsive, irrational thinking (such as feeling contaminated or thoughts of violence) or compulsive, irrational behavior (such as repetitive, obsessive handwashing), the condition is called an *obsessive-compulsive anxiety disorder*.

DIAGNOSING ANXIETY

Anxiety is not always easy to diagnose. The most common diagnostic method is to look for a cluster of symptoms such as those described above. The patient recounts his or her symptoms, and the counselor makes a diagnosis based on his or her clinical impression of those symptoms.

Another method of diagnosing anxiety disorders involves the use of tests such as the Minnesota Multiphasic Personality Inventory (MMPI), which is helpful in diagnosing a variety of mental disorders including anxiety. An anxious individual would score high on scales such as D (Depression) and PT (Psychosthenic). The most widely used psychological test in the world, the MMPI is highly objective and reliable.

A less sophisticated cousin to the MMPI is the Taylor Johnson Temperament Analysis (TJTA), which will also pick up signs of anxiety. One advantage of the TJTA is that it is available for use by pastors in spiritual counseling.

Less reliable (because they are more subjective) but still often helpful are the *projective tests* such as the Thematic Apperception Test (TAT) and the Rorschach Test. The object of projective tests is to determine whether an individual symbolically projects his or her anxiety onto pictures (such as an inkblot) or an object.

Finally, medical tests are also used to aid in diagnosing mental disorders. These tests include Computer Assisted Tomography (CAT scans) and Magnetic Resonance Imaging (MRI), which are like sophisticated X rays of the brain. CAT scans and MRI scans have not proven helpful in diagnosing anxiety disorders but can be useful in diagnosing and eliminating medical conditions that produce anxietylike symptoms (such as physiologically-based schizophrenia resulting from enlarged ventricles in the brain). Another test, Positron Emission Transaxial Tomography (PETT), enables us to examine the local activity of the brain and allows us to follow such biochemical processes as glucose metabolism. Individuals with obsessive-compulsive anxiety disorder seem to metabolize glucose in the frontal lobe of the brain more rapidly than normal, indicating greater than normal mental activity (such as anxiety). For the most part, however, these sophisticated medical tests yield only a limited amount of information and insight regarding the presence of anxiety in an individual.

GOD'S VIEW OF ANXIETY

As Christian therapists, we believe that one of the major sources of anxiety is the fear people have of looking inside themselves, examining negative and conflicting emotions, recognizing sins, and dealing honestly with what they find there. Rather than courageously face the anger, guilt, lust, envy, greed, or resentment within themselves, people bury, suppress, deny, or ignore those moral and emotional realities. At some deep level they know it's there, but they have shoved it out of their conscious minds. The conflict that results between their conscious and unconscious minds is anxiety.

We believe that anxiety is actually a God-given alarm system designed to expose unhealthy emotions and thoughts, so that we can think, feel, and behave in healthy and godly ways. In His infinite wisdom, God wants us to examine our emotions honestly and stop denying our true feelings. Deception is wrong; self-deception is unhealthy. The Holy Spirit uses anxiety to get our attention and to tell us that our inner beings need examination.

Unfortunately, most of us are afraid of the truth. We don't want to look inside and face the pain, disordered thoughts, and unpleasant emotions that lurk inside us. It is a fact of human nature that we want quick, easy solutions—an "anxiety pill"—to make our bad feelings go away. Or we want someone to tell us that our problems are someone else's fault, not our own responsibility. So the normal human response to anxiety is to deny it, fight it, or anesthetize it with drugs (including alcohol, prescription drugs, or illegal narcotics).

God's approach to treating anxiety, however, is to approach this disorder with realism, honesty, and a courageous search for the truth. As Jeremiah 17:10 tells us, "I, the LORD, search the heart, I test the mind." And Jesus, in Revelation 2:23, says that He is the one "who searches the minds and hearts." God knows the thoughts and motives of our hearts. He is the one who can pierce our self-deception and our defense mechanisms, so that the true nature and sources of our anxieties can be brought to the surface. God's approach, which involves uncovering the true sources of our conflict so that it can be understood and treated, is the most effective and successful approach to this emotional disorder.

> ■
> *Anxiety is a curable problem—if the anxiety-afflicted person is willing to take responsibility for his or her cure.*
> ■

ANXIETY AND DEPRESSION

People sometimes confuse anxiety with depression. Though people do sometimes experience depression in connection with their anxiety, there is a difference between the two. In a broad sense, anxiety relates to the future, and depression relates more to the past. Or, put another way, *anxiety is the future superimposed on the present,* and *depression is the past superimposed on the present.* This statement is an oversimplification, of course, since the sources of anxiety, which is a sense of foreboding about the future, are rooted in hidden emotions of the past. This oversimplified distinction, however, does help many people recognize and distinguish between their various feelings and emotional issues.

For example, Jan suffers anxiety as she worries that something may be going wrong with her marriage. She cannot put her finger on a specific problem in the relationship, but she senses something is not going well, and she anticipates the worst. Later, after her marriage ends in divorce (in part because of her anxious behavior, which she did not deal with and resolve), she feels depressed. She feels tremendous loss and grieves the failure of her relationship.

■

Both anxiety and depression are normal reactions that everyone experiences in life. They can become abnormal if allowed to continue for an extended period or if they cause a person to lose control of life or if they prompt a person to hurt himself or someone else.

■

An example of how anxiety and depression are related—and how anxiety can be resolved by bringing hidden emotional issues to the surface—is found in the story of Matt, a young graduate student. Matt came to the clinic to be treated for depression. Like many depressed people, Matt also suffered from anxiety. He had lost interest in his studies and was in a constant state of agitation. Most bothersome were his migraine headaches and insomnia. He got only four hours of rest a night. (An anxious person frequently has problems getting to sleep; a depressed person, by contrast, frequently escapes into sleep, then wakes up in the middle of the night and can't get back to sleep.)

Matt claimed to have no guilt or angry feelings. A standard medical examination turned up no physical abnormalities or deficiencies that would lead to anxiety or depression. Questions about his school work, relationship with parents, and other aspects of his life revealed no insights. But since he was struggling with depression, the clinic doctors knew his problem was linked to something in his past that was still bothering him in the present. And since he suffered from anxiety, the doctors knew he was afraid to look at some negative emotion buried inside of him. But what was it?

Finally, the doctors asked Matt to keep a diary of his dreams, making a note of each dream on a bedside pad immediately upon waking. Dreams often reveal repressed issues and emotions. On his return visit, Matt described a dream in which he was in the backseat of a car; a man and his wife were in the front seat. The car had no top or body, just a frame and seats. The car hit a bump, the man was bounced out, and Matt climbed into the front seat beside the woman and continued driving. The dislodged man ran along behind and finally caught up with the car. Matt got out, and the couple continued on their way.

The meaning of the dream was clear to the doctors, though Matt didn't have a clue what it meant. "Matt," the doctors asked, "have you recently had an affair with a married woman?"

Matt was shaken and astonished. "Yes," he replied. "About six months ago. It's over now, and I haven't seen the woman since."

He had been boarding with a couple while pursuing his studies and had become involved with the woman while the husband was away at work. They had a troubled, insecure, unstable marriage—symbolized in the dream by a car without a top or body—and for a while, Matt had symbolically taken the husband's place in the driver's seat. In the end, as in the dream, Matt was left alone while the couple went on their way together.

"It's so obvious now," said Matt. "But why haven't I felt guilty about the relationship?"

"The fact is, you *have* felt guilty," the doctors explained. "Consciously, you have been pretending you did nothing wrong. You told yourself, 'Their marriage was shaky anyway, the husband never found out, the affair didn't last long, it's over, no harm done.' But deep down, you know it was wrong and harmful. You know that you

THE COMPLETE LIFE ENCYCLOPEDIA

betrayed this man's trust and took advantage of this woman's vulnerability. You didn't cause the problems in the marriage, but you did complicate their problems. You have been consciously hiding from a sense of guilt that, subconsciously, you know is there."

Identifying Matt's hidden emotional conflict was an important first step in resolving his anxiety. Matt had come to the doctors so that he could get his depression and anxiety "fixed" by medical means. He discovered that he had some difficult and ugly realities to face first. There was guilt in his life, and that guilt had to be resolved. The doctors helped Matt to face and work through his guilt feelings, reinforce his moral convictions so that he would not rationalize and engage in such behavior again, and receive God's forgiveness of sin.

The process followed in Matt's case is the process we generally use at the Minirth Meier New Life Clinics to help people resolve their feelings of anxiety:

1. Help the individual get in touch with hidden emotions.
2. Encourage the individual to ventilate these emotions so that there is no longer any conflict between conscious and unconscious thoughts and emotions.
3. Help the individual to experience forgiveness—both God's forgiveness toward him or her and the individual's own forgiveness toward others who have wronged him or her—so that the underlying emotional issues can be discharged and the individual can become free of anxiety.

Forgiveness is not pretending something wrong didn't happen to you, nor is it pretending that something you did wrong didn't happen. Forgiveness is not a matter of "forgive and forget." Memories are indelibly etched in the biochemical pathways of your brain, and they cannot be forgotten by a simple force of will. Attempts to *repress* memories are unhealthy and actually increase your tendency toward anxiety. Forgiveness involves becoming fully aware of your anger toward someone else or (in the case of our own wrongs, mistakes, and sins) becoming fully aware of your own responsibility and guilt—and then, with full knowledge of the awful truth, choosing not to hold the offense against that person or against yourself, by reason of God's grace through Jesus Christ.

Matt had to recognize his struggle with guilt, admit his sin, receive God's forgiveness, and forgive himself. He could never undo what he had done, but he could experience true forgiveness and go on with his life. Forgiveness enabled him to eventually resolve his anxiety and be healed from his depression.

■

Forgiveness is a decision not to dwell on the memory of the offense or to seek opportunities for revenge.

■

WORRY-FREE LIVING

Each of us has endured feelings of anxiety from time to time. Is worry-free living even possible? Yes—though for most people it will always remain a goal, not an achievement. The antidote for anxiety is facing the truth. As Jesus said (in words that are applicable in so many practical, spiritual, and emotional settings), "The truth shall make you free" (John 8:32). To know the truth about anxiety, you must first dispel some commonly held myths about anxiety.

Myth 1: "Give it time; your anxiety will go away." Emotional disorders may be submerged and repressed for a while, but they don't "go away" without work and insight.

Anxiety is the most common mental health problem in America, yet most people ignore it, deny it, excuse it, or put up with it when they could find real release from it. But curing anxiety takes work, and most of us are lazy. That laziness keeps us from enjoying the rich, healthy emotional life God intended for us to experience. Don't expect your anxiety simply to disappear with time. Rather than healing anxiety, time tends to make it worse. Face it, deal with it, resolve it—and then it will go away.

Myth 2: "It's in my genes. Anxiety is just part of my family tree." Nonsense. You may be able to inherit certain symptomatic ways your body exhibits your inner anxiety (say, a tendency to poor digestion or toward high blood pressure), but you cannot inherit anxiety itself. Anxiety is emotional conflict over real issues in your life. In your family of origin, you may have learned ways to cope with anxiety that are unhealthy, and thus you may find yourself mimicking unhealthy patterns of your parents, but that does not mean you inherited a genetic tendency to anxiety. You have a *choice* as to whether or not you will be cured of your anxiety.

Myth 3: "Anxiety is a sign of weakness." As we have already seen, anxiety is an alarm that something is not right deep inside our emotions. Anxiety can actually be a positive reaction, which God can use to get your attention so that you can repair and fine-tune your emotional life. Properly understood, it's a marvelous mechanism for alerting you to the need for self-examination. Anxiety can be a strength. It is only when you deny or repress anxiety that it becomes a weakness.

Myth 4: "It's a sin to dig up the past." Some people object to doing the work of uncovering the hidden emotional sources of anxiety. "Forgive and forget," they say. "Let sleeping dogs lie." But when you seek to reveal the sources of anxiety, you are not just "rehashing the past." You are trying to find out what hidden issues of the past are continuing to affect you in the present. Often, when issues of the past are buried like land mines, they have to be dug up and defused so that you will quit stepping on them and getting hurt in the present. Past issues may involve your own actions for which you harbor guilt or the actions of others for which you harbor resentment. Once the subconscious issue is forced to the surface of your conscious awareness, you can make a deliberate choice to forgive. And then the healing will begin.

Myth 5: "I/he/she must have a demon of anxiety." It has become popular in some quarters to ascribe a host of human emotional, behavioral, and spiritual problems to demonic activity. As Christian therapists, we believe in the reality of demonic activity in our world, but we also believe it is dangerous and too simplistic to look for demonic activity in every issue we face. The "devil-made-me-do-it" explanation is attractive to some people because it holds out the promise of a "quick fix" cure for deep-seated emotional issues. "If I can only find the right deliverance minister," they think, "I'll be liberated with a prayer and a snap of the fingers."

The Bible makes it clear, however, that we are not just spiritual beings, subject to spiritual disorders as a result of demonic opposition. We are also physical beings who experience medical disorders. And we are mental/emotional beings who are subject to mental/emotional disorders, which need sound, sensible, therapeutic treatment. That is why Paul prays for his friends' wholeness in "spirit, soul, and body" in 1 Thessalonians 5:23. Blaming demons for problems that result from our actions, our choices, our emotional issues, is a cop-out, an easy way out. Overemphasizing demonic activity to the exclusion of personal responsibility or medical resources is a serious and dangerous error.

Myth 6: "Christians don't have emotional problems." Of course they do. Ideally, of course, Christians shouldn't have to suffer depression, shouldn't fall into sin, shouldn't be guilty of materialism, and shouldn't engage in selfish power struggles. But we all know that Christians do. Christians are not perfect; they're just forgiven. And God has given us many powerful tools and resources, from the truths of Scripture to the practical guidance of psychology and psychiatry, to enable us to be healed of our disorders and to grow from our experiences.

As Christians, our most important goal in life is to become more like Jesus. We do this in two ways: (1) we look closely at the life of Jesus; and (2) we look closely at our own lives and compare. Dwight L. Moody once said that the best way to show that a stick is crooked is to lay a straight ruler alongside of it. Jesus is our ruler.

Seeking counseling for emotional issues is not a sign of weak faith. In fact, Scripture encourages us to admit our faults to one another, encourage one another, and pray for one another so that we can be healed (see James 5:16).

As we replace these myths about anxiety with the truth, we will be better equipped to face and disarm our anxieties and to live a rich and joyful life.

SELF-HELP STRATEGIES

There is a range of treatment options for anxiety that, depending on the severity of the problem, range from self-help techniques to intensive medical therapy. Some of these techniques can bring some relief almost immediately; others require a commitment to long-term changes in one's life. All of these strategies for healing can be integrated into a comprehensive coping strategy that can dramatically reduce anxiety levels.

Let's first look at a series of mental and spiritual self-help techniques that can help reduce anxiety or prevent anxiety from recurring:

Meditate Daily

We have seen this truth validated again and again: Scripture meditation works. But there are right and wrong ways to meditate on Scripture. Regularity is one key factor. Spontaneity is another. These two statements

Scriptures for Me___

1. **Assurance of Salvation**
   John 10:27–30; John 6:35–37; 1 John 5:11–13; John 3:16, 18; John 1:12
2. **Assurance of God's Forgiveness**
   1 John 1:9; John 8:3–11; Psalm 103:12–14
3. **Assurance of Answered Prayer**
   1 John 5:14; John 16:24; John 14:13–14; Jeremiah 33:3; Matthew 7:7–8
4. **Marital Conflicts**
   Ephesians 5:22–23; Colossians 3:18–19; 1 Peter 3:1–7; 1 Corinthians 7:1–5
5. **Parent-Child Conflicts**
   Deuteronomy 6:4–9; Ephesians 6:1–4; Colossians 3:20–21; Proverbs 13:24; Proverbs 29:15
6. **Loneliness**
   Hebrews 13:5; Matthew 28:19–20; Psalm 139:16
7. **Anger**
   Ephesians 4:26–27; Leviticus 19:17–18; Romans 12:15–16; Proverbs 15:1; Proverbs 19:12; Ecclesiastes 7:9; Colossians 3:8; Matthew 5:21–24
8. **Bitterness**
   Hebrews 13:12; Ephesians 4:31; Acts 8:23; Proverbs 14:10
9. **Forgiving Others**
   Ephesians 4:32; 2 Corinthians 2:7; Luke 6:37; Matthew 6:14; Mark 11:25
10. **Overcoming Depression**
    Psalm 42:5, 11; Psalm 43:5; Genesis 4:6–7; John 14:1
11. **Trials**
    James 1:2–5; 1 Peter 1:6, 7; Job 23:10; Romans 5:1–5; Philippians 1:27; 1 Peter 4:12–19
12. **Suffering**
    2 Corinthians 4:7–18; 2 Corinthians 1:3–4; 2 Corinthians 12:7–10; Hebrews 12:5–11; Romans 8:28–29; Romans 5:15; John 9:1–3; Mark 5:21–42; 1 Peter 1:3–9
13. **Temptation**
    1 Corinthians 10:12, 13; Hebrews 4:15, 16; Proverbs 4:12; James 4:7, 8; Proverbs 8:32
14. **Anxiety**
    John 14:27; Philippians 4:6–8; Matthew 6:25–34; Psalm 27:1; Psalm 27:14; Psalm 34:4; Psalm 56:3

may sound contradictory, but they are not. It is important to build daily habits of Scripture reading and meditation (that's the regularity aspect). But Scripture meditation should not be just another item on our things-to-do list or it will become a burden, a meaningless exercise. Effective Scripture meditation should have an element of adventure, joy, and spontaneity.

Choose a quiet, relaxed environment, sitting or kneeling in a comfortable place. Don't set a goal (a set number of chapters or verses to get through) for your Scripture reading. Just plan to spend twenty minutes or half an hour reading, listening for God's thoughts, stopping whenever a passage seems especially meaningful. Tailor your reading by choosing passages that address issues in your current life. If you are feeling anxious, seek out passages that offer reassurance and peace. If you feel guilty, meditate on the forgiveness passages.

Relax

We often counsel anxious patients to use a repetitive phrase to help them unwind. This technique can work for you too. At the first hint of anxiety, try breathing deeply and slowly. Each time you exhale, repeat the same phrase. What words work best? Christians often like to use a favorite line of Scripture. Perhaps one of the verses that you've meditated on will hold a special meaning for you. If so, jot it down on an index card and carry it with you to memorize for use during stressful times. Or you can choose a phrase as simple as, "Anxiety is a signal to relax." It's a true statement; it has a certain balance and rhythm. And if you say it over and over whenever you are trying to reduce stress, you'll begin to link those words to the response you want: relaxation.

In a similar way, a relaxing hymn can also be a way to relieve anxiety. One hymn, "Tell It to Jesus," seems specifically written for anxiety sufferers. In the third verse, we find the words, "Do you fear the gathering clouds of sorrow? . . . Are you anxious what shall be tomorrow?" And the hymn's refrain is a soothing repetition of practical counsel for anxiety: "Tell it to Jesus, tell it to Jesus." These words are repeated twelve times in a rhythm and melody that convey a healing, soothing effect.

The titles of many old hymns illustrate that one of the historic purposes of Christian music is to soothe the anxious soul: "Never Alone," "What a Friend We Have in Jesus," "Sweet Hour of Prayer," "Love Lifted Me," "'Tis So Sweet to Trust in Jesus." Even the paranoid King Saul relaxed when David played the harp.

In general, music is a powerful tool for altering moods—both for good or ill. If the sound is loud and the beat is throbbing, anxiety can be heightened. If the melody and rhythm are balanced, they can soothe the listener and calm anxiety. For help in soothing your anxieties, select soothing music with calming words.

Exercise

Exercise helps to relieve anxiety in several ways. First, it provides a diversion for worries. Second, exercise releases not only adrenalin but also endorphins and enkephalins that are natural mood-lifters, according to recent research. Third, exercise helps in the sense that the better your physical condition, the better prepared you are to withstand anxiety.

Talk Through Your Problems

Anxiety often builds because people don't air their feelings daily. A small problem can become a phobia if it's turned inward and allowed to fester. So work to keep lines of communication open in your family (see FAMILY; MARRIAGE). Also, make sure you have someone with whom you can regularly share your emotional issues, openly and honestly—a trusted friend, a counselor, a pastor, a support group, a small group Bible study fellowship. Talking through your problems helps to dispel anxiety surrounding current issues, keeps anxiety from turning inward, and helps you to be more objective about the issues in your life.

Make Time for Recreation and Laughter

It has been said that laughter relieves more tension than crying and is certainly a lot more fun. It is likely that endorphins and enkephalins, which help to raise spirits and overcome anxiety, are released with laughter.

Recreation is also an excellent way to drain off your anxieties. Get away from your usual routine. Take a vacation—or just a one-day or half-day or hour-long minivacation. If you tend to be an anxious workaholic, your vacations are probably just worktimes in a different setting. Try to take vacations that are more oriented to relaxation and fun. The better you are able to relax and "get away from it all," the sooner your anxiety level will decrease.

Have Regular Medical Checkups

Have a medical checkup once a year. Personal health is one of the biggest sources of worry. Much of this anxiety can be relieved by having a good medical checkup once a year or a more in-depth examination if needed.

Limit Worry

As counselors, we come into contact with a lot of professional worriers. Their productivity suffers because so much of their time and energy are sapped by constant fretting. If only they could schedule their worry for a specific time slot, confine it to that period, and not allow it to distract them from other matters! Though it may sound silly, this is a solution that many—particularly many compulsive perfectionists—have found workable. Set aside fifteen minutes in the morning and another fifteen minutes in the evening for active worry. If worries surface during other times of the day, jot them down on a card and deal with them during the designated worry period. By confining active worry to a designated time slot of only 1 percent of a twelve-hour day, you can move much closer to your goal of worry-free living. You'll be more productive during the day, you'll be able to list your worries by priority, and by the time you get around to really worrying over them, they will probably have shrunk in importance, and the cards and the problems can be discarded.

Live One Day at a Time

Jesus, the Great Physician, has a profound word of advice for worriers: "Therefore do not worry about tomorrow, for tomorrow will worry about its own things. Sufficient for the day is its own trouble" (Matt. 6:34). Since God cares for sparrows, wildflowers, and other less significant parts of creation, we know He cares for us and is in charge of the future. Thus we would do well to replace anxiety with living one day at a time.

Anxious people make long lists of things to do, they fret over their lists, and punish themselves when they don't get it all done. A key to worry-free living is to accept the limits of a twenty-four-hour day, to do the best you can with the time God has given you, and to accept God's grace for the things you must put off until tomorrow. As the little red-haired orphan sang in the Broadway musical *Annie,* "The sun *will* come out tomorrow!"

Design an Action Plan

When Mark Twain faced the task of delivering a speech to a standing-room-only audience, he was nearly overcome with anxiety. What could he do about it? He had three options: (1) cancel out and disappoint everyone; (2) wring his hands and compound his anxiety; or (3) write a speech and practice it until it was time to get up and speak. He chose action plan number 3. The point is—*do something* to lessen your anxiety. Don't just fret over your circumstances. If you're worried about failing a test in school, work out a study plan to prepare yourself. If you're anxious about entertaining your husband's boss for dinner, choose a fix-ahead menu, send your children to a friend's house for the night, order a pretty floral centerpiece, and prepare the table hours in advance. Study the options, select a plan—then implement it.

Cultivate the Awareness of God's Presence

The best antidote to anxiety is the knowledge that God is with you. The importance of this fact is underscored in the life of Moses (Heb. 11:27): "He endured as seeing Him who is invisible." For Moses, the reality of God's presence was as tangible as if he could reach out and touch God at any moment. The awareness of God's presence with us provides two benefits in fighting anxiety: (1) His presence is a source of comfort, encouragement, security, and peace; and (2) His presence strengthens us to live in obedience to His will.

Replace Worry with Prayer

Prayer is an important weapon in your fight against anxiety, particularly when coupled with time in the Word, plus insight and feedback from friends. If your worry is linked to a specific fear, then ask God to help you through the ordeal. If your worry is generalized and nonspecific, if you feel tense but you don't know why—ask God for insight. Pray that God will search you and show you what the source of your anxiety is so that you can address it quickly. "If any of you lacks wisdom" or insight or understanding, as James 1:5 tells us, "let him ask of God, who gives to all liberally and without reproach, and it will be given to him."

PROFESSIONAL APPROACHES

Of course, many levels of help are available beyond the self-help strategies outlined above. For some people, the resolution of anxiety requires counseling and psychotherapy in order to get at the core issues beneath the anxiety. So often we are unaware of those emotions or motives that may be trying to force their way up from the subconscious into the conscious. God's spirit may be pushing them up to make us aware of what David termed "secret sins."

Many times the encouragement and counsel available from a good friend, a pastoral or lay counselor, a psychologist, a psychotherapist, or a psychiatrist can put you in touch with the core issues and help you develop a plan to deal with them in a way that will siphon off anxiety. Following are some of the professional treatment options that are available to the anxiety sufferer.

In our experience at the Minirth Meier New Life Clinics, the leading cause of anxiety in most people is guilt. The flesh pulls one way, your conscience pulls the other. When you give in to the flesh, you create guilt—the very emotional conflict that sets you up for anxiety. As you rely on God's presence with you, asking Him to lead you out of temptation, you call a halt to the internal tug-of-war between your conscience and your flesh. And the result is peace.

Insight-Oriented Therapy

We have seen many patients who have anxiety because of deep unresolved issues within. As a result of old wounds, deep emotional hurts and repressed anxieties developed and were never dealt with. Eventually, these emotions accumulated to the point that the patients could not function, yet the emotions were hidden and subconscious, so they couldn't even understand why they had become unable to function. Insight-oriented therapists use approaches that enable people to uncover and ventilate their deep hurts and secrets in a safe setting. The counseling process helps these individuals gain insight into how these deep emotions cause the depression, anxiety, or medical problem today. Throughout the course of their therapy, clients again and again have "Aha!" experiences and say, "So *that's* why I was doing that!" or "So *that's* why this keeps happening to me!" The process of uncovering those buried or secret issues is never easy, but the joy of discovery when an insight is gained is beyond words.

The insight-oriented approach also helps people to see how these issues from the past affect their current relationships, such as when anxiety around a certain individual today may be triggered by unpleasant memories of a similar person in the past.

A counselor who wants to help individuals gain insight often begins by simply letting them talk. The term used in therapy for this venting of emotion is *catharsis*. This often begins with being loving enough to listen to them share the issues from deep within.

Insight does not come easily. *Resistance* often develops because it is painful to see issues inside of us that we do not want to look at. To some degree the brain has very carefully arranged a series of defense mechanisms (see DEFENSE MECHANISMS) to protect us from difficult truths. Yet lying to ourselves about the issues and feelings inside us is profoundly unhealthy.

It has been said that being listened to and understood is one of the most moving of all experiences.

Some of the most common past issues that trigger current anxiety include parental absence, loss of one or both parents through divorce or abandonment, parents who are either overly possessive or too harsh, parents who were either distant or enmeshed, parents who were seductive, birth order issues and sibling rivalry, childhood injunctions such as "be perfect" or "don't succeed" or "don't grow up" or even "don't exist." Some of the common current issues and stresses that trigger anxiety include death of a loved one, divorce or separation, personal injury or illness, loss of a job or other major

93

financial problem, retirement, holiday stress around Thanksgiving and Christmas, poor family communication, marital conflict, and conflict with teenagers.

An insight-oriented counselor helps individuals to work through anxiety patterns by asking questions, reflecting back to them, and repeating key words that they shared to emphasize those concepts and issues that seem to be anxiety-related. The counselor may also offer interpretation, gently explaining and restating some of the individuals' attitudes and behaviors, then waiting to see what kind of resistance or acceptance comes in response.

Through this process, individuals are able to bring issues and emotions—many of which have never before been consciously examined—out into the open where they can be placed in a framework of meaning and understanding. Once the true emotional underpinnings of the anxiety begin to take shape, individuals gain insights that can be profoundly helpful in enabling them to make changes that will resolve emotional conflicts and dissipate the anxiety.

In the hands of Christian practitioners, insight-oriented approaches have an added source of insight to offer: God's Word. Hebrews 4:12 tells us that our primary resource for insight, the Bible, is active, living, and surgically sharp—sharper, in fact, than a double-edged Roman sword. It pierces through to the divisions of soul and spirit and body (joints and marrow) and provides us with an accurate evaluation of our thoughts, including our conscious and subconscious emotions and motives. Verse 13 adds that God sees every heart and that all is open and laid bare before Him.

How should you then respond? As God opens His insights to you, you should be like the psalmist in Psalm 119:59, who says, "I thought about my ways, and turned my feet to Your testimonies." The consideration of your emotions and motives should lead to biblical behavior. The psalmist also implores God to search him and know his heart, to evaluate his anxious thoughts, pointing out any hurtful or wicked way and leading him in ways of eternal significance (Ps. 139:23–24). David echoes a similar prayer in light of his perception of God in Psalm 19:14:

> Let the words of my mouth
>   and the meditation of my heart
> Be acceptable in Your sight,
> O LORD, my strength and my Redeemer.

Reality Therapy

Though insight-oriented therapy is our approach of choice, especially when deep-rooted emotional issues are present, other approaches are sometimes indicated. Reality therapy—a present-day problem-solving approach—is one such approach and may be indicated for several reasons. Reality therapy might be indicated when deep issues are not present or when a person's ego structure is too fragile to stand the painful insights that may emerge.

A therapist may feel that a reality approach—listening, offering practical advice to overcome anxiety, developing a specific plan for dealing with current stress—is the best approach. For example, an anxious individual may need to develop a specific plan of eight or ten things to do daily or weekly for the next month, to see if this would help overcome the anxiety. The plan might include such activities as a daily quiet time,

THE COMPLETE LIFE ENCYCLOPEDIA

calling a supportive friend once a day, a daily exercise program, a balanced diet, or doing one specific thing this week to resolve a painful issue from the past.

Some individuals have acquired habits in their daily living that are perfect setups for depression and anxiety—*and they aren't even aware of it.* For example, a depressed person may be sleeping late, not exercising, avoiding social contact, and drinking alcohol or taking drugs, then wondering why the depression gets worse and worse! The goal of reality therapy is to restructure the individual's life in such a way that behavioral changes bring about emotional improvement.

As Solomon tells us in Proverbs 4:23, "Keep your heart with all diligence, for out of it spring the issues of life." To put it another way, as you think within, so you are (Prov. 23:7). Getting in touch with those hidden emotions and motives that produce anxiety, meditating on Scripture, and allowing God's Word to govern your conscious behavior and your thoughts and motives can go a long way toward providing worry-free living.

Belief System Therapy

We all have belief systems that we either adopt intellectually or accept on a "feelings" level. These beliefs affect our present-day lives and may produce intense anxiety and insecurity. When this occurs, those beliefs need to be revised to fit reality. This approach is sometimes called *cognitive therapy* (or, among psychologists, *rational emotive therapy*).

A number of different faulty beliefs must sometimes be corrected in order to reduce anxiety. With *personalization,* a mother may feel that when her child left a shoe in the middle of the floor, it was an intentional, personal attack on her. With *generalization,* a parent may generalize from a single incident, concluding, for example, that a child who misbehaves today will grow up to be a criminal. With *polarization,* issues are seen as black and white, as when a Christian views his pastor and church as either all good or all bad, not recognizing any "gray areas." With *selective abstraction,* a student may focus on the five points missed during the exam rather than the ninety-five correct points. With *magnification,* a person may view a relatively routine marital conflict as catastrophic. With *arbitrary inference,* an individual concludes that a group of people on the other side of the room is talking about him. All of these faulty beliefs can produce intense anxiety.

Among Christians, faulty religious beliefs can produce anxiety. It is important to understand that these faulty beliefs may be operating at a subconscious or feelings level and may actually conflict with the conscious theological attitudes of the individual:

- "God can never forgive me for some past sin." This belief is refuted by 1 John 1:9 and Psalm 103:12–14.
- "God cannot use me because I am spiritually weak." This belief runs counter to 2 Corinthians 12:9: "For My strength is made perfect in weakness."
- "God will love me more if I do more for God." God's love cannot be earned; Ephesians 2:8–9 tells us that God's love is appropriated by grace through faith, not by works.

A Christian counselor can redirect these false beliefs to a biblical perspective by developing assignments whereby the client can see that his or her religious belief systems are not true.

When the belief system is faulty, the individual's beliefs cause anxiety. In cognitive therapy, these belief systems are challenged, and new, healthy, reality-based belief systems are slowly developed.

Group Therapy

The approaches we've examined are, in our opinion, the three most useful individual therapy approaches (among many) that can be used to treat anxiety. We have found, however, that individual therapy can progress much more rapidly when coupled with group therapy. We see the value of group processes not only in modern counseling but also in the New Testament. God established the importance of the group experience during the first century, as evidenced by the many "one another" passages in the New Testament. Through interacting in the group, an individual can often overcome anxiety by learning needed social skills. He or she may learn to deal with conflicts in the present that symbolize unresolved past conflicts. He or she may gain support and receive a vicarious insight into dealing with anxiety by hearing how someone else overcame a specific similar conflict.

At the Minirth Meier New Life Clinics, we have a saying that applies to a lot of the anxiety problems we see: If you find yourself in a rowboat during a storm, pray hard and row to shore! Worry-free living is attainable if you're willing to pray hard and work toward your goal. How hard and how long you must work depends on how far from shore you are when you begin.

A group emphasis can be especially important in conjunction with insight-oriented therapy. It is often easier for an individual to accept insight from a group rather than from one individual such as a therapist. Groups also enable an individual to receive feedback on his or her honesty, game-playing, evasiveness, denial, and self-deception. The group solution is almost always superior to individual solutions in attacking the problem of anxiety.

WORK TOWARD YOUR GOAL

God wants you to live a worry-free life. When anxiety attacks you, you can identify with the words of Psalm 94:19, "In the multitude of my anxieties within me, Your comforts delight my soul." God makes His comfort and His power available to you so that you can experience healing from the pain of anxiety—but you have to do the work of getting well. Healing from anxiety can be achieved because all things are possible through Jesus Christ.

Assertiveness

Jennie came into the clinic suffering from physical exhaustion and emotional depression. Her cheeks were hollow, her eyes were rimmed with dark circles, her shoulders were stooped. She looked ill. "I can't go on like this!" she said, her voice collapsing into sobs. "I can't get my housework done. I only get four or five hours of sleep a night. They won't leave me alone!"

"Who won't leave you alone?" asked the counselor.

"The pastor and the other people at my church," Jennie replied. "They keep asking me to do this, to volunteer for that. I'm teaching a Sunday school class, I'm on four committees, I'm on the Deacons Board, I'm in the choir, and they just asked me to be in charge of Vacation Bible School this summer! I don't know how I'm going to do it all!"

"Why do you have to do it all?"

Jennie stared at the counselor as if she couldn't believe he even asked the question. "Well, because they asked me! They're counting on me!"

"Why don't you say no?"

That really startled her. "Say no?! How can I say no? They love me! What would they do if I said no?"

"What do you think they'd do if you said no?"

She thought for a long time, but didn't have an answer.

"Do you think," the counselor continued, "that maybe—just maybe—they might go ask somebody else? And that the job would still get done? And that maybe another person would get to experience the joy of serving in the church?"

This idea—that she could actually say no—was a new concept to Jennie. It took time and more counseling before Jennie was able to reprogram her thinking and her behavior to the point where she was actually able to cut back her activities at church to a reasonable level. But in time, she was able to make those adjustments. Her exhaustion and depression were eventually cured, and her appearance improved dramatically. Jennie was able to learn healthy Christian assertiveness.

Fred was painting the trim of his house when his neighbor Ray stopped by. "What are you doing, Fred? You just had your house painted two weeks ago."

"I know," said Fred, "but the fella who did the work didn't do a very good job, so I'm giving it another coat myself."

"How much did you pay that guy?"

"Well, I was supposed to pay him fifteen-hundred, but—"

"Gee, Fred, that seems a little steep for a job this size."

"But I ended up paying him two-thousand."

"What?! You paid him five-hundred *more* for a lousy job? Why?"

"Well," said Fred, setting his paint brush down and looking sadly at his house, "when he finished the job, I asked him why it looked all blotchy. He said, 'Don't worry, it'll look great when it dries.' So I paid him the fifteen-hundred and he left. But when the paint dried, it looked even worse. So I brought him back and showed it to him, and he said, 'Sure enough, it needs another coat. I'll give you a break on the second coat—just five-hundred dollars.' So I paid him, and he said, 'I'll be back tomorrow.' Well, he never showed up, and now he won't return my calls."

"So what are you gonna do, Fred?"

"I'm gonna paint my house," Fred replied sheepishly. "I guess he sort of took advantage of me."

"Yeah," said Ray, shaking his head. "Like that vitamin salesman sort of took advantage of you. And those guys who sold you the time-share condo in Elko, Nevada. Fred, when are you gonna wise up and quit being a doormat?"

Dr. Paul Meier knows how people like Jennie and Fred feel. There was a time in his life when people frequently took advantage of him. "I had a hard time saying no to anyone, because I thought I should do whatever anybody asked," he recalls in his book *Don't Let Jerks Get the Best of You* (Thomas Nelson, 1993). "In our church, the attitudes of Jesus were taken out of context and taught with a 'letter of the Law' approach. For example, we were told that if somebody attacked us, we were to turn the other cheek, no matter what the situation might be. Likewise, we were taught that if someone wanted us to 'walk an extra mile' for any reason whatsoever, we were to do it without questioning the other person's motive.

"It wasn't until years later, however, that I learned a Christian should turn the other cheek or walk the extra mile if he is being slapped or hassled *for being a Christian*. The biblical text does not teach that we are to become masochists who allow people to abuse us whenever a whim suits them. But as a young boy, that's exactly what I thought—turn the other cheek and walk the extra mile, no matter what. It was no wonder, then, that I became a prime target for [people] who liked to take advantage of me" (p. 81).

Fortunately, Dr. Meier was able to come to an understanding that though the Bible teaches that we are to be humble, it does not teach that we must become masochists or doormats. The Bible also affirms that we are to be assertive.

Assertiveness is a widely misunderstood concept. Many people equate assertiveness with being selfish, pushy, or aggressive. But true assertiveness is not abrasive or harmful. Assertiveness may be defined as "the ability to state your own needs or defend your own personal worth or convictions firmly, without devaluing the needs and feelings of others." As we examine the life of Christ, we find a Man who was completely humble, yet side by side with His humility was a bold quality of assertiveness. There were times when He withdrew from His ministry to the crowds in order to meet His physical and spiritual needs for revitalization, times when He said no to the demands that were placed on Him, times when He asserted His own human worth and confronted those who sinfully slandered him, times when He defended His convictions and His message with clarity and straightforward candor. He was always sensitive to the deep needs and feelings of those around Him, but He was not a masochist. He was courageously, lovingly assertive.

And He is the example for how we are to live our lives.

ASSERTIVENESS VERSUS MASOCHISM

The opposite of assertiveness is *masochism*—a word that, for many people, conjures up the idea of a form of sexual aberration. But that's not the kind of masochism we are talking about. As we use the word here, *masochism* means "the tendency to set oneself up to be hurt, victimized, exploited, pushed around or taken advantage of." Masochism is self-defeating behavior that a person may indulge in either consciously or unconsciously. It is the tendency to allow oneself to be used or abused by others, whether their imposition is well-intentioned or predatory.

Why do so many people fall into the trap of masochism?

Some people, like Dr. Meier, were brought up believing that to be a good Christian is to be a masochist. It is their Christian duty, they mistakenly think, to volunteer for everything, to say yes to everything, to expend every ounce of energy in Christian service without any thought to their own physical and emotional needs.

98

Another reason people fall into masochism is *shame*. People with masochistic tendencies have what Dr. Meier calls "holes in their souls," emotional deficits caused by abuse of one kind or another in their lives. If an individual is making masochistic decisions today, it may be owing at least in part to how he or she was brought up. The abuse may not have been as radical as sexual abuse or physical violence; it might have been as subtle as occasional childhood incidences of being shamed, blamed, or being ignored by parents. Whatever the source, the individual emerges into adulthood with what we call a *shame base*.

In every person's shame base are deeply buried pockets of false guilt that make him or her feel unworthy, without significant value, so that he or she does not feel entitled to enjoy the fundamental good things of life—happiness, career satisfaction, a healthy marriage, the right to say yes or no. When we talk with patients who have masochistic tendencies, these basic rights sound foreign to them. They say things like, "Some people may have the right to these good things, but I don't. I don't deserve them." Any traumatic experience can and usually does cause a tremendous sense of shame in an individual, which leads to feelings of false guilt. In fact, all people who have been abused tend, to some extent or another, to blame themselves for getting abused. They actually feel that they deserved the abuse.

Shame not only causes masochistic people to feel unworthy or incapable of asserting their own worth, needs, and convictions, shame also causes people to crave the acceptance and approval of others. Many people allow themselves to be exploited, thinking that by doing so they will be liked by those who exploit them. But all too often, when they allow themselves to be exploited, the very people they are trying to please end up losing respect for them—and their own self-esteem ratchets downward one more notch.

HOW TO BE ASSERTIVE

When phrasing your "I" message, think through the situation carefully and don't exaggerate. The key to using "I" messages is to put the responsibility for your own feelings on yourself. "You" messages accuse, demean, and attack the other person. "I" messages assert your own feelings and convictions.

Many Christians have come into the clinic with the legalistic idea that Christians have no rights at all. This, however, is simply not true. The Golden Rule clearly teaches that we should treat others as we would want others to treat us. To violate the Golden Rule, then, violates the right of other persons to be treated with the human dignity that God accorded to us all. Whenever we treat people with less respect and honor than the Golden Rule demands, we violate their God-given rights—and vice versa.

In many places the Bible speaks directly of your rights, or at least strongly implies that you have certain rights—for example, the right to sexual relations with your spouse (see 1 Cor. 7:3–5). Scripture makes it plain that you have the right to be treated honestly. Proverbs tells us "a false witness will not go unpunished, and he who speaks lies will not escape" (Prov. 19:5). The right not to be subjected to violence is set forth in such passages as Exodus 21:18–27. The Bible also condemns gossip and slander (see Lev. 19:16), which implies that you have the right not to have your character attacked and disparaged.

Unfortunately, human beings violate each other's God-given rights in many ways. What do you do with your anger or hurt when one of your God-given rights is violated? You could passively accept the abuse. Or you could aggressively explode in

99

anger (see AGGRESSION; ANGER). But neither of these is a healthy or biblical option. The best option is to *be assertive*. In other words, you should verbalize your angry feelings, making sure at the same time that you "speak the truth in love."

In his letter to the Ephesian Christians, Paul urges believers toward unity and deeper knowledge of Christ in order that they might become perfect (mature) and achieve the stature and fullness of Christ Himself. Paul doesn't want Christians to be children, tossed to and fro by every wind of doctrine or by the abusive trickery of human beings. Instead, he wants Christians to *speak the truth in love* so they can grow up and become like their Head, their Example, Jesus Christ Himself (see Eph. 4:14–15).

And Paul's counsel extends far beyond matters of doctrine alone. The phrase "speak the truth in love" is excellent advice when you seek the best way to respond when you are angry, when your personal worth has been devalued, when your physical, spiritual, and emotional needs are being denied, or when your convictions are being belittled. How, then, do you "speak the truth in love"? The following are four keys to assertive communication:

1. Major on the majors. All too often, we get ourselves embroiled in heated arguments, expending enormous amounts of emotional energy on issues that simply don't deserve it. The first rule of assertiveness is to major on the majors, not on the minors. Reserve your emotional energy for issues that really matter. For example, it is trivial for spouses to argue over the color of socks the husband wears, but it is legitimate to address annoying social habits.

2. Use "I" messages. Verbalize your message gently, respectfully, and tactfully. To speak the truth in love means using "I" messages rather than "you" messages. (See ANGER for examples of "I" messages and "you" messages.) "You" messages convey blame, and blame causes people to react defensively. You can send these same "you" messages as assertive "I" messages.

3. Be careful of your tone of voice. Be aware that your tone of voice helps create an attitude of mutual respect. If the other person becomes hot, loud, and contentious, your natural tendency will be to match that person in volume and wattage. Instead, make a conscious choice to soften your voice, to bring down the level of the confrontation. As you do, the other person is likely to respond to your modulation, and the anger level of the confrontation will likely subside to a manageable level. Speaking the truth in love means, in part, speaking with a loving tone of voice.

4. Forgive. Recognize that you cannot control the other person's response. Your assertiveness may not resolve the problem or win the other person over to your point of view. When that happens, forgive the person and move on (see FORGIVENESS). Don't nurse a grudge. Let go. Get on with your life.

| SELF-TEST | # Are You a Masochist? |

The following test was designed by Dr. Paul Meier, in concert with the more than three hundred therapists of Minirth Meier New Life Clinics across the country. It is designed to help you test your tendency to allow others to abuse or exploit you.

Before you use this test, understand that some people can suffer mild to severe abuse during childhood and beyond and still manage to make the emotional and mental choices necessary to avoid significant masochism. You may score very low on the following test, but it will still be a valuable experience. In general, the higher you score on the Masochistic Tendencies Test, the more likely it is that you have a number of conscious or unconscious (deeply buried) masochistic tendencies—and the more intensely you will need to work in order to build an assertive attitude and communicating style into your life.

Test yourself first, then, if you wish, go back and apply the questions to your spouse or other significant person in your life. Rate each statement from 0 to 3 as follows:

0 = Never
1 = Rarely
2 = Sometimes
3 = Often

____ I tend to see myself as having been a victim in repeated situations in my past.

____ Sometimes I ask my friends for advice; then when they imply I should or could do something to protect myself from an abusive situation I use the words, "Yes, but . . ." to excuse myself from following their advice.

____ I tend to be late to meetings and appointments.

____ When my feelings are hurt, I have a tendency to pout.

____ I have a tendency to procrastinate.

____ When people ask me to do things I don't really want to do, I'll purposefully do an imperfect job so they won't ask me to do that again the next time.

____ I tend to stay so busy that I never get caught up.

____ I have trouble saying no to people who ask favors of me.

____ I feel that if people could read my private thoughts they would reject me.

____ I have tension headaches or migraine headaches.

____ I tend to get physical illnesses more readily than the average person.

____ I tend to volunteer for too many activities (such as car pools, church jobs, committees, organizations).

____ I seem to have lingering feelings of guilt or shame.

____ When we go out to eat, I wait for others to choose which restaurant to go to, even if I don't prefer that kind of food.

____ When we go to restaurants, I tend to pay for more than my fair share or even pick up the entire tab.

____ I have some compulsive tendencies, such as overeating, spending too much, workaholism, excessive volunteerism, excessive handwashing, excessive exercise, excessive television watching, excessive prescription drug use, churchaholism, hoarding things, or any sexual compulsion.

____ I have suffered physical abuse of some sort in the past ninety days without reporting it to the police.

____ I have been a victim of some form or forms of sexual harassment or abuse in the past ninety days and the perpetrator has suffered no consequences for doing this to me.

_____ I have been a victim of some form of verbal abuse in the past seven days without telling the abuser how angry I truly feel about it.

_____ I feel sorry for myself for the suffering I experience now or have experienced in the past.

_____ When I was growing up, my parent of the opposite sex tended to be prejudiced against (or condescending toward) members of my sex.

_____ One or both of my parents tended to give me food or money as a love substitute.

_____ I seem to crave attention.

_____ I have either a father-vacuum (craving male attention), a mother-vacuum (craving female attention), or both.

_____ I felt as if I had to perform to get one or both of my parents to accept me.

_____ I spent an average of thirty or more hours per week in day-care centers during my preschool years.

_____ One or both parents tended to break promises to me.

_____ My parents relied on me to help settle their disputes.

_____ I feel lonely or abandoned.

_____ I was compared unfavorably to one of my siblings or friends.

_____ My parents gave me too many chores and responsibilities growing up. I was almost an extra parent.

_____ One or both parents imposed legalistic or rigid rules on me.

_____ My parents criticized each other in front of me.

_____ While I was growing up, one or both of my parents made decisions for me that I should have been allowed to make for myself.

_____ One (or both) of my parents verbally abused me by attacking my character.

_____ One (or both) of my parents slapped me in the face or slugged me during my growing up years.

_____ One (or both) of my parents sexually harassed and/or abused me in any of the following ways: overt sexual acts, sexual innuendos, treating me as a substitute mate in subtle ways, sexual teasing.

_____ One (or both) of my parents was unable or unwilling to attend my special activities as I was growing up (e.g., sports performances, musical recitals, birthday parties, PTA, graduations).

_____ My parents seemed to be unable or unwilling to seek ways to develop genuine warmth and love for each other.

_____ My parents seemed unwilling or unable to communicate their true emotions to each other in an assertive but loving and tactful way.

_____ One (or both) of my parents was unhappy.

_____ One of my parents was a masochist, and I seem to act more like that parent than the other one.

_____ One (or both) of my parents expected me to excel in a certain area (such as academics, sports, popularity, music) that he or she felt inferior in when he or she was growing up.

_____ One (or both) of my parents told me in verbal or nonverbal ways that I would not succeed in life.

_____ My parents were unwilling or unable to take the time and effort to have regular meaningful religious discussions or devotions with me when I was growing up.

_____ I find it difficult to feel intimate with God the Father.

_____ I felt like a scapegoat in my family—as if one (or both) of my parents was taking his or her anger out on me for some reason.

_____ One (or both) of my parents implied nonverbally or even verbally that I was an "accident," or implied other "don't exist" messages.

_____ I have difficulty remembering much of my childhood, particularly below the age of ten.

_____ I have been verbally, physically, financially, or sexually abused by one or more nonparents, such as a sibling, friend, coach, teacher, pastor, neighbor, stranger, counselor, baby-sitter, or relative.

Now add up your score to see in which category of masochistic tendencies you fall:

0–30	Few, if any, masochistic tendencies
31–70	Mild masochistic tendencies
71–100	Moderate masochistic tendencies
101+	Severe masochistic tendencies

If, through this test, you find a strong indication of masochistic tendencies, then make it a point to consciously, deliberately practice being assertive for the next thirty days. Continue working on communicating firmly, honestly, yet lovingly your personal worth, your needs, and your convictions. Practice saying no when people make demands on you. If you see improvement during that time, then keep it up!

But if you do not see improvement, consider going a step further and getting counseling for help and insight into how to conquer your masochistic tendencies.

Attention Deficit Disorder

Donna was ready to pull her hair out. Her son Timmy, age seven, was (as she put it) "a little wild man." He wouldn't obey, he wouldn't follow directions, and he bounced from mischief to mischief so fast that Donna couldn't finish cleaning up one of Timmy's disasters before he set off another. He also exhibited an explosive temper and became massively frustrated over the tiniest irritations.

Timmy was Donna's third child. Her first two children had been quiet and well-behaved. Donna and her husband were strict but fair and loving Christian disciplinarians, yet none of the disciplinary methods they had successfully used with the first two children worked with Timmy. No matter how they tried to structure Timmy's behavior, he would not obey or even pay attention to them.

The first glimmering of a diagnosis of Timmy's problem came when his first-grade teacher called Donna in for a conference. "Timmy is a very bright boy," the teacher began, "one of the brightest in the class. But he does not get his work done. I've been keeping him in during recess so he can finish his work, but I don't think that's a solution. In fact, I believe all that is going to do is undermine his confidence and his self-esteem. Everyone's out playing, and he's inside, and that's bound to make him frustrated."

"Well, what would you suggest?" asked Donna.

"I would suggest you take him to a psychologist for an evaluation. There may be some problem that can be corrected."

So Donna and her husband brought Timmy to a Minirth Meier New Life Clinic, where his medical problem was quickly diagnosed: *attention deficit disorder,* or ADD.

The popular term for ADD is *hyperactivity,* but the most precise designation is "attention-deficit hyperactivity disorder." The causes of ADD are not completely understood, but researchers have identified three likely sources:

1. An overactive reticular activating system. The *reticular activating system* (or RAS) is a specialized structure running throughout the brain stem. Its function is to monitor incoming sensory information and to relay important stimuli to the higher centers of the brain. If the RAS is overactive, the individual becomes overstimulated by incoming sensory information. That information floods the higher centers of the brain so that the individual is not able to focus on one piece of information before being overwhelmed by the next. The result: decreased attention span, edginess, hyperactivity, and irritability.

2. An underactive reticular activating system. Paradoxically, an underactive RAS is considered a far more common trigger for ADD than an overactive RAS. An individual with an underaroused RAS experiences *stimulation hunger.* The desire for more stimulation triggers hyperactive behavior as the brain struggles to drink in more information. Thus, when certain stimulants are given to a hyperactive child, the brain gets adequate data from normal behavior and the hyperactivity ceases. The drug most commonly prescribed for ADD is Ritalin, a stimulant that calms hyperactive behavior and increases attention span. Ritalin has proven to be a highly effective therapy for ADD, although the dosage of the drug must be carefully fine-tuned by the physician to the patient's individual needs.

3. Dopamine imbalance. Another potential cause or contributing factor behind ADD is an imbalance of a brain chemical, the neurotransmitter dopamine.

The diagnosis of ADD must be made very carefully. Not all "hyperactive" children have ADD, which is a biologically based problem. In some cases, so-called hyperactivity (which may include behavior such as tantrums, disobedience, ignoring instructions, hitting, kicking, and other forms of acting out) may actually be the result of a combination of learned behavior and poor discipline techniques. Hyperactive behavior may be caused by medical factors, psychological factors, or a combination of both factors. If biological factors are the problem (for example, a malfunctioning RAS or a dopamine imbalance), medication is needed. If learning is the problem, new child management skills are required. If both learning and biology are involved, medication and management techniques must be used in combination.

Behavior Modification

Behavior modification is a process of changing the way a person responds through his or her actions *(motor response)*, thinking *(cognitive response)*, and feelings *(emotional response)* to both external events and internal emotions. When a person tends to respond to painful memories or stressful events with negative, self-defeating behavior (called *maladaptive behavior*), that behavior can often be systematically, gradually changed by the application of behavior modification techniques.

Behavior therapy emphasizes changes in the patient's overt behavior. The therapist helps the client to set specific goals that will aid in his or her own progress. Behavior modification works particularly well with phobias and obsessive thinking (see FEARS AND PHOBIAS and OBSESSIVE-COMPULSIVE DISORDER). Behavior modification methods generally involve changing a person's behavior either by altering the consequences of that behavior or by changing the steps that lead up to that self-defeating behavior. Rather than changing the unconscious mind, behavior modification seeks to alter the external behavior and, by establishing new behavioral routines and habits, to eventually alter the mind and emotions as a result.

One way of changing the consequences of a self-defeating behavior is called *extinction,* which is the elimination of reinforcement so that a given behavior will decrease. For example, a patient may have a somatoform disorder—a series of physical complaints for which no medical cause can be found. Suspecting the patient's problem to be *hypochondriasis* (a tendency to imagine oneself having a major disease, based on minor or nonexistent symptoms), the counselor may instruct the client's family and friends to ignore the client's complaints of pains and other symptoms and only pay close attention to the client when he or she expresses feelings of improving health. On a subconscious level, this nonreinforcement of negative behavior, coupled with active reinforcement of positive behavior, often brings about a gradual improvement in both the behavior and the thinking of the client.

Aversion therapy is another form of behavior modification through altering consequences. It focuses on the negative consequences of self-defeating behavior (punishment). Alcoholics have sometimes been treated with mild but unpleasant electrical shocks when they taste alcohol. The idea is to develop a phobia or aversion reaction to the smell and taste of the beverage. This treatment can be effective, but the individual must genuinely want to overcome his or her addiction. The aversion reaction can quickly extinguish if the alcoholic individual chooses to go back to his or her drinking.

Modeling is a form of behavior modification that involves observing and imitating desired behavior. It is often used in group assertiveness training, where shy individuals are taught to take greater initiative and become more outgoing. The leader of the group may display an assertive response, then give each participant a turn at imitating the assertive behavior. The participant is then affirmed and praised by the leader and by the group.

Other forms of behavior modification include *desensitization,* a common treatment for phobias in which the client is exposed to the source of his or her fear so that he or she will overcome that fear, and *contracting,* in which the client and counselor agree on a specific plan or goal between counseling sessions and the client is held accountable for keeping that plan or achieving that goal.

Blended Families

Scott and Meg found love the second time around. She had two daughters; he had a son. Both were determined to make their second marriage work. In the weeks before their wedding, they talked about the new life they were going to build together. It was going to be the best of all possible worlds, with a family life as warm and serene as an *Ozzie and Harriet* rerun, yet with all the magical, romantic sparkle of a fairy-tale happily-ever-after ending.

Dream on!

Scott and Meg were vaguely aware that Meg's older daughter, Karin, age fifteen, was unhappy with the new marriage, but they were too wrapped up in the excitement of their romance to give much attention to their children's feelings. They assumed Karin would get used to the new arrangement and everything would work out all right. After all, the other two kids, both younger than Karin, seemed to welcome the idea with excitement and enthusiasm. Karin would come around eventually—so they thought.

But on the day of the wedding, Karin shocked everyone by showing up at the wedding wearing a black armband.

In the reception following the ceremony, Scott took Meg aside. "I didn't know Karin was taking this so hard!" he said worriedly.

"She's just at that age," Meg explained, trying to sound a lot more confident than she felt. "She'll get used to our new family. She'll have to. Don't worry about it."

Scott did worry, however, and so did Meg. But as they jetted off to begin a beautiful, idyllic honeymoon in the Caribbean, their worries fell behind them. It was a beautiful fantasy week together. At the end of that week, they returned home.

And encountered cold, hard reality.

Meg discovered that Scott's son didn't like the way she cooked, the way she kept house, or her family rules. "That's not the way Mom did it" was the refrain she heard over and over again.

Scott discovered that he and Meg had very different parenting styles and that his new stepdaughters had absolutely no regard for his standing as new head of the household. In fact, they barely spoke to him or acknowledged his existence. And if he tried to discipline them or exercise any parental authority over them, he found he was opposed not only by the daughters but by Meg herself!

The *Ozzie and Harriet* dream started turning into a stressful, conflict-ridden nightmare. Before a full year of marriage had passed, Scott and Meg were afraid that their marriage—and their new family—would rattle apart like an old Tin Lizzie. "Now I know why they call it a 'blended family,'" Meg groaned as she and Scott sat in their counselor's office. "I feel like someone took the five of us, tossed us in a blender, and punched the PUREE button!"

At the Minirth Meier New Life Clinics, we believe the term *blended family* is a misnomer. Families are always *blending,* never fully blended. The process of blending parts of two pre-existing families together into a brand new family is much more difficult than it looks from the outside. A second family functions much differently than a first family and contains unique dynamics, issues, and problems that would never arise in the first marriage.

FIVE STEPS TO A STRONG BLENDING FAMILY

The Brady Bunch scenario is a myth. Mom and Dad don't just come together with their respective broods and instantly become one big happy family. Blending and becoming a strong, whole, healthy family is a five-stage process:

1. fantasy
2. reality
3. crisis
4. adjustments
5. acceptance

Let's examine each stage in turn.

Stage 1: Fantasy

When two previously married people come together and fall in love, they enter a fantasy world. Often, to the woman, her new man is a knight who has come to rescue her from the misery of toiling and caring for her family alone. And the man is happy and honored to ride to the fair lady's rescue and be her hero.

The children of both parents are likely to react in one of two ways during this fantasy courtship period: (1) they may resent the prospect of a new stepparent, seeing this new person as an intruder attempting to take the place of their absent parent; or (2) they may actually welcome the idea and look forward to the seeming return to normalcy of having two parents in the house once again.

During this fantasy stage, nobody is looking very far down the road. The stepparent is expecting to be welcomed into this new arrangement by the stepchildren. Nobody is envisioning the conflicts, jealousies, power issues, and rivalries to come. Even as the storm clouds begin to gather, the adults shrug it off as temporary adjustment jitters.

If you embark upon the adventure of a blending family without recognizing that the rules have changed the second time around, you could be headed for heartbreak and disaster.

After all, the new union is only a few months old, and everyone is just settling in. Everything's going to work out fine, just fine.

Fantasy.

But why doesn't it *feel* fine? Why do new families often seem to split into conflicting loyalties? Why do ex-mates continue to have so much annoying influence on families? Why do ex-husbands and ex-wives keep stirring up trouble? Why do stepkids suddenly begin to resent their stepparents? Weren't they getting along great at first?

The fantasy stage is beginning to crumble, giving way to reality.

Stage 2: Reality

The realization begins to set in: *I didn't just marry a person, I married a whole family—including an entire set of values, family traditions, unspoken family rules, family history, and extended family members that I never counted on when I was in the fantasy stage!* Now we're getting down to reality.

The most common blended family scenario involves a divorced man, whose biological children still live with his ex-wife, marrying a divorced woman with children of her own. This mom and her kids have been together as a unit, functioning on their own, for a period of months or years. Together, they have gone through the trauma of divorce; they have been forged into a team that has learned to function without a man in the house; they have learned their roles and now operate on a common set of rules and expectations. Though Stepdad is now theoretically included in their family unit, he frequently feels like the odd man out. Openly or covertly, the children will continually run to Mom to protect them from this guy who's not really their father.

The reality stage is also the point at which children of either parent come to grips with the death of a dream. Ever since Mom and Dad split up, they have been secretly cherishing what is called a *reconciliation fantasy,* the hope-against-hope that Mom and Dad will someday get together again and everything will be as it was, happily ever after. The remarriage has written *finis* to that dream. Life has changed forever. It will never go back to the way it was. Children are often left to grieve this enormous loss alone. And because children have little understanding of how to process and share their feelings, those feelings will often be acted out in ways that parents find perplexing and even horrifying: a well-behaved kid may turn hateful, sullen, noncommunicative, angry, or depressed and may begin playing one parent against the other.

The stepchildren will also begin to test the stepparents during this time. Being the outspoken critics they are, children won't hesitate to say, "That's not the way my mommy did it," or "You're not my daddy. I don't want *you* to do it." It's normal for a child to long for the home environment into which he or she was born and nurtured. It is a deep, primal yearning. When a stepparent moves into the picture, the absent biological parent, whether living or dead, takes on an aura of sainthood. The stepchildren naturally compare the stepparent with the natural parent—and the stepparent usually comes in second. Bad memories of the absent parent fade away, and the golden memories are preserved in amber. The natural parent emerges as the unattainable perfect parent, and the stepparent ends up with a shabby, imperfect image by comparison, no matter how good and well-intentioned he or she is in reality.

During the reality phase, new issues emerge between the husband and wife. The wife may not have realized, as she entered into this new marriage, how much autonomy she was giving up. After her divorce or bereavement, she has learned that she can parent on her own and she's discovered inner resources of strength and confidence she never knew were there. Now she has to go back to sharing authority, consulting on decisions, and dealing with differences of opinion. She may not consciously resent her new husband, but she may unconsciously sense that he is encroaching on her turf.

The husband, meanwhile, has his own set of problems. He wants to be accepted, to be seen as the good guy, a buddy, a pal. He may know better than to think he can replace his stepkids' biological father, but he at least wants to help make their lives better and he wants to be accepted. Instead, they hate him or ignore him, they accuse him of favoring his biological kids, they place him on a probation that seems never to end. At the same time, he's trying to manage conflict with his ex-wife (and her new husband), trying to maintain a relationship with his biological children, and trying to deal with the guilt of feeling he has failed those children. He actually has two parental roles to juggle, and he feels he's doing a terrible job with both.

One of the biggest underlying (and hidden) issues of the reality stage is *the struggle for control*. Dad wants to assume his leadership role as the mentor, administrator, arbitrator, and disciplinarian of the family, but Mom and her kids resist his "intrusion." The control issue rears up in thousands of family decisions: how to budget, what clothes are appropriate, what entertainment is appropriate, where to attend church, whose family to be with on the holidays, where to go on vacation, and on and on. This battle for control is waged on an unconscious level, and few if any family members are conscious of what the dynamics and emotional issues really are, which adds to the frustration.

The stage is now set for the next crucial step in the blending family adventure.

Stage 3: Crisis

This is the make-or-break stage for most blending families. Unfortunately, few families seek counseling until they feel the intense pain of the crisis stage—if then. We recommend that *all blending families be in counseling from the very beginning, even before the marriage*, so that all members of the family can express and understand their feelings and gain insight into the new family structure they are becoming a part of. By the time families reach the crisis stage, it is sometimes too late.

In the crisis stage, everyone's frustration has grown to a very uncomfortable level. There is a great deal of anger being expressed. The stepparent is locked in an intense competition with the children for their natural parent's attention and affection. An "us-versus-them" mood has started to settle in. There is an intense fear throughout the family that this marriage, like the previous one, is now deteriorating. Insecurity is rampant.

Here's where we find out if the marriage will disintegrate or if Mom and Dad will commit themselves to doing whatever it takes to make their marriage and their family strong. If they are unwilling to go into counseling and honestly face the pain of their issues, they will probably never gain the insight they need to understand what is happening to them. But if they are courageous, if they love each other and their children, they will make any sacrifice, they will endure any amount of work and emotional discomfort, in order to make their blending family work.

Stage 4: Adjustment

If the parents do their job and face their issues, the family will come through the crisis and work to make the adjustments that they learn (through counseling) must be made. Those adjustments include:

Negotiation of roles. Every member must figure out where he or she fits in and what is expected. This requires open, honest, conscious negotiation of roles. Parents and stepparents may legitimately ask, "How much parenting should I do? Should I step in? Should I step back?" Kids may ask, "Who do I obey? What are the rules I have to follow? Has anything changed? How am I supposed to relate to this new person in our lives?"

Relationship building. Relationships should not be rushed but should be built carefully and patiently over a long period of time. At this point, family members are learning to understand and trust each other. The stepparent is learning to ease into his or her role, and the biological parent and children are learning to accept the stepparent.

We all know that relationships are built out of fond memories and Kodak moments. But we sometimes forget that relationships are also built out of conflict and crises. Conflict forces people to "get real" and deal with each other in an honest way, at the level of feelings and reality.

Validation of family rules, traditions, and customs. The new parent in the family learns to respect the existing rules and traditions of the rest of the family, and the rest of the family learns to include the newcomer in the writing of a new family history.

Validation of the new family unit. Everyone in this blending family remembers the first family with a sense of wistfulness and longing. For a long time, this new family has felt a bit artificial and unreal compared with the "real" family that doesn't exist anymore. It takes time, but eventually the blending family comes to a new consensus: "This is our family now. It offers its own environment of love, validation, and security. Maybe everything's going to be okay after all."

Stage 5: Acceptance

If the marriage survives and all the family members adjust to one another, the blending family will have reached the stage called *acceptance*. The blending family has become a *family*, period. The major issues have been worked through. The members of the family have learned to accept and incorporate each other into their world.

But acceptance extends beyond the four walls of the blending family's home. It extends to grandparents and in-laws—and even to the ex-wife and ex-husband who still have a foot in the door because of an ongoing relationship with the children. It is only natural for a stepparent to want to build a hedge around the family and say, "This is our family now. Everyone else—keep out!" But the children need to relate to their biological parents, biological grandparents, biological aunts and uncles and cousins. Once everyone has learned to accept the new family system in all of its rich facets and connections and relationships, the family will begin to experience real peace and stability.

Issues will still arise. Conflicts will still erupt. That is normal in any family, blending or not. But generally, there will be an atmosphere of love, mutual support, and peace. And that is the goal of every blending family.

Faced honestly and with a loving concern for everyone involved, family conflicts can actually become tools for bringing all the members of the family closer together.

PRACTICAL STEPS TO A SUCCESSFULLY BLENDING FAMILY

Here are some practical steps couples can take to build a strong, healthy blending family:

1. Find out everything you can about blending families. Get counseling early on in the relationship—preferably before the marriage takes place. If possible, seek out a therapist who specializes in blended family issues. Read books on blended families. Contact the Stepfamily Association of America, Inc., 215 Centennial Mall South, Suite 212, Lincoln, Nebraska 68508–1834, for information.
2. As much as possible, resolve major issues (discipline, roles, rules, and so forth) *before* marriage.
3. Focus primary attention on strengthening the marriage relationship. Schedule time to be alone together at least once a week, preferably more often. This doesn't slight the needs of the children. The best thing parents can do for their children is to model a healthy marriage relationship and to give the children the security of knowing their parents' marriage is stable.
4. If possible, begin your new marriage in a neutral setting. Relocate to a new house and start fresh. This gives everyone in the family a sense of starting a new adventure, with new roles, rules, and relationships. A neutral setting helps to reduce turf battles, since there is no previously existing turf to protect.
5. Encourage all participants in the new family, children and adults, to express feelings openly in a constructive way. Parents should set an example by being honest about their own emotions.
6. When conflicts arise, settle them openly. Encourage honest communication. When approaching disagreements, take the position, "We are all in this together. How will we resolve this situation so we can all grow closer and stronger as a family?" Remember that conflicts can be catalysts for deepening relationships and building understanding.
7. As parent and stepparent, agree in advance on rules and discipline. Support each other in front of the kids, and settle any parenting disagreements in private. Don't give the children a place to drive a wedge between you. Present a united parental front.

The Brady Bunch is a myth. Blending families takes hard work and a strong constitution. Expect it to take at least three or four years for everyone to settle in. Pray over your new family relationships, be patient, and ease into your new role. The blending family experience is an adventure, and adventures are not always fun while they are happening to you.

But adventures are filled with lessons, excitement, and rewards. We wish you and your new family joy and success in your blending family adventure.

Boundaries

Eric does nothing when his friend Brian makes passes at his wife, Shelly, even though Shelly has asked him to talk to Brian. "He doesn't mean any harm," says Eric. "Besides, he's my friend. I don't want to make him feel bad." Eric has failed to draw a clear, protective boundary line around his marriage relationship.

Margaret is recently divorced, following the discovery of her husband's multiple affairs. She now tells anyone who will listen about her husband's treachery, and even of their sexual problems. She has even talked about these issues with her thirteen-year-old daughter. If she feels a need to ventilate her feelings, she should do so with a therapist, support group, or close friends. Instead, she shares them with people she has just been introduced to. And she shares them with a child who is not emotionally equipped to process such information (this is a form of abuse called *emotional incest;* see ABUSE). Margaret has failed to maintain boundaries of discretion with regard to information that is no one's business but her own.

Tom makes his wife, Elaine, the butt of jokes in front of other people. To maintain the upper hand in their relationship, Tom sometimes tells some of Elaine's most embarrassing secrets to others, right in front of her. He belittles his children and destroys their self-esteem with his sarcasm and name-calling. He is systematically destroying the protective boundaries that should exist around his family.

Jodie allows everyone else in her life to set her agenda. Though she is now in her thirties and married, her parents continue to control her view of herself, making her feel guilty and inadequate if she doesn't respond to their demands. Her friends take advantage of her and continually prevail upon her to set aside her schedule so she can do favors for them. Her husband is physically and sexually abusive of her, engaging in forms of sexual behavior that not only offend her sense of propriety but cause her humiliation and physical pain. Yet Jodie submits without a whimper to all of these indignities from friends and family. She needs to learn how to draw clear, healthy boundaries in all her relationships.

Boundaries are emotional lines of demarcation that we place around ourselves and our family members to create a zone of safety and security. Boundaries enable us to form healthy relationships in which people understand who they are, how they should act, and how others should behave toward them. Within healthy boundaries, we establish our personal identities and maintain our individual integrity. In short, boundaries tell us where "I" ends and where "you" begins.

Personal boundaries are essential to our spiritual and emotional well-being, serving as warning alarms when someone threatens, exploits, abuses, or encroaches on us. Unfortunately, some of us have damaged and distorted boundaries in our lives, which cause us to be repeatedly victimized and steamrollered by the people around us. These distortions in our boundaries are frequently the result of boundary violations during childhood: overprotection, overcontrol and enmeshment; verbal, emotional, physical, or sexual abuse; or neglect and lack of love.

DIFFERENT KINDS OF BOUNDARIES

There are various forms of boundaries that, taken together, serve to define one's personal identity and sense of security and safety in relationships.

Physical Boundaries

Physical boundaries define one's personal safety zone. A person with healthy physical boundaries is able to say, "I will not allow you to touch me in that way. I won't allow you to physically abuse me. I won't allow you to sexually exploit me." That is why one of the best ways to protect children against sexual abuse is to teach them that they have clear boundaries and that they should not allow anyone to touch them in certain ways or certain places on their bodies.

A person with healthy physical boundaries feels fear, anxiety, or anger when those boundaries are violated. A person with distorted or damaged physical boundaries will blame himself or herself for these feelings when others exploit or abuse him or her. In our clinical experience, we tend to find poor physical boundaries in people who repeatedly drift into physically or sexually abusive relationships.

Emotional Boundaries

Emotional boundaries define a protective safety zone around one's feelings, self-esteem, and relationships. Healthy emotional boundaries serve to deflect negative thoughts about oneself and negative behavior (insults, attacks, criticism, and abuse) from others. A person with unhealthy emotional boundaries, however, allows negative self-talk (see SELF-TALK) and the criticism of other people to control his or her self-esteem.

Spiritual Boundaries

Spiritual boundaries define the territory of our relationship with God. A person with healthy spiritual boundaries has an intellectual and emotional understanding of God's love, grace, and affirmation (see "What Is Your Image of God?" under FAITH). As a result, this person feels a strong sense of purpose, meaning, and self-worth in his or her life.

Tragically, many people have a damaged sense of their spiritual boundaries. In some cases, it is because they were raised in religiously abusive environments in which they were taught that God is a stern, unforgiving, critical Judge, and they failed to experience the tender love of God in their early years. Perhaps their parents used the threat of God's wrath and eternal damnation as a means of manipulating and controlling them. Perhaps they had physically or sexually abusive parents who used God as a weapon of punishment: "God will punish you if you don't do what I want. 'Honor your father

113

and mother,' the Good Book says, and you won't be honoring me if you say no to me."

Many people have their spiritual boundaries violated later in life by manipulative religious leaders who say, "God speaks to me, and He is telling me what you should do in your life." A person with healthy spiritual boundaries will respect the Scriptures and the leading of the Holy Spirit but will be suspicious of the so-called authority of those who claim to speak for God.

SIX STEPS TO HEALTHY BOUNDARIES

1. Learn God's appraisal of yourself. Your worth comes from God, not from the approval of others. God offers you His grace, not condemnation, when you make mistakes. As you immerse yourself in His truth about yourself as disclosed in His Word, you will gradually strengthen your spiritual boundaries, and as your spiritual boundaries improve, your other boundaries will be strengthened as well.

2. Be honest with yourself and others about your feelings. People with distorted physical and emotional boundaries tend to be out of touch with their own feelings. When they ignore the warnings their feelings are sending them, they leave themselves vulnerable to mistreatment. Do you feel anxious or uncomfortable when someone touches you or speaks to you in a certain way? Then you should admit that feeling to yourself and require that person to move back out of your personal space. "No," you should say, "I will not allow you to behave toward me in this way. You can change your behavior or you can leave, but I will no longer allow you to insult me or abuse me." With practice and perseverance, you will gradually become more sensitive to those "fire-alarm" feelings that God built into you to protect you from abuse.

3. Be honest with yourself and others about your needs. Think about your needs. If you have a busy schedule, perhaps you have a need for more cooperation and help with household chores from your spouse and children. If you are under a lot of stress, you may have a need for more time alone. If you are feeling alone, you may have a need for greater communication with your spouse or your best friends. If you are unhappy with your sexual life, you may have a need for greater honesty and communication about sexual issues with your spouse. Get in touch with your needs; then take the initiative to state those needs and allow others to know your boundaries.

4. If there is a person who is continually violating your boundaries, plan a strategy for confronting that person. If it is a severely abusive relationship, involving ongoing sexual or physical abuse to you or your children, *get out of that relationship now.* Find a shelter, talk to your pastor, talk to a counselor, stay with a trusted friend where you won't be found by the abuser, but *get out now.* Your safety and the safety of your children overrides all other concerns.

If the violation is exasperating but not dangerous to you (for example, a parent who continues to manipulate you, tries to control your decisions, and monopolizes your time and emotional energy), then make a plan to talk honestly with that person about setting new boundaries in the relationship. Tell that person what you need—no more manipulation, no more intrusiveness, more time to yourself, for example—and make it clear where the boundaries will now be ("You can't call me after nine o'clock anymore," or "You can't talk to me about that subject; if you do, I will turn around and walk away").

5. Practice assertive communication in dealing with people who violate your boundaries. Be firm and focused on the issue. Keep your communication brief and to the point. If the other person brings up side issues or old grievances, just go back to your main point, restate it, don't budge from it, and don't get drawn into a messy argument. If the other person tries to bait you, just be quiet and look the other person in the eye and wait out the silence. Above all, stay calm. When you lose your temper, others control you; when you keep your temper, *you* are in control.

6. As you redraw the boundaries in your relationships, steel yourself against a sense of loss. There is a certain amount of comfort we draw from being emotionally dependent, enmeshed, and controlled by other people. Consciously we may hate it, but subconsciously we crave the security of being a child, of letting others make decisions for us and take responsibility for us. But to be emotionally and spiritually healthy, you must take up the responsibility of your own adulthood. As you make mature choices and draw healthy boundaries in your relationships, you will experience a growing sense of confidence and strength in your self-esteem.

How Healthy Are Your Boundaries?   *SELF-TEST*

Place a 1 next to your answer to each of the following questions (a scoring key follows):

T___   F___   I often feel guilty about not doing enough for my parents or my spouse.
T___   F___   I feel responsible for making other people happy—my parents, my spouse, my children.
T___   F___   I often share personal information with other people that is none of their business.
T___   F___   I feel uncomfortable making my own decisions in life.
T___   F___   I often go along with the plans of others, even when I want to do something else.
T___   F___   I often feel I must explain or defend the actions of my parents or my spouse to other people.
T___   F___   My parents discouraged me from moving away from home.
T___   F___   I do a lot of work for other people, but I hate to ask anyone to do a favor for me.
T___   F___   I wish I didn't have the responsibilities of an adult.

Place a 2 next to your answer to each of the following questions:

T___   F___   When people criticize or insult me, I accept what they say as true and feel bad about myself.

T__	F__	I often think about mistakes I've made and feel bad about myself.
T__	F__	I feel afraid of God.
T__	F__	My parents frequently shared intimate secrets with me.
T__	F__	I was the favorite child of one of my parents.
T__	F__	My parents did not want me to date or marry.
T__	F__	One of my parents seemed overly interested in my sexuality and my body.

Place a 3 next to your answer to each of the following questions:

T__	F__	One of my parents preferred my company to that of his or her spouse.
T__	F__	I was physically, sexually, verbally, or emotionally abused as a child.
T__	F__	I have been in two or more relationships where I have been physically abused, sexually abused, or made to feel like "a nothing."

Add up the numbers in the "T" column.

If you scored from 0 to 5, you probably have fairly secure emotional and spiritual boundaries.

If you scored from 6 to 9, you probably are experiencing a significant distortion in your emotional and spiritual boundaries; you should work on clarifying those boundaries and creating clearer safety zones in your relationships.

If you scored 10 or more, there is a strong likelihood that you have a deeply rooted distortion in your emotional and spiritual boundaries. We would encourage you to seek counseling for your emotional and spiritual issues and for help and insight in strengthening the boundaries in your inner self and your relationships.

Burnout

Most of us take better care of our cars than our own bodies. Ignoring our bodies' warning signals, we push ourselves and push ourselves until our gauges reach "E" for Exhaustion. Inevitably, we run out of gas—physically, emotionally, and spiritually—and our lives grind to a halt.

That is when we reach a state called *burnout.*

Burnout is a loss of enthusiasm, energy, idealism, perspective, and purpose. It is a state of mental, physical, and spiritual exhaustion that goes far beyond mere discouragement. It is a form of "bottoming out," of reaching the end of our rope.

Unfortunately, many of us are so used to running on empty that we don't even realize we're experiencing burnout. We've just learned to accept it.

THE SOURCES OF BURNOUT

We have treated many cases of burnout at the Minirth Meier New Life Clinics, and out of all those cases a pattern emerges that gives us a profile of the burnout-prone person.

Type A Personality

Type A individuals are hard-driving, excessively competitive, and achievement-oriented. They feel pressured to be perfect in order to feel good about themselves. They tend to emphasize quantity rather than quality, having a deep need to accomplish more in order to feel appreciated—and it's a need that can never be fully satisfied. They continue to work harder and harder to get feedback they can never obtain. They tend to beat themselves up when they fail and to brood over past performance failures.

Type A individuals wake up in the morning and write out lengthy "Things to Do" lists. If they get 95 percent of the tasks accomplished by the end of the day, they will still feel angry and discouraged because of that nagging 5 percent. Their self-talk usually takes the form of rules and "oughts": "I must do this; I should do that; I ought to do this." Unable to live up to these unrealistic expectations, feelings of failure and discouragement follow, moving them toward burnout.

Anger

Anger is a major contributor to burnout. People with all types of personalities occasionally get angry and stuff their anger. But perfectionists are the most burnout-prone of all. Perfectionists typically grow up with parents who expect too much. They are usually (but not always) firstborn. No matter what they did for their parents, it wasn't quite enough. Replaying those childhood "tapes," the perfectionists feel that, no matter what they do for the Lord, they should be doing more.

Perfectionists get angry with themselves and others for not being perfect and feel guilty over their anger. Since unresolved anger is a sin, they convince themselves they're not angry, consequently stuffing their anger. Ninety percent of the time they don't even know they're angry; they call it frustration or hurt, or give it some other label. Holding anger in is one of the chief causes of burnout.

Bitterness

Closely linked to unresolved anger as a cause for burnout is bitterness or harbored resentment. We all get hurt, but when people harbor it, brood over it, or don't resolve it, they're asking for trouble. Explosive pressure builds up inside. At some point, the safety valve has to blow, and they tumble into burnout and depression.

> ### The Warning Signs of Burnout
>
> - **Decreasing ability to function or perform**
> - **Detachment or withdrawal from people**
> - **Excessive, chronic fatigue (lack of energy)**
> - **Depleted motivation ("I don't feel like doing anything")**
> - **Exhaustion**
> - **Boredom**
> - **Cynicism**
> - **Increased impatience and irritability**
> - **Feelings of being unappreciated**
> - **Negative changes in work habits and relationships**
> - **Increased paranoia (feeling suspicious, distrustful, apprehensive)**
> - **Disorientation and confusion**
> - **Inability to concentrate**
> - **Physical complaints (headaches, backaches, stomach problems)**
> - **Depression**
> - **Suicidal thoughts**

Unfulfilled Expectations

Unfulfilled expectations include unwritten "rules" people make for others, defining how they should behave and relate to them. The trouble is they can't control other people. When their expectations are not met, they feel cheated and angry.

People have unrealistic expectations of themselves as well, unrealistic goals and dreams they want to achieve and unrealistic notions of the kind of joy they should be receiving from the things they do. Once they discover that the reward is not what they expect, they become angry at themselves, at others, and at God.

Wrong Perspective

The media seduces people into trying to lead the lives they see played out on their TV screens. But that's not reality. Life's problems aren't resolved in thirty minutes. Scripture tells us we should expect to encounter trials. God will enable us to endure, but we can't expect it to happen between commercials. It takes time. Life is difficult.

Too Much Stress

We live in a world filled with changes and stress points. If there are too many too fast, or too many unresolved over time, burnout may result.

AVOIDING BURNOUT

Burnout affects the whole person—body, mind, and spirit. In order to avoid or overcome burnout, you must address all three dimensions.

Recognize the importance of keeping in good physical shape. A regular exercise program, along with a balanced diet and adequate rest and leisure time, are essential for keeping the body ready to withstand the stress that brings on burnout.

Express feelings appropriately. Don't bottle up emotions; sooner or later, the cork has to explode. Maintain a good support system of friends (a small group Bible study that practices high accountability, deep koinonia-fellowship, and unconditional love can be invaluable resources). Verbalize and share emotions, both laughter and tears.

Choose tasks well. Know your limitations and choose tasks that fit within them. Don't constantly aim at goals beyond your capabilities.

Have a proper perspective on work and relationships. Everyone has different priorities, situations, pressures, and problems. Though we all have the same 168 hours per week to use, every person divides those hours up differently. Set up a balanced set of priorities and commit yourself to keeping them; then periodically reevaluate them to make sure they are realistic.

Deal with intimidation well. Strive to be like Paul, who gave this response to those attempting to intimidate or criticize him: "It is a very small thing that I should be judged by you" (1 Cor. 4:3). Look for the kernels of truth in criticism, but don't fall apart because of it. You can survive without having everyone's approval. There will always be critics, but if in your own heart you feel you're doing God's will, then stand strong, having your sufficiency in Him. If you try to be all things to all people, you are well on the way to burning out.

Base your self-worth on who you are, not what you do. From early childhood, many people are taught that they are commodities in the marketplace, only valuable when they're producing. But in actuality they are always of tremendous value. You are worthwhile because of your relationship with God and your identity with Christ. Your worth is in who you are in Christ rather than in what you do.

Develop an attitude of humility. This involves a day-to-day awareness of your human limitations and your total dependence on God.

Spend time daily in quiet time with God and Scripture memorization. Joshua 1:8 talks about how to have prosperity and success: "This Book of the Law shall not depart from your mouth, but you shall meditate in it day and night, that you may observe to do according to all that is written in it. For then you will make your way prosperous, and then you will have good success." This is a powerful tool in avoiding burnout.

Paul's goal, as expressed in Colossians 1:28, was to present every person complete in Christ. That should be your own personal goal as well: to be complete and balanced in all areas. Why? Because God wants you to run with endurance the race He has set before you—not the rat race the world sets before you. It boils down to a matter of stewardship. Are you going to continue to run on empty until you burn out? If you do, you'll have to drop out of the race, and that's not what God wants for your life.

Burn out? Or finish the course? The decision is yours.

Am I Headed for Burnout?

If you're not too tired or hassled, why not take a minute and do one more thing today: take this burnout quiz. Check the statements that are true for you.

____ More and more, I can hardly wait for quitting time so I can leave work.
____ I feel as if I'm not doing any good at work these days.
____ I am more irritable than I used to be. I'm thinking more about changing jobs.
____ Lately I've become more cynical and negative.
____ I have more headaches (or backaches or other physical symptoms) than usual.
____ I often feel hopeless, like saying, "Who cares?"
____ I drink more or take tranquilizers just to cope with everyday stress.
____ My energy level is not what it used to be. I'm tired all the time.
____ I feel a lot of pressure and responsibility at work these days.
____ My memory is not as good as it used to be.
____ I don't seem to concentrate or pay attention as well as I once did.
____ I don't sleep as well as I used to.
____ My appetite is decreased these days (or I can't seem to stop eating).
____ I feel unfulfilled and disillusioned.
____ I'm not as enthusiastic about work as I was a year or two ago.
____ I feel like a failure at work. All the work I've done hasn't been worth it.
____ I can't seem to make decisions as easily as I once did.
____ I find I'm doing fewer things at work that I like or I do well.
____ I often tell myself, "Why bother? It doesn't really matter anyhow."

_____ I don't feel adequately rewarded or noticed for all the work I've done.
_____ I feel helpless, as if I can't see any way out of my problems.
_____ People have told me I'm too idealistic about my job.
_____ I think my career has just about come to a dead end.

Now count up your check marks. If you agree with a majority of these statements, you may be approaching or already experiencing burnout. We suggest you make major stress-reducing changes in your lifestyle or seek professional help.

Career Issues

There is something noble and holy about honest, hard work. When we work, we exhibit one more facet of God's image, which was embedded in us at creation; we follow the example of the One who worked for six days, then rested. Work, according to the Bible, is God's means of keeping our body and soul together, of putting bread on the table, of making responsible provision for ourselves and our families. "The laborer is worthy of his wages," says 1 Timothy 5:18, and, "If anyone will not work, neither shall he eat," says 2 Thessalonians 3:10.

As all of us together work and grow the economy, we make it possible for other people to have jobs and we make it possible for spending, purchasing, and charitable giving to take place. As Ephesians 4:28 tells us, "Let him labor, working with his hands what is good, that he may have something to give him who has need."

Work also builds our self-esteem and gives added meaning to life. Work creates value—either a tangible value (a product) or an intangible value (a service)—and that value we contribute to our society by our work helps to make the world a better place. Whenever we work, we add value and strength to the economy. In fact, we *expand* the economy by our work—even if only by a small amount.

All work, from digging ditches to running corporations, is good and noble. Once we catch a glimpse of the sacred nobility and worth of our jobs, we will begin to transform that "9 to 5 grind" into a blessing—almost a sacrament. Jesus is our standard of excellence. Our goal in our lives and our careers is to please not only our earthly boss but also our Heavenly Boss, our Lord Jesus, just as Paul says in Colossians 3:17, "And whatever you do in word or deed, do all in the name of the Lord Jesus, giving thanks to God the Father through Him."

THE HIDDEN KEY TO CAREER SUCCESS

It's a cutthroat, win-at-any-price world out there. So if you want to win in the business world, you have to cheat, right?

Wrong. In fact, it is our conviction that the hidden key to success in any career is *integrity*.

Thomas Watson, Jr., former chief executive officer of IBM Corporation and one of the most respected business leaders of the century, observed in *Fortune* magazine that, given the choice between integrity and team loyalty in a worker, he prefers integrity every time. "If a manager does something unethical," said Watson, "he should be fired. I did this in perhaps a dozen cases when managers broke rules of integrity. The company was invariably better off for the decision and the example."

Integrity means never cheating or cutting corners, even if you can get away with it, even if you are pressured by people or circumstances to do so. Integrity means telling the truth, keeping your word, being honest about your motivations and your agenda, and taking full responsibility for your foul-ups. Integrity means never compromising your values, your principles, your faith, or your conscience. Integrity means taking a stand for what is right, regardless of the cost and the political or peer pressures.

Pleasing God should be our number one career goal. We should seek to present ourselves approved to God, workers who do not need to be ashamed. Our paycheck awaits us in eternity: His pat on the back for a job well done and His words, "Well done, good and faithful servant. . . . Enter into the joy of your lord" (Matt. 25:23).

King Solomon was a wise man—and a fabulously successful man. He constructed an immense temple to the Lord, made of stone and cedar overlaid with gold, at a cost that would probably exceed five billion dollars in today's terms. He ruled over the most peaceful and prosperous period of Israel's history. After the completion of the temple, God said to Solomon, "Now if you walk before Me . . . in *integrity* of heart and in uprightness . . . then I will establish the throne of your kingdom over Israel forever. . . . But if you or your sons at all turn from following Me . . . then I will cut off Israel from the land which I have given them" (1 Kings 9:4–7).

Time passed, and Solomon failed to walk in integrity. He began to compromise his integrity, and, seduced by women who worshiped false gods, he began to build altars to alien gods. His lack of integrity spread to his son Rehoboam, who succeeded Solomon as king. Rehoboam became a cruel and hated despot, without integrity or love for God. The once-prosperous nation of Israel fell into poverty and social chaos. The temple built by Solomon was plundered and defiled.

What was true for Solomon is true for us today. Integrity leads to success. Compromise leads to ruin and disgrace.

As you look around you, it may well appear that integrity is a rare and vanishing quality. The pressures to compromise your integrity may come from your boss, your coworkers, your suppliers, or your customers.

If you operate on the basis of integrity, you will have greater self-respect and self-esteem. You'll have the joyful experience of knowing that every dollar you earned was an honest dollar, and you'll be justifiably proud of the things you have achieved and acquired through honest, hard work.

You may in fact be able to realize short-term gains by compromising your integrity, but in the long term, your sins will come back to haunt you. Unethical behavior has a way of catching up with us and dishing out to us what we deserve. Most sectors of the business world are really close-knit communities, and the word on people of low integrity has a way of getting around.

In his book *Integrity Selling* (Doubleday, 1987), master salesman Ron Willingham observes, "The kind of person you are sends loud and clear signals to people. . . . That is why integrity, honesty, and genuine concern for your customers and their needs

121

powerfully influence your ability to develop trust with people! . . . Sooner or later most people will get the message about the level of integrity I have. And they often get the message pretty quickly."

So integrity *does* pay in the long run. But even so, that is not our primary reason for practicing integrity in our careers. Our ultimate goal as Christians is not just to do what *works* but to do what's *right*. Even if there is a price to pay for integrity—a lost sale, a lost promotion, a lost job—we choose to be people of integrity so that we can face ourselves in the mirror each day and so that we can face God in eternity and hear His words, "Well done, good and faithful servant."

Tips on Maintaining Integrity in Your Career

1. If possible, seek to work for a boss with integrity. People who have integrity tend to appreciate and reward integrity. People without integrity will be constantly pressuring you to compromise your values—and that leads to conflict and stress.

2. When hiring, seek out employees of integrity. Remember that "a dog who brings you a bone will also take it away." In other words, an employee who cuts corners in order to bring you more business will just as likely cut your throat to take business away from you.

3. Practice integrity in the small things, and the big issues will take care of themselves.

Many years ago, a father received a letter from his college-age son. "Hey, Pop," the son wrote, "this letter is free. They didn't cancel the stamp on your last letter to me, so I used it again." Later, the son received a letter back from his father. A postage stamp was stuck to the top of the letter and a black **X** was drawn across the stamp. Beneath it, the father wrote, "Dear Son, your debt to the United States Government has been paid." This father knew the meaning of integrity in the small issues of life, and his son remembered that lesson when the big issues came along.

FINDING AND MAINTAINING CAREER SATISFACTION

Ray was making more than $150,000 a year as the CEO of a medium-sized electronics manufacturing plant in California. He was a conscientious "culture-manager"—an executive who carefully cultivated a warm and cooperative spirit within the ranks of his workforce. The owners of the company, however, were not interested in a positive, motivated workforce. They were interested in squeezing every possible nickel and every possible minute and every possible drop of sweat and blood out of their workforce. Though he was clearly successful in running a highly profitable company, Ray found himself increasingly at odds with the owners. His bosses were verbally abusive and contentious.

At his annual physical, Ray's doctor warned him that stress was taking its toll on his stomach lining and his blood pressure—and Ray knew exactly where that stress was coming from. It was also taking a toll on his family relationships. And it was sapping the joy from his life. Finally, Ray made a decision—a carefully thought-out decision that was based on the facts and on his values, not on emotion. He decided to quit.

He gave his two-weeks' notice, and the owners—in a ridiculously hostile and self-defeating move, which of course was typical for them—ordered Ray to clean out his desk and "beat it."

Ray could have stayed right where he was. His stomach lining was in peril, but his job and income were secure. Instead, he decided to make a career move. Ray took a much-needed two-week vacation, then spent the next two months on a careful, aggressive job search. Today, he manages a small software company. He makes half as much money as he used to—and he's ten times happier.

Studies indicate that employees who choose to hang on to their jobs out of a desire for job security are more prone to depression, burnout, illness, poor job performance, and absenteeism than employees who have chosen a career path they truly enjoy. It's a good idea to reassess your current career and career goals periodically. Are you in a job that provides career satisfaction and a sense of well-being? Or are you in a job that makes you feel emotionally frustrated, mentally stressed, and physically unwell? If you are paid a million dollars for a job you hate and that is killing your body and your spirit, then you are being underpaid.

As you examine your career goals, acknowledge that money is an issue but not the only issue. Ask yourself: "Does my job require me to do things that violate my values? Am I putting my abilities and strengths to their best use? How are my relationships with the people I work with, both above me and under me? How secure is this position, given the economy and the corporate climate? What opportunities am I missing? What would I really *like* to do? And why am I not doing it?"

It may be that you don't have to change careers in order to find true job satisfaction. You may only need to make changes in the career you already have to reduce your stress level and find fulfillment. Here are some specific steps you can take to maintain your satisfaction over the long haul:

1. Keep your perspective. Don't fall into the trap of thinking you are the only person who can do your job. That's the myth of the "indispensable man" (or woman). Once you begin to feel that you can't leave the job for a few days for a well-deserved vacation, you have set yourself up for defeat and burnout. Make sure you get the time-outs you need to stay physically invigorated and emotionally, spiritually, and mentally motivated.

2. Focus on skills and persistence, not hours. Some people fall into the rut of working fourteen-hour days, believing that workaholism is the key to success. Workaholism is the key to self-destruction and self-defeat. Focus on doing your best, staying at your task, and setting achievable goals. This will enable you to pace yourself and maintain your enjoyment of working.

3. Delegate responsibility. Utilize the skills of people around you. Recognize and reward talent. If you try to do it all yourself, you set yourself up for frustration when the job turns out poorly, gets done late, or doesn't get done at all.

4. Learn to say no. Obviously, you can't refuse an order from a higher link in the chain of command. But very often, people in the business world take on a greater workload—and greater stress—than their job really demands. You don't have to accept every opportunity and every project that comes your way. Be realistic about your stamina, work capacity, and the number of hours in your day. Be willing to say, "I think I'll pass on this one."

5. *Maintain stability zones.* If there is stress and upheaval in your career field, you will be better able to ride it out if you are able to maintain calm oases of stability in the other areas of your life. Avoid a big lifestyle change, such as moving to a new house. Maintain good marital communication, so that you have a supportive family to come home to. Spend time with caring friends, especially Christian friends in a small Bible study fellowship.

Remember, a time of great stress is often a poor time for decision making. If you feel anxious and pressured about the possibility of becoming unemployed, you may jump too quickly into the wrong job. Or you may make as big a mistake in the opposite direction: in the grip of anxiety and "analysis paralysis," fearful of making a wrong move, you may overanalyze every opportunity that comes your way and miss the one with your name on it. The key is to make decisions that are controlled by your rational mind, informed by the facts, covered with prayer. Avoid making decisions that are clouded or driven by emotions.

■

We live in a society in which the workforce is increasingly mobile, and today's corporations are coming to understand that people desire a greater sense of fulfillment from their jobs. People are looking not only for a good salary but for what business consultants call a "psychological paycheck." What do you need to do in order to find career satisfaction? Switch careers? Or just switch gears and remove some of the stress factors from your present job?

■

JOB ANXIETY AND JOB PERFORMANCE

Sometimes pressures, worries, rapid change, conflict, and unresolved problems on the job generate such a high level of anxiety within us that it colors our self-image and makes us feel inadequate and incompetent. Our self-worth plummets. We become emotionally paralyzed. Our work suffers. We wonder, *What is happening to me?*

What is happening is a specific and treatable psychiatric problem that often interferes with workplace performance. This problem is called an *adjustment disorder.* When a person responds to stress with negative, self-defeating behavior that goes beyond the normal and expected reaction, this behavior is called a *maladaptive reaction.*

There are a number of kinds of adjustment disorders. An *adjustment disorder with depressed mood* is a disorder in which the principal manifestations include tearfulness, sadness, feelings of hopelessness, and a depressed mood. There is also an *adjustment disorder with a conduct disturbance,* in which the individual displays disruptive and inappropriate behavior such as reckless driving, fighting, shirking legal responsibilities, and deliberately missing work. There is also an *adjustment disorder with physical complaints,* including fatigue, headaches, and backaches that are not medically diagnosable. An *adjustment disorder with an anxious mood* presents itself with symptoms of restlessness, worry, jitteriness, and specific or nonspecific dread about the future.

Adjustment disorders can cause individuals to withdraw and isolate themselves from others in social and workplace situations and impair functioning in the workplace (nonperformance, nonattendance, errors, sloppiness, inability to follow directions, inability to get along with coworkers).

124

Over time (if left untreated), the anxiety of an adjustment disorder becomes self-reinforcing because of a mechanism called *negative self-talk* (see SELF-TALK). The person broods over a series of false, destructive, often irrational statements about his or her own worth, competence, and value to God, to others, and to self. Negative self-talk can erode a person's self-image to the point that significant clinical depression develops (see DEPRESSION).

Severe anxiety, depression, and adjustment disorders usually respond quite well to professional treatment, including counseling and medical treatment. Less severe cases of anxiety and adjustment disorder in the workplace, along with issues of self-worth and self-esteem, can often be improved by following six practical steps toward a healthy self-concept:

1. Allow for human flaws and imperfections in yourself. Don't focus on your negatives.
2. Make a decision to praise yourself for a good effort, regardless of the results.
3. Set realistic goals for yourself, and give yourself credit for partial success toward your goals.
4. Avoid catastrophic thinking. Don't exaggerate the negatives in situations.
5. Share with trusted friends your accomplishments, realistic appraisals of yourself, and your feelings in dealing with life's obstacles.
6. Affirm others and compliment them on their achievements; they may return the affirmation, and that builds confidence.

How rewarding is your career right now? Only you can answer that question. And if the answer is, "Not very," then only you can do something about it.

DEALING WITH A DYSFUNCTIONAL BOSS

One of the most common problems people experience in the workplace is dysfunctional bosses—managers and executives who generate misery and antagonism through excessive control. Some bosses are overcontrolling micromanagers who honestly feel everybody needs their help. They look over their employees' shoulders, offering suggestions and generally make a nuisance of themselves to the workforce while losing precious productivity for the company. These bosses mean well, but they cause more problems than they solve.

There are other bosses, however, who create much the same level of chaos—but not through good intentions. They manipulate and control others because they feed on the sense of power it gives them. Such bosses are apt to demand that their people work overtime on short notice for no extra pay or pressure and criticize those who would dare to put their families ahead of long hours at the office. They seem to take pleasure in pushing their employees to unrealistic limits, always trying to squeeze more profit out of an overstressed workforce. Their management style often produces high turnover, high absenteeism, and reduced long-term productivity (although they can often achieve high short-term productivity by terror and intimidation). These "bossy bosses" come in varying degrees of "bossiness." Some may feel a bit guilty after sounding off with yet another "shape-up-or-ship-out" tirade, but they'll do it again soon enough if they feel it's necessary to boost production.

The worst bosses of all are the controlling, dominating, abusive ones who feel no guilt at all for their behavior. These are the *sociopathic* bosses. Sociopaths are selfish,

125

uncaring, lacking in empathy or conscience, and quick to rationalize their own faults and to shift the blame onto others. Sociopaths are unreliable, untruthful, unpredictable, and insincere. They view themselves as brilliant and others around them as "chumps" and victims to be exploited or bullied. Sociopaths come in all shapes and sizes. It's easy to diagnose the average incorrigible career criminal as a sociopath, but sociopaths can be found in all walks of life. Some—as you may know through bitter experience—are bosses. Not only do they feel no guilt, they actually derive an emotional high from abusing others.

Closely related to the sociopathic boss is the narcissistic boss. Narcissistic people are extremely self-centered and insensitive to the feelings of others. They have an exaggerated sense of their own importance, exploit people for their own ends, and spend a great deal of time fantasizing about their own power, success, and brilliance. Narcissists believe they deserve special favors but show no inclination to return them.

Sociopathic and narcissistic bosses are often offenders in cases of sexual harassment. Some may get their emotional high from exercising power and control in the sexual realm. They pick out women in the workplace who they think will be passive and vulnerable to their attentions, and then they "test the waters" with a smutty joke, a sexually loaded compliment, a boast about their own sexual prowess, or a pat or fondling touch. If the woman employee does not appear offended, he proceeds to even more blatant behavior and propositions. If the woman employee does confront or resist his first advances, he may pull back ("Hey, don't be so sensitive, I didn't mean anything by it!") and seek another victim. Or he may threaten the woman with reprisals to her job security if she doesn't "play along." Any woman who doesn't succumb to his harassment can expect some sort of reprisal in her career sooner or later, even if he seems to back off at first. Sociopathic and narcissistic personalities have long memories, and they make a point of getting even.

What should you do if you find you are working for a dysfunctional boss?

First, if your boss attacks you, stay calm. If accused or blamed, keep your responses brief, calm, cordial, and respectful. When a dysfunctional person rants and bellows at you, and you respond in a calm, controlled fashion, he or she is likely to start looking and feeling foolish. Don't use sarcasm. Sarcasm is an invitation to a fight, and a sociopathic boss would probably love to get you into a fight that you can't win.

Second, avoid falling into the victim role. Sociopaths are always looking for victims, and if you appear intimidated or passive, you will only invite their abuse. Meet the individual eye to eye and don't flinch. Answer directly and as levelly as possible. Even if you show emotion—a quavering voice, trembling, or even tears—you can still demonstrate by your determined attitude and your rejection of abusive behavior that you are not a victim.

Third, consider confronting this person—but consider very carefully. If he or she is *mildly* dysfunctional, you *may* be able to confront this person gently but firmly. But understand that confrontation, however gentle, may lead to increased tension and conflict, stepped up harassment, demotion, or even firing. Don't attempt such a course without a lot of consultation with people who understand the situation. Recognize that you are taking a big risk in even gently addressing the subject with this individual. (For specific guidance in how to confront, see "Rules for Caring Confrontation" in CONFLICT AND CONFRONTATION.)

Fourth, if necessary, *escape*. Odds are, the best course is to remove yourself from the situation. If you are being systematically abused by a sociopathic or narcissistic boss, then you are being subjected to emotional and mental damage by a person who is operating within a framework of almost incurable evil. Don't assume you can change this person or win him or her over. *Get out.* Seek a transfer to another department, if possible. Or seek a new job. Of course it's not fair that the abuser stays and you have to leave, but we are not discussing what is fair. We are discussing what is ultimately in your best interests. And the best thing for you, if you are working for a massively dysfunctional boss, is to *get out now*—especially if this person is subjecting you to sexual harassment.

Should you report the sexual harassment? Ideally, the answer is yes. By exposing an abuser in the workplace, you may save a lot of other people from being similarly abused. But understand that there is a price to pay for reporting the abuse. The abuser will likely lie about you and smear you to remove blame from himself. People may misjudge your motives and side with the abuser. Others who have been similarly abused will be reluctant to come forward. Before you take such a step, before you even discuss the issue with anyone else at your workplace, get counsel from an attorney who has experience in sexual harassment matters. If you act hastily, without qualified legal advice, you may do yourself a great deal of harm, and end up handing a victory to the abuser.

LOSING A JOB

One of the most painful experiences in life is the experience of being laid off or fired from a job. The emotional and relational effects of an involuntary termination include:

- financial uncertainty
- damage to self-esteem
- emotions of anger, fear, shame, depression, and denial

Your first (and often the hardest) task after you have been fired is to tell your family. Don't put it off; that only makes it harder. Some suggestions: tell your spouse first, and do it in person, not by phone. Then tell your children. Then tell a few close friends who can support you, encourage you, and pray for you.

Be prepared for the emotions your family will go through—including many of the same emotions you feel, such as anger and fear. Adolescents and teenagers will be concerned about such issues as whether the family will have to move or if their college plans are imperiled. Reassure your family that your unemployment situation is temporary, that you are developing a job search strategy, and that you are trusting that God is in control of your situation.

One of the paradoxical problems of a job loss is that it tends to produce the very emotions and behaviors that can sidetrack or defeat your job search. Just when you need your confidence level at its highest, your self-esteem has taken its hardest blow. There are a number of self-defeating issues that you should consciously deal with in order to succeed in your reemployment strategy.

Guilt and Anger

You are likely, at this time, to be down on yourself for losing this job. That emotion of guilt can keep you from mobilizing to get back in the job force and can cause you to perform poorly in job interviews. Anger toward your former employer can also hurt you in interviews. If an interviewer detects resentment toward your previous employer, the interview will likely end at that point. *Solution:* Seek counseling or a support group or even a close friend—someone who can absorb your negative emotions as you ventilate them, reflect positive affirmation back to you, and help you to get into a healthy emotional frame of mind so you can function at peak emotional performance.

Depression and Low Motivation

Depression kills your enthusiasm and causes you to withdraw into isolation. Depressed people find it hard to get up in the morning and attack the job search with needed energy and positive attitude. *Solution:* Focus your thinking forward, to the endless opportunities ahead of you, not backward to regrets and hurts. If necessary, seek professional help to deal with your depression.

Fear of Rejection

No one enjoys hearing "no" or getting that "thank you for your interest in our company, but . . ." letter. But rejection is just part of the process that leads to acceptance and a new career. Don't take it personally. Don't take rejection as a sign that you are "no good." Every employer must sort through a number of qualified candidates to select the one he or she thinks is best. It may have been a very close call between you and the person selected. If you don't get this job, you'll get another. *Solution:* Steel yourself to keep moving forward with your job search strategy, regardless of rejection. Don't let rejection stop you from going out and trying again.

Lack of Good Planning and Effort

Many people feel entitled to a few weeks off to mope around the house; then, when they finally get around to it, they approach their job search halfheartedly and haphazardly. This is a big mistake. *Solution:* Take one day off (at most!) to think and regather your emotional energies, then immediately begin your job search at 8 A.M. the very next day. Keep in touch with your industry, talk to people who know what's going on, and read the trade publications. Your job search must become your full-time job, so attack every task with all your energy. Set clear, achievable objectives ("I will send out five letters this morning and attend one interview this afternoon") and bend all your efforts toward meeting those objectives.

Desperation

Being out of work can fill you with fear and desperation. Savings are running out, bills are mounting, credit cards are going unpaid. When you go into interviews, your anxiety and desperation are written all over your face—and you don't get the job. *Solution:* Make sure you get on a payroll—any payroll—as soon as possible, while continuing your job search. Get a night job flipping hamburgers or driving a forklift if you have to, so you can keep looking for your new career during the day. Working and bringing in a paycheck will raise your self-esteem, lower your anxiety level, and enable you to feel more confident in job interviews. (You don't have to put your "survival job" on your résumé.)

THE JOB SEARCH PROCESS

There are a number of sources of jobs and job information and approaches to take in searching for a new job.

Employment Services

A wide range of employment services are available to people in search of a new job or a different career path. Here's a list of services to guide you through the maze:

1. Career counselors are professional counselors who have earned a degree in counseling (or a related field). This training qualifies them to administer psychological tests, train people in job search strategies, and help people develop their own career plans.

2. Career consultants are career counselors who may or may not have the same academic credentials as career counselors. These professionals generally charge by the hour.

3. Employment agencies help companies fill job openings in the low to medium salary range (generally below $50,000 per year). Depending on the job, either the employer or the employee pays the fee. A reputable employment agency does not receive payment until after the placement is made.

> The key to success in using job placement or career assistance services of any kind is to recognize that your success depends upon you. An employment service can get you through the door, but it can't guarantee you a job. Once you are in the interview, you have to sell yourself.

4. Executive recruiters ("headhunters") are employed by companies to find qualified candidates for executive positions, usually in the $50,000-and-up range.

5. Corporate outplacement firms are retained by corporations to give a range of job search assistance services (such as career counseling, skills and personality assessment, résumé preparation, interview preparation, and job search training) to management and executive level employees who have been laid off or terminated. Normally, the company pays a fee of between 10 and 15 percent of the employee's salary at termination.

6. Retail outplacement firms or *career marketing firms* provide services similar to those of corporate outplacement firms, but the individual pays the fee for his or her own career search services. Fees are usually collected up front, and though these firms usually provide valuable help and insight, there is rarely a "money-back guarantee" if the job search is unsuccessful.

Résumés and Letters

A good résumé is an important tool in an effective job search, but many people place too much importance on the résumé and not enough on other aspects of the search. It is easy to get a thousand résumés out in the mail, but most employers get hundreds of these "junk-mail" résumés, and they routinely go in the "round file" unread. You should have a résumé ready to send an employer on request, or to send in response to "Help Wanted" ads that specifically state, "Send résumé to box so-and-so." But there is a better way to contact prospective employers by mail: *write a letter.*

First, make sure your letter goes to the right person. Address it to an individual who does hiring, not just "Dear Sir or Madam." Do your homework, ask around, make

129

A Warning to Job Hunters

Beware of high-pressure sales pitches from career assistance services. There are some retail employment or outplacement firms ("retail" means that you, not the employer, pay the fee) that use deceptive claims and strong-arm sales tactics to lure desperate people into buying their services. Also, beware of any company that promises dazzling, high-paying career opportunities overseas—such opportunities are practically nonexistent today, and such companies are frequently fronts for scams. (Most countries try to fill positions with their own nationals rather than American expatriates, unless there is a need for an extraordinarily high skill level, such as a nuclear physicist or neurosurgeon.)

Whenever possible, seek out firms that do not require up-front fees. Some reputable firms require payment up front (with fees ranging from $1,000 to $10,000), but you can *always* tell a company that has confidence in its ability to place you by the fact that you don't pay until you get the job. To locate a good employment service firm, don't just go to the firm with the largest Yellow Pages ad. "Network" your way to a firm that gets results. Talk to people who have changed jobs, and talk to employers and find out which firms they routinely deal with.

some phone calls, chat with the receptionist. Remember—the person you want to reach may not be the director of human resources but the manager or executive in charge of the specific department you want to work in. The human resources director may not know how shorthanded they are down in the Widget Design Department and might trash your letter without a second thought—but if the head widgeteer reads your letter, he or she might say, "This is the person we need on our team!"

Keep your letter short—no longer than one page. Make it interesting, and make yourself fascinating, so that the prospective employer has a reason to keep reading. Write an opening paragraph that conveys enthusiasm, and which sets you apart as someone special. Demonstrate your competence, energy, and an understanding of the business you wish to join. You may want to send the letter as a cover letter to your résumé. But if you are making an unsolicited "cold contact" with a prospective employer, then you are probably better advised to send the letter only, no résumé. The letter, being brief and to the point, is more likely to be read that way.

Now, about that résumé: the look and feel of a résumé can be as important as the content. It represents *you,* and it should make a good first impression. Your résumé does not necessarily have to dazzle 'em with fancy ad agency graphics, but it should be clean, crisp, and professional, offset printed or laser printed on good quality stationery. Desktop publishing allows you to produce a nicely typeset product at a low cost, and storing your résumé on a floppy disk allows you to update and revise your résumé easily or tailor it to the wants of different prospective employers or career fields. Some résumé tips:

- Write a "scannable" résumé; make sure your most interesting qualities and qualifications can be discovered in the first fifteen or twenty seconds of skimming (that's all the time most employers give a résumé that crosses their desk). Have an objective friend scan your résumé draft, then tell you what he or she remembers as your stand-out feature. If he or she can't name your key selling points, rework your draft and try it on another friend.

- Be brief. Don't overwhelm the reader with minute details of duties for each position. Focus on duties that relate to the field you are targeting.
- Don't stretch the truth. Be honest. Expect your prospective employer to check references.
- Don't clutter your résumé with unnecessary information (such as height, weight, marital status, and children's names).
- Avoid buzzwords and insider jargon that may not be understood by your prospective employer (particularly if you are considering a new career path).
- Highlight special skills, particularly skills that can add to a company's bottom line.
- Proofread; misspellings can greatly undermine a good first impression.
- Use type to highlight and emphasize. A LONG LINE OF ALL-CAPS IS HARD TO READ, SO USE CAPITALS SPARINGLY. **Boldface type** and

italic type can be useful in highlighting important facts, organizing information, and making the résumé easier to scan. Use white space to keep the page from looking too crowded, gray, and hard to read. Use bullets (•) to set off items in a list.

Robert Half, in his "Resumania" column for the National Business Employment Weekly *(Oct. 2, 1988), told of receiving a résumé from a job applicant along with a cover letter that began, "I know you are looking for a jalapeño-hot financial executive." After listing his qualifications, the applicant concluded, "Well, you have my basic taco. Want some guacamole? Sour cream? Better call soon, 'cause I'll be snapped up fast!" Said Half, "I reached for the Tums." The moral of the story is don't be too cute in an attempt to draw attention to yourself. A better way to stand out is to send your letter or résumé by Federal Express. It gets there fast, and that red, white, and blue package commands respect.*

Interviewing

The job interview is the linchpin of the job search process. Half of the interview takes place in the first ten seconds after you walk into the room: your first impression. You should be appropriately dressed and groomed (and don't neglect your breath!). You should have a poised, upright stance, a warm smile, a strong (but not overly aggressive) handshake, and open, confident body language (avoid hand-wringing, nervous tapping, or any other gestures that convey that you are ill at ease). When you speak, avoid clichés and annoying mannerisms ("uhhhh," "you know," and the much overused "basically").

In preparing for the interview, try to think like an employer. Be aware of the company, its products and services, its top people, its image. Think about what kinds of topics could be covered and be as prepared as possible. Think about how you might handle difficult questions. Think about the strong points you want to get across. Think about questions you want to ask.

In the interview, convey enthusiasm, excitement, and a positive attitude, but without giddiness. Be upbeat. Smile. Use your natural sense of humor. Allow the interviewer to complete questions; don't interrupt. If you are asked a question you don't understand, don't bluff. Ask for clarification. Feel free to pause a moment to gather your thoughts and frame your answers. If you are asked "trick questions" or if the interviewer seems to be adversarial, don't lose your cool, don't become defensive. Stay calm and answer the question to the best of your ability. Avoid coming across as canned; seek to be spontaneous and fresh. Be prepared but not overprepared.

If the interviewer asks what salary range you are looking for, be honest and forth-right and *don't sell yourself short*. Have a figure in mind. Even if you are on the high side, you won't necessarily be knocked out of the running by an answer in the interview. There is still a salary negotiation process ahead, and the company may have some flexibility. Always remember: in an interview, you should *never* raise the issue of salary first; always let the interviewer raise the subject of money.

Your final words in the interview will have the most impact, so be prepared with a brief closing statement that underscores your competence and enthusiasm.

If the Job Search Drags On . . .

Sometimes the job search seems as though it will never end. When the challenge turns into an ordeal, when it becomes clear that a 100-yard dash has turned into a nightmarish 100-mile marathon, you easily become depressed and your motivation fails. You start to question your self-worth and your marketability as a job candidate. When you reach these depths of discouragement, you often encounter other crises; you may hit a financial bottom, encounter tax problems, experience conflict with your spouse or hassles with your children. When two or more crises gather at the same time, you can become emotionally paralyzed, virtually incapable of carrying on in your job search.

Here are some principles that can help you keep moving forward when it seems that your job search is going nowhere:

1. Stay active. Are there leads and contacts you didn't pursue the first time around? Are there letters and phone calls you haven't followed up on yet? Go back to them and keep reaching out through your network of contacts. You may need to go back to the basics of your job search strategy and start over again. That's okay. Just stick with your strategy and don't get out of the job search mode. Keep moving!

2. Stay positive. Easier said than done, right? But you have to keep your PMA (Positive Mental Attitude) humming or you won't reach your goal. Keep in touch with your support network (counselors, mentors, friends, prayer partners), and soak up the encouragement and coaching they offer you. Read motivational literature. Read your Bible and bathe your mind in God's affirming love for you.

3. Maintain a balanced perspective. It is common to experience mood swings during an extended ordeal of joblessness. One day you're thinking, "That job's got to be just around the corner," and the next day, "It's hopeless! I'm a failure!" Try not to assume the worst. If necessary, take a couple days to pull back and reflect on your situation. Maybe you're just too close to the problem to see the answers. Pray, meditate, relax, and recharge your batteries—then hit the ground running and keep sprinting for the finish line.

REDUCE STRESS, INCREASE SUCCESS: MEDITATE

What word characterizes your career right now? *Success?* Or *stress?*

A moderate amount of stress is a good thing. Stress can motivate you to work harder and achieve more. Stress can put a razor's edge on your performance and propel you toward your peak effectiveness.

132

Too much stress, however, and your performance suffers. Your concentration falters. You make mistakes. You become anxious, dissatisfied, angry. Still more stress, and you topple into depression and stress-induced physical illnesses. More stress, and you are immobilized and sick.

But career stress doesn't have to defeat you. You can make stress work for you. To do that, you have to gain a clear picture of yourself and the stressors that weigh you down. You have to gain new perspective and new strength every day to go out and meet the challenges of the workplace.

The key to success, and to managing stress, is *meditation*.

One of the most fascinating studies on the value of "meditation" was conducted in 1974 by Herbert Benson, M.D., a professor at Harvard Medical School. (Dr. Benson's study was secular in nature, and his definition of "meditation" differs somewhat from what Christians practice as meditation. To Dr. Benson, meditation is a process of quiet reflection and introspection, whereas biblical Christians generally use the word *meditation* to refer to a process of reflection on Scripture, prayer, and listening to the "still, small voice" of the Holy Spirit.)

Dr. Benson wrote an article in the *Harvard Business Review*, July–August 1974, titled "Your Innate Asset for Combating Stress." He chose a business journal rather than a medical journal so that he could target the stress-management needs of overworked businessmen and women. In his article, Dr. Benson, a cardiologist, described some of the bodily changes that take place in times of stress, including higher blood pressure.

In our everyday lives (such as in the workplace), stress produces changes in our body responses and readiness. These changes, which prepare our bodies for action, are called "the fight-or-flight" response. Dr. Benson notes that this response produces "coordinated increases in metabolism, oxygen consumption, blood pressure, heart rate, rate of breathing, amount of blood pumped by the heart, and amount of blood pumped to the skeletal muscles." Stimulated by the body chemicals adrenaline and noradrenaline, all these physiological changes work together to produce a coordinated response to a perceived threat (the source of the stress). This response enables us either to "fight" or to "flee" in situations we perceive to be potentially dangerous, either emotionally or physically. Dr. Benson observes that "although the fight-or-flight response is still a necessary and useful physiologic feature for survival, the stresses of today's society" have caused it to be overused. This overuse of the fight-or-flight response often leads to chronic high blood pressure, heart attacks, and strokes (which

Meditating Your Way to Career Fulfillment

The following is a method of Scripture meditation that is used and recommended by Dr. Meier and many other doctors at the Minirth Meier New Life Clinics:

1. Meditate in a quiet place.
2. Choose a comfortable position—but not lying down (people tend to go to sleep when they lie down!).
3. Relax your whole mind and body.
4. Pray that the Holy Spirit will lead you and open to you His truth, which you can apply in the practical situations of your life and your career.
5. Read consecutively through the Bible, but don't place any legalistic mandates on yourself (such as, "I must read three chapters a day," or "I must get through Zechariah by the end of June").
6. When a verse impacts your thinking and emotions, offers comfort, or confronts your complacency, stop and ponder that verse. Pray over it. Roll it over in your mind. *Meditate*.
7. As you meditate on that principle from Scripture, consider ways to integrate that concept into your everyday life and into your career life.

As you follow this discipline over time, you will begin to see changes in your attitude and behavior. You will begin to gain God's perspective on your life, your problems, your career, and the stressful aspects of your life. In time, meditation will change your thinking—and it will change the way you respond to issues and to people at work.

account for over 50 percent of all deaths each year in the United States). According to Dr. Benson, as many as a third of all Americans suffer from high blood pressure—many of them business executives.

What is Dr. Benson's solution? Meditation. He compares the benefits of various forms of meditation, including Zen, yoga, transcendental meditation, and progressive relaxation. Most of these techniques proved to be beneficial to health and produced the *opposite* effect on oxygen consumption, respiratory rate, heart rate, blood pressure, and muscle tension from what the fight-or-flight stress response produces. Instead of an unhealthy stress response, meditation produced a healthy "relaxation response." He found that for any meditation technique to produce this healthy response, it must have four features:

1. a quiet environment (no noise or music)
2. a comfortable position (to reduce muscular effort to a minimum)
3. a mental device (a repeated thought on a single topic or a word to free oneself from thoughts or worries)
4. a passive attitude (a quiet disregarding of distracting, intrusive thoughts rather than an attempt to fight those thoughts, which often makes them intrude even more)

Some years ago, after reading that article, Dr. Paul Meier heard Dr. Benson lecture at a symposium on meditation therapies in St. Louis. Benson stated that since his 1974 article appeared, Harvard psychiatric researchers had discovered *the same beneficial responses in Christians* who pray meditatively or who meditate on single principles or phrases from the Bible. Patients with high blood pressure were taught to meditate on Scripture twice a day for twenty-five weeks—and the result was clear: both the diastolic and systolic pressure readings were reduced in those patients.

Stress cannot be eliminated from your work environment—nor should you want it to be eliminated. You want a reasonable level of stress working for you, motivating you, pushing you toward greater excellence and success. Meditation is a powerful tool for managing stress and for helping you develop into the kind of person God wants you to be.

Childbirth

Pregnancy, and especially a first pregnancy, can be an anxious experience for a woman. Many women feel ambivalent about their pregnancy and may alternate between periods of joyful anticipation and gloomy apprehension. Then, mistakenly thinking it is wrong or abnormal to have negative feelings about their pregnancy, they may experience feelings of guilt or even repression of feelings. If a woman represses or denies her negative feelings toward her pregnancy, she may experience changes in her body chemistry that could be unhealthy for herself and the baby.

The healthiest approach to our feelings is to get in touch with them, acknowledge them, ventilate them by talking about them, and resolve them so that they no longer have the power to hurt us. It is important for women to discuss their ambivalent feelings regarding their pregnancy with the caring, trusted, understanding, nonjudgmental people in their lives. It is to be hoped that the husband can be this kind of empathetic listener. Parents, friends, counselors, and other significant people in a woman's life can also fulfill this role.

It is especially helpful for a woman to be able to talk to other women who have gone through the same experience. In pregnancy, a woman's emotional and spiritual needs should be met in normal ways to ensure a healthy emotional climate in the family when the baby is born. Also, the father has emotional and spiritual needs that should not be neglected during this time. God's ideal plan is for a child to be born into a spiritually and emotionally healthy family so that he or she can be spiritually and emotionally nurtured and protected through the tender growing years of life.

The development of a child's personality begins at conception. The human personality is constructed upon the physical and mental foundation that is laid (in a genetic sense) by both parents and (in a spiritual sense) by God. From the moment of conception, many factors contribute to the makeup of that child's future life: the mother's nutrition during pregnancy (daily protein, calcium, and iron can contribute to sound physical and mental development in a newborn); use or avoidance of certain drugs, alcohol, and tobacco (all of these substances can have damaging effects on a baby in the womb); and the emotional state of the mother. If a woman experiences significant emotional problems or distress during pregnancy, and talking those feelings through with close friends and family fails to resolve those problems, it is best for her to see a professional counselor who can help her uncover and neutralize her hidden emotional issues so that they can no longer hurt her.

LABOR AND DELIVERY

"The miracle of birth" may seem like a trite and overused phrase, but it is absolutely true. Birth is a fascinating miracle that demonstrates the careful, providential planning of our loving God.

We tend to think of labor as something that takes place in and by the body of a woman, and it is. But amazingly, it is the baby who actually (in a biochemical sense) seems to control the process of labor. The baby produces a hormone that triggers the onset of labor, and once labor begins, this hormone controls the course of labor.

The first stage of labor (*stage one labor*) is that which takes place from onset to the full dilation (opening up) of the cervix. The purpose of stage one labor is to enlarge the region that the baby must pass through so that birth can take place without injury to the baby or the mother. It begins with regular, painful uterine contractions about twenty to twenty-five minutes apart and gradually increasing in frequency, with the discomfort spreading from the back to the lower part of the abdomen. Contractions last approximately fifty seconds, and between contractions the uterus relaxes completely. As labor progresses, the contractions become more forceful and frequent until, near the end of stage one, they last about a full minute, with only three minutes or so between contractions.

The first stage of labor is preceded or accompanied by three physical signs of labor: (1) the expulsion of a mucous plug (the *operculum,* which protects the uterus throughout pregnancy) from the cervical canal; (2) the passage of the "bloody show," a small quantity of blood; and (3) the rupture of the "bag of waters," a gush of clear water from the vagina. If the water breaks before labor begins, labor will automatically commence soon afterward. Otherwise, the water will break sometime during the course of labor.

Stage two labor is from full cervical dilation to complete delivery of the baby. At the beginning of stage two, the contractions of the uterus change from purely involuntary physical action to a part physiological, part psychological urge to bear down, push, and expel the baby out of the body. The woman becomes very focused in her concentration on the task at hand. Uterine contractions continue once every minute or two minutes, and last a full minute. The baby's head descends through the birth canal, turns to the side without assistance, and emerges from the vaginal opening, followed soon afterward by the shoulders and body.

Once delivered, the baby's respiratory passages are aspirated so that he or she can breathe. The umbilical cord is clamped, and the baby is now separated from the life support system that tied him or her to the mother's body. The baby is still dependent, but now instead of the linkage of the umbilical cord, this child is linked to the mother by her love and nurturing care. Within a few moments after delivery, the child takes his or her first breaths of independent life, and the flesh of the baby goes from a bluish gray to a bright, oxygenated pink color. Breathing may be irregular at first (this is normal), but soon a regular pattern of breaths is established, punctuated by the most beautiful sound in the world: a baby's first cry.

Stage three labor is from complete delivery of the baby to complete delivery of the placenta, or afterbirth. The miracle of birth has been accomplished.

When Is a Cesarean Section Necessary?

A cesarean section should be performed only when vaginal delivery is believed to carry the greater risk, such as in cases involving:

- improper positioning of the baby (such as a "breech" or bottom-first rather than head-first position);
- *placenta previa,* in which the placenta covers the cervical opening;
- a pelvic outlet too small for the baby's head to pass through;
- physical distress of the baby; or
- problems with the health of the mother, such as diabetes, heart disease, pelvic tumors, or a negative obstetric history.

CESAREAN SECTION

In some cases, childbirth may be accomplished by means of a surgical procedure called *cesarean section.* An incision is made in the mother's lower abdomen and uterus, and the baby is delivered directly through that incision, bypassing the birth canal. The uterus and abdomen are then surgically repaired. In later pregnancies, babies may be delivered either by vaginal delivery or by another "C-section" procedure. Cesarean sections are routine and safe, though surgery entails somewhat more risk than a vaginal delivery.

THE COMPLETE LIFE ENCYCLOPEDIA

PAIN MANAGEMENT IN LABOR

Whether birth is experienced as a warm and wonderful experience or as an ordeal of pain and anguish depends a great deal on the expectations of the delivering mother. Although uterine contractions are anything but gentle and the experience does entail a very real experience of pain, a woman who enters labor in a positive, eager frame of mind can have a much more positive experience of labor and delivery.

Pain can also be greatly ameliorated by the use of analgesics (painkillers). Many women choose not to use any drugs because they do not want to dull the experience of childbirth. It is no mark of weakness if, during the intense onset of labor, a woman changes her mind and asks for some medical help in controlling the pain. Labor pain can, in some cases, be a distraction from the joyful process of giving birth. Appropriate pain medication may, in some cases, actually help the mother to experience the childbirth process more fully and positively.

Painkilling analgesics may be given by mouth, injection, inhalation, or conduction (epidural injection). Available medications include:

> ## Joy Out of Pain
>
> The pain of childbirth, though real, passes quickly. As Jesus said in John 16:21, "A woman, when she is in labor, has sorrow"—and the word *sorrow* in the original language can mean emotional heaviness, physical pain, or even annoyance—"because her hour has come; but as soon as she has given birth to the child, she no longer remembers the anguish, for joy that a human being has been born into the world." The true miracle is that birth brings *joy* out of the pain and travail of labor.

- Mild analgesics and sedatives given during the early stages of labor to help a patient relax and, during protracted slow labor, sleep. During intermediate stages of labor, meperidine (trade name: Demerol, a narcotic analgesic) may be given by injection to ease the pain of labor.
- Inhalation analgesics, such as nitrous oxide and oxygen may be used to manage the patient's response to pain.
- Conduction or *epidural analgesia* is the injection of an anesthetic directly into the epidural space of the spinal cord, resulting in instantaneous, total relief of pain. These injections are usually made at the small of the back (the lumbar region). If the injection is made at the lower end of the spinal cord (the sacral region), the procedure is called *sacral epidural analgesia*. Conduction anesthetics are only administered by specially trained anesthesiologists.
- A *pudendal block* anesthetic is an injection into a nerve in the lower rear region of the pelvis. It is often used to reduce pain during delivery without affecting the sensation of uterine contractions, so that the delivering mother is able to cooperate fully with her body's sensations and actions in the process of moving the baby through the birth canal.

BREAST-FEEDING

Most physicians agree that breast-feeding is preferable to bottle-feeding, especially during the first few months of life. Most hospitals encourage and accommodate bringing

137

mothers and babies together for breast-feeding. Babies do not need or receive much milk from their mothers during the first few hours after birth, but they do receive in mother's milk a fluid substance containing antibodies that protect them against infections. Mother's milk is superior to cow's milk in the quality of its protein and its sterility. And mother's milk provides something that infant formulas can never provide: emotional warmth for both mother and baby. Certain hormones released in the mother by breast-feeding serve as a natural tranquilizer and help the mother's body return to its prepregnancy shape.

POSTPARTUM DEPRESSION

■

Not only is breast-feeding better for the baby, it also helps the mother regain her prepregnancy figure!

■

Postpartum depression affects about 90 percent of new mothers and normally occurs during the first week following childbirth. Onset may even occur soon after delivery. The letdown most women feel after delivery is normal and no cause for worry. The reasons for postpartum depression include hormonal imbalances, family or social pressures, emotional stress, and physical exhaustion. Also, any emotional problems the mother may have had going into her pregnancy are bound to be magnified following childbirth.

Consider what the new mother is going through: she has experienced a physically exhausting ordeal, she has lost blood, she is anemic, and she now has to lose sleep while working hard day and night to change and feed a baby. Those around the mother need to make sure she takes care of herself, gets plenty of help with the baby, receives good nutrition, and gets as much sleep as possible. Though the situation is usually very draining at first, the baby will normally settle down to a regular schedule within a few weeks. If the baby is still not functioning on a reasonable schedule after two months, the mother should consult a pediatrician for help in placing the demanding infant on a schedule.

In rare cases, postpartum depression can become a true depressive illness involving insomnia, irrational fears, irritability, crying, guilt, and even rejection of the baby. In such uncommon and extreme cases, women may need medical and psychological treatment, including antidepressants and long-term counseling to help them accept the role of motherhood. In the even more rare cases where a depressed mother actually poses a danger to herself or her baby, psychiatric hospitalization is necessary. A woman who is prone to such severe and dangerous forms of postpartum depression should avoid future pregnancy.

BIRTH DEFECTS

Sometimes a birth presents a serious challenge to a family. God has arranged the birth process in such a way that most abnormal fetuses are miscarried in the first three or four months of pregnancy. Miscarriages occur in about 20 to 25 percent of all pregnancies. Some babies, however, are born with birth defects, such as *Down's syndrome* (formerly called "mongolism"), a congenital defect involving mental retardation and physical abnormalities. Without entering into a theological discussion over God's direc-

138

tive or permissive will, we must recognize that God does allow such births to occur. Psalm 139 says that we were designed by God in our mother's womb and that the blueprint for this design was drawn even before conception. We cannot know the mind of God (see Deuteronomy 29:29), but we do know that God is love and that He is able to work all things—even human pain and suffering—together for His good purpose (see Romans 8:28–29).

The parents of a newborn with birth defects should receive support and counseling to help them move through the stages of grief (see GRIEF AND LOSS). A family may have to decide whether to put a severely retarded child into a specialized care environment or to keep the child in the home. There is no clear-cut one-size-fits-all answer to this question. Some specialized care facilities for severely retarded children enable children to receive special training, with the parents visiting as needed. Many loving parents place their handicapped children in special facilities in the knowledge that they will receive better continuous care than can be provided at home; others are thankful they kept their handicapped children in their own homes, regardless of the disruption to family life.

Codependency

Not long after the publication of a Minirth Meier New Life Clinic book on codependency, *Love Is a Choice* (Thomas Nelson, 1989), the doctors of the clinic took up the subject on its daily radio talk show. One woman called in and said, "I had always thought our family was pretty normal. Now, listening to you, I realize we are codependent—or as you sometimes put it, dysfunctional. What should I do?"

Dr. Frank Minirth, cofounder of the clinic, replied, "I know how you feel. In our discussion, we forgot to make a very important statement: *All* families are somewhat codependent or dysfunctional. That's natural, since none of us are perfect. All of our parents have made some mistakes. They passed some of their pain on to us, and we'll pass some of that pain on to our own children. But there are steps we can take to heal the root causes of our codependency and to break the generational cycle of codependency."

That is the key issue that faces all of us who struggle with the issue of codependency: becoming whole and creating whole, healthy families.

WHAT IS CODEPENDENCY?

Codependency is living the myth that we can make ourselves happy by trying to control people and events outside ourselves. Put another way, codependency may be

139

broadly defined as "an addiction to people, behaviors, or things." A sense of control, or the lack of it, is central to everything a codependent does and thinks.

Codependency is an epidemic. Roughly one hundred million Americans suffer the effects of codependency today. We can gain better insight into how codependency operates in our lives by examining the traits of codependent individuals:

1. Codependents are driven by one or more compulsions. Compulsions are easy to identify if they are considered "bad," such as addictions to drugs, alcohol, sex, physical abuse of others, or eating disorders. Other compulsive behaviors, though equally real, are difficult to identify: workaholism, spendaholism, success addiction, compulsive neatness, compulsive overachievement in school, and so forth. The people who do engage in these behaviors are rarely seen as addicts; they are praised and *admired* for their actions. Few people would rank any of the seemingly "positive" addictions of these people alongside drug abuse or sex addiction, but the root causes of all these addictions are much the same. Compulsive and addictive behaviors are largely rooted in codependency.

2. Codependents are bound and tormented by the way things were in the dysfunctional family of origin. No one grows up in a home where all needs are met all the time. But in more severely dysfunctional families, the pain is increased and it is likely to pass from generation to generation—though it often takes a different form. One person may be a compulsive drinker; the child of that person may grow up to be a compulsive rescuer and volunteer.

3. Codependents typically have very low self-esteem. They have received few, if any, affirming messages from their parents or primary caregivers during childhood. They see themselves as empty and inadequate, as if they are missing something that everyone else around them has. Codependents look to others for approval, thinking (usually at an unconscious level), *If only I could get other people to approve of me, then maybe I would start to feel good about myself.*

■ *Codependency does not improve with time. In fact, time only tends to make codependency worse. If you have problems with copdependency, there are steps you can take to help reverse your descent into misery, but only you can take them. No one can walk the road of recovery for you.*

■

4. Codependents typically feel that their happiness hinges on the behavior of others. They unconsciously strive to fix the unhappy aspects of their past and present lives by manipulating people and events. If they felt unloved and abandoned as children, they may be compulsively perfectionistic as parents to compensate for the unresolved pain of the past. Emotionally healthy people accept the past as it is, recognizing that it is futile to try to control other people or change events that have already taken place.

5. Codependents feel inordinately responsible for others. Many try to avoid their own pain by taking on other people's problems. If a best friend's marriage breaks up, the codependent thinks, *I should have been able to help my friends solve their problems.* Codependents can't manage their own lives successfully—much less everyone else's—so they end up feeling guilty about everything.

6. Codependents' relationships with spouses or significant other persons are marred by a damaging, unstable imbalance between dependence and independence. God created us to be both dependent and independent. In the end we are ultimately responsible for our own welfare. No other person can be expected to care for all of our needs. On the other hand, God created within us the need for companionship, both with Him and with friends and family. Codependents constantly find themselves at extremes in their relationships. It's either "I can't live without you" or "I don't need you or anyone else."

THE COMPLETE LIFE ENCYCLOPEDIA

7. *Codependents are masters of denial and repression.* Counselors never cease to be amazed at how effectively denial works. One of the first questions put to patients at the Minirth Meier New Life Clinics is, "Could you please tell me about your childhood?" People invariably respond with words such as, "I grew up in a pretty good home." Then they proceed to describe some terribly abusive home situation. The denial that helped them survive childhood almost always stands in the way of their healing as an adult. (See "Denial" under DEFENSE MECHANISMS.)

8. *Codependents worry about things they can't change and often keep struggling to change them.* Codependents cling to a strong set of "if only's": If only I could have managed the children better my husband wouldn't have blown up like that. If only I could make my wife love me, she wouldn't run around with other men. Codependents just don't buy the truth that we can't control other people.

9. *Codependents' lives are punctuated by extremes.* Codependents may be highly respected and considered wise and spiritual in public and raging, verbally abusive, demanding tyrants in private—say, in the workplace or in the family. Those who see only one side of a codependent's life might find it hard to believe that the other extreme also exists in the same person.

10. *Codependents are continually looking for the missing ingredient in life.* Codependents struggle through life like a car running on fumes, sputtering along in search of a gas station. The messages of worth and dignity they missed in childhood have left a big empty space. In despair they look outside themselves to find meaning and purpose in life.

Individual and Family Codependency Assessment

If you suspect you may have codependent tendencies or that there may be issues of codependency in your family, take the following test. Check the statements that are true about your life and the lives of your family:

Part 1: Self-Assessment

_____ I can't stand to be alone.

_____ I am a perfectionist.

_____ I am driven by the approval of others.

_____ I feel desperate when I cannot gain the approval of other people.

_____ I find myself making decisions based on how they will affect other people and rarely consider myself.

_____ Many times I feel obsessed by a need for total order in my life.

_____ I put work first, above anything.

_____ I find myself adjusting to my spouse's needs rather than communicating my feelings.

_____ I do not experience anger.

_____ I overeat often.

_____ I am constantly wondering what other people think of me.

_____ I cover up my feelings so others won't realize what I really think.

_____ I am afraid that if others really knew me they would not like me.

_____ I am constantly trying to figure how to stay ahead in my relationships.

_____ I cover up my feelings of self-doubt with drug or alcohol use.

_____ I can't say no when I am asked to do a favor or serve on a committee.

_____ When I begin to feel sad or angry I go shopping, work harder, or eat.

_____ I tell myself it shouldn't hurt so much when others let me down.

_____ I often feel I need to change the way other people behave.

_____ I need everyone to be happy with me so that I can feel good about myself.

_____ I need others to be strong for me without requiring anything from me in return.

Part 2: Family Relationship Assessment

_____ I frequently doubt that I really know my children.

_____ My child has become secretive and withdrawn.

_____ My spouse and I continually promise to spend more "quality time" with the kids but we never seem to get enough time.

_____ There is a consistently high level of busyness in our household.

_____ On an average week, there are at least two or more evening meals at which the entire family is not gathered.

_____ Someone in our family (adult or child) uses alcohol or some other mood-altering drug, whether illegal or by prescription.

_____ One or more members of my household is constantly at war with another member or members.

_____ My child or children seem to avoid one parent and attach excessively to the other.

_____ I am intensely interested in and involved in my work, my homemaking, my church work, or my community service.

_____ The sexual dimension of my marriage has drastically diminished since we were first married.

_____ I or my spouse has taken sexual expression outside of marriage (an affair, prostitution, pornography, and so forth).

_____ Our marriage is in trouble (one or both of us is seriously considering divorce).

Part 3: Assessment of the Children

_____ One or more of my children has been diagnosed (by a doctor or therapist) as hyperactive.

_____ One or more of my children has begun displaying patterns of "acting out" with baby-sitters, school officials, or other authorities—showing defiance to adults, disrupting group situations and classes, bullying, using foul language, or making rebellious lifestyle and dress choices.

_____ My child struggles to be perfect.

_____ My child suffers persistent or chronic physical health problems which can't be medically explained (headaches, fatigue, frequent recurring illness).

_142_

_____ My child seems to love disrupting the family.

_____ My child gets along better and more easily with adults than with other children.

_____ One or more of my children has great difficulty separating from me.

_____ I have been getting questions or negative feedback from people outside my immediate family regarding my children's grades or conduct.

If you were to come into a Minirth Meier New Life Clinic for counseling, we would ask questions which would unmask the kinds of issues dealt with in this assessment. No one family will display all the above problems, but a dysfunctional, codependent family is likely to reveal a number of symptoms listed in this assessment.

If you checked three or more statements in Parts 1, 2, or 3, then there are probably issues of codependency operating in you, in your family system, and in your children. The more issues you checked, the greater your need for dealing with codependent issues and tendencies. We would encourage you to seek counseling so that you can examine and resolve these issues in your life and your family, and so that you can break the cycle of codependency in time to raise emotionally whole and healthy children.

THE TEN STAGES OF RECOVERY

Following are the stages of recovery from codependency and some steps you can take toward that recovery.

Stage 1: Exploration and Discovery

Be willing to explore your life and discover clues about why you are the way you are. Write a short history of your life, with significant facts and events that occurred at various stages in your life: births, deaths, divorces, beginning school, moving, tragedies, hurts. What patterns do you see? What unhealthy relationships? What painful memories? What incidents that caused you shame?

Stage 2: Relationship Inventory

Bring your relationships into clear and deliberate focus. Don't pass judgment on events in your life by calling them right or wrong. Don't dismiss any memory that comes to mind as irrelevant or too embarrassing to handle (that could be denial or repression at work). Be thorough and be honest with yourself. Take stock of relationships in the following areas:

Father: Was he distant? Abusive? Absent? A workaholic? An alcoholic? Weak? What was he like?

Mother: Was she distant? Or did she smother you with her love? Did she affirm you or tear down your self-esteem?

Opposite sex: Were you frequently exploited in relationships with the opposite sex? Did you have unhappy experiences? Painful experiences? Rejection?

Authority figures: Did you have problems with teachers? Coaches? Bosses? Do you remember incidents that caused you to feel fear, shame, or anger?

Present relationships: How do your present family members, friends, and business relationships make you feel about yourself? If unmarried, what is your dating life like? Are there any shame issues involved in your present-day relationships? Abuse? Exploitation? Control? Are you rescuing anyone? Do you feel abandoned by anyone?

Self: Are there things you don't like about yourself? Are you self-critical when you make mistakes?

God: Do you project your father's negative characteristics onto God? Do you blame God for bad things that have happened in your life? Are you angry with God? Do you feel God is angry with you? Do you feel forgiven or unforgiven?

Stage 3: Addiction Control

If you are codependent, then you have an addiction. It may not involve alcohol or drugs, but you are addicted to something. Unhealthy relationships. Controlling others. Work. Success. Spending. Something. You are caught in the addiction cycle, and every time you indulge your addiction, you incur more consequences, more guilt, and more shame from your addictive agent. Your self-esteem falls, and you descend even deeper into the addiction cycle. In order to break the cycle of addiction and move out of your codependency, you must break free from your addiction. (See "The Addiction Cycle" under ADDICTION.)

Once a substance or behavior has become an addiction in your life, the only solution is abstinence. If the addictive agent in your life is an unhealthy relationship, you must build clear, healthy boundaries in that relationship (see BOUNDARIES). If it is compulsive controlling or workaholism or a substance abuse problem, then you must get into a recovery group and allow the recovery process to pull you out of that addiction and back to sanity. Your recovery from codependency requires that you free yourself from the control of an addiction.

Stage 4: Leaving Home and Saying Goodbye

Many people spend years of their adult lives trying to accomplish the task of leaving home. It means untangling yourself emotionally from parental expectations and your own desire to have a cozy, secure place to run to when life in the real world becomes too hard. It's time to grow up and take your place in the world as a full-fledged adult. That means saying goodbye to Mom and Dad and to false symbols of security. It may even mean saying goodbye to deceased parents—closing the chapter on their emotional abuse or their predictions about you or their control over you. You don't have to seek the approval of your parents anymore.

Stage 5: Grieving Your Losses

It's important to be able to grieve well and to grieve thoroughly. Your losses will continue to affect your life until you have grieved them fully. You must move through the stages of grief (see GRIEF AND LOSS). But understand: grief follows its own timetable. It is not a linear process. You may reach the sadness stage, then find yourself suddenly back in anger. This is normal. Be patient with yourself and recognize that each time you recycle through the stages, the process becomes a little easier—and you make a little more progress.

Stage 6: New Self-Perceptions

If you grew up in a dysfunctional home, you received many negative, distorted messages about yourself. These messages play and replay through your mind, controlling your life and coloring your perceptions. To some codependent people, the simple statement, "I have permission to live," may come as a welcome revelation—and a startling new self-perception. To break free of codependency, you must replace the old self-defeating messages with new affirming messages of your worth in God's sight. "Therefore," says Paul in his masterful statement of a new self-perception, "if anyone is in Christ, he is a new creation; old things have passed away; behold, all things have become new" (2 Cor. 5:17).

Stage 7: New Experiences

The next step in your recovery from codependency is to create new experiences based on your new perceptions about yourself, about other people, about life in general. These new experiences will not be bound by issues from your past. These new experiences may include restructuring your relationships (new boundaries, new expectations, new freedom from being controlled or abused). They may include new forms of behavior—talking about your anger instead of either stuffing it or exploding. They may include becoming more active rather than passive—reading books on parenting, for example, instead of drifting through your role as a parent. Or being more assertive in conflict situations. Or standing up to the interference of intrusive parents. Or becoming a more involved and affirming parent to your children.

Stage 8: Being Reparented

Deep inside every codependent is a personality that still thinks and reacts as a child. That emotional child within stays with us for life. It is the part of us that is still most sensitive to the pain of our dysfunctional family. That child within requires nurture and healing—a process that is known in recovery circles as "reparenting." Reparenting fills the holes left by an emotionally deficient upbringing. You can't go back and demand that your parents make it all up to you, but you can find new sources of love and affirmation to fill those parenting roles. You can experience reparenting in three ways: (1) reparenting yourself, affirming yourself, giving yourself positive messages; (2) being reparented by another person or support group (a counselor, a mentor, or a support group); (3) being reparented by God, through prayer and meditation, particularly in the affirming passages of Scripture.

Stage 9: Relationship Accountability

Being accountable to others is an essential part of your recovery. When you make yourself accountable, you increase the probability that you will follow through on your goals. You may build an accountable relationship with other members of a support group or small group Bible study, with a counselor or therapist, with a mentor or sponsor. In that relationship, you ask others to hold you accountable for whatever goal is important to you, and you meet with that person on a weekly basis, or maybe even more frequently. Some suggested areas of accountability:

- "Please hold me accountable to allow no one to physically or verbally abuse me this week."
- "Please hold me accountable to keep myself pure from immoral or unethical behavior this week."
- "Please hold me accountable not to rescue anyone this week."

Every time you meet with that person or group, they will ask you about your progress in meeting that goal—and you will answer honestly and fully. Knowing that you have that question staring you in the face week after week gives you a great incentive to stick to your goals.

Stage 10: Maintenance

This is your last step on the climb to recovery. Looking back at the previous stages, you can see how far you've come and what it's taken you to get to this point. You've endured a lot of pain and done a lot of hard work. You've learned a lot about yourself. You have crawled out of the pit of codependent shame and despair, and now you want to stay out of that pit. So you work on maintaining your recovery by:

- balancing your time and avoiding extremes;
- meeting your physical, emotional, and spiritual needs; and
- maintaining balance in your relationships.

Don't forget to make God a central part of your recovery. He is present and powerful to help you in your recovery journey. He offers the security of knowing you are loved and affirmed. You cannot master your addictions, but He can—if you surrender to Him. You surrender to Him day by day, piece by piece of yourself, until He finally has all of you. This is the great paradox of the Christian gospel: our loss becomes our gain. We give up everything; we gain everything. We release our brokenness in order to gain wholeness.

Personal disciplines are an important part of maintaining your recovery. These disciplines include an ongoing accountable relationship; journaling; and a regular devotional time.

If your spouse or other members of your family are unwilling to participate in your recovery process, don't despair. A close relationship with God will help you to continue to love and forgive them. And the emotional support you receive from your church, your support group, your counselor, or your network of healthy and recovering friends will keep you on track in your own lifelong journey of recovery.

See also ADDICTION; DYSFUNCTIONAL FAMILIES

Compulsive Behavior

Compulsions are irrational urges or actions that people have difficulty controlling. Compulsions often act counter to people's conscious will. Individuals may consciously want to live sober, moral, guilt-free lives, yet they may repeatedly find themselves struggling against compulsions to drink or abuse drugs, to engage in illicit sex, and to become involved in behavior they know is going to leave them feeling guilty and diminished in their self-esteem.

We say that compulsions are irrational because they urge people to commit acts they know will be harmful to them, yet they do them anyway. In compulsive behavior, the conscious mind (the seat of the will) is engaged in a losing battle with the unconscious emotions (the seat of the compulsion). When compulsive behavior becomes habitual and reaches a level where the person is unable to stop engaging in that behavior—either because of physical dependency on that behavior (such as drinking or drug abuse) or a psychological dependency on that behavior (such as compulsive perfectionism or workaholism)—that behavior is called an addiction (see ADDICTION).

A person who is struggling in the grip of a compulsion can understand the feelings expressed by the apostle Paul: "For the good that I will to do, I do not do; but the evil I will not to do, that I practice. . . . But I see another law in my members, warring against the law of my mind, and bringing me into captivity to the law of sin which is in my members. O wretched man that I am! Who will deliver me from this body of death?" (Rom. 7:19, 23–24).

Compulsive behavior is also a feature of the *obsessive-compulsive personality*. Obsessive-compulsive people are marked by inflexibility and a compulsive drive to achieve perfection (see PERFECTIONISM). They tend to be obsessively preoccupied with order, scheduling, details, and rules to the point that they lose sight of the original goal they had in mind for all of this orderly, tightly scheduled, minutely detailed effort. Obsessive-compulsive people are prone to a number of compulsive behaviors, such as workaholism, control addiction, compulsive overspending, compulsive hoarding, and compulsive religious legalism.

When anxiety and other emotional issues push an obsessive-compulsive personality into an *obsessive-compulsive disorder* (OCD), the compulsive behavior often takes on a bizarre character. Notice the two components of OCD: obsession and compulsion. An obsession is an irrational thinking pattern; a compulsion is an irrational pattern of actions. So, for example, an individual might become obsessed with thoughts of contamination, which would then produce the compulsion of repetitive hand-washing. Or, a Christian might become obsessed with doubts about his salvation and his acceptance by God, and this obsession would produce the compulsion of repeating a religious phrase over and over or performing some self-punishing act of self-atonement over and over. OCD is a form of neurotic mental illness and requires professional psychiatric treatment.

Compulsions, however, are not in and of themselves a sign of mental illness or serious dysfunction. Compulsions are extremely common, and most of us can identify with one form of compulsion or another: compulsive overeating, sexual compulsions (from recurring impure thoughts to sexual addictions), gambling compulsions, compulsive perfectionism, workaholism, compulsive volunteerism.

Compulsions are usually a means of avoiding some unpleasant reality. Compulsive individuals avoid dealing with the actual unconscious conflict (such as guilt or a painful childhood memory) by retreating into compulsive behavior. Once compulsive individuals courageously face their emotional issues, free themselves from guilt, and purge the pain of their childhood through therapy and support (such as is found in a support group or recovery group), the compulsion loses its power over them. And once that

■

Most people who behave compulsively are polyaddicted—that is, they struggle with more than one compulsion. The compulsive overeater may also be a spendaholic or a rageaholic, although some compulsions may be in various stages of remission.

■

■

The only cure for compulsive behavior is insight into what drives that behavior.

■

147

unconscious compulsion has been disarmed and removed from power, the conscious will (which Christians should progressively give over to God's control) will be back in the driver's seat of their lives.

Compulsive Overeating

"Doesn't everyone overeat sometimes?"

"Around the holidays, I always eat till I'm as stuffed as a Thanksgiving turkey! That doesn't mean I have a problem, does it?"

"Why do I eat all the time? Because I'm hungry all the time, that's why!"

"I binged in college—before exams, whenever I broke up with my boyfriend, or whenever my roommate got a care package."

"I'm on the new 'Seafood Diet.' Whenever I 'see food,' I eat it!"

These frequently heard comments typify the confusion many people feel about their weight and their eating habits. Eating is an aspect of our lives that is fraught with gray areas. If you know you are addicted to drugs or alcohol, your choices are very clear: Stay completely away from those substances if you want to stay in control of your life. A recovering alcoholic must choose to either drink or not drink; there's no middle ground. A recovering drug addict is either completely drug-free or not.

But everyone has to eat.

You can't simply quit eating like a smoker quits smoking or a drinker quits drinking. Moreover, every person's need for food is highly individualized. So where do you draw the line? How do you know if X amount of food is just right and Y amount is too much? How do you know if you've got a problem with compulsive overeating?

Many of us tell ourselves, "Yes, I'm overweight—but it's not because I overeat. I'm just big-boned. Oh, and I probably have a slow metabolism, too. Besides, it's probably genetic. My whole family is overweight." Perhaps there are biological reasons for your weight problem. But you should be aware that people who are overweight because of physical, biochemical, or metabolic reasons are in a very small minority. *The vast majority of overweight people have gotten this way because they have a compulsive drive to eat too much.* This does not mean that compulsive overeaters are lazy or lack character or are weak-willed. It simply means that they have emotional issues that compel this behavior. Compulsive overeaters need to gain insight into these emotional issues in order to gain control over their eating patterns.

Some Christians—particularly those who have never had a weight problem—prefer to write this behavior off as the sin of gluttony. Addictive behavior, they believe, is something that happens to non-Christians, or to Christians who are not very spiritual. But though the process of recovery from a food addiction does require reliance upon God, there is much more to compulsive overeating than just "gluttony." The problem of compulsive overeating has its roots in deep emotional issues of pain and guilt. It is often related to instances of abuse or some other traumatic event in the life of the compulsive overeater.

The Minirth Meier New Life Clinics do not define a *compulsive overeater* as a person who weighs a given percentage or number of pounds over an ideal weight. The compulsive overeater may be a few pounds or a few hundred pounds overweight. The issue is not how much the person weighs but why he or she eats. We focus on the subconscious causes of the obsessive urge to eat. We ask the question, "Why is this person eating? Is it because he or she is *physically* hungry? Or is it because he or she is trying to satisfy an *emotional* hunger?"

Compulsive overeaters are usually not aware of the real reasons they eat. They often *think* they eat because they are hungry and may say, "I'm hungry all the time." In fact, however, it is not a physical sensation of an empty stomach that drives their behavior. It is an *emotional emptiness*. For compulsive overeaters, food is an *addiction*. Just as alcoholics build an intense emotional dependence upon alcohol in order to feel good inside, compulsive overeaters become dependent upon food in order to feel good inside (see ADDICTION).

That is why diet books, diet drinks, diet pills, and other diet programs and paraphernalia almost always fail. They attack the symptom (being overweight) but they do not address the root cause (emotional dependence or addiction). Unless compulsive overeaters are able to identify and understand the reasons *why* they overeat, they will never be free of an emotionally dependent relationship with food.

Why Do I Eat?

If you are trying to discover whether or not you are a compulsive overeater, take this self-test. Answer YES or NO to the following questions:

YES	NO	
___	___	Do you eat when you're angry?
___	___	Do you eat to comfort yourself in times of crisis and tension?
___	___	Do you eat to stave off boredom?
___	___	Do you lie to yourself and others about how much you have eaten or when you ate?
___	___	Do you hide food away for yourself?
___	___	Are you embarrassed about your physical appearance?
___	___	Are you 20 percent or more over your medically recommended weight?
___	___	Have significant people in your life expressed concern about your eating patterns?

____ ____ Has your weight fluctuated by more than ten pounds in the past six months?

____ ____ Do you fear your eating is out of control?

If you answered YES to two or more of these questions, there is a strong likelihood that you have a problem with compulsive overeating.

BINGEING

What is that nameless monster that drives you to eat a whole package of cookies before you're even home from the grocery store? Or to gobble down an entire half-gallon of ice cream secretly after your family has gone to bed? Overeaters need to understand the dynamics that cause their eating compulsion before they can become free of this addiction.

Of course, not all compulsive overeaters binge. Some people are "stuffers." They tend to overdo it at the dinner table. Others are "grazers." They do most of their overeating between meals, snacking and noshing at a steady rate throughout the day. But some of the most common compulsive overeaters are "bingers."

Bingeing, as with most addictions, tends to be chronic and progressive. It may start somewhat innocuously, but over months and years there is an inexorable progression. The bingeing may have started out just as a recreation or even as a celebration. Then bingers begin to binge on weekends, then nightly, and somewhere in the addiction progression, they realize that there is more bingeing than real living going on.

Not all compulsive overeaters follow this pattern. Bingers may be very disciplined dieters 99 percent of the time. Then, like an alcoholic on a "lost weekend" toot, they will "go off the wagon" and indulge without letup for a few minutes, hours, or even days. This binge may be followed by another period of days or weeks of moderation—then another binge.

The emotional pattern of bingeing is easy to trace: You binge once, then feel guilty about it. You resolve never to binge again. You keep that pledge for a few weeks or even months. Then something happens—either something to celebrate or something to console yourself over—and you bring out the food. Maybe you didn't plan to binge, but once you got started, there was no stopping you until you became downright sick. Again you feel guilty. Again you pledge: "Never again." But the next time you break that pledge, you don't try to resist the temptation. You think, "What the heck? Just one more binge. I deserve a few moments of happiness." Then more guilt. Another pledge. But the guilt makes it easier to give in the next time, because you already feel bad about yourself. You already see yourself as a hopeless binge-addict. And with each new binge, it takes less and less temptation to trigger the compulsive behavior.

Some people engage in a pattern called *bingeing and purging,* in which a binge is followed by self-induced vomiting or abuse of laxatives to get the binged food out of the system before it can be assimilated by the body. Bingeing and purging is a very

150

dangerous practice that can result in a number of extremely serious health problems and even (in extreme cases) death. (For a complete discussion of bingeing and purging, see ANOREXIA NERVOSA AND BULIMIA.)

THE ROLE OF DENIAL

Denial is an inability to see the truth about oneself. In a sense, it is a lie people tell themselves, which, once they have told it, they cling to and believe. The more serious the addiction, the stronger the denial. It is impossible for people to take control of their eating habits until they have penetrated their denial and admitted the truth about themselves.

One form of denial is "magical thinking," a tendency to approach issues with the unrealistic belief that some "magic pill" can take one's problems away. "If I can just find the right diet," you may tell yourself, "if I can just discover that elusive magic formula, my weight will just slip away." Magical thinking is what sells fad diet books and supermarket tabloids. But magical thinking denies the fact that recovery from any addiction, including food addiction, requires facing the truth about yourself and then acting on that truth in a courageous and disciplined way.

TWELVE REASONS FOR COMPULSIVE OVEREATING

Denial Statements

- "I can lose this weight anytime I want to. I just don't choose to diet."
- "I eat just like everyone else. My metabolism is just slow, and my family is large-boned."
- "I just can't lose weight after a pregnancy."
- "My doctor says I have to lose this weight, but what do doctors know? If weight doesn't get me, it'll be cancer or pollution or falling under a bus. Better to go out eating a chocolate fudge sundae."
- "When I'm ready to lose this weight, I can buckle down and do it by willpower."
- "There's no connection between food issues and the relationships in my life."
- "You tell me I eat out of anger. But how can I be angry at my husband? I have him on a pedestal! I don't feel I deserve his love, so how could I blame him?" (Anytime one partner is on a pedestal, we find anger. Like children on a seesaw, if one is up, the other has to be down.)
- "I've never felt pretty. It's hard to imagine that God wants me to have a body that's healthy and attractive."
- "I'm not denying anything! I really don't have a problem!" (This is denial of denial itself!)

Denial statements keep the addiction cycle going round and round. Until we are able to face the truth about ourselves, it is impossible for any doctor or any diet to help us. As Jesus said, the *truth* will set us free.

Compulsive overeating is a response to external pressures and internal urges that arouse a craving for food that has nothing to do with physical hunger. Following are the twelve most common reasons for compulsive overeating.

Reason 1: Cultural pressures. We are constantly bombarded by cultural pressures, messages from the world around us—especially the advertising world. Advertisers for restaurant chains and snack foods beguile us and shout at us to "Eat, eat, eat!" Meanwhile, sleek Vogue models and hawkers of assorted diet products shame us with the message, "Be slim, slim, slim!" Flip on the TV, and you'll see ads for Sara Lee and Ultra Slimfast back to back. Psychiatrists call these push/pull messages, double-bind messages, paradox messages, or best of all—"crazy-making messages." Do these messages work? How many times have you seen a TV commercial for ice cream or Coca-Cola and thought, "Yes! Just what I need!"—and then headed straight for the refrigerator?

151

We are literally *surrounded* by signals that trigger our desire to eat, and then—after those signals have caused us to gain ten, twenty, fifty pounds—along comes another set of signals that trigger our shame and tear down our self-esteem: "Look at how *fat* you are!" Then we feel so bad inside that we have to binge again and anesthetize our pain with cookies and candy bars. It's a vicious cycle—as vicious as any cycle could be.

Reason 2: A subconscious desire for protection against love and intimacy. This may sound irrational, but there is actually a survival-instinct form of logic at work in the subconscious mind. We frequently see people in our clinic who have built a protective barrier of fat around themselves, and in most cases they have done so in response to some traumatic event in their lives.

With her strikingly pale blue eyes and peach-like complexion, Stephanie would not only be attractive but stunning—except that she is a hundred pounds overweight. In fact, photos of Stephanie when she was twelve or thirteen show her as cute, slender, with the signs of lovely femininity just beginning to bloom on a healthy, athletic young frame. In counseling, Stephanie revealed that it was at about this time that she began to be sexually abused by her stepfather. Although it was years before she understood it, she now realizes that the pounds of flesh she wrapped around her were to prevent any other man from invading her boundaries as her stepfather did when she was a young adolescent.

The same thread runs through many different stories. Greg grew up overmothered and intimidated by the opposite sex, so he wears his three-hundred pound body as a protective covering so he won't have to deal with his sexuality. Lynn never had a weight problem until Ted, her fiancé of four years, broke their engagement and married another woman; in place of romantic passion, she now has a passion for chocolates, and she wears the heavy result of all those chocolates like a bullet-proof vest around her heart, so that no one will ever get close enough to hurt her again.

The sexual dimension of compulsive overeating should not be overlooked. For many people, compulsive overeating is part of a subconscious effort to deny, repress, or obscure their sexuality. The more body fat one acquires, the less conspicuous the body's sexual areas become. If one is heavy enough, sexual activity, because of either diminished aesthetics or simple mechanics, becomes unpleasant, if not impossible.

Sometimes the food itself—not just the body fat—becomes a shield against intimacy. Compulsive overeaters tend to become obsessed with food. This is true even of compulsive dieters: all they think about is the food they are supposed to be eating, the food they are not supposed to be eating, the food they are craving, the food they will reward themselves with if they can only lose five more pounds, and on and on and on. They are on a roller coaster, losing ten pounds, then gaining twelve, then losing eight. They worry before every meal: "What should I eat? Will I be hungry afterwards if I eat that?" If they overeat, they are obsessed with guilt for hours. This endless obsession with food starts to crowd out other life issues—and other *people*—and this, in fact, may be their subconscious goal.

Reason 3: A craving for immediate gratification. We are all born self-centered. If we mature under the care of loving, disciplining parents, we will gradually grow out of our self-centeredness. But if we are not lovingly disciplined and if our parents do not

THE COMPLETE LIFE ENCYCLOPEDIA

set a good example, we will probably continue in an immature pattern of selfishness. We will demand instant gratification: "I want what I want when I want it—and I want it now!" The adult who is "addicted" to instant gratification will eat whenever he or she feels a craving for food. That craving may have nothing whatever to do with physical hunger, but with emotional issues.

Selfishness often leads to an exaggerated sense of competition. Even children who are otherwise cooperative toward their siblings will aggressively compete for food. They will complain, "Hey! That's my cookie!" even if there are three more on the plate. The instinct for food is so basic that people will subconsciously compete for food by taking larger portions than they want.

This underlying cause for overeating can be particularly difficult to detect because people often cover their selfishness with a veneer of unselfishness. Many "instant gratification addicts" will volunteer their time helping people in hospitals, in schools, or at church—then go home and binge in secret to satisfy their urge for self-gratification.

The craving for instant gratification is often especially keen in people from dysfunctional families. Having grown up with inadequate emotional gratification in childhood, they tend to be emotionally dissatisfied as adults. They discover that they can find instant gratification in a package of Oreos or a freezer full of Dove Bars. The gratification that food provides, of course, is temporary—so the "instant gratification addict" must return again and again to the pantry or refrigerator for another "fix" of food. Underlying this recurring cycle of craving/gratification/craving/gratification is an emotional hunger that goes completely unsatisfied. This person doesn't understand that what he or she *really* craves is not temporary gratification but the lasting *satisfaction* that comes from building relationships, achieving goals, and finding meaning and purpose in life.

Reason 4: Using food as a tranquilizer. Each time a person eats, the brain stimulates the production of brain chemicals called endorphins, which are natural painkillers, relaxants, and pleasure stimulators. Endorphins are naturally produced and are designed by God to help the human body deal with pain and stress and to produce a sense of well-being. Certain activities, such as laughter, sexual excitement, eating, and aerobic exercise, stimulate the production of these chemicals. Endorphins, however, are also chemically similar to narcotic drugs such as morphine, and they produce similar results—including addiction.

It is normal, after eating a good meal, to feel placid, tranquil, and even anesthetized as a result of endorphin production in the body. But the compulsive overeater can become dependent on his own endorphins and the state of tranquility and anesthesia that food-induced endorphins cause. So to refer to compulsive overeating as a "food addiction" is not an overstatement. There is a clear analogy between compulsive dependency on food and chemical addictions such as alcoholism or morphine addiction. The difference for the food addict is that the chemical is produced right inside his or her own brain.

Reason 5: Using food to avoid facing anxiety and the truth about oneself. Anxiety is a generalized sense of unease. Often, people feel anxious on a conscious level because of emotional issues that are disturbing them on a subconscious level. The anxiety a person feels may actually be fear of discovering the truth about the hidden memory, thought, emotion, or motive that is operating on a subconscious level. For some people, that anxiety is the trigger for compulsive overeating.

For example, Rick feels an intense subconscious rage toward his father because his father is emotionally cold, distant, and unaccepting toward Rick. Yet Rick also bases his sense of self-worth on his father's acceptance. Rick's father is successful and respected, and Rick consciously wants to be like him. So Rick keeps telling himself what a "great guy" his father is, while denying the evidence of his feelings: his dad is really a self-centered, manipulative, unfeeling sociopath who does not know how to love his son. Because Rick has consciously patterned his life after his father, he has a conflict: he cannot consciously face his own anger toward his father without lowering his opinion of himself and his goals. This conflict produces anxiety.

How does Rick deal with his anxiety? By stuffing it with food. Whenever Rick sees a self-centered, manipulative father portrayed on television or sees an incident involving a selfish father in public, he becomes overwhelmed with a craving for food. He eats to quell his hidden, denied rage, and to keep from having to look at the truth about himself and his relationships.

Reason 6: Using food to punish oneself or others. People sometimes become angry with themselves over some sin, mistake, or failure. Disgusted with themselves for having had an affair or for losing a job or for failing in school, they respond by punishing themselves and making themselves overweight. They sometimes find it less painful to hate themselves for being overweight than to get in touch with their true anger. The weight, then, becomes the scapegoat. This is a form of using compulsive overeating as a defense against anxiety and facing the truth about oneself.

This is the trigger that drove Sherri's compulsion to overeat. "I don't deserve to be pretty," she said, although she had been strikingly beautiful as a teenager. "By staying fat, I can punish myself." But what had Sherri done that she felt she needed to be continually punished for? She was recovering from addictions to several substances and behaviors, including food, alcohol, extramarital sex, anger, and spending. In fact, she had gained a great deal of freedom and control in every one of these addictions but one: her compulsion to overeat. She held on to this one addiction to punish herself for having acted out these other addictions in the past. She felt she had run up a debt of guilt, so being fat was her way of paying off that debt.

Others eat compulsively to punish their spouses or parents for disappointing them, nagging them, or dominating them. *I'll show you,* they think (subconsciously, if not consciously). *I'll make you ashamed to be seen with me!*

Reason 7: Using food to relieve depression or stress. People who are depressed frequently suffer from repressed anger and an unconscious desire to take out revenge against others or against themselves. Many are perfectionists who inwardly resent themselves for not being perfect. Emotions of resentment and anger cause important brain chemicals, serotonin and norepinephrine, to be depleted from our brain cells. These are the chemicals that enable electrical impulses to fire across the synapses of our brain cells. These chemicals enable us to think, to feel good, and to move. When these chemicals are depleted, we lose energy, positive mood, and motivation.

This depletion of brain chemicals can cause people to gain weight as they become less active while continuing to eat at their former levels. Conversely, many people who develop serotonin or norepinephrine depletion actually lose their appetites, and some even develop anorexia.

Reason 8: Using food as a weapon of rebellion. Some people become so tired and frustrated with trying to live up to a perfect body image or following the rules and dictates of others that they may use overeating as a way of asserting their independence. *You may control these other aspects of my life,* they think, *but I will control what I eat!* Usually, this kind of "control" takes the form of out-of-control eating.

Tori rebelled against the perfectionistic standards imposed by her rigid and legalistic husband. Sure, she lived up to his standards in every other area. Both Tori and her husband were high achievers: he was a lawyer, and she was a CPA. They owned an expensive home, drove expensive cars, and sent their children to expensive schools. But Tori could not control her urge to binge. Finally, her husband sent her to a Minirth Meier New Life Clinic for counseling. She came reluctantly and resentfully. On two separate visits, she damaged the car she was driving—significantly, it was her husband's car!—while pulling into the parking lot of the clinic. She was intimidated by her husband, so rather than expressing her anger directly to her husband, she acted it out by damaging his car—and by making herself fat. Only when she began to understand the emotional forces that triggered her compulsive overeating did she begin to resolve her anger and her weight problem. (Her driving improved too.)

Reason 9: Using food to express the need to control one's circumstances. Control is a major issue for children of dysfunctional families. In families with alcoholic or abusive parents, children grow scared, wary, and defensive. Since so many aspects of their lives are out of their control—for example, whether or not they will be hit or molested tonight, or whether or not their parents will assault each other again—they look for areas of life where they can experience some measure of control, safety, and certainty.

As these children grow older, these patterns remain. The adult children may feel that the area they must control is money, so they become either misers or spendaholics. Whether they hoard or spend, they are in control of their money. Or they may choose food as the area in which to exercise control, so they eat whatever they can in order to say, "In this area of my life, I'm the boss"—even though it is the compulsion to overeat, not their own will, that soon masters their lives.

Ironically, many compulsive overeaters are overdisciplined. They tell themselves, "If I just had more willpower, I could beat this food issue. I could make my diet work with a little more willpower." But willpower is not the answer. Attempting to solve the problem purely by self-control and force of will usually results in defeat and even worse bingeing when this approach fails.

Reason 10: Having a faulty body image. A faulty perception of one's own body can lead a person to compulsively overeat (or, in the case of anorexics, undereat). It is amazing the degree to which many people are able to disregard or deny what they see in the mirror. One patient came to a Minirth Meier New Life Clinic weighing nearly four hundred pounds. When the doctors asked him about his weight, he said, "Well, yes, I am a little overweight. I suppose I really should get back on my diet and lose a few pounds this summer." Another patient, who was seeking recovery from codependency and a serious eating disorder, had such a distorted body image that she could not pick her own picture out of a family photo album.

The more serious an eating addiction is, the less accurately a person sees himself. An accurate body image is an important first step toward controlling a compulsion to overeat. As one seriously overweight comedienne once remarked, "I've just found the perfect diet! You can eat anything you want as long as you eat it in front of a mirror—*naked*." Until compulsive overeaters are able to see the truth about their own bodies, they will probably continue to gorge themselves to death.

Reason 11: Feelings toward food which were formed in childhood. People often inherit or develop harmful attitudes about food at their parents' dinner table. Some examples:

For Justin, the dinner table was a shooting gallery. Each night his father would sarcastically "shoot down" Justin or one of his siblings. As a result, Justin learned, "My nurturing isn't going to come from Mom and Dad. So I'll just dig into this food for my emotional, as well as physical, sustenance."

Vicky's parents were obsessive about every child in the family leaving a perfectly clean plate. So the compulsions of the parents were passed down to the children. Vicky vividly recalls times when she could not or would not eat her brussels sprouts or her liver and onions—so she was forced to sit alone at the table for hours. These episodes lasted on into her adolescence. Now in therapy as an adult, Vicky realizes that an unhealthy message was drummed into her as a child: "You must eat! You must eat!" That message continues to be a major factor in her compulsive overeating habits today.

In almost every family, food is part of most family celebrations—and there is nothing wrong with that. But for the compulsive eater, almost anything can become reason to celebrate—and reason to binge. "I learned from my parents," recalls Larry, a thirty-year-old compulsive overeater who still lives with his parents. "You eat to celebrate when you feel good, and you eat to console yourself when you feel bad. If I got a raise at work, Mom would say, 'Let's celebrate!' And she'd fix me my favorite: pork roast with baked potato and sour cream. If I had a bad day at work, she'd say, 'Oh, Larry—I know what will make you feel better!' And she'd fix me my favorite: pork roast with baked potato and sour cream!"

Reason 12: Using food to satisfy one's hunger for love. Most overeaters use food to satisfy their "love hunger," their need for emotional nurturing. Some feel empty inside because they never received the love they needed when they were children. Some feel empty inside because of divorce or a broken romance or the loss of someone close to them. But food can never satisfy our hunger for love.

At the Minirth Meier New Life Clinics, we often use a simple illustration to remind people that there is a big difference between an empty heart and an empty stomach and that the two must never be confused. That illustration looks like this:

■

Some people overeat to please their parents. Dr. Paul Meier shares his own story: "I grew up in a German home. And, like all good Old World eaters, we put butter on everything. Sometimes I used to food my butter rather than butter my food! Mom was a great cook who spent a lot of time preparing really fine meals and desserts when all four of us kids were home. She was pleased to see us enjoy her cooking. It made her happy if we asked for seconds or thirds. So I grew up overeating to please my mom. It wasn't anything she consciously desired or that I consciously desired, but it became a type of codependency."

■

Food can fill—and overfill—the stomach, but it can never reach the human heart.

■

THE COMPLETE LIFE ENCYCLOPEDIA

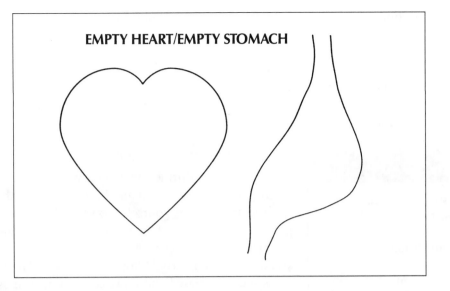

EMPTY HEART/EMPTY STOMACH

Whenever we feel the desire to eat, the question we should ask ourselves is, "Where am I truly hungry? Is my stomach hungry? Or is my *heart* hungry?" The answer to that question will determine whether we will feed on what truly satisfies, or merely gorge ourselves by stuffing a "hungry heart."

What causes a "hungry heart"? Every human infant is born with a need to be loved. Children who grow up with loving, emotionally available parents will have their hearts filled with love by the time they reach adulthood. As adults, they can then fill the hearts of their loved ones—including their own children—with love.

But children who grow up deprived of a heart-filling childhood emerge into adulthood with empty hearts—emotional vacuums waiting to be filled. But if love is not available, what will these people try to fill their empty hearts with? In the case of compulsive overeaters, the stuffing of choice is food. But no matter what people use to fill the emptiness of their hearts—whether food or work or sexual pleasure or anything else—none of it touches the heart. In fact, the more effort they direct toward their stomachs, the less emotional energy they have to invest in those things that *truly* fill the human heart.

HOW TO FILL A HUNGRY HEART

What does your heart truly hunger for? Love and affirmation. Notice that *neither* of these important ingredients of a happy life can by picked up with a fork, chewed, or swallowed. But these *are* ingredients you can find, experience, and place in your heart where no one can take them away.

Where to Find Love

You can find love and acceptance from a number of valid, healthy sources. First, meditate in the Scripture passages that speak to you of God's unconditional love for you.

■

Neither food nor work nor sex nor any other substance or behavior is love. And love is what the heart hungers for. The key to overcoming your compulsion to overeat lies in learning how to feed your hungry heart what it truly wants.

■

157

Second, find a group of people—a small group Bible study, a support group, or a recovery group—where you will be unconditionally loved and accepted as you work on your recovery.

Third, make a commitment to love and forgive yourself for any mistakes you have made. Blame and guilt beat you down and make you feel unloved and unacceptable. Practice seeing yourself as God sees you, forgiving yourself as God forgives you, and loving yourself as God loves you.

■

> ### Meditate on God's Love
>
> - "I am loved with an everlasting love" (Jer. 31:3).
> - "I am beloved and chosen by God" (Col. 3:12; 1 Thess. 1:4).
> - "I am holy and without blame before God" (Eph. 1:4).
> - "I am accepted in Christ" (Eph. 1:6).
> - "I am forgiven; all my sins are washed away" (Eph. 1:7).

Where to Find Affirmation

You can be affirmed in several ways. First, replace any negative messages you may have received with positive messages about yourself. You may have been subjected to the abuse of negative messages throughout your childhood: "You never do anything right!" "I wish you'd never been born!" "You're so stupid!" These messages must be erased and replaced with new messages, based on God's view of you as stated in the Bible.

Second, restructure your lifestyle and relationships in a way that reflects an affirmation of your personal worth. If you have felt unworthy to enjoy an exciting

■

sexual relationship with your spouse, give yourself permission to ask your spouse to meet your sexual needs. If you have felt unworthy to be adequately paid at work, give yourself permission to go to your boss and say, "I believe my performance in this job justifies a raise." If you have felt too inadequate and unworthy to have warm, caring friendships in your life, decide that you will give yourself permission to talk to your friends and say, "I have a need for more closeness in my friendships."

Third, reparent yourself. Extend compassion to your "inner child" (see INNER CHILD). Make this statement to yourself, repeat it, and meditate on it: "I was wounded as a child, and I can't make the hurt go away. I can't change the past. But I know this pain will heal, and I will protect myself from further abuse. I have permission to trust again. I have permission to love myself. I have permission to accept myself as a beautiful creation of a loving God. I have permission to express my emotions—anger, joy, fear, hope, sorrow, happiness. I have permission to express my sexuality according to God's beautiful plan. I have permission to experience intimacy in relationships. I have permission to join a new supportive family of my own choosing, so that I can be unconditionally loved and affirmed."

Fourth, seek reparenting from others—a support group, a sponsor or mentor, a therapist, or a trusted friend. Choose someone who will truly affirm you unconditionally (if you choose someone from your present family or family of origin, you may fall back into old codependent family patterns). Ask that person to meet with you, pray with you, and affirm you on a regular basis.

Fifth, seek reparenting from God. Pray to God and listen quietly for His answer to come to you in your stillness. Read His Word. Experience what it means to have a heavenly Parent who is all-loving, all-accepting, all-affirming. True intimacy with God satisfies like no earthly relationship can.

THE PATH TO FREEDOM

The path to freedom from compulsive overeating consists of ten courageous steps:

Step 1: Be sure you have identified all your addictions. Most people who behave compulsively are polyaddicted. The compulsive overeater may also be a spendaholic or a rageaholic, although some compulsions may be in various stages of remission. Take stock of your compulsions and addictions. Get in touch with the various substances and behaviors you use to mask or anesthetize your emotional issues.

Step 2: Be sure you have broken through denial. Denial is a valid defense mechanism that God has given us to help us get through the first terrible shock of grief and loss. But denial becomes pernicious and unhealthy when it settles in and you use it to whitewash reality and obscure your pain. You must face your addiction squarely and say, "I am not just 'big-boned.' I'm not just 'a little overweight.' I have a serious food addiction, and it is out of my control."

One of the best ways to be absolutely certain that no vestiges of denial linger is to fully acknowledge your addiction in writing. Take a clean sheet of paper and write a letter to yourself. Tell yourself what you are addicted to, why you are addicted, and what you plan to do about it. Say, "I am food-dependent, and I want to surrender this addiction. I will do everything in my power to achieve total recovery." Sign and date the letter. One patient of ours actually mailed the letter to herself. She reported that three days later when the letter arrived in her mailbox, she was able to read it from a fresh viewpoint. This gave a big boost to her recovery process.

Step 3: Be sure you have identified your trigger foods and situations. What foods do you run to for emotional comfort? For relaxation? For an anesthetic against pain? What foods do you daydream about? What situations make you eat most? What situations tend to trigger a bingeing episode? What situations do you dread and get through by overeating?

Every addiction has its "triggers"—situations that fill the addict with an almost irresistible urge to reach out and grab an "addictive agent," a substance (alcohol, drugs, food) or behavior (workaholism, religious addiction). For you, that trigger food might be sugar or chocolate or French fries. You know that just one nibble can set off an uncontrolled binge that won't end until you are practically passed out on the floor from stuffing yourself. Your trigger situations may be family gatherings, office parties, grocery shopping, a fast-food restaurant, a Chinese food buffet, a salad bar, or going to the movies.

Once you have identified your "triggers," avoid them. Don't stock "trigger foods" in your pantry. Plan your travel so that you never have to go near that restaurant that

---

Affirming Messages from God's Word

- "I am set free" (John 8:31–32).
- "I have abundant life" (John 10:10).
- "I am a saint" (Rom. 1:7).
- "I am free of shame and condemnation" (Rom. 8:1).
- "I am a joint heir with Christ" (Rom. 8:17).
- "I am being changed and conformed to the image of Christ" (Rom. 8:28–29; Phil. 1:6).
- "I am a temple of the Holy Spirit" (1 Cor. 6:19).
- "I am a new creation" (2 Cor. 5:17).
- "I am God's workmanship" (Eph. 2:10).
- "I can do all things through Christ" (Phil. 4:13).
- "I am victorious" (Rev. 21:7).

Meditate daily in these messages so that they can reprogram your thinking about yourself.

---

has been your Waterloo so many times in the past. Avoid the popcorn-scented halls of the theater; rent the movies you want to see at a video store. People who go to the grocery store on an empty stomach tend to buy everything in sight; plan your grocery trips for immediately after dinner, and you will be better prepared to resist temptation.

Step 4: Be sure you have enlisted your family's support. One of the most common causes of diet failure is family sabotage: the husband who brings home his wife's favorite ice cream, children who beg for fresh-baked cookies, the mother who prepares the dieter's favorite fattening food. Be forewarned and forearmed. Stock your refrigerator with watermelon or low-fat yogurt to eat instead of ice cream. Buy the kids packaged cookies of a kind you don't like. Ask your spouse to prepare recipes from the Minirth Meier New Life Love Hunger series: *Love Hunger* by Dr. Frank Minirth, Dr. Paul Meier, Dr. Robert Hemfelt, Dr. Sharon Sneed, and Don Hawkins (Thomas Nelson, 1990), *The Love Hunger Weight-Loss Workbook* by Minirth, Meier, Hemfelt, and Sneed (Thomas Nelson, 1991), *The Love Hunger Action Plan* by Sneed (Thomas Nelson, 1993), or *Gentle Eating* by Stephen Arterburn, Mary Ehemann, and Dr. Vivian Lamphear (Thomas Nelson, 1993).

Step 5: Be sure you are dieting for the right motives. Do not start a diet to win love or approval. Don't diet for your husband or your mother or your boyfriend. Be sure you are doing this for yourself, or you will be subconsciously angry and resentful toward the person you are dieting for, and that suppressed anger can trigger a "rebellion binge" and sabotage your progress. A healthy attitude for dieting is "I am lovable and loved just as I am." Then you will be free to lose weight for yourself.

Step 6: Be sure you have set reasonable goals. Though some surveys suggest that as many as 90 percent of Americans consider themselves overweight, only 25 percent are, in fact, significantly obese. Cultural pressures tend to make us feel fatter than we really are. Set your own goal for weight loss, make sure it's an attainable goal, and don't allow fashion models or soap opera stars to distort your body image. Set goals in workable increments. You want to lose thirty pounds? Try setting three ten-pound goals, and give yourself a reward (a nonedible reward!) as you reach each ten-pound goal.

For most people dieting at home, a loss of two pounds per week is a reasonable goal. However, it is perfectly normal to lose faster at the beginning of your diet, perhaps five pounds in the first week or two, then slow to only a one-pound drop the next week. For this reason, many doctors recommend you not weigh yourself every morning. A temporary plateau in weight loss can be devastating to a dieter's morale and precipitate a binge. Slow and gradual weight loss is most effective and most healthful because it allows your body to adjust to new levels.

Step 7: Be sure you understand the medical risks of being overweight. The medical complications of obesity include cardiovascular problems (increased risk of stroke, heart attack, and heart failure); cancer (especially of the colon, breast, and uterus); gall bladder problems; pancreas problems; diabetes; joint, tendon, and back problems; pregnancy compli-

How Much Should You Weigh?

There are many theories on the subject of acceptable weight, plus insurance company charts and the "pinch an inch" test. But Dr. Frank Minirth has a much simpler formula to suggest as a guideline. "Women," he says, "should weigh one hundred pounds, plus five pounds for every inch of height above five feet. For men, weight should be one hundred and six pounds plus six pounds for every inch above five feet." (Of course, this is a general guideline, not an absolute.)

cations; increased surgical risks; and premature aging. Understanding these medical risks can enhance your motivation to lose weight.

Step 8: Be sure you have your doctor's approval before you diet. A diet is a lifestyle change, and any lifestyle change—even a healthy one—will put stress on your body. Therefore, it's important that you have a physical examination before you begin dieting. Risk factors to watch for include heart attack or stroke history, blood clotting history, liver or kidney disease, cancer not in remission, acute psychiatric disorder, and diabetes. Even though being overweight is less healthy than losing weight, these disorders place patients at a much greater risk during the weight loss program. It is important that such patients be monitored to make sure that the diet does not result in dangerous nutritional imbalances (such as a deficiency of potassium or folic acid).

Step 9: Be sure you understand why diets haven't worked in the past. Some of the popular diet programs of the past have been unbalanced, unhealthy, or simply outrageous. For example, the Beverly Hills Diet suggested: "Don't eat potatoes; they turn to vodka in your stomach." Others, however, such as Weight Watchers and the Love Hunger plan, offer a sensible, reduced-calorie method of losing weight.

Step 10: Be sure you truly want to be free. In order to achieve long-term mastery over your weight, you must want it enough to be willing to break the emotional and spiritual bonds that you may have befriended. When this is done, you will truly have gone on your last diet. You will be able to live in peace and freedom with your body and your appetite.

Conflict and Confrontation

Contrary to popular belief, conflict is not necessarily bad. In fact, conflict can be a powerful tool for strengthening relationships and solving problems. When two people or two groups enter into an experience of conflict, many positive results can emerge— if the people involved in the conflict understand how to manage conflict in a caring and constructive way.

Conflict is painful. It brings out anger, fear, and anxiety—all emotional experiences most of us try to avoid. But there is something very beautiful and positive about conflict when it is managed in a healthy way. When conflict functions at its best, you see people fully engaged with one another, passionately taking a stand for their convictions, struggling to hear and to be heard, human beings communicating and connecting with each other across the gulf of their individuality and aloneness.

Conflict is a natural part of living in an imperfect world. We see instances of creative, constructive conflict in the Scriptures—and we see instances of strife and division. Many of the letters of the apostle Paul were written specifically to address conflict in the church; without conflict, those letters of the New Testament might never have been written.

Learning to manage conflict is a skill that requires commitment, emotional maturity, and experience. Conflict management is a skill that can be refined with practice.

THE TEN RULES OF CARING CONFRONTATION

1. Learn to separate major issues from minor issues. Conflict sometimes gets out of control because people major in the minors. Life is too short to spend it fussing over inconsequential problems. Moreover, when we get embroiled in conflict over minor issues, it often means that the real issue is hidden from view.

For example, a husband and wife get into a knock-down, drag-out argument when the husband fails to take out the kitchen garbage. The garbage is a minor issue, and it is only a symbol of the real but completely hidden issue for each of them. For the husband, the hidden issue is that he feels his wife pushes him around by nagging him about the garbage. "Just let me take out the garbage when I get around to it," he says. "Why do I have to drop what I'm doing just because you demand to have the garbage taken out *right now?*" Deep down, he feels his prerogatives as an adult, as a grown man, are being taken away from him and he is being treated like a child. Although he doesn't consciously recognize it, he unconsciously views the situation in symbolic terms: his wife assumes the parent role and he becomes a little boy whose own agenda is not important.

For the wife, the conflict also has a hidden, symbolic dimension. She spends two hours arguing about garbage and how it smells bad and attracts gnats, about how it's unsightly and unsanitary, and about how her husband doesn't have any sense of pride in keeping their house clean—but she never talks about the *real* issue, because it is hidden from her conscious view. She feels as if her feelings and her needs are not valued by her husband—not just in the kitchen, in the issue of garbage, but in the bedroom and in many other aspects of their marriage. The issue is not garbage, but her ignored feelings and unmet emotional needs. Until she and her husband get in touch with the real issues of their marriage so that they can talk those issues through and find real understanding, they are going to continue getting into conflict after conflict over inconsequential problems.

Groups, too, often get hung up on inconsequentials. Churches, committees, businesses, and families often get embroiled in big-league fights over minor-league issues. Why? Because there is a hidden issue that everyone in the group fails to recognize consciously. Or because there is an issue that everyone knows about but fears to talk about. For such conflicts to be resolved, someone in the group must have the insight and the wisdom to recognize that unnamed issue and the courage to name it out loud. That person must also have the courage and persevering love to endure the group denial

---

The Positive Results of Conflict

- Problems can be creatively solved by merging the concerns and points of view of all sides.
- People from both sides can learn to appreciate, understand, and accept other points of view.
- People can grow and change.
- Relationships can be strengthened as tension and distrust give way to harmony and understanding.

---

that is likely to result once that issue has been laid bare. Before the conflict is resolved, that insightful, wise, courageous person may have to endure the verbal attacks of those who, at a subconscious level, want to keep that issue hidden.

2. When conflicts arise, confront them as soon as possible. Once it is clear that conflict exists and the issue needs to be confronted, deal with it openly, forthrightly, and head-on. The longer you wait to get a matter off your chest, the bigger and more intractable the problem becomes. Time tends to magnify resolvable grievances into unresolvable grudges. The emotions behind the conflict gradually build up pressure until, when the lid finally comes off of the cauldron of conflict, it comes off explosively rather than constructively.

People often come to the Minirth Meier New Life Clinics for help in dealing with bitter conflicts over issues that are years old. The feelings surrounding these conflicts are often very intense. But as counselor and client begin examining together the core issues of the conflicts, our clients often come to a point where they recognize that the ■ issue was not originally as big and explosive as it eventually became. Time has a way of magnifying molehills into mountains as anger festers, as insults and offenses accumulate, as attitudes harden. If the issues had been confronted as soon as they occurred, many years of misery could have been spared.

3. Stick to the subject at hand. In times of conflict, people want their case to be as big and convincing as possible. They gather all the ammunition they can think of, dredging up side issues, past issues, character issues, any kind of issue they can think of to hammer the point home: "And another thing . . . !" "And what about the time that you . . . !" "And that's not all . . . !" Soon the conflict is a confusing maze of charges and countercharges. By the time the conflict has collapsed of its own weight, completely unresolved, both sides are sullen and resentful—and neither side can remember what started it all off! The stage is set for even more painful and confusing bouts of conflict to come.

In the life of Paul we see conflict between two great men of New Testament faith, Paul and Barnabas. These two Christian brothers wrestled with each other over the next step in their missionary journey. Out of their conflict came a creative solution: Paul went one way, Barnabas the other. There is no indication in Scripture that one was right and the other wrong. They just didn't see eye to eye, and they agreed to disagree—and they each went in a different direction. And with them, the Gospel also spread in two different directions. Out of their conflict came an expanded influence for the Gospel of Jesus Christ.

■

Conflict can't be constructively resolved by hopscotching from issue to issue. Stay focused on one issue, resolve it, and get on with the business of living.

4. In times of conflict, avoid generalizing; be specific. Avoid words such as "always" and "never." Instead of, "You're always so careless," it is more constructive to say, "I was disappointed with the way you cleaned the garage yesterday. You left a pile of trash in the corner and the floor wasn't swept." Generalizations tend to be received as a personal and injurious statement about somebody's character. Generalizations cause defenses to go up. But if you make specific statements about a specific issue, people are often able to be more objective. "Yes," they may say, "I guess I didn't do that job as well as I usually do." When you deal in specifics, the other person is able to reflect, *This is not a personal attack on my character. This is an observation about one job I didn't do well. I can accept this critique without being personally affronted.*

5. Avoid personal insults and character assassination. Keep the conflict focused on the issues, not on personalities. Avoid behavior or comments that put the other person on the defensive. Demonstrate that your true allegiance is to a relationship, not to an issue.

163

Seek to care more about the person you are confronting than the tasks, rules, agendas, quotas, and results you are debating. No matter how intense the conflict between you and another person, that person should never leave that conflict feeling he or she is not valued by you.

6. Express real feelings; avoid intellectualizing. Many people, in times of conflict, retreat into philosophical exchanges of ideas. They mask their feelings with cerebral-sounding theories: "I think you are just projecting your latent hostilities onto my behavior." Intellectualizing is a form of denial ("I'm not angry; I'm actually quite calm and rational about this matter") and dishonesty ("I won't let you see that you are really getting to me and making me mad"). In times of conflict—especially when family relationships or friendships are involved—it is important that feelings be honestly (but appropriately) expressed: "I feel angry when you come on so dogmatically and attack my beliefs." "I feel hurt when you ignore me." "I felt embarrassed and ashamed when you made those jokes about me in front of our friends."

Of course, expressing feelings means taking a risk. We make ourselves vulnerable to a person who may not accept our right to our feelings. "Oh, it's ridiculous to feel that way," the other person may respond, trying to shrug off and invalidate your feelings. When that happens, you may calmly assert your right to your own feelings. "This is the way I feel," you might say. "I'm not asking you to like the way I feel or identify with the way I feel. I'm not saying you should feel the same way I do. I just want you to know that when you do such-and-such, I tend to feel a certain way. I'm hoping that you will be considerate enough of my feelings to make an attempt to change your behavior in this regard. I care about your feelings, I want to hear how you feel, and I hope you will care about my feelings as well."

When you generalize, people have a hard time understanding what it is that you want them to change in their behavior. But if you are specific, you give them something concrete to deal with. Whether the other person agrees with you or not, you can help to focus and manage the level of conflict by being specific.

7. Demonstrate unconditional love and affirmation, but avoid patronizing. One of the biggest mistakes people make in times of conflict is trying to be affirming but coming off sounding patronizing and condescending.

For example, Pastor Jones is in conflict with Elder Smith. After a church board meeting, Pastor Jones takes Elder Smith aside and begins by saying, "There's something I need to talk to you about—but first, I want to tell you I think you're really doing a great job on the church board. You're always so involved and vocal, and your thoughts are always so well-organized and focused. You're doing one terrific job with the Stewardship Committee, and that report you gave tonight was a class act." And on and on and on, praise upon praise. Meanwhile, Elder Smith is fidgeting uncomfortably, his defenses are going up, he is growing more wary and tense as the suspense mounts. Elder Smith knows that Pastor Jones did not take him aside just to heap praise upon him—and he is waiting for the other shoe to drop. Pastor Jones thinks he is softening the blow when in reality he is tightening the spring!

A better approach would be to meet the issue head-on, while surrounding it with a commitment to the relationship and to unconditional love: "Elder Smith, I have something to discuss with you. This won't be easy for either of us, but I respect you enough to give it to you straight. I care about you, and I'm committed to our relationship as Christian brothers. Here's the problem I have. . . ." Notice, there's no sugarcoating in these words, but there is a clear statement of respect and unconditional love. In this

164

approach, Elder Smith doesn't feel he's been "set up" with a lot of compliments, only to be "shot down" later with criticism.

8. Demonstrate empathy and reflective listening. Put yourself in the other person's place. If you must confront another person, consider how you would like to be confronted if you were in the same place. Listen to what the other person is really saying—and also listen for feelings. Don't just unload, seek to learn and to be responsive to the other person's issues and emotions. When the other person speaks, really listen, don't just think about the point you want to make.

Also, listen reflectively. Mirror back what the other person says to you, restating his or her feelings in your own words: "I hear you saying that you are angry because you don't think it was right for me to spend money on that item when our budget is so tight." This serves two purposes: (1) it helps the other person feel he or she has been heard, and (2) it helps you to understand the other person's thoughts, feelings, and issues.

9. Affirm publicly, confront privately. Avoid raising difficult issues with your spouse, children, employees, friends, fellow church members, and the like in front of other people. Rebuking and confronting people in public brings humiliation, embarrassment, and shame. It destroys self-esteem and relationships.

10. Confront to heal, not to win. Seek growth, not intimidation. There is a saying that "a man convinced against his will is of the same opinion still." The word *convince* comes from a Latin root word meaning "to conquer." If you are trying to convince, you are trying to win, to conquer, to vanquish your opponent. Chances are, even if you win the argument, you will lose the relationship. Seek a solution in which both sides come out as winners. Seek a stronger relationship, greater understanding, and a healing resolution. Seek to learn, change, and grow from the conflict as much or more as you want the other person to learn, change, and grow. As the conflict moves toward the resolution stage, tell the other person what you have learned about the issue, about the other person, or about your own mistakes and motivations.

In any conflict, the only real winners are the ones who learn how to manage that conflict to bring about a positive, constructive resolution. When we approach conflict with courage, honesty, and love for the other person, conflict is no longer the enemy of relationships. It becomes our ally.

■

Don't go for a slam-dunk, one-sided victory; seek genuine peace and understanding in your relationship.

■

Contentment

Dr. and Mrs. Paul Meier have a plaque in their home that reads, "All I want in life is a little bit more than I will ever have!" That sign serves as a reminder of the futility of materialistic cravings and of God's plan for Christians to live contented, well-adjusted lives.

In the mid-1970s, while Dr. Meier was a professor of pastoral counseling at Trinity Seminary near Chicago, he was offered a high-paying opportunity to leave his seminary position and become the administrator of a psychiatric clinic. "I admit I had materialistic urges," Dr. Meier recalls, "and largely because of the salary that was offered, I decided to take the job at the end of the school year." But then something happened that shook Dr. Meier's life: his friend and fellow Trinity professor, Paul Little, was killed in a automobile accident.

"Paul was a very dedicated man of God," said Dr. Meier, "a man with a real heart for bringing people to Christ. I went to his funeral, and Leighton Ford preached the message. Dr. Ford spoke about the importance of being able to reach a point where you can look back over your life and know that your life has counted for Jesus Christ. As I listened, I was deeply convicted and moved. At that moment, I was filled with a certainty that God wanted me to turn down that high-paying position with the psychiatric clinic and to accept another offer to teach full-time at Dallas Theological Seminary at a much lower salary. I heard clearly in my mind the words of Jesus in Matthew 6:33: 'But seek first the kingdom of God and His righteousness, and all these things shall be added to you.'"

It was hard for Dr. Meier to let go of the financial security represented by the clinic offer, but he knew what God wanted him to do. His only question was what his wife would think. But when she heard his decision, she responded, "I'm so glad! That's exactly the decision I was hoping you would make!"

Dr. Meier went to Dallas Seminary, where he worked with Dr. Frank Minirth to structure some new counseling courses. Later, Dr. Minirth and Dr. Meier founded the Minirth-Meier Clinic (now called the Minirth Meier New Life Clinic), which has since become the largest Christian psychiatric clinic in the world and has branch offices in 50 cities across the United States. "I came to the Dallas area," Dr. Meier reflects, "expecting to pursue my ministry as a modestly paid seminary professor—but God opened up opportunities I never dreamed of, and which I would probably have never had if I had pursued the higher-paying position. I have learned that God really knows what He is doing in our lives, and I have learned the importance of contentment."

HOW TO BE ABASED, HOW TO ABOUND

What is the secret to great riches? According to the apostle Paul, the secret is contentment. "Now godliness with contentment is great gain," he wrote in 1 Timothy 6:6. In our practice at the Minirth Meier New Life Clinics, we have seen this principle in action over and over.

Many rich, powerful, notable people have come to our clinics for help with deep emotional and relationship problems. Not only did their money and possessions not help them to feel satisfied, but their pursuit of material success was actually at the root of many of their problems. In fact, we find that almost three-fourths of the marital conflicts we deal with at the clinic are focused on money (usually involving a power struggle over how it should be spent). At the same time, some of the happiest and most well-adjusted people you will ever meet are people of very modest means.

Does that mean it is wrong to have money and material possessions? No. As we examine the Scriptures, we see that some of the godliest men in the Bible were also some of the richest: Abraham, Isaac, Jacob, Joseph, David, Solomon, Job, and Joseph of Arimathea, who gave his own tomb for the burial of Jesus. We also see that those who have the ability to make money and the generosity to give it away have a spiritual gift—the gift of giving (see Rom. 12:8). Barnabas, the missionary companion of Paul, was evidently such a man, because at the end of Acts 4 he is shown selling a piece of land and contributing the proceeds to the church.

But the Scriptures also teach us that we are not to place our hope for security in money, nor to set our ambitions on acquiring possessions. The apostle Paul told the Philippians that it is possible to experience contentment regardless of our material circumstances. "I have learned in whatever state I am, to be content," he said. "I know how to be abased, and I know how to abound. Everywhere and in all things I have learned both to be full and to be hungry, both to abound and to suffer need. I can do all things through Christ who strengthens me" (Phil. 4:11–13).

THE SOURCE OF DISCONTENT

Contentment is a rare commodity today, even amid the vast abundance of our society. The average middle-class family enjoys a level of luxury, comfort, diverse entertainment, and an array of foods that the kings and nobles of past ages never even dreamed of—yet few people of any economic class are content. Why are so many of us discontented, even with all that we enjoy today?

For many people, that discontent and dissatisfaction is rooted in a hunger for individual meaning and significance. In Ecclesiastes 4:4, Solomon describes the empty quest that so many people today continue to pursue: "Again, I saw that for all toil and every skillful work a man is envied by his neighbor. This also is vanity and grasping for the wind." Today, men and women compete for that top job in that fast-track career. They want the status of having a Lincoln Town Car and a Mercedes in the driveway of a custom-designed home right on the lake. They want to be envied by their neighbors, and they toil away, clawing and scratching for meaning and significance—and in the end they find they are grasping at the wind.

The pursuit of material things can choke out our faith. Intent on grabbing our share of "the American dream," we place ourselves in bondage to MasterCard and Visa, we bring home truckloads of clothes and electronic gadgets and furniture—and then we worry ourselves into an early grave trying to figure out how to pay for it all. This pursuit of material things chokes our joy, our emotional health, and even our faith. As Jesus said, "Now the [seeds] that fell among thorns are those who, when they have heard [the Gospel], go out and are choked with cares, riches, and pleasures of life, and bring no fruit to maturity" (Luke 8:14). The pursuit of the "almighty dollar" tends to tighten the noose of worry around our necks. We choke the contentment and joy right out of our lives by making money our motivation for living.

> ### Keeping Up with the Joneses
>
> In our research and counseling experience at the Minirth Meier New Life Clinics, we have found that the frantic quest for status and significance is generally rooted in a struggle with feelings of inferiority. We compete with the Joneses in a desperate struggle to prove our significance against a background of feeling insignificant and without value. God never intended us to seek our significance and our contentment in things. He designed us to seek our contentment in *Him,* and we will never be happy until we abandon our mad pursuit of things and find our rest and our significance in His love and affirmation of us.

167

ABUNDANT LIFE

How, then, can we find true contentment?

First, trust Jesus Christ as your Savior. Tell Him that you are trusting by faith in His death on the cross and His resurrection to give you significance and to pay the penalty for your sins.

Second, commit yourself to making Jesus Christ the Lord of your life. Make a decision to let go of your effort to make your own significance out of status, possessions, and success, which are nothing more than grasping at the wind. Commit yourself to seeking first the spiritual kingdom of God and His righteousness—godly behavior and a godly attitude of contentment.

Money plays a part in life. It pays for necessities and luxuries. But money is not what life is truly about. No matter how much money we amass, no matter how much prestige and status we gather to ourselves, we will still feel insignificant and dissatisfied at a deep level of our being if we don't find our rest in the true Source of all contentment.

Third, recognize that your true significance comes not from things but from your position as a child and heir of Christ and from your lifestyle of service to Him. God has pronounced us to be significant—so significant that He sent His Son Jesus to die in our place. This amazing truth is the true source of our significance and contentment, not a shiny car or a corner office or a Rolex watch.

Fourth, whenever you are tempted to compare your situation with someone else's, to grumble or feel resentful and discontented, or to blame God for the fact that things aren't going your way in life, consider "counting your blessings." It may sound trite, but it can be very helpful to take a piece of paper and write down the blessings of God that you have taken for granted heretofore: your relationship with God, your health, your job, your friends, your family, your home, your freedom, and your possessions.

Fifth, develop a balanced, biblical perspective on earning, spending, saving, and giving. Read the article on FINANCES. Enjoy the material and spiritual blessings God has showered on your life. Remember the words of Jesus in John 10:10: "I have come that they may have life, and that they may have it more abundantly." And focus on making Paul's attitude your attitude: "For we brought nothing into this world, and it is certain we can carry nothing out. And having food and clothing, with these we shall be content" (1 Tim. 6:7–8).

Control Addiction

Richard came to the clinic for help because his world was spinning out of control. He was a real estate developer and was considered to be one of the most successful people in his community. But in the past few years, his life had started to come unglued. "I've sunk a lot of money into this big commercial development," he said, "and frankly, it's not going well. We started this project before the economy started to sour on us, and now there's a chance the whole thing could go south on us—millions of dollars. At the same time, my children are teenagers, and you know what that means. The hair, the clothes, the rebellion—I mean, my son wears an earring, for crying out loud! And then there's my wife, who feels she needs a career outside the home, all of a sudden. I mean, what does she want?"

Looking back into Richard's past, the therapist found a man who had been fairly happy most of his life—academically successful in college, captain of the football team, an engineering degree from one of the top schools in the country, the owner of his own commercial construction business before he was thirty. "Back then," he reflected, "I was really in control of my life. But now?" He sighed heavily. "Things are sure getting out of hand."

Richard had been happy most of his life, while he was in control. Only when he started to lose control did the pain of his emotional addiction to control become apparent. What Richard's counselor helped him to understand was that he was a person who felt a compulsive need to be right, to be in control of people and events. And he needed to understand that his need for control was disrupting his most important relationships in life.

He had always been a controlling father, but lately his kids had begun to realize that they could rebel against his control—and they could win. His controlling tendencies had created a great deal of marital conflict over the years, but finally his wife had had enough. She was tired of Richard and his controlling behavior—so she was spending more and more time away from home, working at an outside job to escape his control.

■

As you look over the list of blessings God has given you, your heart's attitude will probably change from one of resentment to one of praise and gratitude.

■

PEOPLE WHO MUST CONTROL

Most of us, to some degree or another, like to be in control. For some of us, the ability to take command, to organize, and to exercise leadership is a positive strength in many arenas. But that strength can quickly turn into a disastrous weakness when it disrupts our most important relationships—family relationships, friendships, business relationships, church relationships. At the point where our urge to control becomes compulsive, unrestrainable, and destructive to our relationships, we call it a control addiction.

THE CHARACTERISTICS OF CONTROL ADDICTION

Control-addicted people are often unaware that they have a problem—or that they create problems for other people. They tend to be so convinced of the correctness of their opinion, their methods, and their priorities that they can scarcely tolerate anyone or anything that would contradict them. They tend to feel driven by a sense of duty or "oughtness"—"I must do this; I ought to do that." They generally act superior on the outside while feeling inferior on the inside.

169

Do I Have a Control Addiction?

You may be wondering if you have a control addiction. If so, take the following quiz, which is adapted from the Minirth Meier New Life Clinics' book *Imperative People: Those Who Must Be in Control* by Dr. Les Carter (Thomas Nelson, 1991). Check the statements below that apply to you.

____ I hate to admit my weaknesses, even if they seem obvious to others.

____ I get irritated when other people make mistakes.

____ I tend to use words like *should, ought, must, can't* when I'm talking to other people.

____ I tend to do an important job myself because someone else might not do it right.

____ I'm uncomfortable with ideas that are different.

____ I am annoyed and upset more often than I'd like to be.

____ Once I have formulated an opinion, I don't tend to change it.

____ I stay away from people whose opinions are different from mine.

____ When I'm working on a project, I often become so focused that I get irritated when people interrupt me and I tend to snap at them.

____ I get impatient when other people can't understand what needs to be done.

____ I would rather let people have a false favorable impression of me than be open and vulnerable.

____ When someone tells me about a personal problem, I feel I have to provide a solution.

____ I use silence to punish those who disappoint or disagree with me.

____ Before starting a project, I dwell on it constantly to be sure I'll do it just right.

____ When someone else is in a foul mood, it puts me in a foul mood too.

____ Critical thoughts come to my mind more often than I would like.

____ When someone confronts me about my opinions or beliefs, I immediately begin to formulate a rebuttal.

____ I have a mental list of standards people should meet before I accept them.

____ I sometimes resent having to do so much for my family.

____ I am uncomfortable when others share very personal emotions with me.

The average person will check at least a few of these statements. If you checked fewer than five, you are very serene and composed—or else you need to see yourself more positively. If you checked five to eight statements, you are probably fairly normal. If you checked nine or more statements, you are a likely candidate for unnecessary emotional stress and tension—and you exhibit signs of a strong need to control. Your controlling tendencies are going to create problems for you and the people around you. They will continually interfere with your relationships, and with your happiness and self-esteem.

A control addiction is treatable and curable. Control-addicted people can free themselves from the need always to be right; they can give themselves and others the freedom to be human and to make mistakes. The key to recovery lies in (1) understanding the addiction and (2) yielding that addiction to God for healing.

SEVEN CONTROL-ADDICTED THOUGHTS

In *Imperative People* (Thomas Nelson, 1991), Dr. Carter lists seven thoughts that are typical of most control-addicted people.

1. "I emphasize performance over relationships." This attitude drives the behavior of many corporate managers and executives. This is bottom-line, net-net thinking. People and their feelings are unimportant. The product—delivered on time and under budget—is the only consideration for the control-addicted person. Tragically, many people carry this attitude over into their families as well, demanding a just-so performance from both children and spouse, creating pain and destroying relationships in the process.

2. "I'm uncomfortable with ideas that are different from mine." Any relationship will function more smoothly if the two people in the relationship have compatible ideas, goals, and values. But compatibility doesn't mean sameness. Many control-addicted people demand sameness from family members and friends and may even become irate when talking to a stranger about some point of disagreement on, say, religion or politics. They feel that accepting a person whose ideas are "wrong" amounts to condoning the person's "wrong" ideas—so the person and his ideas must be rejected as a package. Control addicts have to be right.

3. "I try to control as much of my life as possible." Many compulsive controllers try to tell themselves, "I don't try to control people, I exercise leadership." The fact is, leaders lead by inspiring and motivating others to follow. Controllers demand conformity and obedience and often use bossiness, shouting, manipulation, advice-giving, or butting in and taking over to achieve their control. They don't trust followers to follow willingly; they make sure the followers conform.

4. "I often feel driven to do something because it's my duty." Control addicts aren't merely committed; they are completely obligated. They feel they do not have the option of saying no to a "duty." This sense of obligation is rooted in a need for such a structured, orderly life that there is no allowance made for choice. Life is either black or white. There is nothing in between.

5. "It is difficult for me to admit my weaknesses." Control addicts don't just gloss over their weaknesses and mistakes; they present themselves to the world as having no flaws at all. They gladly point out the shortcomings of others, but there is no willingness to examine or admit their own. To admit their own shortcomings is to become vulnerable, to be removed from the driver's seat—and that is intolerable to a control-addicted person.

6. "I don't like my emotions—or other people's emotions—to get out of control." Emotions are illogical and subjective—and that means they are not subject to control. When exposed to another person's emotions, a control addict will fidget uncomfortably, and then say, "Can we just get to the point?"

7. "I get irritated when other people make mistakes." Control addicts have high, idealistic expectations of themselves and others. Flaws, even in the minor details, are unacceptable. This trait leads to impatience with others and criticism and faultfinding of their performance. Control addicts often seem to display an air of superiority, impatience, and condemnation over others.

THE CHRISTIAN CONTROL ADDICT

One of the most common problems we encounter in counseling control addicts is that the Christian claim to truth and absolute values often dovetails in a very unhealthy way with the compulsive controller's need always to be right, always to be in control. Christian control addicts have a pronounced tendency to lord their beliefs over others, to behave in superior ways, to be rigid and dogmatic in their beliefs, and to be abrasive in their attempts to evangelize.

To many Christian control addicts, there is no such thing as a "peripheral issue" in matters of faith and doctrine. People who do not believe as they do are heretics or worse. Somehow, these Christians fail to grasp the central importance of humility in the Christian faith. To be truly humble is to recognize that only God has the corner on all truth. Even possessing the Bible as we do, we Christians have to acknowledge that our understanding of the Bible is limited and our interpretation of the Bible may well be flawed in some respect.

The Bible presents the Christian faith as a relationship between a loving Heavenly Father and His children. But to many Christian control addicts, Christianity is a system of rules and regulations. True Christianity is a life of freedom and joy; but the religion of the Christian control addict is often a life of legalism and fear.

It is understandable that many of us would want life reduced to a set of definite rules and easy-to-grasp handles. We don't want to have to deal with gray areas and abstractions and uncertainties. Among the gray areas and uncertainties we must face is the fact that Christians have problems, they get anxious, they get depressed, they experience burnout. Compulsive controllers recoil from such thoughts: "Not me! I don't have emotional problems! That's for the backslidden! That's for people who don't have enough faith!" In a world full of ambiguities and uncertainties, they clutch their brittle, breakable certitudes to themselves, denying the possibility of any human weakness—and shutting off the possibility of healing. James 5:16 says, "Confess your trespasses"—in other words, your sins, your faults, your weaknesses—"to one another, and pray for one another, that you may be healed."

It is so tragic that compulsive controllers tend to miss the healing power of being transparent and vulnerable with fellow Christians. Christian control addicts do not give themselves permission to be human. They cannot experience true Christian fellowship, where everyone in the group of believers discloses his or her inner reality and confesses his or her sins and weaknesses. They are trapped in a mad scramble to appear perfect. But God wants to free compulsive controllers from that trap.

Freedom is His gift, and our inheritance.

YIELDING THE ADDICTION

How can this addiction be cured? It must be yielded, moment by moment. If you are a control addict, you must learn to make deliberate choices:

"I choose to let others be themselves." That means allowing your children to make their own mistakes, to fail, to be human. That means letting your spouse's imperfections slide past without comment, without resentment. That means giving more slack to

your friends, your employees, your fellow Christians. You may have to bite your tongue to keep a word of criticism from passing your lips, while you repeat to yourself, "He's only human. She's only human." In time, it will become easier.

This also means you stop taking over and doing things for other people in the belief that they won't do it right. It means you stop giving advice. It means you stop pushing others to get their work done, to get to an appointment on time, to do their work better. Instead, you positively, affirmingly encourage others to be responsible for their own actions—and you step back and let them make their own mistakes.

"I choose to let me be me." The same grace you are now attempting to give to others you must also give to yourself. When you feel tempted to judge yourself for a mistake, stop. Say to yourself, *I'm only human.* Give yourself the right to make mistakes—even an occasional mistake of briefly relapsing into your old controlling pattern. Pick yourself up and try again. Give yourself the right to make human mistakes.

"I choose to live humbly." No more acting superior while feeling inferior. From now on you don't have to be perfect, you don't have to be the best, you don't have to be right, you don't have to hide your weaknesses, you don't have to maintain an image. When other people express ideas that differ from yours, tell yourself, "I don't have all the truth." Try to see every irritation, every setback, every disappointment in life as a chance to learn more about humility, and in time you will see a pattern of Christlike humility seeping into your life and taking it over.

"I choose to be firm without being controlling." No one is suggesting you should go from being a controller to being a pushover. You can still be firm in your convictions while being open-minded and a good listener. You can be a leader without being a controller. You can be organized without being a fussy hyperperfectionist. So practice being assertively firm without resorting to sarcasm, manipulation, accusations, the silent treatment, or a coercive tone of voice. Read the article on ASSERTIVENESS and practice the principles.

As you seek to turn your control addiction over to God, discuss your issues with a support group or counselor. Ask to be held accountable on a weekly basis for your progress. Pray and meditate on the Bible, and ask God to show you His humility, His grace, and His freedom for your life. Ask God to change your character and reshape you into a person who no longer seeks control but who is controlled by the Holy Spirit. Prepare for a new adventure of change and growth.

And enjoy your newfound freedom.

Dating and Courtship

Rachael was a "good girl," an attractive sixteen-year-old high school junior. Though shy and quiet, Rachael was known for her Christian testimony. She was moderately popular—on speaking terms with (but not socially comfortable with or truly accepted by) the "inner circle," the select group of kids who looked like they just stepped off the set of *Beverly Hills 90210*. Deep down, part of Rachael envied those kids and wanted to be accepted by them, even though she knew that their values were not her own.

Rachael's father—a stern and emotionally distant man who was also a church elder—had warned her about the evil intentions of boys and the perils of dating and the horrible consequences of premarital sex. Rachael had promised Daddy and herself that she would never engage in sex until she was married. Though she had hardly ever dated and had never given her father reason to doubt her moral purity, she felt condemned by her overly suspicious father—and she resented his attempts to control her behavior.

One of the reasons Rachael rarely dated was that her father disapproved of most boys and of dating in general. But when Brent, a young man from the high school group at church, called and asked her for a date on Friday night, she agreed. Daddy knew the boy's family from church, and he readily gave his permission. The evening was to include dinner and a movie, followed by Cokes at the drive-in, then back home before midnight—an ordinary high school date. But Brent didn't take Rachael to a restaurant. Instead, he pulled the car up in front of a big two-story house in an exclusive section of town. There were a lot of other cars parked in front of the house.

"Why are we stopping here?" asked Rachael apprehensively. "I thought we were going to the restaurant."

"Just a little change of plans," Brent replied smoothly. "Nicole's having a party tonight. I thought we could just stop in for a little while. We can get something to eat here and we'll still have time to make it to the movie."

There were no adults at the party—just a lot of kids sitting around the living room, listening to loud music, and drinking vodka out of paper cups. Rachael recognized these kids. They were all from the "inner circle," all the *90210*-type kids. Occasionally, a boy and girl would get up, leave the living room, and head down the hall toward the bedrooms, hand in hand. Rachael was sure she knew what was going on in those bedrooms—and it made her very uncomfortable.

When Brent handed her a paper cup filled with vodka, she at first refused it. She was surprised that Brent, a boy from church, was actually giving her a shot of booze. "It's okay," he said reassuringly. "A little bit won't hurt you." Rachael looked around the room. Everyone was looking at her curiously, as if to see what she would do. Rachael herself could hardly believe what she did next. It was as if a part of her was standing outside her body, watching in amazement as her hands took the paper cup of vodka, lifted it to her lips, and drank. It burned going down, it made her cough, it made her eyes water, but she finished it. Now she *really* felt detached from her body. But she also felt something else. She felt accepted by the other kids in the group. She was a part of them. She was one of the *90210* kids now.

When Brent took her by the hand and led her down the hall toward the bedrooms, she seemed to be floating. On an empty stomach, the vodka had gone straight to her head. She was giddy, and her legs were like rubber. She had never felt this way before. Brent led her to an unoccupied bedroom and eased her down on the bed. Rachael realized what was coming next, and she protested weakly. But then Brent began doing things to her that felt good, and she decided to let him. A few minutes later, she no longer had her virginity. When it was all over, she got up from the bed and rushed into the bathroom, where she spent the next half-hour hugging the toilet bowl, throwing up and crying.

After that night, neither Brent nor any of the other *90210* kids spoke to Rachael or even looked her way again.

THE BEST PROTECTION

Dating is one of the rites of passage from childhood to adulthood. It is a courtship ritual, a process of learning to know and relate to the opposite sex, a process that leads toward romance, engagement, and marriage. Dating has its joys. It also has its pain. And it has its pitfalls, as Rachael found out.

Years later, Rachael explored the pain and guilt of this experience in counseling, and what she discovered bears out a principle that we have seen demonstrated again and again in our clinical experience: The best protection young people can carry with them into the dating experience is not a lot of rules, a lot of warnings, a lot of do's and don'ts. *The best protection is a healthy sense of self-esteem.*

With a strong sense of self-worth, young people can stand up to the common temptations of peer-pressure: drugs, alcohol, and sex. With a strong sense of self-worth, they don't feel they have to compromise or give in just to be accepted. In our experience, it would be safe to say that we never see a young person with healthy self-esteem come in for counseling with a drug problem or guilt over sexual issues. Teenage young people are at extreme risk for many forms of victimization, and they are seldom more vulnerable than while dating. A strong self-esteem is a young person's strongest defense against those risks.

Parents also have a hidden but important role to play in the dating life of their teenage children. Though Rachael herself was responsible for her own moral choices, her father must bear some responsibility for clouding the emotional issue for her in several ways. By being emotionally distant from her, he created within Rachael a "love hunger," a craving for affection that made it that much easier for someone like Brent to take advantage of her by giving her a sexual substitute for affection. And by being stern and controlling, Rachael's father created an unconscious desire for independence within Rachael. When she took her first drink and when she submitted to Brent's sexual advances, Rachael was engaging in an unconscious act of rebellion against her father's control.

Parents must strike a careful balance in relating to their teenage children. Some parents, like Rachael's father, are afraid to let go of their children, and they become overcontrolling. Often, this is an overreaction to guilt the parents themselves feel for having "gone too far" sexually in their own dating experience. Other parents create just as much trouble for their children by being overly permissive. These permissive parents usually have a fear of losing their kids—a fear rooted in their own low self-esteem—so they respond by trying to be "buddies" to their kids instead of parents. They fail to set limits or talk to their kids about the risks of peer pressure, drugs, alcohol, and sex.

(For a more complete discussion of the parental role and ways to build a healthy sense of self-esteem into your children, see PARENTING and SELF-ESTEEM.)

■

When young people begin dating, parents need to strike that delicate balance: setting boundaries without imposing control, building trust without compromising parental authority, giving them a gradually increasing measure of freedom without becoming permissive.

■

A BIBLICAL APPROACH TO DATING

Christian young people should know that the Bible offers guidelines that can be helpful in the experience of dating and courtship. In the Scriptures, we find clear advice as to the kind of people we should date and marry, and the kind of behavior that God expects—behavior that is both moral and healthy. Here are some passages for study, along with the principles we find in those passages:

Genesis 1:27–28 and 2:18–25. In this passage, we see that God created the sexes, and that each sex is (in some sense) incomplete without the other. Each sex helps to meet the other's needs, and both sexes are designed by God to join their lives and their bodies together within the boundaries of a committed marriage relationship. Sex is good and pure within that relationship, and this sexual union was designed and commanded by God even before the entrance of sin into the world. Those who think of sex as somehow intrinsically "unclean" or "sinful" do not understand the biblical view of sex.

Proverbs 5. Young people should listen to the counsel of their parents and should avoid sexual and sensuous temptations. Though a sexual relationship is beautiful in its rightful place in marriage, outside of marriage it is sin, and sexual sins have consequences for the spirit, mind, and body.

Proverbs 31:10–31. This passage lists the desirable qualities of a marriage partner (specifically, in this case, a wife, though these are also good qualities to look for in a husband). Since dating is a ritual of courtship, helping to prepare young people for romance and marriage, it is important that young people begin looking for these same qualities in the people they date. The qualities found in this passage include:

- noble character
- trustworthiness
- helpfulness
- humility
- a servant's heart
- frugality—a wise attitude toward spending and saving money
- an industrious, hard-working spirit
- an ability to plan ahead for possible problems
- generosity toward the needy; lack of self-centeredness and materialism
- building others up rather than tearing them down
- a happy, fun-loving, well-adjusted personality
- devotion to God
- character that is praised and respected by family and others

Many young people, in the process of dating and courtship, have spared themselves a lifetime of struggle by applying this biblical "checklist" to the people they date (as well as applying it to themselves and seeking to become the kind of people described in this passage).

For example, a young man named Jonathan had been dating a young woman named Candi for over a year. He asked her to marry him, and she happily agreed. After their engagement, Jonathan studied this passage in Proverbs and became troubled by some of the disparities he detected between this passage and what he knew of the young woman he intended to marry. So he decided to test a suspicion that this passage had raised in his mind. Jonathan took Candi on a "shopping date," and he invited her to spend as much as she wanted—it was all on him. The resulting shopping spree cost Jonathan over five thousand dollars. "It was money well-spent," he later recalled. "Proverbs 31 describes a woman who is hard-working, thrifty, selfless, and generous to others. I realized that though Candi could be sweet and charming, she was really very grasping, self-centered, and materialistic. I called off the engagement to Candi and later became engaged to a woman who has consciously patterned her life and her character after Proverbs 31. Jill and I have been married for five years now, and we couldn't be happier."

Advice for Daters

Much dating and courtship advice emerges from an understanding of Scripture.

Seek out people who treat others with respect. Does your prospective date or marriage partner respect parents? Friends? His or her own sex, or the opposite sex? Authority figures? The church? God? If not, then don't expect this person to treat you with respect either. Look for signs of dissonance and inconsistency between this person's charming, romancing behavior toward you and the comments and attitudes this person displays toward others. Expect the charm and romance to fade after marriage—and expect to be treated by this person just as he or she treats everyone else.

Avoid people who are overly critical. Matthew 7:3–5 warns against being critical of others. Critical people tend to be *hypocritical* people, and yoking yourself with this kind of person, even for a single date, can be an unpleasant and unproductive experience.

Seek out people who have learned to control selfish, sensual, and materialistic impulses. Passages such as 1 Peter 2:11 and Matthew 6:24 warn against having lust and materialism as our central focus. It is unwise to continue dating a person who is lustful and seductive and who continually makes sexual advances, since the Bible teaches that lust wars against the mind, emotions, and will, making people weak and unstable. It is also unwise to date people who are focused on status, money, materialism, and image, since these values are superficial and unsatisfying and represent a sort of prideful, materialistic lust. Our focus should be on Christ, and in our dating life and courtship, we should seek out people who share that focus.

Seek out people who agree with your values and your perspective on biblical husband/wife roles within marriage. The biblical view of marriage is found in concise form in Ephesians 5:22–33. Because of the last few decades of change in societal attitudes toward gender issues and roles, many people today—including many in the church—do not affirm the roles that are described in this passage. So it is important that these issues be talked about and explored somewhere in the dating and courtship process, before the emotions of romantic attraction make it difficult for both people to be objective about these issues.

1 Corinthians 6:9–20. Our bodies are to be devoted to God, not to pleasing the senses through sexual sin. The key to dealing with temptation is not to fight it, but to flee it (this is crucial, since those who try to fight temptation usually lose the battle). God owns us, Jesus purchased us by His own death, and we should honor Him with our bodies. Sexual sin brings harm and dishonor to our bodies, and to God.

2 Corinthians 6:14. Christians should marry Christians—and thus, Christians should only date Christians. This passage warns against being "yoked together" with unbelievers. This is an area that requires great discernment, as Rachael discovered.

Looking back at her disastrous date with Brent, she realizes that she rationalized that going out with him was okay because he was a boy from her church. She knew her father would approve of Brent for that reason alone, but she also knew things about Brent that her father didn't know—his brash and cocky attitude, his reputation as part of the "fast-lane," *90210* crowd at school, his critical and openly rebellious attitude toward his parents, and the fact that he only attended church to maintain an uneasy truce with his parents and to maintain certain privileges they provided for him (including a car of his own and a lot of spending money). Rachael had known all along that Brent was spoiled, immature, and self-centered—but he was also popular and good-looking. So, to gain his approval, she was willing to go out with him—and give in to him. Today, Rachael realizes that she had rationalized going out with Brent, even though she knew all along that by doing so, she would be "yoked together" (if only for one evening) with a boy who was a churchgoing unbeliever.

1 Thessalonians 4:1–8. God desires that we learn to control our bodies and avoid sexual immorality. Gratifying our sexual desires outside of marriage is an offense against ourselves, against the other person, and against God. These are God's standards, not human standards, and to reject them is to reject God's authority over our lives.

WHAT TO DO ABOUT SEXUAL TEMPTATION

"The Bible is not a book of instruction about sex," says Stephen Arterburn, "but it is very clear on certain sexual matters. As we study what it says to us, we can see that God designed sex and wants us to enjoy sex in a healthy way. He did not include guidelines about sex in the Bible in order to keep us from having fun but to help us to enjoy the gift of sex as it was meant to be enjoyed. Sexual boundaries have a positive purpose in our lives. There is a good reason for two people to come together in marriage, giving each other the gift of their virginity. Sexual sin can be forgiven, but the emotional and spiritual and even physical consequences of that sin often take years to heal. In my counseling practice, I often talk to unmarried young people who are already engaging in a sexual relationship, or who are close to compromising their virginity. There are twelve questions I always ask these people to consider."

The questions Stephen Arterburn confronts unmarried couples with (and he includes both individuals equally in this process) are:

1. Do you think premarital sex will heighten or lessen the meaning of sex in marriage for you and your partner?
2. Do you feel uneasy or guilty during or after sexual intercourse? Could this be the Holy Spirit convicting you?
3. Do you ever rationalize sexual behavior? Do you ever minimize behavior or lie to yourself about the real emotional consequences of your sexual behavior? For example, do you tell yourself it's not really sex and you aren't really losing your virginity if you "only" engage in oral sex or mutual masturbation?
4. Have you examined what the Bible has to say about premarital sex? (See Acts 15:20; Ephesians 5:3; 1 Corinthians 6:13, 18–20; 1 Thessalonians 4:1–8; and 1 Peter 2:11.)
5. Will having sex before marriage enhance or hinder your relationship with God? Your usefulness to God?
6. Are you sure you are both equally committed to each other?
7. Are you completely convinced that this person is the one and only person for you, forever and ever?
8. Will having sex before marriage enhance or hinder your relationship with each other?
9. Could premarital sex damage your communication with each other?
10. Will it enhance or hinder your respect for, and trust in, each other?
11. Have you considered the possibility of pregnancy resulting from a sexual relationship? What would you do in the event of a pregnancy?
12. What are your motives for having premarital sex? Are they pure?

It's hard to maintain sexual purity before marriage today—especially given the powerful cultural and media pressures of our times. But even though social standards change, God's standards do not, and His standards are based on what is in our own emotional, spiritual, and physical best interests. Couples who maintain sexual purity before marriage tend to be the couples who experience the greatest sexual satisfaction, emotional intimacy, and spiritual wholeness during marriage.

THE IMPORTANCE OF PREMARITAL COUNSELING

One of the most important and frequently overlooked aspects of Christian courtship is the role of Christian premarital counseling. Though it is true that it's hard for starry-eyed, love-struck couples to look objectively at their relationship, premarital counseling by a pastor or a Christian psychologist can often be helpful in enabling couples to see each other objectively—or at least, as objectively as possible under the circumstances! Through personality inventories and counseling, problems can often be identified to prevent couples from making major mistakes before it is too late. In premarital counseling, couples can be assessed in terms of:

God's moral rules are never capricious or arbitrary. They are intended for our good, and we violate those rules at our own peril—and the peril of the ones we claim to love.

- their degree of commitment to God and to each other;
- whether their decisions are being made on the basis of objective consideration and commitment or on the basis of emotions;
- their willingness to love and accept each other, recognizing that no one is perfect;
- the true character of their love, whether it is essentially physical (eros), emotional (phileo), or Christlike and spiritiual in nature (agape); and
- their ability to view each other clearly and without illusions.

A counselor can also help the couple to learn and practice good techniques for communication, both sharing and listening; good techniques for managing conflicts; and a good, healthy, biblical basis for a satisfying sexual relationship. A counselor can point the couple to quality Christian resources on marriage-related subjects, and can make sure the couple has adequate information on sexual anatomy, birth control methods, and good lovemaking techniques—including the relational and emotional preparation for a satisfying sex life that takes place not only in foreplay but throughout the day. Common sexual problems in marriage, such as premature ejaculation or low sex drive, may also be covered in counseling.

"Couples who are considering marriage need to understand not only the joys of marriage, but the demands of marriage," says Dr. Paul Meier. "Each partner needs a way to assess his or her own personality and maturity level, as well as that of the prospective mate. Many couples enter marriage without any objective understanding of each other. 'We love each other!' they say. 'Isn't that enough?' No. Starry-eyed attraction is not enough, as half of all marriages attest when they end in divorce.

"In counseling, we use the Bible as our basis for assessing such factors as spiritual maturity, commitment, and Christlike unconditional love. And we use personality inventories that enable couples to discover their personality type and that of their partner, so that they can see how these two personalities fit together and how they conflict. The point is not to scare two people off from each other, but to help them objectively identify potential problems and make healthy adjustments before and during marriage."

Some of the results counselors look for in personality assessments are areas where two people seem to clash, as well as areas where two people fit together too well. Extreme differences in personality suggest potential areas of conflict that are likely to arise again and again. Extreme complementary fits between two partners—for example, if one person has a consistently low self-evaluation and the other a consistently high self-evaluation—suggest that these two people are in an unhealthy, codependent state, where each feeds off of the personality weaknesses of the other. These results will be shown to the couple and discussed, with an emphasis on how these issues may affect the marriage over the years.

Dating and courtship should be fun and pleasurable experiences, filled with the excitement of exploring new territory in relationships. These experiences entail some risks, but if young people are made aware of biblical and psychological guidelines, and if they are protected by a strong sense of spiritual empowerment (through prayer and an understanding of Scripture) coupled with a strong sense of healthy self-esteem, they stand an excellent chance of safely navigating the perils of dating and courtship, and arriving safely in the harbor of a satisfying Christian marriage.

See also MARRIAGE; SELF-ESTEEM; SEX AND SEXUALITY; and SEX EDUCATION

Day Care

As Christian parents, we have been entrusted by God with an awesome responsibility. Psychological researchers estimate that approximately 85 percent of the adult personality is formed by the time a person is six years old. Clearly, those first six years of life are crucial. The way in which we, as parents, train our children during those crucial years, together with the influences we expose them to and the environment we place them in, will have a tremendous impact on their character, emotional development, and mental health.

We live in an era in which parental choices are becoming increasingly difficult. Many families are finding that being a two-income family is not just an option in today's economic climate, it is a virtual necessity. Reluctantly, many parents are leaving their children in the custody of day-care centers during these first six crucial years. Are these parents harming their children by placing them in day-care facilities? Certain self-proclaimed "experts," making the rounds of the daytime TV talk shows, have claimed that children actually benefit from the day-care experience because they are provided with learning experiences they would never get at home. But is this true?

Certainly there are some day-care centers that are adequately staffed with qualified, caring people. But these well-run, well-programmed centers tend to be so expensive that it hardly pays for the mother to work. One of the qualities a child most needs to experience during those early formative years is attention, and for a child to receive adequate attention in a day-care environment there should be at least one personable, caring, involved staff member for every three or four toddlers. Day-care centers that maintain such a high staff-to-child ratio are rare indeed!

"I have read many studies that detail the emotional damage that children often experience in day-care facilities," says Dr. Paul Meier of the Minirth Meier New Life Clinics. "But studies and statistical surveys are one thing. Personal experience is quite another. And the personal experience my wife and I had with a day-care facility some years ago tells me all I need to know about the day-care issue.

"My wife and I had about four hours' worth of shopping to do, and we couldn't get our regular baby-sitter. So—as a last resort—we took our two-year-old son to a neighborhood day-care center. This facility had a very good reputation and came highly recommended. We signed our son in, gave him a big hug, and left him in the hands of a very gracious and friendly woman who took him by the hand and led him out of the waiting room. We waved goodbye and left.

"Hours later, when we returned and called for our son, the staff couldn't locate him. They said, 'Why don't you just go back into the children's area and see if you can recognize him?' So we did—and we were shocked by what we saw. The children's room was neat, brightly painted, and scattered with the usual assortment of nursery-

181

room toys. Around the room were a number of recesses holding small bunks. A few children were in the middle of the room, playing with toys, but most were in these recesses, sitting on their bunks, staring at my wife and me just like prisoners staring out of their cells or animals staring out of their cages. They all looked so sad and alone. It was plain to see that many of them were daily 'inmates' of this facility: they were dropped off, and they reported to their 'cells' where they waited until they were picked up again.

"The most urgent and immediate problem, however, was that our son was not in the room. Frantic to find him, we went outside and searched the grounds, calling his name, and suddenly we saw him. Our defenseless little two-year-old was playing in a nearby parking lot while cars drove back and forth within a few feet of him. We snatched him up, just thankful he was still alive. Apparently, he had simply wandered out of the day-care facility without anyone noticing. I still shudder to think what might have happened—and this was one of the better day-care facilities, with a comparatively competent and caring staff!

"I'm not saying our day-care experience is typical," Dr. Meier concludes. "I'm not saying day-care facilities are bad or that the people who run them are bad people. But day-care workers, however well-trained and well-intentioned, cannot replace the home in terms of love, care, supervision, and individualized attention. In an imperfect world, we are sometimes presented with a poor range of options to choose from, but I am convinced that day-care is the least attractive option for raising toddler-age children."

DAY CARE: WHAT HARM CAN IT DO?

Most day-care centers pay workers little more than minimum wage, which means it is hard for these facilities to attract and keep a well-trained, highly motivated staff. The majority of staff people in day-care environments have little background in child development or childhood education. Most facilities have a very poor adult-to-child ratio, which means few children receive any individualized attention.

Studies indicate that children who experience mother-child separation and many caregivers early in life are more likely to develop an "affectionless character," an inability to experience deep, lasting relationships and an inability to empathize with the feelings of others. This syndrome is often damaging to many adult relationships, including emotional intimacy in marriage.

Children in day-care centers do not have one adult assigned to them as a teacher and caregiver. They have many caregivers, and there is often a lot of turnover within the caregiving ranks: one staff member leaves, another comes aboard. During this critical time of life, when personality and the basic ability to trust are being formed, children should have the opportunity to bond with a few continual caregivers—mother, father, grandparents, older siblings. Children are supposed to learn that they can trust these people, that these caregivers will not abandon them.

In a day-care center, however, the child sees many largely anonymous caregivers. They come, they stay a while, and they abandon the child. This engenders a distrust that interferes with the child's early development and may also hinder relationships later in life.

Does this mean a child raised in a day-care environment will automatically grow up emotionally harmed and relationally dysfunctional? No. Many children who are raised under extremely adverse circumstances grow up to be amazingly well-adjusted. And many who are raised in comparatively normal circumstances develop chronic depression, phobias, schizophrenia, and other mental or emotional problems. The human brain is an amazingly complicated instrument, and it is acted upon by a vast array of influences and factors. However, as we examine the clinical research and the individuals who come into our clinic for treatment, we can recognize definite trends. Children who are "farmed out" to day-care facilities for a large part of their early childhood tend to be likelier candidates for emotional problems in adulthood than are "homegrown" children.

ALTERNATIVES FOR MOTHERS WHO HAVE TO WORK

Some women really do need to work, and they have carefully made sure that they are working for the right reasons. They can say, firmly and convincingly, "Without my paycheck, our family is sunk for sure. This is not about buying a new boat or a big-screen TV. This is about being able to keep the lights turned on and putting a plate of beans on the table every night for my kids." Perhaps their husbands are low-paid or just laid off. Or they may be divorced, separated, or widowed. They truly have no choice.

If you are in that situation, we want you to know that we understand how hard it is for you, and we know you are doing the very best you can under difficult circumstances. Full-time mothering would be your first choice if you had a choice—but you are in a sink-or-swim situation, and your children's welfare depends on your ability to bring home a paycheck. We affirm your courage in doing a very difficult thing—going to work every day—out of your deep love for your children.

Still, there may be other alternatives for you and your children besides traditional day-care options. Some possibilities for you to consider:

Seek out a one-woman, small-scale, in-home nursery. Often called a home-based day-care facility, this option allows your child to experience a steady one-on-one relationship with another adult who will be able to respond to your child's unique personality and individual needs. It is also usually less expensive than group care. To find a home-based facility, place a notice in your church newsletter, ask friends for referrals, and contact your local social service agency to find out which home-based facilities are licensed in your area. Don't assume, however, that

---

Mother Care or Day Care?

Before going to work and placing her children in a day-care facility, a mother should consider these questions:

- Do I have to work—or am I choosing to work? Do I have any other options available to me?
- Why am I working? Economic survival? To raise our standard of living? To fulfill myself? To meet cultural role expectations? (Clearly, our culture praises working women and demeans those who choose the role of mother and homemaker.)
- Do my children need a higher standard of living right now? Or do they need a full-time mother?
- Are there any other income sources we could draw upon that would enable me to stay home with my kids—at least until they are old enough to go to school?
- After factoring in all my expenses—day care, new wardrobe, transportation, lunches, and so forth—does it really pay me to work?

---

a licensed facility is guaranteed safe or desirable for your child; only you can make that determination by careful checking and interviewing. Talk to the home facility operator, being candid about any questions or concerns you may have. Make sure the operator of the home-based facility takes in no more than three or four children. Inspect the home for safety features, such as "child-proofing" and smoke detectors.

Talk to your pastor. Ask: "Is there anyone in the church whom I could pay to care for my children while I'm at work? Is there a church-based Christian day-care facility in the area?" (This is still a compromise rather than a solution, but a Christian staff is more likely be genuinely concerned with the needs of your children than the staff of a profit-making secular facility.)

Search your motivations. If one of the reasons you want to work is that you feel you need a vacation from twenty-four-hour-a-day parenting, then you could probably benefit just as well from an occasional break. Staying home day after day, doing all the household drudge-work while taking care of several small children is a tough job, one that most people would find extremely taxing and demanding. So, instead of sending your kids to day care five days a week, make a commitment to take a break from your routine a couple days each month. Find someone qualified to take care of the children while you catch a little hard-earned R&R. The children may also benefit from the break by learning to be less dependent and by learning that they are distinct individuals, not just extensions of you.

WHAT ABOUT THE GUILT?

It is common for a woman to experience feelings of guilt when she first goes out to work full-time and leaves her children in a day-care center—and even when she just takes a little time for a "mother's day out" program. If you have honestly examined your reasons for working, and you are sure that this is something you need to do as a matter of economic survival, then you have no objective reason to feel guilty. However, it is possible you are feeling some false guilt. You may also experience feelings of frustration, anger, and resentment toward other women who seem to have it easier than you do. If you are having trouble dealing with the emotions of working and leaving your children in a day-care environment, here are some steps you can take to resolve those emotions:

1. *Confess your feelings to God and to another person or persons.* Pray and honestly admit your feelings to God. Find a support group for mothers or single parents where you can be supported and accepted as you work through your feelings.

2. *Learn to separate authentic guilt from false guilt.* Authentic guilt is an alarm, alerting you to unhealthy or sinful behavior in your life. It signals that you need to change some aspect of your life. If you have chosen to go to work and leave your children in day care so that you can find more excitement and fulfillment in life or so that you can have some extra spending money for clothes and shoes, then any pangs of guilt you feel are probably real. But if, after carefully examining your motives, you feel you have made the most realistic decision possible, then you are feeling false guilt. The source of your feelings may come from expectations derived from your own childhood, or from

unconscious comparisons you make between yourself and other mothers, or from criticism you receive from people who don't understand your situation.

Whatever the source of those feelings, it is helpful to sort through them and to understand that they are not reality-based feelings. They will still recur from time to time, but as you keep telling yourself, "I'm doing what I need to do out of love for my family," those feelings will eventually lose their power over you.

3. *Seek creative ways to spend time with your child.* Can you work staggered hours or job-share so that you can free up more time with your child? Are there special crafts projects you can do together? Minivacations you can take together? Picnics? Walks in the park or just around the neighborhood? Think of ways to intensify the connectedness between you and your child during the time you have together.

4. *Seek to make constructive changes in your life.* If you feel trapped by a low-paying, long-hours, inflexible-schedule job right now, recognize that change is possible. While keeping that job, scour the want ads and stay in a "networking" mode until you find a job that is better suited to the "child-friendly" lifestyle you want to achieve. Your community college may offer weekend adult education courses (in computers or management skills) that would enhance your skills and marketability to employers.

Day care is clearly an unhappy compromise that some mothers must reluctantly accept. But even with the constraints of your economic situation, you do have choices and options that can help to limit the negative effects of day care.

Death and Dying

"I go through my day never giving the slightest thought to death," Alan reflected. He was a robust man in his mid-forties, with just a touch of gray at the temples. "I enjoy my life, my work, my family, my recreational pursuits. I never give death a second thought—except very late at night.

"Occasionally I'll have trouble getting to sleep. You know, maybe a cup of coffee too late in the evening or maybe too much adrenaline from an exciting day, whatever. But I'll be lying in bed, awake at one, two, three in the morning. And it's funny, but what my mind always seems to settle on during those dark hours just past midnight is the thought of my own death. I'll think, Someday it's really going to happen. I'm really going to die. It may be a long, painful death or it may come suddenly. I could be just a heartbeat away from a massive coronary. When death comes, I won't have any say in the matter. My senses will shut down, my thoughts will stop, my heart will stop, it'll be all over. And while I lie there, imagining my own death, I start to shiver, and my throat constricts, and it's suddenly hard to breathe. And the only way I can deal with it is to jump out of bed, wringing with cold sweat, and go into the living room and flip on the TV. I have to get my mind off it somehow.

"I'm a Christian," Alan concludes. "I believe in heaven. I don't think death is the end, just a gateway to a better life. But I like the life I have right now, and the thought that I'm someday going to have to give up this life—even though heaven is on the other side—is something that scares me no end."

Alan's experience is not unique. He illustrates a problem and a challenge that we all face. One of the most important tasks you will ever undertake in this life is the task of coming to terms with your own death. And in order to accept your own inevitable death, you must come to a place where you have accepted your one and only God-given life.

ONLY ONE LIFE TO A CUSTOMER

In our counseling experience, we often find that people who have significant problems accepting the inevitability of their own deaths have failed to accept some aspect of their present lives or their pasts. They may be experiencing an exaggerated fear in the area of finances or a relationship; or anger and bitterness over mistreatment they suffered earlier in life; or depression and guilt over some area of perceived failure in life.

Again and again as counselors, we see people who, as the end of life approaches, have clearly been unwilling or unable to come to terms with either their life or their death. One example is the couple in their eighties who refused to make out a will or make any other preparations for a final distribution of their estate. In fact, they actually began to hoard their money as the inevitable end approached. That is why we occasionally see stories in the news of an elderly person who lives in seeming poverty, collecting aluminum cans in a shopping cart during the day and eating canned cat food for dinner—yet who is discovered to have a hundred thousand dollars hidden under the floorboards when he or she dies. The irrational thinking behind such behavior is "If I can just hoard enough money so I can feel financially secure, I won't have to face the loss of my money or my life."

Others practice a different kind of "hoarding": they try to hoard their health. They become vitamin fanatics, they read all they can find about longevity, they buy out the health-food store and try all the life-extension fad diets in the supermarket tabloids. They may even arrange to have their bodies quick-frozen in liquid nitrogen in the hopes of being revived like a frosty Lazarus after a cure is found for the illness that killed them. This kind of fanatical preoccupation with physical health and longevity is a form of denial. "If I just remain vigilant about my health," goes this irrational thinking, "I can keep my health forever. I'll never have to die." Meanwhile, the mortality rate for the human race remains 100 percent, no matter how fit and healthy we may be.

While some may cling to their money or their health, others cling to a relationship, often with a son or a daughter. The overinvolvement of an enmeshed relationship is likely to be magnified as a person approaches death. It is as if this person reasons, "If I can just cling closely enough to my son or my daughter, I will be able to draw on his or her youth to carry me through. I can't really lose everything as long as I can cling to this relationship."

Still others cling to wilted, faded dreams of a future that will never be. Such people are said to be living a contingent life—a life that is contingent upon "if and when." They are always waiting for life to start. In youth, they think, "When I graduate from high school, I can really live." In college, they think, "When I graduate from college, I can really live." After college, they think, "If I can just find the right person and get married, then my life will really begin." And on and on and on, with the final contingency being, "When I retire . . ." Finally, they reach a point where they realize that fifty, sixty, seventy years have gone by and they are still waiting for life to begin. The person who lives a contingent life never admits, "This is my life, and I will enjoy it now."

The key to serenity and emotional security as we live out our lives and approach our deaths is to recognize that there is only one life to a customer, and this is it. Life is not a dress rehearsal. Those who fail to come to grips with this fact tend to live in a world of denial and unreality. When the inevitability of death finally crashes into their lives—a serious heart attack, a diagnosis of inoperable cancer, or some other "death sentence" from nature—such people tend to get stuck in the process of grieving the loss of their own lives. They may get stuck in anger and bitterness and spend their last days raging at God and others. Or they may get stuck in bargaining, desperately pleading with God to release them from the natural fate that awaits the entire human race.

There are few greater tragedies in life than coming to the end of life and saying, "My life is ending—and I haven't even lived yet."

DEATH: THE GREAT MOTIVATOR

Before he became known as one of the greatest of all American novelists, Jack London was a vagabond. Leaving school at age thirteen, he drifted from job to job—illegal oyster harvesting in San Francisco, seal hunting in the north Pacific, working in a jute mill, and prospecting unsuccessfully for gold in the Yukon. During his time in the Yukon, he was snowed in and forced to spend four lonely months in a tiny cabin, waiting for spring to come. During that period of isolation, London had a lot of time to think about his life. He realized he had been busy, he had traveled a lot, but he had accomplished nothing of any value in his life. As soon as the spring thaw arrived, London returned home to California, finished his education, and devoted the last eighteen years of his life to a writing career. During that time, he produced 190 short stories, 22 novels, 5 plays, 28 poems, and more than 200 newspaper articles—an enormous creative output from a man who died all too soon at the age of forty. He devoted himself so intensely to his work that one would almost think he knew how short his life would be.

Jack London had a philosophy that he summed up in these words: "I would rather be a superb meteor, every atom of me in magnificent glow, than a sleepy and permanent planet. The proper function of man is to live, not just exist. I shall not waste my days in trying to prolong them. I shall use my time."

How about you? Are you making your life count for something lasting and important? Are you conscious of how little time you have left on this planet—and are you doing everything possible to make each moment count? Death is coming for all of us. A frightening truth? No. Properly viewed, this is a truth that can energize us and motivate us, just as it did Jack London.

"Every moment of life is valuable," observes author and time-management expert Dennis Hensley in his book *How to Manage Your Time*. "Once time is gone, it's gone forever. You can't buy it back, borrow it back, bribe it back, or even pray it back. A wasted moment is irretrievable" (Warner Press, 1989). We all have a limited amount of

Once we begin to see death as a great motivator, helping us to make the most of our days, then we will cease to see death only as an unhappy end to life. Death becomes nothing more than a (no pun intended) deadline.

187

time in which to get all of our living done. When we become fully aware of that fact, then life becomes a precious commodity, something to be treasured and savored. This truth should completely alter the way we live our lives and approach our deaths.

Does this mean that death should become a lash at our backs, driving us to work harder, to push ourselves into exhaustion trying to get everything done before we die? No. In fact, workaholism is really just another means some people use to avoid the reality of death. Many workaholics feel that if they just keep constantly busy, then unpleasant realities like death will just go away. We're not suggesting that the awareness of the transient nature of life should turn us into compulsive work-addicts. Rather, it should motivate us to do everything we do to the fullest: we should work and achieve, but we should also relax, enjoy recreation times, enjoy our family and our friends, and enjoy nature, drinking in every experience with enthusiasm and gusto because life is short and must be used well and enjoyed deeply.

What Is Your View of Death?

How do you view death? Which of the following statements describes your attitude and feelings toward death?

- "I am fully prepared for my own death whenever the time comes."
- "I look forward to saying hello to God."
- "I know that Jesus has saved me from my sins and that I will live with Him forever."
- "I'd rather die now than live another year with this physical suffering."
- "I'd rather die now than live another year with my memories and my emotional suffering."
- "Death is the absolute horror, the final end. I would do anything to avoid my death."
- "I am afraid of death because I don't know what lies on the other side—heaven, eternal separation from God, or simply nonexistence. It is the uncertainty that scares me."
- "I fear death because I don't believe God can forgive me. I am afraid of God's judgment."

If you are afraid of death, there are two possible explanations for your fear: (1) you may not have resolved all of your fears about living; and (2) you may not have made peace with God. Your fear about death may result from one of these reasons or a combination of both.

FEAR OF DEATH

In our counseling experience, we often encounter people who are committed Christians, who believe in the reality of heaven, and yet who are haunted by a strong apprehension about death. We usually find that a person who has such a strong fear of death often carries an unresolved, unconscious fear of living.

Intellectually, we all know that death is unavoidable. Emotionally, however, we don't really believe we're going to die. We spend our lives in denial of death. Deep down, we are convinced that there's got to be some way to dodge the Grim Reaper, and we'll find it before our time comes. The great American novelist and playwright William Saroyan expressed this belief in 1981, as he phoned a last message to the Associated Press from his deathbed in a California hospital: "Everybody has got to die, but I have always believed an exception would be made in my case. Now what?"

People seek (on an unconscious emotional level) to evade not only physical death but also the symbols of impending death: age lines in the face, deteriorating health, failing eyesight and hearing, and the loss of a driver's license. They cling to the frayed and faded symbols of youth and deny the evidence of the approaching end. They often fall into attitudes and behaviors that, at an unconscious level, represent a way to dodge the fast approach of death. These attitudes and behaviors include:

Hypochondriasis. Hypochondriacs constantly imagine illnesses or inflate existing illness. The symptoms are real, but they are caused by emotions and stress, not a physical problem. Hypochondriasis is called a somatoform disorder, an apparent illness or condition that is characterized by physical symptoms for which there are no organic findings. It is common for gerontologists—doctors who specialize in treating the aged—to have to sift through a number of vague but dramatic somatoform symptoms in order to diagnose true medical problems.

The unconscious reasoning of the hypochondriac is "If I'm vigilant to all my symptoms, I'll be able to outmaneuver death. No terminal illness is going to sneak up on me! I'm paying attention to every twinge and creaking joint!" Hypochondriasis is also a way to grieve one's death before it arrives. The hypochondriac is able to experience death in bits and pieces over a long period of time, moaning and complaining about each one as he or she prepares for "the big one." Clearly, hypochondriasis is not a healthy way to grieve one's mortality, because it compounds one's fear, bleeds away one's happiness, and escalates one's anxiety. Hypochondria is what we call a maladaptive response (that is, self-defeating and unhealthy behavior) to the inevitability of death.

Bitterness, anger, and cynicism. Tragically, these emotions are quite common among the elderly. We all have the choice to determine our own attitudes, but some people, as they approach death, seem willfully bent on rejecting serenity and clutching their resentment. It is as if they view an accepting attitude as a form of surrender, an admission of defeat. Bitterness, anger, and cynicism become a way of avoiding the reality of death. By raging against the unfairness of life, death, and God Himself, people are able to avoid having authentically to mourn and feel the sadness and loss that their death brings. The resentful response is yet another maladaptive response to the inevitability of death.

Suicide. People may kill themselves quickly or slowly, aggressively or passively. It matters little whether a person uses a bullet or simply stops eating or refuses to take prescribed medication. As bizarre as it may sound, suicide is often a way people choose to dodge the inevitability of death. There is actually a certain "irrational logic" to it. Why does a person choose to die in order to avoid the reality of death? To accept death's reality means to accept the brevity and transience of life. In other words, the person who accepts death is able to appreciate and cherish every remaining morsel.

The attitude of the person who can accept and savor the remaining moments of life is illustrated in a passage from Ray Bradbury's classic novel of midwestern Americana, *Dandelion Wine.* In that book, Great-Grandma is on her deathbed with her family gathered around her. "I've tasted every victual and danced every dance," she tells them. "Now there's one last tart I haven't bit on, one tune I haven't whistled. But I'm not afraid. I'm truly curious. Death won't get a crumb by my mouth I won't keep and savor. So don't you worry over me. Now, all of you go, and let me find my sleep" (Bantam, 1964).

That is not just a beautiful scene in a novel. In our clinical experience, we have seen many people who were able to approach their own deaths with such an attitude. That kind of acceptance of life and death is beautiful to behold. Those who accept the transitory nature of life are good stewards of every waking moment, and they live sensibly and they die confidently. But many people take the attitude that "The brevity and impermanence of life is so frightening and distasteful to me that the only way I can handle it is to shorten it deliberately. If I can't master life, I'll just take life and death into my own hands." They selfishly inflict death upon themselves and misery upon their loved ones.

Flight. Greg had been married forty-five years when he suddenly left his wife. Even Greg himself was unable to explain why he abandoned his wife. Finally, after weeks of counseling, the hidden source of his flight from marriage came to light: he was terrified of death. Greg had never made peace with his mortality. This problem went back to his childhood, when Greg saw how hard it was for his father to say goodbye when his wife—Greg's mother—lay dying of cancer. Now Greg was running away from marriage because he was afraid of having to say goodbye to his wife. Flight is yet another maladaptive attempt to dodge death. Have you made peace with your own mortality? Like Greg, you may have absorbed unhealthy attitudes toward death and dying from your parents.

Ron, a client at the clinic, recalls hearing his father say on more than one occasion, "When a man stops working, he stops living." Ron's father died less than two years after his own retirement, fulfilling his own grim prophecy. Decades later, when Ron himself reached retirement age, he joked about his father's attitude, but he didn't take it seriously. Ron was looking forward to retirement.

Yet, just a year into his retirement, Ron's wife became alarmed. Ron was gaining a great deal of weight, had dropped his favorite recreational pastimes, and was turning into a couch potato, headed for a massive stroke. Finally, she confronted Ron with the fact that he was living out his father's legacy. Ron denied it but agreed to go into counseling where he discovered that it was true. He was neglecting his health in an unconscious effort to conform to the legacy his father had passed down to him. In counseling, Ron made a decision not to live out an old family legacy. Instead, he determined to rebuild his enthusiasm for life, and he launched himself back into his old pastimes and interests, while developing a number of new interests.

> *Once you become free of the self-defeating compulsion to dodge your death, you are truly free to live your life. Once you accept the reality of death, you can enjoy the reality of living.*

FINAL ARRANGEMENTS

In the previous section, we noted that, if you are afraid of death, there are two possible explanations for that fear: (1) you may not have resolved all of your fears about living; and (2) you may not have made peace with God. Now we look at the second of these explanations. What does it mean to make peace with God? It means that you:

> *For some people, the moment they settle the matter of life and death by committing their lives to Christ is a moment of intense emotion and spiritual uplift. But most people experience that moment as a quiet, conscious, deliberate decision that takes place without any fanfare. Both experiences are equally valid. Don't be disappointed if your prayer of commitment was not accompanied by a blinding light, such as the apostle Paul experienced when he met Jesus on the road to Damascus. We all meet God in our own way.*

- recognize that you are a sinner and that you need God's forgiveness in your life (see Romans 3:23)
- recognize that Jesus Christ, the Son of God, died on the cross in payment for your sins (see Romans 6:23)
- trust Jesus Christ as your Savior and Lord of your life (see John 1:12)

Once you have made your peace with God, you can begin to look at death in a different way from before. The relationship of death to life is completely transformed. Once you viewed death as an interruption of life that invalidates life and erases all of

Last Wishes

It is advisable, particularly if you do not wish to be subjected to heroic life-extension measures, to make your wishes known. There are several ways this can be done:

1. A Durable Power of Attorney. With a durable power of attorney, you appoint someone to act on your behalf in regard to medical treatment. This legally appointed individual has the right to accept or refuse certain life-support measures for you in the event you become incapacitated. This document should be drawn up by an attorney in your state, and should name a person you trust with your life. Make sure this person clearly understands your wishes regarding medical treatment in an extreme case.

2. A Living Will. This is a legal document that states your wishes regarding medical treatment. It contains instructions, made in advance, so that doctors will carry out your wishes in the event you are unable to make decisions on your own. Most states have laws allowing individuals to leave a living will that can be invoked in the event of a terminal illness. Some states also allow the instructions of a living will to be invoked if the individual is in a "persistent vegetative state" and not expected to regain consciousness.

A living will is a much different document than a last will and testament in that it is not so much a document to be probated and interpreted by a court as a permission form, allowing a doctor to take or not take certain actions, and giving that doctor a formal release of liability. A living will, then, should be given to your doctor for safekeeping, not to an attorney. However, you would be wise to have your living will reviewed by an attorney before entrusting it to a doctor.

Though the doctors of the Minirth Meier New Life Clinics believe there are situations in which it is best to allow a patient to die a natural and dignified death, we are ethically opposed to any form of physician-assisted suicide. Therefore, if a patient is clearly not viable without artificial means (such as a respirator), we would support a decision to remove the artificial means of life support. However, we would not support a decision to take a person off oxygen and feeding tubes, since these are not "heroic" or "artificial" in any sense. Oxygen and feeding tubes are easily administered, and the deliberate withholding of oxygen and food from a patient constitutes killing that patient, not merely permitting death to naturally occur.

Your own wishes should be clearly stated in your living will. A blank living will document may be obtained by contacting the Older Women's League (OWL), 1325 G Street NW, Lower Level B, Washington DC 20005 (209-783-6686), or Concern for the Dying, 250 West 57th Street, New York NY 10107 (212-246-6962). Also, the National Right to Life Committee, which opposes euthanasia, offers a document called "Will to Live: General Presumption for Life," which instructs doctors to make every effort to prolong your life. If that is your wish, contact your local chapter of National Right to Life for information on obtaining a copy of "Will to Live."

Last Wishes—Cont'd

3. A "Do Not Resuscitate" (DNR) Order. Many hospitals offer patients who are terminally or chronically ill the option of signing a DNR. The signed DNR is placed in your file, and hospital personnel are made aware of the order. Then, in the event of an emergency in which you would normally be placed on a respirator or be given cardiopulmonary resuscitation (CPR), these attempts to revive you are suspended.

No advance order is foolproof. If you go into cardiac arrest or stop breathing, the attending doctors may be unaware of a DNR or living will and may resuscitate you against your express wishes. They can hardly be blamed for not taking the time to look up such orders in the event of an emergency. A physician's first instinct is always to save life.

---

life's joys and meaning. Now that you are joined to God by faith, it becomes clear that death does not invalidate life. Death completes life! Death brings life to a successful conclusion.

Does peace with God and the joy of approaching heaven remove every last shred of fear from the prospect of dying? Not in every case, certainly. Dying entails a sudden or gradual extinction of the body processes and sometimes (though not always) involves pain. It is normal to fear the pain, weakness, and immobility that sometimes precede the moment of death itself. Yet it is important to place that pain in a proper perspective. For the Christian, death is not the end but a passage, a crossing-over from one life to another life. It is a form of rebirth, and just as physical birth involves fear, pain, and (ultimately) joy, so does the process of being reborn through death into a new life in the presence of God. He is with us in the process of death, calming our fears, easing our pain, and fulfilling our joy in eternity.

For the person who has made peace with God, death can be a beautiful release from chronic pain, from blindness or deafness, from paralysis, from the indignities and humiliation of a debilitating illness, from confinement to a wheelchair or a hospital bed.

As you look ahead to the approaching moment of your death, making peace with God is the single most important "final arrangement" you must make. But there are other "final arrangements" to be considered before you can truly feel that your life can come to a successful conclusion.

First, you must make peace in your relationships. Words that need to be said must be said—words of love, words of apology, words of forgiveness. It is time to bring order out of disordered relationships. It is time to say your goodbyes to those you have always cared for in life.

Second, you must put your house in order. If you haven't already done so, you should prepare a last will and testament. One-third of Americans die intestate (without a will), and if that happens to you, the disposition of your estate is impersonally decided by a judge, not by you. In many states, a spouse will be awarded only one-third of your estate, and children receive two-thirds, unless you leave instructions to the contrary.

Revelation 21:4 gives us this assurance about the life beyond death: "And God will wipe away every tear from their eyes; there shall be no more death, nor sorrow, nor crying. There shall be no more pain, for the former things have passed away."

192

Wills should be drawn by attorneys, who charge a fairly modest fee for an average estate (usually around $300 or so). That is a small price to pay to make sure every aspect of the will is handled properly. If you really can't afford the attorney's fee, simple will forms are available at stationery and office supply stores—but be aware that by writing an amateur will, you may make costly mistakes or overlook tax advantages to your estate that a lawyer would point out. By the time your mistakes are discovered, it's too late to come back and fix them!

Third, you must give instructions regarding your medical care during the dying process. What sort of medical care would you want if, for example, you were in a coma and unable to breathe on your own? Would you wish to be placed on a respirator, or would you rather slip away at that point?

Fourth, you must make plans for the final remembrance of your life. A funeral is a time of grieving, but it should also be a time when the successful completion of a life is celebrated. Discuss with your spouse or the closest person in your life what you would like your own funeral to be like. Also, listen to that person's feelings on the subject. A funeral is a time when the bereaved gather to say goodbye to someone who has passed away, but it is also a time when a person who is leaving this life can say goodbye to those he or she leaves behind. It is an opportunity for you to make a final statement of love and encouragement to your loved ones. That statement could be kept as a part of a living trust or could be placed in the care of a pastor or close friend, to be read at the funeral. It can be a very healing and treasurable experience for the grieving to hear a warm personal statement of joy and peace from their departed loved one during the memorial service.

Death is inevitable, but the fear of death is not. Once we have settled the intimately connected issues of both life and death, then we can say with the apostle Paul in 1 Corinthians 15:54, "So when this corruptible has put on incorruption, and this mortal has put on immortality, then shall be brought to pass the saying that is written: 'Death is swallowed up in victory.'"

Decision Making

In the mid-1970s, while a professor at Trinity Seminary near Chicago, Dr. Paul Meier was offered a high-paying opportunity to become the administrator of a psychiatric clinic. At about the same time, he was also offered a full-time teaching position at Dallas Theological Seminary—at a much lower salary than the administrative position. According to the world's logic, there should have been no contest: Dr. Meier should have chosen the higher-paying position. But as he was praying and reflecting on his decision, the words of Jesus in Matthew 6:33 kept coming to his mind: "But seek first the kingdom of God and His righteousness, and all these things shall be added to you."

His decision: he took the lower-paying position at Dallas Seminary, where he worked closely with fellow professor Dr. Frank Minirth. Just one among many of the happy consequences of that decision was the founding of what is today known as the Minirth Meier New Life Clinics, a network of mental health clinics in over fifty cities across the United States.

One of the most difficult issues for Christians is that of decision making and discerning God's will. Christians are not called to make decisions in the same way as the rest of the world. Yes, we are to examine our options and apply the rational, logical minds God has given us. But sometimes, as Dr. Meier can attest, we are called to go beyond mere human logic, to transcend pure cost-benefit analyses, and to make decisions that—by the world's values—make no logical sense.

How do we find God's leading when that leading is outside the realm of rational, bottom-line thinking?

DECISION MAKING AND OUR EMOTIONS

Some Christians believe that God leads through emotional impressions. Others suggest that God actually sends certain bodily sensations to reveal His will to us. But how reliable are such impressions and sensations? Haven't many Christians been led astray by their emotions? Is it valid to trust feelings and impressions when discerning God's will?

A careful study of the Scriptures shows us that emotional impressions can come to us from three very different sources:

1. God. Throughout the New Testament, we see that God gives to us such positive emotions as comfort in times of anxiety, joy in times of trouble, love and compassion for people who mistreat us, and peace that passes human understanding. These positive emotions, which God brings to us even when our circumstances would dictate feelings of gloom, despair, and hopelessness, give us the strength to persevere and make courageous decisions that would otherwise be humanly impossible.

When we rely on emotions and impressions, it can be extremely difficult to determine where those emotions and impressions are coming from, and that can lead us into major mistakes. We can and should take our feelings into account as we make decisions in our lives, but the problem is that most of us, whether we realize it or not, make most of our decisions on the basis of emotion.

2. Satan. In passages such as Ephesians 6 and 2 Corinthians 10, Paul describes Satan as throwing mental "darts" in an attempt to create emotional delusions ("imaginations") and obsessions ("strongholds"). The satanic strategy is to use our emotions against us, to paralyze and immobilize us with fear, anxiety, and depression. God does not want us to be limited by our negative emotions. That is why Paul writes, "For God has not given us a spirit of fear, but of power and of love and of a sound mind" (2 Tim. 1:7).

3. Self. In the Garden of Gethsemane, hours before the cross, Jesus faced a terrible decision: Should He save Himself or should He accept the horror of the cross? From within Himself, an emotional revulsion arose against the awful suffering of the cross. But Jesus would not be deterred by His inner emotions. Instead, He made a decision that contradicted His feelings: "Not as I will, but as You will" (Matt. 26:39). All of us, sooner or later, are faced with decisions in which we feel our emotions tugging us one

194

way while God is calling us another way. That is when we must pray, along with Jesus, "Not as I will, but as You will."

Bert Decker, CEO of Decker Communications and author of *You've Got to Be Believed to Be Heard* (St. Martin's Press, 1993), has a favorite saying: "People buy on emotion and justify with fact." In other words, we human beings have a tendency to make emotion-based decisions, then gather all the facts we can to fool ourselves into thinking that our emotional decision is really rational and logical. For example, we tell ourselves that the car we're buying is really sensible and will save us a lot of money, when the real reason we want it is the sleek styling and the colorful computer displays on the dashboard. By basing important life decisions (marriage, choice of college, choice of career, major purchases) on emotion while fooling ourselves into thinking we are being "objective," we open ourselves up to major mistakes and major disappointments.

HOW CAN I MAKE A GOOD, SOUND, GODLY DECISION?

Emotion-based decisions should be avoided. We can and should take our feelings into account, but feelings should only be one small factor among many that we should weigh in making important decisions in life. Here are some suggestions for making wise decisions:

Apply sound, reasoned judgment. Since God has given us sound minds, let's use them. Reason, logic, and analysis can only take us so far. God may call us to go beyond logic in pursuit of His will, but we should never throw logical thinking out the window without at least examining our decision from a commonsense point of view.

Study God's Word. The Bible not only reveals God's will to us, it also searches out denial, self-deception, and self-will within our own inner selves. "For the word of God," says Hebrews 4:12, "is living and powerful, and sharper than any two-edged sword, piercing even to the division of soul and spirit, and of joints and marrow, and is a discerner of the thoughts and intents of the heart." In any decision-making process, Scripture should be consulted early, in order to avoid moving in a direction that is out of step with God's will. Scripture is a powerful corrective to emotional thinking and hidden, self-deceptive intents and motivations.

Seek God's will through prayer. When we pray, we should not only talk to God, we should also listen. Our attitude should be that of young Samuel in 1 Samuel 3:10: "Speak, for Your servant hears." The Spirit of God comes to us gently, quietly, and we must listen carefully for the still, small voice of His Spirit (see 1 Kings 19:12).

Seek the counsel of other wise people. The purpose of seeking the counsel of others is to take a reality check, to see if others see our decision from any angles we are missing. We should seek to be challenged and held accountable. We should ask others to help us penetrate any denial and illuminate any blind spots we might have regarding this decision. We should beware of gathering and sorting through the counsel of others only to have them ratify a decision we have already made; that is a very common (and potentially disastrous) form of self-deception.

Beware of rashness or impulsiveness. The apostle Peter was by nature an impulsive individual. He found it easy to jump out of a boat in the middle of a storm and start walking across the water to Jesus—but his impulsiveness wasn't enough. Soon he began to sink into the water, and Jesus had to reach out and lift him back into the boat. Walking on water is a bold, daring, impulsive thing to do, and many Christians are attracted to such impulsive actions, believing they are acts of faith when really they are acts of foolishness and spiritual pride. The bigger question for such Christians is the same test Peter faced and failed: Can you follow Jesus on dry land, where there is no spectacular feat of faith, no miracle to be performed, no rashness or impulsiveness involved? Can you steadily, soberly follow Jesus on a day-to-day basis? Peter rushed to Jesus on the water, but when he was on dry land, says Mark 14:54, he followed Jesus "at a distance." Consistency and unspectacular faithfulness is much better than rashness or impulsiveness in discerning and following the will of God for our lives.

■

As we seek to understand what God is saying to us through our circumstances, we should be open to the possibility that God is saying neither "Go" nor "No" but rather "Wait."

■

HOW DO I KNOW IF I'VE MADE THE RIGHT DECISION?

Sometimes, when we have made a decision, we will experience doubt about whether we have really made the right decision. Sometimes the best decision is to reverse a decision that we do not have peace about. If we continue to be overwhelmed with worry and a feeling of unease following a major decision, it may be wise to wait and reconsider the matter.

Taking Cues from Scripture

Scripture can help us either to confirm or to reconsider a major decision. Many years ago, Dr. Francis Schaeffer hovered uncertainly over the decision as to whether or not he should open a youth retreat in the mountains of Switzerland. Then, in his devotional studies, he came upon Isaiah 2:2, which read

Now it shall come to pass in the latter days

That the mountain of the LORD's house
Shall be established on the top of the mountains,
And shall be exalted above the hills;
And all nations shall flow to it.

Taking this as a nod from the Lord, Schaeffer built his retreat, named L'Abri, and young men and women streamed to it from all over the world to be encouraged and discipled in the Christian faith.

Confirmation or reconsideration of a decision may also come from circumstances. In both the Old Testament (such as the story of Gideon's fleece, Judges 6) and the New Testament (such as the doors of opportunity that would open or close during Paul's missionary journeys in the book of Acts), we see believers looking at circumstances and making decisions accordingly. Sometimes He opens the doors wide, and there is no question what His will is for our lives. More often, however, He will lead us to wait, to pray, to reflect before making a decision.

Another important fact to understand about God's will: His plan for our lives is not true or false, pass or fail. It is a menu of choices, many of which are equally valid. We have counseled people who become dangerously obsessed with finding God's one and only will for their lives. It is as if God's plan is an elaborate maze that we must thread, and in which one wrong step spells utter and final disaster. The truth is that life is much more varied than that, and God is gracious. If we fall off the path, He wants to set us right again and keep us moving forward.

In times of crisis, opportunity, and decision, the one thing we need above all else is wisdom. And the Bible tells us that the source of true decision-making wisdom is God Himself. "If any of you lacks wisdom," says James 1:5, "let him ask of God, who gives to all liberally and without reproach, and it will be given to him."

<hr />

Defense Mechanisms

We all need an escape from the stresses of everyday life. Sports, recreation, hobbies, travel, TV, movies, a good book—these are all forms of escape we use to "get away from it all" for a little while. A short-term break from our stressful routine is healthy and good for us.

But there is another form of escape from reality that can often be quite emotionally harmful to us and can bring damage and distortion to our relationships. This form of escape is called a defense mechanism.

HOW DEFENSE MECHANISMS HELP US—AND HURT US

Some defense mechanisms (such as denial) are actually protective systems built into our mental and emotional makeup by a loving God, and they are designed to help us get through a terrible shock, such as grief and loss. They also help us to cope, in a short-term way, with anxiety and frustration. But these defense mechanisms can become self-defeating and unhealthy when they settle in, muffling the alarm messages of our emotional pain and preventing us from dealing realistically with our emotional problems.

Defense mechanisms alter our perceptions of reality. In many ways, defense mechanisms are games we play with the rules of reality, in which we rig the rules so that we always win. If we feel guilt, we rearrange our perception of the situation in order to transfer our guilt to someone else. "It's not my fault; it's his fault or her fault." We

197

rationalize our behavior and justify our actions so that we can live with ourselves. We ignore or deny our selfishness and sin. The self-deceptive power of defense mechanisms and sin is described in Jeremiah 17:9: "The heart is deceitful above all things, and desperately wicked; who can know it?" Selfish motives can creep into our lives and influence us without our being aware of them. Even some of our "good deeds" may actually spring from hidden, self-deceptive motives that are selfish and sinful.

God never intended defense mechanisms to become long-term parts of our personalities. When you look at the grief process first described by Elisabeth Kübler-Ross, you see there is a progression that begins with a defense mechanism: (1) denial (that's the defense mechanism); (2) anger; (3) depression; (4) bargaining and magical thinking; (5) sadness; and (6) resolution and acceptance. When a major tragedy occurs, the brain's first defense is to go into denial and say, "No! There must be some mistake! This can't be happening!" Denial is a *temporary* protective covering for the mind. Avoiding the reality and pain for a short time allows us to regroup in order to handle the adjustments to come. These feelings of numbed confusion are normal and even necessary as we move through this stage and progress toward a place of resolution and acceptance.

But if we get stuck in denial and keep playing that defense mechanism over and over again, we will never recover from our grief. We will remain emotionally crippled and trapped in unreality. Consciously, we may be "protected" from the truth, but we know the truth on a subconscious level. This conflict between the conscious and subconscious minds is one of the primary sources of human anxiety.

If they are not penetrated and disarmed, defense mechanisms eventually settle into a state of long-term self-deception, resulting in anxiety and other emotional disorders. To overcome our defense mechanisms, it is important to know what they are, what forms they take, and the subtle and deceptive ways they operate within us. Our goal is to live realistically and courageously, for that is the pathway to true emotional and spiritual health. Armed with an understanding of our defense mechanisms, we can recognize them when they arise, face the truth they attempt to obscure, and make healthy adjustments in our thinking and our behavior so we can live happy, secure lives.

DEFENSE MECHANISMS AND THE BIBLE

Throughout the Bible, we see that the innermost part of human beings is referred to as the mind and "the heart." The Bible pictures "the heart" as the essence of human personality, intellect, emotions, and will. This is why Solomon warns us to guard our hearts "with all diligence" (Prov. 4:23). This also explains Jeremiah's observation that God searches and tests the heart, an observation verified by Solomon (see Jeremiah 17:10; Proverbs 21:2). And David tells us that it is critically important for us to gain insight into the hidden emotions and motives of the heart; he writes, "Search me, O God, and know my heart; try me, and know my anxieties; and see if there is any wicked way in me, and lead me in the way everlasting" (Ps. 139:23-24).

Sometimes we need other people—professional counselors and therapists, or friends in a support group—to hold up a mirror to ourselves and help us to penetrate our defense mechanisms. This is the role the prophet Nathan played in the life of King David, who had committed adultery with Bathsheba and had arranged the murder of her husband, Uriah. Because of his defense mechanisms, David was living unrepentantly and was in serious danger of hardening his conscience and his heart against God. Nathan approached David and confronted him with the truth of his sin, penetrating his emotional defenses, and bringing him back to repentance and reality. (See 2 Samuel 12.)

Following his repentance, David recorded his feelings in Psalm 51:6, where he prayed, "Behold, You desire truth in the inward parts, and in the hidden part You will make me to know wisdom." David's statement reflects our desperate necessity to be honest and reality-based in our inward emotions and motives. He goes on to pray, "Create in me a clean heart, O God, and renew a steadfast spirit within me" (v. 10).

That should be our goal as well.

Psychological researchers have identified at least forty different defense mechanisms. Let's take a look at some of the more common ones:

Denial

Many of our thoughts, emotions, memories, and motives are stored below the level of our awareness, in the unconscious mind. The conscious mind fights to keep these thoughts, emotions, memories, and motives away by lying to itself. This defense mechanism is called denial. An example of denial is when alcoholics lie to themselves and convince themselves that they don't have a problem, that they can quit drinking any time they want. Let's examine how denial works.

Karol is in her early thirties. She is pleasant, friendly, even bubbly. If you met her, you'd never suspect she is unhappy. But when asked about her family life, she becomes evasive, preferring to discuss her social and church activities. When pressed about her relationship with her parents, she shrugs and says, "I came from a good home. I had a nice childhood." Karol isn't lying to us when she says that. On a conscious level, she really believes it's true.

Karol's sisters, however, tell quite a different story. Her father was physically and verbally abusive to Karol and her sisters. As a child growing up in this environment, Karol learned to get beyond the pain by acting friendly and pretending that the negative issues in her life didn't matter. She learned a pattern of denial that followed her into adulthood.

When Karol comes into counseling, it's not because she has a problem with denial. She doesn't even recognize her denial. On a conscious level, she actually thinks she had a normal, "okay" childhood. But she has come for treatment of a generalized state of anxiety, and she is becoming increasingly fearful of people in authority in her church and in her workplace. In counseling, the closer she comes to real insight into the sources of her anxiety and fear, the more agitated she becomes. Her defense mechanism starts working overtime to protect her from the truth about her childhood.

Finally, in a moment of "breakthrough," a painful memory comes flooding back into her mind. It is a scene of her father raging and hurting her—and she realizes that faint echoes of this memory were actually resonating in her relationships with present-day authority figures at work and at church. Soon, more memories of pain come flooding in, and a more realistic image of her childhood begins to assemble. It is painful to recall these events, but it is also cleansing and liberating. Now she understands why she has been so anxious and fearful and that these emotions are a product of past issues. Her denial has been penetrated and replaced with healing truth.

Repression

More subtle and more general than denial, repression occurs when "unacceptable" ideas, feelings, impulses, or motives are automatically banned from conscious awareness. We all use repression at some point and to some degree, and an element of repression occurs in all other defense mechanisms. For this reason, it is often called the "granddaddy of all defense mechanisms."

Repression can sometimes be useful in the short term. God gave us the ability to file some thoughts and memories away so we wouldn't have to deal with everything consciously at all times. If we did, an information overload would eventually short out our neural circuits. But when we repress things in unhealthy ways, it may be because of something we cannot accept, perhaps something from childhood that was too painful or a behavior we practice that is so disgusting to us that we pretend it's not there. This can be a springboard to a host of other problems, such as depression.

Suppression

Suppression is the avoidance of an uncomfortable issue or emotion, usually because the timing is not right to deal with it. Unfortunately, many people never find the "right time," so they never deal with those issues and emotions.

People who use suppression tend to be more aware of their inner conflict than those who use repression. They may consciously reason, "I don't have time to deal with this right now, so I'll put it aside and get back to it later." For example, if a husband and wife have an argument and she points out some areas that he finds very threatening, he might say, "I know we need to talk about that, but I've had such a hectic day that I'm just worn out. Let's talk about it when we're not so tired." This might be okay—if they ever got back to it. But generally, people who practice suppression always have an excuse for why it's not a good time. Suppression is sometimes referred to as emotional procrastination.

Rationalization

Rationalization is closely linked with denial. It's the mind's defense against embarrassment, disappointment, and other situations that cause feelings of anxiety. The mind changes its viewpoint so that the individual's feelings are no longer in conflict with the situation.

A young man defeated in his bid for the senior class presidency might cover his crushed emotions by rationalizing the defeat. "I really didn't want to win anyway," he might say. "If I had won, I would have had to go to meetings all the time. I'd much rather be free to have fun my last year in school."

Rather than facing the pain of rejection and the hurt of losing something he worked very hard to gain, he revises his point of view. This way, he emerges a winner after all. He deludes himself into thinking he actually got what he wanted.

Intellectualization

Intellectualization is popular among people who suffer severe feelings of low self-esteem. Intellectualization is a means by which individuals avoid the awareness of inferiority feelings and other unconscious conflicts by the excessive use of intellectual vocabulary, thinking, and discussion. They retreat from emotion by surrounding themselves with philosophical or academic discussions. Such people often look down on those who are less intellectual than themselves.

A successful self-made man whose parents were not able to send him to college may feel inferior to colleagues who have an assortment of diplomas on their walls. To prop up his ego, he might speak in obscure, philosophical terms and use "dollar words" where "twenty-five-cent words" would be quite sufficient. He works hard to impress others as a means of impressing himself. To prove his refined taste, he might surround himself with expensive works of art, and he might become a visible supporter of the local symphony and museum.

Although these activities seem positive on the surface, they are motivated by a self-defeating effort to hide the truth from himself and others. People who use intellectualization as a defense mechanism often have difficulty making close friends because they are afraid friends will discover the truth about them. Also, potential friends are often put off by the smoke screen of lofty talk and boastful terms.

Reaction Formation

A person using reaction formation aggressively projects the opposite image of what he really is. Reaction formation involves a lie that the person tells not only others but also himself. On one level, the person knows the ugly reality. On another level, the person is able to say to himself, "I'm really a good person. See how hard I crusade against evil!" In a way that defies rational explanation, this individual is able to compartmentalize these two conflicting aspects of himself. This conflict invariably produces great anxiety.

An example of reaction formation is the pastor who preaches vehemently and convincingly on such issues as sexual purity and integrity but is involved in sexual immorality in his private life. Somewhere within himself, he separates his public preaching from his sexual activity and his deception of his wife and others. He may borrow other defense mechanisms, such as rationalization, to seal off the compartments of his inner being ("My wife refuses to meet my needs, so my affair is justified, and has nothing to do with the really terrible sexual sins I preach against"). As a result of this inner compartmentalization, he sees himself as faultless and not as a hypocrite.

People use projection as a way of easing their guilt feelings. Projection allows the sinner to see himself as the good guy, and to tell himself that it is the other people who are the problem, not him. It is common for people to attribute their own anger, perfectionistic tendencies, jealousy, deceptive behavior, pride, and other sins, emotions, and character flaws onto others.

Yet, at some deep level of his being, a part of him recognizes the conflict, and this conflict creates anxiety. As his conflict and anxiety grow, his preaching against sexual impurity may actually become more strident and intense.

Other examples of reaction formation: the man with homosexual tendencies who projects an image of a macho ladies' man; the child molester who projects the image of a defender and friend of children; the person who projects an image of being a model parent while depriving his or her children of love and attention in private.

Projection

Projection involves attributing one's own impulses, emotions, or wishes to another person, then passing judgment on the other person for having that emotion.

201

A husband who is fearful about keeping up with the financial demands of maintaining a business and household but feels it's unmanly to have such feelings, may project his own feelings onto his wife. He might say, "You're never happy. It doesn't matter how hard I work or how much money I bring home, you are never satisfied." He judges his own emotions by projecting them onto his wife, where they are at arm's length. Clearly, projection is unhealthy for one's own emotional well-being, but it can be equally destructive to one's most important relationships.

A more extreme and destructive form of projection is called delusional projection, which can cause a person to lose touch with reality.

Displacement

Displacement involves transferring an emotion from its original object to a safer, more acceptable substitute. For example, a man who is criticized by his boss feels belittled, unappreciated, and angry. Unable to express his anger at work for fear of retaliation, he comes home and castigates his wife, punishes his children, or kicks the dog. A person practices displacement whenever he or she becomes angry and slams a fist into a wall or (preferably) a pillow.

Somatization

Somatization means expressing some emotion, frustration, or anxiety in bodily ways. A person who is unwilling to admit being angry or anxious turns those emotions on his body and develops ulcers, chronic headaches, or diarrhea (just to mention a few). It's much easier to tell a friend, "I'm just not feeling well today; I have a splitting headache," than to admit, "I'm really mad," or "I'm really nervous about how this situation is going to turn out." Not everyone who has a physical ailment is somaticizing. But when people have a constant, steady stream of physical symptoms, there may be some emotional issues that are being pushed down, resulting in real illnesses that are stress- or anxiety-induced.

Regression

Regression occurs when individuals faced with current conflicts revert to an earlier stage of emotional immaturity, where they felt more protected from life's stresses.

This defense mechanism is frequently seen in children who experience the "trauma" of new siblings arriving home from the hospital. The child has unconscious fears—first, about his mother being in the hospital, and then about the new brother or sister demanding so much of Mom's time once she gets home. So he suddenly begins to wet the bed or soil his pants, even though he's been potty-trained for some time. Or he may revert to baby talk or thumb-sucking to get Mom's attention away from that new baby.

Other Defense Mechanisms

As previously mentioned, there are at least forty different defense mechanisms that have been identified by psychological and psychiatric researchers. Other significant defense mechanisms include:

Fixation. This defense mechanism is similar to regression except that, instead of returning to an earlier stage of emotional development, the person remains at the level of development he or she was in when the trauma occurred. For example, an adult individual who is fixated in an adolescent stage may completely neglect his family in favor of watching ball games on TV or reading comic books.

Distortion. Persons reshape their external reality to suit their inner needs. Often distortions involve grandiose delusions and hallucinations such as hearing voices that no one else can hear.

Schizoid fantasy. Persons find reality so painful that they escape through excessive daydreaming.

Isolation. Common among compulsive people who have very strict consciences, this mechanism allows unacceptable emotions such as anger, lust, or greed to be split off from conscious thoughts.

Phariseeism. Persons become increasingly self-righteous and think they are better than others because of what they do or don't do religiously. Their motivation is to avoid becoming aware of their own shortcomings.

Defensive devaluation. Persons criticize others as a way of convincing themselves that they are better than others. Unconscious inferiority feelings are covered by this defense mechanism.

Passive-aggressive unconscious behavior. Persons who have repressed hostility toward some authority figure "get even" in a nonverbal, passive way such as pouting, procrastinating, acting inefficiently, or spreading secretive rumors about the resented person.

Withdrawal. Persons who tend to be introverted deceive themselves about an anxiety-producing conflict by physically removing themselves from the situation.

Sarcasm. Persons with suppressed hostility toward themselves or others sometimes ventilate that hostility without being aware of its existence by making critical jokes about themselves or others.

Undoing. Individuals may carry out unconscious acts in order to negate previous mistakes, in order to be able to believe the earlier mistakes never happened. For example, a Christian might criticize and berate a fellow Christian, then go out of his way to compliment that same person the next day without consciously remembering the earlier incident. This is an unconscious attempt to erase guilt that is felt at an emotional level.

Sublimation. An individual unconsciously channels unacceptable drives (such as hostility or lust) into acceptable channels (exercise, housework, creative endeavors). Although unconscious sublimation is not as unhealthy as many other defense mechanisms, a healthier approach would be to work on becoming consciously aware of those unacceptable feelings, work to deactivate them (through counseling and support groups), pray about them, and consciously redirect one's emotional energies.

FOUR STEPS TO PENETRATING YOUR DEFENSE MECHANISMS

Defense mechanisms are usually much easier to diagnose in other people than to recognize in ourselves. We can clearly see when someone else is denying the truth or shifting the blame or rationalizing some negative action. But our vision becomes clouded when we look within. We can say we're searching for the truth about ourselves, but we have difficulty being honest in our quest. Sometimes we need professional help to point out which defense mechanisms we're using and what truths these mechanisms are attempting to hide.

Let us suggest four practical steps to uncovering and penetrating the defense mechanisms that prevent you from achieving full emotional wholeness:

Step 1: Ask God to reveal your defense mechanisms to you. Pray the prayer of the psalmist: "Search me, O God, and know my heart; try me, and know my anxieties; and see if there is any wicked way in me, and lead me in the way everlasting" (Ps. 139:23–24). Agree with God that your defense mechanisms are deceptive and self-defeating, and tell Him that you want to know the truth about yourself. Claim the forgiveness He has promised in 1 John 1:9.

Step 2: Establish a relationship of accountability with someone you trust. This may be your spouse, a mentor, or another same-sex friend. Choose someone who will not let you get away with self-deception. If someone asks you to hold him or her accountable, realize that it is a serious commitment. Keep in mind that your goal is to speak the truth in love so that the other person can "grow up in all things into Him who is the head—Christ" (Eph. 4:15).

Step 3: Be aware of your circumstances and your response. It is often helpful to keep a journal in which you record events, feelings, and responses. Read back over your journal from time to time to see if you notice a pattern.

Step 4: Meditate on God's Word. Jesus promises in John 8:32, "And you shall know the truth, and the truth shall make you free." Instead of relying on self-deception, choose to rely on the truths of God's Word and the freedom they bring.

Defense mechanisms are a form of deception, and we should commit ourselves to penetrating that deception and facing the truth. Deception keeps us in bondage and prevents us from reaching our God-given potential, but the truth—God's truth about ourselves—truly does set us free.

Depression

Susan sat in the counselor's office, tightly clutching her purse in her lap. "I thought I was just sad," she began. "I've been divorced for two, almost three years now, and I've been sad a lot since the divorce. But this isn't just sadness. I know that now."

"Why do you say that?" asked the counselor.

"Because of what I did when I found . . ." She trailed off.

"Go on. What did you find?"

"I was cleaning out the bedroom closet. And I found his Bible."

"Your husband's Bible?"

"Yes," she said. Tears welled up in her eyes, but her jaw was clenched. The counselor could see that Susan was right: there was sadness here but something else as well.

Anger. Intense anger. The tears spilled from her eyes, ran down her cheeks, and trailed along her tightly set jaw. "I looked at it and I thought, This is his Bible. He used to read that Bible, and still he could run around behind my back, have an affair, and then leave me for another woman. You know, doctor, to this day, he still claims he is a dedicated Christian and that I was the one who drove him away. My husband the adulterer thinks he's a saint!"

"What did you do? After you found the Bible?"

"I picked it up and I threw it against the wall as hard as I could. It was old and the spine was cracked, and it hit that wall and a bunch of pages came out of it and fluttered to the floor. And I looked at the pieces of that Bible and I just started screaming at them. I don't know what I said. I just screamed and screamed."

Additional counseling revealed that Susan was suffering from an unresolved grief reaction following her divorce. Her grief had settled into a depression. She had assumed she was just sad. She wasn't aware of the intense anger she carried inside until the Bible-throwing incident. After thorough analysis, it became clear that she was intensely angry with her husband because of his sin against her, which he compounded with his self-righteous hypocrisy. But it took a long time for Susan to understand that she was also angry with God. The thought that she might actually be angry with God filled her with terror. "No," she insisted again and again, "I could never be angry with God!" But as she examined her life—her abandonment of daily devotions, her inability to attend church, the Bible-throwing incident—she came to realize it was true.

The Bible in the closet symbolically represented not only her hypocritical, adulterous husband but God Himself—the God she had trusted and who had mysteriously allowed her to be deeply wounded by a shattering divorce. Why had God not forced her husband to repent? Why did God not punish him for what he had done to her? After all her years of faithfulness to God and her husband, why had they both hurt her so much? All of these questions and all this anger had been denied and repressed for almost three years.

And now Susan was in the grips of a deep depression.

But once she was fully aware of her repressed anger toward God, she made a decision to turn her anger and her entire life back over to God. She asked His forgiveness. She wept. And she resumed her daily devotions and church involvement. It wasn't easy, but with time and gradually increasing insight into her emotions, she was able to conquer her depression.

AN EMOTIONAL EPIDEMIC

Today, about 5 percent of the total population is medically diagnosed with depression, and many times that number experience depression but will never get the help they need. In fact, the majority of all Americans will experience serious depression at one time or another in their lives.

Depression is the number one mental health problem in America. At the Minirth Meier New Life Clinics, we see more cases of depression than all other emotional problems combined.

Depression can strike any age group, but it is most common in people in their forties and fifties. Depression occurs two times more often in women than in men and is three times more prevalent in higher socioeconomic classes than in lower classes (proof, if proof was ever needed, that money doesn't buy happiness).

Most people tend to think of depression as a long-term, deep sadness. But the reality is that depression has much more to do with anger than with sadness. People also tend to think of depression as something that takes place in the mind and the emotions. And while that's true as far as it goes, depression also has a powerful and destructive effect on the body. As psychiatrists, we tend to see people who are severely, clinically depressed—that is, they are so depressed that their emotional state is manifesting itself as an array of physical problems in the body.

Depression's Greatest Danger

Depression is the number one cause of suicide, and suicide is the tenth leading cause of death in the United States. Thus, it is clear that depression can be a life-threatening illness. If you or someone you know is experiencing severe depression, along with suicidal thoughts, then you need to understand that it is extremely important for a potentially suicidal person to obtain immediate professional help. The pain of depression is intense, but that pain can be alleviated, and the depression can be cured. A life of joy and peace is possible, even if you can't imagine it now.

There is a saying that suicide is a permanent solution to a temporary problem, and this saying is true. The pain of depression is temporary, and once that depression has been treated, life can be beautiful once again. Don't let a momentary pain-based decision rob you or someone you love of the years of laughter and happiness that God still has planned. (For a more complete discussion of this issue, including the ten warning signs of suicide, see SUICIDE.)

Although not everyone will experience the kind of serious depression that we treat all too often at the Minirth Meier New Life Clinics, we all encounter some degree of depression from time to time. We know from our clinical experience that this emotional suffering is not only treatable but preventable. In the remainder of this article, we will show you how to recognize depression, how to recover from it, and how to keep it from returning.

THE WARNING SIGNS OF DEPRESSION

Many people suffer the debilitating pain of depression without even realizing the nature of their disorder. They think they have a purely physical illness. Or, like Susan, they think they are merely sad. The warning signs of clinical depression fall into five broad categories:

1. moodiness
2. painful thinking
3. anxiety

4. physical symptoms
5. delusional thinking

Let's look at each of these categories in turn.

Moodiness

Moodiness is the category of symptoms that most people associate with depression: a sad facial expression, frequent crying or moping, downcast features, and a look of exhaustion and discouragement. In the grip of depression, people often lose interest in their personal appearance, and the seriously depressed individual frequently appears unkempt. Some try to hide their depression by smiling (there is even a name for this behavior: smiling depression). The smile, however, usually looks artificial and thin; the depression shows through.

Psychiatrists and psychologists call this category of symptoms sad affect (in this sense, the word *affect* is pronounced with the emphasis on the first syllable; it refers to the general mood a person projects by his or her facial expression, verbal communication, and body language).

Painful Thinking

Another category of warning signs of depression is painful thinking. Many persons who have experienced both severe physical pain and severe emotional pain will tell you that given a choice, they would take the physical pain any day. In fact, one man recalls that after the sudden death of his teenage daughter, the pain of his depression was so intense that it actually produced physical pain. It was as if every nerve ending in his body was jangled. He couldn't get into a car or sit in a chair or be tapped on the shoulder without experiencing waves of physical pain—but this pain originated in his broken heart.

Painful thinking often centers around guilt—either authentic guilt (the result of actual mistakes and sin) or false guilt (blaming oneself for actions and consequences of which one is innocent or that could not be helped). If the depressed individual could think realistically and objectively, he would realize he is taking on responsibility for acts that are beyond his control.

Painful thinking causes a depressed person to be introspective in a very self-defeating, self-blaming way. The individual will agonize over past mistakes, about "what ifs" and "if onlys," and will frequently wallow in guilt even when totally innocent. This individual will also take an exaggerated view of his problems, and will bitterly condemn himself or others for those problems. In the vast majority of cases, this person feels completely helpless and boxed in by his problems, and his perception of those problems is usually out of proportion to reality. The depressed individual is usually pessimistic, distrustful, angry, preoccupied with his own resentment and emotional pain. He is so self-focused and inwardly focused that his concentration, attention, and memory are impaired. He is angry about the past, negative about the present, gloomy about the future, and he is convinced that his external problems and internal pain are destined to go on forever.

The depressed person who is caught up in painful thinking usually loses motivation and interest in previously enjoyable activities. He begins to avoid people, and this self-imposed isolation serves to increase the pain and bitterness of the depression. The depressed individual usually becomes indecisive and humorless, and a candidate for suicide.

Anxiety

Anxiety and depression often occur together (see ANXIETY). The depressed individual often develops signs of anxious, irritable behavior. He may seem tense, nervous, and agitated. Whereas many depressed people sit and stare at the walls for long periods of time, the person with combined depression and anxiety may have trouble sitting still.

Physical Symptoms

Another category of warning signs of severe depression is physical symptoms (medical doctors call them physiological concomitants of depression). Negative mental and emotional activity in the brain stimulates the production of brain chemicals that affect body functions. Sleep is affected; in some cases, the individual has trouble getting to sleep, but more often the individual awakens in the middle of the night and can't get back to sleep. During waking hours, body movements usually decrease, and a stooped posture and signs of physical exhaustion may appear. Appetite and body weight are affected (both are usually diminished, though not always). Digestion is affected (diarrhea, constipation, or alternating bouts of both). Sexual interest disappears. Tension headaches, dry mouth, rapid or irregular heartbeat are frequently observed. In women, the menstrual cycle may stop *(amenorrhea)* or become irregular *(dysmenorrhea)*.

As a result of these physical changes, many people experience hypochondriasis or mistakenly conclude that they have cancer or some other serious illness. In fact, they would often rather have such a purely physical illness than a set of symptoms arising from emotional conflicts.

Delusional Thinking

Another major—and extreme—category of symptoms is delusional thinking. This category is comparatively rare and only occurs in cases of very severe depression. A person afflicted with delusional thinking cannot sort fantasy from reality. His delusions may be paranoid in nature: he may think people are conspiring against him or talking about him. Or his delusions may be grandiose in nature: he may think he has received a special gift or a special message from God. Common symptoms of delusional thinking are auditory hallucinations (hearing voices that accuse, blame, or give orders) and visual hallucinations (seeing things nobody else sees).

Swift intervention and treatment (usually in a hospital) can usually restore a person to normalcy. Available therapy includes antipsychotic and antidepressant medications, daily psychotherapy, and biblical encouragement. Even with treatment, however, a small percentage of people with delusional thinking do become permanently psychotic. Fortunately, most clinical depressions do not reach the psychotic stage.

CLASSIFICATIONS OF DEPRESSION

Depressive disorders are sometimes classified according to their sources—that is, according to whether the source of the depression is primarily external or internal. The first form of depression, *endogenous depression,* comes from sources that are entirely within the individual, such as a chemical imbalance in the brain or a physical disease. The second form of depression, *exogenous depression*, is caused by a person's reaction to external stress factors, such as a major relationship conflict, financial disaster, or major grief response.

Depressive disorders are also classified according to the symptoms they produce. If these symptoms interfere with an individual's physical well-being and his relationships, the disorder is called a *depressive neurosis*. Depressive neuroses are quite curable by means of professional psychotherapy. If a person shows signs of considerable anxiety along with moodiness, painful thinking, and slow body movement *(psychomotor retardation)*, he is said to have *agitated depression*. This is also highly curable.

If a person has some of the previously mentioned symptoms plus delusional thinking or hallucinations, he has a *psychotic depression*. Psychotic depression is more difficult to treat but is usually curable if caught early. Some psychotic depressions harden into lifelong schizophrenic disorders, which are not curable by current methods. Someday, we hope, a breakthrough cure for this category may be found.

Psychological depression in children is common following a major loss or disruption in life—the loss of a parent, a pet, or a beloved object, or even a move to a new house. Depression in children often takes the form of withdrawal, prolonged sadness, and a marked increase or decrease in the child's activity level. Treatment includes counseling and possible low-dosage medication with antidepressants.

Psychological depression in adolescents is different from adult forms of depression in many ways. It comes disguised by a different set of symptoms. Depressed teenagers may become irritable, hostile, and rebellious. They may be experiencing significant guilt feelings. Because adolescent depression is disguised by a different set of symptoms, it often goes unrecognized and undiagnosed. Teenage depression can be treated by antidepressant medications, which normally lessen the symptoms within about two weeks. Medical treatment should be followed by counseling that involves the entire family so that distorted family communication patterns can be restored to health.

Psychological depression in the elderly is marked by the same symptoms and is treated in much the same way as other adult forms of depression. What makes depression among the elderly a special situation are the special issues and losses that a person must go through with advancing age. Losses tend to cluster together and take on great symbolic meaning for a person who is approaching the end of his or her own life. (For a comprehensive discussion of causes, symptoms, and treatment of depression in the elderly, see the sections "Emotional Losses" and "Depression" under AGING.)

Postpartum depression is a "blue" feeling or emotional letdown affecting the vast majority of new mothers within the first week or so after delivery. It is caused by hormonal imbalances, family or social pressures, emotional stress, and physical exhaustion. In rare cases, postpartum depression can become a true depressive illness involving insomnia, irrational fears, irritability, crying, guilt, and even rejection of the baby. In such cases, women may need medical and psychological treatment, including antidepressants and long-term counseling to help them accept the role of motherhood. In the even more rare cases where a depressed mother actually poses a danger to herself or her baby, psychiatric hospitalization is necessary. A woman who is prone to such severe and dangerous forms of postpartum depression should avoid future pregnancy.

Manic-depressive disorder (also called bipolar disorder) is a comparatively infrequent illness that, unlike most depressions, is probably genetic in origin. The symptoms of this illness include extreme swings of mood from a delusional, grandiose euphoria (marked by rapid, excessive, excited talking) to severe depression with suicidal tendencies. In the euphoric (manic) phase, individuals are cheerful, ambitious, optimistic, and so uncritically self-confident that their judgment is impaired. They may enter into extravagant, ruinous business deals, start writing a novel, or act impulsively in other ways. They have trouble focusing, and their conversations jump from topic to topic in rapid succession. They display demanding, domineering behavior, and a good-natured joking mood can turn into a stream of hostile, sarcastic insults without warning. Denial is extreme in this phase.

The depressive phase of the manic-depressive disorder is in complete contrast to the manic phase. The individual displays the classic symptoms of depression, including low self-esteem, tearfulness, painful thinking, physical symptoms, withdrawal, guilt, and anger. The manic phase can be successfully treated with lithium salt, and the depressive phase with antidepressant medications. Manic-depressive disorder can only be controlled by medical treatment.

SELF-TEST   What's Your Depression Potential?

The following inventory will help you determine your potential for depression and depression-related problems. Place a check in front of each statement you agree with. A key for evaluating the results appears at the end of this inventory.

_____   1. I feel like crying more often now than I did a year ago.
_____   2. I have lost interest in the things I used to enjoy.
_____   3. I feel blue and sad.
_____   4. I feel helpless a good part of the time.
_____   5. I feel hopeless about the future.
_____   6. I feel that I am not useful or needed.
_____   7. I am losing my appetite.
_____   8. I notice I am losing weight without trying.
_____   9. I have trouble staying asleep through the night.
_____   10. I am restless and jumpy a lot.
_____   11. My mind isn't as clear as it used to be.
_____   12. I have less energy than usual; I tire easily or for no reason.
_____   13. I have lost a lot of my motivation.
_____   14. I have been very irritable lately.
_____   15. Morning is the worst part of the day.
_____   16. I find myself introspecting a lot.
_____   17. I don't like the way I am or I don't like who I am.
_____   18. I think about the past a lot.
_____   19. I have more physical problems (headaches, upset stomach, constipation, rapid heartbeat, etc.) than I did a year ago.

____ 20. People have noticed that I don't do my job as well as I used to.
____ 21. I have recently been thinking that life is not worth living.
____ 22. I think other people would be better off if I were dead.

If you placed check marks in front of at least seven statements OR if you placed a check mark in front of statement number 1, number 2, or number 3, and these symptoms have persisted for at least two weeks, there is a strong possibility that you may be experiencing serious depression. Your condition is treatable and can be alleviated by a professional psychiatrist. It is important, however, that you seek professional assistance before your condition worsens.

Important: If you placed a check mark in front of statement number 21 or 22—regardless of your results on the other statements—you should seek the help of a professional psychiatrist or psychologist immediately. We want to assure you that the feelings you are experiencing will pass and you can be helped to feel better.

GRIEF AND DEPRESSION

Most of us, before we have spent very many years on this planet, discover what it means to experience grief and loss. Our first such experience may be the loss of a pet—or the loss of a parent. A child of divorce knows a particularly painful form of loss—the loss, in many ways, of an entire, secure world. Moving into adulthood, we may encounter losses ranging from a shattered romance to the loss of a job; from the death of a spouse or child to the diagnosis of a terminal illness. Whenever an individual suffers a significant loss, he or she must go through the stages of grief, which were first defined by Swiss psychiatrist Elisabeth Kübler-Ross in her 1969 book *On Death and Dying* (Macmillan, 1991). We have adapted them as follows:

1. shock/denial
2. anger (anger turned outward)
3. depression (anger turned inward)
4. bargaining
5. sadness
6. resolution and acceptance

No one goes through these stages at the same rate or in exactly the same way. This process is called a grief reaction, and you will notice that the third stage in the grief process is called depression (for a more complete discussion of the grief process, see GRIEF AND LOSS).

It is important to understand that the depression component of the grief reaction is not a true clinical depression. It is a temporary stage in a normal process that we all must traverse on the journey from traumatic loss to emotional recovery. This temporary form of depression often bears many of the same features as clinical depression, such as altered sleep patterns, diminished appetite, diminished motivation, crying, feelings of hopelessness, and physical symptoms, but this condition normally passes as the recovery process progresses.

A person can get "stuck" in a stage of the grief process, however. The key stages for the risk of depression are stages 2 and 3. If a person gets stuck in the anger stage or the depression stage, a grief reaction can settle into a true clinical depression.

In the anger stage, the grieving person normally feels anger toward God and other people: "God could have prevented this loss!" "How could my parents have gotten a divorce?" "If he had been more careful, he would still be alive today!" Many people, feeling anger to be a sin (particularly anger toward God), quickly repress their anger and are unaware of it.

In the depression stage, anger turns inward. The grieving person feels guilt—authentic guilt, false guilt, or some combination of the two. Authentic guilt is an alarmlike response to sin in one's life; false guilt is a mistaken sense of responsibility for one's own innocent actions, for another person's actions, or for consequences that were beyond one's own control. When a child feels responsible for her parents' divorce or when a person thinks, "If only I hadn't encouraged him to take the interstate, my husband would still be alive," that is false guilt.

Anger is not a sin, per se. In Ephesians 4:26, the apostle Paul tells us that it is possible to get angry without sinning, but that anger does become sin when we clutch it and allow it to sour into a grudge. The anger that follows a major loss is not sin; it is a normal human response. By God's grace, we can move through our anger to a place of acceptance and forgiveness, but we should not feel guilty for the temporary feelings of anger that are a normal part of the grief response. Any guilt we do feel should be surrendered to God as we ask His forgiveness and His help in forgiving ourselves. Those who are not able to forgive others or forgive themselves, and who feel they must punish themselves and blame themselves for their loss and the feelings surrounding that loss, are likely candidates for true clinical depression.

■

When grief turns into clinical depression, a cure can usually be achieved only through treatment in psychiatric therapy.

■

PROFILE OF A DEPRESSED INDIVIDUAL

The following are some of the symptoms and personality traits commonly seen in people who are depressed. A depressed person may not show all or even most of these traits, but a cluster of a significant number of these traits could be an indicator of depression serious enough to warrant professional treatment.

- worry and pessimism
- low energy; weariness
- sense of futility; feelings of uselessness
- moodiness (sad affect); unhappiness; sadness
- feelings of worthlessness
- feelings of hopelessness
- feelings of helplessness
- thinking permeated by guilt
- dwelling on the past
- despondency and gloom

- agitation and irritability
- perplexity and confusion
- feelings of inadequacy; low confidence; low self-image
- feeling that all endeavors are meaningless and without value
- inability to concentrate
- decrease in body movement (psychomotor retardation)
- decrease in thought processes
- sullenness, bitterness, anger, resentment
- anxiety
- hypochondriasis
- sense of dread, and particularly dread of death
- melancholia
- attention turned completely inward
- paralysis of the will
- belief that morning is the worst part of the day
- decrease in appetite or increase in appetite (usually decrease)
- loss of weight or increase in weight (usually loss)
- coldness of extremities
- insomnia (inability to sleep)
- difficulty staying asleep
- increase in sleep (occasionally)
- decrease in sex drive
- dysmenorrhea (menstrual irregularities)
- amenorrhea (the menstrual cycle stops temporarily)
- hot flashes
- suicidal thinking
- painful thinking
- false guilt or authentic guilt
- dejected or discouraged appearance
- frequent crying
- unkempt or slovenly appearance
- withdrawal
- loss of sense of humor
- living in the past; the future seems bleak
- belief that life is not worth living
- introspection and introversion
- physical symptoms: tension headaches, rapid heartbeat, infections, gastrointestinal disturbances
- feelings of unreality or feelings that one is leaving the body (depersonalization)
- feelings of being unloved and mistreated
- remorse
- difficulty remembering joys of the past
- lack of motivation, initiative, or spontaneity
- halting and uncertain speech
- neckache
- backache

- dryness of mouth
- limp handshake
- craving for love from others
- expectations of rejection
- feelings of isolation
- clinging behavior
- defenses of denial, displacement, introjection, projection, and somatization
- desire to conceal aggression
- feelings of being a "super person" that occur prior to the fall into depression as a manic defense against becoming aware of one's low self-worth
- possibility of paranoia; becoming convinced others are angry at him, even though they aren't; projecting anger onto them much as a slide projector projects a slide onto a screen
- masochism—seeking painful experiences and the security of familiar masochistic patterns
- no enjoyment in recreation
- behavior that causes one to become the object of the anger of other family members

THE SOURCES OF DEPRESSION

What causes depression? A number of internal and external factors can precipitate an experience of severe depression.

Internal Factors (Factors That Are Largely Under Our Control)

In counseling, we often hear the statement, "It's in my genes. Depression is just a part of my family tree." That is nonsense. We may inherit certain symptomatic ways our bodies manifest depression (say, a tendency to poor digestion or irregular menstrual periods), but we cannot inherit depression. Most human depression is caused by the individual's own attitude and behavior and is usually rooted in the way that person deals with anger and guilt.

Other emotional factors that dispose a person toward depression include low self-esteem (feelings of inferiority), loneliness (lack of intimacy with other people), and lack of intimacy with God. It should be noted, however, that even these emotional issues often come packaged with anger and guilt: "I can't forgive myself for the mistake I made." "It's so unfair that I don't have any friends." "I can't forgive God for making an unlovely, unworthy person like me." When we make constructive changes in our thinking and our behavior, depression is usually alleviated.

The fact that we must bear much of the responsibility for our own depression is hard for many people to accept. It's so much easier to blame our parents, our spouses, our bosses, our circumstances, some medical disorder, God, or "bad genes." Though it's true that genetic factors can make some people slightly more susceptible to clinical depression because of depletion of a chemical neurotransmitter called *norepinephrine* (or *noradrenaline*) in the brain, that is only one contributing factor out of many in a case of depression. Many people with norepinephrine imbalances and significant life stresses nevertheless manage to avoid clinical depression. Why? Because they make healthy

THE COMPLETE LIFE ENCYCLOPEDIA

choices in regard to the handling of anger toward life's problems. They choose not to cling to their anger or dwell on their problems.

There are many contributing factors that, taken together, result in depression. Genetics and brain chemistry are relatively minor factors. The level of stress we face is a somewhat larger factor. In many cases, stresses and painful events will pile up in a single period of one's life—for example, a death in the family, a job loss, and a serious illness all within a three-week period. For many people, this would be too much stress at one time, and a person's mental and emotional circuits could overload, resulting in depression. But for most of us, the greatest determinant of whether or not we will develop major depression is not brain chemistry or genetic history or external stress factors; the single most important factor is the choice we make in responding to anger. Depression is a condition that—at least in the early stages—is largely ours to control. To do so, we need two things: (1) insight into how depression works, and (2) the will and desire to make the choices that lead to joy and peace.

> ■
>
> *The single most important factor in whether or not you will develop major depression is the choice you make in responding to anger.*
>
> ■

External Factors (Factors That Are Largely Beyond Our Control)

Now that we have established that the greater proportion of the issue of depression is usually within us and under our control, let's examine some of the external factors that we are often called upon to respond to. These are factors we cannot control. We can, however, to a large degree, control the way we respond to these factors.

Research suggests that the vast majority of depressions are precipitated by life stresses. Notice, we said "precipitated by," not "caused by." A stressful event precipitates or triggers a response. Whether we choose to respond in a healthy way or in an unhealthy way is usually within our control (unless, of course, the stress is so massive and traumatic that the mind is completely overloaded and overwhelmed, a rare situation). The following are some of the precipitating events that often trigger unhealthy responses in people, leading to severe depression:

A major loss. A death, a divorce, a lost job or promotion, a financial reversal, a health problem, a disaster (such as a major fire), an accident—these are examples of losses that often trigger an episode of depression.

A major life change. From time to time, we all undergo changes and situational problems that make us feel anxious and depressed. Usually, we cope with the problem and resolve it before it develops into a clinical depression. But when an emotionally healthy person undergoes a stressful life change and responds by becoming anxious or depressed, that person is said to be undergoing an adjustment reaction. Major life changes are related to losses. A change of residence, for example, may reflect losses of a familiar lifestyle in familiar surroundings, with familiar friends and family members nearby; this is why children in families that frequently move (such as military families) are more susceptible to depression than other children.

Different changes and stress factors impact our lives in different ways. (For a list of different stress factors and an appraisal of how these factors can affect our lives and emotions, see the Holmes-Rahe Social Readjustment Rating Scale in the article on STRESS.)

A trauma to our self-image. An emotionally traumatic event can often be devastating to our self-image and can precipitate depression. Examples of such events: the breakup of a romance or a marriage can cause us to feel rejected and unworthy. The loss of a job or a demotion can make us feel unvalued and incompetent.

Some situations that undermine our self-esteem are self-inflicted and the result of sin. We may see ourselves as people of integrity and good moral behavior until we have an extramarital affair or cheat someone in a business deal. At that moment, we ought to feel defiled and unworthy, and our self-esteem should be diminished until we have repented, made amends, and made sure (by placing ourselves in an accountable relationship) that we will not do it again.

Sometimes a Christian comes into the clinic for treatment of depression and says, "I don't know why I'm depressed. My business is going well, my spouse and I aren't engaged in any conflict, my kids are doing well at home and at school, my health is fine—and yet I've been depressed for two months." We then ask, "What have you been doing these past two months that might be making you depressed?" At this, the client will often get a surprised "how-did-you-read-my-mind" sort of look and say (guiltily), "Well, the truth is . . . I have sorta been having, like, well, an affair, you know, but gee, I didn't think something like that could have anything to do with depression . . . could it?"

Indeed it could, and it often does. But after confessing and repenting of sin, and receiving God's forgiveness and forgiving oneself, the depression usually goes away.

Distorted perspective on life. This is actually a combination of external and internal factors. We live in an affluent and increasingly decadent society filled with many pressures and temptations. (That's the external factor.) It is then easy for Christians to become focused on wrong values, and look at the world with a distorted perspective. (That's the internal factor.) We look at another person's wealth or power or sexual adventurism, and we begin to envy that person and resent our own way of life. In Psalm 73:1–3, Asaph describes the depression he suffered because of a distorted perspective on the world around him: "Truly God is good to Israel, to such as are pure in heart. But as for me, my feet had almost stumbled; my steps had nearly slipped. For I was envious of the boastful, when I saw the prosperity of the wicked." Perhaps you can identify with those words. Your feet are close to stumbling, your steps are slipping near the precipice of envy, anger, and depression as you see the "lifestyle of the rich and infamous" all around you. That distorted perspective is a trick of Satan, who wants us to invest our lives in things that offer temporary excitement but that do not last and do not satisfy. As we pointed out earlier in this article, the richest people in our society are also, statistically, the most depression-prone. If we want to avoid depression, we must begin by having our spiritual priorities straight.

Disordered priorities. There is a hierarchy of godly priorities that, if we observe them, will lead us to greater emotional health. If we ignore them, we open ourselves up to many kinds of emotional and relational problems, including severe depression.

Wrong priorities. God has ordained a healthy hierarchy of priorities. If we get these priorities out of order, then we set ourselves up for major emotional and relational problems. That hierarchy of priorities is:

1. Love God.
2. Love your spouse.
3. Love your children.
4. Love your family of origin (parents, siblings).
5. Love fellow Christians.
6. Love your neighbor.

216

When we start rearranging these priorities, it is easy to see the problems that result. For example, if, as an adult, you place your parents' needs and demands above the needs of your own spouse and children, then you have failed to say goodbye to your family of origin, you remain enmeshed in that family in an unhealthy way, and you deny your own family the support and nurture they need and deserve. If you place the needs of your fellow Christians over the needs of your own family, the result is neglect and passive abuse of your own family (as many workaholic pastors and church volunteers have found when they neglected their families to "serve the Lord"). If you place the demands of your family above your need to maintain a healthy intimacy with God, you ultimately harm yourself *and* your family. When these disordered priorities produce harm in your relationships and your emotions, the result is often serious depression.

Satanic attack. One external factor that Christians often ignore (to their own peril) is satanic attack. Though it is dangerous to be obsessed with thoughts of demonic powers, we should be aware that, as 1 Peter 5:8 tells us, Satan walks about like a roaring lion, seeking whom he may devour. One satanic strategy for immobilizing Christians is to paralyze them with depression. But we are not powerless against Satan. We have the indwelling power of the Holy Spirit to draw upon. If we will confess our sins, bringing our hidden issues and emotions out into the open, God will defend us against satanic attack, and Satan will no longer be able to get at us through that particular chink in our armor.

RECOVERY AND PREVENTION

Now that you have gained some insight into the nature and sources of depression, you can put that insight to work, not only to help you recover but to help you to avoid future episodes of depression. Depression is both treatable and preventable. The following principles will help you with your two primary objectives: getting well and staying well.

1. Accept responsibility for your depression and your recovery. Recognize that the most important factors that affect your depression—your attitude, your anger, your thinking—are under your control. Seek God's help in taking over the reins of your emotions.

2. Commit yourself to thanking and praising Jesus Christ every day. What does this have to do with treating depression? Everything! A daily habit of worship, beginning the moment you rise in the morning, is a great way to set your attitude choice for the rest of the day. We suggest you wake up and thank God for another day in which to enjoy your life, your relationships, and the world God has made. Ask God to help you bring honor to Him by doing something positive for another person (spouse, children, boss, employees, neighbors, strangers, anyone). Pray for joy, peace, self-control, wisdom, and the grace to forgive yourself and others throughout the day.

3. Take time to meditate on God's Word. The human brain is much like a computer. Computers, being made out of silicon chips, are referred to as "hardware," and the programs that run on them are called "software." The human brain, being composed of water and organic material, is sometimes referred to as "wetware." Computers (the hardware type) function on the GIGO principle—"Garbage In, Garbage Out." A com-

■

Though external stress factors can precipitate an episode of severe depression, none of them has to bring on depression. We have a choice as to how we will respond to the problems—and even the traumas—that come our way.

■

puter can only generate output based on the input it receives. Human computers (the wetware type) also function on the GIGO principle.

What kind of input has your brain received? One of the reasons people get depressed is that the wetware computer between their ears has been fed too much garbage, including such messages as: "You are hopeless," "You can't do anything right," "Life will never get better; it's all downhill from here." And then there is the "garbage" of painful memories, feelings of shame, and feelings of anger. This bad programming from the past affects the performance of our wetware computer today, and it leads to self-defeating behavior. It causes us to fall into worry, painful thinking, self-condemnation, and anger. It can even cause us to question our relationship with God.

If you are to get well and stay well, you must make a choice to reprogram that wetware computer of yours so that it begins to think God's way. You must make sure that there is no more "garbage in" if you want to stop the "garbage out" of depression. How do you do that? By regular meditation on God's Word. The Bible gives us a new GIGO—"Goodness In, Goodness Out."

That is bad programming. That is garbage. That is untruth. And, if you are depressed, it is a large part of your problem.

In Romans 12:2, Paul encourages us to be transformed by the renewing of our minds. We renew our minds every day when we breathe in God's goodness by meditating on His Word. This renewal must take place on a daily basis so that the old, bad, "garbage" programming in our brains can be overwritten by new, liberating, positive programming straight from God. As Jesus said, we do not live by bread alone, "but by every word that proceeds from the mouth of God" (Matt. 4:4). That is what we must do: feed on the goodness of God, and let His Word be our source of input from now on.

4. Monitor your thinking. This is another way you can help maintain good programming in the computer between your ears. Critical thinking, angry thinking, resentful thinking, painful thinking, gloomy thinking—all of these negative forms of thinking serve only to reinforce your depression. If you change your thinking, you can begin to change your mood. And the Bible tells us that we can choose what we will think about. "Finally, brethren," says Philippians 4:8, "whatever things are true, whatever things are noble, whatever things are just, whatever things are pure, whatever things are lovely, whatever things are of good report, if there is any virtue and if there is anything praiseworthy—meditate on these things." These words are God's stamp of approval on good mental health and on the power of positive thinking.

5. Purge anger daily. Anger is an industrial-strength toxic sludge. It has to be flushed out of your system daily, or it will build up corrosive deposits on your soul. That's why Ephesians 4:26 counsels us to purge the anger out of our systems on a daily basis: "'Be angry, and do not sin': do not let the sun go down on your wrath.'" Anger that is not purged is soon turned inward, where it becomes depression. No emotion is more deadly and hazardous to our emotional, spiritual, and, yes, even our physical health than the emotion of anger.

6. Don't seek revenge. Many depressed individuals use their depression to get even with family members and manipulate others. Their depression settles like a dark cloud over the whole house, causing everyone in the family to feel bad. By moping and inflicting their moods on everyone else, depressed people sometimes try to get attention, or they may just try to make everyone else as miserable as they are. It often works—but the resulting misery only elevates levels of conflict and anger, creating increased pain for everyone including the depressed individual. There are certainly many healthier,

THE COMPLETE LIFE ENCYCLOPEDIA

more honest, more open ways for people to get what they want—and without creating greater guilt for themselves or others.

7. Develop true intimacy with family and friends. Spend time with your children. Spend time alone with your spouse. Don't neglect relationships with your parents, siblings, and close friends. Resolve conflicts as soon as possible—but make sure they are truly resolved, not just swept under the rug. True intimacy with your family and friends is a key factor in preventing depression, since depression is often precipitated by problems and conflicts in our most important relationships.

Also, make sure you develop close fellowship and friendship with other Christians. We have met very few people who are involved in close Christian relationships who are also depressed. Men need the fellowship of other Christian men; women need the fellowship of other Christian women. Couples and singles all need the celebration, growth, accountability, and just plain fun that comes from being involved in a small group Bible study fellowship or "house church." We need each other in the Body of Christ. Isolation breeds depression; fellowship and close friendship create an environment in which depression simply cannot thrive.

8. Avoid overintrospection and an overpreoccupation with self. Insight and reflection are tremendous tools in combatting emotional problems, but introspection can get out of hand and actually increase the level of depression you are trying to heal. Depressed individuals tend to be overly introspective anyway, and this obsessive rumination often leads to distorted perceptions, exaggerated impressions of your problems, and self-reinforcing negative thinking. Depression-prone people should not spend hours in contemplation of their issues, because they have a built-in tendency to be overly critical and hard on themselves, and they easily lose objectivity. This tendency only reinforces the depression. If you must spend time being introspective, try to limit your introspection to a certain period of the day—and to no more than half an hour. When introspective thoughts arise outside of your scheduled time for introspection, just set those thoughts aside and get on with the business of living.

9. Make constructive changes in your behavior. Your thinking and your behavior are mutually reinforcing. You do what you do because you feel the way you feel and you feel the way you feel because you do what you do. This produces a vicious cycle of self-defeating emotions producing self-defeating actions, actions producing emotions, emotions producing actions, on and on and on. You need to interrupt this cycle in order to overcome your depression. Since it is much easier to change the way you behave than it is to change the way you feel, it is your behavior that you need to focus on the most.

For example, if you are depressed in part because your romantic feelings for your mate have diminished, you can either choose to sit and analyze your feelings and try to produce affectionate emotions within yourself (which, obviously, would not be very productive) or choose to perform some loving, affectionate acts for your mate—giving flowers, bringing your mate breakfast in bed, writing an affectionate and encouraging note. When you choose to love your mate through your behavior, the feelings will follow.

10. Change your self-talk. We all talk to ourselves, whether we know it or not. Though people can speak with their mouths at a rate of 150 to 200 words per minute, we carry on an inner dialogue with ourselves at an astounding rate of about 1,300 words per minute! This inner dialogue is called self-talk. In our self-talk, of course, we

Many people have trouble getting in touch with their angry feelings. It is not uncommon for a patient to say, "What anger? I'm not angry," even though his fists are clenched and his teeth are grinding together. Seek God's help in recognizing, admitting, and purging the poison of anger.

don't actually use words most of the time. We "talk" to ourselves in a high-velocity thoughtstream of images, concepts, and ideas, which, when we want to communicate with another fast-thinking human being, we convert to these slow-moving symbols we call words.

As you monitor your thinking, become aware of the times you think critically, the times you blame yourself, the times you dwell on failures, flaws, and limitations. Listen for the negative voices in your thoughtstream: "I don't deserve to be happy." "I can't hope for more than a minimum wage job." "I'll never be able to change." "I always mess things up." Every time you catch one of those voices in the act of dragging you down, make a conscious decision to refocus your thinking onto the positive aspects of your character, your accomplishments, your growth and progress, and, most of all, your position as a child of God.

(For a more extensive discussion of positive self-talk techniques, see SELF-TALK.)

11. Practice assertiveness. Depression often results when we feel our needs go unmet, other people walk all over us, we can't get what we want, and life has steamrollered us. In other words, depression is often the result of allowing ourselves to be hurt and exploited because we are nonassertive. Consciously, we think, "It's wrong to be aggressive. I don't want to be pushy. I don't want to inconvenience anyone. I don't want people to get annoyed with me." But subconsciously, the thinking goes like this: "My needs aren't important. My feelings don't matter. I'm a big nothing."

When we talk to ourselves through our thinking, we may use either a positive, encouraging "self-talk" tone of voice or a negative, critical tone. The depressed person tends to self-talk very critically, and this condemnation fuels depression. To lift yourself out of your depression, you will need to become aware of your self-talk, and make adjustments to refocus your self-talk into a positive mode.

Though it is wrong to be aggressive and to run over and exploit other people, it is equally wrong and extremely self-defeating to be passive. People who are passive and nonassertive eventually internalize their resentment over being ignored and having their needs go unmet. This internalized resentment becomes depression.

The healthy, balanced approach to meeting the needs and desires in life is to be assertive, to state your convictions and wants in a firm but caring way. (For a more comprehensive discussion of the subject, see ASSERTIVENESS.)

12. Get involved in a daily routine that brings joy and satisfaction to your life. One source of depression is the feeling that your life is disordered and chaotic. Having a daily routine gives order and structure to life. As you choose your daily routine, be careful not to "overbook" yourself. Maintain reasonable expectations of what you can get done in a day. Some suggestions for a healthy routine:

- Devote adequate attention to your biggest time expenditure, earning a living, but avoid the trap of workaholism. Your family needs you much more than they need the things you can buy them.
- Set aside time for prayer and meditation, so that you can maintain a close relationship with God.

Ask God for the gift of laughter.

- Make time for relationship-building with your spouse, including time for fun, communication, and a healthy sex life.
- Make time for relationship-building and training of your children, including time for play, problem solving, family devotions, and involvement in their school activities.

220

• Set aside time for relaxation, entertainment, hobbies, interests, and exercise, which are essential to good physical and mental health.

13. Accept your humanness. When you make mistakes, ask God's forgiveness and forgive yourself. Don't dwell on the mistakes or try to punish yourself. God is more gracious and accepting of ourselves than we are. He knows our imperfections, and He loves us anyway. As we learn to have more of God's perspective on our lives, we will learn to give ourselves more room to be human, more room to make mistakes and learn from them. Those who demand perfection of themselves set themselves up to be disappointed—and they set themselves up for depression.

14. Learn to laugh. Laughter is a natural healer. It relaxes us, and the brain chemicals called endorphins which are released during laughter actually help to improve our mood and decrease our tendency toward depression.

You may ask, "Well, how can I laugh when I'm so depressed?"

First, ask God for the gift of laughter. Brennan Manning, in his book *The Ragamuffin Gospel,* says, "Don't force prayer. Simply relax in the presence of [God] . . . and ask for a touch of folly" (Multnomah, 1985). Laughter is God's gift to us to help us restore a more balanced and positive perspective on life, and even on life's problems and stresses.

Second, learn to laugh at yourself and your problems. Once you begin to accept your own human imperfections, you begin to see how silly it was to be so unrealistically perfectionistic. Once you see how much you were expecting yourself to accomplish and how hopelessly unreasonable your expectations were, you realize how ridiculous it was to set your sights so unbelievably high. Laugh at it, knowing that you'll get it all done eventually, and even if you don't, the sun will still come up in the morning.

Third, seek out releases and escapes that let you laugh. Rent an outrageous comedy from the video store. Watch stand-up comedy on TV. Or if family situation comedy is more your speed, look for reruns of *The Andy Griffith Show* or *The Dick Van Dyke Show* on cable.

Fourth, spend time with friends who make you laugh. Call that old college roommate who always knew how to break you up. Join a small group Bible study where the members know how to have fun and laughter as well as a challenging walk through the Word.

15. Seek professional help. Many people are reluctant to seek appropriate help for their emotional problems. But Christ Himself has said that those who are sick need a physi-

---

Positive Self-Talk

Here are some suggested self-talk statements, derived from positive experience and from Scripture, which you can repeat to yourself whenever negative thoughts arise:

• "God is taking care of me and meeting my needs."
• "I keep score of the good things in my life."
• "I choose to forgive and get on with my life."
• "I'm getting the job done, one task at a time."
• "I am moving toward my goals."
• "I face up to my feelings."
• "My feelings are okay, and I'm getting better."
• "Of course I am important, and my feelings matter."
• "I am loved with an everlasting love" (see Jeremiah 31:3).
• "I have abundant life" (see John 10:10).
• "I am free of shame and condemnation" (see Romans 8:1).
• "I am being changed and conformed to the image of Christ" (see Romans 8:28–29; Philippians 1:6).
• "I am a new creation" (see 2 Corinthians 5:17).
• "I am holy and without blame before God" (see Ephesians 1:4).
• "I am forgiven; all my sins are washed away" (see Ephesians 1:7).
• "I am God's workmanship" (see Ephesians 2:10).
• "I can do all things through Christ" (see Philippians 4:13).
• "I am victorious" (see Revelation 21:7).

---

cian. Even though God used miracles to perform many healings, He also used doctors—and He continues to do so today. There are a number of physical conditions that sometimes contribute to depression, and these medical problems require medical treatment so that the emotional problem can be alleviated. Medical conditions that sometimes contribute to depression include hypothyroidism, hypoglycemia, biogenic amine imbalance, endocrine imbalance, electrolyte disturbances, viral infections, and fatigue.

In many cases, the emotional healing process needs a medical boost. Depression causes imbalances in brain chemicals (called neurotransmitters), and these imbalances fuel and reinforce the depression. This can cause an emotional spiral-down effect as the emotions and the brain chemicals continue to reinforce each other in your brain. Careful use of antidepressant medications can be helpful in restoring the balance of neurotransmitters so that the cycle of depression can be interrupted and you can regain a healthy perspective on life.

In some cases of severe depression, a psychiatrist will recommend that a person be hospitalized so that he or she can:

- receive intensive psychotherapy;
- be continually monitored and medically treated;
- be removed from a stressful environment;
- be protected from suicide attempts; and
- experience a helpful, friendly atmosphere.

A Note on Depression Treatments

At the Minirth Meier New Life Clinics, our inpatient programs never use electroconvulsive ("shock") therapy or addictive medications. Tricyclic antidepressants, such as Tofranil, Elavil, and Sinequan, are nonaddicting and are our medications of choice in treating clinical depression.

Hospitalization is generally less expensive to the patient than prolonged outpatient psychotherapy because hospitalization is generally covered by insurance. Since hospital care is more intensive, a person is often able to return to full functioning performance more rapidly when treated in the hospital than when treated in an outpatient environment.

16. *Work all your strategies simultaneously.* Remember: there are no simple, single-cause answers to depression. Anger, of course, is the root cause of most depression, but the anger problem can be attacked in many ways: by reducing your isolation and loneliness, changing your self-talk, spending time with God, becoming more assertive, and learning to laugh. Though there is no single solution to depression, we believe that there can be no ultimate solution without faith in Jesus Christ and applying the principles of God's Word to everyday living.

Divorce

Ellie doesn't believe in divorce. She doesn't want a divorce. She has grown up thinking that divorce is unthinkable.

But Ellie is divorced.

Ellie's forty-two-year-old husband, David, came home one day and told her he had decided he didn't want to be married to her anymore. He had been carrying on an affair with a twenty-four-year-old secretary at the office, and now he wanted to "legitimize" that relationship by divorcing Ellie and marrying the secretary. No matter what Ellie said, no matter how she pleaded, David had a glib (and completely self-deceived) rationalization for everything.

"I'm not going for marriage counseling," he said. "I don't need counseling, I just need a divorce. Look, I know this is hard for you to see right now, but it's really the best for everybody. I'll have what I want, you and the kids will be taken care of, and the kids are nine and twelve—they're practically teenagers—so they're old enough to handle this without being emotionally scarred. You don't want to be married to someone who doesn't love you anymore. After the divorce, you can go find someone who will be better for you than me. After you've had a chance to think about it, you'll see that this is going to work out just fine."

But things were anything but "just fine." Years later, the dust of their marriage had still not settled. Like nuclear fallout, it just kept coming down. David's second marriage ended in divorce, and his children grew up angry with him, blaming him for the destruction of their family. As a result of his two divorces, David was eventually forced to go bankrupt. Both of the children became chronically depressed, and their grades suffered. The daughter, who was twelve at the time of the divorce, went "boy-crazy" in her early teens, looking for a replacement for her father's absent love; she became pregnant at age fifteen. The son, who was nine at the time of the divorce, attempted suicide at age fourteen. Ellie experienced isolation and loneliness in her church, because fellow Christians condemned her for a divorce she never wanted in the first place.

"This has been the worst ordeal of my life," Ellie says today. "I thought I went through a lot of pain when I was a teenager and my mother died of cancer. But that was nothing like this legal, financial, emotional nightmare I'm going through right now. My children's lives have been ruined, and my own life is spinning out of control. Until you've been through it, you have no idea what it's like."

DIVORCE AND THE BIBLE

Disagreement exists among well-informed, well-intentioned Christians as to how the Bible views divorce. A favorite verse among those who take a hard-line position against divorce is Malachi 2:16: "For the LORD God of Israel says that He hates divorce." But why does God hate divorce? Because He loves people, and He understands—as Ellie has found out—that divorce brings pain and suffering into people's lives. Though our loving God has given to human beings the power of free will, the power to make painful mistakes, He always seeks to warn us and help us to avoid those mistakes.

Moreover, God is gracious. After we have made our mistakes, He wants to heal us from the hurt of those mistakes. He offers forgiveness for sin. Though He hates divorce, He loves and forgives divorced people.

Some Bible scholars feel that the Bible offers no grounds that justify divorce. Other Bible scholars, after examining the Scriptures, conclude that there are justifiable grounds for divorce and remarriage. Matthew 19:1–9 seems to suggest that divorce may be

If you or someone close to you is contemplating divorce, we encourage you to study these Scripture passages for yourself. Develop your own personal perspective on divorce, derived from an intellectually honest study of God's Word.

permitted (but is clearly not commanded) in the case of a spouse's adultery. In verse 9, Jesus says, "And I say to you, whoever divorces his wife, except for sexual immorality, and marries another, commits adultery; and whoever marries her who is divorced commits adultery." (A parallel passage in Mark 10:1–12 omits the "adultery escape clause.") In 1 Corinthians 7:12–15, Paul encourages new believers who are married to nonbelievers to remain married, if possible, but if the nonbeliever insists on dissolving the marriage, the Christian partner in that marriage is "not under bondage" to remain married.

THE FAR-REACHING EFFECTS OF DIVORCE

We tend to think of divorce as the act of dissolving a marriage. But when a marriage breaks up, the effects can be more far-reaching than either partner ever imagined.

Broken Relationships

People are often surprised to discover that when they divorce their spouses, they end up divorcing their friends as well. With the best of intentions, people will promise you, "Your divorce won't change anything; we'll still be friends with both of you." But it's difficult for friendships to continue as they once did. Since married couples generally tend to have other married couples for friends, divorce creates awkward, asymmetrical situations. Many people, feeling they can't be "true" friends to both parties, often choose one over the other—or they back off from both.

Relationships in the church are often strained, though progress in this area is being made in many churches. Some are offering divorce-recovery support groups, to help divorced people cope with the traumatic losses.

Finances

After a divorce, the standard of living for both parties changes drastically. Husbands are often responsible for alimony and child-support payments. Wives find themselves returning to work outside the home, often for the first time in years and frequently at a reduced salary because they have been out of the job market for so long. Meanwhile, someone must pay childcare expenses and the doubled expenses of maintaining separate households. And all of this is in addition to attorneys' fees for obtaining the divorce.

Physical-Emotional Health

In the May–June 1990 issue of *Physician* magazine, an article titled "Divorce, a Hazard to Your Health?" by Susan Larson and David Larson, M.D., M.S.P.H., sets forth some staggering statistics about the health risks of divorce. "In light of current research," they write, "the Surgeon General might also consider warning married couples about the potential health and behavioral risks of divorce. Research studies show that the process of marital breakup and divorce puts people at much higher risk for both psychiatric and physical disease—even cancer."

They cited research that seems to indicate:

- Every type of terminal cancer strikes divorced individuals more frequently than it does married people.
- Premature death rates from a number of diseases are significantly higher for divorced men and women compared to married persons of the same sex and age.
- Divorce is tremendously stressful, and this stress can lower the immune system's ability to defend against physical illness.

The change in relationships and support systems can bring about intense feelings of loneliness, rejection, and isolation, which are often cited as emotional causes for medical problems. And the bitterness and anger that accompanies so many divorces can also destroy people's ability to live happily. If allowed to fester, they can eventually result in depression and rob people of the physical and emotional energy needed to make new lives for themselves.

The Effect of Divorce on the Wife

If there are children involved, the wife is usually awarded custody of the children, and she takes on a new role: single parent. She must become the sole authority figure in a new family unit, without Dad's help.

Her relationship with her husband (now ex-husband) is not over. It is merely changed. Now, it is a business relationship, and for years to come, she must deal with having to transact business—primarily visitation and child support business—with the man who used to be her marriage partner. This new relationship is frequently complicated by the fact that the man she must transact business with is now, in an emotional sense, her adversary.

The wife's responsibilities as a single parent are magnified. She must find ways to make fewer dollars go farther than before. She is now charged with all the household decisions and duties (many of which may have been Dad's responsibility in the past) such as bill-paying, home maintenance, and automotive repair. She may have imagined a simpler life after the divorce, but she has found instead that life has only become more stressful and complicated than ever.

She now has sole responsibility for getting the children to and from school, for taking care of them when they are sick, for getting them to the doctor and dentist, for meal preparation and homework assistance—all of this is on top of a full-time job. She does it all without anyone at home to rely on for support and encouragement.

The emotions of this newfound role can be intense, as Ellie relates. "I'm feeling so afraid," she says. "I feel trapped by all these responsibilities. At one point, after David left, I thought, I'll make the most of it. At least I have my independence back. But now I think, What independence? I'm in a straitjacket! I have no time for a life to myself. I'm going in the hole financially. I'm exhausted all the time. And my friends have turned away from me. This isn't independence. This is a prison!"

The Effect of Divorce on the Husband

In most cases, while his ex-wife and his kids continue living together, often in the same house as before, the father must adjust to an entirely new life in a new, often more modest living space (usually an apartment). He has no one to come home to. His roles as provider, helper, and counselor—roles that have largely defined his identity and shaped his self-esteem—have been removed. Disoriented, he must now carve out a new image of who he is, of what gives him his sense of worth.

He is no longer the primary guide and trailblazer for his children. He is no longer home to tuck his kids into bed or fix their flat bicycle tires or to drive his kids to soccer practice or dance class. If he wants to teach his children how to shoot baskets or build a campfire, he will have to make time for it on alternating weekends, when he has visitation with his kids. No wonder so many divorced fathers become known as "Disneyland dads."

The Effect of Divorce on the Children

The universal experience of every child whose parents get divorced is grief. Children of divorce experience the loss of a balanced parental unit as well as the daily support of a parent. They experience a loss of identity as their sense of security, financial identity and future, lifestyle, and core relationships change. Their fundamental security base is gone. The family has been their entire world, and now that world is crumbling beneath their feet.

Many children of divorce develop a number of troubling fears, including the fear of abandonment. They see Mom or Dad exiting the picture, and they wonder, "If a parent can be expelled from the family, what about me? Couldn't this happen to me too?" When the unity and integrity of their family-world begins to break apart, their own sense of personal safety is threatened.

Children often have a tendency to blame themselves for their parents' divorce. They cannot understand the complexities of their parents' differing values, attitudes, and personalities. To children, particularly small children, parents are godlike beings who do not make mistakes. So if the parents can no longer live together, the child reasons, "It cannot be the fault of these godlike beings. It must be my fault." Children tend to use self-referential thinking, an assumption that everything that happens is somehow related to them or caused by them. The younger the child, the stronger the tendency to blame himself or herself for external events.

Children of divorce have to deal with issues of divided loyalty. They see their parents locked in combat with each other, often demanding that the children take sides. The children, however, love both parents. How can I be loyal to one, they wonder, without being disloyal to the other? This emotional conflict can be devastating to a child.

Another emotional issue children have to deal with in divorce is reconciliation fantasies, in which the children refuse to accept the divorce and instead cling to the belief that "sometime, somehow, Mom and Dad will get back together and we'll be a family again." Children will often act out this fantasy through behavior designed to bring the parents together again. By getting into fights at school, by letting studies slide, or through other forms of disrupting behavior, they try to get both parents to focus on their behavioral problems. They reason (often at an unconscious level) that by doing so, their parents will be reunited.

The old school of thought was that divorce would affect children for a while but that they would "get over it." More and more research seems to indicate that divorce is, in fact, devastating to children. Childhood is a time when basic personality is being formed, when basic identity is being built, when a child's sense of security and self-esteem is being shaped. Because the parents are dealing with their own grown-up issues and trying to adjust to their own sense of loss, they often fail to give sufficient nurturing and attention to their children. Parents may not tune in to their children's feelings of loneliness, isolation, fear, abandonment, anger, guilt, and self-blame. So these children are left to deal with their feelings all alone.

The issues and emotions children experience during divorce have profound, lifelong effects, even if the divorce is "amicable" and "civilized." Children may adopt a peace-at-any-price style of relating, which sets them up for future problems with codependency. Divorce alters the way children perceive the world and affects their ability to trust others and develop close relationships. The traumatic effects of divorce follow children throughout their lives, which is why we see so many adult children of divorce support groups springing up these days: grown men and women are continuing to deal with the residual pain they experienced as children when their parents split up.

PREVENTING DIVORCE, HEALING YOUR MARRIAGE

Recognizing the far-reaching effects of divorce on your most important relationship should motivate you to explore every possible avenue to heal the marriage. Here is a ten-step plan for preventing divorce:

1. Commit yourself to Christ. Commitment to Christ is the first step in committing yourself to the healing of your marriage. The law of Christ is the law of unconditional love. If you are truly obedient to Jesus Christ and His commands, you will unconditionally love the person you have married, and you will do the things that lead to healing and strengthening the marriage.

2. Commit yourself to the marriage. Approach marriage with the attitude, "What can I give?" rather than "What can I get?" If you focus on what you can get, you will weaken your commitment to the marriage. Many couples enter into marriage feeling that if it doesn't work out, if their wants and needs are not met, they'll just abandon ship. God wants you to look on marriage as a covenant. Though there will be some failure in any marriage relationship, you are still expected to maintain that covenant. A couple must determine not to allow any obstacle to hinder or discourage them from making positive changes in their marriage. Each must be willing to work, to accept the pain of growth, and to change individually for the good of the relationship. The endurance and strengthening of the marriage must be top priority.

3. Honestly examine issues and personality differences. The best time to do so, of course, is before the marriage takes place. If you discover areas of incompatibility in time to prevent the marriage from taking place, you can avert the pain of divorce that may well come later. A number of psychological tests are available that can be used to reveal potential blind spots. People sometimes see their future mates as being perfect. But after they say, "I do," the blinders come off, reality sets in, faults begin to appear, and they become disillusioned. Soon they are headed for divorce court. Premarital counseling is valuable in avoiding some of these potential pitfalls.

If, however, you are already a year or ten years or twenty years too late for premarital counseling, you can still examine issues and personality differences in the marriage and seek to resolve them, understand them, and accommodate them. Many personality and incompatibility issues that seem so destructive at first can be reframed and reinterpreted during marriage counseling so that instead of seeing your mate's differences and contrasts as evidence of incompatibility, you can see them as traits that complement and complete what is lacking in your own personality. You will probably need professional counseling, however, in order to gain the needed insight into these issues and personality differences.

4. Learn to enjoy marriage. Marriage is a wonderful thing. In our society we've been deceived into thinking that marriage is dull, boring, and confining. It's human nature to focus on the negative. In marriage we also tend to focus on the comparatively few points of disagreement rather than on all the many areas we have in common and can enjoy with each other. Think about good memories, happy experiences, activities you enjoy doing together, times when you have experienced laughter and joy together. Then explore ways to recapture those experiences and rekindle the enjoyment of your marriage together.

5. Focus on behavior; avoid overdependence on feelings. Feelings are fickle. The romantic feeling we call "love" will come and go. That's normal. But if two people will focus on loving behavior—that is, if they show mutual respect, value each other's opinions, listen to each other's feelings, and treat each other with dignity—then the loving feelings will come again. Instead of worrying about feelings, focus on behavior.

6. Commit yourself to positively resolving conflict. Acknowledge your own contribution to the pain of your marriage, and commit yourself to ending the cycle of blame. Don't seek the source of your own misery in the actions of your spouse. Learn how to confront lovingly and fight fairly in your marriage. (See "Rules for Fighting Fairly" in the article on MARRIAGE.)

7. Seek to reduce the stress factors in your marriage. What kinds of factors intrude upon your marriage? Too many church commitments? School commitments? Other activities? Do you or does your spouse make too many commitments during the holidays? Are you or is your spouse a workaholic? Do you allow too little time for relaxation and refreshment in your personal life and your relationship together? Has overspending created financial stresses that need to be resolved? All of these stress factors can create marital frustration and increase the tendency of people to want to "bail out" of a stressful marriage.

8. Assess the level of sharing in your relationship. Seek to improve communication by sharing more honestly and constructively and by actively listening to your spouse. Commit yourself to meeting each other's needs through a two-sided process of give and take. What are your needs? What are your spouse's needs? More affection? More frequent sexual release? More help and support with household work? More support for your parenting role? Assess those needs, share them together, and commit yourselves to meeting them.

9. Consider the consequences of divorce. People often think that everything will be solved by a divorce. In counseling, we often see people who clearly have their hearts set on divorce and are only going through counseling to "jump through the hoop" on their way to their real goal: ending their marriages. They have not really counted the costs of divorce to their spouses, their children, their friendships, and even to themselves.

(For a more complete discussion of ways to strengthen your marriage relationship, see MARRIAGE.)

10. Renew your marriage by mutually agreeing to a renewed marriage contract. A contract is an agreement between two parties, setting forth the boundaries and responsibilities of a relationship so that both parties can succeed and move forward. You may not agree on every point in your agenda, but with a renewed marriage contract, you can agree upon the areas where you will agree to disagree and tolerate each other's feelings and priorities. A renewed marriage contract is not a quick fix to a damaged marriage relationship, but used as a complement to, and continuation of, a marriage counseling process, it can create a framework of understanding and cooperation that will enable you to heal your marriage.

SURVIVING DIVORCE

But what if—for whatever reason—divorce cannot be avoided? Or what if divorce has already taken place? "I wish I knew before my divorce what I know now," you might say, "but that doesn't help me. I need to know how to deal with life as it is right now. I need some insight into how to survive the pain and upheaval of divorce."

The pain of divorce is much like the pain of bereavement. In fact, for many people, divorce is actually worse than bereavement. However painful, death brings a sense of finality and closure, and the grief process is often infused with happy memories of the departed that help to sustain the bereaved person. But divorce—with its pain, conflict, and emotional turmoil—goes on for years. The bickerings and the legal battles are often revived years later around issues such as property rights, custody, visitation, child support, and financial settlements. Being legally divorced—as many divorced people have discovered—is not the same as being emotionally divorced.

One of the most important steps in surviving divorce is to deal with the toxic emotions that divorce stirs up. Perhaps the most toxic of them all is anger. It's only natural that you feel angry over events that have taken place in the course of your divorce. But in order to get on with your life and restore a healthy sense of balance and perspective, you need to move past your anger. If you get stuck in anger and bitterness, those hostile emotions will spill over and touch everyone close to you, including your children. (For more insight into healing yourself of bitterness and anger, see the articles on ANGER and FORGIVENESS.)

Understand, however, that forgiving does not mean being a doormat. Don't let your ex-spouse take advantage of you, especially in areas that affect the welfare of your

---

The Renewed Marriage Contract

1. An opening statement of affirmation; at least one attribute each person admires and appreciates in the other
2. A statement of the extent of each person's commitment to the marriage
3. A promise of fidelity
4. A statement of faith, embracing:
   a. each person's individual statement of faith
   b. clearly stated common ground
   c. statement of tolerance (and limits of tolerance)
5. A statement recognizing old, dysfunctional hidden agendas (such as, "You will take care of me") and a commitment to keeping all future agendas open, honest, and healthy ("We agree to be mutually supportive")
6. A sexual contract, including:
   a. recognition of difficulties or shortcomings in present sexual relations
   b. steps to improve relations and/or explore new techniques
   c. details of frequency, if frequency is an issue
7. Details of everyday life (request for romantic nights out) established through a process of give and take (be specific)

(Adapted from *Passages of Marriage* by Minirth, Newman, and Hemfelt [Thomas Nelson, 1991].)

---

children. If he or she violates your divorce decree in important areas such as child support or visitation arrangements, confront your spouse or contact your lawyer. Without spite or vengefulness, but with a respect for yourself as a person and with a sense of responsibility for your children, require that your ex-spouse keep court-ordered commitments and agreements. In the long run, it can actually be an act of "tough love" and caring to require your ex-spouse to keep commitments in a way he or she may have not done during your marriage.

Another toxic emotion that is common to the divorce experience is guilt. In all likelihood, you do bear some responsibility for the breakup of your marriage. But God does not want you to beat yourself up over those mistakes. He understands that you are a human being and that human beings make mistakes. That is why He has provided a way of cleansing for our sins and mistakes. Confess your shortcomings to God and allow Him to cleanse you, forgive your sin, and give you a new start in life. Then forgive yourself. Take the lessons you have learned from this experience and promise yourself not to make the same mistakes in the future.

Now that you are single again, accept your new status, live in the present, and focus on building a brighter future. Make time to repair your damaged emotions through prayer, reflection, reading, and meditation. Make your relationship with God your number one priority. Get involved in a Bible-teaching church and a small group Bible study.

You may also derive a great benefit from joining a support group or Bible study focused on issues of divorce, singleness, or single parenting. The purpose of such groups is not to meet new people, date, and leap into a new relationship (almost always a big mistake!), but rather to give you support, encouragement, and positive reinforcement so that you can courageously shoulder the burdens of your new life. Be wary of snatching the false security of a relationship on the rebound.

Above all, if you want to survive the divorce process—and particularly if you are a parent and want to raise emotionally healthy children—work hard to maintain a good relationship with your ex-spouse. You may say, "How can I do that? My ex is unreasonable! My ex is vicious, spiteful, vengeful, and tries to undermine me at every turn!" This is often the case in divorces. But you still must try to ease the tension and build a working relationship, particularly if there are children involved. You do this not for your ex-spouse's sake but for your children's sake, for your own sake, for your own emotional well-being.

It doesn't matter who initiated the divorce or whether the problems in the marriage were your fault or the other person's fault. That's old news. The issue that needs to be addressed today is "What can I do to make my life better now? What can I do to speed my recovery from the trauma of this divorce?" To recover, you have to move beyond blaming, beyond bitterness.

The path to forgiveness is the path to recovery.

GRIEVING YOUR MARRIAGE

How do you get to forgiveness? You must go through the process of grief. Forgiveness is the final stage in the grief process that was first mapped by Swiss psychiatrist

Elisabeth Kübler-Ross in her book *On Death and Dying.* In the years since that book was published, we have found that the grief process applies not only to the loss that is suffered when someone dies, but also to many other forms of loss, including the loss of a marriage. As we have adapted the Kübler-Ross model, there are six stages in the grief process of divorce:

1. Shock and denial. Your spouse says, "I want a divorce," and you say, "No, you can't mean that. Sure, we've got problems, but things are really not that bad. We'll get counseling. We'll work harder. We'll fix the problem. But everything's going to turn out fine in the end." But things do not turn out fine. The marriage continues to head for destruction, like a ship steaming toward a reef in the storm, yet you just can't seem to see it or acknowledge it. That is denial.

2. Anger. Once you start to realize that your spouse is serious about the divorce, the result is often anger, coupled with blaming. "It's your fault! If you weren't so stubborn, if you would just change, everything would be okay!" Anger is a defense against having to acknowledge your own responsibility in the breakdown of your marriage. Anger is an outward-projected emotion, unlike guilt, which is directed inward. Anger tosses blame like a hot potato into the lap of the other person, saying, "Our relationship is crumbling, I am in pain, and I refuse to accept the blame for this mess! I'm throwing it back at you! You are responsible! When you come to your senses, then this marriage will be fine, just like it used to be."

> **Gaining Perspective**
>
> As you reflect and meditate, and as you work on your issues through the group recovery process, seek to develop an objective perspective on the mistakes you have made in your marriage—not a perspective that says, "I'm so terrible, I was so bad, I was so stupid," but a perspective that says, "Here are the mistakes I made, and this is how I will learn and grow from those mistakes." Take responsibility for your new life and your own happiness.

3. Depression. Depression is anger turned inward—so it is not surprising that the depression stage usually follows the anger stage in the grief process. Depression usually comes intertwined with guilt—a miserable, self-condemning sense that you have failed, you have sinned, you have ruined the marriage, you have ruined your life, and you will never be happy again. The depression stage is a temporary phase in the grief process, but it can turn into true clinical depression if you get "stuck" in this stage and fail to continue working through your grief over the loss of the marriage (see DEPRESSION).

4. Bargaining (and magical thinking). In this stage, you may bargain with God, or bargain with your spouse, or bargain with friends to intercede with your spouse, or bargain with your children to let your spouse know how miserable you are. Even if the marriage was miserable, you fear change and disruption even more, so you beg, plead, and bargain to have the marriage restored. You may engage in magical thinking such as, "If I only pray hard enough or give money to the church, God will restore my marriage," or "If I just give myself a complete makeover or do something to make my mate jealous or take up an exotic new interest to make myself more fascinating, then my mate will come back to me and call off this divorce."

5. Sadness. Once you are finally able to let go of anger and bargaining, once you realize that nothing is going to save this marriage and that the divorce is really going to happen, then you settle into sadness. Sadness is the appropriate response to sad events. You deal with sadness by shedding tears. But eventually sadness ends. Unlike chronic depression, sadness comes, you live through it—and then it goes away.

6. Forgiveness, resolution, and acceptance. Once the stage of sadness has passed, you reach the culminating step in the grief process, which has been your goal from the beginning: forgiveness, resolution, and acceptance. This is what the Bible calls "the peace that passes understanding."

At this stage, you survey the ruins of your marriage and say, "This marriage is over, but I am going to be okay. I no longer blame or judge my ex-mate. I no longer condemn myself. I no longer plead with my mate or with God to restore what cannot be restored. I accept my new life, I forgive myself and my ex-mate, and I'm ready to start rebuilding."

Forgiveness is the only way to freedom from the pain of the past.

THOUGH THE MARRIAGE IS OVER, PARENTING GOES ON

When divorce cannot be avoided, it is up to the divorcing couple to make the most of a very imperfect situation. As we established earlier, divorce inevitably has negative consequences for everyone involved—and especially for the children involved. This is a tragedy. Yet the job of parenting goes on for both parents, even after the marriage has ended. Both parents have a responsibility to raise their children in as healthy and secure an environment as is possible under these circumstances.

Though the harmful effects of divorce cannot be eliminated completely from children's lives, those harmful effects can be softened if the parents are willing to make constructive changes in their attitudes and behavior toward each other and toward their children. Even after a divorce, children can grow up feeling loved and affirmed by both parents, and the damage to their self-esteem can be healed to a large degree. But in order for that to happen, both parents must attempt to understand divorce from a child's perspective.

Over and over in our counseling experiences at the Minirth Meier New Life Clinics, we see parents engaging in behavior that is extremely harmful to the emotional makeup of a child. If you are involved in a divorce and there is no hope of reconciliation, at the very least you must be sure to avoid such behavior as:

- Engaging in a vicious, destructive custody battle in which the child is used as a pawn to get even with the other parent.
- Slandering or expressing hostility toward the other parent in front of the child. For example, "The reason we're breaking up is because your father is a liar and a cheat!" Or "Your mother destroyed this marriage by her sin, and God will punish her for being unfaithful!"
- Asking the child or manipulating the child into spying and reporting back on the other parent.
- Pumping the child for information about the other parent.
- Attempting to purchase the child's loyalties through lavish gifts.
- Getting back at the other parent through the child by deliberately violating that parent's rules or wishes.

For Your Child's Sake

Here are some positive steps you can take to help overcome the negative effects of divorce in your child's life:

- Model effective communication. Talk about things in your life that you are enthusiastic about. Talk about interests you have in common with your child. Ask relationship questions: "How are you feeling? This divorce has been hard for me; how are you handling it?" Avoid questions with one-syllable answers ("yes," "no," or "fine"). Ask questions that require thought, feelings, or description: "How did it feel, scoring that goal at the soccer game?" "Tell me about your new boyfriend." "What's your science project about?"
- Tune in to the child's behavioral messages. Children often act out rather than verbalize feelings. Instead of immediately punishing or shutting off irritating behavior, "listen" to the behavior and try to discover the underlying feelings that need to be resolved.
- Be careful to validate, not discount, your child's emotions and thoughts. Even if you feel the child's thinking is inaccurate, say, "I can sure understand how you would feel that way." Help the child to feel significant, not shunted aside.
- Maintain your own parenting style, but avoid undermining or contradicting the parenting style and rules of the other parent.
- Discipline firmly and lovingly. Many parents, out of guilt over the divorce, become overindulgent. This leads to greater problems and insecurity in the child. Children interpret consistent, fair discipline as a sign of love and security.
- Stay actively involved in your child's life, even if you are the "absent" or "noncustodial" parent. Attend your child's school and sporting events. Make visitation a priority. Don't feel visitation must be overprogrammed or overscheduled; allow plenty of time for relaxing and conversing with your child.
- Avoid punishing the other parent by playing games with visitation or child support payments. If you engage in that kind of irresponsible behavior, you will only be hurting your children.
- Relate to your ex-spouse on a businesslike level. Be cordial, polite, and friendly. Keep promises and commitments. Be on time for visitation appointments. Make child support payments on time.
- Join a support group for single parents or divorced fathers. Find a source of validation and support for the issues and emotions you are experiencing. Contact your pastor or therapist for referral to a group in your area or for advice on starting a group.
- Pray for wisdom, guidance, and strength to carry you into this new phase of your role as a parent.

Instead of tearing down the other parent, do everything you can to affirm and build up that parent in your child's eyes, even if the words want to stick in your throat, even if you know that the other parent is trying to tear you down. Affirming the other parent is not something nice you're doing for him or her; it is something therapeutic and essential you are doing for the emotional health of your child. Your child will eventually be able to see that you are trying to do what's right in a difficult situation (though it may take time for him to gain that perspective), and he will respect you for trying to make the divorce as easy on him as possible.

Instead of blaming your ex-spouse for the sins of the divorce, tell your child, "We both tried to make our marriage work, and we both made a lot of mistakes. We know that everybody in the family has been hurt, and it hurts most of all to know our children have suffered. Even though we will not be together as a family anymore, I will always love you and so will your other parent." Also, make sure that your child understands that he is not to blame for the divorce: "This divorce is a decision we are making as adults. We know this decision hurts you, and we are sorry. But we want you to know that we are making this decision because of problems between us as husband and wife. This is a grownup problem, and you are not to blame."

Your child should also be given permission to be loyal and loving toward both parents: "It's okay for you to love both of us, even if we can't get along. I won't get mad at you if you love your other parent. I want you to love your other parent." You should have such conversations with your child early in the divorce process, and you should reinforce and repeat them from time to time.

WHAT ABOUT REMARRIAGE?

Admit it to yourself: you failed the first time in marriage. That's not a statement of blame but a statement of fact. Accept the fact of your failure, learn the lessons of that failure; then—if you feel that the time is right for remarriage—apply those lessons to your new marriage. Make constructive changes so that you don't fail a second time. Here are some practical guidelines regarding remarriage:

- Avoid making any major life decisions (a major move, a career change, and above all, a new marriage) in the first two years after your divorce. The grief process takes at least that long, and often longer. You run a serious risk of marrying on the rebound—that is, marrying not because you are truly in love but because, subconsciously, you are seeking to restore a familiar, comfortable situation. Rebound romances are one of the reasons second marriages have less than a 30 percent chance of surviving five years or more (for third marriages, the odds drop to 15 percent).
- Go slowly. Give yourself and your children time to work through your issues and grieve your divorce. Listen to your children's feelings about your possible remarriage.
- Pray about the relationship. Ask God for the ability to see your feelings and motivations clearly and honestly. Pray for the wisdom to know if you are entering remarriage for the right or wrong reasons.
- Seek premarital counseling before you remarry. Take the personality profiles your counselor offers, and examine the results seriously and objectively. Don't go into another marriage with the idea, "What can go wrong? We love each other!" That's what got you into trouble the first time.

234

- Make your new marriage your number one priority. Focus on making this marriage work. If you do, then relationships with children, church, work, and friends will fall into place. Join forces with your spouse against all internal and external threats. Make a decision to bond yourselves together in unconditional love.

(For additional insight into the issues of remarriage, see BLENDED FAMILIES.)

HOW SHOULD CHRISTIANS RESPOND TO DIVORCED PEOPLE?

Ellie, whose story we sketched for you at the beginning of this article, is a Christian woman who doesn't believe in divorce, who doesn't want a divorce—yet who is divorced. It was not her idea. It was not her choice. It was simply her fate. She did everything she could to save her marriage, but her husband simply wasn't willing.

As a result, Ellie has been shunned by many of the Christians in her church. "I'm not a 'perpetrator' of divorce," she says. "I'm a victim of divorce. My husband left me for another woman. So why am I treated like a leper? Why am I isolated in my own church? Why am I no longer allowed to teach Sunday school? Why won't my old friends have me over to dinner anymore? When my children were dedicated in this church, the entire congregation stood and pledged to help me raise my children in the nurture and admonition of the Lord. Why won't anyone help me with my children when I really need the help, now that I'm divorced?"

Ellie asks some very probing questions. She has been victimized twice—first by her adulterous husband and again by her uncaring church. According to the Bible, the church does have responsibility to help meet the needs of women and children in distress. For example, James 1:27 says, "Pure and undefiled religion before God and the Father is this: to visit orphans and widows in their trouble, and to keep oneself unspotted from the world." Technically, perhaps, Ellie is not a widow and her children are not orphans, but Christians are not supposed to duck their spiritual responsibilities by reason of a technicality. The spirit of the passage is clear. Ellie and her children are deserving of all the respect, love, and caring that the church is required to give them under the law of Christ—which is the law of unconditional love—and under the commitment that the congregation has made to them.

Divorced people, whether they initiated the divorce or are the unwilling victims of divorce, have gone through one of the worst of all human experiences. Many have undergone more grief and stress than those who are widowed. Their children are undergoing intense emotional upheaval. God hates divorce, as Malachi 2:16 says, but the reason He hates divorce is because He loves people. God hates the pain that divorce brings upon men, women, and their children. And He also hates the additional pain that some Christians inflict on their divorced brothers and sisters in Christ.

We have made it clear in this article that we do not condone divorce. We have made it clear that the Bible does not condone divorce. We have made it clear that divorce carries with it many painful, destructive, and far-reaching consequences that begin with the two people who are severing their relationship and then ripple out into many other lives, especially the lives of their children.

But having said all that, we have to acknowledge that our God is a God of grace and forgiveness. He is a God who restores broken lives and heals broken hearts. If God is in the business of accepting, forgiving, healing, and restoring, then we, as members of His church, must be in that same business too. Fortunately, many churches today are seeking to meet the spiritual, emotional, and practical needs of divorced people and single parents. An increasing number of churches now offer support groups, classes, and special services for people who are single again.

We are all human. We have all "blown it" in different ways. The ground is level at the foot of the cross. Those who have gone through a divorce need to be forgiven, and they need to forgive themselves. The church is a place where hurting people are loved, welcomed, and integrated into a body of people who are all recovering sinners.

If you are in a position similar to Ellie's, feeling set aside and rejected by your church because of your divorce, we encourage you to seek out a church family where your issues will be understood, your personhood will be respected, and your needs will be ministered to. There are many churches that would be privileged and honored to stand with you and to help you through your process of recovery from divorce.

Scripture makes it clear that God hates divorce and that He permitted divorce only because of the hardness of the human heart. Divorce was not part of His plan for marriage. "Therefore," Jesus said in Matthew 19:6, "what God has joined together, let not man separate." God does not give us these instructions just to make us miserable. Quite the contrary, He does so because He knows that by following His instructions, we will live happier, more fulfilled lives. Our goal for marriage must always be "until death do us part."

When imperfect people fail to achieve that objective, our goal must be to offer them Christlike grace, acceptance, and forgiveness.

Dysfunctional Families

Robert and Brad came from very similar backgrounds. Both grew up in lower-middle-class families in Oakland, California. Robert's family moved there in the late 1950s from a little town in the Texas panhandle. Brad's family moved there in the early 1960s from Kentucky. Robert's dad worked in the shipyards, and so did Brad's. Both recall observing at an early age how their families lived meaningless lives—working all day, coming home at night, watching TV in cramped, smoke-filled apartments, boozing, arguing and fighting, the children being punished or berated without love.

Robert grew up to be much like his father. Dishonorably discharged from the Navy after an incident involving a drunken brawl and going AWOL for a week, Robert went to work in the shipyards. When the recession and defense cutbacks forced him to be

236

laid off, Robert, his wife, and his four children lived on unemployment benefits. When those benefits ran out, he lived on welfare. He is an alcoholic, his children have been removed from his home three times by Child Protective Services because of his angry, abusive nature, and the police have been called to his apartment on several occasions to intervene in domestic problems between Robert and his wife.

Brad, by contrast, took his life in a completely different direction. At the age of nine, he made a decision that he was never going to be like his father or anyone else in his family. He didn't want to live out a meaningless existence, alternating between pounding rivets in a steelyard and boozing in front of a TV in a smoke-filled apartment. At that early age, he started going to the library and reading all the books he could find on business and success. Brad worked his way through junior college, and his grades were so stellar that he won a number of scholarships and acceptance into Harvard Business School, where he earned an MBA. He went to work in an electronic products firm, where he rose high in the company. Another firm, recognizing Brad's talent and ambition, hired him away and made him CEO, with a corporate limousine and Lear jet at his disposal. Several years later, he left that company, started his own Silicon Valley computer products company, made it successful, sold it for a fortune, and started another company, which has become equally successful. Brad has been profiled in *Business Week, Fortune,* and the *Wall Street Journal.*

You would never know to look at them that both Robert and Brad came from almost identical beginnings. Both are products of dysfunctional families. One of the ironies of dysfunctional families is that the children of such families tend to go to one extreme or another, either faithfully reproducing the dysfunctionalism of childhood or getting as far from their dysfunctional roots as possible.

WHAT IS A DYSFUNCTIONAL FAMILY?

When a machine, such as a toaster or a television set, doesn't work the way it was intended to by its designers, we say that it is "malfunctioning." When a family doesn't work the way it was intended to by its Designer, we say that this family is dysfunctional. Those prefixes, *mal* and *dys,* both mean "bad" (*mal* is Latin, *dys* is Greek). The Designer of the family is God, and He designed the family to be a safe, nurturing enclosure where a husband and wife would come together, bring children into the world, love them, teach them, build their confidence, shape their character, enable them to mature, and eventually release them into the world as secure, happy, functioning adults. That is how a functional family is supposed to work.

Since people are imperfect, families (which are made up of people) are imperfect too. There has never, in all of human history, been a family that was fully functional as God intended. The first dysfunctional family was the household of Adam and Eve, a family in which we see classic symptoms of dysfunctionality—denial, blaming, and scapegoating—in the way Adam and Eve respond to God after eating the forbidden fruit. Their children, Cain and Abel, were the first murderer and the first murder victim in human history. Because of sin, the family has never operated in the fully functional way God intended from the beginning. Thus, all families are, to a greater or lesser degree, dysfunctional. Some, however, are only mildly dysfunctional, in which case we consider them to be essentially "healthy." Others are massively dysfunctional; it is in such families that a host of emotional problems, codependency, addictions, self-defeating behaviors, abusive behaviors, and personality disorders arise.

Moreover, dysfunctional families tend to produce dysfunctional children, who grow up to create another generation of dysfunctional families. Thus, the cycle of dysfunctionality goes around and around, producing generation after generation of pain and emotional suffering.

A dysfunctional family can be identified by a number of distinguishing features. Every dysfunctional family will have some of these features but may not have all of them.

Active Abuse

Active abuse may include verbal violence, battering, beating, or sexual molestation. Some of these forms of active abuse are illegal, some are not—but all are destructive. (For a detailed discussion, see ABUSE.)

Passive Abuse

Passive abuse is more subtle and harder to detect, but it is also extremely damaging to its victims. Passive abuse is characterized by a lack of emotional involvement and investment in the lives of one's children. Forms of passive abuse include workaholism, perfectionism, emotional coldness or distance, chronic marital conflict, divorce, depression, or even death. The inclusion of such issues as divorce, depression, and death in a list of forms of passive abuse does not imply condemnation of those who are divorced, depressed, or dead. Often, these situations cannot be helped. Still, these issues affect children deeply and tend to have roughly the same effect on a child's emotions and personality as the other forms of passive abuse listed above. (For a more detailed discussion of passive abuse, see ABUSE.)

Emotional Incest

Emotional incest is a form of abuse in which the parent relies upon the child to fulfill adultlike roles and responsibilities. Parent and child roles are reversed. Emotional incest is not usually sexual in nature, as the name would seem to suggest, although it can lead to sexual incest in some extreme cases. In emotional incest, the parent often goes to the child for counseling or emotional nurturing or relies on the child to carry out household duties or seeks to be "babied" by the child in some way. (For a more detailed discussion of emotional incest, see ABUSE.)

Unfinished Business

Sometimes a child is expected to achieve the unrealized dreams and goals of a parent. It may mean that the child is expected to carry on the family business, or realize an achievement that the parent aspired to (and failed in), or attend the same university the parent attended. The child is pushed in a certain direction because the parent wishes to experience vicariously the rewards he or she failed to achieve through the successes of the child. Children who are forced to carry out the unfinished business of their parents often become depressed and dissatisfied in life, even if they are successful in the field that their parents have chosen for them. They think, "I never got a chance to be what I want to be. I was forced to live somebody else's life."

Negative Messages and Low Self-Esteem

Either overtly or subtly, a dysfunctional parent expresses messages to his or her child that convey a negative image of the child's own personal worth, of the world, and of life in general. As a result, the child's sense of self-worth, confidence, and optimism about succeeding in life are undermined or destroyed. These messages may be verbalized statements such as, "You're worthless! Get out of my way! I wish you had never been born! How can you be so stupid! Why do I even bother with you?"

Often, however, these messages are not stated directly. Instead, they are stated through behavior—and actions can speak just as loudly, if not louder than, words. These negative message-sending behaviors include suicide threats or attempts, emotional abandonment or distance, chronic depression or joylessness, or abuse.

Distorted Roles

People in dysfunctional families tend to settle into one of several kinds of roles within the family. These roles tend to be extreme and well-defined and serve to perpetuate unhealthy dynamics in the family. These roles also tend to substitute for honest communication. As long as everyone stays in his or her role and carries out his or her function in the family, the unspoken reasoning goes, we do not have to face the fact that something is wrong with our family.

All of these roles are essentially enabler roles. That is, when every person plays his or her dysfunctional part, the dysfunctional behavior of the entire system is enabled to continue. The victim enables the persecutor to continue persecuting. The persecutor enables the victim to continue to be victimized. The hero enables other family members to continue on with their addictions and their irresponsible behavior, because he or she is always there to clean up the mess and prevent those family members from having to deal with the consequences of their actions. The scapegoat gives everybody someone to blame for the family's problems.

People often respond to their roles in different ways as they become adults. In the story at the beginning of this article, we looked at two men, Robert and Brad, who both came from dysfunctional families. In their families, both Robert and Brad played the role of hero—rescuing family members from their self-inflicted problems, cleaning up their messes, covering up the family's shame, fixing the family's mistakes. As they grew older, Robert and Brad began to deal very differently with their roles in the dysfunctional family system.

Brad became a driven, success-oriented workaholic. At the base of his personality was a subconscious need to continue his hero role into adulthood. At some hidden level of his personality, he was actually trying to redeem his dysfunctional family of origin through good works and achievement.

As Robert grew up, he reacted against his hero role. He was tired of carrying the burden of his family's needs, demands, and emotions. He was tired of covering up the shame of his family. Finally, he embraced the hard-drinking, meaningless lifestyle in which he was raised. If anything, he succeeded in sinking even lower than his father.

The Roles People Play

People often play one of the following distorted roles in the drama of the dysfunctional family:

Hero: This is the responsible personality in the family. This person, often a child, is rewarded for good behavior and good work. He or she often takes over a parental role in the family that the parent himself or herself has abdicated. This person cleans up after the alcoholic parent. He or she fixes the meals and does the laundry when the parent is too depressed to function.

Scapegoat: This is the person who is viewed as the rebel and troublemaker in the family. Whatever problems the family has, the scapegoat gets the blame.

Mascot: This person is the cheerleader, the cute and funny attention-getter, the one who tries to dispel or mask the family's pain by laughing, joking, or trying to get everyone to cheer up.

Lost child: This person is the loner. Considered likeable enough—but generally unnoticed—by everyone else, this person shies away from the limelight for fear of attracting negative attention.

Placater: This person is the smooth talker who tries to spread oil on the family's friction. He or she has a knack for saying the right words at the right time, to make it all better when things go wrong.

Martyr: This is the self-sacrificing soul who will do anything to make things work out for everybody else. This person will sacrifice his or her own needs, wants, and happiness, even to the point of taking undeserved blame or abuse, in order to alleviate family tension.

Persecutor: This person intimidates others, blames others, prosecutes and persecutes and generally accounts for much of the open misery of the dysfunctional family. He or she always knows what's wrong with the family, and never hesitates to say so. Rage and anger are the continual undercurrents in this person's makeup. Everyone walks on eggshells around this person.

Victim: This individual actually accepts the role of victim, thinking, "Bad things just happen to me. It's my lot in life. I probably even deserve it. I guess I'll just be an unhappy person for the rest of my life."

Enmeshment or Disengagement

Dysfunctional families often involve extremes in relationships—either extreme closeness or extreme distance. When family members are too close, when a parent treats a child as an extension of his or her own personality, then we say that this family is enmeshed. In an enmeshed family, children are often not allowed to grow up and leave home. They are often discouraged from forming attachments or interests outside of the family. A family that is enmeshed is a family with too few boundaries.

Other families go to the opposite extreme, to disengagement. In a disengaged family, the family members isolate themselves into their own little worlds. They live under the same roof, but there is no real communication taking place—no sharing of thoughts or feelings, no intimacy or self-disclosure, and in many cases, no love.

240

Secrets

Dysfunctional families are families that keep secrets. The secret may be Dad's incestuous involvement with his daughter. Or it may be brother Jason's drug habit. Or it may be Mom's affair. In many dysfunctional families, there are rules about secrets: "There are some things we just don't talk about. We don't talk about it among ourselves, and we certainly don't talk about it outside of this house!" Secrets are shameful. Dysfunctional families will do anything to cover up their shame.

Suppressed Emotions

In dysfunctional families, real emotions tend to be denied, suppressed, and repressed. If one family member demonstrates the audacity and the temerity to express honest anger or honest hurt—particularly if that emotion is directed at some family secret—other family members are quick to pounce on that emotion and make it go away. Examples:

Daughter, in pain, tears streaming down her face: "Mother! I'm trying to tell you that Daddy is hurting me! For years he's been forcing me to have a sexual relationship with him!"

Mother, smiling vaguely: "Oh, you don't know what you're saying. You're too young to know about such things. Here, dear, have a cookie."

Or this:

Son, red-faced with anger, smashing a china saucer on the floor: "Why won't you listen to me? I'm trying to tell you I can't stand the way you treat me like a little boy! I'm thirty years old, and you won't let me grow up. You won't let me leave this house! You keep manipulating me with your phony heart condition and your whining about being lonely without me! I tell you, I hate you for not letting me become a man!"

Father: "I won't allow you to speak to your mother and me like that. Now, get a broom from the pantry and clean up that mess, then go sit on your bed. When you've calmed down, you can come tell us you're sorry for blowing up, and we won't say another word about the matter."

Dysfunctional families use very twisted forms of communication in order to keep people in their roles and keep family secrets hidden.

Codependency

Codependency is the act of living out the myth that you can make yourself happy by trying to control people and events outside of yourself. Codependents are driven by one or more compulsions, such as an addiction to drugs, alcohol, sex, abusive behavior, workaholism, spendaholism, compulsive overachievement in school, and so forth. Codependents typically have low self-esteem and feel their happiness hinges on the behavior of others. They feel inordinately responsible for the needs and happiness of other people, and they worry obsessively about things they can't change—and they frequently try to change them anyway. (For a thorough discussion of the subject, see CODEPENDENCY.)

Addiction

Addiction is a compulsive or physical dependence upon a substance, person, or behavior that provides a temporary sense of well-being. The gratification that comes from indulging an addiction never lasts long, but the destructive effects are both long-lasting and far-reaching. The focus of an addiction—the substance, person, or behavior upon which a person may form an excessive dependency—is called an addictive agent, and the list of addictive agents includes (but is not limited to) drugs, alcohol, sex, work and success, controlling behavior, money, rescuing behavior, toxic relationships, and perfectionism. (For a more complete discussion of this issue, see ADDICTION.)

MAKING DYSFUNCTIONAL FAMILIES FUNCTIONAL

Dysfunctional families are families that have learned to respond to stressful events, painful memories, and unpleasant emotions in negative, self-defeating, maladaptive ways. The maladaptive patterns that govern the dysfunctional family are difficult to change and correct. The members of the dysfunctional family have learned their roles and their coping techniques. They know the dysfunctional rules by heart: "We get rid of pain in our family by denying it. We get rid of blame and shame by scapegoating it onto our rebellious son. We deal with anger by changing the subject. We do not need family therapy, because that would expose the truth, and the truth is painful, so why don't we just go on like we've been going on and everything will be all right and we'll all be happy, okay?"

As a result of this denial and maladaptive behavior, the misery of the dysfunctional family grows worse and worse—and the cycle is perpetuated into the next generation. Dysfunctional families can be healed.

The term *dysfunctional family* is a kind of catch-all for a range of family problems that must be attacked individually and collectively in order for family healing to take place. The following keys to healing dysfunctional families contain referrals to other articles in this encyclopedia that will give you insight into the various factors and dynamics of the problem of dysfunctional families. The keys to healing dysfunctional families are:

- *Seek professional help.* If you are in a dysfunctional family, you already know that you are probably the only one in your family who sees the need for help. The rest of your family "just doesn't get it." They are in denial. Do what's best for you. Get the help and insight you need to break out of the dysfunctional pattern of your family. As you grow stronger in your recovery, ask your counselor or therapist how to penetrate the denial and the maladaptive defenses of your family, so that they can learn to honestly face the truth about themselves. Denial is too strong and long-established dysfunctional patterns are too deeply entrenched to try to heal the family without professional help.
- *Stop addictive and codependent behavior.* Addiction is a product of the dysfunctional family pattern, but it also serves to perpetuate that pattern. In order for healing to begin, the cycle of addiction must be interrupted. The attempt to gain happiness by controlling people and events must be turned off. (For a comprehensive discussion of this issue, see ADDICTION and CODEPENDENCY.)

- *Build new patterns of family communication.* Family secrets must be brought out into the open. Dysfunctional rules about family communication must be changed. People who have repressed and denied their painful memories and toxic emotions must learn how to ventilate these feelings honestly and constructively. (For insight into healthy patterns of family communicating, see FAMILY.)
- *Learn how to deal honestly and constructively with anger and other emotions.* It is crucial to be able to express anger without exploding; to be healed of the bitterness and resentment that result from active or passive abuse; to be able to forgive and get on with the business of living. (For an in-depth discussion of these issues, see ABUSE, ANGER, EMOTIONS, and FORGIVENESS.)

And remember: blended families can be dysfunctional families too. (For insight into the unique relational and emotional dynamics that can arise in second marriages, see BLENDED FAMILIES.)

Emotions

As a doctor making rounds in a hospital, Dr. Frank Minirth became acquainted with a severely depressed patient, a man in his seventies. He had no major physical illness, no cancer, no heart disease, no diabetes, nor any other life-threatening medical condition. He was simply very depressed. Every day, Dr. Minirth would look in on him, and every day when he left, this patient would say, "Goodbye, Dr. Minirth." The man wasn't saying goodbye for the night, he was saying goodbye forever.

"I did everything I could think of," Dr. Minirth recalls. "I tried to encourage him and cheer him up, I tried to help him develop a more positive outlook on life, but every night he would say goodbye, as if this was the last time I would ever see him."

One night, at around 3 A.M., Dr. Minirth got a call from the night duty nurse, telling him that this patient had died. Dr. Minirth was surprised. "Died? What did he die of?"

"We don't know," the nurse replied. "We can't figure it out. He just died."

Reflecting on the man's death, Dr. Minirth concludes, "It wasn't disease that killed him. It was emotion. Emotions have tremendous power to affect our lives. Positive emotions can enhance our lives and make us healthier. Negative emotions can make us sick. Emotions can do anything. They can even kill." What are these familiar yet mysterious forces within each of us called emotions?

From a psychological perspective, an emotion is a feeling that tends to produce an impulse toward a certain kind of behavior. Psychologists and psychiatrists call the emotional aspect of our experience the *affective* or *feeling* part of our experience. The word *affect* (pronounced AF-fect) refers to our emotional makeup.

243

Emotions are commonly categorized as either positive or negative. *Positive emotions* are pleasant feelings, or feelings that tend to produce healthy behavior. They include happiness, elation, excitement, wonder, surprise, and enthusiasm. *Negative emotions* are unpleasant feelings, or feelings which tend to produce unhealthy behavior. They include anger, worry, fear, disgust, sadness, loneliness, and depression.

THINKING, FEELING, AND PHYSICAL WELL-BEING

Our emotions are closely related to the way we think. Certain ways of thinking naturally produce either positive or negative emotions.

Negative thoughts—ruminating on past failures and painful memories, feeling pressured by current stresses, or contemplating future disasters or problems—arouse not only negative emotions but negative biological responses. These negative responses include increased blood pressure, increased gastric juices in the stomach (which can lead to ulcers), heart disease, and coronary artery disease. The lungs can be affected, resulting in asthma attacks. The hypothalamus can be affected, which in turn depresses the body's immune system. These symptoms all belong to a class of health problems called *psychosomatic reactions.*

If negative thoughts can produce a negative impact on the body, it should not be surprising that positive thoughts can positively impact the body. Positive thinking can lead to the release of neurotransmitters (such as serotonin and noradrenaline), which stimulate clearer thinking, a relaxed mood, and a pleasurable sense of well-being. Positive emotions actually help to improve the functioning of the immune system, which helps to protect us from cancer and infections. Thus, emotions can have a powerful role to play in either extending or shortening our lives. At the Minirth Meier New Life Clinics, we believe that if it were not for negative emotions—particularly the sin-related emotions such as guilt—human beings could routinely live to be over a hundred years old.

The word psychosomatic *does not mean, as many people think, that "it's all in your head." It means that the mind, emotions, and body are interacting in such a way that a psychological problem is being manifested as a physical problem. Psychosomatic problems are real medical manifestations produced by psychological struggles.*

The linkage between our thinking, our emotions, and our bodies is recognized in the Bible. Throughout the Bible, we see that references to deep emotions are actually references to specific body organs. Whereas we sometimes speak today of emotions as being (in a metaphorical sense) a "visceral response" or a "gut reaction," both testaments of the Bible make a literal connection between an emotional response and the visceral organs—a clear suggestion that the inner workings of the body are powerfully affected by our emotions. For thousands of years, the Bible has proclaimed what medical science is only recently coming to recognize: thinking, feeling, and physical well-being are inextricably intertwined (see Genesis 43:30; Philippians 1:8; Philemon 7, 20; and 1 John 3:17–19).

Many stress-related, anxiety-related, depression-related, and psychosomatic illnesses could be prevented if we could only understand and receive God's assurance of peace, love, acceptance, and forgiveness. That is why Proverbs 3:8 tells us that trusting in God results in "health to your flesh, and strength to your bones."

The Bible also recognizes the importance of thinking on positive things, so that our emotional, spiritual, and relational life will be positively affected. "For as he thinks in his heart," says Proverbs 23:7, "so is he." And Paul, in Philippians 4:8, agrees that what we think about is extremely important: "Finally, brethren, whatever things are true, whatever things are noble, whatever things are just, whatever things are pure, whatever things are lovely, whatever things are of good report, if there is any virtue and if there is anything praiseworthy—meditate on these things."

In our culture in recent years, there has been an increasing emphasis on feeling and a decreasing emphasis on thinking. During the climactic moments of the film *Star Wars,* many people viewed it as a statement of deep philosophical truth when Obi-Wan Kenobi whispered to Luke Skywalker, "Trust your feelings, Luke!" Years later, people are still trusting their feelings rather than using their God-given abilities to think and reason. People no longer ask you, "What do you think?" They ask, "How do you *feel* about that?" People marry because of feelings, not a well-considered commitment, and when the feelings lose their intensity, they move on to a new relationship.

Christians, unfortunately, are no exception to the growing antirational, overemotional mood of our culture. Many demand that Christianity be more than a commitment to Christ; it must be an exhilarating experience. If they do not "feel God's presence" in their lives—that is, if they are not on a continual emotional high—they conclude that the reality of their faith has departed. The result is a undependable faith that is continually being tossed about on waves of emotion like a rowboat on a stormy sea.

Throughout the Bible, there is a much greater emphasis on knowledge than on emotion. In fact, the Greek word for "feeling" is used only two times in the entire New Testament, whereas the word for "knowledge" appears almost five hundred times. Yet it would be an overreaction to suppose that feelings have no place in the life of a mature Christian. We find many specific emotions expressed and underscored throughout the Bible, from rage to fear, from elation to depression, and we see behavior ranging from ecstatic dancing to the wailing of deep despair. One of the most profound and revealing verses in all of Scripture is that little two-word statement in John 11:35, "Jesus wept."

When we are in the grips of negative emotions such as anger, fear, or grief, we may wonder, *Why did God give us emotions? What possible function could they serve? Wouldn't we be a lot better off if we didn't have to experience so many painful emotions?* The fact is that our emotions—including our so-called "negative" emotions—serve a positive function.

Guilt serves as a warning that there is sin and self-defeating behavior in our lives. *Fear* can serve as a self-protective warning that we need to remove ourselves from, or defend ourselves in, a dangerous situation (this is the "fight or flight" response that is a part of both human and animal behavior). *Grief* is a natural result of any loss (the loss of health, the loss of a career, the loss of a cherished dream or goal, the loss of a life), and it helps us to readjust to the new situation that follows that loss. *Anger* is an outward-directed emotion that enables us to project emotional energy onto someone or something that is creating harm. Anger is useful in motivating us to set right something that is wrong, such as when Jesus displayed anger in chasing the money-changers out of God's Temple—a case in which Jesus was angry not for Himself but for an injustice against God.

Just as the positive emotions—joy, elation, wonder, excitement—can help to improve and even prolong our lives, the negative emotions can also be beneficial in our lives, so long as they don't take over. Through an understanding of the range of our emotions and their effect upon the body, we begin to see the wisdom of God's design of the human body and the human inner being.

The key to understanding the biblical view of emotion is recognizing that our emotions are God-given; they are valid—yet they were never intended to rule our lives or overrule our reason. Feeling and thinking must go together in order for us to be whole human beings. People who feel but cannot think are no more healthy than people who think but cannot feel.

COMMUNICATING EMOTION

During the past few decades, many psychological and encounter group movements in our society have advocated total ventilation and expression of anger and other negative emotions. This "say how you feel" approach operates on the theory that keeping emotions "bottled up" is unhealthy. "Stuffing" our emotions can result in increased emotional issues, psychosomatic illnesses, or self-defeating behavior such as engaging in denial.

Though we agree that it is important that emotions be expressed in order to achieve good emotional health, we have treated many survivors of the "let it all out" approach to emotions. We can attest to the fact that there is nothing healthy about exploding and attacking other people every time we feel frustrated. This approach destroys relationships and wounds people—and we find that it actually does little to promote health and release in the person who explodes. In fact, once a person begins to "ventilate" by raging and blowing off emotions, that person frequently becomes more hostile and angry, not less.

Anger should be released—but it should be released carefully, caringly, and under controlled conditions. Anger that is explosively unleashed is a dangerous and destructive force. But anger that is expressed in a controlled way, with a view toward making constructive changes in a relationship, can be a powerful force for healing relationships. The healthy expression of emotion should emphasize one's own feelings, not blame toward the other person for what he or she said and did. One should say, for example, "When you did such-and-such, I felt angry," not "You made me angry." A healthy response to emotions requires that we take ownership of, and responsibility for, our own emotions. Yet such a statement also recognizes the validity of confronting those who hurt us with the harmful effects of their actions.

One of the most underappreciated aspects of the expression of emotion is the *nonverbal communication* of emotions. There are many ways in which we communicate, and words are just one of those ways. We communicate through facial expressions, gestures, tone of voice, and body movements. The very same words can be given many different shades of meaning depending on whether they are whispered or shouted, whether our facial expressions appear open and sincere or sarcastic and smirking, whether our eyes are hard with anger, wide with delight, or glistening with tears.

Paralanguage is one aspect of nonverbal expression that deals with those aspects of communication that involve voice qualities apart from the actual words we say, such as pitch, volume, intensity, and rate of speech. *Eye communication* serves to establish emotional intimacy or distance. *Body cues* indicate emotional states. A forward-leaning posture, for example, indicates involvement and attention, whereas a rigid, arms-folded posture indicates skepticism, wariness, and dislike.

We often send mixed and contradictory messages with our words and our nonverbal communication. In fact, this is one of the most common family communication issues, and one that often leads to great pain and unhealthiness in relationships. Most of us only place conscious attention on our verbal communication while ignoring our nonverbal communication. Yet those who see and hear us often find our nonverbal communication more persuasive and "louder" than our words.

In research conducted in 1971, UCLA professor Albert Mehrabian determined that 55 percent of the impact of our personal communication is made by our facial and body movements, 38 percent by such vocal elements as tone of voice, pitch, and volume, and only 7 percent of the impact was made by the words themselves. Clearly, nonverbal communication has an overwhelming (and much underrated) impact on the way we communicate emotions. If we want to communicate our feelings effectively, then we must learn to tune in not only to what we are saying but to how we are saying it. Our verbal and nonverbal messages must have congruence and consistency.

If, for example, we wish to communicate love, acceptance, and forgiveness to our children, we should not say, "I forgive you" or "I love you" with a stern expression, a standoffish posture, and folded arms. We must say it tenderly, with a touch or a hug, with a loving and caring expression. If we send our children a positive verbal message surrounded by a negative nonverbal message, we may be fooling ourselves, but we will not fool them about our real feelings. Such conflicting messages do enormous emotional damage to our most important relationships.

WHY DO CHRISTIANS HAVE EMOTIONAL PROBLEMS?

Many Christians have the unrealistic expectation that being a Christian should be a guarantee against emotional problems. The flip side of this unrealistic expectation is the idea that whenever a Christian does experience emotional problems, it must be because of sin or a lack of faith. Though some emotional problems can be traced to guilt feelings resulting from a pattern of unconfessed sin, there are many reasons that Christians have emotional problems, including reasons that have nothing to do with their spiritual state. Those reasons include genetic factors, environmental stress, medical problems and physical health, and traumatic events such as the loss of a loved one or the loss of a career.

The importance that genetic factors play in personality types and emotional problems has only recently begun to be understood and appreciated. For example, studies of schizophrenia reveal that children of schizophrenic parents have a higher incidence of schizophrenia *even when raised in a healthy home away from their parents,* which indicates that heredity, not environment, is the primary factor in this emotional illness.

Sometimes there are factors that affect our emotional health over which we have no control. Still, the encouraging fact about our emotions is that most of the emotional issues we face are rooted in factors that we *can* influence or control.

Many Christians fail to understand the responsibility they have for their own emotional well-being, even following conversion. They think, *If Christians have the Holy Spirit living within them, if they have a power and a new life within them at the moment of conversion, shouldn't God simply heal all their mental and emotional problems at that time?* There is a profound (but common) misunderstanding at the heart of this question. The Bible teaches (and modern psychology tends to affirm) that human beings consist of three dimensions, body, soul, and spirit. At the moment of conversion, our spirit is made new, but the soul is not made new. The soul must gradually be changed and developed over time—and our mind and emotions are a part of the soul, not the spirit. That is why Paul says in Romans 12:2 that our minds must be gradually transformed by the continual, day-by-day renewing of our minds. This transformation is an ongoing process involving prayer, time spent in the Word of God, and time spent in fellowship with other Christians. In cases involving deep and painful emotional issues, such as situations involving abuse, trauma, or addiction, Christian counseling or psychiatry may be needed in addition to these spiritual disciplines.

A healthy Christian understanding of our emotions is summed up by A. W. Tozer in his book, *That Incredible Christian:* "The emotions are neither to be feared nor despised, for they are a normal part of us as God made us in the first place. Indeed, the full human life would be impossible without them" (Christian Publications, 1964).

See also ANGER, ANXIETY, DEPRESSION, GRIEF AND LOSS, GUILT, HAPPINESS, JEALOUSY, and LONELINESS

The Biblical Prescription for Happy Life

Many of the problems we face can be avoided if we follow the biblical prescription for a happy life. Most of the emotional problems we treat at the Minirth Meier New Life Clinics are rooted in feelings of guilt, anxiety, and stress. And most of the treatments we prescribe for these problems involve having the individuals make behavioral and attitude changes that are consistent with the biblical prescription for happiness:

- Stop sinful behavior.
- Let go of resentment and practice forgiveness.
- Purge anger on a daily basis.
- Increase reliance upon God through prayer.
- Increase understanding of God through reading His Word.
- Reduce stress through regular meditation and reflection (quiet time).

Failure

Babe Ruth was the home-run king of the New York Yankees during the 1930s. But he was also a man who knew about failure.

The Yankees were in the final game of a hotly contested season. This game would decide if the Yankees would win the pennant or not—and the game was so close it went into extra innings. The opposing team was leading by one run at the bottom of the thirteenth inning. Babe Ruth, "the Sultan of Swat," had failed miserably that day, striking out every time at bat.

As he stepped up to the plate for the last time that day, there were two men out and a runner at first. A home run would win the game, another out would lose it. He swung twice and missed twice—two strikes. Everything came down to the next pitch. He swung . . .

And knocked it out of the park! The Yankees won the game, and would later go on to win the World Series.

After the game, reporters asked him what was going through his mind when that last pitch was coming over the plate. He might have been thinking about all the other times he struck out. He might have been thinking about how humiliating it would be if he failed one more time, just when the chips were down. He could have been listening to those voices which said, "You can't pull it off. You'll never make it."

But his answer to the reporter's question was very simple. "I was thinking the same thing I always think when I'm up to bat. I was thinking about hitting a home run."

We all know what it feels like to fail. We've all experienced "the agony of defeat" in life, in school, in athletics, in business, in the performing arts, in relationships, perhaps even in marriage. One of the worst effects of failure is that it shakes our confidence, it makes us *feel* like failures—and when we feel like failures, we often *act* like failures. The result: a vicious cycle, a self-fulfilling prophecy, one failure begetting more failures.

It is good to want to win, to want to excel, to reach for the brass ring. But for some people, winning is everything. They don't just *want to* win, they *have to* win in order to have any sense of value, meaning, or significance in life. The problem for most people who are this driven to win is that no matter how much they win, it's never enough. They are never satisfied. While achieving goal after goal, they still feel like failures. Why? Because they have set their sights on the wrong goal, on a goal that can never satisfy.

MAKE FAILURE WORK FOR YOU

Jerry's father was a successful business owner—and a stern, unloving man. Throughout Jerry's childhood and adolescence, his father continually pushed him, drove him, and berated him for not working hard enough, for not being smart enough, for not measuring up. On more than one occasion, Jerry's cheeks burned with shame and anger as he heard his father tell him, "You'll never amount to anything!"

When Jerry was still in college, his father died of a sudden heart attack. After graduation, Jerry joined a small, successful company and quickly worked his way up the ranks. Within four years, he resigned and started his own company, which became quite successful. He sold that company and started another, and it also prospered. Everything Jerry did throughout his twenties and thirties was a major success.

And every day of his life he felt like a failure.

No matter what Jerry did, no matter how much he accomplished, he heard a voice from the grave telling him, "You'll never amount to anything!" His father was dead, and there was no way he could reach out, rub his father's nose in his own success, and say, "I showed you! I succeeded! I proved you wrong!" So he spent every day trying to prove himself a success, while feeling like a failure.

What Jerry had to learn—and what most of us have to learn—is that there is a more important standard of success than that which Jerry strove for, a more meaningful standard of success than the one inflicted on Jerry by his father. God's standard of success is the truest standard of all. He does not measure us according to our bank account or the car we drive or the neighborhood we live in. He measures us according to our character, according to the truest reality of our innermost selves. His standard is rich in grace. It is not a standard based on what we can achieve by our own blood, sweat, and tears, but a standard based on *who we are* because of the blood of Jesus Christ.

Once we have learned to redefine success in God's terms, we have automatically redefined failure. No longer does failure—even a failed business or a failed marriage—mean we have reached the end of ourselves. Now that we see failure from God's perspective, it becomes clear that failure is just another opportunity for growth.

Turn Failure into Strength

Our failings can be converted and transformed into strengths. That is the healing and reinvigorating message of Psalm 84:5–6:

> Blessed is the man whose strength is in You . . .
> As they pass through the Valley of Baca [weeping],
> They make it a spring.

That must become our perspective on failure: take a valley of sorrow and turn it into a spring. Whenever you fail, learn from your failure. Make failure work for you.

EIGHT STEPS TO TRUE SUCCESS

As you read this article, you may be thinking, *That makes sense—on a thinking level. But at a feelings level, I still see myself as a failure. How can I change the way I feel? How can I start feeling and thinking and behaving like a success?* Here are eight suggested steps to authentic success:

Step 1. Recognize your true status in Christ. We all want to feel significant, that our lives count for something. Some of us seek our sense of significance in things that have no eternal value: a bit of power in the corporate pecking order, a bigger salary than the next guy, marrying the "right" person, becoming a big wheel in the church. In comparison to the significance that God offers us, all of these status symbols are paltry and tarnished. In the Bible, God tells us that we have *true* and *lasting* significance simply by being in a relationship with Him. We are the children and heirs of the living God, we are ambassadors of Christ, we are a royal priesthood. No earthly status symbol can hope to match our significance in Christ.

Step 2. Recognize that God can best use you when you are weak. God is in the business of taking failures and using them to achieve His purposes. A prime example is Peter, who denied Christ three times after promising to stick to Him like glue. It is clear, as you read Peter's story, that he felt like a complete washout. But Jesus was not through with Peter. He had a job for him to do, despite his failure. In fact, Peter was probably especially valuable to Jesus *because* of his failure and the important lesson Peter had learned. That is why Jesus, in John 21:15–17, asked Peter three questions that parallel the three denials of Peter: "Simon, son of Jonah, do you love Me?" Each time, Peter replied, "Yes, Lord, You know that I love You." So Jesus told Peter, "Feed My sheep." After Peter's failure, Jesus reinstated him and made him the leading apostle of His newly founded church.

Whatever your failure, God wants to reinstate you and use you for His glory. God's message to each of us in our times of weakness is "My grace is sufficient for you, for My strength is made perfect in weakness" (2 Cor. 12:9).

Step 3. Seek the support of other Christians as you recover from a major failure. Find people you can trust, such as members of a small group Bible study, a support group, or a professional counselor. Seek out a safe haven for yourself where you can experience emotional release, accountability, and support. Above all, you need a place where other people can hold up a mirror to you and show you who you really are, caringly and objectively. A group of caring Christians can provide you with a "reality check" so you can become more objective about your failures. Through their feedback, you can gain insight and encouragement and the strength to persevere and succeed.

Step 4. Stop listening to "failure messages." Remember Jerry? His father told him, "You'll never amount to anything." That was his "failure message," and it played over and over in a continuous subconscious loop. What are the "failure messages" that play in your mind? Whatever they are, it's time to shut them off.

If you experienced an abusive or painful childhood, chances are there are some failure messages playing very loudly in the back of your mind, telling you that you are

---

The Educational Value of Mistakes

One of the top CEOs in the country tells the story of a department head of his company who made a two-million-dollar mistake. "This poor fella came into my office," the CEO recalls, "and told me why he should be fired. He was head of purchasing for our company and he said, 'I was moving ahead so fast on this project and I was so gung-ho that I failed to qualify the vendor we were buying material from. The stuff this vendor shipped was poor quality, but we used it anyway because we were running late. It turned out terrible, and now we're going to have to get new material from another vendor and run it all over again.'

"I said, 'Gee, that sounds bad. What did this whole fiasco cost us?'

"He hung his head and groaned, 'About two mil.'

"I whistled and said, 'That's an awful lot of money. Would you ever do a thing like this again?'

"He said, 'Absolutely not. Next time around, I'd make sure I knew the vendor could deliver quality material. . . . Of course, after a mistake like this, I guess there isn't going to be a next time, is there?'

"I said, 'I just paid two million dollars so you could learn a valuable lesson. Now, why would I fire you and give some other company the benefit of your experience? Just get back to your office and make sure it doesn't happen again.'"

We all make mistakes, but the important thing is to see the *educational value* of those mistakes. Failure gives us feedback for change and growth. Failure seasons and matures us. Failure prompts us to reassess our actions and to redirect our steps. Through each failure, we learn and we become more of what God wants us to be.

251

incapable of success or that you don't deserve to succeed. These messages are setting you up for failure and making you feel like a failure even amid your greatest successes. You may need the help of a counselor or psychiatrist to help you turn off those messages. If so, begin by praying about your past, asking God to give you wisdom to understand your past and courage to delve into it. Then get the professional help you need. Professional counseling can help you learn how to stop sabotaging your success and your relationships and how to rechannel your thinking into more successful directions.

Step 5. Act like a success. People who feel like failures usually behave like failures. They avoid the eyes of other people, they have weak handshakes, they walk and sit in slumping positions. When you assume the air of a failure, people will presume that you are a failure—and they will treat you like one. You'll fail to get the job, the promotion, or whatever it is you really want.

Start employing the stance and behavior of a successful person. Believe in yourself, and others will believe in you. Show that you value yourself (as God values you) by your upright posture, your confident smile, your strong voice. Behave like a success, and people will treat you like a success—and soon, success will come your way.

Step 6. Refuse to let others make you feel like a failure. Many people make the mistake of allowing others to be in charge of their feelings and their self-esteem. For example, Ted, a midlevel sales manager, was continually berated on the job by Derek, his superior. "Your division is the worst in this company!" he said on several occasions. "You're always under quota. If you don't shape up, Ted, we're gonna have to figure out some way to get along without you." Fearful for his job, Ted worked himself into exhaustion, trying to raise his own sales figures and those of his division, but his numbers were never good enough, according to Derek.

Ted was shocked when Derek was suddenly fired and it came out that Derek had been browbeating and intimidating *all* his sales managers, telling them that they were *all* the worst in the company. Many had quit in discouragement, and that had hurt the company, leading to Derek's firing. It turned out that Ted was the top sales manager in the entire company! Amid his success, he had allowed a tyrannical and incompetent superior to make him feel like a failure.

After three years of marriage, Moira's husband, Gardner, began to attack her self-esteem. As weeks went by, his criticism of her became more frequent and more scathing. "Just look at this house!" he'd say. "Look at what a terrible mother you are! How can you let our son live in an environment like this? If you don't get your act together, I'm taking Mick away from you and getting a divorce!" In panic over this threat, Moira tried to meet Gardner's incredibly high standards of housekeeping, cooking, childcare, personal appearance, and sexual performance—but he was never satisfied. Finally, he left her. He didn't take their son away, as he had threatened, but he did file for divorce. And then Moira found out from a friend that Gardner had been carrying on an affair for almost a year. All of his criticism of her had been nothing but a rationalization for his own adultery. Moira vowed never again to put another person, even a husband, in charge of her own self-esteem.

Step 7. Develop and maintain a sense of perspective—and a sense of humor. Failure pushes us to emotional extremes. We look at the ruins of our plans and goals, and we say, "I'm a complete failure! My whole life is messed up! I can never recover from this!" There is always hope, though we may need help—the help of a support group or professional

252

counselor—in order to regain our hope and a balanced perspective on our situation. The viewpoint we should work to maintain is "I messed up because I'm human, but God is helping me to overcome this and learn from it. I am persevering, I am growing, I am making positive changes in my life."

Perhaps the best strategy for regaining our perspective on life and on failure is a well-tuned sense of humor. Ecclesiastes 3:1 and 4 say,

> To everything there is a season,
> A time for every purpose under heaven. . . .
> A time to weep,
> And a time to laugh.

Immediately after a major setback, we may—with justification—feel like weeping. But a time must come when we are able to reflect on the bigger picture and to lighten up, to laugh. Let's not take ourselves too seriously. Let's live, laugh, and enjoy life. The Bible teaches in Proverbs 17:22, "A merry heart does good, like medicine." Don't forget to take your medicine. Don't forget to laugh.

Step 8. Be sure to learn—and apply—the lessons of your failures. Reflect on your mistakes—not to ruminate or wallow in them but to pick them apart and analyze them so that you can extract valuable lessons from them. Ask yourself, Why did this failure happen? Was I too hasty? Did I procrastinate? Did I fail to plan adequately? Did I fail to listen to advice? Did I fail to take "worst case scenarios" into account? Are there character traits in my personality which sabotage me in my relationships or in my career?

After you have learned all you can from your mistakes, take those lessons and formulate a plan for the future. It can be helpful to keep a journal or diary in which you write down principles, insights, and lessons that you have learned in life. Read over your journal from time to time and see how you have grown over the past year or several years. Also, record your goals and plans in your journal and refer back to them often for motivation and inspiration.

PERSISTENCE!

The world knows of Thomas Edison and of his more than one thousand patents for various inventions, including the electric light bulb, the phonograph, and the motion-picture projector. But people rarely stop to think of all the failures he experienced along the road to those successes. On one occasion, Edison and his associates were working in their New Jersey laboratory, trying to perfect an invention and meeting up with failure after failure. Finally, one of Edison's assistants threw up his hands and said, "What a waste! We've tried over seven hundred experiments, and every one was a failure! We're no better off than when we began!"

"Oh, yes, we are," Edison replied with a buoyant smile. "We know seven hundred approaches that won't work. We're getting closer all the time!"

That is an attitude of persistence, and that attitude is a necessary ingredient for overcoming failure and achieving success. The moral: *Don't give up! Hang in there! Keep trying!*

■

Thomas Edison often remarked that many people who failed in life simply didn't realize how close to success they were when they gave up.

■

"He who has begun a good work in you," says Philippians 1:6, "will complete it until the day of Jesus Christ." God won't give up on you, so don't give up on yourself! Because our God is eternal, failure is never final. You can overcome, and you will.

Faith

Valerie came to the clinic with symptoms of depression and anxiety. She sat down in the therapist's office and described her feelings and some of the stresses she had been dealing with lately. After listening intently for about half an hour, the therapist posed a question. "Tell me about your relationship with God," he said.

"Well," Valerie responded, "I'm very active in my church. I teach Sunday school, and I'm on the deacon's board. In fact, there are some weeks when my church work is practically a full-time job, with committee meetings, special events, and all."

"That's very commendable," said the doctor, "but I was actually more interested in your personal relationship with God."

"Well," she said, uncertainly, "I was raised in the church. My parents were very devout."

"That's an excellent heritage to have," replied the doctor, "but that's still not what I meant."

She frowned. "No?"

"No. What I'm really getting at is . . . How do you relate to God on a personal, intimate basis?"

Valerie looked back at the therapist with eyes that looked frightened, even trapped. "I—I—Well, I mean, how can anyone have, you know, a *personal* relationship with Somebody you can't even see?" she said, stammering. "I mean, God is so—well, *different* and *distant*. How can you have an intimate relationship with Somebody who's—" She waved her hand toward outer space. "—who's *out there* somewhere?"

As Valerie and her doctor talked together, it became clear that—despite all her busyness for her church, despite her religious upbringing—she really had no relationship, no intimate connection to God. Her view of God as a vague, distant Somebody "out there somewhere" was a major component of her emotional problems. She was working busily, sometimes even to the point of exhaustion, doing things for the church and ostensibly for God, yet she had no sense of who God was, whether God loved and accepted her, and whether or not any of the activities she did counted for anything. She was actually trying to please God and win His love through her activities. Though she had heard words like *grace, forgiveness,* and *the love of God* all her life, she had no real understanding of what these words meant in her own life. She had never internalized the love of God and applied it to her own experience.

In the weeks that followed, Valerie's eyes were gradually opened to a whole new undiscovered realm of spiritual experience. She encountered the amazing love and grace of God and found it was actually possible to know Him as a Person and a Friend. She committed her life to Christ, and today she continues to grow in an ever-deeper adventure of faith.

WHAT IS FAITH?

According to the Bible, *faith* is not religion. Faith is a *relationship*. It is a living, dynamic interaction between ourselves and God. Faith is our response to an initiative that God made to us while we were lost in our sin. He demonstrated His love to us by giving His Son, Jesus, to take the penalty for our sin upon Himself. Our response involves three steps:

1. We must recognize that we are sinners and that we need God's forgiveness in our lives (see Romans 3:23).
2. We must recognize that Jesus Christ, the Son of God, died on the cross in payment for our sins (see Romans 6:23).
3. We must trust Jesus Christ as our Savior and Lord, committing ourselves to live the rest of our lives for Him (see John 1:12).

Many people make a connection between faith and feelings. They think that if they don't experience a feeling of excitement or religious passion, then their faith must not be real. It is important to understand that the foundation of faith is not feelings, which are changeable. The foundation of faith is God's Word, which never changes. Those who place a greater reliance upon feelings than upon God's Word tend to have an erratic, undependable faith that rises and falls with every mood. But those who base their faith upon trust in God's Word have an unshakable foundation.

The assurances that God gives to those who place their trust in Him are firm, reliable, and all-encompassing. "And I give them eternal life," says Jesus in John 10:28, "and they shall never perish; neither shall anyone snatch them out of My hand." In Romans 5:8–9, Paul writes, "But God demonstrates His own love toward us, in that while we were still sinners, Christ died for us. Much more then, having now been justified by His blood, we shall be saved from wrath through Him." And Jude verse 1 describes Christians as being "preserved in Jesus Christ."

People fail us at times, but we can always seek refuge in God. We are comforted by His constant presence, as Psalm 139:7–12 tells us. We are reminded of God's enduring love in Psalm 136 and of His redemptive power in Psalm 129. Of course, learning to trust God may be a progressive process for you, especially if your ability to trust has been damaged by an incident or pattern of betrayal, abuse, or dysfunctionality in your childhood or recent past. But you can learn to be vulnerable and to open your heart to God's invitation.

Don't feel that you have to plunge into a relationship with God before you are ready. If you only feel capable of getting to know God a little at a time, that's okay. Just be sure to give as much as you can give to what you do understand about God. Be honest with Him. If the prayer of your heart is "God, I only half-believe in You, I still have many doubts," then say that to God. He doesn't desire our flowery words or our lofty speeches, but He does desire our honesty and our earnest desire to know Him. Hebrews 11:6 tells us that the only way to know and please God is through faith and that He will reward those who diligently seek Him.

FAITH AND EMOTIONAL PROBLEMS

Many secular psychologists and psychiatrists view faith as a hindrance to emotional health. They have seen cases of people with religious obsessions and compulsions, or children who have been threatened with fire and brimstone by emotionally abusive parents, or people who have acted out strange and even dangerous behaviors because they were instructed to do so by "the voice of God." It is important to understand that these are all manifestations of *religion,* interacting with emotional illness. These are not manifestations of *genuine faith.* Religion is a structure of doctrines, practices, and traditions that may or may not involve authentic faith. But pure faith in Jesus Christ is not a religion, it is a *relationship* of trust between ourselves and Christ.

Many of the individuals who have had a major influence on the fields of psychiatric and psychological research have failed to understand the differences between faith and religion. Sigmund Freud concluded that the reason people became Christians was that they were looking for a cosmic father figure. Carl Jung believed that people became Christians because they were responding to a symbolic "archetype" of God. Abraham Maslow believed that people became Christians as part of a peak religious experience, an intense emotional and spiritual event that confers a sense of overwhelming meaning and validation upon a person's life.

We believe there's a certain amount of truth to all of these interpretations. Freud and Jung were correct to the extent that human beings do have a "God-shaped void," an inner need for communion with an infinite, Heavenly Father—not a mythical being, as Freud would have us believe, but a real Father-Creator, a loving Person with whom we can have intimate fellowship. And Maslow was correct to the extent that many Christians (though certainly not all, and not even most) do describe their conversion experiences as being very highly charged with emotion and an intense feeling of being joined to the Infinite; the emotional component of faith is important but certainly not central (see EMOTIONS).

In our experience at the Minirth Meier New Life Clinics, we have found that genuine faith—far from hindering emotional health—is a major component of emotional health. Again and again, we have found that many emotional problems have a spiritual basis and require a spiritual solution. Some of the spiritual causes of emotional pain include:

A pattern of sinful behavior. Sin produces guilt, emotional instability, depression, and anxiety. Much of the emotional pain we treat at the clinic is the direct consequence of sexual sin, abortion, financial misdealings, lying, and so forth. People often compound their emotional issues by engaging in even more sinful behavior in an attempt to anesthetize their emotional pain. Authentic guilt and mental anguish are the normal responses of those who sin and do not repent of that sin and turn to God. When we see the emotional aftermath of sin, it is easy to understand why 1 Peter 2:11 tells us that the sins of the flesh "war against the soul."

Christians do sin; God does not expect moral perfection from imperfect human beings, even after their conversion. Yet any Christian who willfully practices sin—that is, anyone who engages in a pattern of sin without experiencing guilt and depression—should question the sincerity of his or her commitment to Christ and should immediately repent and recommit his or her life to Christ (see 1 John 3:4–10; 1 John 1:9; and Psalm 103:12–14).

False guilt. Though authentic guilt serves a positive purpose in our lives—that is, it awakens us to the existence of sin and the need to repent—many of us also experience false guilt, a sense of condemnation that arises either because of judgments that other people impose on us or judgments we impose on ourselves. In most cases, false guilt is part of a pattern that begins in childhood when unforgiving, rigid parents excessively punish the child. This child grows up convinced that anything less than superhuman perfection is failure, and since he cannot be perfect no matter how hard he tries, he grows up feeling guilty and inferior.

This neurotic condition of false guilt can usually be relieved only as the afflicted individual is immersed for a long period of time in the truths of the Bible that speak to the love, acceptance, forgiveness, and grace of God. In time, with counseling and daily Scripture study, a person can be helped to see that God does not expect His children to live perfect, sinless lives. He only wants us to trust Him and do our best to seek His will on a daily basis.

The Christian "Power System"

Although we are Christian psychiatrists and counselors at the Minirth Meier New Life Clinics, we do not require that people profess a faith in Jesus Christ before we will treat them. In fact, we have treated persons of all religions, as well as agnostics and atheists. Many of these people respond to treatment and recover their ability to function normally. However, we have seen quite clearly that Christians tend to derive more benefit from therapy, and that Christians seem to recover more quickly and more fully than non-Christians. There is a reason for this: Christians have the advantage of a "power system" that non-Christians don't have. The source of this "power system" is threefold:

1. Christians have the Bible as a final authority to direct their behavior. The Bible is our guidebook, and the rules are clear. Statements such as "Thou shalt not commit adultery" are not intended to ruin our fun but to protect us from self-defeating and self-destructive behavior.

2. Christians have the Holy Spirit as a source of comfort, guidance, wisdom, and encouragement in times of emotional stress. Through the Holy Spirit, all the vast resources of the Creator-God of the Universe are alongside us, available at a moment's notice.

3. Christians have God's assurance of forgiveness. The greatest single source of emotional pain is guilt, a sense that one's life has been forever stained by sin. The knowledge that God has cleansed that stain and removed our guilt from us, as far as the east is from the west, is the most liberating and healing experience any person can know. But this assurance of forgiveness is unique to Christianity. Apart from faith in Christ, it is impossible to experience the fully cleansing experience of God's forgiveness.

Alienation from God. A feeling of alienation from the love of God is a major source of emotional problems. Reconciliation to God—which includes finding a sense of God's love, forgiveness, and acceptance—is the only complete answer to this emotional pain. To be complete persons, as God intended and designed us to be, we must commit ourselves completely to Him. That is why we find this commandment in Matthew 22:37: "You shall love the LORD your God with all your heart, with all your soul, and with all your mind." Loving God with all of one's heart means to love Him affectionately, with the emotions. To love God with all of one's soul means to love Him with the will, according to one's knowledge of Him. To love Him with all of one's mind means to love with a sense of total conscious awareness of Him and commitment to Him. We have found that people who have this kind of total commitment to and loving relationship with God tend to have far fewer emotional problems than most people.

WHAT IS YOUR IMAGE OF GOD?

At one time or another, most Christians experience some hindrance in their faith because of dissatisfaction or disappointment with God. Many of us find it hard to admit to others—or even to ourselves—our displeasure with God. Yet this is one of the most common issues we deal with in our clinical experience.

Even people who would not describe themselves as dissatisfied or disappointed with God often feel frustrated by a lack of closeness to God and a confusion about who God really is. Intellectually, they may know all the doctrines and all the confessions of the church, but they are frequently unable to sense God's presence in their hearts and in their lives.

What we are describing is a problem that many sincere believers experience, a problem that hinders their faith, robs them of joy, and impairs their emotional health. This problem is called *a distorted image of God.* By "image of God," we don't mean God's true image as it is revealed in the Bible. We are referring here to a person's individual conception of God and experience with God at a given point in his or her life. The way God is portrayed in the Bible is not subject to distortion, but your own inner understanding of God can easily become distorted because of a number of factors in your life. Distortions in your image of God may arise because:

- You misunderstand what the Bible says about God.
- You blame God for problems and hurts caused by other people or by your own sins and mistakes.
- You have been influenced by the destructive and anti-Christian ideas of our secular culture.
- You unconsciously identify God, our Heavenly Father, with an abusive or unloving earthly parent; that is, you project the negative qualities of your mother or (more often) your father onto God.

Whatever the source of your distorted image of God, the result is a set of messages that play and replay in your mind and prevent you from loving God and sensing His love toward you:

"I don't know if I can trust God."

"God loves some people more than He loves me."

"God isn't fair."

"God is too controlling. He just wants to spoil my fun."

"God can't forgive someone like me."

"God enjoys watching me suffer."

"God won't love me unless I pray just the right way."

"God won't love me unless I'm perfect and sinless."

The result of these distorted ideas about God is that He becomes like a stranger to you. You are prevented from having a fulfilling faith relationship with Him because these false images of God prevent you from trusting Him.

The Origin of Distorted Images of God

Your image of God develops and changes over your lifetime. It is continually shaped and reshaped by new learning experiences, new emotional experiences, by joys, sorrows, triumphs, and traumas. Sometimes your individual conception of God moves closer to His true image; sometimes it regresses and becomes more distorted. Though God and His Word are unchanging, your experience with God is dynamic and continually changing.

For most of us, our image of God is most powerfully shaped during childhood. To be sure, part of our image of God is derived from the things we are taught about God during our formative years through our parents, Sunday school and church, parochial education, and so forth. But for most of us, the things we were consciously taught about God have not influenced us nearly as much as what we were unconsciously taught about God by the example of our parents. People who had distant, unloving parents tend to view God as remote and unloving. People who had abusive, rageaholic parents tend to see God as dangerous, angry, and unpredictable. People who had critical, judgmental parents tend to grow up fearing the judgment of a stern, ominous God. Not surprisingly, those who had loving, caring, nurturing parents have the best chance of experiencing a healthy relationship with a loving God.

Yet even if we have been given a good foundation for a healthy image of God in childhood, events that take place in adolescence and adulthood can arise that wound us and damage our image of God. If a trauma takes place in our lives—a painful disability or the death of a loved one—we may ask, "Why did God allow this to happen?" If we are diagnosed with cancer or if we lose a job, we may wonder, "Why is God punishing me?" What we are doing, in such cases, is attributing a negative event to God, then generalizing from that event and concluding that since God allowed or caused this event, He must be unjust, or vindictive, or sadistic.

The correction for this distorted image of God is to recognize several truths to be simultaneously at work in our lives: (1) God loves us, and does not want us to be hurt; (2) we live in a fallen world in which bad things can and do happen; (3) when bad things happen, it does not mean that God caused or willed those events, or that God does not love us; and (4) God promises to help us in times of suffering but has not promised to remove us from all suffering.

The Personality Factor

People also develop distortions in their image of God as they project their own personality traits onto God. For example, a demanding perfectionistic individual is likely to see God as strict and judgmental. A tenderhearted individual is likely to see God as gracious, indulgent, and even soft on sin.

And there are other ways our individual personality makeup can affect our view of God. Our personality—which, put simply, consists of our mind, emotion, and will—is what makes each of us a unique and distinct individual. Though we are each unique, there are certain personality categories we tend to fall into, and our relationship with God will be affected, either positively or negatively, depending on our personality type.

For example, an *obsessive-compulsive personality* tends to be driven, perfectionistic, uncompromising, anxious, and preoccupied with strict moral standards, analysis, and doubting. It is common for obsessive-compulsive people to doubt their salvation and to wonder if God has abandoned them. They seem to require frequent reassurance that they are truly loved by God.

The *histrionic personality* tends to be emotional, extroverted, dramatic, and spontaneous. Histrionic individuals tend to experience an unstable, vacillating relationship with God, based on the feelings of the moment rather than on the promises of the Bible. When emotions run high, God is seen as a loving Friend. When emotions dip low, the histrionic may direct feelings of anger toward God.

The *paranoid personality* is characterized by an exaggerated sense that "everything happens to me." This individual will interpret general events, and even events that befall other people, as being specific attacks aimed at him or her. If a loved one gets cancer, the paranoid personality says, "God did this because He's angry with me." This individual is often wary in his approach to God, thinking, "God is out to get me."

The *neurotic personality* is prone to anxiety and will tend to reshape memories and beliefs in such a way as to reduce the level of anxiety. This individual, then, will tend to invent his or her own image of God so as to reduce that anxiety level and provide a greater sense of control over life.

(For a more comprehensive discussion of this issue, see the article on PERSONALITY TYPES AND DISORDERS.)

Treatment of a Distorted Image of God

Left untreated, distortions in our image of God lead to emotional damage and spiritual impairment. We will find it increasingly difficult to accept the wisdom and comfort of the Bible and the Holy Spirit. As 2 Corinthians 7:1 tells us, "let us cleanse ourselves from all filthiness [or impurities] of the flesh and spirit, perfecting holiness" out of reverence for God. His will for us is to grow in an ever-increasing expression of the fruit of the Spirit, as described in Galatians 5: love, joy, peace, patience, kindness, goodness, faithfulness, gentleness, and self-control. Over time, a distorted image of God tends to produce the opposite traits within us: loneliness, depression, anxiety, impatience, bitterness, resentment, distrust and doubt, callousness and indifference, and self-centeredness.

The following is a ten-step plan for healing your distorted image of God, adapted from *Please Let Me Know You, God* by Dr. Larry Stephens of the Minirth Meier New Life Clinics (Thomas Nelson, 1993):

Step 1: Do not evaluate God on the basis of your understanding. God is infinite, but we are finite. That is why Proverbs 3:5 counsels us, "Trust in the LORD with all your heart, and lean not on your own understanding." Our tendency in times of pain or confusion is to pray, "God, You owe me an explanation!" We must learn to exchange this demanding attitude with an attitude of trust and humility: "Lord, I don't know why You have allowed this in my life, but I will choose to trust You no matter what happens."

Step 2: Avoid basing your image of God on negative experiences in your life, past or present. People and circumstances may have hurt you, but God does not hurt you. He is a healer. He loves you. He is on your side.

Step 3: Avoid basing your image of God on the example, behavior, or ideas of others. Parents, teachers, pastors, evangelists, authors, doctors, mentors, and fellow Christians are all human and fallible. You can learn a great deal by talking, listening, interacting, and observing other people, but you should never make any other person a basis for your image of God. The only valid sources for determining who God truly is are the Word of God, the Spirit of God, and the example of the Son of God, Jesus Christ.

Step 4: Avoid basing your image of God on your feelings—especially your negative feelings. Emotions go up and down, but God and His truth never change.

Step 5: Make a decision to place your unconditional trust in God. You may not always *feel* like trusting God, but feelings are not the issue. What really matters is that you have made a conscious _decision_ to trust God. Base your beliefs and your behavior on that decision, not on your feelings. As Dr. Stephens says in his book, "It's easier to act your way into a new way of feeling than to feel your way into a new way of acting. . . . Concentrate on living your life as if you trust God, and the feelings of trust will follow."

Step 6: Evaluate your image of God regularly. Make appropriate adjustments in your thinking whenever you detect distortions. Spend time with the Bible every day so that its truth about God can permeate and saturate your thinking.

Step 7: Focus on the biblical truth that Jesus is God and the character of God is the character of Jesus Christ. Many people fragment their image of God, saying, "I like Jesus, but I find God the Father kind of forbidding and scary." Jesus came to reveal the character of God to us. Whatever we see in the character of Jesus is true of the character of God the Father. "He who has seen Me," says Jesus in John 14:9, "has seen the Father."

Step 8: Read your Bible and pray daily, regardless of whether you feel like it. Prayer and Bible study are spiritual disciplines that require a daily commitment—and that pay daily dividends. You may not feel like maintaining a devotional life right now, but if you *make* a commitment and *keep* that commitment, regardless of your current feelings, a time will come when you will not want to miss a single day with the Lord.

Step 9: Don't allow your personality to dictate your experience with God. Your personality type can be a hidden source of distortion in your relationship with God. But if you recognize that your doubts about God are owing to obsessive-compulsive tendencies, or that your anxiety about God's caring for you is owing to neurotic tendencies, then you can make allowances for these personality tendencies, and you will experience less emotional pain. Understanding your personality type can arm you with the perspective you need to overcome the problems and emotional deficits that personality types often cause.

Step 10: Seek healing in your self-image. If you have a negative self-image, you may begin to confuse the way you view yourself with the way God views you. This distortion can cause you great emotional pain. The more you are able to forgive and accept yourself unconditionally, the less distortion you are likely to feel in your relationship with God.

FINDING MEANING IN LIFE

We all long to know that our lives matter, that we are not just using up space and killing time on this planet until it's time to die.

In his book, *In Search of the Heart* (Thomas Nelson, 1993), Dr. David Allen talks about the spiritual discoveries he has made while working with drug and alcohol addicts at the Minirth Meier New Life Clinic in Washington, D.C. Although it is his job to help his clients along the road to recovery, he often finds that he gains insight into his own spiritual journey by watching his clients struggle to find healing and meaning in life. It is common for recovering addicts to announce, "I'm in recovery," but Dr. Allen says his patients are more likely to announce, "I'm in discovery."

"They are saying," Dr. Allen explains, "that they are in a different stage from when they first recovered from their problems and addictions. In fact, discovery is available to anyone who is searching for a deeper meaning in life—searching for his or her heart."

The journey of faith truly is a journey of discovery. We all long to understand our place in the scheme of the universe. We all want to discover the meaning God has for the all-too-brief interval that comes between the moment of our birth and the moment of our death.

Money doesn't provide meaning. Neither does fame or power or pleasure or success or achievement. People seek after these things as if they are the be-all and end-all of life, but once they have acquired them, they still feel empty. We have seen this truth proven over and over, as many a wealthy, successful businessman has come into the clinic and said, "I should be satisfied with my life. Look at everything I have—a ton of money, a beautiful home, a wonderful family, a powerful place in the business world, a corner office, and the respect of my peers. So why do I feel so empty all the time?" Even the rich and famous are starved for meaning and in need of spiritual discovery.

Within each of us, behind all the defenses and pretenses, beneath all the emotional bandages we have wrapped around our hearts for self-protection, there is a unique living spirit, our deepest and truest identity, a one-of-a-kind self that has been made in the image of God, and which yearns for communion with God. As Saint Augustine wrote in his *Confessions* (J. W. Edwards, 1946), "Thou hast made us for Thyself, and we shall ever restless be until we find our rest in Thee."

SELF-TEST | Am I Searching for Meaning?

Are you in search of discovery and a deeper sense of meaning in life? To find out, take the self-test that follows, which is adapted from Dr. Allen's book, *In Search of the Heart.* Check the statements that apply to you.

THE COMPLETE LIFE ENCYCLOPEDIA

_____ I sometimes fear disclosing my true self to another person because that person might abandon me.

_____ I don't like to be alone. I'd rather be with other people who affirm me.

_____ I tend to overreact to events.

_____ I try to please others, which may be my way of establishing my meaning and identity.

_____ I love my spouse or friend and at the same time tend to hate him or her. (Psychiatrists call this a "close ambivalent attitude," both desiring and rejecting another person at the same time.)

_____ I am tired and fed up most of the time.

_____ I sometimes feel very depressed.

_____ I'm often afraid to trust someone.

_____ I have no meaning in life.

_____ I sometimes back away from a relationship because I feel the other person might try to control me. (We call this "fear of engulfment.")

_____ I need a drink at night to relax.

_____ I use food to make me feel better.

_____ I use drugs when I am depressed.

_____ I blame myself for a lot of the problems in our family.

_____ My life seems empty and boring.

_____ I often don't have much motivation to do anything.

_____ I feel empty inside.

If you checked one or more of the above statements, your emotional issues and problems may have their genesis in a deep need for discovery and meaning in life.

Our spiritual journey is a lifelong process, and each individual travels that journey in his or her own way. At many points along the road, we will make discoveries and experience the exhilarating and profound "Aha!" of deep insight. The moment of discovery may occur as we contemplate the wonder of creation, or as we stumble onto a brilliant nugget of truth in God's Word, or as we find some newly revealed glimmer of truth reflected back to us in a conversation with a friend. That moment of discovery gives us a sudden explosive revelation of a major truth, or of God's love, or of the peace and joy that is available to us even in times of pain and turmoil. And in that moment of discovery, we encounter a little bit of God's meaning and eternal plan for our lives.

As believers and followers of Christ, we have a Companion on our journey of spiritual discovery. This Companion knows the way, and He guides us along our journey. We are not just aimless wanderers in search of truth. We are being _led_ closer to the Truth, step by step and day by day. The One who is the Way, the Truth, and the Life is guiding us deeper into Himself. He is revealing to us our ultimate meaning as He directs our steps.

Though every individual's spiritual journey is, by definition, a unique and private experience, there are a number of steps you can take to ensure that you are moving forward and following the leadership of Jesus Christ as you go:

■

Amid all our busyness, our impossible schedules, our frantic quests for fun and excitement, we must find time for discovery, for taking that journey deeper into God, deeper into our hidden selves, deeper into true meaning.

■

1. Acknowledge the lordship of Jesus Christ. The real journey begins once you have acknowledged that He is in control of your life. Jesus is not only our Guide and Counselor along our spiritual journey. He is our purpose for living every day.

2. Dedicate your life, wholly and solely, to God. "I beseech you therefore, brethren, by the mercies of God," says Romans 12:1–2, "that you present your bodies a living sacrifice, holy, acceptable to God, which is your reasonable service. And do not be conformed to this world, but be transformed by the renewing of your mind, that you may prove what is that good and acceptable and perfect will of God." Presenting yourself as a living sacrifice to God is like handing Him a blank check and saying, "Here's the rest of my life. Do with it as You wish." You cannot find God's truest, deepest meaning for your life while you are busily conforming to this world and its temporary, perishing values. True meaning can only be found in the good, acceptable, perfect plan of God for your life.

3. Make a decision to discover your spiritual gifts. Your spiritual gifts are some of the most important aspects of yourself. By discovering your spiritual gifts, you discover who you are in Christ and how He wants to use you. You will discover your gifts as you:

- Study the Scriptures and learn all we can about spiritual gifts. (See especially Romans 12:4–8; 1 Corinthians 12 and 14; Ephesians 4:8, 11–12.)
- Get involved in a local church, using your gifts for teaching, witnessing, helping, serving, leading, and meeting practical needs.
- Get involved in a small group Bible study that practices close fellowship, affirmation, and accountability. God uses other believers to recognize and affirm the gifts in each of us.

4. Spend regular, daily time in prayer, reflection, and studying God's Word. In those special quiet times with God, particularly as you are still and listen intently to God's voice speaking within you, He is able to reach you, to heal your hurts, to calm your fears, and to give you a deeper understanding of His purpose in your life.

Through your commitment to excellence, to integrity, to caring for others, and to working hard for every nickel you earn, you become "salt" and "light" in our culture. You show that Christians are different from the rest of the world—and it's a difference that other people want and that attracts them to the Truth.

5. Seek ways to offer up every aspect of your life, including your career, to God for His use. Many Christians become frustrated with their careers, thinking, "God isn't using me here. I'm just spinning my wheels. If only I had made a choice early in life to be a pastor or a missionary, then God would be able to use me." But that's just not so! God doesn't want a church full of pastors and missionaries. He has an eternal purpose in mind for construction workers, secretaries, housewives, bankers, musicians, social workers, and ditchdiggers too! You can find creative ways to express God's presence in your life through your career.

The apostle Paul was a tentmaker by trade, but his truest calling was his calling from God. He knew how to combine his earthly occupation with his vocation for Jesus Christ. Even in prison, when his options were so limited, he made the best of his circumstances, writing many of the letters which are today a large part of our New Testament. If you feel "imprisoned" by your circumstances right now, consider what it was like for Paul to be shut up in a literal prison of iron bars and stone walls. Even

THE COMPLETE LIFE ENCYCLOPEDIA

facing death, his life had meaning and purpose. "For to me, to live is Christ," he said in Philippians 1:21, "and to die is gain."

As you set out on your own journey of spiritual discovery, here are some questions to consider as you pray and seek God's continuing, deepening presence in your life:

"Where is my life headed?"

"What am I living for?"

"What will I leave behind after I am gone?"

"What am I doing now that will be of significance in eternity?"

"Have I made my life fully available to God?"

For us as believers, the ultimate meaning in life is knowing that we belong to Christ, and He is able to use us to accomplish His eternal purpose. He is the Lord, and we are His servants. The way we spend our days, and even our moments, can have an impact on lives that will resonate down the centuries and on into eternity. When God's purpose becomes our purpose, then we have discovered the greatest meaning that can be found in life.

FAITH AND GOD'S WORD

Do we truly appreciate the amazing resource God has given us in His Word? Many of us have copies of the Bible in various translations, sitting on bookshelves, gathering dust. We take our Bibles to church on Sunday mornings—but what about the rest of the week? We say that this Book is God's supernaturally revealed message to the human race, but if that is so, do we spend an appropriate amount of time each day reading that miraculous message?

As evangelical Christians, we believe the Bible to be inerrant (without error) and inspired by God. The apostle Paul writes, "All Scripture is given by inspiration of God, and is profitable for doctrine, for reproof, for correction, for instruction in righteousness" (2 Tim. 3:16). That term *inspiration* literally means that Scripture was "God-breathed." Paul is describing a process by which the Holy Spirit supervised selected human authors as they composed and set down God's revelation to the human race. As you read through the books of the Bible, you can sense the individual personalities of the writers. God used these individual personalities as He poured His message through them. God's thoughts flowed out onto the original manuscripts without error, and then God preserved this book so that it could be accurately handed down for our instruction and encouragement today.

We know that we can trust the Bible as God's Word for a number of reasons:

1. The Bible contains many prophecies that have been fulfilled to the last detail. For example, there are more than three hundred specific Old Testament prophecies regarding the coming of the Messiah, and Jesus fulfilled all of those prophecies with amazing precision.

2. The reliability of the Bible has been affirmed by the most reliable and credible person who ever lived, Jesus Himself. On a number of occasions, He rebuked His own disciples for their slowness to believe the Scriptures. "Sanctify them by Your truth," He prayed in John 17:17. "Your word is truth." In other words,

265

FAITH

He was saying that God's truth, contained in His Word, is the tool for setting His followers apart as dedicated and committed to Him. His truth is the antidote to the toxic lies, both satanic lies and worldly lies, that surround us and attack our thinking.

3. The Bible repeatedly claims to speak for God. In the Old Testament alone, there are more than 3,800 passages in Scripture that make the claim that the Scriptures come from God.

4. Finally, one of the most indisputable evidences of the reliability of God's Word is the fact we see every day in our clinical practice at the Minirth Meier New Life Clinics: this Book has the power to change lives. Again and again, we have seen individuals challenged by the message of the Bible. They have placed their trust in Jesus, who is revealed in the Bible. They have committed their lives to God, whose Word is the Bible. They have not only been saved in a spiritual and eternal sense, but in case after case, story after story, they have been healed of deeply entrenched sinful habits, addictions, emotional pain, dysfunctional relationship patterns, and tortured memories. As 1 Peter 1:23 tells us, we have "been born again . . . through the word of God which lives and abides forever."

The sixty-six books of the Bible have been given to us to lead us to the truth, to steer us away from error, to encourage us to persevere under pressure and stress, and to equip us to serve God. How, then, can we lay hold of this message and build it into our lives? We do so by a process called *meditation*.

Meditation means more than just reading the Bible. To meditate means to reflect, to ponder, and to carry on an inner dialogue with oneself about the Word of God. Meditating on the Bible helps us to internalize its message, and to make it a part not only of our conscious minds but of our subconscious minds, which have a hidden but very powerful influence on the way we feel about ourselves and the way we live our lives.

Scripture meditation not only brings the results we would naturally expect—a deeper understanding of the Bible and a greater appreciation of God's character—it also brings about some surprising positive results in the lives of most people who practice meditation on a regular basis: lower blood pressure and other beneficial body responses, an increased capacity for handling stress and anxiety, a tendency toward longer life, and greater success in careers and most important relationships.

266

YOUR DAILY QUIET TIME

One of the most important aids to a healthy faith and a healthy emotional life is a daily habit of meeting alone with the Lord. This spiritual discipline is called a *daily quiet time*. A quiet time should ideally involve Bible study and meditation (as described on page 266) and prayer.

Here are some suggestions for an effective quiet time:

1. Make your quiet time a regular, daily habit. Choose a time when you can spend time with God, alone and undisturbed (most people find that early in the morning is the best time).
2. Select a special place for your quiet time—your bedroom, your breakfast nook, your office, anyplace where you can spend about half an hour in undisturbed solitude. Turn off the phone or let the answering machine answer it. Don't let anything intrude on your special place and your special time.
3. Keep a notebook or journal of significant Scripture insights, notes, observations, and "Aha!" experiences with Bible meditation and prayer. Also, keep a record of prayer requests, along with answers when they occur.
4. When you pray, be sure to spend time being quiet and listening for the Lord's answers. "Be still, and know that I am God," says Psalm 46:10. Many people make the mistake of only talking to God in prayer and never listening to God in prayer. The quietest part of your quiet time is a time when God can bring important thoughts and insights to your mind that can improve your spiritual life, your emotional life, and your relationships throughout the day, throughout the week, and throughout your life.

This process only takes ten minutes or so in the morning and can be repeated in the evening for maximum results. As you follow this process, you will find you have more power in your life to break sinful habits, rechannel unproductive or self-defeating thinking, defuse anxiety, build confidence and self-esteem, and gain confidence for personal witnessing.

Don't neglect the crucial spiritual discipline of a daily quiet time. God enjoys spending time with you, and if you make your quiet time a priority in your life, you will find you genuinely enjoy spending time in His presence.

> *Time spent in quiet communion with God helps to improve your thinking and tends to improve your activities and relationships for the entire day. A daily quiet time is an integral part of the process described in Romans 12:1–2, whereby we are to be transformed by the renewing of our minds.*

Making the Most of Your Quiet Time

Here are some more suggestions for internalizing God's Word during your quiet time:

1. When you encounter an especially meaningful verse for your life, take time to memorize it. Write it on a card and place it on your bathroom mirror, the dashboard of your car, or your refrigerator. Make it a part of your daily thinking for the next week.
2. Personalize that verse by replacing the appropriate personal pronouns with your own name.
3. Imagine yourself carrying out the instruction and meaning of that verse in the everyday situations of your life.

FAMILY DEVOTIONS

Frank and Beverly had been talking about having family devotions for months, but they never seemed to get around to it. The TV was on, the kids needed baths before bedtime, the phone would ring—there was excuse after excuse, but the net result was that there never seemed to be time in the evening for family devotions. One day, their kindergarten-age daughter, Kristy, spoke up at the dinner table. "At school today," she said, "my friend, Lisa, told me her family does something every night called 'deboshuns' or something like that. They pray together and sing songs together and they talk about things they're thankful for and their dad reads Bible stories to the kids. That sounds like fun. Why don't we do something like that?" Frank and Beverly looked guiltily at each other. And that night, they started a new family tradition. They have rarely missed a night of family devotions since.

Statistics indicate that families that practice a daily devotional time together have healthier marriages and happier home lives. We are all familiar with the statistic that half of all marriages end in divorce. But were you aware that only 1 in 40 marriages ends in divorce when the family attends church regularly? And that only 1 in 400 marriages ends in divorce when the family prays and studies the Bible together?

In addition to our personal quiet time with God, we should also spend time with God as a family. An effective time of family devotions only takes ten to twenty minutes. It can take place in the morning (say, at the breakfast table) or evening (after dinner or before bedtime). Most families find evenings to be less hectic than mornings, when people are rushing to get ready for work and school.

The Scriptures make it clear that faith in God is not for individuals only but was intended by God to be a family affair. In Joshua 24:15, Joshua declares, "As for me and my house, we will serve the LORD." And as Paul said to the Philippian jailer in Acts 16:31, "Believe on the Lord Jesus Christ, and you will be saved, you and your household."

Particularly when small children are involved, family devotions should be kept fairly short, lively, and interesting. As adults, avoid praying long prayers: save your big prayer list for your personal quiet time. Use children's Bible storybooks to relate biblical truth. Avoid using Bible translations that are difficult for children to understand.

Don't be discouraged if some family members resist participating (especially teens or young adults). Be alert to distractions and problems that may arise to interrupt your family devotional habit; some of these problems may be a form of satanic attack on the good thing you are trying to do in your family life. Avoid "preaching" to your children through your prayers ("Lord, please make my children sorry for hurting my feelings today"). Prayer is for talking to God, not lecturing your children.

Avoid becoming frazzled or angry if devotions don't go exactly as you planned. Calmly persevere and try to be a steady influence on your family. If you make a commitment to family devotions and keep that commitment, you will eventually see the enthusiasm grow. You may experience the thrill that Frank and Beverly have discovered: their children are the biggest boosters of family devotions, and they make sure that Frank and Beverly never miss a single evening together with the family and with the Lord!

SELECTING A LOCAL CHURCH

"We are His hands, we are His voice," sings contemporary Christian singer Randy Stonehill. And that is an excellent description of the role of the church. As the Bible describes it, the church is not a building or a denomination, it is a *body*—the Body of

Christ, the visible expression of God's work and God's message in the world. This body is made up of individuals just like you, ordinary people who have tapped into the extraordinary power of God by trusting Jesus Christ as Lord and Savior. Through us, God does His work in the world. Through us, He speaks and witnesses of Himself in the world. We truly are His hands and His voice.

This body is manifested on a local level by assemblies we call *churches*. In these local assemblies, believers meet on a regular basis to worship God, to study His Word, to pray together, to minister together, and to support and encourage each other as they work together to tell the story of Jesus Christ to others in their neighborhoods and throughout the world. In the local church, believers have an opportunity to exercise their spiritual gifts so that they can build up the entire Body of Christ. They also have the opportunity to contribute their resources to support God's work.

Many people, particularly new Christians, find the vast number and variety of churches in our country to be confusing. In some places, you will find three or four churches on a street corner, with signs in front advertising snappy sermon titles, almost seeming to compete with each other for "business." Look in the Yellow Pages of your phone book, and you'll see church ads competing with one another. But you can't pick out a good church the same way you would select a plumber or a dry cleaner. The size of the Yellow Pages ad is no indication of whether it is the right church for you.

All too often, churches are run like businesses, with a board of directors, a CEO (the pastor), and the customers (the people in the pews). But God didn't design the church to be a business. He designed it to be a family—a family of faith. It is to be a place where people can find love, acceptance, and forgiveness, as well as a place where they can be held accountable for their lifestyles and their spiritual progress.

How, then, do you select a local assembly that will meet your needs for fellowship and worship, while giving you a place where you can practice your faith and express your God-given gifts? Here are some suggestions:

1. Base your selection on the right criteria. The *wrong* reasons for selecting a church include:

- "It's close."
- "The church building is so beautiful."
- "It's the church where my relatives go."
- "It has the biggest choir in town."

2. Don't take for granted that it's the right church for you and your family just because of its denomination or its size. As you begin to get serious about a certain church, ask about the church's beliefs and practices. Not every church teaches the essentials of the Christian faith, but the church *you* belong to *should*. Those essentials include:

- the deity of Christ (the belief that Jesus is God)
- salvation from sin by grace through faith in Jesus Christ
- the inspiration and trustworthiness of Scripture
- the practices of baptism and Communion by believers

3. Ask about the programs of the church. Does the church emphasize evangelism and missions; that is, does it place importance on witnessing to the world about Jesus

Christ? Does it have specific programs to meet your needs and the needs of your family? If you have children in your family, does the church have a strong ministry to children and youth? Does the church have strong relational programs of small group Bible study and relational sharing? If you are in recovery, does the church have Christian recovery and support groups to address your needs?

Some people say, "I have Jesus. I don't really need to go to church to be a Christian." But Hebrews 10:24–25 tells us otherwise: "And let us consider one another in order to stir up love and good works, not forsaking the assembling of ourselves together, as is the manner of some, but exhorting one another, and so much the more as you see the Day approaching."

The Christian faith was designed to be lived out not in isolation but in fellowship and community. We need each other in the Body of Christ. We need the support, encouragement, and instruction that take place in a church fellowship. But even church on Sunday nights and midweek is not all there is to our lives together in the Body of Christ. We also need a deep-level faith support system.

YOUR FAITH SUPPORT SYSTEM

Most churches have a Sunday morning "fellowship time" around the coffeepot between services, and this is a good practice. Members get a chance to talk, encourage each other, and meet new people at these fellowship times. But when the New Testament talks about fellowship (using the Greek word *koinonia*), it refers to something much deeper and more intense than chatting around the coffeepot. Fellowship in the early church involved a regular process of:

- praying together, *with* each other and *for* each other
- worshiping and praising God together
- singing spiritual songs together
- confessing faults, sins, and hurts to one another
- holding each other accountable for lifestyle issues, behavior, and spiritual growth—not in a harsh way, but in a loving and accepting way
- confronting sin or denial out of love for each other
- sharing burdens and meeting each other's practical needs

These dynamics characterized the church of the book of Acts, and these dynamics are still a necessary part of the Christian life and the Christian faith. Today, these dynamics are best found and developed in small groups. To find a small group where your faith and spiritual growth can be nurtured, encouraged, and enriched, start by finding a local church that offers small groups. They may be called "fellowship groups," "koinonia fellowships," or "house churches." These groups normally meet on weekday evenings in homes, although some churches have Sunday night small group programs. These fellowships usually contain eight to fifteen people and are built around a Bible study curriculum. They may meet weekly, biweekly, or monthly.

You may think, *I have so much to do, how can I possibly take on one more commitment?* But the support and growth you will experience in your group is so powerful, meaningful, and enjoyable that after you have been in the group for a few weeks, you'll wonder how you ever got along without it!

SHARING YOUR FAITH

One of the most important—and most overlooked—aspects of the Christian faith is the fact that *the best way to hold on to your faith is to give it away.* In other words, share your faith with other people. They need to hear the truth that you have already received.

If you had a cure for cancer, you wouldn't keep it to yourself, would you? Well, then why would you want to keep the cure for sin all to yourself when people all around you are dying in their sins?

One of the most sobering truths of the Christian life is the fact that many people—people we know and laugh with and joke with and work with—are absolutely lost without knowing Christ as their Savior. The

"Easier said than done!" you may say. "I can't witness to people! I get all tongue-tied and knock-kneed!" That's the same argument Moses made when God told him to be His prophetic witness to Pharaoh. That argument doesn't hold any more water now than it did then. You don't have to be Billy Graham to be a witness. You just have to be you, and you just have to be willing.

tragic truth is that most of them don't even know what to do to be saved. They know that they lack meaning in their lives, that they are unhappy and unfulfilled—but they don't know the solution to their problems. You have the cure. Don't hoard it. Give it away. Give it to your neighbor, your coworker, your friend, classmates. Tell them that Jesus died for their sins, that He has risen and has solved their sin problem. Tell them that by His death and resurrection, they now can have the free gift of eternal life. Here is a simple three-point strategy for sharing your faith:

1. *Yield your life to the Holy Spirit.* Pray that He will control you and empower you. Confess and repent of any sin in your life. Ask Him to give you boldness to say the words He gives you to say.
2. *Become a friend to non-Christians.* People find an authentic Christian lifestyle, characterized by unconditional love and acceptance, far more convincing than any words. Find ways to minister to the practical needs of your non-Christian friends. Find ways to be a good helper, a good listener, a hospitable host. In time, they may ask you, "Why are you doing this?" And you can tell them, "Because I want you to know that God loves you."

   Remember, it is not our job to make people accept Christ. Only God can convict people of sin and of their need to trust Christ. Some people that you witness to will reject your message. But the fact that some choose to reject Christ should not be viewed as a rejection of you personally. If people refuse your Gospel, be cordial and continue to be caring.

3. *Once you have earned the right to be heard, speak.* Ask God to give you the words to say, then say them. We have found it is often helpful to ask, "Has anyone ever shown you from the Bible how you can know you are going to heaven when you die?" This will usually give you opportunity to present the basic elements of the Gospel, along with the appropriate Scripture passages for each point. (See the table of "The Basic Elements of the Gospel.") Then, if the person expresses a desire to commit his or her life to Jesus Christ, you may lead him or her in the prayer of commitment that appeared earlier in this article.

"Always be ready," says 1 Peter 3:15, "to give a defense to everyone who asks you a reason for the hope that is in you, with meekness and fear." We should be spiritually prepared. We should have our minds steeped in Scripture and bathed in prayer. We should always be alert to opportunities to share our faith. If we do these things, God will be able to use us, again and again, as channels of His blessing and love to a hurting, lost world.

THE BASIC ELEMENTS OF THE GOSPEL	
GOSPEL TRUTH	SCRIPTURE SUPPORT
Each of us is a sinner.	Romans 3:23
Though God loves us, He must punish sin.	Romans 6:23
God loved us so much, He sent His Son, Jesus, to take the punishment for our sin on Himself.	John 3:16; Romans 5:8
We can receive the free gift of salvation by trusting Christ and turning our lives over to Him.	Romans 10:13

AMAZING GRACE

Amazing grace, how sweet the sound,
That saved a wretch like me . . .

To most non-Christians, the word *grace* is a vague, religious-sounding word of uncertain meaning. To those of us who have tasted God's grace, it is a sweet sound indeed! God's amazing grace took the penalty for sin off of our lives and placed it onto Christ as He hung upon the cross. There the sin problem was dealt with for all time. Once that truth becomes real to us, there can be no more amazing fact in our lives than the awesome, amazing fact of God's grace.

Grace is God's goodness to us, far beyond our ability to earn or deserve it. The grace of God stands in contrast to the system under which most people labor in futility: the system of law, of works, of trying to earn God's favor. This effort is at the heart of legalism, the religion of the Pharisees of Jesus' day. Jesus and the religious legalists were continually at odds—and ultimately, it was the legalists who had Jesus crucified. The legalistic system says, "Work harder! Be perfect! If you don't make any mistakes, if you don't break any of the rules, then God may be willing to accept you." Most of the people around you believe in a legalistic system. They think that if you do enough good deeds, you can go to heaven (often, the idea is that you have to have enough good deeds to balance or cancel out your bad deeds). But people who think this way never have any assurance of salvation, nor any peace that God has accepted them. They can never be sure they've done enough. That is why legalism breeds depression, anxiety, and emotional insecurity.

Grace, on the other hand, proclaims that God loves us unconditionally, freely, even before we love Him, even while we are lost in our sin. We do not have to earn His acceptance. In fact, we *can't*. We are declared righteous *not* because of any goodness on

The meaning of grace has been made easy to remember by this acrostic:

God's
Riches
At
Christ's
Expense.

our part, but on the basis of the infinite merits of Jesus, who died in our place. Our motivation for serving God is not "earning brownie points" with God, not fear of punishment if we don't work hard enough, but *love* and *gratitude* to God for what He has already done on our behalf. Because our focus as Christians is on God's grace, God's unconditional love, God's forgiveness—*not our works*—we can feel completely secure in our salvation. God's love can never be taken away from us.

This does not mean we have freedom to sin without consequences. Sin quite properly produces guilt and anxiety within us, and it produces sorrow in the heart of God. When we have occasion to sin, the fear we have is not that God will withdraw salvation from us but that we have grieved the heart of our loving Father. The solution is to turn about, to confess and renounce the sin, and to accept God's instant and complete forgiveness.

Legalism produces destructive and self-defeating messages in the heart of the religious person: "God is a harsh judge. I must be careful not to anger Him. If life is hard and painful, then it must be God's angry judgment of some sin in my life. God hates sin, so He must hate me when I sin. I'm not doing enough. I need to work harder. I need to be perfect. I must serve God because I am afraid."

Grace produces messages within the person of faith that lead to spiritual and emotional health: "I am loved. I am accepted. God will help me recover from my mistakes. God understands that I fail, and He gives me grace. If life is hard and painful, God will give me the strength to get through it. God hates sin, but He loves sinners like me. I joyfully serve God out of gratitude for all He has done for me."

Grace is the air we breathe. It is life and love and liberty. By grace we are saved through faith. There is no greater news than that!

For related issues, see also GUILT; LEGALISM; PRAYER; RELIGIOUS ADDICTION; SOUL

Family

Say the word *family,* and most people get a mental picture of a typical arrangement—Dad, Mom, and 2.3 children. The old TV show, *Leave It to Beaver*—now *that* was a family: Ward and June, Wally and the Beaver. But what about *The Andy Griffith Show?* Andy was a widower, but the fact that Opie didn't have a ma didn't make Andy, Opie, and Aunt Bea any less a family. And *The Brady Bunch?* Well, that was a family and a half!

The point is that families come in all shapes and sizes.

The family was designed by God to provide a safe, nurturing enclosure where children could be conceived, born, raised, loved, encouraged, instructed, and ultimately released to form their own families. The story of how God designed and created the first human family begins in Genesis 2, immediately after the story of the creation of the world. Clearly, God places great importance on the family. In fact, the Bible makes it clear that caring for the needs of one's own family comes before all else: "But if anyone does not provide for his own," says 1 Timothy 5:8, "and especially for those of his household, he has denied the faith and is worse than an unbeliever." If God places such overwhelming priority on the well-being of the family, then so should we.

Tragically, we have seen many Christians who failed to grasp the priority that the family is supposed to have in God's plan. Missionaries and pastors seem especially prone to placing "the Lord's work" over the needs of spouse and family. Often driven by obsessive-compulsive tendencies, many "professional Christians" neglect their own families while they run off and minister to the needs of parishioners' families. Placing "the Lord's work" ahead of their own families, they forget that their families are "the Lord's work" too.

■

God did not intend the family to be merely a group of people who are genetically related to one another. A true family, as designed by God, is also a group of people who are bound together by love, understanding, and a covenant to care for one another and defend one another. When the family functions this way, then children grow up secure and strong, able to trust other people and able to trust God.

■

Your family is your safe harbor in stormy times. It is your repository of memories from the past and dreams for the future. The most important relationships of your life are formed in the family. The highest joys and deepest sorrows of your life are lived out in the family. Even as an adult, your identity—father, mother, provider, counselor, instructor, mentor, disciplinarian, helper, protector—is hammered out in the family. The greatest lessons of your life are learned there, and the meaning of your life is discovered there.

Most of us take our families for granted. We give little thought to the complex mechanics that enable a family to function—or cause it to dysfunction. Clearly, this dynamic entity that is so important in our own lives and to God's plan should not be taken for granted. To have a healthy family, we need to understand how families work.

PASSAGES OF A FAMILY

Every family goes through *passages*—stages of growth, change, and maturation.

Stage 1: A family begins as a couple.

Stage 2: The couple's life is dramatically changed by the arrival of the first child. Amid the joys of new parenthood come the added responsibilities, the stress, and the shock of suddenly being "tied down" by a child. As the child grows, new issues emerge. By age two, this tiny individual is exerting a will and engaging in power struggles that are completely out of proportion to his or her diminutive size. Parents must negotiate with each other how to deal with these parent-child conflicts and must arrive at a common approach. To achieve their own selfish ends, kids will try to divide the parents. The power struggles and stresses of this stage are often hard on a marriage and on the entire family. It is important for the parents to check the state of their marriage relationship and to renew their commitment to each other for the sake of the entire family.

Stage 3: In a few more years, the family again undergoes a major change as the children begin school, as family members begin to drift off in different directions, and as life becomes more hectic. Children are being exposed to more outside influences and bringing home new behaviors and attitudes that make us wonder, "Where did they learn *that?*" Some fathers tend to abdicate parental responsibilities and relegate them to the mother during this time—but that is a major mistake. This is a crucial time for the formation of a child's conception of who God is, and since the father has an extremely important role in shaping that conception (see "What Is Your Image of God?" under FAITH), the father needs to be very much involved in child-rearing duties.

Both parents and children need to experience stable relationships during this wobbly passage in the life of the family. For the sake of the entire family, it is important for the parents to continue to focus on the needs of their marriage, including sexual needs. Children should be put to bed at a decent hour so that parents can enjoy and fulfill each other emotionally and relationally. The best way to meet the needs of the children is to make the marriage relationship priority one.

Stage 4: As the children reach adolescence, a new stage takes place: the stage of turmoil. There is emotional turmoil, teenage rebellion, and the turmoil of hormonal changes, to be sure, but there are other forms of turmoil during this passage as well: more events to transport the kids to; more expenses for clothing, activities, and school; dating issues and questions about sex; scholastic and peer pressures; more choices for the young person to make, more conflict for the family to endure.

One of the most important functions of this passage of family life is to help the children in their process of *individuation* (moving to independence and adult individuality). Consciously or unconsciously, they look to the parents for models as they attempt to carve out their own personal identities. During this time, teenagers will try on different forms and degrees of independence, like trying on new clothes to see how they fit. As they chafe and chomp at the bit, raring and bucking for a semblance of adulthood while still clinging to a measure of childlike dependence, the level of family conflict will inevitably rise.

The crises and stresses of this passage in the life of a family can tear a marriage apart—or the marriage can actually grow stronger as parents learn new strategies of cooperating and coping together. The parents will tend to view the teenager and teenage conflicts in the family to be the sole problems in the family. Yet there are likely to be hidden issues in the parents' marital relationship that are going ignored and unresolved at this time. It is important for the parents to take stock of their ongoing relationship needs and to be sure that:

- They are functioning together as a parenting team, consulting and agreeing on parenting strategies.
- They are focusing on their individual and mutual needs in the marriage and continuing to make their relationship priority one.
- They are helping their teenage children along in the individuation process, balancing privileges with added responsibilities.
- They are dealing forthrightly and openly with the teenagers' emotional and physical changes and sexual curiosity and interests. Teenagers, particularly teenage boys, will normally experience strong sexual feelings and fantasies, and though they should be given firm guidance regarding abstinence, their sexual feelings should be acknowledged and affirmed as normal, so that they don't feel "weird."

Stage 5: The emptying of the nest is another difficult passage in the life of a family. It is the end of an era. Children, who for decades have been the focus of family life, now take flight. Mom and Pop are forced to deal with each other again, not as partners in parenting anymore but purely as companions. Can their relationship survive this passage? Can they reestablish intellectual, emotional, and sexual intimacy?

There are advantages and joys to this passage: increased leisure opportunities, coupled with a greater measure of privacy, make communication and enjoyment of the marriage easier to achieve. There is a bond of shared history, a backlog of shared memories to draw upon and enjoy. There are traditions to preserve and build upon. The children have moved out of the house, but they still consider it home, a harbor to return to, and the parents must preserve it as a museum of memories, a place of warmth and love. Another passage of family life is looming on the horizon, a pleasurable and enjoyable passage that signals that the family is entering an entirely new generational cycle:

Stage 6: Grandchildren.

WHAT DOES A HEALTHY FAMILY LOOK LIKE?

There are seven factors that can consistently be found in families that are mentally, emotionally, and relationally healthy. These factors are:

1. love
2. discipline
3. consistency
4. example
5. clear family hierarchy
6. clear family communication
7. clear family rules

Let's examine each of these factors in turn.

Love

This word *love* is subject to many definitions in our culture, so it's important to be clear on what we mean by love. We are *not* talking about the counterfeit, smothering love of an overenmeshed parent–child relationship. Nor are we talking about the indulgent love of overprotective parents who fail to discipline their children or expose them to the challenges of life. Parents who, in the false name of "love," neglect to discipline their children actually cause their children to feel *hated* rather than loved. As Proverbs 13:24 says, "He who spares his rod hates his son, but he who loves him disciplines him promptly."

What, then, does authentic family love look like?

Authentic love offers positive reinforcement and attention. Many children who rebel or misbehave do so because that's the only way to get attention from their parents. Children hunger for attention and stimulation. If they can't get the attention they need through good behavior, they'll get it any way they can. Parents who frequently affirm and positively reinforce their children for good behavior and good character qualities will tend to see those qualities grow and increase in their children.

Authentic love makes every person in the family feel significant, even the youngest child. The common parental tendency is to ignore children, to be impatient with their questions and interruptions, to patronize them with an "Uh-huh" or an "Oh, really?" when they are not listening to them at all. And, if they are honest, most people will have to admit that there are times when they patronize their spouses as well. To make others in the family feel significant, we need to stop whatever else we are doing, look the other person in the eye, and attentively interact with that person. It is helpful to restate what the other person has just said so that we ourselves internalize that statement and truly hear it and so that the other person *feels* heard, *feels* valued, and *feels* significant.

> ### Authentic Love
>
> Authentic love requires that we:
>
> - love God;
> - love ourselves (in a humble way, not a narcissistic way);
> - love our mates;
> - love our children; and
> - love the people around us.

Authentic love passes the test of 1 Corinthians 13. There, the apostle Paul describes a kind of love that is unconditional, and is rooted in the will rather than in changeable feelings. He writes (verses 4 to 7):

> Love suffers long and is kind; love does not envy; love does not parade itself, is not puffed up; does not behave rudely, does not seek its own, is not provoked, thinks no evil; does not rejoice in iniquity, but rejoices in the truth; bears all things, believes all things, hopes all things, endures all things.

Authentic love demonstrates love for the children by ensuring that there is genuine love between the parents. Unhealthy parent-child relationships almost always result when there is a lack of emotional satisfaction, sexual satisfaction, and unconditional love between mother and father. As the apostle Paul writes in Ephesians 5:25–33,

> Husbands, love your wives, just as Christ also loved the church and gave Himself for her, that He might sanctify and cleanse her with the washing of water by the word, that He might present her to Himself a glorious church, not having spot or wrinkle or any such thing, but that she should be holy and without blemish. So husbands ought to love their own wives as their own bodies; he who loves his wife loves himself. For no one ever hated his own flesh, but nourishes and cherishes it, just as the Lord does the church. For we are members of His body, of His flesh and of His bones. "For this reason a man shall leave his father and mother and be joined to his wife, and the two shall become one flesh." This is a great mystery, but I speak concerning Christ and the church. Nevertheless let each one of you in particular so love his own wife as himself, and let the wife see that she respects her husband.

This passage also indicates that authentic family love entails healthy self-love. Verse 28 says, "he who loves his wife loves himself." Loving ourselves in a healthy way is essential to healthy marital love and healthy family love.

Authentic family love involves a healthy sense of self-esteem, healthy intimacy in the marriage relationship, healthy intimacy with children, and healthy intimacy with God. This kind of love establishes a sense of emotional and relational security.

Discipline

The word *discipline* comes from the same root word as the word *disciple*. The goal of discipline is to disciple our children and enable them to become mature individuals who are spiritually strong and emotionally healthy.

There are many techniques available for disciplining children. We should not forget that discipline is a positive concept. It should include positive reinforcements such as praise ("You did a great job cleaning your room!"), affirmation of character qualities ("I can see that God is helping you to grow and become a very caring and thoughtful person"), and attention ("Let's go read together" or "Let's play catch in the backyard").

But there are clearly times when discipline calls for negative reinforcements: a suspended privilege, time out in a corner or on the child's bed, or a spanking. In recent years, spanking has fallen into disfavor in parts of our culture. Some people even equate spanking with child abuse. Even though many adults have a hard time distinguishing between spanking and child abuse, children instinctively understand the difference when one or the other is applied. At some level (although not always at the conscious level), a child knows that a genuinely caring spanking is administered in love, and that child can sense whether a given blow was a loving "rod of discipline" or an abusive "rap in the mouth."

Spankings are administered thoughtfully and reluctantly; they are administered in sorrow, not in anger; they are surrounded by a calm and patient explanation as to the reason for the spanking; they are over quickly; they are administered only under circumstances where the child needs to be alerted to dangerous behavior ("I spanked you because you need to learn not to run out into the street") or open rebellion, to break a stubborn will.

Child abuse is administered haphazardly, impulsively, and angrily; it is an act of hostility and impatience, not love; it is excessive in force and duration; it is administered in order for the adult to vent hostile emotion and is just as likely to be in response to a minor or imagined slight as to a genuine behavior problem.

The Bible clearly calls for spanking as a form of punishment for young children. It becomes less and less appropriate as the child gets older, and should be used rarely if at all after age nine or ten. Spanking should occur immediately after the offense (though the adult should be careful not to lash out in anger), so the young child will associate the spanking with the offending behavior. The older a child becomes, the more responsive he or she will be to nonspanking forms of discipline, such as the suspension of privileges.

Consistency

In a healthy family, parents present a united front, using the same rules and consistently enforcing those rules so that discipline and boundary lines are predictable, not capricious. This enables everyone in the family to feel more secure.

Psychological research suggests a link between emotional illness and the way a person was disciplined as a child. Importantly, that link involves not the *severity* of the discipline but the *consistency* of the discipline. A child who gets away with a given act

278

on some occasions and then is severely disciplined for the same act on other occasions tends to grow up feeling insecure and unsure of where the limits of behavior are drawn. If one parent is too harsh and the other too lenient, this also contributes to insecurity within the child.

Husbands and wives won't always agree on parental styles and strategies, but those disagreements should *never* be aired in front of the children. Parents should support each other in front of the children and disagree only in private. Parents should discuss their disagreements and arrive at a compromise or solution. Future incidents should be dealt with consistently.

Consistency also applies to our demonstration of acceptance toward our children. Though we may not always accept our children's *behavior,* we must always help *them* to feel accepted, not rejected. Children grow up feeling insecure if they are made to feel favored at one time but rejected or in disfavor at other times. Even when a child is being disciplined, it is possible—in fact, it is essential—for the child to understand that your love and acceptance continue to be unconditionally offered and expressed.

Example

In many families, parents set standards for their children that they themselves don't keep. "Do as I say, not as I do," is a prescription for raising resentful, emotionally unhealthy children. In the end, children will generally do what we do rather than what we say.

Linda used to preach to her three children about the evils of smoking. "Just look at me," she'd say, puffing smoke from her mouth and nostrils, "I have tried to quit smoking for years, and I can't. It's a filthy, disgusting habit, and I can't break it. Someday these things are probably going to give me cancer. The best thing for you to do is not to start. If I ever catch one of you kids with a cigarette between your lips, you're going to wish I hadn't." Her children were young then; they're in their twenties today—and they are all heavy smokers.

Art is another parent who came to the clinic for treatment of his alcoholism. "I don't like this alcohol problem," he said, "but at least I'm a good parent. I discipline my kids, make them go to church two times on Sunday and once on Wednesday. I make them read their Bibles every day and do their homework every night after school. I don't let them watch TV in the evenings—too many beer commercials."

"How often do you go to church?" the counselor asked.

"Me? I don't need church."

"I guess you read your Bible a lot, then."

Art's brow furrowed. "Well, uh, not exactly."

"What do you read, then? If you want your children to spend so much time studying, you must think reading is a very important way to spend your time. What books have you read lately?"

Art seemed surprised. "Books?"

"You don't read books?"

"Well, I've got this alcohol problem, you know, so I mostly just sit down in front of the TV and polish off a fifth of whiskey."

"So you want your kids to go to church, read their Bibles, read other books, and avoid TV and alcohol. Is that right?"

"Right."

"But you aren't interested in setting an example for them? You just want them to do what you say and ignore what you do?"

"Now, wait just a doggone minute!" Art said, his anger rising. He was offended at the counselor, but the counselor was trying to save this man from doing what so many other parents had done: try to parent by edict rather than by example.

"Oh, that they had such a heart in them," says God in Deuteronomy 5:29, "that they would fear Me and always keep all My commandments, that it might be well with them and with their children forever!"

Clear Family Hierarchy

In our clinical experience, we find that the majority of neurotics come from homes where there was no father or where the father was weak-willed and emotionally impotent and where the mother was domineering. This doesn't mean that children of single-parent homes *have* to grow up emotionally ill. In many cases, people have no choice but to provide as secure and stable a home life as possible under the conditions of single parenting. We do not condemn single parents; on the contrary, we commend single parents for taking up the challenge of being good parents and providing good homes under what are clearly not the best of circumstances. (For more specific counsel on single parenting, see "Single Parenting" under PARENTING.)

It is no longer socially fashionable or politically correct to say that men should have the leadership role in the home. It is still, however, quite biblical to say so. In Ephesians 5:23, Paul writes, "For the husband is head of the wife, as also Christ is head of the church." The principle that wives are to be submissive to husbands applies even to non-Christian husbands. In 1 Peter 3:1, the apostle Peter writes, "Wives, likewise, be submissive to your own husbands, that even if some do not obey the word, they, without a word, may be won by the conduct of their wives." This does not mean a wife should be a doormat or a punching bag for an abusive husband. It does not mean she is never to confront her husband for sinful behavior. But it does mean that the husband, under ordinary, nonabusive circumstances, has a leadership role in the family, and the wife is not to undermine or usurp that leadership role in any way.

Modern society is placing increasing pressure on women to assume equal or superior authority in the family. Both the Bible and clinical experience agree: this is a prescription for family disaster. If you feel prompted by friends, family members, or social pressures to overturn God's plan for fatherly leadership in the family, remember that Romans 12:2 counsels us to "not be conformed to this world." We are not to allow this world to squeeze us into its mold. Only when we stand by biblical convictions are we able to "prove what is that good and acceptable and perfect will of God."

In a healthy family, there is a clear hierarchy. Dad provides loving, sensitive leadership, listening to input from Mom and the rest of the family. He honors Mom and encourages the children to honor her as well. Mom and Dad put each other first; then they work as a mutually supportive team to raise and love their children.

Clear Family Communication

In a healthy family, individual family members are given permission to think and express their own thoughts and feelings. Each family member's individuality is recognized and celebrated. Communication within the family is clear and free of distortions, such as double meanings, sarcasm, denial, and manipulation. When communication is clear, honest, and open, people learn they can trust each other.

Does clear communication mean that there is no conflict? No. Conflict is inevitable in any family, including healthy families. But conflict is much easier to manage when everyone is operating on the basis of honesty and openness. When there are hidden agendas and suspicions, conflict festers into bitterness. Fights get started and people don't even understand what the issues of the fight really are. Honest communication enables conflict to be managed more fairly and constructively.

Clear Family Rules

Every family operates on the basis of rules—both spoken and unspoken assumptions about how family members are to think, behave, and communicate. In a dysfunctional family, the rules are mostly hidden and unconscious. Though extremely powerful, the rules are seldom consciously examined.

In some families, the rule is "Nobody is allowed to change. Everyone must stay exactly the same." A timeless conformity is imposed on the family. All individuality and growth and new interests are immediately kiboshed.

In other families, the rule is "Nobody is permitted to make friends or maintain interests outside the family." This rule maintains a status quo of unhealthy enmeshment.

In other families, the rule is "We do not talk about that subject." The family is required, as individuals and as a unit, to practice denial about a painful, uncomfortable subject. If anyone brings up the unpleasant subject, that person is ostracized or punished in some way until he or she comes back in line with official family denial.

There may be rules governing family communication, such as, "The children don't talk to Dad; the children talk to Mom, and Mom talks to Dad." There may be rules governing family coalitions: "This is our secret, and your daddy must never know about it." There may be rules governing family secrets: "You know better than to talk to outsiders about Mom's 'problem.'"

Family secrets can be especially damaging. There is enormous destructive power in secrets. They are like emotional land mines, lurking below the surface and just waiting to explode if somebody takes one misdirected step. Often the people who are "in the know" regarding a family secret will form a coalition against those who don't know, and the result will be tension and conflict with people who haven't any idea what the fuss is all about! When certain issues, events, and opinions are off limits, then it's time to overhaul the family communication system.

In a healthy family, the rules are flexible, discussable, and subject to change. An effort is made to examine and reexamine the family rules openly.

STEPS TO A HEALTHY FAMILY

We now know what the passages of a family are and what a healthy family looks like. But how do we get to the healthy stage? What specific actions can we take as individuals and as marriage partners and parents to make our home a happier, healthier home?

Step 1: Suspend the blame cycle. One of the favorite sayings of recovery authority John Bradshaw is, "No one is to blame. Everyone is responsible." We must learn to quit

> *When a family honestly admits, faces, and discusses its problems, that family is demonstrating courage and good emotional health. In the long run, the issues that hurt us the most are the issues we deny, repress, and refuse to discuss.*

blaming, while making everyone responsible for making the family a better place in which to live. When family members assign blame, the family experiences unproductive pain. When family members shoulder responsibility for the family's health and happiness, productive changes begin to happen.

The all-too-common response to problems in a family is for family members to deny responsibility for their own actions and the family's health. Another all-too-common response is to sling blame in other directions to take the heat off of oneself. It's always easier to point out the faults of other people than to look within and say, "I messed up."

A person who is blamed feels attacked. The normal human response to being attacked is for defenses to go up. Common psychological defense mechanisms include denial, rationalization, suppression, intellectualization, reaction formation, and more (for a complete discussion, see DEFENSE MECHANISMS). The person who is blamed will, instead of analyzing the blame to see if there is any truth in the accusation, seek to evade the blame through a psychological countermove. He or she will also be more likely to go on the attack and throw the blame off onto someone else. Now you have the basis for a major conflict.

To parody Barney the Purple Dinosaur, "I blame you, you blame me, we're a messed-up family." The cycle of blame *must* be suspended or it will keep on going round and round.

When there is a family problem, the healthy approach is to say, "We have a problem here, and no one is really to blame for it. The issue is not *Whose fault is it?* but *How are we going to fix this problem?* Let's all work together on it. Let's all find ways in which we can contribute to the solution. Let's all make some behavior changes and attitude adjustments. Let's all take responsibility for making this family happy and healthy."

Step 2: Acknowledge your contribution to the pain. Most of us find it easy to tell a family member, "The problem with you is . . ." It's a lot harder to say, "*I'm* part of the problem." But that is exactly what Janice learned to do.

"Rich," said Janice to her husband, "I've been blaming you for the conflict we've been having. But as I think back, I'm beginning to realize that I've been making a big contribution to the problem. You know what an angry, controlling rageaholic my dad was. An explosive temper, a critical spirit, always laying into me for one thing or another. Well, when we have been at odds over how to discipline Kim, I have been reading you the same way. I've felt that you were exploding at me, trying to control me—"

Rich immediately became defensive. "I wasn't trying to—"

"I know you don't see yourself as explosive or controlling, and you may be right," said Janice. "That's the whole point. I'm saying that the problem may be me. I think that when we get into an argument or a discussion about these issues, my unconscious mind starts to flash on Dad, and I see *him* standing there instead of you. And there's the possibility that you come on stronger and more controlling than you realize. Right at this moment, it's hard to be objective, but I'm trying to be. I want to take my share of the responsibility for this relationship and this family—and I want to fix my side of the problem, okay?"

"Yeah," said Rich. "Okay. Me too."

At that moment, both Rich and Janice began to gain a better handle on their conflict, and though it was not the last fight they ever had, their conflicts became increasingly more manageable after that.

282

When we acknowledge our contribution to the pain, we engineer a reversal in the dynamics of conflict and pain. Instead of focusing on each other as enemies, we focus together on the problem. We become a team, allies committed to defeating the conflict, not antagonists committed to defeating each other.

Step 3: Commit yourself to recovery and healing. If there is conflict or pain in your family relationships, then openly verbalize or write out your commitment to recovery and healing. State the issue that you are willing to work on. Allow other family members to hold you accountable for change. This is especially important if there are family problems involving addiction or codependency. In that case, the commitment should include a statement such as, "I am committed to attending a Twelve Step recovery group three nights a week so that I can make progress in overcoming my compulsive behavior." Another commitment that may be necessary is the commitment to seek professional counseling.

Step 4: Make emotional intimacy with your spouse a top priority. When there is a low level of sharing and communication between partners in a marriage, each partner usually has reasons for holding back, and those reasons usually involve blame for the other partner. Once we have stopped the cycle of blame, we can deal with the level of intimacy between the partners.

Do we talk about real issues? About feelings? Is there emotional closeness between us? Do we do enjoyable things together? Do we spend time together just holding each other? Is our sex life mutually enjoyable?

Does either one of us feel shut out? Frustrated? Misunderstood? Not valued or listened to? Not accepted?

The answers to these questions say a lot about the level of sharing in the relationship. The better and freer the level of sharing between Mom and Dad, the healthier the entire family will be.

Step 5: Set healthy boundaries. Boundaries are the protective emotional shields we use to define the shape and limits of our relationships. We place boundaries *around* our family as well as *within* our family, around ourselves. We use boundaries to say, "This is who I am as an individual. This is who you are as my spouse. This is who you are as my child. This is who we are as a family."

Some families wrap themselves tightly within a thick, thorny, hedgelike boundary that keeps all the family members inside and the rest of the world outside. In such a family, Mom and Dad have no close friendships beyond the family circle. The children are permitted no outside interests or outside friendships. Everyone in the family sees every other member as an extension of himself or herself. This kind of family arrangement is called *enmeshment*. There is no room for individuality or independence. This is a very unhealthy situation, and it produces emotionally stunted children who are unable to individuate and liberate themselves from the family when the time comes to leave the nest. In enmeshed families, one or more children often stay home well into their twenties or thirties and never seem to become full-fledged adults.

Other individuals or families fail to maintain adequate boundaries. Every individual in the family needs adequate boundaries that say where "I" end and "you" begin. When the *emotional* boundaries between a parent and a child are inadequate, the result can be emotional incest. When the *physical* boundaries between parent and child are inadequate, the result can be sexual incest or physical abuse. When there are inadequate physical boundaries around the family relationship, the result may be an adulterous affair. (For a more comprehensive discussion of this issue, including the various kinds of boundaries and the "Seven Steps to Healthy Boundaries," see BOUNDARIES.)

Step 6: Seek out and eliminate stress factors. One of the issues that can make a family unhealthy in a hurry is *stress*. We can't control all the stress factors that affect our families, but there are a surprising number of stress factors that are under our control. We simply need to recognize them and deal with them.

What is the stress factor that is inflicting pressure on your family? Too many commitments and an overscheduled pace? Friction from unresolved conflicts? Behavioral issues such as addiction or codependency? Financial burdens? These are all issues that can be dealt with and removed as stress factors in the family.

Extended-family stress factors can be reduced by creating firmer boundaries. Confront Aunt Gladys about her meddling comments. Ask Mom and Dad Jones not to call after ten o'clock. Inform your brother that you can't afford to lend him any more money. It takes assertiveness to draw clear boundaries in family relationships, but the rewards in reduced family stress can be immense.

Step 7: Commit yourself to a process of clear family communication. If you have a tendency to use sarcasm or double meanings, if you often send double messages (saying one thing with your words while sending the opposite message with your tone of voice or body language), or if you have a tendency to operate with hidden agendas, secrets, or manipulation, then you need to learn new ways of communicating. You may need to surrender your compulsive drive to control people and situations (see CONTROL ADDICTION). You may need to work through your defense mechanisms (see DEFENSE MECHANISMS). You may need to learn how to appreciate and celebrate the other personalities and opinions in your family, even when they contrast with yours.

> ### Easing Financial Stress
>
> Financial stress factors can be removed with creativity and energy. A too-costly home or that expensive boat (otherwise known as "a hole in the water you throw money into") can be sold, and the lifestyle can be scaled back. It may be that just six months to a year of working an extra weekend job would be all it takes to retire that credit card debt. Less eating out. Deferring the new furniture purchase. Brown-bagging to work. Simpler, less materialistic Christmases. There are many ways to reduce financial stress—if we are willing to look for them.

If this sounds like a difficult task for you, then consider getting counseling for these issues. Most likely, it would be best if your entire family went into counseling together. With the help of a professional counselor, unhealthy communicating patterns—patterns that are completely disguised and hidden from the family members themselves—can be recognized, brought out into the light, examined, and dismantled. Healthy communication strategies can be put in their place.

It may be painful to face the issues that have been denied and hidden for so long, but it is no more painful than allowing those issues to fester. Open communication about issues and feelings is the key to disarming conflict, rebuilding trust, revitalizing hope, and rekindling love. Bring those issues out into the light.

Demonstrate the courage and caring to communicate clearly and truthfully with the most important people in your life.

A HEALTHY FAMILY IS A WORK OF ART

The Bible is a book about a great family, the family of faith, whose Father is God Himself. It is through the example of earthly parents that children first learn about their

Heavenly Parent, God. The family is a child's proving ground, where he or she is trained to take a place in society. In the family, we learn how to interact in relationships, how to function in our various roles including gender roles, how to get along with others, how to relate to people with different views and personalities, and how to respect the rights and feelings of others.

This is a sobering and challenging perspective on the family. Clearly, there is more to a family than sharing meals and watching TV together under the same roof. There is something noble, something wonderful, something transcendent about the family. When we become willing to undertake the hard work of making our families more healthy, more functional, and more loving, then we have created something beautiful, something of lasting value.

A healthy family is a work of art. It is something we create, working from a blueprint drawn by God.

See also DYSFUNCTIONAL FAMILIES; MARRIAGE; PARENTING

Fears and Phobias

In his book *You've Got to Be Believed to Be Heard* (St. Martin's Press, 1993), Bert Decker reported that some years ago the *Times* of London conducted a survey on fear. The survey question: "What are you most afraid of?" People were allowed to list their three top fears. The results of the survey were surprising.

What would you think would be the number one fear among all the people surveyed? Do you think it might be the fear of death? If so, you would be wrong. The fear of death was way down at number seven. Only 19 percent of those surveyed listed death as one of their greatest fears.

What about fear of illness? Certainly everyone fears getting cancer or diabetes or Alzheimer's disease, don't they? They do, but that's not the number one fear. Fear of illness is down at number six, with 19 percent listing it as one of their top fears.

Fear of deep water? That was number five, with 22 percent.

Fear of financial disaster? Number four, with 22 percent.

Fear of insects and spiders? Number three, with 22 percent.

Fear of heights? That's a big one, number two, with 32 percent—but it's still not the number one fear.

What, then, was number one? What one prospect inspired more apprehension, more dread, more horror than death and illness combined? More than deep water, bankruptcy, bugs, and dizzying heights? What one fear was cited by 41 percent of those questioned?

The answer is at the end of this article.

HEALTHY AND UNHEALTHY FEARS

Fear is an unpleasant emotion—one of the most unpleasant emotions we will ever experience. Because it is unpleasant, we classify fear as a "negative emotion." But even so-called "negative emotions" serve a positive function in our lives. There is such a thing as healthy fear.

When fear is realistic and based in the facts regarding some threat in our lives, fear actually helps us. It is a vital mechanism for survival, because it prepares us to deal with danger. Fear triggers a number of physiological responses that are designed to make us move faster and be stronger so that we can meet the challenge of a deadly adversary. Reality-based fear is perfectly healthy. If you stand on the shoulder of a busy freeway while cars whiz past at 65 miles an hour, your reality-based fear tells you not to cross the freeway. If another man walks out into the freeway, humming to himself, reading a newspaper as he walks, then it is clear that he is not afraid. Yet, despite his emotional serenity and calm demeanor, he is in far greater danger than you are, trembling and biting your nails back on the freeway shoulder.

Fear is a natural, protective response to danger. Out of concern for our well-being, God designed us with the capacity to be afraid. But when the thing we fear is unreal, or when the terror we feel is completely out of proportion to the actual size of the threat, then that fear is unhealthy. Unhealthy fear places strange and unrealistic thoughts in our minds. Those thoughts trigger physiological reactions such as:

- rapid heartbeat
- irregular heartbeat
- hyperventilation
- shortness of breath or difficulty in breathing
- difficulty swallowing
- choking sensation
- weakness in the limbs
- sweating
- chest pain

- dizziness, vertigo, or fainting
- trembling
- numb or tingling sensations
- blurred vision
- nausea
- diarrhea
- hot flashes or chills
- fear of going insane or losing mental control

The fear we experience—and the bodily reactions that accompany the fear—may be the result of facing an armed mugger on a dark street or seeing a mouse run along the floor. The mugger is a real threat. The mouse is unpleasant and unsanitary but is hardly a threat. Extreme fear in the face of a real threat is *healthy* fear. Extreme fear in the face of a minor or nonexistent threat is *unhealthy* fear.

Some of the fears we experience are related to "threats" that are highly intangible, such as the fear of being criticized by others, fear of losing love, fear of poverty, or the fear of conflict. One of the most common fears is called *performance anxiety*. This is the fear of making an embarrassing mistake while performing in the presence of an audience, such as while giving a speech or singing in public. Performance anxiety can even strike us when our audience is only one person: when a person becomes anxious and fearful about performing badly during sexual intercourse, it frequently interrupts the feelings of passion and becomes a self-fulfilling prophecy.

PHOBIAS

We are all afraid of something. And most of us fear things that are not worthy of the time and emotional energy it takes to be afraid. Even though God assures us that He will give us the strength we need to face any situation, we are often ruled by fear rather than faith.

For some of us, unhealthy fear becomes rampant in our lives. Our fears become so extreme and so focused that they take the form of an emotional disorder called a *phobia*. A phobia is an irrational fear that is centered on a specific kind of situation, object, or activity. Phobias tend to be disproportionate to the potential danger, and reasoning with a phobic person ("See, the spider is in a jar. It can't hurt you.") has little or no effect. Phobias are beyond logic and beyond voluntary control.

Some typical phobias: Margaret has a phobia called *agoraphobia*, literally "the fear of the marketplace," a fear of open places and a fear of leaving home. Margaret might as well be a prisoner in a penitentiary, for she has not been out of her house in two years.

Jerry witnessed (but was not involved in) a terrible automobile accident when he was twelve. He was shaken by the sight of blood and dismembered bodies. He even watched a boy his own age die before an ambulance could arrive. Now in his thirties, Jerry is afraid of being in an accident, and he has never learned to drive a car.

Phobic people will go to great lengths to avoid the objects, places, and situations that provoke their fear. They may intricately route a trip hundreds of miles out of their way just to keep from driving over bridges. Or they may change jobs in order to avoid getting into an elevator. Intellectually, they know that their fears are ridiculous, they know that they are living a joyless existence, but they are powerless to conquer their fears. Phobic people rely on others to do for them what they are afraid to do for themselves. Soon, friends and family get tired of their dependency and their irrational, clinging behavior.

The "Phobias" table on pages 288–89 lists several phobias that people deal with. Some, such as the morbid fear of high places (acrophobia), are easy to understand. Others seem strange and almost laughable to those who have never been in the grip of an intense phobia. All of these disorders are very real.

Even in the face of dangers, problems, and an increasingly anxious world, we can cling to the fact that God is with us and He is able to supply all our needs, regardless of our circumstances (see Philippians 4:19).

ATTACKING AND OVERCOMING OUR FEARS

It is amazing how frequently the phrase "fear not" appears in the Bible. "Fear not" is God's message again and again to Abraham, Isaac, Jacob, Hagar, Moses, Joshua, Isaiah, Daniel, Mary and Joseph, Zacharias, the shepherds, Simon Peter, the apostle John, and the apostle Peter. "Are not five sparrows sold for two copper coins?" asks Jesus in Luke 12:6. "Do not fear therefore; you are of more value than many sparrows" (v. 7).

Here is a six-point strategy for dealing with fear:

1. Try to limit fear-inducing mental input. Many of us experience more fear than we need to by needlessly exposing ourselves to influences that make us afraid. Surveys show that people who watch large amounts of television are significantly more fearful

PHOBIAS	
PHOBIA NAME	MORBID FEAR OF
acrophobia	high places
agoraphobia	leaving familiar places
algophobia	pain
anthophobia	flowers
arachibutyrophobia	peanut butter sticking to the roof of the mouth
astraphobia	thunder and lightning
belonophobia	pins and needles
claustrophobia	confined places
decidophobia	making decisions
entomophobia	insects
ergophobia	work
erthyrophobia	blushing in public
gephydrophobia	crossing bridges
heliophobia	sunlight
hematophobia	sight of blood
hydrophobia	water
iatrophobia	doctors
lalophobia	speaking
monophobia	being alone
mysophobia	dirt, contamination
necrophobia	dead bodies
nyctophobia	darkness
ombrophobia	rain
pathophobia	disease, suffering

PHOBIA NAME	MORBID FEAR OF
phonophobia	speaking aloud
photophobia	strong light
taphophobia	buried alive
trichophobia	hair
toxophobia	being poisoned
xenophobia	strangers
zoophobia	animals

and pessimistic than those who watch little or no television. And it's not hard to see why, when television programs tend to feature violence and disaster above all else. One of the worst offenders is TV news, which tends to focus only on bad news. Watching TV news tends to give you an image of the world that is more bleak and negative than the world really is. Yes, it's important to stay informed, but is it really important for you to know about every car wreck and street-corner stabbing that took place in the last twenty-four hours? If you tend to be fearful, it might be advisable to limit your exposure to such influences.

2. Counter your fears and other negative emotions with positive self-talk (see also SELF-TALK). Most of our fears result from unhealthy ruminating on faulty beliefs or negative thoughts. So, if we replace faulty beliefs or negative thoughts with positive thoughts, healing has a chance to take place. The Bible encourages us to practice positive self-talk. In Philippians 4:8–9, we are told to think on things that are noble, lovely, and pure, "and the God of peace will be with you."

3. Prayer is a crucial component of your strategy to conquer fear. God wants you to trade your fears and anxieties for trust in Him. "Be anxious for nothing," says Philippians 4:6, "but in everything by prayer and supplication, with thanksgiving, let your requests be made known to God." When you relinquish your fear to God, He gives you a peace that cannot be explained—the peace that passes understanding.

4. Monitor your fear responses. Be aware of the times when your fear and anxiety levels rise and when they fall. When fear sensations rise, remember that these feelings come and go. Knowing that these feelings will pass enables you better to cope with them.

5. Focus on behavior, not feelings. Make an effort to continue normal functioning, even when your fear level rises. When you endeavor to behave normally, normal emotions often follow. You don't have to be emotionally comfortable in order to function. Keep moving forward with your life despite your fears, and your fear level will probably subside.

6. Replace fear with love. 1 John 4:18 tells us, "There is no fear in love; but perfect love casts out fear." When God's love controls your life, fear can no longer control you. When you examine the contrasts between love and fear, it is easy to see why "perfect love casts out fear."

LOVE AND FEAR	
Love . . .	Fear . . .
. . . is focused on others.	. . . is focused on protecting oneself.
. . . thinks no evil.	. . . broods over potential evils.
. . . focuses on the present.	. . . frets over the future.
. . . moves us toward involvement with others.	. . . forces us into withdrawal and isolation from others.
. . . is based on fact and on faith.	. . . is based on emotion.
. . . is the highest expression of our humanness and Christlikeness.	. . . is a base, instinctive reaction that we have in common with the animals.
. . . is a mark of a Christian who trusts God.	. . . is a mark of doubt and a lack of faith in God.

As we clearly see in these comparisons, the opposite of fear is not courage, but *love*. As we pray, we should ask God to perfect us in love. Christlike, unconditional love is a powerful antidote to the toxin of unhealthy fear.

THE FEARS OF CHILDHOOD

Fear is an important part of the healthy development of every child. In fact, fears are necessary for growth, and a child cannot develop emotionally without working through his or her fears.

There are normal fears that children experience during each stage of growth, and they are usually resolved before the next stage begins. Sometimes, however, these fears persist into subsequent growth stages, often resurfacing in new forms. If they are not resolved in childhood, these fears can remain lodged within the child and later emerge as adult emotional problems such as depression, anxiety, bitterness, timidity, and procrastination. These emotional problems rob an individual of joy and satisfaction in life and impede the individual's ability to function effectively.

By helping a child face and work through fears, parents can help the child deal with a variety of emotions and problems in life. Yet parents usually feel inadequate to the task of helping a child deal with his or her fears. "I don't know what to do," say many parents. "I don't know what to say. What if I make a mistake? What if I say something to make my child's fear worse instead of better?" But we have the assurance of 2 Timothy 1:7 on our side: "For God has not given us a spirit of fear, but of power and of love and of a sound mind." Childhood fears are a major worry for caring parents, but God enables us to deal with any issue life throws our way.

290

One common mistake parents make in trying to deal with a child's fears is that they try to solve the child's problem. The parent cannot do that. The child must resolve his or her own fear. The parent should be alongside the child as a source of comfort and guidance, so that the child knows he or she does not go through the fear alone.

Here is a six-point strategy for helping your child work through his or her fears:

1. *Know your child.* Spend time with your child. Talk to, read to, travel with, relax with, and above all, *play with* your child. The medium of play is a great way to get to know what your child thinks and how your child feels. Children often use play to reenact and resolve their own fears and to work through relationships with others. Play gives children an outlet for physical and emotional energy, and for expressing their innermost fears and concerns. By listening to and observing your child at play, you will gain valuable insights into his or her conflicts and fears.

Reading to your child is another way of getting to know your child. Unlike television, which supplies images as well as stories, books allow the reader and listener to create their own mental pictures, and to place themselves in the story. Through stories, a child exercises his or her imagination and power of identification with the characters in the drama. Through mentally and emotionally processing the drama, children are often able to work out conflicts and fears. As you discuss the story with your child, sharing your own responses and feelings, the child often is able to open up and share feelings and fears you would never have learned about any other way.

2. *Allow the child to take responsibility for his or her own feelings.* Parents sometimes try to take over for their children, saying, "I'll lie down with you until you go to sleep." But that's not what the child hears. The nonverbal message of the parent's behavior is, "I'll stay with you to make sure the monsters don't get you. Your fears may come true. This situation even scares me." Instead of being reassured, the child experiences even greater anxiety.

Shining flashlights into closets, opening drawers, looking under beds, can sometimes help to temporarily allay fear, but exposing a fear as logically unfounded does not in any way resolve the fear. Instead, let the child know you are nearby and you are willing to talk about the fear. Here are some specific actions you can take to be alongside your child as he or she works to resolve the fears:

- Alter the situation. If there are specific conditions that contribute to the child's fears, make constructive changes in those conditions. Make changes in the decor or arrangement of the child's room. Make changes in the child's schedule. Altering the situation can alter the child's thinking about his or her fears and interrupt the cycle of thinking that triggers the fears.
- Talk with your child.
- Make sure your child gets plenty of sleep.
- Use music as a calming influence.
- Use recreation to encourage a positive emotional balance and a healthy sense of happy weariness at bedtime, so that sleep comes easily.
- Take vacations. Sometimes a change of pace will interrupt the child's habitual responses and speed the healing process.
- Make sure there is plenty of laughter and fun in the life of the family.

- Have the child medically checked. Some medical problems can create fearlike symptoms in a child's behavior. Also, certain medications (asthma medicines, for example) can produce anxiety and fear symptoms.
- Pray *with* your child and *for* your child. When your child expresses fear, stop right there and pray together. This provides an opportunity for parent-child bonding and spiritual teaching.

3. *Avoid dismissing the child's fears.* A common parental response to a child's fear is "There's nothing to be afraid of! Just get back in bed and go to sleep!" This message hardly reassures the child. Instead, it says, "Your feelings are insignificant. Go away."

Parents commonly confuse a child's *fright* with a child's *fear.* Fright is the symptom, the physiological response, the statement which says, "Mommy! Daddy! I'm scared!" But the fear is what underlies and provokes the fright response. Children have deep fears that they are unable to verbalize, and that surface in the form of fright responses—monsters in the closet, shadows on the wall, bad dreams. The fears are the real issue, and you should always address those fears, not dismiss them.

4. *Address the child's fears from his or her perspective, not your own.* Listen nonjudgmentally to the child's feelings, allow the child to be afraid, and demonstrate empathy. An empathetic attitude says, "I know you are scared. I was scared when I was your age, too. Tell you what, I'll walk you to your bed and sit with you for a few minutes. We'll talk for a bit, and then it's time to sleep." This statement communicates to the child that his or her feelings are real and they are validated—but also that they are survivable. It says, "I understand how you feel, and I'm here alongside you, but I can't resolve your fears for you. That's your job, but I'm here and you will be safe."

5. *For deeply embedded fears, seek professional help.* A professional counselor or therapist can help you develop and implement such therapeutic approaches as:

The Fears of Childhood

INFANT-TODDLER FEARS

- Fear of abandonment
- Fear of being overpowered
- Fear of losing parental love and approval
- Oedipal fears (competition with the same-sex parent for the love of the opposite-sex parent)

LATE PRESCHOOLER FEARS

- Fear of the power of "big people" to inflict hurt
- Fear of nightmares and night terrors

GRADESCHOOLER FEARS

- Fear of competing and losing in life
- Fear of being insignificant and without value
- Fear of sexuality

TEENAGE FEARS

- Fear of growing up
- Fear of liberation and independence
- Fear of new situations and new challenges

- *Desensitization.* Repeated exposure to increasingly intense levels of the feared stimulus can often help reduce fears. For example, a child who fears dogs might be shown pictures of dogs, then be given stuffed plush-toy dogs to handle, then be shown dogs in a pet-store window, then be allowed to touch a friendly dog. This approach not only deals with the surface symptom (fear of dogs) but the deeper fear as well (fear of being overpowered).
- *Positive reinforcement.* This involves praising (reinforcing) the child when he or she courageously faces the feared situation: "You did great! It was scary, but you faced it and you won! You are really a champ!"

292

- *Extinction.* The opposite of positive reinforcement, extinction involves refusing to give undue attention to the fear symptom. This works in situations where the fear symptom is used by the child in an unconscious effort to gain attention. By ignoring the fear symptom, you promote its extinction.
- *Assertiveness training.* This technique is especially helpful for shy children. Though the underlying fears must still be resolved, assertiveness training helps to relieve the surface symptoms and also builds self-esteem. Assertiveness training is best done by a professional.
- *Insight-oriented approach.* Anxieties and fears operate on three levels: (1) individuals feel anxious about feelings and experiences from the past, (2) individuals feel anxious about present problems and experiences, (3) individuals are afraid of the fear itself; once they have experienced one anxiety attack, they are fearful of future attacks. You can help to defuse these fears by:

Reflecting the child's emotions. Restate in your own words what the child is expressing: "I hear you telling me you're scared, that you feel like crying. I know it's scary when you have to be away from your mother for a while."

Gently confronting the child's denial, so he or she can be in touch with authentic feelings. Be *very* gentle. For example, "You said you're not afraid of visiting the doctor, but the way you're wringing your hands and biting your lip, I can see that you're feeling anxious."

Self-disclosure. Share your own feelings and experiences, particularly times when you were afraid as a child. You can admit to adult fears as well, but make sure you don't share issues that are beyond the child's ability to handle. You should not convey to the child that your fears are out of control or that you feel you are unable to control the situation. Though it can be very freeing to a child to know that adults have fears too, the child also looks to you for security.

6. Practice consistent discipline. Parents sometimes feel sorry for the fearful child, so they indulge or make allowances for the child. This does not do the child any favors, particularly where fears are concerned. Firm, loving discipline actually helps to dispel such childhood fears as:

- fear of losing parental love or approval
- fear of not knowing where the boundaries are
- fear of not being able to successfully grow up

Discipline reassures your child that you care, that boundaries are clear, and that you will be there to guide him or her toward healthy, successful adulthood.

THE NUMBER ONE FEAR

One last thing: As promised at the beginning of this article, here is *the number one fear* among people surveyed by the *Times* of London:
Fear of public speaking.

293

What the Bible Says About Fear

The following passages can be a source of comfort and strength in times of fear:

"Be strong and of good courage, do not fear nor be afraid of them; for the LORD your God, He is the One who goes with you. He will not leave you nor forsake you. . . . do not fear nor be dismayed" (Deut. 31:6, 8).

"Whenever I am afraid,
I will trust in You" (Ps. 56:3).

"But You, O LORD, are a shield for me . . .
I will not be afraid of ten thousands of people
Who have set themselves against me all around" (Ps. 3:3, 6).

"The LORD is my light and my salvation;
Whom shall I fear?
The LORD is the strength of my life;
Of whom shall I be afraid? . . .
Though an army may encamp against me,
My heart shall not fear;
Though war may rise against me,
In this I will be confident"
(Ps. 27:1, 3).

"I sought the LORD, and He heard me,
And delivered me from all my fears" (Ps. 34:4).

"God is our refuge and strength,
A very present help in trouble.
Therefore we will not fear"
(Ps. 46:1–2).

"He shall cover you with His feathers,
And under His wings you shall take refuge;
His truth shall be your shield and buckler.
You shall not be afraid of the terror by night" (Ps. 91:4–5).

"Whoever listens to me will dwell safely,
And will be secure, without fear of evil" (Prov. 1:33).

"When you lie down, you will not be afraid;
Yes, you will lie down and your sleep will be sweet.
Do not be afraid of sudden terror,
Nor of trouble from the wicked when it comes;
For the LORD will be your confidence,
And will keep your foot from being caught" (Prov. 3:24–26).

"The fear of man brings a snare,
But whoever trusts in the LORD shall be safe" (Prov. 29:25).

"For I, the LORD your God, will hold your right hand,
Saying to you, 'Fear not, I will help you' " (Isa. 41:13).

"Do not fear, for you will not be ashamed;
Neither be disgraced, for you will not be put to shame;
For you will forget the shame of your youth,
And will not remember the reproach of your widowhood anymore" (Isa. 54:4).

"Do not fear, little flock, for it is your Father's good pleasure to give you the kingdom" (Luke 12:32).

"Peace I leave with you, My peace I give to you; not as the world gives do I give to you. Let not your heart be troubled, neither let it be afraid" (John 14:27).

"For you did not receive the spirit of bondage again to fear, but you received the Spirit of adoption by whom we cry out, 'Abba, Father'" (Rom. 8:15).

"For I am persuaded that neither death nor life, nor angels nor principalities nor powers, nor things present nor things to come, nor height nor depth, nor any other created thing, shall be able to separate us from the love of God which is in Christ Jesus our Lord" (Rom. 8:38–39).

"Be anxious for nothing, but in everything by prayer and supplication, with thanksgiving, let your requests be made known to God; and the peace of God, which surpasses all understanding, will guard your hearts and minds through Christ Jesus" (Phil. 4:6–7).

"For God has not given us a spirit of fear, but of power and of love and of a sound mind" (2 Tim. 1:7).

"So we may boldly say: 'The LORD is my helper; I will not fear. What can man do to me?'" (Heb. 13:6).

"There is no fear in love; but perfect love casts out fear, because fear involves torment. But he who fears has not been made perfect in love. We love Him because He first loved us" (1 John 4:18–19).

Finances

"A feast is made for laughter,
And wine makes merry;
But money answers everything."
Ecclesiastes 10:19

As Christians, the things we treasure most are to be stored in heaven, not on earth (see Matthew 6:19–21). But the Bible also has a lot to say about treasury matters right here on earth. God understands that we have to provide food and shelter for ourselves and our families, and in His Word we find God's plan for money management—a plan that is as valid and practical today as it was two thousand years ago.

Financial worries are rampant these days. Personal debt is at an all-time high. People who once took their jobs for granted now worry about the effect that corporate "downsizing" and "restructuring" will have on their futures. How can people plan their financial futures under such uncertain conditions?

The Bible's principles for money management give us a sound, flexible plan that fits any economic conditions—bull market or bear, high inflation or low, expansion, recession, or depression—even a monetary collapse! The most important biblical principles for money management are:

1. Everything you have belongs to God.
2. Give back to God first.
3. Avoid going into debt.
4. Live within your means.
5. Save and invest.
6. Set long-term financial goals.
7. Have fun money.

Here are some of the advantages of following this biblical prescription:

- People who follow these guidelines will accumulate interest on investments instead of paying out interest on debts. Thus, even in times of high inflation, the people who follow these principles will see their net worth increase while the net worth of everyone around them is being eaten up by rising prices and interest.
- If this prescription is advantageous in the comparatively hard times of high inflation, it is doubly advantageous during good economic times, since these principles result in lower spending, lower interest payments, and greater money set aside for emergencies and financial freedom.
- Many analysts look at the continuing fiscal irresponsibility of an overspending Congress and at such fiascoes as the savings and loan bailout, and they conclude that a day of financial reckoning is coming to America, and to the world. If there is a monetary collapse, then it will be those who are spending less than they earn, who have savings, and who have avoided debt who will be in the best position to weather those times.
- Also, if a monetary collapse were to bring political and economic upheaval to our society, those who survive emotionally and spiritually will be those who truly understand that everything belongs to God.

Clearly, God's Word is as reliable in matters of money as it is in matters of faith, spiritual truth, and emotional wholeness. Let's take a closer look at each of these biblical money-management principles.

Principle 1: Everything You Have Belongs to God

God is sovereign. He is Lord of the whole earth, of everything in it—and of everything you own. Our culture views material wealth this way: "I worked hard for it, I paid for it, I've got a bill of sale, and it's mine, all mine." A biblical view of material wealth is "God owns it, and I manage it." There is a name for the biblical view of

296

material wealth. It's called *stewardship*. As Christians, we are stewards or caretakers of God's resources.

What does this mean in practical terms? It means, first of all, that since everything we have belongs to God, then every spending decision we make is a *spiritual decision*. We recognize the spiritual implications of our tithes and offerings. But we should also recognize that there is a spiritual dimension to every transaction we make, every time we write a check or "pass the plastic," every time we visit an ATM machine or sign a mortgage contract. This means that whenever we make a spending decision, we are saying in effect, "This is the decision God Himself would make in the same circumstances."

You might say, "Oh, now I really feel guilty!"

This is not meant to make you feel guilty. Remember, our God is a loving and generous God. He doesn't want us to live as ascetics. He gives us an abundance so that we can enjoy life and share our good fortune with others. It is not a sin to enjoy a restaurant meal or to own a VCR or to live in a nice house—unless you sense that God is telling you not to do so. When we view our spending decisions from a spiritual point of view, we shouldn't feel guilty, we should feel liberated. If we spend regular daily time listening to God in prayer, then we will likely be qualified to make spending decisions that reflect God's values and priorities.

The second implication of stewardship is that since everything is God's, He can take it back whenever He wants, and that's okay. It's good to have material possessions, but we should hold them loosely. When God wants them back, we should offer them willingly. If we clutch God's possessions as if they were our own, then how can He ever trust us with more?

Principle 2: Give Back to God First

We want to keep our credit rating. We want to keep the power turned on. We don't want someone to cut our credit cards in half. So every month we pay our bills. But there is one bill that many of us forget to pay, or only pay sporadically. The tragic thing is that this is the bill we should be paying first, before all others.

The first check out of our checkbook every month should say, "Pay to the order of God." God deserves and expects the firstfruits of our labors, the very first part of our income. "Honor the LORD with your possessions," says Proverbs 3:9–10, "and with the firstfruits of all your increase; so your barns will be filled with plenty, and your vats will overflow with new wine." Since God owns all that we have, it is only reasonable that He expects us to return a portion to Him. But God is gracious. He actually promises a *reward* for our giving. He promises to provide for us with such an amazing abundance that it is beyond our imagining.

The issue is not the dollar amount. The issue is the condition of your heart. The issue is trust and faith. Do you trust God enough to stretch your giving right now? Do you believe His promises are real and valid today? What does your giving say about your relationship with your Heavenly Father?

How much should we give? Ten percent? More? The Old Testament standard was a tithe, 10 percent. But if we applied all the legalistic formulas that were used in Old Testament times, we find that the average Israelite often gave as much as *22 percent* of his income to God! But the Christian is not bound by legalism. The Christian is under grace. And one of the beautiful qualities of God's grace is that it expands our thinking.

God wants to *stretch* our trust in Him, and our expectations of ourselves. He wants us to discover that He is able to do far more through us than we can imagine. He wants us to explore His amazing, gracious love toward us, so that we can learn to rely on Him completely for our spiritual, emotional, and yes, our financial needs. Ten percent of the gross (before taxes!) is a good place to *begin* with God. But what if you are only giving 5 percent right now? Or 1 percent? Or only putting a dollar in the collection plate every other week? Then start right where you are and start growing your commitment. To whatever you are giving right now, add 1 percent—then watch what happens. In a few more weeks or months, as your faith increases, add another percent.

Once you have decided to stretch out in faith and increase your giving to God, you have another decision to make: To whom do you give the money? At the Minirth Meier New Life Clinics, we believe that a Christian's giving priorities are:

1. Give to the local church first. The church is our Lord's most visible and foundational expression of His body in the world.
2. Next, give to parachurch organizations—missionary organizations, Christian radio ministries, Christian colleges and universities, evangelistic and social action ministries such as Campus Crusade for Christ, World Vision, the Billy Graham Evangelistic Association, Inter-Varsity Christian Fellowship, Youth for Christ, and so forth.

Remember: When you give, you are not giving to God. You are giving *back* to God. This attitude will help you to give gratefully and cheerfully, not from your leftovers but from the firstfruits of your labors.

Principle 3: Avoid Going into Debt

Debt is a national epidemic. Roughly 80 percent of Americans carry a debt load in excess of their assets. And the average American couple pays 25 percent of gross income to debt service—*not counting payments on the home mortgage.* The issue is credit cards, heavily financed automobiles, and other forms of consumer credit. The problem is only getting worse. Now that you can put groceries and fast food on a credit card, some people will actually be paying interest on hamburgers and cartons of eggs *years* after they are eaten and forgotten.

The fallacy of debt is the attitude that "I don't want to wait until I've earned it. I want it now." Debt is not the real problem, just a symptom of greed or ignorance or a narcissistic attitude of entitlement. Any time you overextend yourself in order to satisfy some short-term need or craving, you have entered into debt. The way to financial security and peace of mind lies in making a commitment to avoid debt. Of course, by making such a commitment, you agree that you will be content in having less of the world's goods than the people around you have. But "godliness with contentment," the apostle Paul wrote in 1 Timothy 6:6, "is great gain."

Five Kinds of Debt

1. Credit card debt. Credit card debt makes no responsible economic sense whatsoever. Credit card companies charge interest rates that once were the exclusive domain of loan sharks. These little plastic wonders enable us to spend money we don't have, and as we carry the debt over, month after month, year after year, we end up spending still more money we don't have to pay the exorbitant interest. Industry estimates show that using a credit card every month will lead you to spend about a third more money to live than if you spent only cash. Clearly, large amounts of credit card spending represent a poor stewardship decision.

2. Consumer debt. This is debt used to finance automobiles, major appliances, furniture, and so forth. Again, the goal is to spend money we don't have, and the result is poor stewardship.

3. Mortgage debt. This form of debt is no longer as surefire as it once was. Mortgage debt only makes sense if the home you buy appreciates in value and if you can be reasonably certain of repaying the loan. These days, real estate does not automatically appreciate as it once did. In fact, real estate today often *loses* value. And in today's job market, one's ability to repay the loan is also less certain than it was some years ago.

4 and *5. Investment debt* and *business debt.* These forms of debt can make economic sense, depending on the same general criteria that we applied for mortgage debt. The investment or business asset should be appreciating in value and there should be a strong confidence in the ability to repay the debt.

When we take on debt, we make a solemn commitment to pay back the debt. There is an important spiritual principle at work here. "The wicked borrows and does not repay," says Psalm 37:21. As Christians, we are not to live as the wicked do. We do not have the option of reneging on our debts. God calls us to keep our commitments and to pay our debts.

Principle 4: Live Within Your Means

What do you live for? Most Americans live to spend. They organize their lives and careers around acquiring material possessions, creature comforts, and status symbols. Most of their discretionary spending goes toward luxuries and toys—and adults *do* have their toys, ranging from computers to video equipment to sporting equipment to four-wheel-drive vehicles to power boats. Then, to help themselves feel better about all of this conspicuous consumption, they will send a few leftover shekels to the United Way.

But God expects us as Christians to exercise control over our lifestyles and their spending. We are not to be like the rest of the world; we are not to have the values of the rest of the world. Self-control is not only a virtue, it is one of the fruits of the Spirit that, according to Galatians 5, *all* Christians are to have. God tells us that our lifestyles should not gratify the flesh and the senses but should build us up in the Spirit. "For he who sows to his flesh," says Galatians 6:8, "will of the flesh reap corruption, but he who sows to the Spirit will of the Spirit reap everlasting life."

Steps to a Self-Controlled Lifestyle

As you make a commitment to live a self-controlled lifestyle, there are several steps you must take:

Step 1: Commit to live within your means.

Step 2: Determine what your means are. How much money do you have each month, after setting aside taxes, giving to God, mortgage, and other fixed expenses? How much money do you actually have discretion over?

Step 3: Determine how much money you have truly been spending. The best way to do this is to keep a diary for two or three months in which you list every check you write, every credit card purchase, every cash transaction, then put this information into categories (food, entertainment, travel, and so forth). This sounds like a terrible pain—and it is. But it's the only way to get an accurate picture of your real spending patterns. You can't get an accurate picture by just going back through your checkbook—there are too many places where money leaks out through credit cards and cash purchases. After gathering this information, you can form a clearer picture of your true spending patterns. Using computer programs such as Quicken, Microsoft Money, or a good spreadsheet program, you can actually create a visual picture using bar graphs and pie charts.

Now you are ready to begin budgeting.

Step 4: Budget. Make a plan for how much you would *like* to spend, versus how much you have actually been spending. In that budget, lay down some rules about the way you spend money. You may see, from your spending diary, that a lot of money leaks out of your planned spending through unplanned use of the credit card. Make a decision to restrict credit card use to certain kinds of purchases where you need records for tax purposes or for absolute dire emergencies. Otherwise, pay cash. Paying cash is a great way of imposing responsibility on yourself. Cash is tangible, visible, and it is easy to see when there is no more money to spend. With credit cards and even, to some extent, checks, money is just a lot of unreal numbers that you never really think about. You are much more prudent when spending "real money."

As you make a concerted effort to live within your means, you will see your expenses go down. Your lifestyle may be less consumption-oriented, but that doesn't mean you will be less happy. You will actually be happier, because you will finally have your life and your finances under control. When our lives show evidence of *one* of the fruits of the Spirit, self-control, the other fruits of the Spirit, such as joy and peace, tend to follow.

Principle 5: Save and Invest

The Bible affirms the work ethic and the thrift ethic. If we work hard, save well, and invest prudently, we will have financial success. And if we share with those who have need, we will please God. "He who tills his land will be satisfied with bread," says Proverbs 12:11, "but he who follows frivolity is devoid of understanding."

How do we "till our land" in today's world? By saving and investing. Here is how it works. If, at age 25, you begin saving $1,000 per year (only $2.74 per day), then forty years later, at age 65, you will have put away only $40,000—but with interest and compounding at a rate of 12½ percent per year, *you will actually have accumulated $1,000,000!* On just $1,000 a year for forty years, you would become a millionaire. Of course, in the early part of the 1990s, interest rates have not been that high, so let's recompute this example at only half that rate. At 6¼ percent interest you would need to save $2,000 per year—which is only $5.48 per day—in order to become a millionaire by age 65.

A wise savings and investment plan should include the following features:

1. Elimination of credit card and consumer debt. This stops the "hemorrhaging" of your capital through high interest rates.
2. Maintaining a "sinking fund"—an amount equal to one month's living expenses in an interest-bearing checking account. This gives you "liquidity" (that is, instant access to your money) in the event of an emergency.
3. Investing up to six months' living expenses in an interest-bearing money market fund. This is also a high-liquidity source of money for longer term emergencies (a job loss or temporary disability) or larger purchases (notice the advantage of not having to borrow). If this account is drawn down for emergencies or purchases, it should be replaced as quickly as possible.
4. Maintaining as many diversified long-range investments as possible for major emergencies and for retirement. Since the Tax Reform Act of 1986, real estate investments are much chancier than before, and many real estate properties go down in value, causing your investment to diminish rather than grow. We suggest an investment program involving some combination of tax-free bonds, mutual funds, Treasury bills and notes, many of which can be sheltered in a tax-deferred retirement plan. Before you invest, consult with an accountant for the best way to invest significant sums of money. Always be aware that, as a rule of thumb, the higher the interest or return that is promised, the greater the risk that you could lose some or all of your original investment. Highly speculative investments, such as commodity futures, should be avoided unless you are extremely knowledgeable and have a very high tolerance for financial risk.

For an ongoing education in the field of investing, we recommend you subscribe to publications such as *Money* magazine and the *Wall Street Journal*.

Principle 6: Set Long-Term Financial Goals

There is an old saying, "People don't plan to fail, they fail to plan." Not knowing where you want to go with your financial future can get you nowhere fast. How do you set long-term financial goals? Here is a goal-setting plan:

1. First set goals for the short term: giving goals, tax obligations, debt elimination goals, and accumulation goals.
2. Next set goals for the medium range: How much will you need for your children's college education? Do you plan to start your own business, and if so, how much will you need? Meet these goals with low-risk investments.

3. Set goals for retirement and financial security. Meet these goals with low-risk investments.

4. After the short-, medium-, and long-term goals have been met—that is, after you have investment programs running for each of these goals—then and only then are you free to speculate in more aggressive, more risky investments such as aggressive mutual funds, the stock market, or the commodities market. These kinds of investments are clearly not for everyone and should not be attempted by people who are financially or emotionally ill-suited to take the risk.

The important thing to remember is to create a strategy and stay with that strategy to avoid getting pulled off course into unwise or ill-timed investments or risky speculation.

Principle 7: Have Fun Money

After all we have just said, you may think, "Being a good steward of God's money sounds like hard work and no fun. We won't have any money for enjoyment, and life is going to be just plain boring."

Absolutely not!

God wants us to enjoy life. In John 10:10, Jesus said He came so we can have an abundant life, and in Deuteronomy 6, God promises the people of Israel a land of fruit and nice homes and prosperity. God wants us to use His resources for enjoyment—not recklessly but responsibly and gratefully.

The best way to use fun money is with activities that build family relationships and family memories—a date with your spouse, a vacation with the family, a weekend trip. Fun money should also be used to buy relationship-building gifts—flowers for your spouse or a game for the family to play on a rainy weekend. When spending fun money, always use cash and always focus on relationships.

Jesus said that those who are faithful in the small things will be given greater responsibility. You may think, *I'll never have much money to manage.* But the fact is, if you manage what you have well, it can become more money—and it may well be that God, in response to your excellent stewardship, will give you added responsibility and added money to manage. It is in our fallen nature to resist undertaking the discipline of good stewardship, but if we follow these biblical guidelines for responsible money management, we will discover that discipline does not lead to bondage. It actually leads to freedom.

Fitness and Health

The Lord did such a marvelous job of "knitting" you together that it's almost impossible to separate your physical system from your emotional system and spiritual well-being. The health of one directly affects the other two. So, in order to keep ourselves emotionally healthy and spiritually balanced, we need to develop our physical stamina. And, believe it or not, we need to develop our management skills—skills for stress management, diet management, and fitness management.

Every man, woman, and child is a manager. Each of us has control of, authority over, and responsibility for his or her own physical, mental, and spiritual health. The human body is a finely tuned, meticulously designed, God-given machine, and it needs to be carefully maintained. It is composed of some 10 billion nerve cells, more than 200 bones, 60,000 miles of blood vessels, more than 650 voluntary muscles and countless involuntary muscles. Our lungs inhale and exhale 500 cubic feet of air per day, and our hearts pump 2,000 gallons of blood per day.

What kind of care are you giving *your* magnificent human machine? A body that has been carefully supervised can often withstand the challenges of disease and stress for much more than seventy years. Certainly, there are health factors that are beyond our control—factors such as genetic makeup, gender, accident, and just the plain old ravages of time. But there are also many factors that are within our control: habits, attitudes, sleep, stress level, diet, exercise, recreation, and spiritual growth. When we effectively manage these factors, we dramatically increase our odds of feeling better and living longer.

Managing a balanced lifestyle is a big responsibility. It comes down to choices. These are choices you have to make for yourself. The choices that must be made for your personal fitness and balanced lifestyle come down to two major areas of life: exercise and diet. Let's examine each of these areas:

EXERCISE

What is the function of exercise? Exercise builds muscle—that is, lean body mass. Our muscles use more calories than fat tissue, so exercise helps us not only to lose weight but to maintain an ideal weight. Exercise improves body toning and strength, increases the body's metabolism (which means faster calorie consumption), and decreases calcium loss (which helps guard against osteoporosis). Aerobic exercise—that is, exercise that increases heart rate and respiration and gets more oxygen into the bloodstream—strengthens the heart and lungs, reduces blood pressure, lowers blood cholesterol and triglycerides, increases energy levels, and decreases appetite. Studies show that consistent aerobic exercise enables us to maintain a more positive outlook and increases our productivity and mental acuity, thanks to the heightened release of endorphins (a neurotransmitting chemical) in the brain.

Basic aerobic exercises include:

Fast walking. Walking is much kinder to muscles and joints than running, but for an aerobic workout, you must push yourself, and stay with it. Set a speed goal of one mile in fourteen minutes or less—and walk continuously for at least half an hour. Walking burns about 350 calories an hour, suppresses the appetite, improves digestion, relieves stress, and increases alertness by supplying more oxygen to the brain. Best of all, it can be enjoyed by nearly everyone and requires no special equipment, strength, or talent.

Cycling. Another sport with a low level of joint stress. For a good aerobic workout, you must cycle at fifteen miles an hour or more. Outdoor cycling is best and most enjoyable, but stationary bikes also provide a great exercise benefit.

Make Exercise Part of Your Lifestyle

Here are suggestions for making exercise part of your lifestyle rather than an added chore:

1. Set realistic time goals. You can see results in weight reduction and increased body tone by exercising just half an hour, three times a week. Don't set too ambitious a goal, or you may lose heart and drop out. To make sure you stick by your commitment, take an aerobics class or work out with a friend. By making an instructor or friend aware of your goals, you create an atmosphere of accountability—and accountability is a great tool for keeping you focused on your goals.

2. Pick a regular time for exercise. Most people find a morning routine to be advantageous and easy to stick to. Exercising before dinner is another good choice, since it suppresses the appetite and speeds up the calorie-burning mechanism called metabolism. Thirty minutes of aerobic exercise causes the metabolic rate to remain elevated for several hours afterward.

3. Take advantage of every exercise opportunity. Take the stairs instead of the elevator. When you go to the store, look for a parking place at the back of the lot instead of close to the door. Do housework, yardwork, and gardening with enthusiasm! With a little thought, you can make exercise a lifestyle rather than a chore.

Swimming. The best sport of all to avoid bone and joint pain. You can either swim laps for an aquatic aerobic workout or attend an aquatic aerobic class at a local gym or health club.

Jogging and running. Running gives you a complete, fast aerobic workout but causes greater stress on bones and joints. A running program should not be started until you have had a complete physical checkup and have obtained good comfortable running shoes and cool running clothing.

Aerobic dancing. This is an excellent way to improve your cardiovascular fitness, lose weight, and have fun. Try low-impact dance workouts if you are concerned about joint problems.

In short, any sustained exercise that keeps your heartbeat elevated for at least twenty minutes is an aerobic workout and will benefit your body. Other forms of aerobic exercise include handball, racquetball, tennis, cross-country skiing, skating—even mowing the lawn.

■

The easiest way to know if you are having an aerobic workout or not is sweat. If you're not sweating, you're probably not working hard enough.

■

DIET

People often wait until they have health problems to change the way they eat. After they're diagnosed with high blood pressure, they decrease their salt intake. After they suffer colitis, they learn the value of fiber. But good eating habits now can prevent disease later.

Rather than going on a diet, it's smarter to fix the diet you're on. If you do choose to go on a special diet, lose weight slowly. Don't go on crash diets or prolonged fasts, and don't take diet pills. Try not to let every meal become a process of denial or indulgence.

People who have been the most successful in keeping weight off after dieting have usually had:

- a critical moment that stopped their cycle of dieting and overeating, such as a health scare or traumatic social situation;
- an understanding of why they were overweight, including psychological reasons—experiences from their childhood, habits, fears, or needs (see COMPULSIVE OVEREATING);
- a learning stage, slowly building one small victory on the foundation of another;
- enough self-discipline and self-forgiveness to get through the toughest, later stages of dieting (if they slip up, they don't berate themselves; making lifestyle changes often involves two steps forward and one step backward); and
- permanent changes in behavior, attitudes, values, and thinking.

Here are some common-sense suggestions for a diet that will work together with your exercise plan in helping you to be fit and healthy:

1. Maintain your weight. Avoid bizarre diet plans, which produce yo-yo results. Focus on a balanced food intake and exercise to make you healthy.

2. Limit fat consumption. Dietary fat has been linked not only to heart disease and stroke but also to increased incidence of cancer of the colon, breasts, ovaries, pancreas, prostate, and rectum. Particularly unhealthy are animal fats and so-called "tropical oils" such as chocolate, coconut, and palm kernel oils.

3. Increase consumption of complex carbohydrates. This group includes fresh vegetables, fruits, whole-grained and enriched cereals, potatoes, and legumes. Foods rich in complex carbohydrates also supply vitamins and minerals and are an efficient source of energy, essential fiber, and water.

4. Avoid foods high in cholesterol. Cholesterol-rich foods include egg yolks, liver, kidneys, crawfish, hot dogs, sausages, and whole-milk dairy products.

5. Eat less sugar, avoid added salt, and limit caffeine intake. Also, avoid alcohol.

6. Drink plenty of water. We recommend 16 ounces, four times a day. Drink sixteen ounces before each meal and one hour before bedtime.

7. Fast and pray. Here is a biblical prescription that is just what the doctor ordered. Forgoing two or three consecutive meals a week has many health benefits, plus powerful spiritual benefits when coupled with prayer and Bible study. Fasting cleanses and rejuvenates us physically as well as emotionally and spiritually.

EXERCISE AND EAT WELL FOR LIFE!

You *can* change your life. You can learn to eat well, while having fun and feeling better with good aerobic exercise. Start taking good care of your magnificent human

305

machine, and it will give you many years of faithful, dependable service. A body that has been carefully managed through adequate exercise and good diet will reward you with increased energy, greater mental agility, and greater enjoyment in life.

Plan for fitness success. Then stick to your plan and watch it happen!

Forgiveness

I forgive you!

Forgiveness is a word Christians love to talk about. It's a beautiful word to say and hear; but applying it in real-life situations is sometimes a different story. Forgiveness is a painful process. When we've been wounded, it's hard to forgive the one we deem responsible. We often think, *Why should I? He doesn't deserve to be forgiven.* And that's often true. But God commands us to forgive, and disobeying that command can have serious emotional and spiritual ramifications for our lives—and serious physical ramifications too.

BITTERNESS KILLS

The emotion of bitterness (holding grudges) depletes brain amines called *serotonin* and *noradrenaline,* causing clinical depression. If the depression remains untreated for too long, the person may become suicidal. Bitterness can be directed toward oneself (for making a mistake, for not living up to our unrealistic expectations), toward others, toward God, or toward some combination of all of these. Individuals whose serotonin and noradrenaline are depleted awake in the middle of the night and can't get back to sleep, experience memory and concentration problems, feel tired during the day, get headaches, and may lose or gain weight.

This extended bitterness can also reduce natural antibodies, increasing one's susceptibility to infection. A spirit of bitterness can even contribute to heart attacks or strokes.

Anxiety disorders may also result from unresolved bitterness. Anxiety is a fear of facing the truth about one's own thoughts, feelings, and motives (see ANXIETY).

Paranoid disorders are another result of unresolved bitterness. The more people suffer growing up—the more they're verbally criticized, ignored, put down, or abused—the more bitter and paranoid they become. Paranoid individuals feel inferior but compensate by fooling themselves into thinking they're actually supremely important. They may act as if they are the best at everything or the most knowledgeable in every subject. In extreme cases, they may become delusional and even dangerous to themselves and others, requiring medication to help correct the dopamine imbalance that is a part of their paranoia.

306

REVENGE BELONGS TO THE LORD

We refuse to forgive because of vengeful motives. We want to play God, and we want revenge—someday, somehow. We want the one who has hurt us to experience as much pain as we feel—or *more*. But Romans 12:19–21 cancels out our right to revenge. Paul writes,

> Beloved, do not avenge yourselves, but rather give place to wrath; for it is written, "Vengeance is Mine, I will repay," says the Lord. Therefore "If your enemy is hungry, feed him; if he is thirsty, give him a drink; for in so doing you will heap coals of fire on his head." Do not be overcome by evil, but overcome evil with good.

Paul's theme in these verses is *Give revenge over to God.* This doesn't mean that we ignore injustice or that we don't defend ourselves against the evil actions of evil-intentioned people. We have a biblical right to defend ourselves against abuse. God does not expect us to be doormats. But He does expect us to respond justly and graciously, even as we are defending ourselves and confronting abuse. When we seek revenge, we are overcome by evil. But when we seek justice and forgiveness, we vanquish evil with good.

Some people try to live by the old saying, "Forgive and forget." That is a saying we never use at the Minirth Meier New Life Clinics. We are to forgive—but not forget. If we forgot every injury and injustice that was ever done to us, we would never learn from them. Some things should never be forgotten. They should be dealt with, worked through, forgiven—but remembered as a warning not to get into the same situation again.

When people attack us and abuse us, it is wrong and unhealthy for us to simply absorb that abuse, then pretend it never happened. Why? For several reasons:

- Attempting to forget the wounds of the past is emotionally unhealthy; it is an act of repressing or denying emotion. Repression and denial tend to produce emotional disorders such as depression and anxiety.
- When we attempt to forget acts of abuse against us, it is frequently a sign of passivity, rooted in low self-esteem. It is a way of saying, "I don't count, my feelings don't count, I am worthless. Go ahead and wipe your feet on me. I will just try to forget it."
- When we attempt to forget acts of abuse against us, we excuse the abuser, whereas the loving thing to do would be to confront the abuser and seek to change his heart and behavior. We do people no kindness in allowing them to remain in their sinful, destructive behavior patterns. According to Matthew 18:15–17 and Galatians 6:1, if we care about people, we should lovingly stand up to them and confront their sin (see CONFLICT AND CONFRONTATION).

We see how the apostle Paul dealt with an abusive person in 2 Timothy 4:14–15. There he writes, "Alexander the coppersmith did me much harm. May the Lord repay him according to his works. You also must beware of him, for he has greatly resisted our words." Note that Paul took the same advice he gave in Romans 12:19–21, leaving vengeance to God: "May the Lord repay him."

I believe Paul forgave Alexander, but he also learned from his experience. He had set some healthy boundaries in his dealings with Alexander. His warning to Timothy was "Watch out for this guy. Don't trust him. He hurt me once, and he may hurt you." There are abusive people in this world, and we should not allow them to continue abusing us. And—as much as is in our power—we should prevent them from hurting others too.

Forgiveness does not mean you have to cozy up to an abusive person and become fast friends. Nor does it mean you become a doormat and allow him to wipe his feet on you. Nor does it mean you let an abuser mistreat you. Forgiveness does not mean you have to have warm fuzzy feelings about the other person. In many cases, forgiveness does not even mean you have to reconcile with the other person or have any contact with that person again. Here is what forgiveness *does* mean:

Forgiveness means making a choice. You probably don't *feel* like forgiving—and you don't have to. Forgiveness is an act of the will. It's a decision you make for your own sake, to restore your life and your emotions to good health.

Forgiveness is not an act of self-sacrifice. It is an act of healthy, biblical self-love. People who harbor bitterness and grudges allow others to revictimize them whenever they brood over past hurts. The abuser is in control of the bitter person's emotions. When you forgive, you free yourself from the abuser's control. You become free, and with that emotional freedom comes emotional health and well-being.

Forgiveness is completely up to you. Some people say, "I'll forgive when she apologizes." That's not forgiveness. True forgiveness can forgive even those who are totally unrepentant. You have the power to forgive right now, regardless of what anyone else says or does.

Forgiveness does not equal reconciliation. It takes two to reconcile but only one to forgive. The abuser may not want your forgiveness and may never repent. So what? Even if others are wrong and sinful, we can be right and emotionally whole. In many cases, reconciliation would actually be harmful—as in the case of a woman who is repeatedly abused by a violent husband who refuses to change. In such cases, we can still forgive. We can remove both the abuser and bitterness from our lives—and that is a choice that is both healthy and pleasing to God.

Forgiveness is an ongoing process. Few people are able to forgive, then wipe the offense out of their minds. Every time the offense comes back to mind, it must be forgiven again. But as you continually, resolutely forgive each remembrance of the offense, your thinking and feelings will gradually be regrooved until a time comes when the old memories no longer return—or if they do, the pain of those memories will be gone. The task of forgiving will have been completed, and you will be at peace with the past.

CLEARING THE ANGER HURDLE

To reach forgiveness, we must first clear the anger hurdle. Do Christians have the right to be angry? Yes. The Bible acknowledges that we do—though the Bible also tells us how to handle anger appropriately (see ANGER). Christians are human. And human beings get angry virtually every day. Often it's over minor things, such as being cut off in traffic or getting behind someone with too many items in the supermarket express line. We use words like *frustrated, hurt, irritated,* and *perturbed,* but they're all synonyms for *angry.* We use these words because we're taught from childhood that anger is not acceptable.

Can you remember when you were three or four years old? You were probably more in touch with your anger than you are now. Actually you were more in touch with *all* your emotions. When you felt love for your parents, you put your arms around their knees and gave them a big hug. When you were sad, you cried. When you were angry you said, "I'm mad at you!" If you had healthy loving parents, they gave you a hug and said, "Thanks for letting me know how you feel. Let's sit down and talk about it." They honored your feelings, acknowledged your right to have your own feelings.

But if you received negative messages about your anger as a child, you may have learned to lie to yourself about your feelings and to shield yourself with defense mechanisms such as denial or repression (see DEFENSE MECHANISMS). That is one reason you may spend so much of your adult life denying that you are angry, yet feeling depressed.

So what should you do to clear the anger hurdle? Here are some steps you can take:

1. Stop and analyze your anger. Don't just express it impulsively as soon as you feel it. Anger is always a response to feeling that some right has been violated, so ask yourself: Which of my rights is being violated? Am I justified in being angry over this issue? Am I reacting appropriately, or is my anger out of proportion to the seriousness of this issue?

2. Speak the truth in love. Notice the three components to that command: speak, truth, love. You don't *stuff* your anger; you *speak* it. You don't speak lies; you speak the truth, even if it hurts. And you don't speak rudely; you speak the truth *in love.* Your goal is restoration, not revenge. We share our anger with the other person *not* to hurt that person but (if possible) to restore the relationship.

3. Verbalize your anger. Avoid using "you should" or "you shouldn't" messages. Say, "I feel angry when you do this," or "I feel angry right now because you said something about me that wasn't true." Own your feelings. Avoid blaming others for the way you feel.

4. Choose to forgive. Forgiveness starts with an act of the will. Biblically, we are to choose forgiveness no matter how the other person responds. If you choose not to forgive, you are only hurting yourself. This doesn't mean that by choosing forgiveness you'll be able to blot out the past, but it does mean you've identified your feelings and you refuse to dwell on them. As you forgive, make sure you allow yourself time to work through these feelings.

FORGIVING IS LOVE'S TOUGHEST WORK

Revenge is natural. Forgiving is unnatural. When someone strikes us, our instant, reflexive response is to strike back. God does not want us to respond to life and its challenges in a *natural* way. He wants us to respond in a *supernatural* way.

One phrase we often hear in counseling is "It's not fair that I have to forgive. My spouse/parent/friend doesn't deserve to be forgiven." And frequently, the person who says this is right. Forgiveness isn't fair. It wasn't fair for Jesus to die on a cross, and it wasn't fair for God to place our sin on His shoulders, and it wasn't fair that we should

Forgiveness is not an act of justice. It's an act of grace and mercy and love.

be forgiven at Christ's expense—but we are grateful for God's grace, mercy, and love all the same!

The people who abuse us and mistreat us don't deserve our forgiveness. But we deserve to forgive. Forgiving others is the only way to be fair to ourselves. When we forgive, we don't do the abuser a favor, we do ourselves a favor.

During one of our clinic call-in broadcasts, as we were spending the entire week on the subject of forgiveness, we received a call from a pastor's wife who was obviously very angry. With a trembling voice she told us how one of the parishioners in her church had been cleaning out the sanctuary and had thrown out large quantities of rare organ music that were irreplaceable. The pastor's wife (who was, of course, the church organist) was clearly distraught. Even though the dumping of the organ music had not been done on purpose, she just didn't know how to get past her anger and grief. So we gave the woman several ideas for dealing with her problem:

First, we suggested she forgive herself for any mistakes she may have made. Perhaps she was angry at herself for leaving the music out where it could be found and tossed out like any other pile of trash. Next, we urged her to go to the person who had tossed out the music and forgive that person in a face-to-face encounter. Then, we suggested that she forgive God for letting this tragedy happen. Finally, we suggested she set aside half an hour each day for the next seven days to feel her anger and grief—to weep, scream, whatever it would take to express her anger over the loss. After seven days she would be far more ready to give up her anger and get on with her life.

That, after all, is the bottom line: letting go of the issue. Forgiving the person who hurt you or violated your rights. Getting on with your life. When anger is kept in the heart, it turns into animosity, hatred, and a grudge that you can bear for years, possibly until you die. (In fact, it may bring on an *early* death!) Moreover, unresolved anger gives Satan a dangerous handle on our lives—and we dare not allow that to happen. As Paul writes in Ephesians 4:26–27, "'Be angry, and do not sin': do not let the sun go down on your wrath, nor give place to the devil."

There is an old line that says, "bury the hatchet . . . but leave the handle sticking up." In other words, forgive halfway—but reserve the right to get even! That's a good description of repressed anger—and a good prescription for anxiety and depression. When God calls us to forgive, He demands that we bury the hatchet, handle and all!

Gambling Addiction

The practice of wagering money on games of chance is as old as history itself. Dice carved from animal bones have been discovered in prehistoric burial caves. The ancient Greeks made bets on games of dicelike astragals, and the ancient Romans seemed to have an obsessive-compulsive fascination with betting on gladiators and chariot racers.

The historian Tacitus observed that the ancient Germanic people wagered not only their money but their freedom on games of chance—and the losers became slaves.

In our society today, people are still gambling, and still becoming enslaved by games of chance. For hundreds of thousands of Americans, gambling is not just an entertaining pastime. It is an obsession, a compulsion, an addiction. Gambling ruins thousands of lives and thousands of families every year. It causes financial destruction, emotional destruction, and destruction to family relationships.

Compulsive gambling is not limited to any economic class. The poor and middle class play the horses or buy lottery tickets believing that this is their only shot at fabulous riches. And we often hear stories of entertainers, sports figures, financiers— people who have amassed enormous fortunes—who have squandered astounding sums in Las Vegas or Atlantic City. Gambling enterprises, whether illegal, legal, or government-controlled, play on the greed and ignorance of people who have no concept of how statistically hopeless the odds of winning truly are.

A preoccupation with gambling disrupts one's personal life, one's most cherished relationships, one's lifestyle and security, and one's career. People who compulsively engage in gambling frequently find themselves falling into other sins and problems such as defaulting on debts or involvement in fraud or forgery to cover gambling losses. Gambling also involves the sin of covetousness. Excessive reliance upon chance in order to make money expresses a desire to possess another person's money without having to earn it. Gambling involves an attempt to "make a fast buck" at the expense of another person.

Though compulsive gambling is an addiction, it is incorrect to say (as some in the recovery and psychology fields have said) that gambling is a "disease" or a "sickness." There is no "gambling virus" that we can "catch" and that forces us against our will to put money on a roulette table or to buy a lottery ticket. The impulse to gamble is strong in many compulsive people, but we all still have the power to choose whether to gamble or not.

People can learn to conquer their gambling addictions, but it is crucial that they begin to take full responsibility for their own actions, their own choices, and their own recovery. The Twelve Step organization Gamblers Anonymous (GamAnon) has chapters in many cities; see the white pages of your telephone book for a meeting near you. Also, many churches offer Christian Twelve Step groups and may have a group for either gamblers or people struggling with compulsions in general. The process of recovery from gambling addiction is very similar to the process for recovery from other addictions such as alcoholism, drug abuse, and compulsive overeating.
See also ADDICTION and COMPULSIVE BEHAVIOR

Gender Identity Disorder

Gender identity disorder involves feelings of dislike for one's own inborn maleness or femaleness. One form of gender identity disorder is *transsexualism*. A transsexual is an individual who wishes to live as a member of the opposite sex. This disorder usually

311

surfaces in childhood, prior to puberty: a boy wishes to grow up to be a woman, hates his male genitalia, and desires the traits of a woman; a girl with this disorder may insist she is a boy and may desire or claim to have male genitalia.

Individuals with a gender identity disorder are emotionally confused or experiencing conflict in their view of themselves. In young adulthood, individuals with this disorder may complain about having to wear the clothing of their own gender and may participate in activities usually associated with the opposite sex. Some are so repulsed by their own genitalia that they have their bodies cosmetically and surgically altered to resemble the opposite sex.

Some gender identity confusion is common during the emotionally turbulent years of adolescence, and the vast majority of people come through this time with their inborn gender identities intact. A certain percentage of young people, however, manifest homosexual preferences.

Homosexuality is a behavior choice made by an individual to practice sex with someone of the same gender. Female homosexuality is usually referred to as *lesbianism.* Parents are understandably concerned for their children and want to understand the factors that would tend to cause a person to develop homosexual or lesbian tendencies. Some research suggests a link between genetics and homosexuality, which would tend to support the gay advocacy's contention that people are *born* either heterosexual or homosexual: "it's in the genes." Clinical experience, however, tends to indicate that environment plays an even more important role.

Male homosexuality seems to occur most frequently when the son has an absent or detached father in childhood and spends a great deal of time with his mother. As a result, he identifies sexually with his mother and may even develop her mannerisms. Yet he will also crave the attention and affection of his absent father. During the adolescent years of raging hormones, this often results in homosexual temptations. These temptations are not the fault of the young person, but it is important that the individual understand that he has a choice to yield to or resist those temptations.

Many young people yield to occasional homosexual urges in adolescence but go on to heterosexual lifestyles and orientations in adulthood. Shame and guilt over these youthful episodes, however, tends to persist, causing some men to become involved in multiple heterosexual extramarital affairs in order to prove to themselves that they are not homosexuals.

A *lesbian* is a female who engages in sexual relations with another female. The sources of her disorder may be an absent or workaholic mother, which produces a tendency to identify more with her father. She may develop his mannerisms and model her sexual identity on his, even though she craves the attention and affection of her absent mother. As an adolescent, confusing her need for emotional nurture with eroticism, she manifests lesbian tendencies. Again, as with male homosexuals, the key element in her behavior is not one of temptations or urges but the element of choice. She has the power to choose to act out these urges or not to. Homosexuals who choose to act on their homosexual urges are no less responsible for their behavior than heterosexuals who act on their heterosexual urges outside of marriage.

Many adolescents with gender identity disorder can be helped and enabled to make healthy emotional choices that will cement their sexual orientation in the direction of heterosexuality. Many adolescents are confused about their gender identity, but they are not yet full-fledged homosexuals. They are at a crossroads. This confusion may lead them to experiment with homosexual behavior, and, with time and experience, they may become compulsively addicted to homosexual or lesbian behavior. But with love, understanding, and counseling, confused young people can often be spared a lifetime of emotional pain and sexual shame.

Before his death due to AIDS in 1988, Jerry Arterburn (Stephen Arterburn's brother), told the story of his painful struggle with homosexuality in the book *How Will I Tell My Mother?* (Thomas Nelson, 1990). In the revised edition, Stephen added a section to the book describing the possible early indicators and psychological sources of male homosexuality. These factors include:

- He has been labeled a sissy.
- He has feminine interests.
- He prefers female playmates.
- He dislikes traditionally male games.
- His parents wanted a girl.
- He is dressed in feminine clothing. (His parents' desire for a girl leads them to cross-dress him.)
- He frequently expresses the wish to be a girl.
- He has a weak relationship with his father.
- He has difficulty forming opposite-sex relationships in adolescence.
- He was molested by someone of the same sex at an early age.

In our clinical experience, we have repeatedly seen these factors in the early lives of homosexual men, and we have also seen many of these factors mirrored in the early lives of lesbians:

- She has been labeled boyish or a tomboy.
- She has male interests.
- She prefers male playmates.
- She dislikes the forms of play that girls traditionally enjoy.
- Her parents wanted a boy.
- She is dressed in boys' clothing.
- She frequently expresses the wish to be a boy.
- She has a weak relationship with her mother.
- She has difficulty forming opposite-sex relationships in adolescence.
- She was molested by someone of the same sex at an early age.

It is important, however, that parents not overreact. Certainly, a child with just one or two of these factors is not destined to become a homosexual. Many perfectly healthy boys, for example, simply have no interest in throwing a football or swinging a bat. And many children who manifest most or all of the above factors grow up to be heterosexual in adulthood. If your child's sexual orientation is a matter of concern to you, based on observing some of the above factors in your child's life, you should:

1. *Discourage mannerisms of the opposite sex.* Do so gently, not angrily or hysterically.

Current secular, "politically correct" thinking suggests just the opposite: *encourage* the "obviously homosexual" child to explore homosexuality and become comfortable with a homosexual orientation; this approach, however, leaves the child alienated from the heterosexual world and from God.

2. *Provide the child with a strong same-sex role model.* The child is looking for same-sex adult approval and a clear same-sex example to pattern his life and behavior after. If the child is encouraged to spend significant time with a strong same-sex role model (a stepparent, friend, relative), the child may be able to identify with that role model before his or her sexual orientation is settled in the direction of homosexuality.

3. *Clarify scriptural mandates.* The child needs to hear from an early age that God disapproves of homosexual behavior. Though our society speaks in a babble of discord on this issue, the Bible is crystal-clear. Make it plain to your child that God does not hate people; rather He loves all people and wants to spare them from the pain and suffering that homosexual behavior brings.

Broad warnings against sexual immorality are found in 1 Corinthians 6:13–20 and 1 Thessalonians 4:3–6. Specific warnings against homosexual behavior are found in Romans 1:21–32; 1 Corinthians 6:9–10; 1 Timothy 1:8–10; Jude vv. 6–7; and Leviticus 18:22. These passages should be placed in a context that affirms God's love for sinners and His ability to redirect the lives of sinners. The promise of God's unconditional love and forgiveness is beautifully expressed in Psalm 103:8–13; Jeremiah 31:34; and Isaiah 43:25. In John 8:1–12, we find the story of how Jesus forgave a woman who was guilty of sexual sin—but He also held her accountable to "go and sin no more." When we explain God's view of homosexuality to our children, we must be careful to present the full range of His personality, both forgiveness and justice, both grace and truth.

4. *Be supportive.* Unconditionally love your child. Blaming and shaming undermines self-esteem and tends to reinforce the emotional forces that lead to sinful or self-defeating behavior patterns.

5. *Seek counseling.* This issue is too complicated for parents to handle alone.

It is important, in viewing the issue of homosexuality, that Christians be able to separate the sin from the sinner. Many Christians are extremely harsh and unloving toward people who struggle with homosexual tendencies, having little compassion for the dysfunctional family issues or abuse that created the underlying pain of their sexual orientation. Many Christians condemn homosexuals and call AIDS "God's curse" upon the sin of homosexuality. Some understanding is needed. Homosexual behavior is sin, according to the Bible; homosexual tendencies are not. A homosexual orientation is a disorder, much like schizophrenia is a disorder. We do not condemn the schizophrenic for his disorder, nor should we condemn the homosexual.

We believe that the AIDS plague is a *consequence* of homosexual sin, just as herpes

---

Treatment and Counseling for Homosexuals

Adult homosexuality and lesbianism are difficult, but not impossible, to treat. Professional treatment and counseling are available through the Minirth Meier New Life Clinics (1-800-NEW-LIFE), and through Exodus International, P.O. Box 2121, San Rafael CA 94912 (1-414-454-1017). Christian support groups are available through Homosexuals Anonymous Fellowship Services, P.O. Box 7881, Reading PA 19603 (1-215-376-1146). Church education programs are available through Desert Stream Ministries, 1415 Santa Monica Mall, Suite 201, Santa Monica CA 90401 (1-213-395-9137).

and syphilis are consequences of heterosexual sin and heart disease and cancer are consequences of the sin of gluttony. This doesn't mean that God actively curses those who acquire any of these diseases. All behavior entails consequences; for every action, there is a reaction. God's biblical warnings against sexual sins may, in one sense, be viewed as not only moral laws but rules of good health and hygiene. If we confine our sexual activity to the safe enclosure of marriage, we virtually guarantee that we will not contract certain diseases.

Those who condemn others for their sins should recall Jesus' treatment of the woman caught in adultery (John 8), as well as C. S. Lewis's statement in *Mere Christianity* (Macmillan, 1960): "The sins of the flesh are bad, but they are the least bad of all sins. All the worst pleasures are purely spiritual: the pleasure of putting other people in the wrong, . . . of power, of hatred. . . . That is why a cold, self-righteous prig who goes regularly to church may be far nearer to hell than a prostitute."

Grief and Loss

Surely He has borne our griefs
And carried our sorrows;
Yet we esteemed Him stricken,
Smitten by God, and afflicted.
Isaiah 53:4

Grief is one of the most painful emotions we will ever experience. Grief is our reaction to the loss of someone or something intensely important to us. When we have made a major emotional investment in a person, an ambition, a dream, or a possession, the loss of that emotional investment brings immense sorrow and pain.

One of the most profound and revealing verses in all of Scripture, John 11:35, is an image of grief: "Jesus wept." In those two words, we get a searing glimpse into the heart of Jesus—and by extension, into the heart of God the Father. Our Lord is moved by loss, just as we are. He demonstrated His grief through His tears at the grave of His friend, Lazarus.

Some people are uncomfortable in the presence of another person's grief. They may have the idea that there is something wrong, shameful, or sinful about grieving. A Christian who has just lost a close loved one may find himself or herself accosted by some well-intentioned but misguided soul who will say, "You shouldn't cry, you shouldn't grieve. Your loved one is with the Lord, in a much better place. You should be celebrating, not weeping." People who say such things misunderstand both the Scriptures and the emotions of grief and loss. If Christians shouldn't cry or grieve, then why did Jesus Himself weep at the tomb of Lazarus?

In the first-century church at Thessalonica, there were people who were grieving the loss of loved ones. These early Christians had been taught by Paul, yet many were uncertain about God's plans regarding the Second Coming of Christ. They wondered if those who had died were going to be received into heaven when Jesus comes again. In their uncertainty and confusion, many of them grieved and sorrowed with the same hopelessness and despair that were commonly expressed at pagan funerals. So Paul wrote to them about the way they expressed their grief, and he clarified his teaching about the Second Coming of Christ. "I do not want you to be ignorant, brethren," he said in 1 Thessalonians 4:13, "concerning those who have fallen asleep [died], lest you sorrow as others who have no hope."

Some Christians today will pluck that verse out of context and say, "You see? The Bible says we're not to grieve, we're not supposed to feel sorrow when a Christian dies." But that's wrong. Of course we will feel sorrow when a loved one dies, or when any other major loss occurs. We will feel sorrow, we will grieve, but, as Paul told the Thessalonians, we will not grieve in the same way as those who have no hope. The Christian hope transforms the nature of our grief, but it does not take all grief away. It is normal to grieve. What's more, it is *healthy* to grieve. It is a clinical fact: those who fail to grieve their losses completely tend to have emotional problems later.

THE STAGES OF GRIEF

Whenever a person suffers a significant loss, he or she must go through the stages of grief, which were first defined by Swiss psychiatrist Elisabeth Kübler-Ross in her 1969 book, *On Death and Dying* (Macmillan, 1993). We have adapted those stages as follows:

1. shock and denial
2. anger (anger turned outward)
3. depression (anger turned inward)
4. bargaining
5. sadness
6. forgiveness, resolution, and acceptance

No one goes through these stages at the same rate, or even in exactly the same order. But these stages do give us a useful road map of the grief process so that we can better understand what is happening to us in the aftermath of a major loss. Let's examine these stages in detail.

Shock and Denial

A loss occurs. Stunned and shocked, the person who has suffered this loss either refuses or is unable to believe what has happened. When bereaved people describe their initial feelings after a loss has taken place, the vast majority say something like, "This can't be happening! This isn't real!" That is denial.

When Francine answered her door one evening, she found a uniformed officer on her porch, hat in hand, a somber expression on his face. "Ma'am," he began, "it's my

Bringing your honest feelings to God is one way to work through those feelings and come to a place of resolution.

THE COMPLETE LIFE ENCYCLOPEDIA

duty to inform you . . ." And he proceeded to tell Francine that her college-age daughter had been killed in a head-on collision on the interstate north of town. Francine's only response for the next two hours was denial. "There must be some mistake," she said, smiling. "You've driven all the way out here for nothing, officer. If anything had happened to my daughter, I would know. Maybe a friend borrowed my daughter's car, or—well, there could be a million perfectly logical explanations for this mistake. But I just know that nothing could have happened to my daughter." Not until Francine was shown her daughter's body at the morgue was her denial finally penetrated so that her real grieving could begin.

There is nothing wrong or unhealthy about the denial stage of grief. A short period of denial protects us mentally and emotionally, so that we can get through the shock of a loss and adjust ourselves to the fact that the loss really did take place. Denial prepares us for the next stage of grief.

Anger

This stage involves anger turned outward, directed at someone other than oneself. It is not uncommon for people to feel angry with the person who died. "How could she leave me like that?" Or "Why wasn't he more careful?" This stage also tends to involve anger toward God for allowing the loss to occur. In situations in which the loss is brought about by someone's sin or mistake—for example, a drunk or negligent driver or a murderer—there will be blaming and intense anger directed at the perpetrator.

Again, there is nothing unhealthy about this stage of the grief process. Anger is a natural, healthy, God-given mechanism for dealing with pain and loss. Paul told the Ephesians, "Be angry, and do not sin: do not let the sun go down on your wrath" (4:26). In other words, be aware of your anger: acknowledge it, deal with it, then release it. God even understands when, in our grief, we are angry with Him, and He wants us to bring our honest feelings to Him in prayer. As you read through the Psalms, the story of Job, and the writings of Isaiah, Jeremiah, Ezekiel, Hosea, and Habakkuk, you find that some of the greatest people of faith have wrestled with anger toward God.

Your best resources for working through angry emotions are:

- prayer and writing a letter to God
- talking through your emotions in a grief support group
- talking through your emotions with a counselor
- talking through your emotions with a close, empathetic friend

If you allow anger to settle into your soul and fester, it becomes a poisonous emotional sludge called bitterness. The poison of bitterness can destroy your soul. But if you choose to face your anger and honestly work through it, you will be able to continue moving through the grief process.

When You Are Angry with God

If you are angry at God for allowing a loss in your life, express your feelings to God in prayer. Or do as the psalmist did: write God a letter. In Psalm 13:1–2, David expresses his anger to God:

How long, O LORD? Will You forget me forever?
How long will You hide Your face from me?
How long shall I take counsel in my soul,
Having sorrow in my heart daily?

Or listen to these feelings poured out by the prophet Habakkuk (1:2):

O LORD, how long shall I cry,
And You will not hear?

Depression

In most cases, outward-directed anger turns inward and becomes depression. The grieving person often feels guilty—guilty over being angry with God and others, guilty that he or she did not do something to prevent the loss, guilty over regrets: "I wish I had said, 'I love you,' more often." Or "I wish I had kissed him goodbye that morning." Or "If only we hadn't fought before she went out the door that last time." The guilt we feel may be authentic guilt over some sin or failure, but more often when people grieve they experience *false guilt*. This is guilt we feel over actions we couldn't have foreseen or failures that weren't our fault or regrets that are not reality-based. Grief tends to distort our perceptions, and when our thinking is distorted, we easily fall prey to false guilt.

One of the most tragic and needless forms of false guilt we see in cases of grief is when a parent loses a child to an accident or an illness such as leukemia and then agonizes, "Why did God take my child? What sin did I commit? What did I do to make God angry with me?" It is important that we understand that when loved ones die, it is not because God wants to punish someone else for sin. Disease and death are a predictable part of life in a fallen world, not a judgment for sin in the lives of those who survive.

This kind of false guilt is the result of what is called *self-referential thinking*. It is the error of thinking that everything that happens in life is somehow connected with, or directed at, oneself. In a way, self-referential thinking is a form of self-centeredness. If you think about it logically, you have to ask yourself, "Why would a loving God punish an innocent child for the sins of someone else?" The answer: He wouldn't. We are not the center of the universe, and all of life's events do not revolve around us. When loved ones die, it is not our fault. It is just something that happens in an unjust, fallen world. To take on the responsibility of another person's death, when we had nothing to do with that death, is to think self-centeredly and to take on false guilt.

Whether our guilt feelings are authentic or false, they are a form of anger that we turn inward against ourselves. When this happens, we become depressed. It is important to understand that the depression stage of the grief process is not true clinical depression. This depression is a *temporary stage* in a normal process that we all must take on our journey to recovery from grief. This temporary depression displays many of the symptoms of clinical depression: altered sleep patterns, diminished appetite, diminished motivation, crying, feelings of hopelessness, and physical symptoms. However, if we do not resolve our guilt and learn to forgive ourselves, this stage can turn into true, long-lasting clinical depression.

The principal warning sign of clinical depression in this situation is *a lack of progress in dealing with the loss (being "stuck")*. A long grieving period—several months to even two or three years—is not unusual or unhealthy in and of itself. During that period, however, there should be *some* progress in moving through the grief stages. There should be a gradual resumption of relationships with friends, involvement in life, and improvement in mood. If the individual remains emotionally paralyzed, withdrawn, and nonfunctional, then he or she may be sliding into a deep clinical depression. Clinical depression is a potentially life-threatening problem and requires treatment by a professional psychiatrist.

318

If someone you know shows signs of clinical depression, encourage that person to undergo a full medical evaluation. Be alert to any distorted or painful thinking by that person, as evidenced by such statements as "Everyone would be better off without me" or "I'm just in the way." Be alert to any expressions of suicidal feelings, and don't hesitate to discuss those feelings, calmly and honestly. Avoid expressions of shock or judgment; be empathetic and understanding. If the individual appears to have a suicide plan, take positive action. Remove any means of suicide from reach and contact a therapist or suicide prevention agency *immediately* (see SUICIDE).

In the normal progression of the grief process, the temporary depression stage passes, giving way to the next stage.

Bargaining

We normally think of bargaining as a stage one passes through while grieving one's approaching death owing to a terminal illness: "God, if You'll just take away this cancer, I'll do anything You want!" But a form of bargaining can also be observed as people grieve a loss that is already finalized: "God, what do I have to do to get rid of this awful grief? How can I go on like this? God, just take away my depression and my sorrow and I'll do anything You want!"

Sadness

Sadness is a normal consequence of letting go of bargaining. It is clear that the situation will not change; our grief is going to go on. Having accepted this reality, we sink into a deep sadness. Not depression—this stage is not marked by anger or guilt. We are simply sad. And that's okay. We deal with sadness by shedding tears. We get out the picture album or the home movies and we cry our eyes out. Sadness is miserable—but not as miserable as depression and not as wrenching as bargaining. Eventually sadness diminishes. As we look at the old pictures and remember the old events, we sometimes smile and even laugh. We realize there are many good memories to enjoy. There is still an ache of sadness, but the sadness can be lived through.

Forgiveness, Resolution, and Acceptance

The forgiveness, resolution, and acceptance stage is the goal of the grief process. In this stage we discover what the Bible calls "the peace that passes understanding."

Don't expect to arrive at Stage 6 and to be able to say, "I'm glad that's over! No more sadness or depression for me!" Our emotions don't travel in a straight line. They zigzag. There will be times ahead when you feel a resurgence of anger, a recurrence of sadness, a reversion to depression. Painful emotions will come and go, but each time they return, they will be less intense and less prolonged. As the normal pace and emotional state of your life resumes, your grief feelings will occupy less and less of your heart and mind.

Not everyone makes it all the way to forgiveness, resolution, and acceptance. Some get stuck in the anger stage; unable to get past blaming God for their loss, they sink into a state of bitterness from which they never recover. Others get stuck in depression, as the normal emotions of the grief reaction trigger imbalances in brain chemicals, causing the depression to reinforce itself. Most people can work through the stages of

You can't go under, over, or around the grief process. The path to grief recovery leads straight through the emotions of grief.

319

grief with the caring support of family and friends. But when people get stuck in one of the stages of grief, they may need additional help from a psychologist or psychiatrist to regain their momentum toward resolving their grief.

Covering up or repressing your grief is a sign not of spirituality but of unhealthy denial, and it is a choice that often leads to long-term depression. If you feel shattered and immobilized by the loss of a loved one, the loss of your health, the loss of a job, the loss of your reputation, the loss of a relationship, or the loss of your mate's faithfulness, then consider finding a Christian counselor who can help you uncover your feelings and work through the stages of grief.

THE INTENSITY OF GRIEF AND LOSS

Sometimes people will respond to loss in ways that seem disproportionate. A minor loss may appear to be grieved more intensely than a major loss. We see this and we wonder, *Why?* Many factors affect a person's reaction to a loss.

The Timing of the Loss

When losses come bunched together, they can overload a person's ability to respond to them. A series of minor losses may be more emotionally devastating than a single major loss. A person might respond to one loss by saying, "That was a terrible loss, but I'll survive." That same person, by the third or fourth loss, may say, "Life is just too painful. I can't handle this anymore."

The Meaning of the Loss

After a serious financial loss, Fred was forced to give up his large house in the suburbs and move to a much smaller condo. Even though the condo was nicely furnished and offered a perfectly comfortable lifestyle, Fred became depressed over the loss of his house—not because of the house itself but because of what it symbolized: the loss of his status, his sense of success, his self-esteem. He had invested all of his emotional energy into that house, and once it was gone, he felt a major portion of himself was gone. "Your life is over" was the message he read in his circumstances— and that message left him deeply depressed.

The Upsetting of Life's Equilibrium

If a major loss occurs during a time of relative calm and stability in life, it will be painful but probably endurable. But if a major loss occurs at a time when a person is already emotionally off-balance due to financial problems, emotional stresses, family conflicts and the like, then that loss could well topple him or her off the tightrope.

The Circumstances Surrounding the Loss

If we lose someone close to us due to a sudden, unexpected accident, we will process that loss differently than if we lose someone after a long battle against cancer or some other chronic disease. A sudden loss may trigger a more intense anger stage in our

A Grief Survival Guide:
How to Keep Moving Toward Recovery

Here are some suggestions to help you continue your own journey toward recovery from grief and loss:

- Don't be ashamed to express your emotions. Talk through them or cry through them. Find a friend you can trust to be a good, supportive listener and prayer partner.
- Say goodbye. Many people find it comforting to verbalize their goodbyes during the meaningful ritual of a funeral service. If you have lost someone close to you, take a last look at the final earthly resting place of your loved one and say it aloud: "I love you. I'll miss you. Goodbye." These words, like a period at the end of a sentence, express your acceptance of the finality of your loss, and can help to accelerate your healing process.
- Maintain your spiritual lifeline. Read the Bible and pray, telling God honestly how you feel and listening for His answers.
- Avoid making major decisions (a major move or job change, for example) during the first year of a major bereavement. Avoid romantic involvements for a while. Your thinking processes may be confused or distorted during this time, and your grief-impaired judgment may lead you into major mistakes in life.
- Maintain adequate nutrition and physical exercise during your grief process. A strong body contributes to clear thinking and an improved emotional state. Poor nutrition and lack of exercise are often factors in prolonging and deepening depression.
- Stay involved with friends and family. Make an effort to reconnect with familiar routines and interests. Take a grief recovery class or join a support group. Travel and visit places you have always wanted to see. Enjoy your family's companionship, but don't lean too heavily on relatives for your needs.
- If you have lost a spouse, learn to do things for yourself that your spouse used to do. This means you may need to learn a new skill, such as cooking. Or maintaining the car. Or keeping house. Or balancing the checkbook and paying the bills. But as you do these things, you will gain a new and healthy sense of mastery over life.
- Write a letter to God or to your loved one. Say exactly what you are feeling. If you never got a chance to say goodbye to the one you love, then say it in the letter. You may even want to save the letter and read it over in the years to come.
- Treasure memories and mementos. Some people, in the intense stages of grief, will put all reminders of a loved one in a box and take them to the Salvation Army. Then, when they move into the sadness or acceptance phases, they will wish they had kept something as a memento. Avoid making hasty decisions about your memories. Mementos help keep warm memories alive.
- Find a way to minister to other people, particularly people who are grieving. One of the best ways to overcome grief is to transform your pain into help and healing for others. In the process, you will find yourself getting involved in life, in the world, and in the lives of other people again. It's hard to sit and mope when life offers the satisfaction of helping and healing other people.

grieving, as we think, "How could God allow this? My loved one had so many good years of life to experience—and now it's all cut short!" A loss that takes place over time tends to be grieved over time. By the time a loved one dies of some lengthy disease, we have already gone through most or all of the stages of grief, and death may seem more of a release and a relief than a cosmic unfairness.

By understanding the factors that affect the intensity of the grief process, we can be more understanding of our own grief experience and more supportive of those who are going through the grief process.

Supporting Others Through the Grief Process

Here are some suggestions for helping a friend or family member through the grief process:

- Offer your quiet, supportive presence. If you don't know what to say, that's all right. Don't say anything. Just be there with a hug or a squeeze of the hand.
- Encourage the grieving person to talk about the loss. Invite the individual to share memories, whether happy or sad.
- Listen nonjudgmentally. Don't be shocked by anything the individual shares, even anger or guilt. Don't say, "You shouldn't say that" or "You shouldn't feel that way."
- Encourage the individual to remain connected with a support system (church, Bible study, grief support groups or classes).
- Encourage the individual to maintain healthy routines and functioning: friendships, activities, personal hygiene, spiritual pursuits.
- Pray with that person. Pray in brief, simple, authentic statements, not lofty religious-sounding phrases.
- Be there for your friend or family member over the long haul, not just during the first few days or weeks. Many grieving people hear the words, "If you need anything, just call me." But people who are grieving won't call you. You need to call them. Be proactive in ministering to the needs of people who are grieving.

Whether you are grieving or standing by someone who is grieving, remember that life moves in cycles. Grief comes, it wounds us, but it eventually subsides. As Ecclesiastes 3:1 and 4 says,

> To everything there is a season,
> A time for every purpose under heaven. . . .
> A time to weep,
> And a time to laugh.

This time of weeping will pass. Someday, it will be time to laugh and enjoy life again.

Guilt

Kitty Dukakis, wife of former presidential candidate Michael Dukakis, traces many of her addiction problems and low self-esteem to the false guilt she carried for most of her adult life. At age eighteen, Kitty learned that her mother was an illegitimate child adopted by a couple Kitty had always thought to be her natural grandparents. Her biological grandmother had given up Kitty's mother on one condition: that she herself be allowed to live with the adoptive couple and function as her own daughter's nurse.

When the truth was finally revealed to her by a cousin, Kitty confronted her mother with the obvious question, "Why did you keep this from me?" Her mother shrugged and said, "Well, now you know."

Kitty recalls the moment of truth as one of the most devastating moments in her life. She felt she had been living a lie, that her mother was guilty of an enormous breach of trust, and that somehow the result was that she, Kitty, was less than she appeared to be. Her self-esteem plummeted. Within a year she began using amphetamine pills that she discovered in her mother's room. It was the beginning of an addiction that haunted her for twenty-six years.

Although much of Kitty's guilt was false guilt that really belonged to another generation, she claimed that guilt as her own and carried it for many years. She lived out the truth of that old slogan of the recovery movement, "We are only as sick as our secrets." Time and a successful marriage didn't ease the guilt; if anything, Kitty's guilt escalated, and her self-esteem eroded. After her husband's political defeat by George Bush in 1988, Kitty's addiction secret came out. She entered a recovery program, and in the process of her recovery, she realized that if her husband had won the White House, the pressure of being First Lady might have sent her out of control.

"Michael was good enough to be president, for sure, but was I worthy to be his partner?" she said in her autobiography titled *Now I Know* (Simon & Schuster, 1990). "In my despair, I turned to alcohol."

Guilt affects people in different ways. Guilt immobilizes and defeats some people, paralyzing them with toxic messages of unworthiness and blame. Guilt compels and drives other people to overcompensation and overachievement in a futile effort to prove that the guilt messages that play and replay in their minds aren't true.

AUTHENTIC GUILT AND FALSE GUILT

When we trust Jesus Christ as Savior, the blame for our sin has been removed, the charges against us have been dismissed. Our slate has been wiped clean. As Christians, we stand before God forgiven, unconditionally accepted, and declared completely righteous by God. That doesn't mean we will never sin again, but it does mean that we have appropriated God's grace, by faith in Christ, to cover our sins and grant us pardon.

Why, then, do so many Christians have so much trouble with feelings of guilt?

The answer lies, in part, in the way we define *guilt*. One dictionary defines guilt as "the *fact* of having committed a breach of conduct, especially violating the law and involving a penalty" and as "a *feeling* of culpability or blame." Notice the differences in these definitions: the *fact* of guilt and the *feeling* of guilt. They are not one and the same. The fact of guilt exists whenever we violate God's Word. The fact of a person's guilt or innocence exists whether that person *feels* guilty or not. A hardened sociopathic personality is capable of committing the most brutal, hideous crimes imaginable without any feelings of guilt whatsoever. The fact that a sociopath feels no guilt has no bearing whatsoever on the fact of his guilt.

Guilt feelings come in two varieties, *authentic guilt* and *false guilt*. As Christians, we recognize that God uses feelings of authentic guilt in our lives to protect us from moral, emotional, spiritual, and physical harm. Authentic guilt creates in us the uncomfortable awareness that we have violated God's moral law. Authentic guilt is produced partly by the conviction of God's Holy Spirit and partly by the conscience God has designed into us. Many secular psychiatrists, however, beginning with Freud and continuing to the present day, would disagree that there is such a thing as authentic guilt. Freud theorized that *all* guilt is false guilt, and as such is always unhealthy. From both the Scriptures and from clinical experience, we can see that Freud was very much mistaken on this point.

How, then, do we determine if what we are feeling is authentic guilt or false guilt? One way is to ask ourselves whenever we experience pangs of guilt, "Have I violated a clear statement or command of God's Word?" If we have not, then our feelings of guilt are probably based on erroneous information and false assumptions. As a child, you may have been exposed to the old rhyme, "Step on a crack, break your mother's back"—and you may have actually felt a twinge of guilt whenever you stepped on a crack in the sidewalk! Clearly, this is false guilt, rooted in silly superstition. There is no sin involved, no violation of any command in God's Word.

But authentic guilt is rooted in the objective fact of God's Word, and this feeling of guilt performs a valuable function in our lives. At the Minirth Meier New Life Clinics, we sometimes liken authentic guilt feelings to an engraver's acid. The engraver uses small amounts of acid to etch a pleasing design into polished metal. The acid smooths out rough edges and defines delicate lines. Acid becomes a medium for producing a beautiful work of art.

In a similar way, God uses small amounts of guilt in our lives to cleanse us of our sins and help us rid ourselves of character defects. The guilt serves as a warning signal, which alerts us that we are doing things we shouldn't be doing and that our lives are moving in directions that aren't good for us. Authentic guilt, like acid, is a powerful, positive force that God, the Master Engraver of our lives, uses in small measured doses. We are His work of art, and guilt is just one of the tools He uses to shape and sculpt our lives. Like acid, guilt burns, it hurts; but if we are pliable in God's hands, if we learn to listen to guilt and respond to what God is trying to tell us, then the acidlike guilt we experience can help to make us the kind of people He wants us to be.

The problem many of us have is that we have not learned to listen to the message of authentic guilt. We don't just let God etch our lives with small doses of acidlike authentic guilt. Instead, we leap into an entire vat of an acid we call *false guilt,* and we immerse ourselves in this corrosive, destructive emotional substance. As the acid of false guilt eats into us, it creates an emotional residue of false guilt, which we call a *shame base*. Out of this shame base comes all sorts of self-defeating, dysfunctional behavior: self-blaming, self-shaming, codependency, addiction, obsessive-compulsive behavior, and sin.

Equally destructive is the fact that our preoccupation with unnecessary guilt tends to obscure our recognition of legitimate sources of guilt. We are so obsessed with false guilt that we don't even recognize those dysfunctional aspects of our lives that need to be confessed and released through the process of recovery.

For example, Dan is a workaholic parent, driven to overachievement by the false guilt messages inflicted on him years before by an abusive father. Now he neglects his own children in order to devote himself body and soul to his work. Yet when his wife confronts him about the harm he is doing to his children, he vehemently denies that his compulsive behavior is hurting his family at all. Here we find one of the paradoxes of guilt: the very people who carry around massive loads of *false* guilt often live in denial regarding the *authentic* guilt they carry.

In 1 John 1:9, we read, "If we confess our sins, He is faithful and just to forgive us our sins and to cleanse us from all unrighteousness." So we go to God in prayer, we confess our sins—yet the guilt feelings remain. Why is that? It is because *we have not forgiven ourselves*. God tells us that, as far as He is concerned, we are forgiven. He has wiped the slate clean. So the condemnation we continue to feel is our own grudge against ourselves! God says we are righteous, according to his forgiving grace, but we insist on punishing ourselves.

When we insist on shouldering a load of false guilt, we give Satan room to work in our lives. Satan's job is to accuse us of sin, to make us fear God's punishment. Satan wants to immobilize us and paralyze us by making us feel unworthy of a relationship with God. But we are not unworthy; Jesus has covered us with His own worthiness, and that makes us worthy. We are free to live for Jesus because Jesus died for us. So let us free ourselves from bondage to false guilt. Because Jesus died and rose again, the fact of our guilt has been wiped away.

■

Feelings *of guilt* without the fact of guilt have no valid reason to exist.

■

How Much Guilt Are You Carrying?

How about you? What kind of guilt are you carrying? To help you diagnose your own guilt level, place a check mark in front of any of the following statements that you identify with.

____ Gloom and doom are my specialty. I can out-worry anybody.

____ I apologize all the time. I misread people's reactions to me and fear that I have angered or disappointed them. "I'm sorry" is one of my favorite phrases. "It's all my fault" is another.

____ I don't know how to respond to a compliment. Rather than say, "Thank you" when I'm complimented, I usually negate the kind words by mentioning my shortcomings.

____ I feel fragmented. Because I overcommit myself and say "yes" too often, I feel pulled in a dozen directions.

_____ I frequently overwork myself so I don't have time to dwell on my guilt.

_____ I worry that God is keeping score. I hear people talking about the love and forgiveness of God, but to me God is watching my mistakes and figuring out how He's going to punish me for my wrongs.

_____ I feel I constantly have to justify my right to exist. No matter how much I've achieved, I feel inadequate.

_____ I don't deserve to be happy.

Each of these statements is typical of guilt-ridden people. If you checked two or more of them, you are probably carrying excessive guilt.

THREE STEPS TO GUILT REDUCTION

The best way to overcome false guilt is to understand it for what it really is. The more we grow in an appreciation of God's grace, the more we will understand that we have no right to condemn ourselves. Only God has that right—and His judgment of all who believe in Jesus Christ is a judgment of righteousness. As Christians, we are called to live by grace, setting goals that are attainable, refusing to compare ourselves with others, choosing to forgive ourselves daily and starting each morning afresh instead of beating ourselves down for failing to achieve inhumanly perfectionist standards.

We can reduce the level of guilt we experience—both authentic guilt and false guilt. Here is a three-step guilt reduction plan:

Step 1: Practice regular moral self-examination and confession. The Christian practice of accountability and confession goes back to the beginnings of the early church, and it has been adapted as Step 5 of the Twelve Steps of Alcoholics Anonymous: "Admit to God, to ourselves, and to another human being the exact nature of our wrongs."

We often suggest that our clients say a prayer that King David prayed as he confessed his sins of adultery and murder:

> Have mercy upon me, O God,
> According to Your lovingkindness;
> According to the multitude of Your tender mercies,
> Blot out my transgressions.
> Wash me thoroughly from my iniquity,
> And cleanse me from my sin.
> For I acknowledge my transgressions,
> And my sin is always before me. (Psalm 51:1–3)

By admitting our sins to God, by admitting our sins to ourselves, and by admitting them to one other trusted human being, we penetrate our denial, we come to a truer understanding of ourselves and our weaknesses, and we guard ourselves against future sin. When the Twelve Steps say that we admit our faults "to another human being," that person could be a close friend, a psychologist, a pastor, or a sponsor in a recovery program. As we take the lid off our lives and air out the sins and flaws we have kept locked up inside, our burden of guilt begins to dissolve. Through the forgiveness and

Whatever your sin and guilt, it probably does not exceed David's sin of adultery, lying, and murder. God forgave David for these sins because David was truly repentant, and He will forgive you. His promise to you is, "Though your sins are like scarlet, they shall be as white as snow" (Isa. 1:18).

THE COMPLETE LIFE ENCYCLOPEDIA

acceptance of those individuals to whom we confess, we receive God's love and absolution from sin. We experience the blessing of relief and release from guilt.

Step 2: Make amends to those we hurt. Making amends means saying we're sorry. But it also means repentance and restoring (wherever possible) what we have taken as a result of our sins and mistakes. If we have stolen, we must repay and replace what we have stolen. If we have lied, we must set the record straight and commit ourselves to a lifestyle of truth.

There are some situations in which the best way to make amends is to stay out of another person's life. Dr. Meier once counseled a woman who was a recovering sex addict. She had seduced many men and had even caused one couple's divorce. During counseling, she was overcome with grief and guilt over her sin, and she announced that she was going to look up each man she had seduced and apologize. Her intentions were good, but Dr. Meier knew that if she carried out her intentions she could endanger her recovery. The men involved might misread her attempt at renewing contact, and by reviving memories of her past sins, she risked sliding back into her sex addiction and destructive behavior. Dr. Meier convinced her that the best plan under the circumstances was to avoid any contact with these men.

Step 3: Embrace a new lifestyle that avoids guilt. If there are areas of your life that present continual stumbling blocks and that lead you into sin and guilt, make a decision to turn your back on those areas. Here, the line from the Lord's prayer is extremely apropos: "and lead us not into temptation, but deliver us from evil." As we renew a commitment to live lives of total integrity, uncompromising truth, extravagant unconditional love, and cheerful forgiveness, offering immediate apologies and making full amends, we will just naturally have less reason in life to feel guilty.

There is a great sense of relief as we turn our guilt over to God. The cross of guilt is too heavy a burden for any human back to bear. We can't carry it on our own. We were never intended to. And we don't have to. We don't have to bear our own crosses, because Jesus has already done that for us. We only have to confess our guilt to Him, and He will remove it from our shoulders.

See also SHAME

■

If you have any question whether you should or should not contact someone to make amends, you should consider getting the advice of a wise friend or professional counselor.

■

Happiness

THE MINIRTH MEIER NEW LIFE GUIDE TO A HAPPY, HEALTHY LIFE

1. Commit your life to Jesus Christ. True, lasting happiness is impossible apart from God. If you want to be happy, start with a sober truth: recognize that you are a sinner and that Jesus Christ died for your sins. This truth leads you to the joyous truth that by trusting in Jesus, you can be saved from your sins. Salvation is a choice, and only you can make it. (For a complete explanation of God's salvation plan, see FAITH.)

2. *Commit yourself daily to serving and glorifying Jesus Christ.* If you really desire happiness, then start each day with joy. The moment you wake up and arise in the morning, give thanks to God for another day to serve Him. Pray that God will use you that day to bring honor to Him by serving others, beginning with your own family, then extending to those you see in your neighborhood and your world throughout the day. Pray for opportunities to tell others about Jesus Christ—then watch for those opportunities and use them.

3. *Spend time each day meditating on God's Word.* "Your word is a lamp to my feet and a light to my path," says Psalm 119:105. God's Word lights our way through a world of darkness. If you want to be happy and healthy, then follow the light of God's Word. Meditate on it daily, and apply its practical truths to your everyday life.

4. *Purge anger from your life on a daily basis.* Don't nurse your grudges; get rid of them. Anger that is allowed to settle in your soul turns to a toxic emotional sludge called bitterness. Don't let bitterness take up residence in you. Flush the anger out of your system every day, just as you would flush the gunk and rust out of your radiator on a regular basis. Effective management of anger is essential to true happiness. (For a complete discussion of this subject, see ANGER.)

5. *Don't get caught in the sin trap.* Sin causes guilt, grief, anxiety, and depression. Lying, financial misdealings, sexual sin, and other forms of sin may seem like a shortcut to pleasure and happiness. In fact, there is a television commercial for *Playboy* magazine that makes this exact claim: a bevy of Playboy "bunnies" looks seductively into the camera and announce, "We have the secret of true happiness." By happiness, they mean sexual pleasure through pornography. This kind of "happiness" is a trap. The true road to happiness is not the road of sin. As Proverbs 4:14–15 tells us,

> Do not enter the path of the wicked,
> And do not walk in the way of evil.
> Avoid it, do not travel on it;
> Turn away from it and pass on.

6. *Spend time with your family.* You need time alone with your mate, and you need time with your children. You also need time with extended family, with parents, siblings, grandparents, and other close relatives. Don't fall into the "quality time" myth—the idea that a little "quality time" is more important than a quantity of time. Would you accept the same reasoning from a restaurant who served you a "quality meal" consisting of a one-inch cube of succulent prime rib, a leaf of endive, and a crumb of rare, aged Roquefort cheese? These are quality ingredients, right? But they are hardly a meal. Relationships need nurturing as well—*quality* nurturing and *quantity* nurturing. If you want to be happy, build strong family relationships. Give the ones you love the gift of your time.

7. *Cultivate close friendships.* If you want to be happy, experience true koinonia-fellowship with a few other Christians. Deep, lasting friendships are rare in this life—most of us will only have at most a half dozen truly close friends. These are the people

THE COMPLETE LIFE ENCYCLOPEDIA

you will share the good times and the hard times with. These are the people you'll share true feelings with. You'll laugh with them—and at times you'll cry with them. You will counsel each other, comfort each other, and help each other grow to become more like Christ. In friendships, your goal should not be to have many friends but to have a few who know you well. "There is a friend," says Proverbs 18:24, "who sticks closer than a brother." That kind of intimacy in a friend is one of the essential keys to a happy life.

8. *Glorify God and seek satisfaction in your daily routine.* God doesn't call every Christian into full-time Christian work. Those of us who have "regular" jobs are not second-class citizens of the kingdom of God. Some Christians are called to preach sermons and feed starving children for the Lord. But most of us are called to dig ditches and lay bricks for the Lord. All work is holy if it is done for the Lord. We can pray as we work. We can glorify God as we work. We can serve God as we serve our employers with dedication, enthusiasm, and a commitment to excellence. God will reward His good and faithful servants, both in this life and the life to come. And there is enormous happiness and satisfaction in that.

One of the most effective ways we can honor God is to honor Him with our daily routine.

But our daily routine is more than just the work we do. Our daily routine is the list of priorities we follow every day. Those priorities should include:

- intimate quiet time with God, including prayer and Scripture meditation
- time for relaxation
- time for relationship-building with one's mate
- time for relationship-building with one's children, including time for play, problem solving, devotions, and spiritual training
- time for ministry

9. *Do some act of kindness or service for someone this week.* Ask God to lead you to one person who needs a touch of God's grace and God's love. Then be observant and ready when God presents you with an opportunity to serve, counsel, or witness. Service to others and to God is one of the greatest sources of happiness there is.

10. *Respond, don't react.* There's a big difference between responding and reacting. A reaction is an unthinking reflex following a stimulus. When someone verbally attacks you, and you attack back, that's a reaction. When someone attacks you and you have the presence of mind to turn that attack aside with a soft word, that's a response. People who learn how to respond to situations in a Christlike manner instead of reacting instinctively and emotionally are people who are in full possession of themselves. They have moral authority in situations of conflict. They are effective in achieving their goals. They are happy people.

11. *Maintain godly self-esteem.* God has commanded us to love other people as we love ourselves. How, then, can we truly love others if we hate and blame ourselves? The Bible says that Satan's role is to be an accuser, so if we accuse and berate ourselves all the time, we are just carrying out Satan's work! In order to carry out God's work, we must have God's view of ourselves. We must see ourselves as forgiven men and women who are being restored to the image of God as the character of Christ is gradually formed within us.

The paradox of low self-esteem is that, though it might seem like a form of humility, it is actually a form of self-centeredness. The person who is constantly blaming and hating himself is spending a lot of time in self-absorption. But when we love ourselves in a healthy way, we are not self-centered. We are free to devote our attention to the needs of others.

(For a more comprehensive discussion of this subject, see SELF-ESTEEM.)

12. *Practice positive self-talk.* We all talk to ourselves every day. For many of us, that inner dialogue consists of a stream of defeatist, negative, critical, angry, self-blaming thoughts. We hold grudges against others and become bitter. We hold grudges against ourselves and become depressed. Read Philippians 4:8 and see the kinds of things God wants us to meditate on and the kind of self-talk we are to practice. Our focus is to be on the things that are noble, just, pure, lovely, praiseworthy, and of good report. When that is the kind of self-talk we practice, we are focused on the thoughts that lead to happiness.

13. *Understand your feelings, but focus on behavior.* It's important to understand why you feel the way you feel, why you are anxious or depressed, why your self-esteem is low. But don't forget the even more important role that your behavior plays in the way you feel. Often, the best way to change the way you feel is to first change the way you behave.

14. *Accept the fact that no one is perfect.* People often make themselves very unhappy with rigid expectations of perfection they place on the world and on people around them. They have no tolerance for sin or mistakes. They are hard on themselves, making completely unrealistic and outrageous demands on themselves, then spiraling into depression when they are unable to meet their own demands. Instead of demanding perfection from yourself and others, learn to benefit from your mistakes, and let others benefit from their mistakes. Lower your expectations—and you will be a happier person.

15. *Be assertive, not aggressive, not passive.* Aggressive people are angry, unhappy people, and they make everyone around them unhappy. Passive people go through life with other people's footprints on their unhappy faces. Both aggressive people and passive people tend to become bitter and depressed. The people who truly go through life as happy, healthy, effective, well-adjusted people are those who are *assertive.* They speak up and ask for what they want or what they need. They confidently state their convictions. They gently and courteously confront the unjust actions of others. They believe their own feelings are important, but they value the feelings of others as well. If you want to be happy, be assertive. (See ASSERTIVENESS.)

16. *Accept responsibility for your happiness.* In fact, if you wish to be happy, accept responsibility for all your emotions. Many people want to make the rest of the world responsible for their feelings. "You make me mad," they say, ignoring their own power to choose how they will respond in a given situation. "Life is unfair," they complain, ignoring the fact that life is unfair for everybody, but many people, even under the worst of circumstances, choose to be happy anyway. We cannot control all our circum-

---

Feelings Follow Behavior

Holly was worried about her marriage. "I don't feel I love Jordan anymore," she said. "I don't know where they went, but my feelings for him are just gone. And I don't think he feels anything for me, either." Holly wanted to rekindle love between herself and Jordan, but she didn't know how. We told her: focus on behavior. Do loving things for your husband. "But I don't *feel* like doing loving things," she protested. "Do them anyway," we told her. She did—and something amazing happened. As she acted out loving behavior toward Jordan, the feelings came back. For both of them. And they couldn't be happier.

---

stances, but we have much more power over our own emotions than we often care to think. We would rather scapegoat than shoulder the responsibility for our happiness. Those who are truly happy are those who have accepted the responsibility for their own feelings.

Headaches

"You must help me!" thirty-five-year-old Joan exclaimed. "I've had migraines for several years now. I've tried various medicines. But I'm not better, and my job and home life are suffering. I simply must have help!"

Dr. Minirth listened intently. "I love a challenge," he said, "and I've had success in tough cases before." Joan's eyes brightened.

Headaches are the most common of all types of pain. In a year's time, about one in six Americans visits a doctor specifically for headaches. More than 90 percent of all people have headaches, and almost 25 percent of them have experienced a severe form. More than half a billion dollars per year is spent for over-the-counter pain-relief drugs.

Research reveals that people have probably always been plagued with headaches. Our early ancestors cut holes in the heads of people with headaches. The idea was to relieve the pain by driving out the demons that caused the pain. The great physicians Hippocrates and Galen both described migraine headaches. And ancient Greeks and Chinese also struggled with head pain. Some of their remedies actually had some merit—the equivalent of aspirin and narcotics.

Modern science has brought relief through better understanding of the causes, preventive measures, and improved medications, but headaches still prevail.

Is Joan's plea for relief echoed by you or someone you know? There is help and hope! Headaches can be successfully attacked from all three dimensions of our humanity: body, mind, and spirit. As Joan and Dr. Minirth talked, he shared with her a number of medical, psychological, and spiritual principles that he believed could change her life . . . *and they did.*

One month later, Joan returned to Dr. Minirth's office and reported, "I can never thank you enough. My headaches have almost stopped, and my whole life is going so much better!"

By learning these same principles, you can control and prevent your headaches and improve your life as well.

MEDICAL HELP FOR HEADACHES

When you are suffering from a headache, people may tell you, "It's just a headache; don't worry about it." But you do worry. When your head is throbbing, you can hardly think of anything else. Headaches occupy your mind, your time, and your energy. They diminish your job performance. They can even affect your relationships.

An interesting fact about headaches is that the brain itself does not feel pain. It has no pain receptors. Headache pain is related to pressure on other structures such as the vessels, cranial nerves, sinuses, and the covering of the brain. In order to treat a headache adequately, we have to know what kind of headache it is and how it is affecting these structures and causing the pain.

The right medical help can make all the difference in the world. Even minor adjustments in medicine, diet, or lifestyle can make a difference when combined as part of a comprehensive approach. The most appropriate treatment depends on the type of headaches you have. The approach for someone who has one headache per month is very different from the approach for someone who has had a headache every day for the last month.

Headaches are actually a form of chronic illness. Any headache problem should be evaluated by a medical doctor, especially headaches that:

- are accompanied by convulsions;
- follow a blow to the head;
- bring on mental confusion;
- start suddenly in an older person;
- change in frequency, intensity, or character;
- are aggravated by coughing;
- awaken the sufferer at night;
- are localized to a certain part of the head;
- are accompanied by fever or numbness;
- require increasingly large doses of over-the-counter medications for relief; or
- interfere with the sufferer's lifestyle or occupation.

Headaches can be indicators of major health problems, so don't ignore these warning signs.

A family physician, internist, general practitioner, or neurologist can help you evaluate and diagnose the sources of your headaches. The exam would probably include a medical history followed by a thorough physical examination, with an emphasis on the neurological aspect (affecting or affected by the nerves in your head) to be sure there aren't any abnormalities. Further evaluation could involve a CAT scan (computerized axial tomography, or a computerized X ray of the head), an MRI (magnetic resonance imaging), or an EEG (electroencephalogram), which tests brain waves. A new test, the NMR (nuclear magnetic resonance scan) allows doctors to see small areas of the brain.

If headaches involve tension or muscle contraction, some of these complicated, expensive tests may be avoided, with the doctor focusing instead on checking the history of stress or anxiety. There also seems to be a relationship between recurring headaches and allergies, histamine, congestion, and even barometric or altitude pressure.

Joan's medical evaluation included a medical history, physical exam, a battery of laboratory blood tests on different systems in the body, a urinalysis, and a heart tracing (electrocardiogram, or EKG). Further tests depended on the initial findings.

332

EVALUATING A HEADACHE

Joan had originally come to our clinic, despondent and depressed, because she could no longer cope with her headaches. At her first meeting with Dr. Minirth, she answered a series of questions:

- How long have you had headaches?
- Where is the pain located?
- How often do you have them?
- Do you have more than one type of headache?
- Have they changed in character lately?
- Are they sharp or dull?
- What time of the day do they start?
- How long do they last?
- Are they mild or severe, acute or chronic?
- Have you tried any medicines for relief?
- Are there any other symptoms?
- Do you have any medical illnesses?
- Are you currently under stress, or have you recently had a trauma?
- Have there been any changes in your appetite? (This question helps to establish the severity of the pain.)

There can be enormous variations among different kinds of headaches, so we want to know exactly what the headache feels like and where it is localized. The answers to all these questions help us to identify the specific type of headache so we can develop a specific treatment.

VARIOUS KINDS OF HEADACHES AND THEIR SYMPTOMS

Tension Headaches

- Can be chronic; steady pressure or pain.
- Worse during times of stress.
- Usually located in the front and/or back of the head (bilateral).
- Constant bandlike pressure lasting for hours or days.
- May be worse at the end of the day.
- May recur regularly for weeks, months, or years.
- Most common of all headaches.
- Usually begin after the age of ten.
- Muscles tighten in the face, neck, shoulders, or jaws.
- Sufferer can continue to function.
- Common causes: standing in long lines, conflict, taking a test, driving in heavy traffic, noisy environment, etc.

Migraine Headaches

- Throbbing or pulsating severe pain.
- Frequently just on one side of the head (unilateral) but can be bilateral or switch sides.
- Often accompanied by nausea and vomiting.
- Recur at irregular intervals (days, months, years).
- Build over minutes to hours to a steady pain that persists for two to twenty-four hours.
- Pain tends to be around the eyes.
- Can be incapacitating to the point that the person can't function in normal routines.
- Tend to be hereditary (60 to 70 percent of the cases).
- Sometimes have neurological effects such as weakness of an arm or leg.
- Related to vessel constriction and dilation.
- A quiet, dark environment can speed recovery.
- Afflict women three times more often than men.
- Often begin in one's twenties and fade in the forties.
- Seeking medical attention is important.
- Lifestyle may trigger migraines: skipping meals, becoming stressed or fatigued, exercise, smoking, or sleeping late.
- More frequent in perfectionistic, compulsive personalities.
- Certain foods containing chemical substances may trigger migraines in some people. Other triggers are allergies, air pressure changes, and pollutants.
- Classic migraines are usually preceded by an aura (visual disturbances) where the visual field is reduced or there may be flashing lights that look like starbursts or wavy lines.

Cluster Headaches

- Occur in clusters of short duration, usually without warning (as often as twelve to fifteen times a day for periods of up to ninety minutes).
- Pain is on one side of the head (unilateral), usually behind the eye.
- Pain is severe and steady (the most excruciating of all headaches); often occur at night.
- May disturb vision and involve nasal congestion and tearing.
- May be triggered by alcohol, smoking, specific foods, stress, or glare.
- Often no family history.
- Predominantly in middle-aged men (ages thirty to fifty).
- Pain begins abruptly, lasting less than two hours (and may occur daily at the same time).
- Clusters come in bouts of days to weeks and recur at intervals for months to years; remissions can last a year or more.
- Sufferer should seek medical attention.
- Clusters tend to be more common in the spring and fall; there may be a link to histamine.

Headaches of Head Trauma

- Constant dull ache with superimposed throbbing.
- Usually occur within a day of injury to the head.

- May be localized.
- Associated problems are: trouble with memory, concentration, emotional instability, irritability, equilibrium.

Headaches Associated with Vascular Disorders
- Can be caused by: anoxia, aneurysm, hemorrhage, hypertension, vasculitis, stroke, visual malformation, lupus, temporal arteritis, basilar artery, and others.

Headaches Associated with Nonvascular Disorders
- Can be caused by: meningitis, brain tumor, cyst, abscess, subdural hematoma.
- Worse with excessive coughing, changing head position; double vision.
- Usually accompanied by other neurologic symptoms (loss of coordination or strength) because of the increased intracranial pressure.
- Sufferer should seek medical attention.

Headaches Associated with Chemical Substances (or Withdrawal from Chemical Substances)
- Excessive use of alcohol; hangover headache may relate to the alcohol's effect of dilating vessels, histamine release, or breakdown products of the alcohol.
- Food allergy headaches.
- Caffeine withdrawal (common).
- Birth-control pill headaches.

Headaches Associated with Systemic Infection
- Can be caused by: syphilis, tuberculosis, fungal infections, herpes, almost any disease that can cause fever.

Headaches Associated with Metabolic Abnormality
- Hypoglycemia (low blood sugar); in such cases, the previous meal may not have provided enough protein, carbohydrates, or fats to maintain normal blood-sugar levels. Eating healthy between-meal snacks may help.
- Hunger headache.

Pain Associated with Diseases of the Head and Neck
- Eye disorders, glaucoma, refractory error. (Sufferer should consult an eye doctor.)
- Arthritis of the cervical spine.
- Lesions of the teeth, tongue, ear, or throat.
- Jaw joint dysfunction (clicking or popping noise, bilateral pain, limited movement, tenderness).

Trigeminal Neuralgia
- Pain above the temporal area (temples), usually in older people.
- Burning and aching in the temples.
- Often triggered by certain actions such as a light touch or a yawn. Pain lasts a few seconds to a minute or two but is intense. Pain may strike very infrequently

or as often as several times a day. Trigeminal neuralgia (also called tic douloureux) responds very well to carbamazepine (Tegretol).

- More common in women.

Hypertension Headaches

- Traditionally thought to occur upon awakening but can occur at other times as well.
- Most hypertension (high blood pressure) has no symptoms at all; that's why it's known as the "silent killer." However, if the blood pressure is extremely high (over 180 systolic and over 100 diastolic), headache pain may be present.

Cough Headaches

- Distinctive, brief, severe, bursting after a cough.
- Often occur in middle-aged men.

Lumbar Puncture Headaches (Spinal Tap)

- Self-limited.
- Many who have had lumbar (back) punctures can attest to this pain.

Allergy or Sinus Headaches

- Allergies from pollens, dust, feathers, animal hair, or foods can cause headache pain. Skin tests are helpful in determining specific allergies.
- Common cause: allergic rhinitis or hay fever.
- Common organic headaches are caused by acute sinus infection (blocked sinus drainage resulting from colds, allergies, or bacterial infections).

Toxic Headaches

- Countless chemicals can cause headaches.
- Exogenous—chemicals originating from without the body, such as pesticides, preservatives, smog, polluted water, insecticides, fuels, paint, cleaning fluids.
- Endogenous—chemicals originating within the body, such as from a viral or bacterial source (can be severe).

Sex or Exercise Headaches

- Rare, painful.
- May be related to excitement, increased blood pressure or heart rate.

Postseizure Headaches

- Headaches often occur after a grand mal seizure.

THE PSYCHOLOGICAL DIMENSION

Certain psychological patterns have been shown to produce headaches. The head is like a command post for the whole body, so it makes sense that it's where the pain zeros in when there's turmoil or stress.

It's often easier for a person facing a conflict and other problems to focus on his or her body than on emotions. In a way, to have medical problems and physical symptoms is more socially acceptable than to talk about uncomfortable and powerful emotions. It's more acceptable to say, "I'm sick today. I have a bad headache," than to talk about the anger or fear that's simmering inside.

Clearly, anxiety can contribute to tension in muscles and can cause pain. And Dr. Paul Meier suggests that probably 90 percent of people with chronic headaches have repressed anger or some kind of conflict or stressful emotions. But many people don't recognize that anything other than the headache is going on in their minds and emotions. You have probably seen what happens when a cat becomes hostile or afraid. Its back muscles bunch up, its spine tenses, its fur bristles. What you may not know is that when you feel anger or fear, you experience very similar physiological changes in your musculoskeletal structure and your skin.

The Emotional Headache

"I once had a hospitalized patient," recalls Dr. Minirth, "who had been plagued with severe headaches for almost ten years. But she had almost no awareness of her emotions. I would look at her and the anger or worry would be written on her face. 'You seem upset about something,' I would say.

"'No, I'm not,' she would respond. 'I'm okay, but I'm having a bad headache.'

"'I knew better. 'I'm wondering,' I would say, 'yesterday when you got that phone call from your husband, when he said he wanted you to come back home, what were you feeling?'

"'I wasn't feeling anything.'

"She was completely out of touch with her feelings. Whether she was experiencing anger, fear, shame, anxiety, guilt, or even love, she was not allowing her conscious mind to receive those emotions—but they were there, affecting her physically, triggering her pain. It was my job to get her to own up to her feelings. Once she began to understand her emotions, she began to make progress toward relieving her headaches."

GAIN INSIGHT AND CHANGE YOUR THINKING PATTERNS

Personality seems to have a lot to do with headaches. Perfectionistic, driven, overly conscientious, ambitious, or rigid individuals tend to be the most vulnerable to headaches. If they can't meet their own unrealistic expectations, they feel anxious; their muscles tense up, and suddenly they realize that there is a sharp or dull or throbbing pain attacking their heads (see PERFECTIONISM).

Through counseling, Joan discovered she was one of these headache-prone perfectionists. What about you? Do you relentlessly pursue hard work? Are you unable to relax? Are you meticulous, overly controlling, or competitive? Are you a chronic worrier? Are you on a collision course like Joan? If so, one of the strategies you need to adopt in attacking your headache is to change your thinking pattern. Remind yourself that you want to walk with Christ and that you don't have to have everyone else's love and approval. You don't have to be perfect or successful at everything.

Our thinking patterns are deeply grooved by years of habit, and it's not easy for us to change. We think at a rate of between four hundred and twelve hundred words per minute. If we continue to repeat obsessive, headache-producing thoughts to ourselves, then we will certainly have headaches! But the mind can be reprogrammed. We can control what we think about.

Here is the Bible's prescription for healthy thinking—and, as it turns out, for headache prevention:

> Be anxious for nothing, but in everything by prayer and supplication, with thanksgiving, let your requests be made known to God; and the peace of God, which surpasses all understanding, will guard your hearts and minds through Christ Jesus. Finally, brethren, whatever things are true, whatever things are noble, whatever things are just, whatever things are pure, whatever things are lovely, whatever things are of good report, if there is any virtue and if there is anything praiseworthy—meditate on these things (Phil. 4:6–8).

TREATING THE PAIN

Prevention is the best medicine. You may be able to reduce the chances of developing headaches in the first place if you:

- get seven or eight hours of sleep each night;
- eat at regular mealtimes (don't skip breakfast!);
- avoid smoking and smoky environments;
- avoid drinking alcohol and overeating; and
- exercise regularly to improve your circulation and reduce stress.

If a tension headache does strike, try this simple relief: stop what you're doing and try to relax. Lie down, take a warm bath, or put a warm or cool cloth on your head. Massaging the scalp, neck, face, and shoulders can also bring relief.

Stress reduction and lifestyle changes are long-term goals, but dietary changes are also helpful. Some foods contain chemical substances that may trigger headaches in susceptible people. Try to reduce or eliminate these from your diet: aged cheese, alcohol, bacon, pods of broad beans, chicken livers, any foods with large amounts of monosodium glutamate (MSG, often used in Chinese food), chocolate, and citrus fruits and juices (orange, lime, lemon, grapefruit). Also eliminate coffee (both caffeinated and decaffeinated), tea, bologna, salami, pepperoni, summer sausage, smoked fish, hot dogs, nuts, onions, yogurt, avocados, bananas, meat tenderizer, soy sauce, and eggs.

If these measures fail, pain relievers are available.

CHANGING BEHAVIOR, REDUCING PAIN

Joan didn't have to keep suffering. Excellent medical help is certainly available today. But to be fully effective, medicines must be used in conjunction with emotional, behavioral, and spiritual health care. Dr. Minirth made it clear to Joan, "I will do the

338

A Guide to Prescription and Nonprescription Headache Medications

Because of possible side effects and other concerns, medication should be used with great caution and discernment. Used inappropriately, medicine will not produce the desired results, and can even be dangerous.

The medical treatments for headaches fall into several categories. Non-narcotic pain relief medicine has been around since ancient times. The Romans, Greeks, and American Indians used the bark of the willow tree for pain relief.

Aspirin (or salicylate, which is found in many trees and other plants) has sold more than any drug in history. (Forty billion aspirins are consumed each year in America.) Coated aspirin are designed to cause less stomach irritation but may be less effective because of decreased absorption. Aspirin, like other medicines, can have significant side effects (ulcers, ringing in ears, Reye's syndrome in children, poisoning, etc.). However, aspirin has generally proven safe for most people and is often the first choice for management of mild to moderate headaches.

Tylenol (acetaminophen) has been used extensively for controlling headache pain.

Nonsteroidal anti-inflammatory drugs (NSAIDs) have also been used successfully. NSAIDs include Advil and Motrin (ibuprofens); Anaprox, Naprosyn, Feldene, Clinoril, Tolectin, Orudis, Nalfon, Indocin, Voltaren, and Meclomen have also been used extensively. These can have side effects such as stomach irritation.

Narcotic pain medicines (codeine, morphine, Demerol, Talwin, Percodan, Vicodin) have also been prescribed. They can be extremely effective but unfortunately are addictive and can produce a dependency. They are used with great caution by most doctors today, especially for chronic headaches, as they can actually increase the pain through a phenomenon called rebound and withdrawal state. At our clinics, we rarely prescribe any controlled narcotic medicines for headache pain.

Ergotamine (Gynergen, Bellergal), like caffeine (Cafergot is caffeine plus ergotamine), is a vasoconstrictive agent that has brought relief to many individuals with migraine headaches. It should be used only to abort acute attacks. Though it is not addicting, ergotamine (along with caffeine) is one of the most often abused drugs by people with chronic headaches. Used regularly it exacerbates the condition, causing withdrawal headaches. Midrin, a drug similar to ergotamine, has successfully been used to abort and prevent mixed headaches (headaches with multiple causes and multiple symptom sets). It is probably less effective than ergotamine but may have fewer side effects.

Antidepressants (Elavil, Tofranil, Sinequan, and Norpramin) have been used with excellent results in reducing the intensity and frequency of pain in some individuals with chronic headaches. Low doses actually treat the underlying serotonin factors.

Beta blockers such as propranolol or Inderal are used to help prevent vascular headaches. But don't use them if you have certain heart problems, diabetes, asthma, or are pregnant.

Prednisone is sometimes prescribed for cluster headaches.

Minor tranquilizers (such as Serax, Librium, and Klonopin) may relieve tension and muscle strain and decrease headaches. Sansert has been used to prevent mi-

"I encourage headache sufferers to schedule no more than about 80 percent of their waking day," says Dr. Minirth, "and leave the other 20 percent for the unexpected. People say they can't get everything done in that time, but they can. With the remaining time, they can either relax or use that time to handle unexpected situations or chores. People are always amazed at the relief that brings to their lives!"

best I can with your medicines, but it is the medicine in conjunction with a whole-person approach that can make a difference. By a whole-person approach, I mean we will involve individual counseling, group counseling, a diet and exercise program, and spiritual encouragement. A medical approach will help. A psychological approach will help. But either alone is not enough. We are going to work on all of the headache-producing factors in your life at once. We'll start with the behavioral factors."

Dr. Minirth began by prescribing a series of relaxation exercises for her neck and head, plus breathing exercises for anxiety. Also, he worked on her need to become more assertive, which would help her to manage her anger and stress levels. No longer could she stuff her feelings, because those feelings had a way of "unstuffing" themselves and emerging as headache pain.

Joan also learned that she could rearrange her daily schedule to allow more time for rest, leisure activities, and humor. Laughter, she discovered, relieves as much tension as crying—and it's a lot more fun! She formulated a new behavioral plan that included specific times for exercise, relaxation, friendships, sleeping, and healthy eating. She learned to devote more time to enjoyable conversation, Scripture memorization, reading a good book—all simple common-sense approaches to decreasing stress and increasing positive moods. She started the new plan immediately and watched closely to see if the headaches decreased each week.

Dr. Minirth's suggestions made an important difference for Joan. Feelings *can* be trained to follow behavior. But a focus on behavior must come first.

CHRIST: THE GREAT PHYSICIAN

Christ wants us to have a good life. He doesn't want us to suffer needlessly. He wants us to be healthy so that we can be effective in life and so that we can reach out

340

and help others. He wants us to be still and know that He is God. Christ is supreme and sovereign—even over headaches.

"The single thing that impresses me the most, above anything else," says Dr. Minirth, "is how much Jesus Christ loves us. He loves us immeasurably. Immensely. I cannot overstate it. His love must be our driving force in life. As we immerse ourselves in that love and internalize it, we can't help but become healthier spiritually, emotionally, and physically. And that means fewer headaches. He is the Great Physician, and His love is the greatest medicine."

Headaches can respond to medical treatment. Or to psychological treatment. We have seen people get better even by resolving their spiritual problems. But the best treatment of all is one that addresses *all three* dimensions of our humanness: body, mind, and spirit.

For a comprehensive discussion of the causes and cures of all forms of headaches, read *The Headache Book* by Dr. Frank Minirth (Thomas Nelson, 1994).

■

Headache prevention is not just a matter of finding the right pill. More important, it's a matter of living the right way.

■

Home Schooling

Home schooling has become an increasingly popular option among American parents in recent years, and particularly among Christian parents. The primary reason for the growing interest in home schooling is a growing dissatisfaction with public schools. Parents see a number of alarming trends in the public schools, including:

- decreasing test scores and declining academic standards
- increasing school violence and gang activity
- increasing availability of dangerous drugs on or near school campuses
- declining standards of discipline
- declining moral standards and values
- elimination of all traces of Judeo-Christian influence from schools, even such nonsectarian influences as the Ten Commandments
- increasing use of public schools for social architecture and liberal/humanist indoctrination
- use of the schools as a place to disseminate "values-free" sex education, and as a place to make abortion and contraceptives available to young people

Clearly, there are enormous problems facing public schools and American parents. But is home schooling the answer to those problems?

ADVANTAGES OF HOME SCHOOLING

There are situations in which home schooling is the most desirable way to educate children. One such situation is on a foreign mission field. In past decades, missionary

341

children have often been sent to boarding schools, frequently hundreds of miles from the parents, for nine months out of the year. This practice represented an extreme hardship for both missionary parents and their children, but many missionary parents were willing to endure this situation out of a belief that it had to be this way in order for them to serve the Lord. We have since witnessed some of the tragic fallout from this practice, as these missionary children have grown to be bitter, angry, atheistic adults who feel they were rejected by their parents during their formative years.

Being a missionary is a high calling from God. But as Christians, we must recognize that our first and utmost calling from God, whether we are missionaries or not, is rearing emotionally and spiritually healthy children—children who feel loved, accepted, and secure in their position as children of God and children of godly parents. As a result, more and more missionaries are choosing to educate their children at home. Clearly, this is a much healthier option than the old missionary boarding school option that has damaged many young lives.

Here in America, however, we have many more options available to us than do missionaries on the foreign field. If the public school in your district does not meet your child's needs, it may be possible to get an interdistrict transfer to another school. Also, there are many excellent private schools, including Christian schools, that could provide a healthy learning environment for your child—at a cost. There are home school cooperatives, where a number of parents band together to provide an environment that is a hybrid between home schooling and private schooling. And then there is traditional home schooling, in which the parent acts as teacher.

Research suggests that most home-schooled children adjust well to school when they eventually enter it. Many, in fact, excel academically and in leadership qualities. Home schooling usually requires only about two or three hours of the adult's time per day, and a number of excellent Christian home school curricula are available at Christian bookstores. Home schooling allows the parents to have control over the values content of the curriculum and to make spiritual instruction part of the daily routine.

If parents are willing to make the regular time commitment and if they are qualified to assist and tutor the child in the various subjects that are covered in the curriculum, home schooling has a number of advantages that deserve consideration. However, parents need to be aware that home schooling involves much more than simply handing a child a workbook to fill out. Home schooling is a serious commitment and should not be approached lightly.

DISADVANTAGES OF HOME SCHOOLING

There are a number of serious drawbacks to home schooling that should be seriously weighed before a decision is made to home school. The disadvantages of home schooling include:

Absolute commitment required. Many parents enter into home schooling with the best of intentions but without realizing how many distractions, interruptions, and detours there can be in a day. Many parents fail to give adequate oversight and attention to their home-schooled children. Occasionally, a home-schooled child falls far behind his public-schooled peers because the parents are not keeping their commitment to make the child's education a top priority.

Lack of socialization with other children. One important factor that public schools provide that home schools cannot is a place for social development. By interacting in a society of thirty or so other students, elementary school children develop a sense of belonging. They learn responsibility and social skills by participating in group experiences at school. Interaction with nonparental authority figures and with children is very healthy for school-age children. So is group play during recess periods. School is very important in helping children develop a sense of society, acceptable social behavior, and a healthy sense of self. It is difficult for any home school to provide all of these benefits.

Excessive dependence. Some home-schooled children become so comfortable in the cozy, familiar surroundings of the home that they develop an excessive dependence upon the parents and the home. When the time comes for them to start testing their independence, they cling to the nest.

A self-defeating strategy for school phobia. Home schooling is sometimes used by parents of a child with a school phobia. A school-phobic child is afraid to go to school and stay there all day. A possible reason for school phobia is immaturity; the child may not be mentally or emotionally ready for formal schooling. In such cases, home schooling for a year or two *may* be an acceptable stop-gap to help prepare the child for school.

In the majority of cases, however, the school phobia is not related to immaturity but to an overdependence upon the mother. In these cases, the parents of the school-phobic child were overprotective during the child's preschool years. The school-phobic child is frequently an only child or the youngest child among several children. The parents in these cases have generally spoiled the children and resisted their growing up; the children have learned conscious or unconscious manipulation techniques in order to avoid having to make the normal passages and transitions (including the transition of entering school) that lead to adulthood. In such cases, home schooling is the worst possible way of responding to a school phobia, since it allows the child to avoid a necessary life challenge and transition.

The loving parent should place the child in school and not allow the child to stay home under any circumstances. If there are fears that underlie the child's school phobia, the entire family should undergo family counseling so that the child's underlying fear can be brought out into the open and disarmed. It is essential to determine the reason for the phobia. If the problem is lack of experience with other children, the child can be placed in a home or preschool environment with planned interaction with other children. If overdependence is the problem, then the overprotective parent should seek counseling. If the child's fear is owing to conditioning or trauma (for example, having witnessed bullies intimidating other children on a schoolyard), then the parent may attend school with the child a few times, gradually diminishing the time spent with the child, until the fear is extinguished. (See "The Fears of Childhood" under FEARS AND PHOBIAS.)

ALTERNATIVES TO HOME SCHOOLING

Christians have many valid concerns regarding public schools. However, before making a decision to home school, Christian parents should consider a number of alternative options. In our public school systems, you will find many dedicated teachers and administrators, including many Christians with clear biblical values and a genuine love for teaching and for their students. Many of these fine people feel they have been abandoned by parents who would rather pull their children out of the system than try to work within the educational system to make it better for all students.

Making the Most of Your Child's Education

Whether you choose home schooling, private schooling, or public schooling for your child, there are several steps you can take to help ensure a good education for your child:

- Be actively involved with your child's education. Be aware of your child's schoolwork and homework. Make sure your child is being adequately challenged, and that he or she is gaining a sense of confidence and mastery in the subjects being studied.
- Talk to your child about school. Be aware of any fears or problems he or she is dealing with—insecurities, lack of confidence, intimidation from other children, peer pressure, and so forth.
- Give your child a solid grounding in the Christian faith, in values, in mo-

rality, and in sexual responsibility. Make sure your child has many opportunities for spiritual and moral instruction through family devotions, Sunday school, youth club, vacation Bible school, Christian summer camp, and so forth.
- Make sure your child receives an adequate, biblically-based sex education. Your child should have the accurate facts about sex (appropriate to his or her age level) by about age eight to ten.
- Make sure your child is accurately, adequately armed with information on the dangers of drug abuse.
- Be aware of political and social issues affecting education. At the very least, be a responsible voter. If at all possible, be a concerned activist.

For some Christians, home schooling may be the best choice. But as Christian parents, we should also consider the possibility of rolling up our sleeves and getting involved in the public schools and working to change them for the better, not only for the sake of our own children, but for the sake of all children. We can become involved by volunteering to help in the classroom, by volunteering to participate in the parent-teacher organization at school, by attending school board meetings, and by running for elective office (such as school board member).

We cannot shield our children from all the harmful influences of the world—nor should we. Rather, we should be helping our children learn how to be strong and stand firm in a non-Christian world. The Bible teaches that as Christians we are to be *in* the world but not *of* it. This is a perspective we should teach our children as well, and it is difficult to model this concept to our children if we have taken them out of the world and put them into a home-schooling environment.

Whether you choose to school your children at home or send them to public school, your goal should not be to shelter your children from the world, but to help them become salt and light in the world, and to make the world a better place in which your children can live and grow.

Impulse Control Disorders

Impulse control disorders are a subclass of obsessive-compulsive disorder or OCD (see OBSESSIVE-COMPULSIVE DISORDER). OCD is a neurosis marked by the repetitive experience of unwanted thoughts and impulses (an obsession), which leads to behavior that the individual consciously does not want to engage in (a compulsion). Often, the unconscious purpose of the obsession is to help the individual repress a painful thought or memory.

What sets an impulse control disorder apart from other OCD behavior is the fact that the compulsion results in socially undesirable manifestations called *impulsions*. The individual feels a psychological release after committing the act. Other forms of OCD—repetitive hand-washing or repetitive checking of door and window locks to make sure the house is safe, for examples—are self-defeating and often painful, but they are not socially undesirable per se. Examples of socially undesirable impulsions include:

- Kleptomania—compulsive stealing owing to an obsession with stealing, without any regard to a need for, or valuing of, the object being stolen.
- Exhibitionism—extreme attention seeking; the exhibitionist behavior may be of either a sexual or nonsexual nature.
- Pyromania—the compulsive act of setting fires for neurotic reasons; the pyromaniac is fascinated by the sight of flames, and sets fires without apparent motive such as harming others, causing property damage, or collecting insurance money.
- Voyeurism—secretly watching other people undress or engage in sex.
- Intermittent explosive disorder—uncontrolled acts of violence or property destruction that are completely out of proportion to any external stress or provocation; the individual may explode in rage over an innocent remark or other neutral incident.

People with impulse control disorders find it extremely difficult to stop themselves from engaging in their disordered behavior, much as they may consciously want to stop. When not engaging in their impulsive behavior, they are often reserved, conformist, indecisive, with exaggerated feelings of guilt and low self-esteem. Sexual maladjust-

345

ments are common in such individuals. Treatment of impulse control disorders involves psychiatric care and usually requires many years of effort in order for the individual to achieve control over his or her impulsions.

Infidelity

"Honey, where's the checkbook?" asked Michelle, standing outside the door of the bathroom.

"I just stepped out of the shower," said her husband, Brian, from behind the door. "I'll look for it as soon as I throw some clothes on."

"I can't wait for you to throw some clothes on, Brian," said Michelle. "The gardener's at the door right now and he wants to get paid."

"But can't you just wait one—"

"It's probably in your briefcase," said Michelle. The briefcase was on the bed, just a few steps away. She went to it and flipped the snaps open.

"What did you say?" asked Brian, his voice muffled behind the bathroom door.

"I said it's probably in your briefcase. I'll look."

"Huh? My briefcase? No! Wait! Don't open that briefcase!"

But Michelle already had the briefcase open. She found the checkbook. And she found something else. A letter, scented and written in the flowing script of a woman's handwriting.

The bathroom door flew open, and Brian came stumbling out, wrapped in a towel, his eyes wide and his face red. "Michelle, wait, don't . . ."

Brian saw that Michelle had the letter in her hands. *That* letter.

"Michelle, honey, I can explain . . ."

Michelle said nothing. She looked at Brian with eyes that seemed haunted. Then she looked back at the words on the page, the words in that flowing feminine script:

My darling Brian,

  I probably shouldn't put these feelings down on paper. I mean, what if they were ever read by the wrong person? But I can't help it. I simply had to tell you thank you, thank you, thank you, for last night, the most wonderful night of my life . . .

The words began to blur. Michelle turned the page over and read the signature. *Celia.* She had met Celia at the office Christmas party. Pretty, blonde, and ten years younger than Michelle. A teardrop splashed on the page. Michelle set the letter down in the briefcase where she had found it, then looked up. Brian had turned around and was slowly walking back into the bathroom. He closed the bathroom door behind him with a soft *snick.*

Michelle's world would never be the same.

WHY DO AFFAIRS HAPPEN?

One of the most tragic facts about infidelity is that it is so unbelievably common. It happens all the time. Infidelity even affects Christian marriages with numbing frequency. It destroys trust. It destroys relationships. It destroys families and leaves behind a trail of wounded spouses and wounded children. Some shocking facts about infidelity:

- Approximately 40 percent of married men will be unfaithful at some time during their marriage.
- About 15 percent of married men admit to having a *series* of adulterous affairs during their marriage.
- About one-third of all married women will have an affair at some time during their marriage.

Why do people have affairs? The reasons run deeper than mere sexual hunger. There are a number of contributing factors that tempt some people to violate their marriage vows.

Money and Power

This is primarily a man's issue. As a man's income increases, so does the likelihood that he will commit adultery. In fact, according to a 1986 survey, approximately 70 percent of men earning $70,000 or more have had affairs. This affirms Jesus' warning about the snare of riches: "It is easier for a camel to go through the eye of a needle than for a rich man to enter the kingdom of God" (Matt. 19:24). With increasing wealth come growing power, pride, and hunger for acquisition. The powerful, wealthy man becomes accustomed to getting what he wants. He becomes bored with what he has, and he wants more: a more expensive car, a more lavish house, a more adventurous sex life.

For some men, life becomes a series of conquests; some are boardroom conquests, some are bedroom conquests. In many cases, the issue is a sense of *entitlement:* corrupted by his growing power, a man becomes accustomed to having others give him what he wants, which often makes him demand more. It is common for a man who feels a strong sense of entitlement in other areas of his life to extend it into the sexual realm. When his infidelity is discovered, the powerful man with a strong sense of entitlement will often feel more defensive than remorseful. "A man in my position has certain needs," he may say. But needs are not his issue; demands are.

Loneliness

Many people, both men and women, feel lonely in their own marriages. Women are especially vulnerable to this issue. There is a yearning to be accepted and loved, and the lonely man or woman looks for this acceptance and love in a sexual liaison. In such cases, people who are lonely may not be the aggressor in the affair, but either consciously or unconsciously they send out signals that they are lonely and available. Such people often find themselves being exploited and used by sexual predators.

> *Couples who are happy with their sexual and emotional relationship rarely have reason to violate the boundaries of their marriage.*

Frustration and Dissatisfaction

Marital dissatisfaction often leads to extramarital affairs. When there is poor communication, emotional issues get swept under the rug. Sexual frustrations have a chance to mount. One partner begins to look around and think, "Now *there's* someone I could be happy with." On an emotional level, infidelity usually begins within the marriage, as the partners turn away from each other and allow distance to grow between them. By the time the affair begins, the husband and wife are already estranged from each other to some degree. An "emotional divorce" has taken place, even though both partners continue to live under the same roof.

Excessive Neediness

Many people reach for a substitute sexual and emotional partner when they feel their sexual and emotional needs are not being met at home. This is not in any sense a legitimate excuse for infidelity, but it does help us to understand the motivation for this behavior. People who engage in adultery because of excessive neediness offer such excuses as:

- "My needs and my feelings were never taken seriously."
- "I needed someone to care about *me*."
- "Is it so wrong to want a little kindness, a little touching, a little affection?"
- "My spouse was always grouchy and rejecting. My lover was always sweet and accepting. I ask you, what kind of choice is that?"
- "My spouse was so critical, always nagging, I just had to get away."
- "My spouse is always so self-absorbed. I got tired of being ignored, and I found someone who made me feel important."

In all of these statements there is a rationalization of sin. But there is no legitimate excuse for sin. However, by listening to these statements, it at least becomes easier to understand what motivated and tempted these individuals to sin.

Anger

We tend to think of anger as an emotion acted out with shouting, arguing, slamming doors, or violence. But anger is acted out in a wide variety of behaviors, including sexual behavior. Infidelity is frequently an act of rebellion and revenge against the injured spouse, even though the offending spouse may not be consciously aware of his or her anger. Many unfaithful spouses, when their infidelity is exposed, become defensive about their actions, claiming that their adultery was justified because their spouse denied their legitimate needs for sex, affection, emotional support, or affirmation. In most such cases, however, emotional needs and sexual pleasure were secondary, next to the motive of hurting the spouse.

Though it's true that anger can perform a healthy, self-preserving function in our lives, anger must be approached honestly and forthrightly, not through behavior that sabotages relationships. Ephesians 4:26 says, "Be angry, and do not sin." Whenever anger is expressed through sinful behavior, that anger and all other negative emotions are compounded, not resolved. Sin always carries negative consequences. The sin of adultery is *never* justified, no matter how angry a spouse is or what legitimate needs are being denied. The way to resolve these issues is through honest communication, not deceptive and destructive sexual behavior.

Unaccountable Time

When he accepted a call to be pastor of a large church, Stan asked for and received a commitment from the elders that he would have two study days for sermon preparation—no phone calls, no appointments, no interruptions. He would study at a little hideaway, some distance from the church. Two years later, it was discovered that he used his study time and his hideaway to engage in affairs with several women parishioners.

Rosa is a feature editor for a travel magazine, and her work takes her all over the country. She spends a lot of time in hotels and restaurants where she will never be recognized. It all started with "harmless" flirting with strangers. She enjoyed the excitement of doing something forbidden, though she "knew" it would never lead anywhere (that's denial talking). The problem is, it *did* lead somewhere. Now she is psychologically dependent on the "high," the emotional "rush" she gets from these casual affairs in various cities. And it all began with unaccountable time.

Vern is a salesman who is frequently out of his office. He has a flexible schedule and is hard to reach by phone. This makes it easy for Vern to sneak an hour here, a couple hours there, in adulterous relationships with other women. Time spent without accountability often leads to emotional and marital ruin.

Self-Preoccupation

The choice to engage in adultery is ultimately a self-centered choice. The promiscuous individual willfully ignores his or her spouse's needs, children's needs, and the commandments of God in order to gratify the self. Many individuals will rationalize their actions as acts of "love" for the third parties, but once you peel away all the denial and self-deception, you find a core truth: the adulterer was thinking only of the desires and needs of the self.

Accordingly, many situations of adultery involve people with specific personality disorders that are characterized by excessive self-preoccupation. Although people of all personality types are subject to infidelity, the two primary personality disorders that overwhelmingly tend to produce self-preoccupation and adulterous behavior are *the narcissistic personality disorder* and *the sociopathic personality disorder*. The sexual behavior of these personalities is best described as exploitative and predatory. Both narcissists and sociopaths seem to have an uncanny ability to spot potential victims—people who are emotionally vulnerable to their seduction.

Narcissists are extremely self-centered. They lack empathy and are often unable to recognize the pain of others. They have an exaggerated sense of their own importance, and they tend to exploit people for their own ends. Narcissists spend a great deal of time fantasizing about their own power, success, brilliance, and idealized love. Narcissists believe they deserve special favors (a strong sense of *entitlement*), but show no inclination to return them. Narcissists are frequently quite charming and persuasive and may even project a very convincing image of a caring and self-sacrificing person when in fact the opposite is true. Narcissists tend to become involved in multiple affairs, sometimes several at the same time.

■

One key to success in marriage is mutual accountability—and a major danger to marriages is a partner who has a lot of time he or she does not have to account for.

■

349

Sociopaths are much like narcissists in that they are very selfish, uncaring, lacking in empathy, and quick to rationalize their own sins and to shift the blame onto others. Sociopaths are unreliable, untruthful, unpredictable, and insincere. Sociopaths differ from narcissists in that they tend to have little or no plan for their lives, whereas narcissists fantasize greatness for themselves. Sociopaths are virtually without conscience and are unable to feel guilt for their actions.

(For a comprehensive discussion of these issues, see PERSONALITY TYPES AND DISORDERS.)

WHAT TO DO IF YOU DISCOVER YOUR MATE'S INFIDELITY

You may discover your spouse's infidelity as Michelle did, through some accidental arrangement of circumstances. Or someone may tell you. Or your spouse may tell you himself or herself. For most people, learning about a mate's infidelity triggers a grief response, much like the response people have when they learn that a loved one is dying or will soon die. The normal stages of the grief process are:

1. shock and denial
2. anger (anger turned outward)
3. depression (anger turned inward)
4. bargaining
5. sadness
6. resolution, acceptance, and forgiveness

Your first response is shock, numbness, horror, coupled with feelings of denial: "This can't be happening to me. This can't be happening to my marriage, to my family."

Soon after the shock and denial, you will probably feel anger. You may want to scream at your spouse. You'll feel rage. You will wonder, "How could you do this to me? How could you do this to our family?"

Within a few minutes, hours, or even days, you will probably experience anger turned inward—guilt and depression. If you are already a person who struggles with a lot of guilt, self-blame, low self-esteem, or depression, you may very quickly move into this stage, thinking, "It's my fault. I should have worked harder on the relationship. I should have done more." But even a person with very strong self-esteem is likely to feel some guilt and depression over what has happened.

Bargaining is another phase of grieving the loss of trust and fidelity. You may bargain with your spouse: "What can I do to keep you to myself?" Or you may bargain with God: "Lord, I'll do anything if You'll just put our marriage back the way it was."

Eventually, you give up on bargaining, and you resign yourself to the fact that trust has been broken, the boundaries and covenants of your marriage have been violated. Something between you and your mate has been shattered, and it will take a lot of time to rebuild it. And that leads to sadness.

In time, if you and your spouse are committed to rebuilding, if you have plenty of counseling, support, and prayer, you may get to resolution, acceptance, and forgiveness. But that stage is a year to several years away.

One of the first questions that many couples have when infidelity has broken the boundaries of their relationship is: *Should we separate or stay together?* In many cases, separation is an immediate choice. The injured party may, at least during the shock and anger phase, say, "I won't have you around me! I can't stand to look at you! I want a divorce!" These feelings are understandable. In most cases, these angry feelings pass, and the injured party begins to wonder, "Is there hope for us? Can we survive this and stay together?"

In cases in which the affair has been going on for a long time, a period of separation can be helpful in clarifying the situation. The unfaithful spouse may still be emotionally and sexually involved with the third person and may not want to give that relationship up right away. You must send a very clear message to the unfaithful spouse: "I will not tolerate a three-way relationship. End it now; then let's talk." You must not show any toleration or leniency regarding the infidelity. This is a mistake that many injured spouses make, particularly during the bargaining phase of their grief experience. They send signals that suggest, "I want you back so much that I'm willing to put up with some infidelity."

If you don't confront your spouse's behavior in an absolute, zero-tolerance fashion, you encourage your spouse to continue his or her self-centered and destructive behavior. You may doom a relationship that would be otherwise salvageable. Your only hope for saving your marriage and making it a real marriage again lies in forcing your spouse to face the consequences of his or her sinful behavior. In order to achieve this purpose, you probably should separate for a while.

What is the purpose of the separation? Your goal is to reestablish a friendship relationship between you and your spouse. You can talk on the phone or in brief visits, but there should be no sexual relationship with your spouse during this separation. The details of the financial arrangement for maintaining two households need to be worked out. The offending spouse should be held accountable to you and should report on his or her use of time during the separation. The offending spouse should not have any contact with the third person. If the offending spouse objects to any of these arrangements (such as having to contribute to your living expenses), that is an indication of incomplete remorse and incomplete repentance. A truly repentant person does not complain about the consequences of infidelity; he or she accepts the fact that the consequences of sin must be accepted and worked through.

A separation allows guidelines to be established so that trust can gradually be rebuilt. Both sides may need time to get away and think about their lives and the issues that are truly important to them. If the affair was brief, then the separation may also be brief, so long as you are both prepared to work together on your problems and issues both during and after the separation. But if there is evidence that the unfaithful spouse remains entangled in adulterous behavior, the separation should be longer.

The length of the separation depends on the attitudes of the two partners, not on some arbitrary time limit. A separation may last a few weeks or several months, and a counselor should be involved in helping both of you determine the best arrangement for your situation.

Is a separation always required? No. In many cases, the unfaithful spouse has been

■

If you are the injured spouse, you must decide to be a rock, not a doormat.

■

■

The separation should not end until the unfaithful spouse has made a clear commitment to end all contact with the third person. The goal is to reaffirm that the unfaithful spouse has returned, body and soul, to the marriage relationship, and that his or her commitment to the marriage is 100 percent.

■

miserable and guilt-ridden in the adulterous relationship. There may even be a sense of relief at being caught. Now that the affair has been exposed, the unfaithful spouse is willing to work on making amends and repairing the relationship. If the injured spouse is willing and emotionally able to do so, you can remain together and work on your issues under the same roof.

What about the third party? If you have never met the "other man" or the "other woman," then this third person is bound to be a great source of both pain and curiosity to you. What is this person like? Why was your spouse attracted to him or her?

If your unfaithful spouse is truly repentant, he or she should be willing to talk about some of the general facts and circumstances of the affair. It is important that the unfaithful spouse recognize and acknowledge that the affair is over, that secrecy has been removed, and that there can be no secrecy in the future. Admitting the general facts of the relationship are an important step toward closing this chapter. Lurid accounts filled with sordid details are hardly necessary, and would only cause you additional distress and emotional pain.

When Cliff learned of Amber's affair with a coworker in her office, he sat her down and browbeat her, intimidated her, and yelled at her, demanding to know the man's name and address, the times and dates of every encounter they had, the name of everyone who had seen them together, and details of their lovemaking. Amber was scared to death, afraid that Cliff was capable of anything, including murder. "I'll tell you anything you want to know," she said, "but not here. In a counselor's office."

"You don't set the terms here," Cliff growled. "You're the one who was running around, not me."

"I was wrong, and I want to make it right," said Amber through her tears. "But you're scaring me right now. If you want me to answer your questions, you have to be reasonable."

Reluctantly, Cliff agreed to go to a counselor. It was clear to the counselor that Cliff was a vengeful and intimidating man who was not in full possession of himself. He encouraged Amber to share with Cliff in a general way and promised Cliff that there would be additional disclosure in future counseling sessions. In time, Cliff became more reasonable, and the crisis passed. But there was a time when anything was possible.

It is understandable that the injured spouse would want to know everything about the affair, no matter how painful it would be. Yet the person who demands to know every last detail is not responding in a healthy way. In many cases, that person is demonstrating an excessive craving for *control* (see CONTROL ADDICTION).

DO I HAVE TO STAY MARRIED TO THIS PERSON?

Once infidelity is exposed, it is not unusual for the injured spouse to want to end the marriage. This is an understandable emotion. The task of establishing accountability and reestablishing trust with the offending spouse seems like too much work, too much pain. At this point the option of divorce begins to look very attractive. And though few Christians would be quick to justify divorce, an injured spouse is likely to view a four-word phrase in Matthew 19:9 as just the loophole he or she needs (note the added italics):

> Whoever divorces his wife, *except for sexual immorality,* and marries another, commits adultery.

It is crucial to understand that these words spoken by Jesus Himself are a form of permission, not a command. Jesus is not saying, "If your spouse is sexually immoral, you must get a divorce." He is saying that divorce is an option in such situations—and it is up to the individuals involved to discern God's will for their lives.

In this passage, Jesus demonstrates a very keen insight into human relationships and human emotions. He understands that, in some cases of adultery, the injured spouse will be so wounded by the unfaithful spouse's sin that he or she *must* make a new start in order to recover, emotionally and spiritually. But He also understands that in some cases, the emotional and spiritual pain will only be worsened by divorce. At the Minirth Meier New Life Clinics, we usually encourage people who find themselves in such situations to consider the possibility of reconciling and placing God in control of a renewed and restructured marriage relationship. Even if it doesn't work, the couple will know that they did all they possibly could do to save the marriage.

Adultery is, at base, a lifestyle of deception. In order for recovery, restoration, and reconciliation to take place, all deception of self and of others must be burned away. Honesty—the painful, brutal honesty of self-analysis—must take the place of deception. The unfaithful spouse will naturally find it hard to face this kind of soul-baring honesty. In many cases, the injured spouse will also have issues in which repression and denial block honesty. This is where Christian counseling comes in.

A counselor, acting as an insightful but objective neutral party, can help a couple formulate strategies for uncovering the truth, for rebuilding trust, for restructuring boundaries, and for encouraging personal and marital growth. The spouse must *want* to save the marriage. Without that motivation, all efforts to counsel the individual will likely be fruitless. If a spouse declines needed counseling, the other partner should seek counseling for his or her own issues, while making sure that the unrepentant spouse continues to pay a price for being unrepentant. By "paying a price," we do not mean the other partner should nag or punish the unrepentant spouse; rather, he or she should calmly make it clear that the normal marital routine will not be resumed until there is genuine repentance. That means no sexual relationship, at the very least, and it may mean a continued separation.

Though it is impossible to know another person's heart, there are signs that indicate that repentance is genuine. Those signs include:

- Being willing to end the affair fully, freely, and finally. No "tapering off," no fond goodbyes. Over, done with, the end.
- Accepting full responsibility for the affair. Not assigning blame, not taking 50 percent or 75 percent of the responsibility, but taking all responsibility for his or her own actions.
- Being willing to go into counseling.
- Being willing to make himself or herself accountable to the spouse.

A spouse should not be dragged kicking and screaming into counseling, since it is virtually impossible to get positive results from a sullen, resentful, uncooperative client.

SEX AND LIES

Infidelity is about sex. But even more fundamentally, infidelity is about deception. Adulterers have to lie to account for their whereabouts and the use of their time. They have to account for strange phone calls, mysterious credit card charges, and money missing from checking accounts. They have to account for withdrawing, sexually and affectionately, from their spouse.

One of the most common deception techniques used by adulterers is the bluff. Some years ago, a leading presidential candidate dared reporters to follow him around and see if rumors about his sexual indiscretions were true or not. "I guarantee you'll be bored," he said, "because there's just nothing to these rumors." He didn't count on the reporters calling his bluff. They followed him around and got pictures of him cavorting with a blonde—not his wife—on a sailboat and on the Caribbean island of Bimini. The boat was appropriately named *Monkey Business*. At that moment, his presidential aspirations ended.

The most accomplished bluffers in the world are not poker players but adulterers. "What are you accusing me of?" they say with a perfect simulation of wounded righteousness. "Shall I give you a copy of my itinerary every day? Would you like me to phone you every fifteen minutes? How can you think I would ever do such a thing to my family?" Bluffers use these techniques to silence those who are suspicious—and their bluffs all too often go unchallenged.

Adulterers become expert actors and inventive tellers of clever evasions, hedges, half-truths, and bald-faced lies. Operating on the truism that "the best defense is a good offense," adulterers often shift blame onto others (particularly their spouses) in order to shift attention away from their own hidden sins. "As long as I can keep my spouse off balance and defending himself or herself," they reason, "my spouse will never suspect what I'm doing."

Adulterers lie to others, to be sure, but first of all they lie to themselves, using *denial* as a defense mechanism to keep from having to accept the guilt and blame for their actions (see "Denial" under DEFENSE MECHANISMS). Some of the most common lies adulterers tell themselves:

- "This is just a phase I'm going through."
- "After years of marriage, I've finally discovered true love."
- "This doesn't have to change anything; I can love a wife/husband and a lover."
- "Our marriage has been in trouble for a long time. We've been growing apart. It's only natural that I would fall for someone else."
- "I have to see where this relationship leads. I may not find another person like him/her again."
- "I've been under so much stress lately."
- "I deserve to have a good relationship in my life."
- "Okay, I stumbled, but God will forgive me."
- "This is my business. My spouse doesn't know about it, I'm not going to leave my family, so what harm does it do?"

- "It's an addiction. I have a sex addiction. I have a relationship addiction. I have a drug or alcohol addiction. Addiction is a disease, right? I can't be held responsible for an addiction, can I?"

All of these denials are *lies*. Adulterers use these lies and excuses to make themselves feel better about doing something that is clearly, unequivocally, inexcusably *wrong*.

The only way for a marriage to be healed is for both parties to commit themselves to a program of total, uncompromising honesty and integrity. No more half-truths or evasions, no more bluffs, no more self-deception. The offender must be willing to make a full confession without evasions, excuses, scapegoating, blame-shifting, or minimizing: "I did it. I'm 100 percent responsible for my own actions. I have to accept the consequences. I have to make amends." The act of infidelity seems like a terrible wrong to commit against God and against others—and it is. But deception is even more basic to the sin of infidelity. If we make a decision never to deceive, never to equivocate, never to compromise the truth, then we will not be able to engage in adultery. The willingness to deceive always precedes the act of adultery.

THE ROAD TO RESTORATION AND RECONCILIATION

The sex act is an act of emotional fusion that bonds two people together in a way that transcends explanation. Our sexuality is the most powerful language we have in which to express our commitment to another human being. When we express our sexuality within marriage, we produce a sense of significance and security between ourselves and our partner. When we express our sexuality outside of marriage, however, we produce confusion and relational distortion. Sexual expression is the most pure and complete when it is contained within the protective boundaries of a deeply personal, totally exclusive relationship.

When those protective boundaries are crossed, a wound is inflicted that will not heal quickly. It will take a great deal of time, effort, and commitment to bring healing and trust to a marriage that has been so seriously violated. Impatience is the great saboteur of reconciliation efforts. Many couples make the mistake of trying to rush their reconciliation, and important issues get swept under the rug, only to emerge as relationship-breaking problems months or years later. Other couples make the mistake of throwing in the towel, of giving up without even giving it a try. Christlike love hopes and believes all things and is willing to take on the tough job of putting a broken marriage relationship back together again.

Here are a number of lifestyle changes a couple should make in order to experience recovery and restoration of a healthy, trusting marriage relationship:

1. Both spouses should commit themselves to a daily discipline of devotions, both individually and together. This spiritual discipline includes Bible meditation, prayer, and regular involvement in church and a small group Bible study or support group. The more we focus on building the fruit of the Spirit into our lives (see Galatians 5:16–23),

the more genuinely loving and self-controlled we will be. Infidelity is an issue that requires a spiritual approach as well as a psychological approach.

2. The third person must be placed completely off limits. There must be no further contact, casual, formal, or otherwise. The offender must agree to this condition, and the injured spouse must insist on it. This is non-negotiable.

3. The offender must be willing to make an all-out effort to re-earn trust and to win back the affection of the spouse. This means the offender's schedule may need to be restructured so that he or she spends more time involved with the family and less time with work and outside interests.

4. The offender must be willing to make himself or herself accountable to the injured spouse and to a counselor.

5. Communication processes may need to be overhauled so that emotions and issues can be recognized and resolved. A counselor can be very helpful in restructuring family and marital communication patterns.

6. The offender's old lifestyle of deception must be replaced by a new commitment to honesty, openness, accountability, and integrity.

7. The couple should recognize that there is no such thing as a perfect romantic relationship. Instead of looking for an idealized relationship that doesn't exist, they should commit themselves to improving the marriage relationship they already have.

8. The couple must recognize that sexual temptation cannot be eliminated but it can be controlled. Those who are vulnerable to temptation should make a special effort to avoid circumstances, people, and influences (alcohol, movies, cable TV) that tend to stimulate unfaithful thoughts and unfaithful behavior.

9. The couple should recognize the difference between *reputation* and *character*. Reputation is who other people think you are. A reputation may or may not be the reality. Character, however, is who you really are when no one else is watching. Your goal should be to become a person of authentic character, a person who is honest and upright, even when no one else is observing your behavior. "Create in me a clean heart, O God," said David as he was being restored following his sin of adultery, "and renew a steadfast spirit within me" (Ps. 51:10).

The injured party must make a decision to forgive, and to forgive again, and to forgive again. We don't forgive because we feel like it or because the other person deserves it. We forgive because God has forgiven us and because we find emotional and spiritual healing when we forgive. God is able to forgive once and for all, so that our sins are removed as far from us as the east is from the west. Human beings, unfortunately, are unable to forgive so permanently and completely. Anger and bitterness creep back into our minds again and again, so we must forgive repeatedly and continually. (See FORGIVENESS.)

10. The couple should recognize the difference between *forgiveness* and *reconciliation*. Forgiveness should be offered unconditionally. In fact, forgiveness is more important for the injured spouse than the offender. When you forgive, you say, "I will not keep you under my judgment. I will not try to stand in God's place and take vengeance against you for what you've done. I will let go of my grudge against you and get on with my life." You can forgive without reconciling. You can forgive, even if the offender never repents. Forgiveness is unconditional; reconciliation is conditional.

Forgiveness is more important for the injured spouse than the offender.

Many offenders pronounce themselves "cured" a week or a month after the affair is exposed, and any effort to hold them accountable or to impose changes on their lifestyle is met with the accusation, "You just don't want to forgive me!" Offenders need to understand that forgiveness does not mean that everything immediately goes back to normal. Being forgiven is not the same thing as being trusted. Changes have to be made and trust must be re-earned. If an offender is not willing to submit to life changes and a process of accountability, then that offender is probably not fully repentant.

The injured spouse should not be too quick to reconcile if the offender does not demonstrate true remorse and repentance. Some injured spouses reconcile out of desperation rather than forgiveness. They have an excessive dependency upon the unfaithful spouses and are willing to let the unfaithful spouses get away with adultery and to "let bygones be bygones." The problem comes when the bygones haven't gone, when the offender is not fully repentant. It is important for the injured spouse to demonstrate self-respect, assertiveness, and a will to hold the offender accountable. The injured spouse must demand truthfulness and adherence to new rules or else the relationship is doomed to become unhealthy again, and a moral relapse becomes not only possible but probable.

11. Successful reconciliation requires that some aspects of the marriage return to normal and that some *never* return to normal. The daily routines of life should be resumed, so that both spouses can feel that life is moving forward once again. But unhealthy patterns of communicating and relating must forever be disrupted, and new, healthy patterns must be put into their place. A counselor can be an important resource in helping a couple decide which aspects of their relationship should remain and which should go.

12. There must be an end to blaming and accusing. Blame places one person in a superior position and the other person in an inferior position. When the injured spouse loads blame onto the offender, the weight of that blame can be so crushing and painful that the offender can actually be driven out of the marriage. The offender must have hope of a better future in the marriage in order to stay motivated to work on the marriage. If there is nothing in the marriage but blame and pain, the offender may lose heart and opt for divorce.

13. There must be an end to defensiveness. Each side must listen to the feelings, complaints, and needs of the other without jumping in to defend himself or herself. The key to reconciliation is change, and for change to take place, both parties must be willing to consider their own contributions to the problem and be willing to make constructive changes.

14. The couple must confront the urge to control. The injured spouse may exhibit controlling behavior, demanding complete authority over the offender and even punishing the offender. The injured spouse sometimes engages in controlling behavior by bringing the matter up again and again.

The unfaithful spouse may also be controlling, seeking to steer any discussion of problems away from areas that make him or her uncomfortable and seeking to dictate the reconciliation process. A counselor can be helpful in confronting controlling behavior by either side, so that communication will be healing, honest, and productive.

> ■
> *To have integrity is to do the right thing even if nobody else sees, even if it costs you or hurts you.*
> ■

357

15. The couple should "court" or "date" for a while before reengaging in a sexual relationship. There should be a renewed level of communication, nonsexual touching, and affection. Then, once the couple feels comfortable with this new level of emotional interaction, the two of them should get away for a weekend "honeymoon," a romantic interlude to give them a sense of a new beginning and recommitment to their special relationship. Sexual relations should not be renewed if the offender is unrepentant or lacking in remorse. The offender should not be encouraged to think he or she can "have the best of both worlds," sexual relationships both in and out of marriage.

16. The injured spouse should avoid using the affair as "ammunition" whenever he or she is angry. In counseling couples at the clinics, we find that it is not unusual for an injured spouse to continue raising the issue in a vindictive way as long as five, ten, or twenty years later. It is understandable that there would be recurring feelings of anger and insecurity six months, a year, even two years later. But those feelings should diminish, and the injured spouse should make a determined effort to lay the matter to rest.

17. If there is a relapse, the trust issue becomes not doubly difficult but many orders of magnitude more difficult. If the spouse can't be trusted after all the promises, the commitments, the counseling, and the accountability that was established after the first affair was exposed, how can this person *ever* be trusted? Recovery is still possible, but the process is now more complicated, and will take more work and much more time.

If both parties are still willing to work on recovery and restoration, the reasons for the relapse need to be explored. Did the unfaithful spouse lack resolve or sincerity? Did the unfaithful spouse resist accountability? Did the injured mate contribute to the problem by being overbearing or controlling? Did the injured mate demonstrate an excessive dependency that gave the unfaithful spouse a "green light" to return to a lifestyle of infidelity? The offender must not be allowed to play with the innocent spouse's emotions. A counselor is needed in such a situation to clarify issues and to help both parties keep commitments and establish healthy boundaries in their relationship.

God's plan is for two people to be together, committed and faithful, within the protective enclosure of holy matrimony. But people fail and sin. That's when we need the strength of God and the grace of God. Infidelity hurts and it wounds. But the wounds don't have to be fatal.

There is life after infidelity.

Inner Child

"Why do you ask me so many questions about my past?" asked Dave. "The problems I've got are going on right now, not thirty years ago. I came here because I've got a problem with booze and my marriage is falling apart. Now, when are we going to stop talking about when I was a kid and start working on the problems I have *today?*"

THE COMPLETE LIFE ENCYCLOPEDIA

"You don't seem to want to talk about your childhood," said the doctor.

Dave crossed his arms sullenly. "I think I just established that."

"You insist you had a normal, average childhood."

"Sure. Hey, my dad was strict, but he was fair."

"You mean, like the time he threw you down the basement stairs, and then locked you down there for a few hours?"

"I had that coming. Like I told you, he was strict. What are you implying?"

"I'm not implying anything, Dave. I'm telling you straight out that the behavior you describe as 'strict' is a lot more than just 'strict.' It's abuse. It's not normal. It's not average. It's abuse. Not just this incident, but all the incidents you described when I asked you about your dad's discipline style. The time he shamed you in front of your girlfriend. The time he put your hand in a vise to teach you not to steal. The time he burned you with a cigarette. You need to know that most fathers don't do things like that to their kids. And the ones that do can go to jail for it."

Dave jumped to his feet. "This isn't getting us anywhere!" he growled through clenched teeth. "I thought you were going to help me with my problems! All you want to do is talk about the past! There's nothing wrong with my past!"

"Then why are you crying, Dave?"

Dave stopped suddenly. He put his hands to his face, and when he took his hands away and looked at them, he saw tears glistening on his fingers. He sat down heavily, put his head in his hands, and began moaning, crying, rocking back and forth. "Why did you have to ask me about that stuff? I don't want to think about that stuff! I don't want to think about it!"

But, over the next few weeks, Dave thought about it a lot. And he talked about it. In time, he began to get better. He began to experience healing in a part of himself that we call the *inner child*.

WHAT IS THE INNER CHILD?

The concept of the inner child is a model for understanding the way people think and feel. This model is used by psychologists, psychiatrists, and people in the addiction-recovery field to explain how the experiences of childhood have shaped us emotionally into the people we are today. Everyone has an inner child, and God's plan for human development was for everyone to experience emotional nurturing during his or her formative years so that he or she would grow to healthy, confident adulthood, with a good balance between the inner and outer dimensions of his or her personality.

Research shows that about 85 percent of one's adult personality is formed by the time a person is six years old. Clearly, God has made an enormous investment in every person's inner child, with the plan that the experiences of the inner child would shape the adult personality in positive ways. Unfortunately (because of the Fall of the human race described in Genesis, and the resulting entrance of sin into the world), many of our childhood experiences are negative experiences, and they result in negative influences on who we are and how we feel as adults.

The human mind (or soul) is made up of both conscious and unconscious components. Your childhood experiences have a powerful influence in shaping both the conscious and unconscious aspects of who you are. There is a continual conflict between these two dimensions of your being. The unconscious mind attempts to push thoughts and memories into your conscious awareness, and your defense mechanisms fight like mad to keep the most painful and frightening of those thoughts and memories suppressed (see DEFENSE MECHANISMS). The conscious mind avoids pain at all costs and recoils from experiencing painful events and memories all over again.

In a general sense, the inner child may be viewed as the unconscious mind, whereas the outer self may be viewed as the conscious mind. The human soul or mind, then, could be viewed as having an unconscious core (the inner child) surrounded by an outer covering (the conscious mind).

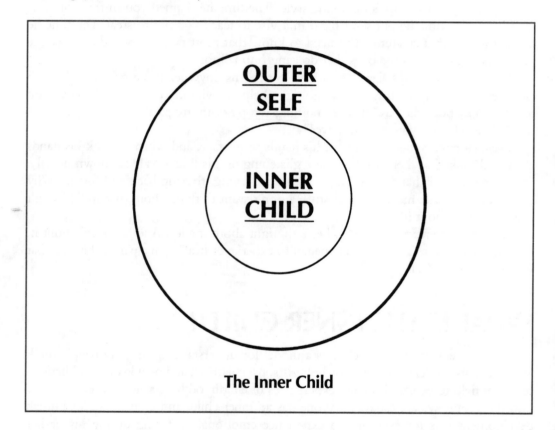

The Inner Child

The inner child is the essential *you* that existed before you began to acquire your roles and identities as son or daughter, student, athlete, dancer, artist, class clown, friend, marriage partner, parent, career person. Before any of these identities were added to you, there was a basic, essential *you*. When you were born, you were nothing but a naked inner child without any outer self at all. You were innocent, curious, naive, uninhibited, spontaneous, and totally vulnerable. You had no defenses, no facades, no image to project.

Soon after birth, however, you began to assemble your outer self from bits and pieces of the world that you experienced. In infancy, you learned you could receive a comforting touch or food by crying. In early childhood, you learned how to get along with other children and how to please adults. As you grew, you learned social norms,

360

behavioral expectations, and ways to manipulate your environment. You learned that in order to avoid pain or shame, you should keep certain parts of your inner self hidden from others. You learned that other people would accept or reject you on the basis of things you said and did, so you began to monitor and adjust your behavior to the expectations of others. Your outer self grew into a complex and elaborate network of responses, inhibitions, attitudes, beliefs, opinions, and conscious projections that enable you to function in the adult world. Whenever you relate to another person in a social situation, you and that person interact with each other's outer selves. The outer self is the self of logic, reason, and rational communication.

But buried within you, surrounded by your civilized, socialized outer self, a living inner being lives. This hidden inner being still throbs and pulsates with the uninhibited desires and appetites of a little child: "I want what I want and I want it *now!*" The inner child is the emotional, feelings-oriented part of you, the aspect of you that loves, hates, fears, rejoices, and feels shame. Some of the most painful problems a person experiences, including depression and anxiety, come about as a result of conflict and disharmony between the outer self and the inner child. The outer self is often unaware of (or out of touch with) what the inner self is feeling, and frequently is at war against what the inner self seeks to express.

It is important that you interact with the world and with other people through your outer self. But many people emphasize their outer selves while denying their inner selves. Still others operate completely on the basis of gushy emotion, without any logic or social restraint at all, and they need to learn how to think and behave with greater clarity and thought. The healthiest people are those who are able to integrate the outer self and the inner child and who are equally comfortable with logical, intelligent action and with genuine feeling, each in its appropriate setting.

■

Both the inner and outer selves are valid and important parts of your whole being.

■

COAXING THE INNER CHILD OUT OF HIDING

When people come to the Minirth Meier New Life Clinics for counseling, they come because there is some sort of stress or pain in their lives. They want the doctors at the clinics to help them turn off the pain and return their lives to a comfortable state. This is a perfectly valid motive for going into counseling or therapy, since it is only natural that people equate the removal of pain with the restoration of health. So the client comes in and begins relating to the doctor through the means of his or her outer self. The conversation usually begins on a logical, fact-oriented level.

The doctor's goal, however, is to help that person move beyond the outer self and to bring the inner child out of hiding. We use a series of exercises and techniques to help the client become aware of his or her feelings. We look at current stress factors in the client's life, we look at family relationships, we look at childhood experiences and events, both traumatic and happy. If all goes well, we start moving inward, closer and closer to the core of this person's being, closer to the inner child.

Often, that inner child, sensing that the light of exposure and truth is approaching his hiding place, begins to panic. Fear and anxiety set in, sometimes emerging through the mediation of the outer self as an outburst of anger or annoyance: "This is pointless! I'm getting out of here!" Or it may emerge as an unemotional, intellectualized statement: "I don't think this is leading anywhere, doctor, but thank you for your time." In either case, we often see patients becoming anxious to resign from treatment just as their issues, memories, and emotions are about to come into view. This is normal, but this is also why it is extremely important for people in counseling to make a commitment to push through the pain and anxiety, so they can keep moving toward wholeness and recovery. It is important to recognize that, in counseling, the emotional pain usually gets worse before it gets better—but once the person gets past the crisis point, he or she will almost certainly experience a tremendous and liberating sense of relief and healing.

Our Lord, being the Great Physician of body, soul, and spirit, wants to heal us wherever we are wounded. If your inner child has been wounded by childhood abuse, trauma, or neglect, He wants you to experience His healing touch.

■

The psalmist tells us that it is critically important for us to gain insight into the hidden emotions and motives of the inner child. He writes, "Search me, O God, and know my heart; try me, and know my anxieties; and see if there is any wicked way in me, and lead me in the way everlasting" (Ps. 139:23–24). There is pain, there are hidden motives, there are worries, and there are buried sins within each of us. The more we uncover these hidden parts of ourselves, the more emotionally healthy we become. There is no part of your inner being that God does not know. He created you, body, soul, and spirit. He created your conscious and unconscious mind. He created your inner child.

■

SELF-TEST   Has Your Inner Child Been Wounded?

To diagnose the state of your own inner child, take the following short self-test and see if you find yourself in the following list of symptoms.

____ Depression
Do you have periods of unhappiness, anger, or guilt that come and go without any logical reason? Are you unhappy more than you are happy? Do you have a history of depression?

____ Anxiety
Do you suffer from sleeplessness, disturbed sleep, generalized nervousness, excessive worry, or anxiety about job performance?

____ Anger
Do you rage or scream or have difficulty controlling your anger? Are your spouse, children, friends, coworkers, fellow church members, or employees intimidated by you?

____ Problems with Relationships
Do you have trouble with current relationships? Have you had frequent breakups? Are there people in your life that you can't live with and can't live without?

____ Fears and Phobias
Are you afraid of everyday situations such as going outside the house, being in crowds, using elevators, flying, driving in traffic, or darkness? Do you ever have unexplained feelings of panic?

362

_____ Perfectionism

Do you demand flawlessness from yourself and others? Do the mistakes and sins of others make you angry and frustrated? Do your own mistakes and sins make you feel guilty or depressed?

_____ Compulsive Behavior

Do you engage in behavior that is irrational, repetitive, habitual, and that you wish you could stop but cannot? Compulsive over-achievement or workaholism? Compulsive gambling or spending? Compulsive overeating? Compulsive religious legalism? Compulsive exercise? Ritualized behavior such as repetitive hand-washing or compulsive neatness? Repetitive checking of doors and windows to see that they are locked? Do you eat when you are not hungry? Are you anorexic? Bulimic?

_____ Addiction

Do you compulsively abuse substances or behaviors such as alcohol, tobacco, illegal or prescription drugs, food, sex, or pornography? Do you use certain substances or behaviors to cope with problems or feel better?

_____ Sex

Do you have multiple sexual partners? Do you continually fantasize about sexual relations outside of marriage?

These symptoms are indications of inner conflicts between your inner child and outer self. Compulsions and addictions are attempts to keep one's inner self hidden from others and from one's own conscious awareness. Depression, anxiety, anger, fears, and relationship problems all signal hidden, unconscious issues that emanate from the inner child and that interfere with the effective, healthy functioning of the outer self. (For a comprehensive discussion of each of these issues that may relate to your inner child, see ADDICTION, ANGER, ANXIETY, COMPULSIVE BEHAVIOR, COMPULSIVE OVEREATING, DEPRESSION, FEARS AND PHOBIAS, and RELATIONSHIPS.)

Understand, _most_ people would check at least one of these statements, because we all experience these symptoms at one time or another. But the more statements you check, the more likely it is that you are experiencing woundedness in your inner child. You may even experience symptoms (such as relationship problems, depression, or fear) that are so crippling that you have difficulty functioning. If so, you could greatly benefit from Christian counseling or psychotherapy or from involvement in a recovery group or support group.

REPARENTING YOUR INNER CHILD

The way to healing your wounded inner child is through a process called _reparenting_. Reparenting fills the holes left by an emotionally deficient upbringing. You can't go back and demand that your parents make it all up to you, but you can find new sources of love and affirmation to fill those holes in your soul. You can experience reparenting in three ways:

1. *Reparent yourself.* You reparent yourself when you extend compassion to your inner child. You can say to yourself, "I was wounded as a child, and I can't change the past. But I know this pain will heal, and I will protect myself from further wounds. I have permission to love myself. I have permission to accept myself as a beautiful creation of a loving God. I have permission to express my emotions—anger, joy, fear, hope, sorrow, happiness. I have permission to express my sexuality according to God's beautiful plan. I have permission to experience intimacy in relationships. I have permission to join a new supportive family of my own choosing, so that I can be unconditionally loved and affirmed."

2. *Allow others to reparent you.* You can be reparented by a support group, a sponsor or mentor, a therapist, or a trusted friend. Choose someone who will truly affirm you unconditionally. (If you choose someone from your present family or family of origin, you may fall back into old codependent family patterns.) Ask that person to meet with you, pray with you, hold you accountable, and affirm you on a regular basis.

3. *Allow God to reparent you.* Pray to God and listen quietly for His answer to come to you in your stillness. Read His Word. Experience what it means to have a heavenly Parent who is all-loving, all-accepting, all-affirming. True intimacy with God satisfies like no earthly relationship can. We suggest you read Deuteronomy 5 and Ephesians 5—6. Insert your name as appropriate, and listen as if God speaks directly to you. Focus on a problem or need and discuss it with God in prayer. Don't worry about formalities and speaking in "thees" and "thous." Just open your heart to Him as you would to a close friend or a loving, attentive, nurturing parent.

We also recommend you read *Healing the Child Within* by Charles L. Whitfield (Health Comm., 1987), *Becoming Your Own Parent* by Dennis Wholey (Doubleday, 1988), and *Reclaiming Your Inner Child: A Self-Discovery Workbook* by Ken Parker (Thomas Nelson, 1993).

Insanity

Insanity is not a precise or useful term to use in psychology or psychiatry. The term has a definition in criminal law, meaning *a condition of mental disorder or defect that is sufficiently incapacitating as to relieve a person of responsibility for criminal conduct.* In psychology and psychiatry, the term has no precise or commonly agreed-upon meaning.

Mental and emotional disorders come in varying degrees and are accompanied by varying arrays of symptoms. We can describe the severity of these symptoms. We can treat the symptoms through counseling, medication, or some combination of both. But there is no therapeutic purpose served by labeling a person as "sane" or "insane." Instead, when we examine a patient at the clinics, we might conclude that this person has,

for example, a *psychotic disorder,* meaning that—because of schizophrenia or a delusional disorder—he or she is out of touch with reality. This is a precise diagnosis that serves a useful therapeutic purpose.
See also ABNORMAL PSYCHOLOGY

Jealousy

O, beware, my lord, of jealousy;
It is the green-eyed monster which doth mock
The meat it feeds on.
                    Shakespeare, *Othello,* Act III, Scene 3

You may know this green-eyed monster called jealousy. That awful twisting sensation deep inside you. The terrible images in your mind. The fear and the distrust.

Where does jealousy come from? Jealousy generally comes from one of two sources:

1. If it is *reality-based* jealousy, it comes from experience. You may have caught a glimpse of your mate's roving eye at the beach or a party. Or there may be subtle signs that you have assembled in your mind that make you suspect your partner is unfaithful. Or your mate may actually have a history of infidelity, in which case feelings of jealousy, distrust, and insecurity are perfectly understandable and normal. (If your marriage is in recovery from infidelity, see the comprehensive discussion of this subject in INFIDELITY.)

2. If your jealousy feelings are *not* reality-based—that is, if you just have an anxious feeling about your relationship, if you feel like hovering around and clinging to your mate, if you get irritable and insecure whenever your mate leaves on a business trip or talks to someone of the opposite sex—then you probably have an emotional issue that needs to be resolved.

What are the causes of jealousy feelings that have no factual basis?

An inability to trust. People who have been abused or exploited as children frequently grow up with a limited ability to trust. Having been frequently lied to or mistreated during the years when their personality was being formed, they now expect to be lied to and mistreated. They may look for evidence that their spouses are untrustworthy, even if no evidence exists.

An inability to trust can also develop in infancy. It is important that infants bond to their mothers very early and receive continual assurance of her presence and care so that they will later become secure and outgoing adults. Infants whose mothers are absent or undependable frequently become overdependent and unable to trust those around them later in life. Children who develop an inability to trust in infancy usually demonstrate their insecurity in the preschool years by clinging to anyone, even strangers. In adulthood, such people are often overdependent and prone to serial relationships.

Fear of abandonment. The most common fears during the infant-toddler years are fear of abandonment, fear of losing parental love and approval, and Oedipal fears (that is, a sense of competition with the same-sex parent for the love of the opposite-sex parent). In a healthy family, children outgrow these fears as their parents reassure them by word and action that they will always be there and so will their love. In some families, however, these fears are reinforced rather than resolved. If there is a divorce or if a parent dies, or if the parents are unloving and emotionally distant, then the fear of abandonment comes true. People whose infant-toddler fears were never resolved in childhood often become insecure, fearful, clinging, dependent, jealous adults. The same fears they had in toddlerhood now reemerge in adult relationships as fear of abandonment by the spouse, fear of losing the spouse's love and approval, and fear of having to compete with others for the spouse's love.

A histrionic personality. Personality type has an enormous influence on emotions, including the emotion of jealousy. One personality type that particularly seems to predispose women to jealousy is the *histrionic personality.* Histrionic individuals have a flair for the dramatic, are highly reactive to other people and situations, and are intensely expressive with emotions. They overreact to minor events and erupt into anger over the slightest irritations. Though they can seem quite charming when it suits them, histrionics tend to sabotage their relationships with others by being demanding, self-centered, inconsiderate of others, manipulative, and helpless. They constantly demand reassurance and attention. They often experience jealous feelings that are rooted in possessiveness, selfishness, and excessive dependence. Histrionics tend to have had poor relationships with their opposite-sex parents (many have histories of abuse), and they have unconscious needs to prove that their mates are just as worthless and untrustworthy as their parents.

A borderline personality. Individuals with borderline personalities demonstrate instability in relationships. Their interactions with other people are intense, and their opinions of other people swing wildly from "You're the most wonderful person in the world!" *(idealization)* to "You're worthless, you're horrible!" *(devaluation).* These wide variations in mood will often produce jealous thoughts and feelings that are not rooted in reality. These individuals are also subject to depression, irritability, anger, and low self-esteem. They cannot tolerate being alone, so if their spouses are away on trips or at work, they will sit at home feeling empty, bored, suspicious, and insecure. Their imaginations will work overtime, and the result will be an intense jealousy.

A paranoid personality. This personality type is characterized by hypersensitivity and an exaggerated sense of "self-reference"—that is, a sense that "everything that happens is directed at me." The commonly accepted conception of a "paranoid" is someone with an acute mental disorder who fancies himself being persecuted by the CIA or some such thing. But we are not talking about anything so extreme as that. There are many people who are functional and generally reality-based in their perceptions yet have paranoid, self-referential tendencies. They tend to interpret all remarks, actions, and events as personal threats. Paranoid individuals tend to hold grudges and experience intense jealousy. Like borderline individuals, paranoid individuals have highly active imaginations, and they frequently imagine scenarios that shift their jealous feelings into overdrive.

An avoidant personality. This individual is hypersensitive to rejection, whether real or imagined. Avoidant individuals tend to be socially withdrawn unless there are strong indications that they will be uncritically accepted. Their self-esteem is very low, and though they are withdrawn, they deeply desire to be loved and accepted. If an avoidant person feels momentarily rejected by the spouse, he or she is likely to interpret that rejection, whether real or imagined, as a sign that the spouse "doesn't love me anymore." This results in jealous feelings rooted in self-hate ("I don't love me, so how can my spouse love me?") and fear of rejection and abandonment.

A dependent personality. Individuals with a dependent personality allow other people to assume responsibility for their life decisions. They have low self-esteem, low self-confidence, and see themselves as inept and helpless. They cling to their mates and feel intense anxiety when alone. Their low self-esteem leads them to wonder how anyone else could love them, and the thought that their mates might cease to love them (and leave them alone and helpless) fills them with panic.

Feelings of jealousy that are rooted in fear of abandonment, an inability to trust, or a personality issue can be alleviated through counseling. It's important that these feelings be resolved, since unresolved feelings of distrust and jealousy lead to behaviors (possessiveness, criticism, nagging, questioning, accusing) that can turn one's fears into a self-fulfilling prophecy. A jealous person often uses jealous behavior in a self-defeating attempt to clutch the spouse closer and possess the spouse. The spouse feels threatened and smothered by this jealous behavior and pulls back, making the jealous individual even more jealous and insecure, resulting in even more desperate attempts to clutch the spouse closer, a vicious cycle that sends the marriage into a tailspin. In effect, the jealous person's attempt to cling actually pushes the mate away.

There are practical steps couples can take together to increase their level of mutual trust and lower any level of jealousy in their relationship. Those steps include:

1. Revive caring behaviors. Make an intentional effort to reromanticize the relationship. Go on dates, hold hands, go for walks together, give each other back rubs or massages, have nice, quiet conversations, say, "I love you."

2. Have fun together. Really have fun. Not just doing grown-up activities like skiing or taking in a concert. Revive the idea of just "playing" together. Go out to the park and swing on the swings. Take a shower together. Dance barefoot in the backyard. Be spontaneous. Do anything that excites you or gives you pleasure. Have *fun.*

3. Write a renewed marriage contract. Include in that contract a pledge of fidelity. A renewed marriage contract is not a guarantee that one spouse won't be unfaithful, but it is one more reminder of the commitment, and one more hedge of protection, safety, and security you can put in place around your marriage. The more secure both parties feel, the less jealousy there will be.

4. Develop a secure, individual identity along with your marriage identity. One of the most common sources of jealousy is an exaggerated, clinging dependence on one's mate (which we call *enmeshment*). The solution is to maintain a zone of secure individuality within the boundaries of the marriage. Learn not to feel threatened if your spouse doesn't agree with you, if your spouse's mood goes up or down, or if you have to be separated from your spouse for a few days. Learn to enjoy your own company.

Jealousy is a poisonous compound consisting of insecurity, anxiety, a controlling spirit, and an overactive imagination. Some people think that jealousy is a sign of love, but they are mistaken. It is a form of fear—the fear that someone we love will stop

■

La Rochefoucauld was right when he said, "In jealousy there is more self-love than love."

■

loving us. If jealousy is a form of fear, then it can't be love, because—as 1 John 4:18 tells us—"There is no fear in love; but perfect love casts out fear."

Perfect love casts out jealousy too.

Learning and Education

"Mrs. Carter? This is Betty Harper, Whitney's teacher. I was wondering if we could schedule a time when we could meet and talk about Whitney's schoolwork."

Mrs. Carter gripped the phone tightly. "Is—Is there something wrong with Whitney's schoolwork?"

"Well, her grades have been slipping. She's not getting all her classwork done, or her homework, for that matter. Whitney's a very bright child, Mrs. Carter, and she's capable of so much. But lately—Well, she seems to be unhappy. I was wondering if you and I could put our heads together and see if we can help your daughter pull out of this slump."

Mrs. Carter was facing one of the most common questions of parenthood: "How do I motivate and inspire my child to learn in school?" Children spend almost a third of their crucial "wonder years," those all-important developmental years, in formal education. Their primary task during the first two decades of life is to *learn*—and not just to learn information and facts, but to learn ways of thinking, ways of perceiving, ways of evaluating. The learning process impacts not only their intelligence and skills but their values, their spirituality, their moral attitudes, and their self-esteem.

The key to a child's success in school is *parental involvement*. Though it is the school's job to educate children, there is much we can do to help the school inspire our children's best learning efforts. Children have not one but two crucial arenas of learning: the school and the home. In fact, *most* of what we have learned in our lives came to us not while we were sitting in a classroom but while we were interacting with other people. In other words, one of the most powerful learning tools we have is the tool of *relationships*.

Children learn through relationships with parents, with siblings, with teachers, with other children, with friends, with extended family, and with God. Long after their report card grades are forgotten, long after they have forgotten what a hypotenuse is, they will remember lessons learned in relationships. They will remember those special teachers who energized them. They will remember lessons learned in those "teachable moments" in the home. They will remember truths and character qualities that were actively modeled to them by parents, mentors, and other role models. There are not just three Rs to a well-rounded learning process; there are four: Reading, 'Riting, 'Rithmetic, and Relationships.

In this article, we will examine several aspects of learning, including:

- how to keep children enthusiastic about learning
- how to meet the special needs of the kinesthetic learner

Parents and teachers must form a team of support and encouragement for the learning child.

The four Rs: Reading, 'Riting, 'Rithmetic, and Relationships.

THE COMPLETE LIFE ENCYCLOPEDIA

- understanding learning disabilities
- understanding adult learning problems

FACTORS THAT AFFECT THE LEARNING PROCESS

There are a number of factors that affect our children's ability to learn and that we can positively influence.

Innate Strengths and Weaknesses

When children's strengths go unrecognized and their weaknesses go undiagnosed, they tend to find schoolwork to be very difficult and discouraging. Even very intelligent children sometimes find themselves labeled as "lazy" or "limited" or "underachievers," and these labels can create lifelong problems with low self-esteem and low self-confidence. These children may procrastinate or avoid difficult tasks and even lose motivation for easier tasks. The challenge for both parents and educators is to identify and utilize those strengths while finding ways to compensate for those weaknesses, so that these children can stay motivated instead of becoming frustrated.

Family and Emotional Issues

Children sometimes lose their motivation to learn when they become emotionally upset over personal conflicts or family problems. Family and emotional problems affect learning in three ways:

1. These issues interfere with a child's ability to concentrate.
2. These issues diminish the child's motivation to learn, and he or she adopts a "what's-the-use?" attitude.
3. Children sometimes use poor school performance as a way of getting attention when they are in emotional pain, when they feel ignored, or when they want divorcing parents to get back together.

Study Environment

Children learn and function better in some environments than in others. It is important to know the best study environment for your child. Some children do better studying in the afternoon, after school and before dinner. Others are more effective studying after dinner. Older children should be given the responsibility of selecting the best time for them and should be held accountable to keep that time. Your child should have a neat, orderly, well-lit place to work (an orderly environment contributes to orderly thinking). Study time should be consistently scheduled, free of interruptions and distractions.

Valid and Invalid Motivation

Sometimes we give our children the wrong message about the motivation for learning. We say, "You'd better study if you want good grades." The child thinks that over and realizes he or she can't taste, touch, or play with a good grade—so what good is it? Grades can be a good indicator of a child's learning progress, but they are not

Learning doesn't end on graduation day. Learning is (or should be) an ongoing process for all adults as well as children.

Every child has strengths and weaknesses that affect his or her ability to learn.

369

always a valid motivation for learning. A better motivation for learning is the joy and excitement of learning itself. We should ask our children, "Tell me something interesting you learned in school today." If your child has a tendency to say, "Nothing" to that question (and many do), then wait until your child discusses something interesting from school and build on that opportunity. When those opportunities arise, enthusiastically interact with your child. Convey to him or her the fact that you are still inspired and excited about new ideas and new concepts. Model excitement about learning, and you will help to build the right motivation for learning in your children.

Self-Confidence

Many children are capable of learning, but they don't *know* they're capable of learning. When children lack confidence in their ability to finish a task, they often choose not to begin it. One of our tasks as parents is to build our children's self-confidence and give them a sense of accomplishment. We do that by letting our children do their own work, so that they can discover their own capabilities. Even when they ask us for help, we can make them assume responsibility and discover a sense of accomplishment. For example, if the child wants to know about space flight, you can say, "Let's go to the encyclopedia and look it up together."

A lack of confidence may come from past failures, or from parental messages that the child is incompetent. A parental message may not even be anything so blatant and deliberate as labeling a child as "stupid." We can send a message to the child that says "You can't handle this" simply by taking over the child's work and making him or her dependent on us.

Let the child do as much as possible for himself or herself; offer help only with hard words or difficult concepts. The more we do for our children, the more we deflate their self-esteem and their belief in their own strengths and abilities.

Children are naturally curious and excited about learning. They *enjoy* the process of discovery. It is a quality designed in them by a loving God. When children lose their interest in learning, it is because of some factor that has dampened their enthusiasm or devalued their self-esteem. Our task as parents is to nurture their natural excitement for learning and to uncover and resolve any problems that would hinder that excitement.

REWARDS AND REINFORCEMENTS

Many parents wonder if it's valid and healthy to reward children for learning. Studies show that rewards (which psychologists call *reinforcements*) can help motivate children and encourage them to develop good attitudes and habits for effective learning. However, rewarding in the wrong way can undermine the learning process.

Some parents try to *bribe* their children with food or toys or money. Bribing children can backfire in three ways:

1. Bribes convey the idea that learning is a chore and should only be done in exchange for payment. Bribes undermine the idea that learning is exciting and fun and that learning is its own reward.
2. Bribes sometimes lose their value. Eventually, the child has had so many toys or ice cream sundaes in exchange for doing homework or getting good grades that the bribe is no longer desired by the child.

3. The child learns to negotiate with you for bigger bribes: "I think an A should be worth five dollars, Dad, not just a measly buck." Learning should not be held hostage by a pint-size negotiator!

The best rewards or reinforcements are those that are the most natural and least tangible. A privilege: "You can watch the Disney Channel after your homework is done." A relational reinforcement: "I'm so proud of you. Let me give you a hug." A place of honor in the family: "We're all so proud of you that you get the 'You're a Hero!' plate at dinner tonight." A surprise: "Guess what? To celebrate your being on the Merit List, we're going out to the ball game tonight!" Rewards should be spontaneous and not given so frequently that they become commonplace. The best rewards are those that involve and enhance the relationship rather than those that are expensive, electronic, or sugary sweet.

THE SPECIAL NEEDS OF TACTILE-KINESTHETIC LEARNERS

Many children have special learning needs. They are not necessarily learning-disabled, but they learn differently than other children. Understanding the learning style of your child is an important factor in helping him to be an effective student. Some children learn best by hearing *(auditory learners)*. Some learn best by seeing *(visual learners)*. And some learn best by moving. Children who need to move in order to learn are called *tactile-kinesthetic learners*. *Tactile* means having to do with touch; *kinesthetic* means having to do with motion. Most schools do a good job of educating students with either an auditory or visual learning preference, but few do a good job with tactile-kinesthetic learners.

All children begin as tactile-kinesthetic learners. They put their whole bodies into the learning process. Most children change their perceptual and learning preference as they mature. The visual learning preference tends to develop around the first or second grade. The auditory learning preference develops around the fifth or sixth grade, preparing the child for the more lecture-oriented teaching methods of junior high school and beyond. A small but significant number of individuals, however, remain tactile-kinesthetic learners for life.

If a child does poorly in school for no obvious reason, it may be because he or she is a tactile-kinesthetic learner or a visual learner. It is important to understand the teacher's style of teaching. If the teacher tends to be a lecturer, then the tactile-kinesthetic and visual learners will be left out. A visual learner needs books, pictures, and videos in order to internalize concepts. A tactile-kinesthetic learner needs motion, touch, and experiences in order to learn.

When a child is unable to assimilate information that the children all around him can assimilate, he begins to see himself as inept and stupid. In order to remove the stigma of being "dumb," such children often choose to excel in the only way they know how: they become very good at being bad. They disrupt the class. They become discipline problems. Very often, the "bad kid" who grins and waves at his classmates as he is being led off to the principal's office is, deep inside, a sad, defeated tactile-kinesthetic learner. He could learn if his parents and teachers understood his learning style—but instead of learning, he is going to go through life thinking he is "dumb" and choosing to be "bad."

Here are some ways you can recognize and help a tactile-kinesthetic learner:

- *Talk to your child.* Ask him or her, "If you could learn the subject any way you want to, how would you like to learn it?" Your child might say, "I'd like to learn how to add and subtract with dominoes," or "I'd like to solve *real* problems with *real* stuff like oranges and marbles, not just do problems on paper."
- *Try different teaching approaches.* Take your child to a museum or the zoo instead of just teaching from a book. Find active instead of static approaches to concepts and lessons. Use board games and interactive, hands-on computer programs to communicate ideas. Build something, sculpt something, paint something together. Use dancing, singing, and other action-oriented means to involve the child and make learning fun.
- *Have your child tested.* There are tests available that, when professionally administered, can definitively assess your child's learning style.
- *Work as a team with your child's teacher.* Most teachers are eager for parental involvement and are aware of different styles of learning. Many teachers are willing and able to vary their teaching styles to accommodate the learning needs of different children. Good teachers truly *want* their students to succeed.

LEARNING DISABILITIES

There are five stages of brain development, and each stage corresponds to the maturation of certain areas of the brain. When these different areas of the brain do not adequately develop at the appropriate stage, a learning disability often results.

Stage 1 involves the maturation of the brain stem, particularly the *reticular activating system* (or RAS), which monitors incoming sensory information and relays important stimuli to the higher centers of the brain. If this brain structure fails to develop adequately by about age three months, the result can be a learning disability in later life called *attention deficit disorder* or ADD (see ATTENTION DEFICIT DISORDER).

Stage 2 begins at the same time as Stage 1 and is also completed at about three months of age. This stage involves the maturation of the four primary areas of the cerebral cortex, which is the thinking and reasoning part of the brain. As these parts of the brain mature, the purely reflex functions of the brain (crying, sucking, grasping) are replaced by more learned and purposeful actions.

Stage 3 takes place at the same time as Stages 1 and 2 but continues to about age five. During this stage, the child learns to fear strangers and prefer familiar people and develops motor skills such as crawling and walking.

Stage 4 involves development of the tertiary parietal region at the rear of the parietal lobe of the brain. This stage is normally completed at about age six or seven (though it may be completed as early as age three or as late as age twelve). This area of the brain compares and relates information that is processed by other parts of the brain, such as the temporal and occipital lobes. Some researchers believe that IQ (intelligence quotient) is primarily a test of this region of the brain. When this area matures, the child is able to begin such higher mental functions as reading, writing, grammar, and logic, and is ready for formal education.

When this part of the brain matures later than average, the child will probably not be able to perform the standard academic functions for his or her age and grade level. This does not mean that the child is retarded or learning-disabled—although he or she may be misdiagnosed as such. Such children should be allowed to wait rather than being forced into an educational situation in which they will perform poorly and develop problems in their self-esteem.

Injuries to the tertiary parietal region during or prior to Stage 4 can produce problems ranging from a learning disability called dyslexia to major mental retardation, depending on the severity of the injury. Problems can also arise if a developmentally immature child is pushed into formal education before he or she is ready.

Dyslexia is a developmental disorder that causes difficulty in learning to read. It afflicts about 5 percent of the population and is more common in boys than in girls. In addition to being caused by damage to the tertiary parietal region (for example, because of injury or oxygen deprivation during birth), dyslexia is also believed to have a genetic cause in many individuals.

Stage 5 occurs in adolescence and involves the development of the prefrontal (or tertiary frontal) region of the brain. This region continues to mature throughout adolescence and is not completely mature in most individuals until almost the mid-twenties. This region of the brain involves planning and judgment.

One of the most important concerns for learning-disabled children is the issue of self-esteem. Learning-disabled children are often held back in school so that they can catch up academically. Children naturally want to remain with their age group and feel singled out when they are held back. If this happens, it is best for children to experience as much normalcy and contact with their own age group as possible. For example, a child who has been required to repeat the second grade in school should still be permitted to attend the third grade Sunday school class with his or her peers, since the concerns of a Sunday school class are spiritual and relational, not academic and developmental.

Regardless of what class a learning-disabled child is in, he or she should be encouraged and inspired to do his or her best work. Many children who are learning disabled in one area (say, verbal skills) may have great academic strengths in other areas (math, for example). The child should be affirmed and praised for those strengths while an attempt is made to compensate for those weak areas.

If a child feels bad about himself for a weak area, say, "There's nothing to feel bad about. Remember, God made everyone with certain talents, and you have some very special talents that you can use for God."

ADULT LEARNING PROBLEMS

Many adults experience problems with learning, continuing education, Bible study, and even concentration during prayer and meditation. Though they may or may not have had learning problems in the past, they find themselves daydreaming, wandering, or unable to focus. There are several possible causes for adult learning problems:

1. Attention deficit disorder. Though this disorder generally affects children, some adults do not completely grow out of it and may continue to have occasional residual hyperactivity and diminished attention span. (See ATTENTION DEFICIT DISORDER.)

2. Anxiety. Feelings of fear, worry, panic, and anxiety cloud our thinking and make it difficult to concentrate. Both current stresses and repressed past emotional issues can contribute to anxiety. (See ANXIETY.)

3. Depression. This problem is most common among people in their forties and fifties but may strike at any age. Poor concentration is one of the main symptoms doctors look for when clinical depression is suspected. Other symptoms of depression include moodiness (sadness, crying, moping), loss of interest in personal appearance, problems with sleep, painful thinking (self-blame, guilt, remorse, suicidal thoughts), anxiety, loss of appetite, digestive disorders, and (in women) irregular or stopped menstrual periods. (See DEPRESSION.)

4. Schizophrenia. Preferring to daydream rather than to live in the real world is an early warning sign of mental illness.

5. Medical problems. A complete medical examination will help you rule out any organic causes for your lack of concentration. A psychiatrist can provide a mental evaluation. Problems with the brain or nervous system frequently can show up as memory lapses or an inability to concentrate and focus. If your doctors find no physiological or mental disorders, seek Christian counseling, which may help you to confront any hurtful memories you may have been carrying since childhood.

Learning should be a lifelong process and goal for us all. We learn more about life, about spiritual reality, and about God as we experience fellowship with other believers and as we study and learn from God's Word. It is there, in the Bible, that life's truest and most applicable lessons are to be learned.

> **Learning is a process of acquiring not only information but insight and wisdom.**

Legalism

A legalistic religious system requires gaining God's acceptance through good works and rigid adherence to a strict moral law. Legalism is the basis of most of the world's religions. In fact, most people have a legalistic notion of Christianity, believing that those who go to heaven are those who live good enough lives.

Legalism, however, runs completely counter to biblical Christianity, the heart of which is *grace*. If legalism were the basis of Christianity, there would be no room for grace. God's acceptance would depend on our own works and righteousness, and Jesus would have died for no reason. Moreover, we would never know any peace or assurance of salvation in a legalistic religious system, since we could never be sure we have been "good enough" to be accepted by God.

Grace is God's unmerited, undeserved favor. God's amazing grace has saved us from the penalty of our sins (eternal death) and has given to us—as undeserving as we are—the assurance of eternal life in heaven with Him. Perhaps the most amazing fact of all concerning God's grace is the fact that He has given grace to us "up front"—before we trusted Him and before we loved Him. We receive His grace by placing our faith and trust in Jesus Christ (see FAITH).

The moment we commit our lives to Jesus Christ as Lord and Savior, we receive total, unconditional love and acceptance. Our sins are blotted out. We are justified and declared righteous because the merit of Jesus Christ covers us and washes away the stain of our sin. Our security in life and in the life to come is based solely on God's unconditional love and acceptance of us—*by grace through faith*—and that can never be taken away from us.

If our relationship is based on faith and grace rather than our own righteousness and good works, then are good works important? Absolutely! As Paul says in Romans 6:1–2, "What shall we say then? Shall we continue in sin that grace may abound? Certainly not! How shall we who died to sin live any longer in it?"

Good works and a godly life are still vital to us and important to God—not because good works can save us. They can't! But as believers, we should *want* to please God—not out of fear of damnation, but out of love and gratitude for our salvation. If we have no desire to live godly lives, then we should question whether our commitment to Christ is really genuine.

Jesus exemplified this truth in his dealings with the woman who was caught in the act of adultery. The legalistic religious leaders brought the woman to Jesus, demanding that she be condemned to death. But Jesus responded to this woman with words of grace. "He who is without sin among you," He said to the religious legalists, "let him throw a stone at her first" (John 8:7). This statement silenced them, for even the most rigid and self-righteous legalist had to confess that there was sin in his life.

Then Jesus turned to the woman and said, "Has no one condemned you? . . . Neither do I condemn you; go and sin no more" (vv. 10–11). He offered her grace—but He also confronted her behavior. She was to leave her life of sin, not so that she could be saved by her own righteous actions, but so that by her new lifestyle she could demonstrate her gratitude to God for His grace and forgiveness.

The tragedy of legalism is that it engenders a great deal of fear, anxiety, insecurity, and guilt. The legalist continually tries to earn God's acceptance, and continually, obsessively frets over the fear that he has not done enough. The grace-oriented Christian can relax and rest in the acceptance and unconditional love of God.

■

True learning changes our behavior, and draws us, soul and spirit, closer to God. As Moses taught the people in Deuteronomy 5:1, "Hear, O Israel, the statues and judgments which I speak in your hearing today, that you may learn them and be careful to observe them."

■

Loneliness

Nancy is a widow in her sixties. She has no financial worries and lives alone in the huge house where she and her husband, Rex, spent forty happy years together. She attends church every Sunday, slipping into the back of the early service and leaving by the side door so that she doesn't have to greet anyone when the service is over. She knows the neighbors on either side of her home well enough to wave and smile, but she never socializes with them. Nancy has a daughter who lives three states away and who calls once a month. People often ask Nancy how she likes living alone. "Fine, just fine," she will say with her brittle smile and sadness in her eyes. "I like being alone. I have a very comfortable life." When Nancy cries, nobody else sees.

Rafer is a successful businessman with a strong handshake and an outgoing personality. Though he's always busy, always on the move, he makes time to be involved in his church, serving as a member of the board of elders. Ask anyone and they'll tell you: "Ol' Rafe has lots of friends, tons of friends! Yessir, everybody likes ol' Rafe." But one day, as Rafer and his pastor were having lunch together, Rafe said something shocking. "Pastor," he said, "there are probably five or six hundred people who think of me as their friend. But I can't think of one person in this world that I could call at three in the morning if I had a real problem. I can't think of one person in this world who is really the kind of friend you read about in Proverbs, the kind that 'sticks closer than a brother.' I'm surrounded by people every day of my life, yet I've never felt so alone."

Ashley is sixteen, a good student, a good kid from a good family. Lately, she's been finding excuses to withdraw from the youth group at church. She feels plain, unlikable, awkward. "There are people who are nice to me," she says, "but they're the same people who are nice to everybody. Nobody wants to be my friend because of *me*. My parents say, 'We're your friends, sweetheart; talk to us about your problems.'" She wrinkles her nose and makes a face. "Yuck! Who wants to have their *parents* as their only friends in the world? Let's face it. I'm homely, I've got all the personality of a potato, and I'll never have any friends. Why does God even bother putting miserable people like me on the planet?"

Nancy, Rafer, and Ashley are three very different people, but they all have one thing in common: they are all very lonely. Loneliness knows no social, economic, or age boundaries. It afflicts people who live in isolation. It also afflicts people who live amid crowds and a fast-paced social whirl. Loneliness is not just the feeling that nobody is around. It is the feeling that "nobody understands, nobody cares, nobody knows the real me."

In Genesis 2:18, after the Lord God created the first man, He said, "It is not good that man should be alone." Truer words were never spoken! We were created and designed to live in relationships and in fellowship with other human beings. We deeply desire to know other people and to be known by them, to have at least one other human being truly enter our lives, to understand our pain, and to share our joys.

THE SOURCES OF LONELINESS

Everyone struggles with loneliness at some point in his or her life. One survey showed that about 25 percent of adult respondents said they had felt very lonely in the preceding few weeks. Teenagers reported an even higher percentage; many teenagers feel rejected or ignored by their peer group, and they believe that no one understands or cares about their worries, fears, and problems. Loneliness is common among young mothers who spend day after day taking care of children and having very little adult interaction. Loneliness is also common among older adults who have experienced losses in their lives—perhaps the loss of a spouse, certainly the loss of many friends over the years, and often the loss of family ties as children move away to pursue their careers. The most common cause of loneliness is *loss* owing to death, separation, or divorce.

Loneliness is epidemic in our changing, mobile society. Every year, about one-fifth of American families move to a new location. The average American changes addresses once every five years. Even if you haven't moved in the past forty years, odds are that many of your neighbors, close friends, relatives, and pastors have—and you are left alone.

Some people erect a wall of loneliness as a defense against rejection. *If I don't make friends,* they think, *then no one will ever leave me, hurt me, or reject me. I will reject the world before anyone can reject me.* Such self-defeating attitudes are usually rooted in childhood and adolescent experiences of rejection; their ability to trust other people has been damaged. In other cases, people who make themselves lonely are people whose childhood developmental needs of acceptance and affection were not met. In still other cases, people who create their own "loneliness zone" are those who never acquired the social skills to make friends.

Loneliness is compounded when we keep our feelings inside. Some of us truly have no one to talk to, but many of us choose isolation by deciding to live by a code of stoic, rugged individualism; or by thinking, "I don't want to burden anyone with my problems"; or thinking, "I don't want to show weakness"; or thinking, "No one wants to hear what I'm going through. I'll just keep it to myself."

People who are not gifted or attractive may be lonely simply because other people are not attracted to them. But the opposite extreme also can result in loneliness. People who are extremely intelligent, attractive, or creative may be very lonely because (1) they work such long hours at their creative or academic pursuits that they miss out on social opportunities, or (2) they are wary in relationships, believing that other people only like them for their looks or their abilities, and not for who they really are inside. In many cases, work and achievement become barriers, preventing these individuals from having to allow other people into their lives.

Diagnosing Your Loneliness

SELF-TEST

The following inventory can help you determine your level of loneliness. Place a check mark before each statement you identify or agree with. Answer quickly, without taking very much time to ponder. If in doubt, check off the statement. Your most immediate response is usually the most accurate.

____ I sometimes hurt inside.
____ I often feel empty inside.
____ I sometimes yearn to be with another person.
____ I sometimes feel restless and bored.
____ I frequently do not feel accepted by a group I am with.

_____ I sometimes feel "I don't belong here."

_____ I frequently worry that others may not accept me.

_____ I occasionally suspect that other people avoid me.

_____ I sometimes feel that others are smarter than I am.

_____ I sometimes feel that others are better-looking than I am.

_____ I sometimes feel that others are more confident and talented than I am.

_____ I wish I could be more outgoing.

_____ I belong to few clubs or organizations.

_____ Even though I belong to one or more groups, I don't really feel a part of them.

_____ Nobody really knows who I am inside.

_____ I feel abandoned, misunderstood, or unsupported by people in my church or my family.

_____ I sometimes do not feel that God is close to me.

_____ My friends have no idea of the problems I'm going through.

_____ I don't want anyone to know I feel sad or lonely.

_____ I spend a lot of hours alone.

_____ I feel that no one can ever really know another individual.

_____ I seldom associate with people my own age.

_____ I often withdraw into daydreaming.

_____ I often enjoy my inner fantasy world more than being with people.

_____ I don't feel I really need friends.

_____ I often feel desperate for friends.

_____ I would rather talk about theories, issues, and intellectual subjects than talk about real feelings.

_____ I sometimes use humor to avoid facing my own loneliness or sadness, or to keep others from knowing how much I hurt inside.

_____ I have many physical aches and pains.

_____ I wish I could be more open about my emotions.

_____ I rarely confront people who have hurt me; I would rather withdraw.

_____ When I'm alone, I sometimes do things I shouldn't—binge eating, drinking, using drugs, watching too much television.

_____ I often feel very guilty.

_____ I often feel angry or sad.

_____ I often think about mistakes I've made; I frequently focus on regrets.

_____ I often help others, but others rarely help me.

_____ I often feel put down by others.

_____ I am often preoccupied with my looks.

_____ I am often preoccupied with work, achievement, and success.

_____ I wish I were more popular.

_____ I was not very popular in high school or college.

_____ I was not very active in social activities in school.

_____ I have not dated much.

_____ I sometimes have trouble trusting others.

_____ I have sometimes used alcohol or drugs to escape from feeling bad inside.

_____ I work hard so I can forget my feelings or so I don't have to be home alone.

378

_____ I have had few friends all my life.
_____ My relationships with others are often stormy and unstable.
_____ I sometimes feel rejected, even by my closest friends.
_____ Others seldom come to see me or call me.
_____ I have often felt inferior to others.
_____ I hate it when people criticize me.
_____ I often criticize others.
_____ I feel that being a leader is a lonely job.
_____ People have told me I'm aloof or "stuck up."
_____ I have trouble forming lasting relationships.
_____ I feel awful when people reject me.
_____ I would like to be around people, but I'm afraid they won't like me.
_____ I don't really want to be around people very much.
_____ I would rather vacation alone than with friends or family.
_____ I often worry about my relationships with others.
_____ When I am with other people, I feel anxious and uncomfortable.
_____ I have sometimes felt so lonely that I had little reason to live.

Now go back and count the number of check marks. A score of 20 or less indicates that you are probably not lonely very often. A score of 21 to 29 indicates that you experience loneliness at times but probably do a fair job of tolerating, managing, and emerging from your loneliness. A score of 30 or more reflects a definite struggle with feelings of loneliness. You should strongly consider implementing the suggestions in the action plan in this article for conquering loneliness. You may also want to consider counseling for any issues in your life that interfere with your relationship with God and with others.

AN ACTION PLAN FOR CONQUERING LONELINESS

Loneliness does not have to be permanent. Properly understood, feelings of loneliness are a "wake-up call," signaling to us that we have important emotional needs that are not being met. The solution to loneliness is to identify and meet those needs. Here is an action plan for discovering our needs and conquering our loneliness:

1. Assess your emotional needs. Are you feeling stressed out and have no one to share your struggles with? Or do you just want someone to know the real you? Do you need someone to confess your sins to, someone to hold you accountable to make constructive changes in your life? Do you lack confidence and need a friend who can help you gain the self-assurance to attempt a major challenge in your life? As you gain a clearer sense of your emotional needs, you will be able to understand exactly what you are looking for in a friend.

2. *Reach out to people who are serious about authentic relationships.* You may ask, "Where do I find people like that?" Answer: Many churches offer small group Bible studies and support groups that are perfectly designed for people who need friends. Contact your pastor and ask about the small group ministries in your church. If your church doesn't offer such groups, find a church that does. The people in these groups are committed to relationships, they are committed to being open and accepting, and they are eager to know and befriend new people. In these groups, people pray for each other, care for each other, get together socially, and express the love of God to one another.

3. *Disclose yourself to a few trusted people.* Don't be embarrassed to go into a group and honestly ask for help. Take a week or two to get comfortable with the group and build your trust level, then let down your walls and let the people in the group see who you really are. And don't just take from the group; give as well. Be a good listener and a good friend. Become involved in other people's lives as they become involved in yours.

4. *Sharpen your social skills.* One of the best ways to get people to take an interest in you is to take an interest in people. Ask people about themselves, about their careers, their children, their interests, their hopes for the future, their faith, how they came to know the Lord. It is always refreshing and enjoyable to meet someone who is truly interested in you, so turn the situation around, become interested in others, and you will soon find yourself connecting with people on a deep level.

5. *Place yourself in new situations.* Take on new interests and activities in which you will get out and meet new people. Volunteer for ministries at church. Get involved in recreation activities through your job or a health club. Look for avenues of community service. Get involved with your local political party organization or with a community club.

6. *Reach out to lonely people.* When you see someone sitting alone at church, sit down and introduce yourself. Ask people out for lunch after church. Find an exercise partner at the gym. Make a point of getting to know your neighbors. Focus on one person at a time. When you give caring and attention, you often receive caring and attention in return.

7. *Turn off the TV.* Television can be like a drug we use to anesthetize our loneliness. People often "zonk out" in front of the TV so they won't have to deal with other people or with their own emotions and issues. Television also reduces the amount of time we have to devote to friendships and social activities. Research shows that excessive TV watching makes people more fearful, distrustful, and cynical—emotional qualities that tend to deepen our isolation and loneliness.

8. *Don't forget to smile.* You'll be amazed how a warm, open, friendly expression on your face can open doors to lasting friendships.

9. *Be patient.* Sometimes people "scare" potential friends away by rushing intimacy, by spilling their entire life story onto shy, reserved people they have just met. Give friendship time to grow. Give people time to learn who you are and that you can be trusted.

10. *Seek friendship with God.* Our Lord is a Friend who understands loneliness. Jesus was subjected to intense loneliness when He was abandoned and betrayed by His disciples at the time of His arrest (see Matthew 26:56 and Mark 14:50). When He was

Human companionship, as important as it may be, cannot fill the place in our lives that was made for God alone.

on the cross, dying, He said, "My God, My God, why have You forsaken Me?" (Mark 15:34).

Within each of us is a God-shaped void, an emptiness that can only be filled by a relationship with God Himself. Until we find our connection with Him, we will always be lonely. If you have never experienced a relationship with God through faith in His Son, Jesus Christ, then you can begin that experience right now. (For a thorough explanation of what it means to know God and how you can begin a relationship with Him, see FAITH.)

If you feel isolated from God, consider the sources of those feelings of isolation. There is a saying, "If God seems distant, ask yourself, 'Who moved?'" God always wants to have a relationship with us, but there are many kinds of barriers that sometimes cloud our relationship with God. Some of us have had negative childhood experiences that cause us to project a negative image onto God; for example, if we had cold, unloving, distant parents, we will likely project an image onto God that is cold, unloving, and distant, even though the Bible presents Him as a loving, tender Father (see the section "What Is Your Image of God?" in the article on FAITH).

We also experience isolation from God as a result of sin. Patterns and attitudes of sin break our fellowship with God because God cannot have fellowship with sin. Adam and Eve even experienced this principle; before their sin, they had close fellowship with God, but after their sin they hid from God. If there is sin in your life, deal with it, confess it, turn from it, and ask God to cleanse your heart. Meditate on Psalm 51, the psalm David wrote after repenting of his sin with Bathsheba. As you pray, take time to be still and listen for God to speak comfort to your heart. Wait—and feel His loving Presence surround you.

Jesus has promised never to leave us or forsake us (see Matthew 28:20). He hears us when we pray. His Holy Spirit comes to us as the Comforter. He is ready and eager to meet with us and have intimate fellowship with us. He gives us a beautiful word-picture of intimate fellowship with Him in Revelation 3:20, where He says, "Behold, I stand at the door and knock. If anyone hears My voice and opens the door, I will come in to him and dine with him, and he with Me."

See also RELATIONSHIPS

Manic-Depression

Manic-depressive disorder (also called *bipolar disorder*) is a comparatively infrequent illness that is probably genetic in origin. The symptoms of this illness include extreme swings of mood from a delusional, grandiose euphoria (marked by rapid, excessive, excited talking) to severe depression with suicidal tendencies.

THE MANIC PHASE

In the manic (euphoric) phase, individuals are cheerful, ambitious, optimistic, and so uncritically self-confident that their judgment is impaired. They experience marked increases in speech and motor ability. The euphoric mood resembles the "high" of a person who abuses amphetamines. During this phase, the individual demonstrates contagious good cheer, though his good mood can turn instantly to irritation and anger if frustrated. At that point, the individual often becomes verbally abusive and caustic and may cause an embarrassing scene.

During the manic phase, the individual's ambition and optimism know no bounds. He bubbles over with enthusiasm, grandiosity, and a vastly inflated sense of his own abilities and talent. The individual's judgment is so impaired that he may sit down and start writing a novel. The result may be completely incoherent, but the manic individual will believe it to be the greatest piece of literature since *Moby Dick.* Or he may withdraw his life savings and sink it all into a crackpot business deal, believing he is going to make millions. He talks rapidly, excessively, switching from topic to topic so quickly that those around him are unable to follow. He may talk loudly and abrasively and sprinkle his high-flying, optimistic dream-spinning with insensitive jokes or hostile sarcasm. In this state, the individual will be intrusive, domineering, and demanding; he will expect others to support his improbable dreams and schemes, and to work as hard as he does to bring them about. He will ruthlessly berate those who oppose his wild plans.

Because of the revved-up state his body and mind are in, the individual will find it hard to sleep during the manic phase. He may call friends at all hours of the night and be surprised to find his friends have all been sleeping. Along with the euphoric mood comes extreme denial. The manic phase may, in fact, be a state of denial that there is an underlying depression at work.

THE DEPRESSIVE PHASE

The depressive phase or episode of the manic-depressive disorder is in complete contrast to the manic phase. The individual displays the classic symptoms of depression (see DEPRESSION), including low self-esteem, tearfulness, painful thinking, physical symptoms, withdrawal, anger, and sometimes delusional thinking. The individual will stop caring about personal grooming and will feel helpless, hopeless, worthless, and discouraged. Feelings of guilt and failure saturate the individual's thinking, and he ruminates on gloomy, self-critical thoughts. Motivation dries up. The individual withdraws from relationships and frequently becomes suicidal—a major concern in such cases.

Physical symptoms may include restlessness, inability to concentrate, sleep disturbance, appetite disturbance, weight loss (or gain), low energy, difficulty in getting started in the morning, constipation, diarrhea, and headaches. Emotional symptoms may include anxiety, irritability, paranoia, and delusions of being persecuted by God or other people because of some sin, real or imagined.

382

TREATMENT

The manic phase can be successfully treated with lithium salt and the depressive phase with antidepressant medications. Manic-depressive disorder can only be controlled by medical treatment.

Marriage

"We've got a silver wedding anniversary coming up in six months," said Gene, "and after all these years I sure thought we'd be a couple of old married folks, all bored and settled in. But our marriage still has more ups and downs than one of those roller coasters at Six Flags. Sometimes, for weeks on end, I'd swear we're still on our honeymoon, and other times it's like the mother of all domestic battles, complete with kitchen utensils flying through the air."

"Now, Gene's exaggerating," said Gwen. "I never threw any kitchen utensils at him. But when it comes to marital spats, we have sure had some doozies. And it can get so confusing. I mean, some of the things we fight about now were problems even before we got married—we just never got them resolved. And then there are the new problems, the changes that take place in our marriage that we have a hard time adjusting to. I never imagined that a marriage could go through so many changes over the years. I never thought I'd be in my late forties and still have to make adjustments in my relationship with Gene."

The situation that Gene and Gwen describe is not uncommon. Few of us go into marriage with any realization of how dynamic and ever-changing the marriage relationship is. Or how many aspects of a marriage that *should* change *don't*. Gene and Gwen came to a Minirth Meier New Life Clinic for counseling after twenty-five years of marriage, but the fact is that *anytime* is a good time to take a good, hard look at the marriage relationship, to understand the passages and changes that a marriage goes through, to understand how marriage communication functions (and malfunctions), and to learn how to work more effectively together as a marriage team.

When people come to one of the clinics for marriage counseling, they usually come because of a painful symptom in the marriage, and they want the doctors at the clinic to fix the symptom so that they will feel better and they can get on with their married lives. The symptom might be chronic fighting. Or problems with (or about) the children. Or power imbalances and family alliances ("us" against "them"). Or there might be emotional problems such as anxiety or depression. Or there might be codependency and compulsive behavior problems, such as chemical dependence or workaholism.

As serious and painful as these symptoms are, they are just the surface stuff, the tip of the iceberg. They are problems, but they are not The Problem. They just signal that something far deeper and more fundamental is not right near the throbbing heart of the marriage. Our goal in counseling is to plumb the depths of these problems, to cut out the tumors, not just put bandages on the marital bruises and abrasions.

THE PASSAGES OF MARRIAGE

The inner workings of marriage can be compared to the dynamics of a softball game. The city league softball player steps up to the plate, shoulders his bat, and watches intently. Here comes the pitch . . .

"It's a solid hit into deep right field!" the announcer screams. The ball is still airborne as the player rounds first. The ball arcs into the tall grass, very deep right field, landing with a thud. The somewhat overpadded and portly fielder huffs and puffs after the rolling ball. The player passes third, homeward bound—but wait!

He failed to touch second!

As his team groans in unison, the runner dashes back to second base and tags up. What should have been a home run now ends up as only a double—all because the runner failed to touch all the bases. Marriage is like that. But in the "game" of marriage, we call the bases *passages*.

When the doctors and counselors at the Minirth Meier New Life Clinics deal with marital issues, we look at three entities: the husband, the wife, and the marriage itself. Is the marriage an entity? Absolutely. It is practically a living, breathing organism. It has life cycles, vital signs, and symptoms of dysfunction, just like a living organism. And we have found that if a marriage is not growing, it's dying, just as with any living organism. When a marriage gets stuck in a passage, it stops growing. And if growth is stopped for a long enough time, death is right around the corner. Growth is critically important to healthy relationships.

Passages are predictable and necessary stages, involving the physical, the emotional, and the spiritual dimensions of the relationship. Through these passages, partners journey toward the lifetime goal of growth as individuals and as a couple.

The Five Passages of Marriage

Not counting courtship, we divide the lifetime of a married couple into five segments. These passages are:

1. Young Love: the first 2 years
2. Realistic Love: the 3rd through 10th years
3. Comfortable Love: the 11th through 25th years
4. Renewing Love: the 26th through 35th years
5. Transcendent Love: 36 years and thereafter

There are five distinct stages through which a marriage must pass. A marriage matures from one developmental stage to the next, from passage to passage, according to the passage of time and the changes that take place in the three entities, husband, wife, and marriage. Remarriages may differ somewhat, because they tend to telescope some passages into a briefer span of time, or extend a passage beyond its normal life span. But on the whole, these passages describe the course of the vast majority of marriage relationships.

As the marriage moves from one passage to another, from base to base toward home plate, it also moves through specific conditions common to the human race: crisis and conflict, intimacy, forgiveness, children, and memories.

Like bases on a softball diamond, each passage must be appropriately dealt with and negotiated if the next one is to count. The tasks that accompany each passage must be completed before the next tasks begin. These tasks are attitude changes and jobs that need to be completed in order to maintain an intimate marital relationship. If a runner skips a base, problems result. If a runner gets stuck on one base, the only way he can leave is by walking away scoreless. That's infinitely less satisfying than making it to home plate, for the aim of the game from the very beginning is to make it home.

WHAT IF YOUR MARRIAGE DOESN'T FIT THE PATTERN?

Remember the age-guessing booth at carnivals long ago? A rather rough-looking man with a four-day stubble would offer to guess your age within three years. If he guessed correctly, he won and you paid him. If he missed, you won and he paid you. And he almost always won. Why? Because age makes itself known in certain ways, and the trained eye can see those ways in every person.

A marriage also ages in certain predictable ways, regardless of the people involved or the circumstances. The same patterns prevail even though yours may be a most unusual union. After all, what is "normal"?

"My wife, Mary Alice, and I know our marriage could probably never be considered normal," says Dr. Frank Minirth. "When we married, we were both in school. I was in medical school, and I studied day and night. She had two more years to complete her degree, so she was studying too. It wasn't a normal start-a-family situation. Her first job was as a teacher in inner-city Little Rock. Definitely not normal! And I worked long days completing my internship. And, of course, there's nothing normal about getting a medical practice started. Yet, despite the nontypical aspects of our marriage, we can look back and see that our marriage did follow the typical passages of marriage. Today, we are happily in our fourth passage of marriage.

The passages of marriage are the common denominators of any marriage. They are universal. They form the Christmas tree on which we hang the ornaments of a life shared together—the joys, the memories, the problems, the emotions, the love.

"There are all kinds of marriage situations. You have Navy marriages where a husband and wife don't see each other for months when the husband ships out. There are couples who run mom-and-pop stores and are side by side every day of their lives for fifty years. There are the special stresses on a marriage when one partner is an over-the-road trucker. Or a top CEO who jets around the world, cutting high-level business deals. When you get down to it, every situation is unique and every couple is unique and every individual is unique. So if all of these aspects of marriage are unique, what is 'normal'? The answer is simple: The *passages* are normal."

How about *your* marriage? Have you successfully completed the passages of your marriage thus far? Are there bases you need to go back and tag? Are there passage-related issues you need to go back and resolve? Could your marriage be happier and more secure if you gave it some conscious examination and work?

If your first marriage ended in divorce, do you now begin to see the underlying reasons why it failed? In most divorces, the marriage-busting trouble comes when one or both partners get hung up in a passage and fail to complete the tasks of that passage.

If you play chess or backgammon, you know that the strategy changes as the game proceeds. Your goals at the beginning of play aren't the same as those at the end. It's that way with marriage too. The original contract ceases to serve and must be rewritten. Every marriage changes with time, just as every individual grows and changes over time. Sometimes, couples use "growth" as an excuse for dismantling their marriage. "We just grew apart," they say. But "growing apart" is no excuse for divorce. When couples see themselves growing apart, they can sit down, examine their relationship, and decide how they are going to grow together.

SUGGESTIONS FOR A HEALTHY MARRIAGE AT ANY PASSAGE

The passages of marriage concept gives us the tool to understand the growth and change that occurs in a marriage relationship.

Before we look at each specific passage in the life of a marriage, here is a list of suggestions that can and should be implemented at any and every stage in a marriage. These suggestions are offered as a guide to help you gain insight into the dynamics of your own marriage relationship.

1. *Commit yourselves to spiritual growth.* It's crucial to grow spiritually as a couple. Study together. Pray together. Find fellowship together with believers. Invite God to have a place of honor in every room of your home, in every arena of your life.

2. *Decide to act as a team.* Don't make a big decision without consulting one another. Questions of finance, child raising, lifestyle, and major purchases all pertain to the marriage partners as a unit, not as individuals. The welfare of the marriage itself depends on harmony in these (and other) areas. Teamwork requires that the team members keep in step, each knowing what the other thinks and does. Sharing decision-making responsibility spins off benefits to the relationship, because the process of making decisions together generates deeper intellectual and emotional intimacy.

3. *Make time to share personal issues.* Couples need to keep each other informed regarding feelings, needs, and perceptions. A day should not go by without at least a quarter hour set aside to discuss important events and concerns, highs and lows, joys and struggles. This openness creates camaraderie and a sense of team spirit ("us against the world," not "me against you") that can carry a couple through difficult times in any passage of marriage.

4. *Confront problems before they have a chance to grow.* People are imperfect, and that means problems will inevitably arise. However, couples can choose to confront problems regularly so that they don't have a chance to turn into crises. Issues should be discussed succinctly, considerately, not in monologues but in genuine dialogues in which both sides listen and wish to hear, learn, and grow.

5. *Avoid controlling behavior.* A controlling spirit can be manifested in many ways, both subtle and overt: possessiveness, intimidation, manipulation, bossiness, pouting, the silent treatment, procrastination, lying, and tuning out. The goal of such behavior is to satisfy our emotional needs to get our way while forcing our mates to react. The result is conflict and resentment. No adult wants to be controlled, and every adult understands what is happening when someone else tries to control him or her. When a marriage becomes a team partnership, competitiveness and controlling are replaced by loving, mutual interaction.

386

6. *Look for common ground.* Some spouses become so immersed in their individual private worlds that a huge gap opens up between them. Spouses should be curious about each other's goals and interested in each other's feelings. One partner should not be expected to have an expert understanding of the other's career, hobbies, and activities, but a working understanding, plus an attitude of support and caring, can be very useful in building common ground for an ongoing relationship.

7. *Maintain balanced time commitments.* Just as plants need water and sunshine, relationships need time for healthy growth. The classic complaint of so many wives is "He's never home!" In recent years, however, as more and more women pursue active careers, we have begun to hear, "She's never home!" Those spouses who are home sometimes misuse the relationship-building time they have at their fingertips, choosing instead to squander it on TV or other time-wasters. There are two ways to spell *love* in a marriage and in a family: L-O-V-E and T-I-M-E.

8. *Minimize stress factors.* There are many invaders seeking to storm the walls of your marriage castle and take your relationship hostage. Don't let them. Beware the invasion of the stress factors. There are many wonderful, worthwhile things that are important, that need your time, and that—if you are not careful to keep them in their place—will suck the blood right out of your marriage relationship. Church commitments. School commitments. Service clubs. Social clubs. Committees. The kids' groups, such as scouts and athletic teams. Volunteer organizations. Once-a-year activities like Thanksgiving, the home and garden show, the fair, or the Christmas pageant. You can't eliminate these stress factors, and you wouldn't want to. But they must not be allowed to take over and occupy the territory that belongs to your marriage relationship.

9. *Accept the fact that there is no such thing as an ideal relationship.* People who have romanticized, idealized images of marriage tend to become disillusioned with the marriage they are in, look for a way out as soon as the going gets tough, and then move from marriage to marriage in search of that elusive "happily-ever-after" storybook ending. When you get married, it's time to get real. The ideal marriage doesn't exist. But two people in a less-than-ideal marriage can always work together to make it a better marriage.

10. *Accept the fact that marriage takes work.* Couples tend to look at other couples and say, "Why can't we be like them? They were made for each other! They're always so in love! They don't have all the problems and pain that we have." Maybe, maybe not. We don't know what goes on behind other couples' closed doors—and we can be thankful that they don't know what goes on behind ours! Some of what we take to be "a marriage made in heaven" may just be a facade. Or the beauty of a given marriage may be real—but if it is, it is almost certainly the result of hard work, commitment, and a willingness to love no matter what the situation. Marriage takes work. The sooner we learn this truth, the happier we will be.

The First Passage: Young Love (The First 2 Years)

The essential tasks that must be accomplished in order to complete successfully the first passage of marriage are:

> ■
> *Regularly sharing feelings and discussing issues is one way we live out Paul's counsel in Ephesians 4:26: "Do not let the sun go down on your wrath."*
> ■

The Major Tasks of the Passages of Marriage

Passage 1: Young Love—the first 2 years

- mold into one family
- overcome the tendency to jockey for control
- build a sexual union
- make responsible choices
- deal with your parents' incomplete passages

Passage 2: Realistic Love—the 3rd through 10th years

- hang on to love after reality strikes
- recognize the hidden contracts in your marriage
- write a new marriage contract
- childproof your marriage

Passage 3: Comfortable Love—the 11th through 25th years

- maintain an individual identity along with your marriage identity
- say the final goodbyes
- overcome the now-or-never syndrome
- practice true forgiveness
- accept the inevitable losses
- help your adolescent become an individual
- maintain an intimate relationship

Passage 4: Renewing Love—the 26th through 35th years

- combat the crisis of this passage
- maintain companionship and unity
- grieve the particular losses of this passage

Passage 5: Transcendent Love—36 years and thereafter

- prepare for retirement
- achieve a transcendent perspective
- accept your one and only God-given life

- mold into one family
- overcome the tendency to jockey for control
- build a sexual union
- make responsible choices
- deal with your parents' incomplete passages

The more conscious couples are of these tasks and what they must do to complete them, the more effective, healthy, and happy they will be in marriage—and the safer the marriage union will be from the threat of conflict, crisis, and divorce. Let's examine each of these tasks more closely:

Mold into one family. It isn't easy to mold two different people from different backgrounds into a cohesive, functional unit. It's especially hard to do so without sacrificing each partner's individuality. The couple must learn to pull up old roots and change old habits and to recognize that "the way we always did it in my family" isn't the only way it can be done. As a couple begins creating their new family system, each partner attempts to put original family patterns behind and begins to reshape their relationship. Finding the new balance is rocky, and the balance is never perfect. Conflict is inevitable, no matter what the ages or backgrounds. Often the couple's ability to handle this conflict is stifled by fragile egos, idealized images of marital bliss, and immaturity.

Overcome the tendency to jockey for control. Most marriages are stormy and tempestuous in these first few years. This can be very disillusioning to a young couple starting out. The idealism of young married love says, "We're not supposed to be fighting. We're just supposed to *love* each other." Thank goodness, then, for young love's most powerful tools for preserving the relationship, *excitement* and *enthusiasm*.

When conflict arises in the relationship, there are many ways a couple can choose to respond, including blaming, grudge-keeping, intimidating, withdrawing, and passive-aggressive undermining. All of these responses are unhealthy and destructive. There are, however, three *healthy* and *constructive* ways for a couple to respond to conflict:

1. compromise
2. agreeing to disagree
3. giving in

This last option is a beautiful gift of love that one partner gives to the other. It is important to note, however, that there should be a healthy level of mutuality in the relationship. It's good if some problems are resolved by one partner giving in—as long as it's not the same partner who gives in every time! In a healthy relationship, both partners serve each other, both partners give, and both partners take.

Build a sexual union. Sex is the most intimate expression of oneself to another human being. It is emotional and physical fusion. During this passage, it is important for partners to discover each other's needs. The husband's needs will often tend to be immediate and physically passionate, whereas the wife's needs will tend to be emotional, affectionate, a desire to be close and to be held. During the first passage, the couple needs to learn to balance his sexual energy with her need for emotional security and intimacy.

The sexual dimension of marriage infuses the entire relationship. Lovemaking means much more than what takes place between the sheets. A couple builds a sexual union by talking together, taking walks together, holding hands, looking into each other's eyes, taking an interest in each other's interests, building a dream of the future together. When a couple takes such an all-inclusive view of their sexuality, the moment of climax becomes more than just the physical release at the end of a sex act; it becomes the beautiful culmination of all of those special, intimate moments that have been shared together throughout the day and throughout the week. (See SEX AND SEXUALITY.)

Make responsible choices. The first two years of most marriages occur during a time when the husband and wife are fairly fresh from the nests of their families of origin. They haven't gained a lot of practical experience in matters such as money management, time management, and relationship management.

A common choice that many young couples mishandle is the choice of a lifestyle. Two people come together from fairly affluent families, and they decide they want to live the same way their parents did, in a big house with two new cars, new appliances and nice furniture. Soon they are in hock up to their eyeballs, and they run to Mom and Dad for a loan to pay for it all. What they didn't realize is that most young couples—including Mom and Dad—start out with next to nothing and build up their net worth over a period of decades. A responsible lifestyle choice for most young couples is to start with an apartment, build up savings, drive a used car, work hard, and dream about the future.

Other choices that need to be made include: How do we make time for our relationship while we work hard to build our dreams? How do we resist the urge to "bail out" when things get tough? How do we maintain individual identity, individual boundaries, while at the same time coming together as a married unit? These are some of the choices that must be made with responsibility and growing maturity.

Deal with your parents' incomplete passages. As we were growing up in our parents' home, we absorbed attitudes and impressions about marriage and husband-wife roles from their example. We assume that our attitudes about marriage (which largely reflect the attitudes of our parents) are "normal" because those attitudes are the only ones we've ever known. Suddenly, we are thrown into a sink-or-swim situation with another person from another family background with a whole different set of attitudes that he or she thinks are "normal" but that we regard as "weird." It's time to reconsider, and to take a hard look at the attitudes and impressions we have absorbed by osmosis from our families of origin.

What passages or tasks did our parents fail to complete? Did they fail to overcome the tendency to jockey for control? Did they fail to learn how to make responsible choices? Did they fail to maintain individual identities? Fail to practice forgiveness? Unless you become consciously aware of these passages in your parents' life where they got stuck or derailed, you are likely to repeat their pattern.

What self-defeating attitudes did you absorb from your parents? "Men don't show emotion or say 'I love you.'" "Women can't be trusted with money." "Sex is a weapon in the battle of the sexes." "Keep your man on a short leash; men can't be trusted." Your parents' attitudes were probably never verbalized when you were growing up, but they were modeled, and you absorbed them unconsciously and uncritically. Now they have to be dug up like land mines, one by one, so that they can be defused. If you don't, they will continue to explode unexpectedly throughout your marriage, wounding both you and your spouse.

What's more, some of those land mines will still be lying around for your children to discover. A key principle of this passage of marriage is *All incomplete passages become unfinished business for the next generation.* If your parents left any unfinished business for you to deal with, then finish it now. Resolve these old issues in your present-day marriage, and make a commitment not to pass them on to your own children.

SELF-TEST

Have You Completed the Passage of Young Love?

Check the following statements that apply to you. This inventory determines if a couple has completed the First Passage. Make your own assessment and any adjustments that are necessary.

_____ I'm willing to bend on issues that have popped up regarding the nitty-gritty tasks of married life: who balances the checkbook, who does the cooking, who scrubs the toilet, and who cleans the kitchen floor.

_____ We have reached agreement on some major control issues.

_____ I'm willing to step out of my old family into this new one. Evidence that I'm maturing into my new role as a partner is:

_____

_____

_____ I have not come as far out of my family as I would like to, as illustrated by this instance:

_____

_____

____ Three things I can do to loosen my ties to my family of origin are:

1. _____
1. _____
1. _____
2. _____
1. _____
1. _____
3. _____
1. _____
1. _____

____ I'm willing to open up into intimacy. One recent instance in which I let myself be vulnerable to my mate is:

_____
_____

____ In this last week, we found time alone together (other than in bed!) ____ times.

____ I can honestly claim that our sex life is open, honest, and enjoyable for both of us, more so than in the beginning.

____ Okay. So I'm willing to admit that my romance with a perfect partner is an illusion. An ideal marriage is a myth. Marriage takes work. As evidence that the statement is true, I offer this incident:

_____
_____

____ I'm willing to pursue romance with my spouse anyway. Three recent instances in which my partner and I made a romantic gesture are:

1. _____
1. _____
1. _____
2. _____
1. _____
1. _____
3. _____
1. _____
1. _____

The Second Passage: Realistic Love (The 3rd Through 10th Years)

The essential tasks that must be accomplished in order to complete the second passage of marriage are:

- hang on to love after reality strikes
- recognize the hidden contracts in your marriage
- write a new marriage contract
- childproof your marriage

This is the transition from La-La Land to the Real World. After about two years of marriage, the observant couple will notice a lot of changes in the relationship, and not all the changes are good.

Hang on to love after reality strikes. These years bring realistic love. Can two people learn to walk together without tripping over each other? The marriage is no longer new. The excitement has probably faded. Partners start taking each other for granted. Sex, emotional intimacy, and communication have probably become familiar by this point. Everything that can be explored about the other person has been explored (at least that's the assumption; the fact is that both partners still have much more they can discover about the other person, if they are willing to look).

Recognize the hidden contracts in your marriage. The hidden agendas, the fine print of the marriage contract, don't surface much during the First Passage. The hidden contract may lie dormant for years, only to be triggered by some random event. It's crucial during this stage that both partners become aware of these hidden expectations, secret pressures, buried motives, and emotional symptoms.

Write a new marriage contract. After the hidden agendas have been unearthed and placed on the table for inspection, it's time to write a new marriage contract, replete with new, open agendas. The goal of a marriage contract isn't to agree on all points. You may reach the decision that you have different agendas and priorities in some areas. In those situations, you may simply have to agree on which issues you will disagree and tolerate each other's points of view. Match what you can and mesh the rest. A renewed marriage contract should contain:

1. Affirmation (state at least one attribute each person admires and appreciates in the other).
2. A statement of the extent of commitment to the marriage.
3. A promise of fidelity.
4. A statement of faith:

   • each person's individual statement of faith
   • clearly stated common ground
   • statement of tolerance (and limits of tolerance)

5. A statement of recognition of old, dysfunctional hidden agendas.
6. Declaration of new agendas to correct dysfunctions.
7. Sexual contract, including:

   • recognition of difficulties in present sexual relations
   • steps to improve relations
   • details of frequency, if frequency is an issue

8. Details of everyday life (for example, a request for romantic nights out) established through give and take. Be specific.

Childproof your marriage. The final task of this passage is to adapt to the changes that happen when little people enter your family. Kids: all-time world-class stressors. The sands of parenthood shift under our feet as rapidly as a newborn child changes. These changes take place in five stages:

■

The danger of this passage is boredom. But boredom isn't inevitable. The couple must find ways to continue exploring the vast undiscovered country of their relationship.

■

- surprise (the first child)
- drifting (school-age children)
- turmoil (adolescent children)
- renewal or death of a relationship (the empty nest)
- joy (grandchildren)

As the children grow, the marriage moves inexorably from reality toward comfort. Marriage is on its way to becoming like a familiar pair of old house slippers. This doesn't mean that all the stresses and perils of marriage are over. Quite the contrary, as we shall see . . .

Have You Completed the Passage of Realistic Love?

SELF-TEST

Check the following statements that apply to you.

_____ Having shared these years together I can honestly look at my spouse and say, "You're someone special. I like you. I still find a fascination with the mystery of who you are. I'm still in love with you."

_____ I can think of three specific features, characteristics, or attributes of my spouse that I still cherish, such as: "You have a sense of humor that always keeps our relationship fresh," "You have deep spiritual values, which have helped sustain us in the most difficult times," or "You have a sexy body. After ten years of marriage I still catch myself watching you walk across the room."

_____ I have seen you in the illusion of courtship. I have seen you in the difficult moments of stark reality. I have come to appreciate the reality of you in mature love, as much or more as in early love. I appreciate the following strengths you have shown in our most challenging crisis.

_____ I appreciate the boundaries we have established with our children. We have reached that special balance between union and separateness in both our individual and couple relationships with each child.

_____ No child in our family feels excluded or favored, and no child has been moved into the position of ally or surrogate with one parent against (or in place of) the other parent.

_____ If children have not entered or remained in this marriage, due to choice, infertility, miscarriage, or premature death, we have both grieved this void.

_____ I now recognize that I entered this marriage with a number of unrealistic expectations of you, and these expectations were the hidden agendas in my emotional marriage contract.

_____ I'm willing to surrender these toxic expectations that I imposed on both of us. I do this without a sense of unnecessary shame because I realize I was doing the best I knew how in our early years. However, I also realize the enormous damage these expectations have inflicted on us. I am actively seeking to suspend them.

_____ Having revoked or amended the toxic contracts that originally brought me to you, I now commit to draft a new contract for our union. The following is a list of new fresh ways I seek to be your partner.

Mentally: _____

_____

_____

Emotionally: _____

_____

_____

Physically: _____

_____

_____

Spiritually: _____

_____

_____

The Third Passage: Comfortable Love (The 11th Through 25th Years)

The essential tasks that must be accomplished in order to complete the third passage of marriage are:

- maintain an individual identity along with your marriage identity
- say the final goodbyes
- overcome the now-or-never syndrome
- practice true forgiveness
- accept the inevitable losses
- help your adolescent become an individual
- maintain an intimate relationship
- write a new marriage contract

As children grow, the marriage continues to change, from reality into comfort. This Third Passage shapes what is to come and serves to renew what has passed.

Maintain an individual identity along with your marriage identity. In the beginning of a marriage, the task is to forge together. By this stage, the task is nearly the reverse: to maintain an individual identity along with the marriage identity. Beware of becoming too dependent on another person, action, or thing. The goal of marriage is a healthy interdependence.

Say the final goodbyes. Though we are adults, holding down our own jobs, taking care of our own families, facing our own challenges, there's a sneaking little part of us that doesn't want to be all grown up. It's a scary world, full of risks and perils, and we still think somebody should be there to protect us if the world starts to beat up on us. For most of us, that "somebody" is Mom and Dad. But by this passage, Mom and Dad are getting on in years, and they are vulnerable to the world themselves. It's time to stand on our own two feet and face the world squarely. It's time to say goodbye to Mom and Dad as our parent-protectors and to say hello to them as equals. We're all adults now.

Overcome the now-or-never syndrome. Disenchantment often sets in during this passage. The now-or-never syndrome begins to hit as a part of the identity issue: Should I make one last grab for an exciting life before life passes me by? Should I quit trying in this marriage? Could there be somebody else out there who could really meet all my needs? Or should I just marry my job? Temptations loom in this passage, but don't let the blahs of the Third Passage discourage you. Instead, find creative ways to reignite your marriage relationship.

Practice true forgiveness. Forgiveness is crucial in both big and small matters. The Lord's Prayer says, "Forgive us our trespasses as we forgive those who trespass against us." Forgiveness does not mean forgetting. It means we choose not to hold on to bitterness. Whenever you remember something that has hurt you in the past, forgive it again and get on with your life.

Accept the inevitable losses. You're really fighting the odds in this stage of marriage. There is so much at stake. So many crises, changes, and opportunities. Couples are facing the realities of middle age and having to accept inevitable losses such as the loss of youth, the loss of vocational dreams, the loss of financial dreams, and the loss of romantic ideals. Those losses sometimes lead people into a dangerous attempt to recapture those lost notions—sometimes through an adulterous affair. The Third Passage is a time for reaffirming commitments and making sure that boundaries are firmly in place around the relationship.

Help your adolescent become an individual. The kids are rapidly changing during this passage. Suddenly, you find yourself living with teenagers—and with turmoil. This stress is natural and necessary for everyone concerned. Make sure that you and your spouse are working together as a team to win this game. Being an effective parent requires that you be an effective marriage partner. Don't neglect intimacy with your spouse as you fight the daily battles of living with teenagers.

Maintain an intimate relationship. Comfortable love is sharing of the soul, including hopes, dreams, fears, shames, joys, and sorrows. It's an easy, comfortable balance between dependence on each other and independence. It's knowing someone else deeply and appreciating him or her anyway.

Write a new marriage contract. A renewed marriage contract can be just as important in Passage Three as in Passage Two. Think about what would go into a renewal of your own contract at this stage of your marriage, whether you've actually reached this stage or not. It's fun to think about the future. Go back through your relationship to remember the romance, memories, and laughter you have experienced together. What specific items might you write into a new contract to promote romance over the next years? What exactly can both of you do to avoid taking each other for granted?

Think about your history. What can you do to deepen and transmit your family history and traditions? Write it all into the contract.

By this time in your life, you have spent more time with your spouse than with your parents. Your history together will be part of the blessing you take into the next passage of marriage.

395

When reality comes nowhere near matching your dreams and aspirations, it must be grieved through. When your dream and reality match or nearly so, celebrate. Celebration is the other side of the grief coin, and it is totally appropriate. If none of your realities come close to fulfilling your original aspirations, ask yourself, "Did I set my dreams too high?" That, too, should be grieved.

SELF-TEST | # Have You Completed the Passage of Comfortable Love?

Dr. Robert Hemfelt, a psychologist with the Minirth Meier New Life Clinic in Richardson, Texas, uses the following exercise in counseling. You can do it yourself at home. Its purpose is to clarify the issues of your marriage and to assess how realistically you see your future relationship. This exercise also provides insight into what you might want to change in your renewed marriage contract.

"I'll give you six categories," he explains. "For each of them, think about the dreams and expectations you started out with in your marriage. Whether they were exaggerations or illusions you harbored, or if those dreams and expectations seem quaint or nonsensical now, write them down. Then write down a brief description of what you see as the reality. How do you view those dreams now? Have you abandoned them? Did you achieve them? Take however much time you need."

Explore your past and present, and catch a glimpse of your future. We've provided answers we typically hear to prime the pump for you. Try to look at both the positives and negatives of your reality.

1. Sexual romance
    Write down your dreams (for instance: "I assumed romance would be similar to what I read in romance novels, continually intense and passionate").
    Now write a description of your marriage as it is now (for instance: "We have had a good relationship. It fulfills me if I rein in my original dream").

2. Finances
    Your dreams (for instance: "I planned to own my own business by this time").
    Now, reality ("I'm an area manager for someone else. But at least I have as much financial security as the job permits. And I can go home and leave my job behind").

3. Sharing with friends
    Your dreams (such as: "I'm outgoing by nature, so I pictured my wife and me with a wide circle of ten or fifteen close couples, and we'd entertain every weekend").
    The reality (such as: "I find it hard to accept that we've got maybe three close couples and one eccentric single as friends. There isn't a lot of close sharing, and my wife is the opposite; she doesn't like to entertain. Frankly, I don't see anything positive here").

4. Dream of children

This category has two parts. One is whether you wanted children and, if so, how your reality matches with the dream. Your dream ("I always wanted to have two children").

The reality ("One of four couples struggles with infertility and we're one of them. My husband is resigned to the fact we won't have biological children, but I'm having trouble with it. So I guess you'd say we're halfway; he's there, but I'm not").

The second part of this category has to do with how your children are turning out. Does that approach the original dream? Your dream ("I wanted my children to share my beliefs").

Reality ("My kids are their own persons. They have at least temporarily rejected some of my beliefs").

5. Spiritual

Your dreams (for instance: "The family I grew up in was constantly involved in church—all of us").

The reality ("My husband is a good man and a Christian. We go to church every week, but it's not the center of our lives. I can't find a church around here as vibrant as my old home church").

6. My spouse in general

Your dreams ("What can I say? She was going to be built like a swimsuit model, earn a Ph.D., and cook like Julia Child").

Reality ("Would you believe she's built more like a boy and didn't graduate from college? But man, can she cook! And I love her and she loves me!").

The Fourth Passage: Renewing Love (The 26th Through 35th Years)

The essential tasks that must be accomplished in order to successfully complete the fourth passage of marriage are:

- combat the crisis of this passage
- maintain companionship and unity
- grieve the particular losses of this passage

Combat the crisis of this passage. The storms of life generate far more than misery and frustration. They trigger very real physiological and psychological changes. You can get sick from too much stress and tragedy in your life, and it is not "all in your head." Your body chemistry shifts, causing physical symptoms and lowering your resistance to disease.

Stress is powerful. Retiring, losing your job, getting sick, even moving to a new home can become major stress factors in this passage of your marriage. Any drastic shift in the status quo upsets more than just your routine. Good changes can disrupt your life as surely as bad ones. Winning the lottery can mess up your life as badly as going bankrupt. Sending a child to college or marrying off a child can be extremely stressful.

The key to surviving these crises is, once again, to become a team—"us against the world," not "me against you." Make a commitment not to blame but to repair and recover. Take responsibility for your own contribution to the pain. Share your feelings openly so your needs can be met, and don't let your anger smolder in resentment. Grieve the pain, do some give-and-take with your partner, and minimize the stressors in your life.

Maintain companionship and unity. Renewing love also means renewing the intimacy of your companionship and unity. Since this is an extremely vulnerable time for infidelity, both partners need to make a conscious recommitment of themselves to the marriage relationship. Both partners should:

- prioritize quality time for intimacy, conversation, vacation, romance, and sex
- make a conscious effort to make amends for wrongs and heal hurts in the relationship
- make a conscious effort to give as well as take, to meet the other's needs as well as make requests for one's own needs

Sexual difficulties will sometimes arise during this passage, often because one or both partners assume that this is the time of life when sex tapers off. In fact, most people can enjoy a vigorous sex life well into their seventies. Unless there is a physiological problem (such as alcohol abuse, diabetes, or medication interactions), sexual problems during this passage usually signal that the couple has not maintained emotional intimacy.

Other symptoms of a decrease in emotional intimacy during this passage of marriage include excessive fighting, power struggles (including the withholding of sex as a weapon or punishment), and physical separation. The good news is that a relationship can be repaired if both partners are willing to do the work of reestablishing intimacy.

Grieve the particular losses of this passage. Losses seem to mount as we move through this passage. Life is full of losses, and to successfully complete each passage you have to come to terms with the inevitable losses of that passage. You may have to say goodbye to your parents as they are laid to rest; to your children as they move away and begin their own lives; to fond dreams that will never come true; to health; to financial security. The key is to invest yourselves in each other right now. Begin laying a foundation for happiness that will take you on into the final passage of your life together.

■

Professional counseling can be extremely helpful in enabling a couple to understand their issues and develop strategies for reestablishing intimacy before it's too late.

■

SELF-TEST

Have You Completed the Passage of Renewing Love?

If you have been married more than twenty-five years, you know that this is a time of either renewal or alienation. Intimacy involves opening up to each other, becoming vulnerable. It also requires learning new things about each other. Use this self-test to help you evaluate your progress toward intimate union and renewal. If you haven't been married this long, the test may give you ideas for invigorating your marriage now and preparing for the future.

1. One of my very favorite romantic moments of our marriage occurred when:

    _____
    _____

    ____   I have talked about that special moment with my spouse since then.

    ____   I have *not* talked about that special moment with my spouse since then.

2. One area in which I see myself slowing down physically is:

    _____
    _____

    ____   My spouse has noticed it.
    ____   My spouse has *not* noticed it.
    ____   I am embarrassed or afraid to talk about it.
    ____   I am *not* embarrassed or afraid to talk about it.
            I compensate for that slowing-down by:

            _____

            _____

3. When I am with friends, the topic I tend to talk about most is:

    _____
    _____

    The human being whom I mention most is _____. If it's not my spouse,
    the reason I don't mention marriage and my spouse is:

    _____
    _____

4. The last time my partner and I did something together was when we: (Something
    active and interactive, not passive. Watching TV doesn't count unless you had a
    spirited, stimulating discussion about the TV show afterward.)

    _____
    _____

    If that activity was more than a week ago, what could we have done more
    recently that we failed to do? What are some opportunities for interaction and
    relationship-building that we should be more aware of?

    _____
    _____

5. Responding to "the empty nest":

    ____   I dread the day our first child moves out (or did so when it happened).

    ____   I eagerly anticipate the day our first child moves out (or did so when it
            happened).

My major reason for feeling this way is:

_____

_____

I have (or have not) discussed these feelings with my spouse because:

_____

_____

6. If my spouse and I lived to be a hundred (with our mental capacities still intact), people would surely ask us, "How did you two manage to stay together so long?" My answer would be:

_____

_____

The Fifth Passage: Transcendent Love (36 Years and Thereafter)

The essential tasks that must be accomplished in order to complete the fifth passage of marriage are:

- prepare for retirement
- achieve a transcendent perspective
- accept your one and only God-given life

You've been together a long time now. True love at last. Look on the changes in this passage as another network of goodbyes and hellos. While this is a handy way to look at life in general and your marriage in particular during any passage, now in these latter days this philosophy pays rich dividends.

Spiritual resolution of the deepest sort, the sort that leads to a true and abiding love of God, comes only when the person has said all the other goodbyes, made peace with his or her mortality, and put away all the false idols that used to be so tempting.

Prepare for retirement. Preparing for retirement means more than making sure you have enough money. You have a lot of lifestyle decisions to make. Do you want to maintain the level of income, activities, and travel you have now? Move up a notch? Or do you want to downsize and simplify your lifestyle and budget? Again, the key is to work together and dream together as a team, prepare to make those dreams a reality—but don't forget to have a Plan B!

Achieve a transcendent perspective. Transcendent love is a profound and peaceful perspective toward your partner and life. It does not mean that you are oblivious to your pain and your losses but that the years have given you the character, the wisdom, and the strength to rise above them. There is not a thing or a person in this life that we will not someday either leave or lose. During these years, we learn to loosen our grip on our treasures and our loved ones. We hold these things loosely so that we can give them freely, willingly back to God, not clutch them like desperate misers. The closer we come to letting life go, the more precious each day becomes. Now it becomes clearer what is truly important in life, and what isn't. That is a truly transcendent perspective.

Accept your one and only God-given life. Part of the task of acquiring a transcendent perspective is learning to accept the fact that you have only one life to live, and then it's over. This final task in the final passage of marriage involves coming to terms with death, recognizing its finality and its swift approach, and accepting your one and only God-given life. For the Christian, death is not the end. Death completes life. It is a new beginning. With this as your perspective, you are finally free to turn your hands and your heart completely to God. If this passage goes well, if you have been building a strong spiritual base throughout your life, then you will experience peace—a transcendent peace, the peace that passes understanding.

Though there are goodbyes to be said in this final passage of marriage, there is something to look forward to. "For now we see in a mirror, dimly, but then face to face," says Paul in 1 Corinthians 13:12, looking forward to death with a transcendent perspective. Face to face . . . with God! Yes, death means goodbye.

But it is also the ultimate hello.

Have You Completed the Passage of Transcendent Love?

SELF-TEST

Consider your own passage of marriage, then check the statements below that apply to you.

_____ I can still give the world something. What I can give the world is:

_____

_____

_____ I can picture myself as an old person and (barring catastrophic illness) I can pretty much estimate what my physical and mental limitations might be. I may not be completely at peace with the vision, but I can see it. Those limitations might be:

_____

_____

_____ God's role in my life, particularly as it relates to death and illness, is:

_____

_____

(For instance, some people feel that God has guided every day of their lives. They are often able to face death well, because they know He has already sustained them through difficult situations and they know He will sustain them again. They trust Him as they trust no one else. Others have very different views of God's role in their lives. What is your view?)

My attitude toward death is:

_____ I am petrified of death. It seems like the final end.

_____ I'd rather die now than live another year of misery.

_____ I am prepared for my own death.

_____ I look forward to saying hello to my God.

_____ I believe Jesus Christ saved me from my sins and that I will live with Him forever.

If you would like to explore the five passages of marriage in greater depth, read *Passages of Marriage* by Dr. Frank Minirth, Dr. Brian and Dr. Deborah Newman, and Dr. Robert and Susan Hemfelt (Thomas Nelson, 1991). Now that we have examined these five passages and have seen how a marriage relationship grows and changes dynamically over time, let's examine some specific areas of the marriage relationship where problems often develop, and where solutions and strategies can be found.

MARRIAGE COMMUNICATION

Getting married is easy. Being married is not.

When two people first get married, they think they are alike. There is an emotional fusion that takes place. It's not uncommon for two young, euphoric, infatuated lovers to say such things as, "I am you and you are me." Intense young love wants to merge and fuse with the object of its desire.

But young lovers, however earnest, are mistaken. These two people are not each other. They are themselves. They are different. And sooner or later, those differences are going to come out. When that happens, disillusionment will take place. The unspoken lament of disillusioned young love is "Something's wrong! We're not each other anymore! You're not me! You have weird ideas and strange attitudes and some habits that are downright disgusting! I've made a big mistake! Let me out of this relationship!"

The problem: the couple didn't understand the value and the beauty of differences. They bailed out in the early stages of the very first passage because they thought that differences meant incompatibility. It's such a tragedy to see a perfectly good and salvageable marriage go into the ash heap just because the partners didn't understand that *it is our differences that make a marriage work*. With their differences, two people complement each other. They make each other complete in those areas where, by themselves, they are incomplete. With their differences, two people sand off the rough edges of each other and make each other more well-rounded as human beings. There is a reason that opposites attract: unconsciously, we look for people who are what we wish we were and who have what we wish we had.

In our marriage adventures, we would all do well to remember that Gallic slogan of love, *vive la différence!* Differences in emotional makeup, in interests, in background, in attitudes, and in abilities can all be valuable assets in a marriage relationship. Other differences, however, such as differences in communication, tend to create disharmony and disunity until we learn how to resolve those differences, how to hear each other more clearly, and how to understand each other more completely.

The most common marital communication problems arise from the differing attitudes men and women have toward communicating feelings. Women commonly complain, "He never talks!" Men almost universally protest, "I do too!" Who's right? They

402

both are—from their own gender-based perspective. In broad, general terms, what a woman means by "talking" is sharing feelings; what a man means by "talking" is sharing facts.

"Sure, I talk," men will say defensively. "I talk about my work, about the problem with the car, about something Rush Limbaugh said on the radio today, about sports, about politics, about a new restaurant I heard about. My mouth is dry as a gourd, I've been talking so much!"

"You see!" women will say, triumphantly. "He yaks and yaks about stuff that doesn't mean anything. But does he *talk?* No! I try to talk to him about the problem with the kids, the decision I have to make about whether or not to go back to school, about what I'm going through now that I'm about to turn forty! He just tunes me out! He doesn't listen, and he doesn't talk!"

Why are men and women so different when it comes to communication? In her book *You Just Don't Understand* (Ballantine, 1990), Dr. Deborah Tannen suggests that women use communication to build relationships, to express the feelings that create the basis of friendships. Men, on the other hand, use communication to get attention, to get what they want. Some would suggest that the differences between men and women are purely cultural and reflect the gender biases that were drummed into us as children. But research indicates that there may be a very real physiological reason why men and women communicate so differently.

The "brain-mapping" research of Nobel-winner Roger Sperry suggests that the left and right hemispheres of our brains operate very differently, with the left being devoted largely to logic, factual analysis, and concrete reasoning, and the right being devoted largely to feeling, intuitive thinking, and creativity. Studies show that the corpus callosum—a cablelike bundle of nerve fibers that connects the left and right hemispheres of the brain—is thicker in women than in men. This suggests that women have more nerve pathways connecting the left and right halves of the brain, and that means there is more communication between these two hemispheres in women than in men. This may help to explain why women tend to be more right-brain influenced in their thinking and men are more left-brain oriented. We were made that way and designed that way so that we, as men and women, could complement each other and supply what the other lacks in thinking and communication styles.

Who's right? Men, with their left-brain concrete logic? Or women, with their right-brain (or, more accurately, whole-brain), feelings-oriented, relationship-oriented thinking? The fact is, it's not a question of who's right or who's wrong. It's a matter of each side learning to understand the other. Most men need to be more sensitive to a woman's way of thinking and feeling—*and* they need to do a better job of getting in touch with and expressing their own feelings. Many women, on the other hand, need to respect the largely male approach to analysis and factual problem solving.

This is not to say that women are illogical or that men are unfeeling machines. Nor should we form conclusions about individual men and women based on these generalizations about gender. Certainly, there have been many women attorneys, scientists, politicians, and doctors who could think circles around their male counterparts. The physiology of the corpus callosum is a good explanation for a statistical tendency in a large population, but it does not account for individual differences.

How, then, should we respond to these clear differences in the way men and women, husbands and wives, communicate? Our purpose should not be to assign blame, but to achieve understanding. Here are some suggestions for approaching marital communication in a healthy, mutually constructive way:

1. *Maintain a realistic perspective.* People often magnify minor situations or take personal offense where no offense is intended. Many marriage partners start from a standpoint of unrealistic expectations and feelings of entitlement: "I deserve . . ." "That's not fair . . ." "You owe me . . ." It's normal to have expectations in marriage, but the people we married are imperfect human beings, and they will disappoint us from time to time. Instead of expecting perfection, we should expect disappointment from time to time, because to do so is only realistic. If we expect occasional disappointment, we may find ourselves being pleasantly surprised.

2. *Celebrate differences.* Tell your partner that you accept him or her with all of those differences and that you are thankful to God for those differences. Affirm your partner's uniqueness. Find ways to reframe your differences as strengths rather than weaknesses.

3. *Remember that listening is communication too.* Too many people think communicating is talking. But some of the most effective communicating we ever do is communicating with our ears open and our mouths shut. Effective communicators listen for feelings, for tone of voice. They listen with the eyes, watching expressions and gestures, reading the nonverbal dimension of the communication.

And as we listen, we should reflect back what we hear, restating feelings and responding to pain. When we nod, give good eye contact, and restate what the other person has said, we show them that we hear—and we also absorb and comprehend *more* of what we hear. This is called *reflective listening* or *active listening*. It can be very healing and clarifying when there is confused or distorted communication going on.

4. *Recognize that marital communication is hard work.* We all want a happily-ever-after relationship, but what we all get is a series of communication problems that must be solved. If we are mature and if we are committed to healthy relationships, we will accept the challenge of communicating effectively and patiently, and we will resolve our problems one by one.

5. *Make God a part of your marriage communication process.* When conflicts and communication problems arise, stop and pray together. God has given us His Spirit in order to unify His followers, and that includes those followers who happen to be married to one another! Ask God to make you sensitive to His Spirit and to each other. Ask for the ability to hear clearly what the other person is saying and feeling. Invite God to be at the center of your relationship, and even at the center of your conflicts.

Thank God for marriage. And yes, thank God for the differences between you and your spouse. *Vive la différence!*

Experiencing God's presence helps to keep both partners focused on a healthy, loving, constructive solution to marital communication problems.

RESOLVE CONFLICT IN MARRIAGE BY "FIGHTING FAIR"

All married people argue from time to time. It is not so much the *presence* of conflict that determines the health or dysfunction of a marriage, but rather *how that couple handles conflict and disagreement.* In fact, the way we resolve conflict is more important than the resolution itself. Love and fair play are crucial to a healthy relationship. When two partners are committed to a fair and loving resolution of conflict, growth can take place *even during times of stress and disagreement.* Marital conflict can actually improve the strength of the relationship *if* the goal of the two partners is not "winning" but resolving the issue.

The key to resolving conflict in marriage—in fact, the most important ingredient in any relationship—is *love.* Understand, when we say *love,* we are not talking about a tingly, fuzzy feeling. We are talking about the same kind of love psychologist Norm Wright calls "a perfect commitment to an imperfect person." We are talking about the same kind of love the apostle Paul describes in 1 Corinthians 13:4–7, where he writes:

> Love suffers long and is kind; love does not envy; love does not parade itself, is not puffed up; does not behave rudely, does not seek its own, is not provoked, thinks no evil; does not rejoice in iniquity, but rejoices in the truth; bears all things, believes all things, hopes all things, endures all things.

It is clear from these descriptions that the truest form of love is not a feeling at all. It is a *commitment,* rooted in the will, not the emotions. In fact, when we love the way God calls us to love—volitionally and unconditionally—then we will find ourselves behaving in ways that run completely *counter* to our feelings. Emotionally, we may want to attack; but God's unconditional love calls us to care, to listen, to understand. Emotionally, we may want to withdraw; but God's unconditional love calls us to hang in there, to persevere, to endure our pain in order to bring healing out of conflict.

That is the kind of love we need to resolve the conflicts of marriage. That is the kind of love the apostle Paul enjoins in Ephesians 5:25–33:

> Husbands, love your wives, just as Christ also loved the church and gave Himself for her, that He might sanctify and cleanse her with the washing of water by the word, that He might present her to Himself a glorious church, not having spot or wrinkle or any such thing, but that she should be holy and without blemish. So husbands ought to love their own wives as their own bodies; he who loves his wife loves himself. For no one ever hated his own flesh, but nourishes and cherishes it, just as the Lord does the church. For we are members of His body, of His flesh and of His bones. "For this reason a man shall leave his father and mother and be joined to his wife, and the two shall become one flesh." This is a great mystery, but I speak concerning Christ and the church. Nevertheless let each one of you in particular so love his own wife as himself, and let the wife see that she respects her husband.

One way you live out Christlike unconditional love toward your marriage partner is by choosing to "fight fair" whenever conflict arises. Following are twenty-one practical, proven rules for fighting fair. They were originally designed to help husbands and wives resolve conflict in marriage, but you may find that they apply equally well in other relationships and situations.

■

Feelings may change from moment to moment, but unconditional love "bears all things, believes all things, hopes all things, endures all things."

■

■

Always "fight fair." Implement rules for conflict and abide by them.

■

If you and your partner can implement these rules and abide by them, even when emotions run high and issues become difficult, then you will see growth and healing in your relationship. However, some couples will find that having a set of rules sounds good when there is no fight going on, but those rules quickly fall by the wayside when tempers flare. If you or your partner have trouble handling emotions during times of conflict, we encourage you to seek counseling from a qualified professional.

1. Consider your relationship a long-term commitment, not to be discarded because of one disagreement, no matter how serious it may be.
2. Pray about each conflict before discussing it with your partner.
3. Consider all the factors in a conflict before bringing up the conflict to your partner.
4. Agree always to listen to each other's feelings, even if you consider those feelings inappropriate.
5. Commit yourselves to both honesty and acceptance.
6. Determine to care for each other unconditionally, with each partner assuming 100 percent of the responsibility for resolving the conflict (dividing up responsibility on a 50/50 basis seldom works).
7. Limit the conflict to the here and now. Never bring up past failures, since all past failures should already have been forgiven.
8. Eliminate the following phrases from your vocabulary:

   - "You never," or, "You always."
   - "I can't" (substitute "I won't" or "I choose not to").
   - "I'll try" (usually this means "I'll make a half-hearted effort, but I won't quite succeed").
   - "You should," or, "You shouldn't" (these are parent-to-child statements; you are both equal adults).

9. Limit the discussion to the one issue that is the center of the conflict.
10. Focus on resolving that issue rather than attacking each other. Think of the situation as "us versus the problem," not "me against you."
11. Offer your partner some time to think about the conflict before discussing it (but never put it off overnight).
12. Each partner should use "I" messages, not "you" messages. For example, "I feel angry toward you for coming home late without calling me," not, "You make me so mad when you come home late." We should always take responsibility for our own feelings and responses, even when we confront another person's behavior.
13. Never say anything derogatory about your partner's personality. When we attack another person's character and personality, that person's defenses go up and communication shuts down. Focus on issues and specific behavior; don't generalize and get into personal attacks.
14. Even though your partner won't always be right, consider him or her an instrument of God, working in your life.

15. Never counterattack, even if your partner does not follow these guidelines. If the guidelines are violated, gently remind the other person that you have both agreed to these guidelines.

16. Focus on behavior, not hidden motives. Don't try to read your partner's mind. If you're not sure what was meant by something that was said, ask for clarification.

17. Be honest about your true emotions, but keep them under control. Instead of exploding, say, "I feel angry." (See ANGER.)

18. Remember that the resolution of the conflict is what is important, not winning or losing. If the conflict is resolved, you both win. Remember, this is not a competition between the two of you. You're both on the same team.

19. Agree with each other on what topics are out of bounds, either because they are too explosive, too hurtful, or have already been discussed.

20. Even though your mate won't always be justified in reproving you, recognize him or her as an instrument of God working in your life. Proverbs 12:1 says that "he who hates correction is stupid."

21. Commit yourselves to learning and practicing these guidelines. Agree to call "foul" whenever one of you accidentally or intentionally breaks one of them.

FINDING HELP FOR OTHER ISSUES IN MARRIAGE

Here is where to find other important marriage-related issues covered in this encyclopedia:

For insight into sexual issues, both functional and dysfunctional, see SEX AND SEXUALITY.

For insight into how to deal with adultery in your marriage, see INFIDELITY.

For help in understanding and resolving feelings of possessiveness and jealousy, see JEALOUSY.

For insight into the various aspects of divorce, see DIVORCE.

For insight into how different personality types affect the marriage relationship, see PERSONALITY TYPES AND DISORDERS.

For help in dealing with feelings of bitterness and resentment in marriage, see FORGIVENESS.

For insight into family issues, see FAMILY and PARENTING.

For insight into dealing with stress in marriage, see STRESS.

For an in-depth discussion of the many issues involved in maintaining a happy, healthy marriage relationship, you may consider reading *Passages of Marriage* by Minirth, Newman, and Hemfelt (Thomas Nelson, 1991); *Getting Ready for Marriage,* a workbook by Jerry Hardin and Dianne Sloan (Thomas Nelson, 1991); *Together on a Tightrope,* a book on helping your marriage to survive during times of intense stress, by Dr. Richard Fowler and Rita Schweitz (Thomas Nelson, 1991); *The Intimacy Factor* by David and Jan Stoop (Thomas Nelson, 1993); and *The Pursuit of Intimacy* by Teresa Ferguson and Dr. Chris and Holly Thurman, with Carole Gift Page (Thomas Nelson, 1993).

Memory

Memory is the ability to store and retrieve past experiences in the human mind. Learning, thinking, and reasoning could not take place without memory. The ability to remember plays a significant role in physical as well as intellectual activity. Our memories are a basic component of humanness, and pleasurable memories are a major source of pleasure and emotional security in life.

How we remember remains something of a mystery, although scientists have identified several parts of the brain that seem to be responsible for the storage of experiences and information. Researchers have also determined that there are at least two distinct processes involved in the storing of experiences and information: *short-term memory* and *long-term memory*. Scientists believe that the brain uses a combination of electrical and chemical processes to encode experiential information into stored memories and to decode and retrieve that information at a later time. The exact process by which a memory trace (or *engram*) is impressed upon the nervous system has yet to be identified, though research continues.

Hand in hand with the ability to remember is the ability to forget painful or traumatic experiences, to save some impressions in long-term memory, to allow other impressions to fade from short-term memory, and to ignore some experiences so that the mind does not become overcrowded and overloaded with insignificant memories. Our brains are amazingly equipped to sift, select, organize, and translate the input from our senses so that important impressions can be stored and recalled for later use.

HOW A SIGNAL FROM THE SENSES BECOMES A MEMORY

Information and signals enter our minds through the senses. We see, we hear, we touch, we taste, we detect a fragrance, and the stimulus that affects our senses is converted into a code that is carried as an impulse through our nervous system to the brain. The brain records that encoded signal in a portion of the brain stem that is responsible for sensory-information storage.

As soon as that signal is sent to the sensory-information storage center, a portion of the brain called the *reticular activating system* (or RAS) immediately begins to process and analyze that information for significance. The RAS asks: Is this information important? Urgent? Irrelevant? The processing of this information takes less than a second. If the information is given a low priority by the RAS, the information is recorded over by the next signal and disappears (much like recording over a audio or video tape). If the information is given a higher priority, it is passed on to the short-term or long-term memory centers. The reticular system serves as a traffic cop, letting some signals pass through to the high portions of the brain while blocking other signals.

Another structure within the brain that helps determine how signals from the sense organs should be processed is the hippocampus. Located within the limbic system, the hippocampus acts like the "record" button on a VCR. The hippocampus detects elevated emotions (such as anger, fear, joy, or excitement) and figuratively "presses the button" so that incoming impressions will be recorded in long-term memory. The stronger the emotion, the more the signal is magnified. That's why memories of intensely emotional events (the birth of one's child, one's own wedding day, being in an automobile accident or an earthquake, or hearing news of a major event such as the assassination of President Kennedy or the *Challenger* disaster) are etched so indelibly in our minds.

Paradoxically, the same intense emotions that usually burn memories into our minds can—in extreme cases—interfere with long-term memory. If being in an automobile accident or earthquake is experienced as an extremely traumatic event, the terror of the experience can overload the brain's ability to scan incoming information for possible storage. The individual may misremember the sequence of events or "blank out" the event altogether. In many cases, this appears to be a defense mechanism to prevent the mind from becoming overwhelmed by emotions too powerful to bear. Instead of reliving a horrible moment again and again in the memories, the individual experiences a merciful span of amnesia regarding that traumatic incident in his or her life.

After the brain has assessed the importance of incoming signals, the message may be held briefly (a few seconds to a few minutes) in the short-term memory centers of the brain. Short-term memory holds limited amounts of information for a short period of time. When you look up a phone number in the directory, for example, that information goes into short-term memory. You repeat the number to yourself as you close the book, you dial, and you get your party on the line. Two minutes later, you probably couldn't recall that number to save your life. Studies show that impressions stored in short-term memory fade very quickly. People normally experience about 80 percent recall after three seconds, 40 percent recall after six seconds, and 20 percent recall after nine seconds. As new information enters short-term memory, previously entered information is erased.

Highly significant information may be passed directly from short-term memory to long-term memory in one of two ways: (1) it may be given an additional boost by the hippocampus, when accompanied by strong emotion; or (2) it may be "rehearsed" and repeated in short-term memory, so that it acquires enough mental "momentum" to be passed on to long-term memory. Rehearsal may be deliberate on the part of the individual, as when we read and study a verse of Scripture in order to commit it to long-term memory. Or rehearsal may be involuntary, as when our minds are bombarded by repeated commercials; without even realizing it, we find ourselves thinking, "You can count on me, Sears Roebuck and Company," or "Le'go my Eggo!"

The Complicated Brain

How much memory can one brain store? It's hard to believe, but the truth is that the brain's capacity is virtually limitless. If you doubt this statement, consider this: your brain contains about 100,000,000,000 neurons (nerve cells), and each neuron is connected to surrounding cells by a fantastically complex network of fibers called axons and dendrites. Each of these billions of cells may have as many as 100,000 fibers leading into it from other cells. As a result of this complex circuitry, the number of interconnections among the cells of your brain is actually *greater than the number of atoms in the entire universe!* No wonder astronomer Robert Jastrow calls the human brain "the most complicated object science has ever tried to understand."

Is sheer repetition the best way to store information in long-term memory? No. Studies indicate that memories last longest when they are experienced through a variety of experiences and senses. If, for example, you are studying for a test, you will have more effective recall if you study in a variety of ways, using a variety of media, rather than just repeating the information to yourself. Moving images, photographs, charts, or graphics (particularly if they are alive with color) can greatly enhance recall over information that is delivered in a purely verbal form. When you study from a textbook, use a colored marker to highlight important facts, summarize and restate important points in writing, and outline the material so you can get a comprehensive overview.

If you are speaking before a group and want others to retain your message for a longer period of time, put a lot of expression and animation into your face and voice. Use big gestures, and enhance your presentation with colorful graphics or video clips. Use surprise. Use powerfully emotional stories—either uproariously funny or terribly sad. These emotions will activate the RAS of your listeners and boost your message into the long-term memory centers of their brains.

There is debate among researchers as to whether information stored in long-term memory can be lost. Some believe that long-term memory decays or is gradually "recorded over" as time passes. Others believe that long-term memory is never lost, except through injury or disease of the brain. They point to the recovery of long-forgotten memories under hypnosis and the experience of having one's life flash before one's eyes when death seems near as evidence that the information remains stored for life, even if it is not easily accessible to the conscious mind.

Information stored in our brains is indexed and cross-referenced several different ways. The brain uses associated settings and senses (such as a certain room or a fragrance or a song) to help us recall certain memories. That's why:

- A whiff of perfume will bring an entire memory of some long-ago event flooding back into your mind.
- A man you recognize but can't quite place if you meet him on the street becomes instantly placed if you see him at church, where you normally see him.
- When a thought or idea has slipped your mind, you can often remember it by going back to the room you were in when it first occurred to you.

If there is one mental activity that truly deserves our time and attention, it is Scripture memorization. "Your word I have hidden in my heart," says Psalm 119:11, "that I might not sin against You." When we etch God's Word into the limitless, interconnecting nerve pathways of our brains, we lay a foundation for emotional and spiritual wholeness that will carry us through this life—and beyond.

THE HEALING OF MEMORIES

In recent years, both secular psychiatrists and Christian counselors have been stressing the value of a process called "the healing of memories." This process is based on the psychoanalytical concept that many of us have repressed and buried painful memories, yet those memories continue to reach out from the unconscious mind and

■

Our amazing, God-given power of remembering is too valuable a gift to waste. We fill our memory centers with television programs, trivial facts, sports statistics, and other inconsequentials, and we neglect the Word of God.

■

410

affect our conscious feelings and our behavior today. The goal of this form of healing is to unearth those memories, bring them up into the realm of conscious awareness, reexperience them, release those memories (by forgiving ourselves or others), and get on with life. God is involved in the process through prayer; He is asked as the Great Physician to heal the emotional pain associated with the memory. Sometimes the individual is encouraged to imagine Jesus as being physically present to take the pain away or (in the case of memories of abuse) to physically shield the individual from the abuser.

Healing of memories has been shown to be very effective in cases of trauma and abuse. Not everyone who suffers from painful memories and emotions, however, is in need of such healing. Though this process is sometimes attempted by well-intentioned Christian laypeople after reading a book or attending a seminar, the healing of memories is a process best left in the hands of trained professional counselors. Individuals who do not understand the dangers of repression and denial have sometimes exacerbated the emotional problems of some individuals by attempting to "erase" old memories or "substitute" new memories in their place.

People with painful memories need healing from those memories. But true healing does not come from denying that the painful event happened. Healing comes when we courageously face the reality of our lives and our memories and allow God to take the sting out of those memories.

Mental Health

We are made in God's image. Our minds are patterned after His mind. His image, which was stamped upon us at Creation, is the basis of all mental health.

Though we were created in perfection, sin came into the human race and implanted within each of us the basis for mental and emotional disorders. This is not to say that all mental illness is the direct result of specific sins, but all of the brokenness, distortion, dysfunction, and sickness that we find in our world is, in a general sense, the logical consequence of the entrance of sin into the world.

Yet God, through Jesus Christ, is in the business of restoring our mental, emotional, and spiritual wholeness. He is re-creating His original image in us by conforming us to the image of Christ. The more Christlike we become, the more mentally healthy we will be.

Total health in a whole person requires that one have healthy relationships in three directions:

- inward, toward oneself
- outward, toward others
- upward, toward God

What are the distinguishing characteristics of a mentally healthy individual? The following is a list of some of the most important features to look for. A mentally healthy person . . .

1. Is able to function at full capacity and is physically, intellectually, and emotionally balanced.
2. Is in contact with reality.
3. Is relatively free of anxiety.
4. Is able to adapt to changing situations with self-control and discipline.
5. Is able to tolerate stress and to cope with a wide variety of new situations.
6. Can react to all situations in a realistic way.
7. Exhibits an attitude of confidence in himself or herself, faith in God, and a sense of humor.
8. Has a clear and unwavering purpose in life.
9. Is able to relate well to a variety of people.
10. Is able to accept the legitimate authority of individuals and institutions, and is able to cooperate and perform well on the job.
11. Is able to make and keep friends, and to be a friend to others.
12. Is able to love and be loved.
13. Is able to experience intimacy in close interpersonal relationships, such as marriage.
14. Is able to balance different roles, so that he or she is able to be both interdependent and independent, to care for himself or herself and to offer care to others, to compete and to compromise, to be organized and to be creative, to express logical thought and to express feelings, to follow and to lead—according to the given circumstances of the situation.
15. Is dependable and trustworthy.
16. Is able to focus on others, and is not continually wrapped up in his or her own selfish desires, bitterness, suspicion, and problems.
17. Is capable of expressing and controlling emotion. This does not mean that emotions are repressed, but rather that behavior is under control.
18. Is satisfied with his or her maleness or femaleness, is able to enjoy an active and satisfying sex life within marriage, and is concerned with helping his or her partner to enjoy emotional, spiritual, and sexual intimacy.
19. Is spiritually balanced. A mentally healthy Christian is engaged in Scripture study and meditation, prayer, fellowship, worship, and witnessing. A lack of balance can be seen in many Christians who are overly emotional (too much feeling, not enough objective truth) or who are overly doctrinal (too much emphasis on rules and formulas, not enough on feeling and spirituality). Christians should seek a balance within their own souls, and within the body of Christ.
20. Is able to enjoy a positive, satisfying relationship with God, coupled with a steady growth in character and emotional maturity.

THE FRUIT OF THE SPIRIT

In Galatians 5:22–23, we find a list of qualities called "the fruit of the Spirit." It is interesting to contrast these qualities with the symptoms of mental and emotional disorders and dysfunction:

THE FRUIT OF THE SPIRIT	SYMPTOMS OF POOR MENTAL HEALTH
Love	Bitterness, Resentment
Joy	Depression, Low Self-Esteem
Peace	Anxiety, Guilt
Longsuffering (Patience)	Dissatisfaction
Kindness	Suspicion, Selfishness
Goodness	Denial, Defensiveness
Faithfulness	Infidelity
Gentleness	Anger, Rage
Self-Control	Addiction, Codependency

When Christians read the Bible and maintain a daily dialogue with God through prayer, it is not only an indication of mental health, it is also a major reason for good mental health. In addition to these fundamental spiritual disciplines, Christian counselors and psychiatrists can also be helpful in uncovering and resolving problems that hinder an individual's mental health. As we follow God's prescription for good mental health, we experience progressive growth toward the goal that was set for us in Romans 8:29—that we would be conformed to the image of God's Son, Jesus Christ, who is our ultimate model of spiritual truth and good mental health.

See also ABNORMAL PSYCHOLOGY and specific issues such as ADDICTION; ANXIETY; and DEPRESSION

Mind

The mind is the complex interacting network of facilities that makes us what we are as human beings:

- perceiving
- remembering
- thinking
- evaluating
- knowing
- deciding
- relating to others
- reflecting

The mind is a uniquely human facility. Animals perceive, remember, decide, and even relate—but they do not reflect on their own existence and on the existence of their minds, as we do.

The mind does not just perceive. It does not just sense. It apprehends and seeks to understand. It knows and is hungry to know even more. It is aware of itself and aware of other minds like itself, and it seeks to have a relationship and an interaction with other minds like itself. The mind considers itself and devises theories to explain itself. The mind has purpose, and it exerts a will of its own.

In a general sense, what we call the *mind* corresponds to what the writers of the New Testament called the *soul*. The Greek word that we translate as "soul" was *psuche*, from which we get our word *psychology*, the study, knowledge, and science of the human mind. The Bible teaches (and modern psychology tends to affirm) that human beings consist of three dimensions: body, soul (mind), and spirit.

Many Christians are confused regarding the concept of the soul and the concept of the spirit. The Bible suggests that at the moment of conversion, one's spirit is made new but the soul is not made new. The soul must gradually be changed and developed over time. One's mind and emotions are a part of the soul, not the spirit. That is why Paul says in Romans 12:2 that we must be gradually transformed by the continual, day-by-day renewing of our minds. This transformation is an ongoing process involving prayer, time spent in the Word of God, and time spent in fellowship with other Christians. In cases involving deep and painful emotional issues, such as situations involving abuse, trauma, or addiction, Christian counseling or psychiatry may be needed in addition to these spiritual disciplines.

Psychologists and psychiatrists divide the mind into three parts or dimensions:

- the conscious mind
- the subconscious mind
- the unconscious mind

The *conscious mind* deals with whatever one is aware of and thinking about at a given moment. The *subconscious mind* deals with any thought, feeling, motive, or past event that one can call to memory; a person is not continuously aware of subconscious thoughts, but he or she can consciously access them. The *unconscious mind,* however, includes everything recorded in the brain that one *can't* call back to memory at a given moment. The unconscious mind is believed to be the hidden reservoir of at least 80 percent of one's thoughts, feelings, and motivations.

The Bible has a great deal to say about the mind and how it relates to emotional health. Some examples:

Isaiah 26:3 reveals to us the source of true peace: "You will keep him in perfect peace, whose mind is stayed on You." And Luke 10:27 tells us what it means to have

THE COMPLETE LIFE ENCYCLOPEDIA

our minds stayed on God: "You shall love the LORD your God with all your heart, with all your soul, with all your strength, and with all your mind."

Our goal, as Romans 12:2 tells us, is to be transformed by the renewing of our minds, not conforming ourselves to the world, but becoming conformed to the likeness of Christ. We do this, as 1 Corinthians 2:16 tells us, by having the mind of Christ, a mind described by Paul in Philippians 2 as a mind of humility, the mind of a servant: "Let this mind be in you which was also in Christ Jesus, who, being in the form of God . . . made Himself of no reputation, taking the form of a bondservant" (vv. 5–7).

God's will is for all of us to have whole, healthy minds, free of anxiety and fear. "For God has not given us a spirit of fear," says 2 Timothy 1:7, "but of power and of love and of a sound mind."

See also ABNORMAL PSYCHOLOGY; EMOTIONS; and MENTAL HEALTH

Neurological Disorders

Neurological disorders are either temporary or permanent mental disorders caused by a physiological brain dysfunction resulting from disease, aging, chemical imbalance, drug abuse, injury, or genetic disorder. Neurological disorders fall into five major categories:

1. Amnestic Syndrome and Organic Hallucinations. Amnestic syndrome is an impairment of short-term memory caused in whole or in part by brain injury, brain infarction (dying or dead sections of brain tissue), nutritional deficiency, or chronic alcohol abuse.

Organic hallucinations result from such medical factors as seizures or drug abuse (particularly alcohol or LSD).

2. Delirium and Dementia. Delirium is a confused mental state that may include memory and attention problems and disorientation. People afflicted with delirium frequently lose track of time and forget where they are. They may experience visual and auditory hallucinations (sights, sounds, and voices that aren't real). Delirium is often the result of substance abuse and can be life-threatening. Medical treatment in a hospital setting is required in such cases.

Dementia is a serious disorder marked by symptoms that grow increasingly more severe as the illness progresses. These symptoms are caused by irreversible changes in the brain tissue. The disorder begins with seemingly minor symptoms: loss of interests and motivation, minor memory loss, and bouts of depression. With time, these symptoms worsen and additional symptoms appear: slowed or slurred speech, disorientation, loss of balance and mobility, loss of body control. Dementias may develop at virtually any age, although the risk of dementias such as Alzheimer's disease increases dramatically with age (see ALZHEIMER'S DISEASE).

Dementias can sometimes be treated with medications, but there is usually little that can be done to help a demented individual. There are no known cures for dementias.

415

Treatment is often best focused on the family of the victim, so that family members can adapt to the problems associated with the illness and so that feelings of false guilt can be uncovered and dealt with.

3. Organic Delusional Syndrome and Organic Affective Syndrome. Organic delusions are connected to a specific organic factor such as drug abuse (amphetamine, methamphetamine, LSD, or marijuana intoxication). Organic affective syndrome refers to a mood disturbance caused by drugs, hormones, steroid medication, or illnesses such as hyperthyroidism.

4. Organic Personality Syndrome. This condition involves marked personality changes brought on by physiological causes such as brain tumors, brain injury, stroke, thyroid disease, or steroid medication. Personality changes observed in this syndrome include angry outbursts, sexual indiscretions, paranoia, and apathy.

5. Intoxication and Withdrawal. This class of disorders results from intoxication with such substances as alcohol, barbiturates, opioids, cocaine, amphetamines, or marijuana. Even caffeine use (from coffee) can produce severe withdrawal symptoms in some individuals. Withdrawal symptoms result from the cessation or reduction of a specific substance that was regularly used by the individual to the point of intoxication. The most common symptoms of withdrawal are restlessness, anxiety, irritability, sleep disturbances, and inability to concentrate and focus. The withdrawing individual also has an overwhelming urge to resume use of the substance.

Some of these five categories of disorders are the result of aging and natural bodily deterioration. Some are the result of invading illnesses. Others are the result of lifestyle choices, such as alcoholism or drug abuse. We cannot control all the things that happen to us (such as injury or disease), but we can control what we do to our own bodies. Drawing on the power of the indwelling Holy Spirit, the insights of Christian counseling, and the support of other people in a support group or recovery group, you can conquer your addictions before they conquer you.
See also ADDICTION and COMPULSIVE BEHAVIOR

Obsessive-Compulsive Disorder

Jack put his key into the lock of the front door and turned to his friend, a psychologist. "My mother's at a meeting with her women's group at church," he said. "I just wanted you to see this and tell me if you think this is some kind of psychological problem."

"Okay," said the psychologist, intrigued.

The two of them stood on the front porch of the "mother-in-law apartment" behind Jack's own home. Jack's mother had lived there for about five years. Jack turned the key and opened the door, and the two of them walked in. The living room of the apartment was clean and orderly, and there were knick-knacks, photos, and mementos arranged about the room.

"I don't see anything out of the ordinary," said the psychologist.

"Not here," said Jack. "In there." He pointed toward the kitchen.

They walked through the small dining area and stopped dead at the doorway leading into the kitchen. The psychologist whistled. "I see what you mean."

There were sacks and boxes and cans of food everywhere. Stacked on counters, bulging out of cupboards, piled up along the floor. There were cans of beans, fruits, vegetables, soups, corned beef hash, stew, tuna, and much more. There were boxes of pasta, rice, cereal, flour, and cornmeal. Food filled the sink. Food was stacked all the way to the ceiling in places. It was stacked on top of the stove and stuffed inside the oven. Jack and the psychologist just stood at the threshold, looking into the kitchen. They couldn't go inside. The floor was completely covered with stacks of food, and there was no place to walk.

"I asked Mom if she had joined one of those end-of-the-world cults—you know, those survivalists who stockpile food so they'll have plenty to eat when civilization falls. She got real nervous and irritable when I talked to her about it, and she said I was never to go near her kitchen again. I'm real worried. What's going on here?"

"Your mother hasn't joined a cult, Jack," said the doctor. "She has a problem. It's called an obsessive-compulsive disorder."

People with *obsessive-compulsive disorder* (OCD) are plagued by recurrent obsessive thoughts and compulsive behavior so severe that they feel emotional discomfort and their functioning on the job and in relationships is impaired. Obsessive thoughts are ideas or impulses that are intrusive, irrational, and unpleasant. Such thoughts often involve fears of violence or contamination. Compulsions are repetitive, intentional actions that OCD sufferers perform in habitual or ritualized ways, often in response to obsessive thoughts.

Attempts to resist a compulsion often result in feelings of intense anxiety; that anxiety is temporarily relieved by engaging in the compulsive behavior, but it always returns, sometimes compounded by lowered self-esteem caused by the compulsive behavior. Experiences of anxiety and depression are common among OCD sufferers. The compulsive behavior that results from these anxious feelings is often quite bizarre.

Obsessive-compulsive disorder occurs with equal frequency among men and women. The first symptoms usually occur in childhood or adolescence. OCD sufferers usually experience moderate to severe impairment in career and relationships, and the OCD tends to progress over time as the individual gradually becomes dominated by the obsessive-compulsive behavior. Examples of compulsive behavior include compulsive hand-washing, compulsive perfectionism, compulsive hoarding (buying and storing more food or other goods than can be used), compulsive religious legalism, compulsive working and achievement (workaholism), relationship addiction (compulsive attachment to certain people, including abusive people), compulsive dieting, compulsive exercise and fitness training, compulsive rescuing of others, and compulsive sexual behaviors.

Notice the two interrelated components of OCD: *obsession* and *compulsion*. An obsession is an irrational pattern of thinking; a compulsion is an irrational pattern of behavior. So, for example, an individual might become obsessed with thoughts of contamination, which would then produce the compulsion of repetitive hand-washing. Or a Christian might become obsessed with doubts about his salvation and his acceptance by God, and this obsession would produce the compulsion of repeating a religious phrase over and over or performing some punishing act of self-atonement over and over.

Compulsions are not of themselves a sign of mental illness or serious dysfunction. Compulsions are extremely common, and most of us can identify with one form of compulsion or another, such as compulsive overeating or compulsive perfectionism.

Compulsions are usually a means of avoiding some unpleasant reality. The compulsive individual avoids dealing with the actual unconscious conflict (such as guilt or a painful childhood memory) by retreating into a compulsive behavior. When an unpleasant thought tries to push its way up into the conscious mind from the unconscious, the mind uses the compulsive behavior to push the thought back down.

OCD is a form of neurosis. Exposing and disarming the unconscious painful thoughts that produce the compulsive behavior requires the help of a professional counselor or psychiatrist. Successful treatment of OCD has been achieved by approaches such as behavior modification and drug therapy (see BEHAVIOR MODIFICATION).

> *Once we courageously face our emotional issues, free ourselves from guilt, and purge the pain of our childhoods through therapy and support (such as may be found in a support group or recovery group), the compulsions lose their power over us. And once those compulsions have been stripped of their power to hurt us, our conscious wills (which, as Christians, we are progressively giving over to God's control) will be back in the driver's seat of our lives.*

Parenting

Ross is a father of three, with a daughter in high school, a son in junior high, and another daughter who just arrived ("our little surprise") a month ago. "Melissa and I have one daughter who's already looking at college catalogs and applying for scholarships, and we have another daughter in Pampers. We're enjoying it, but we're too old for this! I feel I need a refresher course in parenting. Help!"

Sandra, age forty, is a single parent and a new Christian. "I have kids whose ages are fourteen and nine. As I've been getting more deeply involved with my home Bible study group, I've been seeing how my friends, who are Christian parents, relate to their kids—and I've been increasingly aware of all the mistakes I've made with my own kids. I want them to have the faith I've just discovered, but they were not raised in the Christian faith, and their dad—my ex-husband—is a hardened atheist who always makes fun of Christians. Now my kids are making fun of me for being a 'fanatic.' After all the time that's been lost, how can I help my kids to see my faith is real? How can I get them to want to know the Lord too?"

Max is a dad with a discipline problem. "I've tried lots of different approaches," he says, "but my kids' behavior problems just get worse and worse. Should I spank? Does spanking damage my kids emotionally? Is there a better alternative? What should I do?"

Jeff and Donna are not your typical parents. "We're Christians with a '90s relationship," says Jeff. "We have a fifty-fifty partnership. I'm not the boss, Donna's not the boss. In fact, I'm a house-husband, doing the Mr. Mom thing, while Donna goes out to work. I mean, she has the ability to make more money than I do right now; I'm currently working on a master's degree, so it just makes sense for me to stay home while she brings home the bacon. I'm not threatened by that, and Donna seems to like it fine. But I look in the Scriptures and I see things that bother me a bit. Our situation just doesn't seem to fit the family mold that's described in the Bible. Are we doing something wrong?"

SEVEN VITAL FACTORS FOR A HEALTHY FAMILY

As Christian counselors and psychiatrists, we have worked with thousands of parents at our Minirth Meier New Life Clinics nationwide. From our extensive experience, we have uncovered seven vital factors that we believe are essential to a spiritually, emotionally healthy family. Those seven factors are:

1. a strong spiritual foundation
2. authentic unconditional love
3. honest family communication
4. firm, loving discipline
5. consistency
6. healthy behavioral models
7. biblical leadership roles

In this article, we will explore the role of Christian parenting and how these seven factors enable us to build healthy families and raise happy, secure children.

A Strong Spiritual Foundation

A human being is a complex entity comprised of three interwoven dimensions: body, soul (mind, emotions, and will), and spirit. In order to approach our humanness realistically, we must approach it *holistically*. That is, we must be careful not to carve a human being into various segments and study each segment in isolation. Our level of spiritual health affects the health of the soul and the health of the body. Mental and emotional problems in the soul can make us physically sick and hinder our spiritual progress. Physical problems can make us emotionally upset and depressed, and if we fail to respond in a healthy spiritual way, sickness and injury can cause distortions in how we view God. We must look at the *whole* human being, with all dimensions functioning, interacting, interrelating, alive and dynamic.

As parents, then, our responsibility is to encourage the growth of our children in all three of these dimensions. If there is one dimension that all too often goes neglected, it is the spiritual dimension. As Christian parents, our spiritual responsibility is (1) to maintain a close relationship with God ourselves, and (2) to model and teach our children to have a close relationship with God themselves. Our first order of business as Christian parents is to have a faith relationship with Jesus Christ, as we see in this exchange between a jailer in the city of Philippi and the missionaries Paul and Silas in Acts 16:30–31: "And [the jailer] brought them out and said, 'Sirs, what must I do to be saved?' So [Paul and Silas] said, 'Believe on the Lord Jesus Christ, and you will be saved, you and your household.'"

To believe on Jesus is simply to place your trust in Him as Savior and Lord, to rely on Him for what He has done for you, to accept His death on the cross as the punishment you deserve for your own sins. There is no religious ritual or atonement you can do to make up for your sins. You cannot earn God's forgiveness. All you can do is accept salvation as a free gift of God's grace. It is completely free, and you receive it through faith alone. If you have never placed your trust in Jesus Christ before, you can do so right now. If you would like to know more about how to receive a new life in Jesus Christ, read the article on FAITH.

Once you accept Jesus Christ, you have a tremendous resource available to you that you didn't have before. You have God as your personal heavenly Parent, a perfect role model who enables you to understand your own role as parent more perfectly. Just as earthly parents love and cherish their children, want them to be happy and to be the best human beings they can be, and are there to help their children with their problems, so our heavenly Parent loves us, cherishes us, desires our joy and our growth, and helps us with our problems.

One of the most exciting privileges we have as Christian parents is the privilege of helping our children learn to know and love Jesus Christ, so that they will trust Him as Savior and Lord. The Scriptures tell us that we have a joyful responsibility to teach, train, and bring up our children in the admonition of the Lord (see Deuteronomy 6:6–7; Psalm 78:5–7; Proverbs 14:26; 22:6; Ephesians 6:4).

From the time they are born, our children should find themselves part of a family that practices a totally inclusive devotional atmosphere. There should be sacred music for both children and adults (as well as good secular music); prayer (both regularly scheduled and spontaneous); family devotions; Scripture reading (for children, there should be Bible stories appropriate to their level of understanding); regular church and Sunday school involvement; extra spiritual influences such as Christian camping and vacation Bible school; and, at the center of each parent's life, a total commitment to Jesus Christ as Lord.

Many parents expect the church to meet the spiritual needs of their children. But programs such as Sunday school, vacation Bible school, and youth groups are only intended to reinforce what's going on at home. They are supplements to family spiritual instruction; they are not intended to be the sum total of a child's spiritual training. Children and teenagers hunger for meaning and spiritual truth. If parents abdicate their spiritual responsibility, the child will look elsewhere. The upsurge in cultic and occultic involvement supports this fact.

Children are not property; they are a gift. Your children belong to God. He has entrusted them to you. Be assured, God loves your children far more than you do. He's

Not only we ourselves, but our entire household is affected by our faith in Christ.

It's not a matter of whether you teach your children spiritual values, but rather what you are teaching them. It's not enough to "talk the talk." You must also "walk the walk." Kids can spot a phony a mile away. So our first spiritual duty is to be people of integrity. Are you the same on the inside as the outside? Are you the same at home as at church?

420

LAYING A SPIRITUAL FOUNDATION

PRENATAL CARE	It is never too early to begin giving our children a strong spiritual base. There are even actions we can undertake while a child is still in the womb that will contribute to that child's spiritual health in later life. One of the best ways a Christian mother can contribute to her unborn child's spiritual health is by focusing on her own spiritual well-being. She can listen to soothing Christian music. Take care of her spiritual, emotional, and physical needs. The father can help provide his wife with a calm, supportive, nurturing environment for her pregnancy. There is significant medical evidence that a positive maternal attitude can contribute to the health of the baby, to a reduced chance of miscarriage, and to the prevention of congenital abnormalities.
INFANCY *(birth to 15 months)*	Immediately after your baby is born, you can begin laying a strong spiritual foundation in that child's life. Obviously, an infant cannot understand the plan of salvation, but that child will inevitably be affected by the character and attitude the parents project, which are largely grounded in their spiritual faith. Even in infancy, a child can sense the atmosphere of the home, whether the fruit of the Spirit are lived out there or not. The best possible environment for an infant is a home that is loving, joyful, peaceful, patient, kind, good, faithful, gentle, and self-controlled (see Galatians 5:22–23).
TODDLERS *(15 to 36 months)*	As the child matures, acquiring new experiences and language skills, a very important aspect of the child begins to take shape: his image of God. Here, the role of the father is extremely important, because the child's image of his Heavenly Father is going to be based in large part on the image of his earthly father. This doesn't mean that children with abusive or neglectful fathers are doomed to be unable to know their Heavenly Father, but our clinical experience is overwhelming: children who experienced positive fathering are statistically more likely to have positive experiences with God, and those who experienced negative fathering will be more likely to have difficulty in their faith. It is important, during this phase of the child's development, that he or she feels loved, affirmed, secure, protected, and accepted. Toddlers need to receive positive influences, and care should be exercised in the kinds of television, music, and tone of voice they are exposed to. Toddlers need a lot of touching, hugging, eye contact, smiles, and gentle words. The way we relate to our children at this crucial, formative stage has an enormous impact on the child's later personality and spiritual development.
PRESCHOOLER *(3 to 6 years)*	The child reasons concretely, in black-and-white thinking. Until a child is able to comprehend abstract concepts (on average, at about ten years old), there is little point in trying to reason with him about his conduct. To correct a child's bad behavior or affirm (reinforce) a child's good behavior, the rebuke, physical punishment, hug, or praise must be immediate and directly linked to the child's actions. Children at this age are frequently able to understand that they sin, that they want God to forgive

421

LAYING A SPIRITUAL FOUNDATION—*Cont'd*

PRESCHOOLER *(3 to 6 years)* Cont'd	them, and that they want to live forever in heaven (though their conception of heaven is liable to be extremely vague). By age six, many children are able to place their trust in Christ; in fact, a child's faith may have some advantages over adult faith, since Christ taught that we adults are to become like little children in order to believe and inherit the kingdom. Here again, as in the toddler stage, the father has a crucial role to play in shaping the child's understanding of God.
ELEMENTARY *(age 6 to 12)*	During these years, the child experiences a growing ability to comprehend abstract concepts. He or she experiences a budding conscience and a growing sense of right and wrong. Children identify with the parent of the same sex and model themselves after their parental example. They watch the interaction of the parents between themselves. They pick up subtle messages and begin to gauge their own self-worth. It is important that parents not criticize each other, since by doing so, they tear down the self-esteem of the child who identifies with the criticized parent.
TEENAGE YEARS	As teenagers, our children begin hammering out their own individual identities. They begin thinking about the meaning of their lives, and they want to commit themselves to something important. Conflict is common during these years, and parents need to create an atmosphere in which conflicts are resolved productively and spiritually, while keeping the lines of communication open. Teenagers no longer want simply to absorb the teachings of their parents; they want a faith that is all their own, tested and proven in the laboratory of their own lives. This doesn't mean they will reject your faith, but they will likely test it, evaluate it, doubt it, and question it. All of this is healthy, because while we all want to transmit our faith and our values to the next generation, one of those values is an ability to think for themselves. If our children are able to discover and apply God's truth for themselves in the world they are living in, then they will be much less likely to be conned into cults or false philosophies in the future. (And, as they approach college and independence, we can be sure there are cults and false philosophies laying in wait to entrap them.)

not asking you to be a perfect parent, but He is asking you to be a faithful steward. And in this arena, 10 percent is unacceptable. He's asking for 100 percent.

You may be thinking, "Well, I guess we'll have to start having family devotions every day. I suppose we can schedule in fifteen minutes right after dinner. I'm not sure Johnny can sit still any longer than that."

That's a start, but the picture is much bigger than that. Family devotions should be a 24-hour-a-day proposition. Deuteronomy 6:6–7 tells us, "And these words which I command you today shall be in your heart. You shall teach them diligently to your children, and shall talk of them when you sit in your house, when you walk by the way, when you lie down, and when you rise up."

The Bible tells us to pray without ceasing. This is something children must see modeled in the lives of parents. Let them see that your prayer life extends beyond the

Praying with and for our children is the glue that holds it all together.

422

dinner table, beyond bedtime prayers. As needs arise during the day, pray spontaneously. For example, if you're driving and you see an accident along the side of the road, pray together for those involved in the accident and thank God for protecting your family.

When you pray aloud with your children, keep it simple. A young child may feel awkward and shy about praying if he feels he has to compete with his parent's eloquent prayers. Praying with children communicates that they are just as important to God as adults and helps them see their parents as equally dependent on God. This gives our children a powerful model for spirituality that they will take with them throughout their lives.

Authentic Unconditional Love

Unconditional love is what the original Greek New Testament calls *agape*. It is the kind of love Paul describes in Ephesians 5:25, where he says, "Husbands, love [*agape*] your wives, just as Christ also loved the church and gave Himself for her." The reason we call this kind of love *unconditional* is that it is love that does not change according to conditions such as the behavior or lovableness of the person who is being loved. Unconditional *agape* love involves an act of the will. When Paul says, "Husbands, love your wives," he is giving a command. You cannot command a feeling; but you can command a person's will. Unconditional love is more powerful than any feeling; it is an act of the will, an act of obedience to God.

The first duty of parents is to love *(agape)* each other. They must seek the good of each other. They must affirm each other, show respect to each other, protect and defend each other, serve each other, and cherish each other. One of the best gifts parents can give their children is a secure home in which the two parents love each other unconditionally. Love between the parents enables the children to feel secure and safe. (See MARRIAGE.)

The second duty of parents is to love *(agape)* their children. This means they will discipline their children—not in anger, but in love. Godly, loving parents will build up their children and raise their self-esteem. Loving parents challenge their children and cherish them. Loving parents sometimes have to be tough with their children and allow their children to experience the consequences of their sins and rebellion.

Here again we see the difference between *agape*-love (rooted in the will) and *phileo*-love (rooted in feelings). Feelings-oriented love wants to be liked. When a dad says, "I can't bear to discipline my kids, I want them to like me," he is operating on the basis of feelings, on the basis of *phileo*-love, not *agape*.

Christlike *agape*-love, says psychologist Norm Wright, is "a perfect commitment to an imperfect person." It is the same kind of love the apostle Paul describes in 1 Corinthians 13:4–7:

> Love suffers long and is kind; love does not envy; love does not parade itself, is not puffed up; does not behave rudely, does not seek its own, is not provoked, thinks no evil; does not rejoice in iniquity, but rejoices in the truth; bears all things, believes all things, hopes all things, endures all things.

The world can be a confusing and threatening place. Knowing that God is accessible through a 24-hour prayer hotline can comfort children and offer them security and stability.

There is nothing wrong with love that is rooted in feelings. There is nothing wrong with romantic love (which in Greek is called eros*). There is nothing wrong with family love (*phileo*). But unconditional* agape *love is higher, deeper, wider, and more powerful than any other kind of love. It is also the most beautiful form of love, because* agape *love is constructive; it creates worth and value in those who are loved. It erases sin and guilt and makes forgiveness possible.*

423

Feelings may change from moment to moment, but unconditional love "endures all things."

Honest Family Communication

The apostle Paul describes the basis for good family communication in Ephesians 4:25: "putting away lying . . . 'speak truth.'" Or, as Ephesians 4:15 says, "speaking the truth in love." But how, in a practical sense, do we do that? How do we communicate truth and love at the same time? Here are some basic guidelines for honest family communication:

1. Take time. Don't fall for the myth of "quality time," which for most people means, "I'm too busy with my workaholic pursuits to really spend time with my children, so every once in a while I'll take them on a 'quality time' outing to make up for the way I neglect them all the rest of their lives." Children need more than "quality time." They need a lot of your time. They need to be mentored and discipled. They need to be loved and encouraged. They need to be able to watch your example so they can learn what a man of God or a woman of God is really like. Both boys and girls need a strong relationship not only with the mother but also with the father. Take time in regular family devotions. Take time in heart-to-heart talks. Take time in family games, vacations, and recreational times.

2. Express anger appropriately. Explosive anger destroys relationships. Sneaky passive-aggressive anger destroys relationships. Repressing and denying anger is equally destructive. The solution is to learn to express anger appropriately, to express anger assertively rather than aggressively. (For a complete discussion of this issue, see ANGER.)

3. Express love often. Hug your children and tell them you love them. Love must be demonstrated, and it must be verbalized. Don't ever take it for granted that your children know they are loved. Show them and tell them—*often.*

4. Talk to your children about spiritual things. Talk to them about their relationship with God. Try to win them to Christ when they are young. Help them to experience the love, acceptance, and forgiveness of God through your own love, acceptance, and forgiveness.

5. Take the initiative. When you are wrong, be the first to admit it. Many parents hesitate to say, "I'm sorry," because they think it's a sign of weakness to do so. But asking forgiveness when we have done wrong is not a sign of weakness, it's a sign of strength. It is helpful for our children to see the example of parents who seek forgiveness from their spouses and from the children themselves whenever forgiveness is needed.

6. When there is conflict, fight fair. Parents should resolve conflicts with each other and with children on a basis of love and fairness. (See "Guidelines for Fighting Fair" under MARRIAGE.) These guidelines were devised to help couples deal with conflict, but they can be a helpful standard for *all* family communicating, including communicating with children.

Firm, Loving Discipline

Another essential ingredient of a happy, healthy Christian family is children who are firmly, lovingly disciplined. These children have a sense of protective boundaries. This ingredient is expressed by the apostle Paul in Ephesians 6:1–4, where he writes,

> *A parent who truly loves (agape) will practice tough love when the situation demands. A truly loving parent wants the best for his or her children more than he or she wants to be liked.*

Children, obey your parents in the Lord, for this is right. "Honor your father and mother," which is the first commandment with promise: "that it may be well with you and you may live long on the earth."

And you, fathers, do not provoke your children to wrath, but bring them up in the training and admonition of the Lord.

The exact definitions of words in these verses are instructive. In that phrase "the training and admonition of the Lord," the word *training* means "discipline." The word *admonition* means "training by word." As parents, we are to discipline our children, and we are to verbally instruct and train our children.

But there is a tempering note in these verses. We are not to "provoke" our children to "wrath." In other words, we are not to exasperate our children by disciplining them in an inconsistent, undependable, capricious way. And we are not to place unrealistic, perfectionistic expectations on them that they can never hope to live up to.

At our clinics, we often counsel people who as children were "provoked to wrath," frustrated in their self-esteem, made to feel negative about themselves. We have seen the anger, the depression, the guilt, and the bitterness that these people struggle with. And this is a clear demonstration, if one was ever needed, of the practical wisdom of biblical counsel.

Here are some suggestions for training and disciplining your children:

1. Teach them to memorize Scripture. The Word of God builds character. This is part of the process of bringing your children up in "the admonition of the Lord."

2. Discipline them consistently. Agree with your spouse about disciplinary matters. Avoid indulging your children one time, then landing on them with both feet the next. Focus on disciplining firmly and calmly, not in anger by lashing out. Discipline is training and correcting, *not* getting even with your kids for making you mad.

3. Prepare your children ahead of time to face peer pressure. Your children will be pressured to use alcohol, tobacco, and illegal drugs. They will be pressured to allow themselves to be used sexually. They need to be prepared ahead of time to face and withstand these pressures. One of the best ways to strengthen a child's resolve to stand against peer pressure is to build a child's self-esteem. When he or she feels there is nothing to prove to anyone else, that he or she does not always need attention or acceptance by others, then the child will be able to take a courageous and even solitary stand against the pressures and temptations of the world.

4. Set standards about the company your children keep. This is especially important in the teen years. Young people are often swayed by "ringleaders" and led into temptations they would never face on their own. Know the kids your children "hang out" with. Know where they are and what they are doing. Don't hand your child or teenager a lot of unaccountable time before he or she is mature enough to handle it.

5. Avoid yelling. Calm verbal reproof (linked, if necessary, with spanking) is a biblical discipline technique. That is what *admonition* means. Yelling, screaming, and nagging are unproductive. In fact, a rebellious child will sometimes try to goad you into losing your temper in order to control your behavior. If you lose emotional control, the child wins the battle. Don't let that happen.

6. Spank. Spanking has fallen into disfavor in some parts of our society. Some people confuse spanking with child abuse. "You'll never teach a child anything by

Give your children the gift of your time, so that communication can take place and relationships can grow.

425

hitting him," they say. But this thinking runs counter to two very persuasive facts: (1) spanking is biblical, and (2) spanking works. Properly administered, spanking is nothing at all like child abuse. Child abuse is an act of anger and rage. Spanking is an act of love, and in most cases, the parent spanks reluctantly and with a sense of grief and sorrow, not rage.

Discipline is the most distasteful part of being a parent. Your children are convinced you enjoy making them miserable, yet discipline usually leaves the parent feeling the most miserable of all. "This is going to hurt me worse than it does you" is a statement parents have made for generations, and generations of children have scoffed. But it's true. We would all rather be buddies to our children than disciplinarians, but our children don't give us that choice. Neither does God, who calls us to love our children by disciplining them.

A spanking, a restricted privilege, a long, unpleasant talk—these are not exactly Kodak moments. But they are crucial, formative, life-shaping moments in the lives of our children. If we do our job well, then someday, just maybe, our children will look back over all those moments, and thank us.

Consistency

Children are amazingly resilient. We can make a lot of mistakes as parents, and our children will still probably turn out all right. In counseling thousands of individuals over the years, the doctors at the Minirth Meier New Life Clinics have observed a clear pattern involving the relationship between the way children are parented and the way they turn out as adults. Children from overly strict homes (if the strictness is not *too* extreme) still tend to become healthy, functional adults. The same can be said for children from overly lenient homes (if the leniency is not *too* extreme).

But in all the *criminals* that we have counseled, we have seen a very alarming trend: About two-thirds of those criminals came from homes where at least one parent spoiled the child excessively. The other third came from homes where at least one parent was physically abusive or extremely verbally abusive.

Yet the most significant finding of all was in regard to a special kind of criminal, the one with a *sociopathic personality disorder*. (Sociopaths are people who cheat, exploit, or criminally victimize others without any conscience or remorse.) In virtually every case of sociopathy we examined, we found a background of *parental inconsistency*.

In a healthy family, both parents present a united front. A child is not allowed to play one parent against the other. One portion of the family is not allowed to form alliances against the other. The child knows that he can't get away with asking Mom for a privilege that Dad has already said "no" to. If Mom and Dad have differences regarding discipline or a privilege, they resolve that difference in private, not in front of the kids. Both parents support, defend, and back each other up in front of the children. The message the kids receive is clear: Mom and Dad are a unit. Don't even think of trying to split one off against the other.

In a healthy family, both parents keep their word to the children, and the children are held accountable to do the same. If circumstances change, and it becomes absolutely impossible to keep a promise, the circumstances are explained to the children, and they are asked to be understanding and encouraged to deal with the disappointment in a mature way. But such situations are the rare exception, not the rule. If the parents

In a healthy family, there are clear, consistent rules and boundaries. When those rules are broken or those boundaries are violated, predictable consequences follow in a logical and consistent way.

426

Some Guidelines for Spanking

Spanking should be immediate. "Because the sentence against an evil work is not executed speedily," says Ecclesiastes 8:11, "therefore the heart of the sons of men is fully set in them to do evil." Delaying discipline dilutes its effectiveness. When a mother says, "I'm telling your father when he gets home," the child gets the impression that Mom is weak and ineffectual, that Dad is threatening and someone to be avoided.

Discipline for defiance of authority. When a child breaks the rules to test or violate parental authority, the child needs to be instantly shown that this attitude will not be tolerated.

Spanking should be done in private. Spanking in front of other people inflicts shame on a child and wounds his or her self-esteem.

Link spanking with genuine grief. When a child defies authority or demonstrates untrustworthiness by lying, the parent should be honest about his or her feelings of grief and disappointment—not to manipulate the child, but so that the child will understand that his or her actions cause pain and sorrow to another person. The open expression of parental grief is especially important in dealing with older children and teenagers, who are mature enough to understand the meaning of these feelings. When a child sees disappointment on the face of a parent, he or she realizes that something valuable has been taken away from this important relationship—and the child often learns a lesson from the experience that will last a lifetime.

Spanking should be brief and appropriate, not excessive. Some religiously disordered parents abuse their children in the name of God. They beat their children with rods, belts, or fists. Some cause bruises, broken bones, or bleeding. Child abuse is a terrible, tragic sin, and when children are abused in the name of God, then God Himself is dishonored and children grow up resenting and fearing God.

Spanking is for young children; for older children, other techniques are more effective. A quick spank on the rear with a paddle or hand immediately after an act of defiance is appropriate and effective for young children. Spanking should become less and less necessary as children mature. Spanking becomes increasingly inappropriate as a child approaches the age of nine or ten, when "time out" in a corner or in the bedroom or the loss of privileges (no sweets, no TV, grounding) become effective tools.

Demonstrate love and acceptance before, during, and after the spanking. Hug the child after the spanking. Don't apologize for an appropriate spanking. Spanking is a parental duty and an act of love, not a sin.

Require the child to make amends. If the child is disciplined for causing a loss or damage, the child should be required to make restitution. He or she should dip into savings or do chores in order to understand that there is a cost to his or her actions.

Avoid breaking your child's spirit. We want our children to be independent and well-disciplined, not defeated and regimented. Spanking should be appropriate and not applied too frequently, or the child will either become immune to the pain or will become timid and withdrawn. Avoid punishing severely for expressing emotion; encourage the child to stay in touch with his or her feelings and to express them appropriately instead of explosively. If you spank a child for showing emotion, such as anger, the child will not be any less angry, but he will learn unhealthy patterns of repressing emotion.

promise to be at that soccer game or that dance recital, or if they promise a trip to Disneyworld, they'd better deliver or have a very good excuse. Consistency means keeping promises. Psalm 15:4 says that God honors those who keep their promises, even when it hurts them or costs them to do so.

Healthy Behavioral Models

It is said that character is caught, not taught. So if we want to raise healthy, happy children, we need to model attitudes and behavior that lead to wholeness and joy. Here are some ways we, as Christian parents, can set healthy examples for our children:

1. Build a healthy marriage relationship. Nothing is more instructive and inspiring to children than to see their parents in love, showing consideration to each other, working together as a team, solving problems together, even resolving conflict together. A healthy marriage is the best gift you can give your children, so make that your first priority.

2. Establish healthy priorities. Our children should see us spending time alone with God; taking care of our mental health (through recreation, rest, and reflection); spending time with our spouses; spending time with our children; spending time in service to God; spending time meeting the family's needs for food and shelter. When our children see us living by healthy priorities, they can't help but absorb those priorities as their own.

3. Take responsibility for choices. Some people gripe about life's unfairness, make statements like "I can't do this" and "I have to do that," and blame their problems on other people or circumstances or God. These people produce children who grow up to be just as negative and dysfunctional as they are. As Christian parents, we want to model a responsible, positive attitude toward life. When life is unfair, we ask God for the serenity to accept the things we cannot change, the courage to change the things we can, and the wisdom to know the difference. We refuse to say, "I can't" or "I have to," but instead we say, "I will not" or "I choose to." We make a decision not to blame others or God, but to take responsibility for our own lives and our own happiness. We make a decision to act rather than to be acted upon. When our children see those qualities in us, they are inspired to greater growth and maturity by our example.

4. Serve God in a healthy local church. It is important for children to see their parents using their talents and spiritual gifts in service to God. There are many opportunities for service available to us: teaching Sunday school, singing in the choir, serving in

Ralph Waldo Emerson once wrote, "What you do speaks so loud I can't hear what you say."

When our children see us putting ourselves on the front lines of Christian service, they realize that our faith is important to us, and it becomes more important and real to them.

Some Tips for Managing Your Relationship with Teenagers

During the teenage years, a child's allegiances shift away from family and parents to peers. It becomes more difficult—difficult but not impossible—to maintain open channels of communication with teenagers. This is a risky passage in the life of the family and the life of the teenager. Often, communication between parents and teenagers breaks down without the parents fully realizing what is happening. As teens move into the orbit of friends and increasingly out of the orbit of family, their values, attitudes, and beliefs will be increasingly subject to outside influences.

As teenagers search for personal identity, they take a strong interest in ideals and ideologies. They begin to look for reasons and meanings in life. They are able to reason like adults, although they are less mature. During this time, teens begin finding new role models besides their parents, including teachers and coaches, some of whom may present values and ideas that are at odds with your own Christian values. The result of all these influences is that your child may begin to question your Christian way of life.

It is important not to panic and not to attempt to control your child, since that will only drive your child away. As your teenager questions and explores new ideas and values, it is important to be accepting, patient, and secure. Communicate both love and respect for your teen as a young adult. Teach your teenager why you believe what you believe. Don't ask your children to accept your beliefs blindly, but teach them to think for themselves. God's Word can withstand the test. The key to seeing your teenager through this crisis of questioning is to *keep the lines of communication open*.

Here are some suggestions for enhancing communication with your teenager:

Maintain a habit of family devotions. This is a good time for talking and for letting young people participate. Children will tend to "clam up" as they reach their teen years, and this is normal. Help keep your teens involved by asking each person to share something he or she is thankful for from the day, something meaningful that happened, or something he or she would like the family to pray for. Some families keep a "kitty" handy during devotions, and anyone who refuses to talk during devotions must put a quarter in the kitty. Both children and teenagers have short attention spans, so it's best to keep devotions relatively brief.

Special time with Dad. An involved father is important to a child at every stage of his or her development, including the teenage years. Dads should make time in their schedules (once a week, or at least once a month) to take their teenagers out for a cola or for lunch for a time of staying in touch, one on one.

Family meetings. There should be a regular time (weekly or monthly) when the family can get together and discuss family business, problems, joys, feelings, rules, and complaints. The goal is to keep family communication open so that the family can function as a unit and so that everyone feels included. Issues to discuss might include rules about use of the car or phone, problems with peers, dating, morality, vacation plans, and family decisions.

Some Tips for Managing Your
Relationship with Teenagers—*Cont'd*

Practice discipline that is appropriate for teenagers. Disciplining teens is trickier and requires more sophisticated approaches than disciplining a small child. Spanking should be a thing of the past by the time a child enters his or her teens, since physical discipline of teenagers tends to produce resentment and rebellion rather than submission. New strategies are needed. Parents should move from the physical to the mental/emotional forms of discipline, involving counseling or restricting the teenager. Privileges that may be restricted include use of the car, the phone, the television, the computer, or other home recreational facilities; travel (being grounded); and after-school activities such as sports activities. Teenagers should have as much latitude as possible in choosing friends or dates, but if you are concerned about a given friend or date (for example, if you suspect a risk of alcohol, drugs, or date rape), then you should place firm limits on those relationships.

One key to effective discipline is to look for ways to give the teenager responsibility and to treat the teenager more and more as an adult. Parents should encourage teenagers to use their God-given minds and reasoning abilities to solve problems and get out of bad situations. Teens should also be encouraged to look at life in spiritual terms, and to find ways to apply biblical principles to practical situations in their lives.

leadership, meeting human needs as deacons, becoming involved in visitation or evangelism.

5. Model chastity, fidelity, integrity, and honesty. You want to raise children of integrity, children who will respect their own bodies and emotions, children who will not misuse their sexuality, children who will always value the truth. All Christian parents want these things for their children. If you want that for your children, then *model* those qualities. If you are tempted to betray your spouse, then think how the revelation of your sin would affect your children. Get counseling or have someone hold you accountable to keep yourself pure and your integrity intact. Whatever you want your children to be, you must be first.

Biblical Leadership Roles

It is important for children to see healthy biblical leadership roles being lived out in the home. Here is a checklist of the features of healthy husband and wife roles, drawn from such passages as 1 Timothy 3:2–5; Ephesians 5:22–33; and Proverbs 31:10–31:

The husband's role:

- To manage the family's business, acting as the CEO of the family. He can delegate specific responsibilities, such as paying the bills, but he is ultimately responsible for overseeing the family finances.

- To lead the family's devotional life.
- To love his wife as Christ loves the church.
- To nourish and care for his wife's mental and emotional needs.
- To recognize and utilize his wife's abilities and gifts in running the family so that he and she form a complete team.
- To discipline the children in conjunction with his wife.
- To lead, plan, and make decisions.

The wife's role:

- To submit to her husband's leadership—not in such a way that she loses her identity and worth but so that there are clear lines of authority and responsibility in the home; she is free to express her ideas and opinions, and a loving husband maintains an atmosphere of mutuality and respect in the home.
- To manage the household.
- To care for the family's needs for food and clothing.
- To invest and even work outside the home if she chooses, so long as the physical and emotional needs of the family are met first (see Proverbs 31:13, 16, 24).

Some people believe it is wrong for a Christian mother to work outside the home. The Bible makes no such clear-cut case. There are situations in which the mother may have no choice but to work outside the home, as when she is divorced or widowed. The key is to make sure that the family does not suffer if Mom works.

DISCOVERING YOUR CHILD'S UNIQUE DESIGN

It's impossible to meet the spiritual needs of a child you do not know. Proverbs 22:6 says, "Train up a child in the way he should go, and when he is old he will not depart from it." Some parents assume this means that if we just teach our kids enough Bible verses and take them to church, they won't stray from the faith. But that's only part of the picture. That phrase, "in the way he should go," can also be translated, "according to his own unique character or characteristics." Every child has different strengths and weaknesses. It's the job of parents to discover those unique character qualities and to help the child achieve his or her maximum potential by building on those strengths and compensating for those weaknesses.

Our job as parents is to help our children become the best they can be at who they already are. To do this, we should view our children as *disciples*. The Greek word for "disciple" simply means a learner, a follower, one who is taught. Christ aimed to impart his very life to His disciples. Fathers and mothers "training up their children in the way they should go" should prioritize the "discipling" of their own children, modeling before their children's watchful eyes how a Christlike life is to be lived.

> *Our job as parents is to help our children become the best they can be at who they already are.*

BUILDING YOUR CHILD'S SELF-ESTEEM

Many people confuse self-esteem with arrogance, pride, or self-love. But good self-esteem is actually a very healthy and biblical concept. To have good self-esteem is to understand who we are in God's sight. Healthy self-esteem is like a three-legged stool, and the three legs that support it are three biblical truths:

1. We are created in God's image. There is a grand old hymn that asks the question, Would Jesus go to the cross and give His life "for such a worm as I?" The truth of the Bible is that we are not worms, we are beings who were created in God's own image. Though that image has been marred by sin, it is still a part of who we are, and that image is being gradually restored in us as we grow to become more and more like Christ (see Romans 8:28–29).

2. Human beings are fallen, but not worthless. Sin broke our relationship with God, but it did not cancel out our value to God. He prized us so highly that He sent His own Son to die in our place and redeem us from our fallen and sinful condition.

3. God loves us. It is a message that is so pervasive in Christianity that we sometimes fail to recognize how profound a truth it really is. "Jesus loves me, this I know" is a song we sing from childhood. And the most famous verse in the Bible tells us, "For God so loved the world that He gave His only begotten Son, that whoever believes in Him should not perish but have everlasting life" (John 3:16). Truly, God's love for us is a wonderful basis for healthy self-esteem!

■

Each of our children is different from the others. Each is different from us. Parents need to notice the individual identities of children and to help them live in a way that is consistent with who God made them to be. The child who is creative and artistic, who likes to write stories or draw beautiful pictures, should be encouraged in these artistic endeavors. Special art classes or courses in school should be made available to the child to enhance and magnify those abilities. The child can be built up in his or her own self-esteem as you say, "I see in you a gift for imagining and creating. Remember that God is creative too. He created the entire universe, and He created you. God has given you this gift, and I believe He wants you to use it to bring honor to Him."

■

HELPING YOUR CHILD MANAGE ANGER

One of the most common problems we see in family counseling is a child who sets the agenda for how emotions are managed in the family. Even the best-intentioned parents sometimes find themselves frustrated by their inability to deal with their child's anger. One of the mistakes parents make is focusing on *control.* "How do I control my child's behavior?" is the question parents often ask. But that's the wrong question. The real question should be, "How can I manage my feelings and stay composed *so that these emotions can be positively resolved?*" There are several strategies you can use to manage your own anger and to help your child learn to manage his or her own anger. These strategies, when learned early in life, can serve an individual well on into adulthood:

1. Don't be intimidated by your child's anger. When we respond in fear to a child's anger, we give that child a great deal of power in a battle for control. The alternative is to let our children be human. We as adults have struggles with our emotions, and it's only natural that our children would too. Give the child room to express human emotion, but hold on firmly to your parental authority. Try to recover your objectivity and respond with calm reason and fairness.

Encouraging a Healthy
Self-Esteem in Your Child

Here are some suggestions that will enable you to encourage a healthy sense of self-esteem in your child:

- Say "I love you." Children need to hear these three words. Particularly in their early years, children derive a large portion of their self-worth from how their parents relate to them. If they know their parents love them, children feel they can love themselves in a healthy way.

- When you praise your child, place as much emphasis on *character* as on *achievement*. This focuses the child's attention on the aspect of achievement that is most important. For example, say, "These are excellent grades! These grades represent the maturity, commitment, and perseverance you have shown throughout the school year. I'm very proud of the character you've demonstrated by applying yourself to your work. I can see that God is really producing some wonderful character qualities in your life."

- Praise the child for specific behavior, in order to reinforce that behavior. "I was proud of you for keeping your cool when Mr. Jones yelled at you and accused you of breaking his window," you might say. "I could see that was hard for you, but you are really learning how to control your anger and how not to become defensive when other people attack you."

- Praise with sincerity. Children can spot empty or meaningless praise. Focus on character qualities instead of outward appearances ("You're so cute!") or flattery ("You're so strong—Wouldn't you love to clean out the garage today?").

- Praise in private. When you let your child know you are proud of him or her on a one-to-one basis, the child knows you mean it. These moments build relationships and help the child to feel "special" in a healthy, biblical way.

- Invite your child to share opinions, ideas, and feelings. This helps the child to feel important—not more important than anyone else, but as important as everyone else. Children should grow up thinking, "My thoughts are valid. My feelings are worth expressing." This concept helps the child to experience the sense that he or she is valued.

- Pray with your child. This helps your child to know that he or she is important to you and to God. It is a powerful boost to a child's self-esteem to hear, "Father, thank You for this child. I'm so grateful that You have made him/her a part of our family. I know You love this child so much, so please continue to bless his/her life."

- Answer your child's questions. Encourage your child's questions, because this helps your child to know that you value his or her interests and thought processes. The more your child asks questions and gets good answers, the more confidence your child will have in his or her own intellect and curiosity.

- Give your child your full attention. Parents often have a tendency to be so absorbed in grown-up interests that they only give their children an "uh-huh" or

2. Model healthy communication. That means avoiding sarcasm ("Calm down, or I'll give you something to be mad about!"), authoritarian statements ("because I said so, that's why!"), preaching, yelling (which communicates insecurity), or shouting down your child. As much as possible, listen to your child's thoughts and feelings, but be careful not to allow your child to manipulate you with incessant arguing, interrupting, and rebuttal.

3. Don't major on the minors. Children will get upset over the most trivial issues: what to wear, who goes first, what TV show to watch, why he doesn't get to play right now. Parents easily get drawn into these trivialities and end up arguing for hours over issues that don't deserve thirty seconds of attention. Yes, these issues are extremely important to our children, and we should be careful not to minimize or devalue their feelings. But we should help our children to put these issues into a realistic perspective.

4. Be honest about your own experiences. Let your children know that you experience anger, too—not by exploding at them, but by sharing events and feelings with them. Tell them about strategies and solutions you have learned for dealing with your own emotions. One of the best ways children learn is through the openness and honesty of their parents.

5. Offer spiritual insights with care. Anger management is largely a matter of spiritual maturity. Spiritual understanding is an important factor in managing our emotions. Truths about grace, patience, love, and forgiveness can and should be woven into everyday situations, but if we hit children over the head with religious concepts during a time of anger and confrontation, the result is likely to be counterproductive. Our goal is to give our children the spiritual tools to live more effectively, not just to structure their behavior in a legalistic way. As we help our children apply the spiritual principles of anger management found in the Bible, they will begin to see how practical and applicable the Bible is to everyday life.

Even in times of anger.

UNDERSTANDING THE "IMPOSSIBLE CHILD"

Some youngsters seem impossible to get along with, but often we just don't understand the way they think. Children perceive the world very differently from adults. They don't know how to verbalize their concerns and frustrations, and they operate with limited knowledge and skills. They experience the world on a three-foot-high level—physically, emotionally, and mentally. Until we understand their perspective, it's hard to help them work through their problems.

Many factors affect children's behavioral development, including the family setting and lifestyle, the personality makeup of the child and family members, and the way they perceive relationships and experiences. Kids who misbehave may be simply confused or scared. Because very few children are taught about their emotions—particularly the painful emotions like anger, sadness, and fear—they often express their feelings in ways that are inappropriate.

Children often feel rejected, especially in situations involving divorce, separation, death, a workaholic parent, or parents who are not emotionally committed to each other or the kids. Parents can feed these feelings of rejection without realizing it. Today, family schedules are filled with "have-to" and "want-to" activities. As members spend less and less time together, their relationships become superficial. Feelings of rejection can cause insecurity, low self-esteem, negativism, attention-seeking, hostility, jealousy, and slow conscience development. The way to reverse such feelings is to spend time with our children—an investment that pays dividends for a lifetime.

Parenting styles also affect children's emotional development and behavior. Children of overprotective or domineering parents can become overly submissive, overdependent, and can develop low self-esteem. In this dangerous world, parents need to find a balance in providing reasonable protection and teaching children independence.

Overly permissive parents can produce selfish children who are intolerant, rebellious, and inconsiderate. The lack of discipline can cause kids to be antisocial, lack initiative or spontaneity, and harbor bitterness toward their parents. Children learn more from watching their parents' actions than from listening to their words. Discipline is a way of correcting errors as well as teaching problem solving and effective adapting skills.

Children of perfectionistic parents often lack spontaneity, have overly rigid consciences, and are subject to false guilt and depression.

■

The better we understand the factors that cause an "impossible child" to be "impossible," the more we see how truly possible it is to help the child and train him or her to live positively and constructively.

■

435

WHEN DOES A CHILD NEED PROFESSIONAL COUNSELING?

All children have emotional problems from time to time—fears, anger, disobedience, acting out, and more. How does a parent know if a child's emotional issues are serious enough to warrant professional help from a Christian psychologist or psychiatrist? Following are some guidelines to help you with your decision.

The Age-Inappropriate Principle

Certain behavior may be normal at one developmental stage but clearly abnormal at another stage. When children or teens exhibit behaviors that are appropriate to early stages of development, it is called *regression* and is frequently a response to stress. Some examples:

- bed-wetting
- soiling
- temper tantrums
- separation anxiety (inappropriate clinging to parents)
- adult-level knowledge of sexual behavior
- adult-level sexual behavior

If such behaviors persist, it may be advisable to consult a professional therapist.

Especially advanced behavior in a child may also signal problems. A prime example would be adult sexual knowledge or behavior in a young child, which may be a warning sign that the child has been sexually abused.

The Inherently Unhealthy Principle

Certain behaviors are virtually *always* unhealthy, regardless of age:

- hallucinations
- delusions
- obsessions (particularly morbid preoccupations)
- compulsions
- cruelty to animals
- substance abuse
- fire-starting
- chronic antisocial behavior and trouble with the law

If you observe any of these behaviors in your child, even once, you should contact a mental health professional for his opinion as to whether an emotional evaluation is needed.

The Dramatic Negative Change Principle

A major negative change in a child's mood or behavior may signal a need for professional evaluation:

436

- significant drop in grades
- unmanageable behavior
- dropping old friends and choosing new friends from "the wrong crowd"
- emotional and social withdrawal
- significant weight loss or gain
- sleeping too much or too little
- loss of energy and excessive fatigue
- expressions of worthlessness or self-hate
- apparent difficulty concentrating, thinking, deciding
- depressed or morbid thinking (including thoughts of death)
- suicidal preoccupation or attempts
- excessive negative emotions (anger, sadness, resentment, guilt, anxiety)

The Trauma-Checkup Principle

Traumatic life events sometimes signal a need for professional evaluation, including:

- divorce of parents
- death of an immediate family member or close friend
- any incidents of sexual abuse

If you are not sure if your child's issues are serious enough to warrant professional help, you would be wise to err on the side of safety. It is easier to intervene in a problem at an early stage than to try to reverse a pathology that is advanced and deeply entrenched. If you don't know how to locate a Christian psychologist or psychiatrist in your area, ask your church for a referral.

SINGLE PARENTING

Our hearts go out to single parents. Being a parent is a demanding job even with a partner. For single parents, the demands are not just doubled by the loss of a parenting partner, they are multiplied. Although the average single parent is a divorced or widowed woman, many men find themselves in this position as well (see also DIVORCE; GRIEF AND LOSS). The following are some of the added burdens faced by a single parent, along with some practical solutions:

Earning a Living

Maintaining an income can be a major problem for single parents, and especially for single mothers (who tend to earn less than their male counterparts). Single mothers in particular should ask themselves if there are alternatives to full-time employment outside the home (at least until the children reach school age), such as:

- alternative sources of income
- options for cutting the cost of living
- jobs that can be done in the home
- job-sharing with another single parent

Day Care

We believe day care is a poor option and a last resort. But for many single parents, it may be the only option available. When the issue is economic survival for yourself and your children, you do what you have to. However, there may be some creative day-care options you haven't considered. (See DAY CARE for a comprehensive discussion of these options and other issues.)

The Child's Need for Emotional Bonding

In our clinical experience, we have found that children who have a large number of caregivers in their early years—particularly if there is a lot of turnover among those caregivers—tend to be at much greater risk for later emotional problems than children with only one or a few primary caregivers.

Ideally, you should be that adult in your child's life, but realistically that is not always possible. In such cases, it is advisable to have someone care for your child on a regular, long-term basis, building a relationship and bonding with your child: a grandparent or other relative; a nurse or nanny who will make a long-term commitment to the position; a close friend or neighbor. If you do this, you may experience feelings of resentment and jealousy, since it will seem that you have been replaced. But these feelings have to be set aside (and dealt with in counseling, if need be) for the good of your child. Encourage your child's caregiver to develop a strong love-relationship with your child; then be creative about making time for you and your child to be together when you are not at work.

Illness and Other Emergencies

You will need to have a "Plan B" for those days when your child's caregiver is unable to watch your child, because of illness or for some other reason. It is advisable to have a plan in place so that you can take a day off from work or you can make an arrangement for a friend to be available in an emergency.

Meeting Your Children's Physical, Emotional, and Spiritual Needs

Now that you are parenting alone, the entire burden for meeting your children's needs falls squarely on you. Be sure to maintain healthy habits, such as family devotions, talking to your children about their feelings and problems, and having times of fun and relaxation together.

Meeting Your Own Physical, Emotional, and Spiritual Needs

Take time for exercise, talking through your feelings and struggles, experiencing Christian fellowship and sharing, praying with other Christians and sharing prayer needs, Scripture meditation and personal devotions, and so forth.

Guilt Feelings

Whether you are single because of divorce or loss, and whether you are a mom or a dad, you are bound to experience feelings of guilt, either false guilt or authentic guilt (for a comprehensive explanation, see GUILT). You may feel trapped, unable to handle the new responsibilities that have suddenly been thrust upon you. As a result, you may feel guilty about being inadequate to the role of single parent.

If divorced, you may also feel guilty about the divorce, particularly if you feel responsibility for the divorce.

If bereaved, you may feel guilty and remorseful over things you wish you had said or done (or not said or done) while your spouse was still alive. Or you may feel guilty for not parenting or managing the household as well as your spouse would have. Or for not spending enough time with the kids.

It's important to recognize these guilt feelings, to admit them, and to work through them. Whether or not the feelings are valid, they are real. Evaluate those feelings, evaluate your own behavior, bounce those feelings off a friend, a counselor, or a support group. Admit the mistakes you made, honestly acknowledge your own sins and mistakes, make amends (if possible and if necessary), ask God's forgiveness, forgive yourself, and move on (see FORGIVENESS).

Grief

Whether you are single because of loss or divorce, you are hurting, and you have much to grieve. So give yourself permission to grieve. Grief issues differ in different situations, but the grief process progresses in fairly predictable stages. See GRIEF AND LOSS for a full explanation of the stages you must go through.

The Child's Anger

When a child loses a parent to divorce or death, the biggest emotional burden facing that child is anger. The problem is compounded by the fact that the single parent is going through so much emotion at this time that he or she may not be tuned in to the child's feelings. Single parents will sometimes even rationalize the child's feelings: "My kid's doing just fine, couldn't be better, not to worry. Kids always bounce back from things like this."

But the child is hurting deeply. He may show it, or he may stuff it, but there is anger in this child. His world has been shredded. His security has been ripped away. This child is angry with the absent parent (even if that parent is dead), angry with God, and angry with you.

Your first response may be to try to shut down that anger. "You shouldn't feel like that," you may say. "Come on, get a hold of yourself, chill out." The child's anger makes us uncomfortable, particularly if we have repressed or denied some anger of our own. The child's anger stirs up heat and friction in our little family unit, and that makes us uncomfortable.

Your job, as a single parent, is to face that anger, draw it out, give your child permission to talk, and even permission to express anger.

The Child's Guilt

The death of a parent is not the child's fault. Neither is divorce. But children feel guilty anyway. They can't help it. Children have a tendency to practice *self-referential*

439

thinking. Whatever happens in life, they think it relates to them. For example, if something bad happens in the family, it must be a punishment aimed at that child for something bad he or she did. If there was anger or arguing in the family, it was the child's fault. If the family structure came unglued, it was the child's fault.

Older children can intellectually understand that they are not to blame if the parents get a divorce or if Dad comes down with cancer. But at a deep emotional level, that self-referential thinking can persist for an amazingly long time. You wouldn't expect to find such guilt in a teenager, because teenagers can reason, and this kind of guilt is totally unreasonable—but in counseling, we find it there all the same.

Children need repeated parental reassurance that the loss of the other parent to death or divorce was not a result of anything the child did. A child who has been acting out or misbehaving prior to the loss often feels exceptionally guilty after the loss. He thinks, *If only I hadn't been so bad, Daddy wouldn't have left us.* Or *If only I hadn't been so bad, God wouldn't have punished me by taking Mommy to heaven.* These are unbelievably heavy thoughts and emotions for a child to carry. Our job as parents is to help our children work through those feelings. If the child does not show progress in resolving those feelings, the parent should not hesitate to get the child into counseling.

Sometimes single parents (particularly divorced parents) are treated as second-class parents by others, particularly by legalistic and self-righteous Christians. This is a tragedy and an injustice. There is nothing second-class about any kind of parenthood, including single parenthood. If you are a single parent, we commend you for your courage and your commitment to your child. You have accepted an enormous challenge, and you are meeting the challenge day by day. Even though the need to hold down a job has cut your available hours in half, you are doing the parenting job of two people.

As you continue the task of raising your children to be strong, healthy, confident young people, remember that there is another Parent alongside you.

As you continue the task of raising your children to be strong, healthy, confident young people, remember that there is another Parent alongside you. Draw on His strength and His wisdom to meet the challenges ahead, for He is a loving heavenly Father.

OTHER PARENTING ISSUES

Articles on other specific issues affecting your role as a parent may be found elsewhere in this encyclopedia.

For information on learning and developmental issues, see ATTENTION DEFICIT DISORDER, DAY CARE, HOME SCHOOLING, LEARNING AND EDUCATION, TELEVISION AND OTHER ENTERTAINMENT MEDIA.

Information on emotional issues can be found in AGGRESSION, ANGER, DYSFUNCTIONAL FAMILY, EMOTIONS, GRIEF AND LOSS, GUILT, SHAME.

Spiritual issues: FAITH.

Family dynamics: CODEPENDENCY, DYSFUNCTIONAL FAMILY, FAMILY.

Teenage issues: DATING AND COURTSHIP, SEX AND SEXUALITY, SEX EDUCATION.

Perfectionism

Are you a perfectionist?

"No," you may reply, "I'm committed to excellence!"

We hear a great deal in business, church, and motivational circles about *excellence* these days. And we hear a lot about *perfectionism* in psychological and recovery circles. Excellence is good. Perfectionism is unhealthy. What is the difference?

There is a fine line between a commitment to excellence and an obsession with perfection.

WHAT'S THE DIFFERENCE BETWEEN EXCELLENCE AND PERFECTIONISM?	
EXCELLENCE . . .	**PERFECTIONISM . . .**
Is striving for the best you can do.	**Is striving for an impossible ideal.**
Is realistic.	**Is idealistic.**
Says, "I want . . ."	**Says, "I must . . ." or "I ought . . ."**
Makes requests.	**Makes demands.**
Desires success.	**Fears failure.**
Focuses on process.	**Focuses on product.**
Is free to pursue excellence.	**Is enslaved by an obsession with perfection.**
Is self-accepting.	**Is self-condemning.**
Is accepting of others.	**Is impatient with others.**
Functions in reality.	**Focuses on idealized fantasy.**

Perfectionists are focused on what "ought" to be, on what other people "should" do, on what they "have to" do. They rant and complain about the unfairness of the world. They set goals, but the goals they set are impossible to achieve. They have "Things to Do" lists longer than your arm, and when they fail to get everything done (which is inevitable), they become angry and depressed. If perfectionists go on weight-loss programs, they expect to trim twenty-five pounds in one week. They often

441

fail to get projects finished because they aren't satisfied until the projects are done to perfection.

The strict standards of perfectionists interfere with their ability to get tasks done. They are preoccupied with order, rules, scheduling, and details. Concentrating on the individual leaves of an individual tree, they are unable to see the forest. They insist that others do things their way and tend to have definite beliefs and values. Perfectionists make excellent religious legalists, though their relationship with God may be stormy. Some perfectionistic Christians experience anger toward God, believing that God is too harsh and demanding and that He expects too much of them (they may have had the same stormy relationship with their parents). They are rigidly absorbed in right and wrong and are unable to internalize God's grace. Even if they are intellectually familiar with the concept of grace, they live by the law of legalistic perfection.

Perfectionists tend to have a great deal of trouble with relationships. They are difficult to live with because they impose the same impossible standards on spouses, children, friends, and employees that they inflict on themselves. They continually criticize their spouses for various imperfections. They incessantly criticize their children; then become angry when their children rebel. They become angry with themselves for their own imperfections, which leads to guilt, depression, and diminished self-esteem.

Perfectionists are product-focused, whereas people committed to excellence allow themselves to enjoy the process as well. Perfectionists live in the future, dreaming of the moment when their product will be completed (perfectly, of course) so they can at last be satisfied and content. Yet they postpone decisions and actually starting projects because everything has to be just right when they begin. If the perfectionist does manage to complete a project, there is no satisfaction, no contentment, because (1) it's time to start another project and (2) the product just completed is not as perfect as he had hoped and dreamed.

■

For the perfectionist, happiness is a mirage that seems to recede and vanish the closer he gets to his goal.

■

THE MAKING OF A PERFECTIONIST

Extreme perfectionism is one manifestation of the obsessive-compulsive personality, and most perfectionists are workaholics. Doctors, lawyers, musicians, and computer programmers are particularly prone to perfectionistic, obsessive-compulsive traits. Underlying all the hard work a perfectionist does are feelings of inferiority and self-hate. Believing themselves to be "nobodies," they work frantically to amass power, wealth, and status in vain attempts to convince themselves they are "somebodies."

Studies show a linkage between child-rearing practices and adult perfectionism. Children with excessively strict and harsh parents are more likely to become excessively perfectionistic. During childhood, their sense of self-worth was damaged and they learned to view themselves conditionally. That is, since the child's parents were so strict and demanding, and since they only communicated approval and affection when the child's behavior was perfect, the child learned he could only love himself if he was perfect.

Are You a Perfectionist?

Examine yourself for perfectionistic tendencies. Check the statements that apply to you:

____ 1. I often put off starting projects because I don't have time to do them perfectly.
____ 2. I often think I should have done a certain task better than I did.
____ 3. I have great plans for the future; someday, I will accomplish amazing things.
____ 4. I expect the best of myself at all times.
____ 5. If I can't do something really well, there's no point in doing it at all.
____ 6. If I try hard enough, I should be able to excel at anything.
____ 7. I feel ashamed if I show weakness or foolish behavior.
____ 8. I get upset if I make a mistake.
____ 9. If I do anything that seems "just average," I become unhappy.
____ 10. I refuse to be a second-rate person.
____ 11. In my experience, if you want something done right, you have to do it yourself.
____ 12. I set my standards as high as possible.
____ 13. I am often disappointed with other people's work.
____ 14. I get upset when things don't go as planned.
____ 15. Other people don't understand my desire to do things right.

If you checked 2 or more statements in questions 1 through 5, you probably have perfectionistic tendencies that interfere with your ability to start and/or complete projects.

If you checked 2 or more statements in questions 6 through 10, you probably have perfectionistic tendencies that are harmful to an already low self-esteem.

If you checked 2 or more statements in questions 11 through 15, you probably have perfectionistic tendencies that interfere with your relationships with family members and people who work under you in church or business situations.

The more statements you check, the stronger and more deeply entrenched your perfectionistic tendencies are likely to be. If you checked four or more statements on this self-test, you should consider getting counseling (including a personality assessment) to determine more accurately if you have unhealthy perfectionistic tendencies that could be helped by professional counseling.

You should be aware that most perfectionists deny their perfectionism and defend it as "normal" or "a commitment to excellence" or claim that "people should strive for perfection." Understand that, though it is important and commendable to strive for excellence, it is unhealthy to be obsessed with an uncontrollable drive for perfection.

For a "reality check," have someone who knows you well—a close friend or spouse—take this test for you and answer the questions on your behalf. Compare your answers and the other person's answers. This exercise can be a helpful aid in penetrating any denial you may have regarding your perfectionism.

HOW TO BE HEALED OF PERFECTIONISM

Perfectionism is a very deeply ingrained personality trait. Yet there are conscious steps you can take to recover from perfectionism so that you and the people around you can experience the freedom and serenity of just being "good enough," without having to be perfect:

1. Begin to redefine yourself in terms of balance rather than perfection. Make a conscious decision to demonstrate grace to yourself, to take time to relax, to give yourself room to be human, to make mistakes. Seek to be balanced and healthy rather than perfect.

2. Acknowledge the fact that your worth comes from being made by God, not from being perfect. The root of your perfectionism is the false belief that you are only worthwhile if you are perfect. Work on seeing yourself through God's eyes. The Bible says, "For He knows our frame; He remembers that we are dust" (Ps. 103:14). Does that sound like a God who expects perfection? Of course not! And when we expect perfection, we expect more of ourselves than God does. We actually put ourselves in a higher place of judgment than God, condemning ourselves without mercy while our merciful Heavenly Father pleads with us to accept the free gift of grace, love, and forgiveness that He offers us. It's time to stop playing God with your life; rest in God, accepting the fact that your worth comes from His love for you, not from any accomplishments or perfection of your own.

3. Replace law with grace. As a perfectionistic Christian, you understand grace on an intellectual basis. Now it's time to internalize grace and make it part of your inner, emotional being. Whenever the feeling arises that says, "I must do more, and I must do it perfectly," you must tell yourself, "I'll do my best, and my best is enough." When you feel, "I've failed, I'm worthless," you must tell yourself, "I made a mistake, and I will learn from it and do better next time." When you experience feelings of self-hate and self-condemnation, you must tell yourself, "There is therefore now no condemnation to those who are in Christ Jesus" (Rom. 8:1).

Will it help to tell yourself these grace-oriented truths when those legalistic voices keep shouting at you to be perfect? At first, probably not. But as you keep repeating these truths in your mind over and over again, you will gradually see law replaced by the grace of God in your heart.

4. Let "good enough" be good enough. Perfectionists go through life like Olympic gymnasts seeking a perfect 10 score. Learn to play life like a game of horseshoes: "close enough" still counts. A "good enough" boss is better than a perfect boss. A "good enough" parent is better than a perfect parent. A "good enough" spouse (and a spouse who lets his or her partner be "good enough") is better than a perfect spouse. If you want to be better than perfect, then learn to be just "good enough."

5. Be a person of excellence. Not perfection, excellence. Set goals that can actually be achieved. Focus on the process, especially in relationships. Concentrate on being the kind of boss, spouse, or parent who inspires loyalty, respect, and love—not fear. Seek to be like Christ: merciful, caring, interested in others, and the kind of Man who knew how to pace Himself, how to take a break from the crowds and the pressures, how to relax with good friends.

444

6. Seek God's help in overcoming your perfectionism. Let Him cover you with His love and surround you with His grace. If your earthly parents pushed you to be perfect, let your heavenly Parent teach you about grace, about relaxing, about peace. Ask God to heal you of your perfectionist obsession and liberate you to be the kind of excellent person He made you to be.

Personality Types and Disorders

Personality is the ingrained pattern of one's behavior, thoughts, and feelings that remain essentially consistent through various situations and across a long span of time. In some respects, we will interact in different ways with different people. We will respond in varying ways to varying situations. Yet there are certain tendencies in our thinking and our behavior that will be fairly consistent regardless of the situation.

For those of us who are parents, it is a sobering fact that, according to various psychological studies, *approximately 85 percent of the adult personality is already formed when a person is six years old.* Some of a person's personality is a product of genetics, but a great deal is directly traceable to environment and parenting. How we train our children and interact with our children during those crucial first years will overwhelmingly determine how they will live all the decades that follow. Whether children will be happy or unhappy, healthy or unhealthy, functional or dysfunctional in their adult years will be profoundly shaped before they even enter the first grade.

What is the nature of personality? What makes different personalities? Why are some people dominant and aggressive and others meek and submissive? Why are some people open and friendly and others closed and wary?

The ancient Greeks gave a lot of thought to these questions of human personality. They arrived at four broad personality divisions, categorizing people as *phlegmatic* (emotionless), *choleric* (active and irritable), *sanguine* (happy), and *melancholic* (depressive). Some years ago, one prominent Christian writer attempted to adapt these temperaments to a Christian framework, but most psychologists would agree that these four categories are too broad, simplistic, and imprecise to be of much practical use.

PERSONALITY TESTING

Today, psychologists use personality assessment tests to understand personality. Personality tests can help therapists make diagnostic decisions and can help counselors arrive at the source of emotional issues even when clients are unable to verbalize their

445

feelings and problems adequately. Personality tests are also used as screening devices to identify individuals with psychological disturbances. Employers, churches, and mission boards often find it advisable to detect people who have major personality or emotional difficulties before they are placed in important positions.

The Taylor-Johnson and Minnesota Multiphasic Personality Inventory (MMPI) are commonly used personality tests that help therapists to evaluate and treat emotional problems. The most widely used psychological test in the world, the MMPI is a highly objective and reliable indicator of emotional disturbance, although it affords a relatively poor description of normal personality.

A less sophisticated cousin to the MMPI is the Taylor-Johnson Temperament Analysis (TJTA), which is available for use by pastors in spiritual counseling. Less reliable (because they are more subjective) but still often helpful are the projective tests such as the Thematic Apperception Test (TAT) and the Rorschach Test. The object of projective tests is to determine whether an individual symbolically projects his or her anxiety onto pictures (such as an inkblot) or objects.

COMMON PERSONALITY TYPES

Following are brief descriptions of several personality types. Although a person with one of these personality types can be essentially healthy and functional, these personality types can become so extreme and pronounced in some individuals that they are referred to as *personality disorders* (a comprehensive discussion of personality disorders appears later in this article). An understanding of personality types can be extremely important in helping people experience healing from emotional and spiritual problems. For example, people with the obsessive-compulsive personality tend to have a greater than normal tendency to doubt their salvation and are more subject to anxiety and depression than the norm.

Most people show traits of more than one personality type. For example, a man with an explosive personality might have a tendency to lose all control, explode in a rage, and beat his wife and children. Then, after he calms down, he may exhibit strong traits of the narcissistic personality: being extremely self-centered in an attempt to avoid guilt and prosecution for his crime, narcissistically blaming others (including his victims) for his actions, and rearranging his recollection of events to make himself the innocent party in this story ("Actually, my wife was so mean, so unfair, that I couldn't be held responsible for hitting her; I was really the one being abused in this relationship").

We should be careful not to pigeonhole ourselves or others. A common mistake many people make regarding personality issues is to look at a description of a given personality type and say, "Oh, I must be an obsessive-compulsive" (or some other single personality type). A personality type is a "filter" we place on an individual that makes his or her behavior easier to categorize and understand. But people are complex creations that have been shaped by complex forces. It sometimes takes two or more of these "filters" to make sense of an individual's motivations and behavior.

The simplified summaries that follow are meant not to label anyone but to give a general picture of the many kinds of people who comprise our families and our society. Because each personality type has positive and negative aspects, it's important to be aware of one's dominant traits and keep them in balance. If any of these traits become excessive or inflexible, impairing a person's functioning or relationships, the result may be a personality disorder.

The Neurotic Personality

A neurotic person experiences a great deal of anxiety and the symptoms that accompany anxiety. The neurotic personality is in touch with reality but tends to reshape memories, beliefs, and experiences in ways that will reduce the level of anxiety. The religious beliefs of a neurotic individual are likely to be somewhat fluid; this person will tend to refashion his or her idea of God in any way that will help reduce the anxiety level.

The Obsessive-Compulsive Personality

The obsessive-compulsive is the workaholic personality type. The majority of these individuals are men. An obsessive-compulsive individual is characterized by uncompromising views, perfectionism, constant doubting, drivenness, and an obsession with analysis and strict moral standards. The obsessive-compulsive person may experience recurring unpleasant thoughts and feelings of anxiety. *Obsessions* are irrational thoughts that are repeated many times, and *compulsions* are repeated behavior patterns that result from obsessions.

An obsessive-compulsive tends to be overconscientious, self-sacrificing, overdutiful, and hardworking. Birth order is frequently a factor in producing obsessive-compulsive people: twelve of the first thirteen astronauts were the oldest child in their families and had these traits. Obsessive-compulsives tend to be the most productive individuals for almost any kind of work. They are well-organized, handle facts carefully, and have a strong passion for truth. However, they can be overly strict, rigid, and incapable of relaxing (you'll see them on vacation at poolside, tapping away at their laptop computers). Extreme obsessive-compulsive behavior can be destructive, resulting in workaholism, anxiety attacks, and sleep disorders. These individuals frequently have trouble handling emotions and accepting people unconditionally.

The obsessive-compulsive person tends to fret over the possibility that God has abandoned him or her and to obsess over his or her salvation until he or she finally gains reassurance. After a while, that sense of reassurance will evaporate, and the doubting cycle will begin all over again. This type of person is likely to see God as a demanding parent expecting perfection.

It is helpful for the obsessive-compulsive to focus on relationships and time management, to learn to say no to overinvolvement, and to live one day at a time. He or she also needs to learn to lean on others at times.

The Histrionic Personality

The histrionic personality is the attention-seeking individual. The vast majority of these individuals are women. In many ways, this personality type (which is also called the hysterical personality) is the opposite of the obsessive-compulsive type. This individual is dramatic, extroverted, seductive, and impulsive. She emphasizes feelings rather than logic. She tends to be attractive to the opposite sex, socially popular, vivacious, and charming, though she often sabotages relationships with others by being demanding,

The Lord's message of peace and hope to the obsessive-compulsive workaholic is found in Matthew 11:28: "Come to Me, all you who labor and are heavy laden, and I will give you rest."

447

self-centered, fickle, inconsistent, inconsiderate, possessive, manipulative, and helpless. Often the histrionic has had a poor relationship with her opposite-sex parent (many have a history of abuse), and she may have an unconscious need to prove that her mate is just as worthless and untrustworthy as her parent.

The histrionic personality seeks (or demands) continual approval and praise from others, is overly concerned with being attractive, and demonstrates emotion (ranging from affection to temper tantrums) at the drop of a hat. This type person is typically self-centered and shallow and demands immediate gratification. (Stephanie, the pampered poor-little-rich-girl maid on the TV show *Newhart* is an extreme caricature of the histrionic personality type.)

It is important to understand, however, that histrionic traits are not exclusive to women, nor are they expressed only in sexual seductiveness. Within the Christian community, we also see histrionic individuals who emphasize emotional experiences rather than the objective logic and truth of God's Word. When a histrionic person's emotional state is bright and positive, God is a close, warm, nurturing friend. When that same person becomes angry or depressed, those feelings of anger are often turned against God. The histrionic typically confuses emotionalism with spirituality and is prone to spiritual/emotional ups and downs, sometimes blaming the devil in order to exempt herself from personal responsibility. She becomes religiously grandiose and claims special powers and gifts. Even in church-related activities this type person unconsciously seeks attention. In the individual's prayer life, she often seeks to command God to do her bidding, treating Him more like the genie of the lamp than the sovereign Lord of the universe. She may even become angry with God for not doing things her way and may attempt to "punish" God by neglecting personal devotions or other religious duties.

The Passive-Aggressive Personality

Passive *and* aggressive? It seems like a contradiction in terms. This is how the passive-aggressive personality works: this individual feels resentful that his or her emotional needs have not been met by others, and this resentment is usually felt at an unconscious level. The passive-aggressive individual will frequently deny having any anger or aggression because he or she is not aware of these feelings. Because of low self-esteem and low confidence, he or she will not feel capable of expressing anger in an assertive way. Instead, this individual's aggression will surface in a subtle, nonverbal, manipulative way, so that other people will not recognize and confront the aggression.

The passive-aggressive individual tends to be a chronic complainer. He or she criticizes people in authority without reason and resents even reasonably stated suggestions from others. The individual acts wounded when someone disagrees with him or her or when he or she feels imposed upon. This type of person often believes he or she is doing better work than he or she gets credit for.

The passive-aggressive person engages in a variety of manipulative behavior patterns, including:

Obstructionism: A wife who is angry about something her husband did or said on Saturday night gets even by making the family late for church on Sunday morning. Ostensibly, she can't find her lipstick or her shoes, but this passive obstructionism is actually a concealed act of aggression against her husband (who is probably compulsive about getting to church on time).

Chronic Tardiness: A passive-aggressive individual doesn't like being told what to do, so he or she will often get even by being late for appointments.

Procrastination: The passive-aggressive frequently puts off chores that have been assigned or requested by people he or she resents. For example, a husband resents his wife telling him to mow the lawn, so he keeps finding excuses for letting the grass grow.

Inefficiency: The passive-aggressive individual sometimes does assigned tasks poorly or slowly because he or she resents authority figures. If Bob doesn't like his overbearing, meticulous boss, he may do a certain project inefficiently enough that his boss will give the task to someone else—but not inefficiently enough to get fired. It the boss gets frustrated and takes the project away from Bob, then Bob has achieved the reward he was looking for.

Pouting: Instead of confronting disagreements openly, honestly, and maturely, the passive-aggressive will withdraw and sulk, punishing the other person with silence. The pouting will often be accompanied by denials, which further frustrate the other person: "Angry? What are you talking about? I'm not angry. I'm fine."

These behaviors may seem calculated and deliberately manipulative, but frequently the passive-aggressive individual is largely unaware (at a conscious level) of these hidden motivations and hidden agendas. The passive-aggressive individual frequently comes from a background featuring a difficult relationship with one or both parents, involving a communication pattern in which the parent would give the child or teenager angry or wordy lectures and would disregard or disallow anything the child or teenager had to say. This creates in the child a coping pattern of avoiding direct confrontation and using hidden manipulative ploys to express aggression and resentment.

The passive-aggressive individual would do well to gain insight into his or her hidden emotions, particularly anger. As the individual begins to understand how hidden anger generates manipulative behavior, he or she can gradually replace a desire to control others with a greater ability to accept others as they are.

The Dependent Personality

The dependent personality type exhibits a continual childlike desire to have others provide for him or her, make decisions for him or her, set his or her boundaries, and meet his or her needs. This person has low self-esteem and low self-confidence and sees himself or herself as inept and helpless. He or she clings to other people and is intensely anxious when alone. This person is prone to excessive fear, false guilt, and inferiority; his or her feelings are easily hurt. The dependent person exhibits submissive behavior toward others, is extremely sensitive to criticism (especially when the individual feels he or she has been too forward or assertive), and will often agree with the statements of others even when he or she inwardly disagrees (to avoid the rejection of others). This type person is often overly tolerant of abusive or unfriendly circumstances. The dependent individual is the classic victim personality.

The dependent individual tends to see God as an indulgent Father who does everything for him or her. If the individual is suddenly forced to take some major step in life on his or her own initiative, or if the person is disappointed to discover that God doesn't simply hand over everything as he or she demands, the individual often resents God for being a neglectful parent. The dependent individual would do well to learn assertiveness and appropriate expression of anger (see ANGER; ASSERTIVENESS).

The Independent Personality

The independent personality type is characterized by an excessive resentment of control by outside authority figures. This individual is marked by a rebelliousness that is so strong that the person will often do what he or she does not want to do, engaging in behavior that is actually harmful to himself or herself if by doing so the individual can demonstrate his or her independence from others. For example, an independent man may be planning to drive to his destination via the freeway, but if his wife says, "Take the freeway, it's faster," he will spend an extra hour on the surface streets just to prove his independence from his wife's perceived attempt to control him, even though he only hurts himself by this behavior. The independent personality will often take a minority or antagonistic point of view in a conversation—even a totally absurd and unsupportable point of view—just to prove his or her independence from the group. This person thrives on being thought of as "different" or even "odd."

> The independent personality often struggles in his or her spiritual life because of a tendency to view God—the ultimate Authority Figure—as too controlling or intrusive in his or her life.

The Paranoid Personality

The paranoid personality is the suspicious individual. This personality type is characterized by hypersensitivity and an exaggerated sense of *self-reference*—that is, a sense that "everything that happens is directed at me." The commonly accepted conception of a "paranoid" is someone who believes he is being persecuted by the CIA or spied on by little green men. But we are not talking about anything so extreme as that. There are many people who are functional and generally reality-based in their perceptions, yet they have paranoid, self-referential tendencies. They tend to interpret remarks, actions, and events as threats to them personally. Paranoid individuals tend to hold grudges and experience intense jealousy.

The person of the paranoid type will tend to see God as untrustworthy, hostile, and threatening in a way that is directed specifically toward him or her. This person may be wary and skeptical in his or her approach to God, feeling that "God is out to get me."

The Introverted Personality

The introverted person is shy, withdrawn, and melancholic (depressive). This personality type is believed to be largely the result of a family system in which:

1. The mother dominated and tended to ignore the teenager's presence and feelings, interrupting whenever the child or teenager spoke.
2. The father was generally passive and attentive to the mother and also tended to interrupt and ignore the child or teenager.
3. The child or teenager gave attention and respect to both parents, despite their tendency to ignore and disregard him or her.

Introverted individuals have extremely low self-esteem and tend to be ineffective in life.

The Borderline Personality

The borderline personality is unpredictable. This individual exhibits instability in a variety of areas, such as behavior, mood, relationships, and self-image. His or her interactions with other people are intense, and his or her opinion of other people will swing wildly from "You're the most wonderful person in the world!" *(idealization)* to "You're worthless, you're horrible!" *(devaluation)*. These wide variations in mood will often produce thoughts and feelings that are not rooted in reality. This individual is also subject to boredom, insecurity, depression, irritability, anger, and low self-esteem. He or she tends to be impulsive and hostile in relationships, and these factors inhibit the individual from forming long-lasting relationships. This type person is sometimes physically aggressive and is at risk for alcohol and drug abuse problems.

The borderline individual often feels empty and that his or her life is without meaning. This person tends to vacillate between dependent and independent struggles with God. In the mind and emotions of the borderline individual, he or she will have alternating, seesawing experiences with God. At one time, he or she will see God as remote, absent, invisible, and neglectful; at other times, the person will resent Him as intrusive and overprotective.

The Asthenic Personality

The asthenic personality is a sickly, helpless individual who sees himself or herself as being at the mercy of external factors and forces. This person feels completely incompetent to act on his or her environment; instead, the individual waits for the environment to act on him or her, and the individual hopes for another person to take care of him or her. This behavior is learned at an early stage in life.

The asthenic individual finds his or her continual feelings of helplessness to be very stressful and is prone to many physical illnesses, both real and imagined. Since an important ingredient of happiness is a sense of control and self-direction, asthenic people, who feel helpless and controlled by people and circumstances, tend to be very unhappy.

The Explosive Personality

The explosive individual is emotionally explosive when provoked. He is given to outbursts of temper that are usually frightening and sometimes violent. An extreme explosive personality who has committed acts of violence will sometimes describe the experience as "crossing the line" or "going over the edge." Upon reaching a certain level of anger, it is as though all restraint and control disappear, and the individual may commit acts of mayhem that he later claims to scarcely remember.

The Depressive Personality

The depressive individual has long-term feelings of futility in his or her ability to handle tension at work and in the family. This person is plagued by anxiety and generally feels inferior, hopeless, worried, and rejected. The depressive person is convinced that he or she can't manage life as well as other people, and the individual struggles with negative feelings about himself or herself. This person is subject to depression, memory lapses, and problems with concentration and thinking.

The Cyclothymic Personality

The cyclothymic individual is much like a manic-depressive (see MANIC-DEPRESSION), except that his or her emotional highs and lows oscillate in much slower cycles. During euphoric "high" periods, the cyclothymic is a joker, "the life of the party," everybody's buddy. But during emotional lows, he or she withdraws. These oscillating moods create problems in building long-term, close relationships. The cyclothymic may examine his fears and issues during low times, resolving to make improvements and gain insight into his behavior. The key to long-term improvement lies in learning to make emotional progress during the tempestuous, euphoric "highs."

The Avoidant Personality

The avoidant personality is so called because he or she is socially uncomfortable and tends to avoid people and relationships. The avoidant individual is hypersensitive to rejection, whether real or imagined. This person tends to be socially withdrawn unless there are strong indications that he or she will be uncritically accepted. The avoidant personality's self-esteem is very low, and this individual may devalue his or her own achievements and get discouraged by his or her personal shortcomings. Though this person isolates himself or herself, the avoidant deeply desires to be loved and accepted. If an avoidant person feels momentarily rejected by the spouse, he or she is likely to interpret that rejection, whether real or imagined, as a sign that the spouse "doesn't love me anymore." This results in heightened fear of abandonment.

A person with this personality type may avoid God—and may also see God as an avoider. "God is like everyone else in my life," he might say. "When I need Him, He is not there."

The Schizoid Personality

The schizoid personality, like the avoidant, is sensitive to rejection and tends to withdraw or be indifferent to social situations. Even though the schizoid wants to be accepted by others, he or she chooses solitary activities and rarely experiences strong emotions, such as anger or joy. This individual is frequently unable to feel emotionally close to others.

The schizoid individual often lacks social skills, finding it difficult not only to express intimacy but also to express hostility or assertiveness appropriately. Seen as a "cold fish," the schizoid individual is often indifferent to either praise or criticism from others.

The Schizotypal Personality

The schizotypal personality is somewhat like the avoidant and schizoid personalities. This person may experience magical or autistic thinking, characterized by the belief that his actions or thoughts directly affect the outcome of other people's lives or major events. As a result, he may be afraid that his actions or thoughts will cause problems in people's lives or major events, and he withdraws into isolation and aloofness. He is also hypersensitive and paranoically suspicious.

This individual is viewed by others as odd and peculiar because of his or her hermitlike behavior, weird beliefs, paranoid suspiciousness, fantasy-oriented thinking, eccentric behavior, and often eccentric, unkempt appearance. He or she may display unusual mannerisms. This type of person may talk to himself or herself, display superstitious beliefs, and claim to have special mental or magical powers. Under extreme stress, the individual may become psychotic (lose touch with reality) and engage in behavior that others around him or her will consider "crazy." Many schizotypal individuals are genetically related to true schizophrenics (see SCHIZOPHRENIA), which suggests a genetic relationship to the schizotypal personality. Schizotypal behavior is so extreme that an individual with this personality is generally considered to have a schizotypal personality disorder.

The Narcissistic Personality

The narcissistic individual is self-centered, lacks empathy, and may be unable to recognize the pain of others. He believes he deserves special favors but feels no obligation to return them. The narcissist demands attention and admiration and has trouble accepting criticism.

The Sociopathic Personality

The sociopathic personality is also called the antisocial personality—*not* in the popular sense of the word "antisocial" (meaning withdrawn or socially uncomfortable). In this sense, *antisocial* means "against society." The word *sociopathic* also means "dangerous to society." The sociopath experiences repeated conflicts with other people. He or she tends to be extremely self-centered, irresponsible, callous, and impulsive. This individual cannot empathize with other people and rarely (if ever) feels guilt or anxiety. This type person frequently experiences financial problems because he or she lives for the present instead of planning ahead. This individual lacks ambition, values, and close interpersonal relationships (because he or she is irritable, selfish, and aggressive).

In one sense, everyone is born with some sociopathic tendencies, since we all have a sinful nature. But individuals whose sociopathic tendencies are so extreme as to constitute a personality disorder often become criminals.

A Final Word About these Personality Types

It is important to remember that none of these personality types is totally good or bad. As you become aware of your own personality type, seek a greater understanding of your strengths, weaknesses, and patterns of thinking and behavior. By understanding these personality traits, you may be able to improve relationships at home, at church, and on the job.

PERSONALITY TYPES IN MARRIAGE

Certain personality types seem like oil and vinegar: you always see them together, but they don't mix well. These personality combinations attract each other but produce significant problems in marriage. In counseling, we see many of these same combinations over and over:

The Obsessive-compulsive man and the histrionic woman. The obsessive-compulsive man is dutiful and conscientious and has a strict moral conscience. He is attracted to a woman

453

who is his opposite, his complement—someone who completes in him what he lacks. He finds a woman who is exciting and excitable, emotional and dramatic, theatrical and seductive. These qualities excite him and arouse pleasurable feelings in him.

The histrionic woman, meanwhile, is drawn to the obsessive-compulsive man because of his opposite traits: his steady, stable, logical, fatherly image. Each finds in the other what he or she lacks. He can't feel, and she can't think! But soon the very qualities that drew them together begin to generate annoyance. He gets tired of her theatrics. She begins to view him as a dull, logical "cold fish." Unless they both have the maturity to understand their personality issues, there will be a lifelong battle between conflicting personality traits, or there will be divorce.

The obsessive-compulsive man and the obsessive-compulsive woman. Both partners are likely to be overly perfectionistic, demanding, and critical. They can hardly live with themselves, much less get along with each other. If their obsessive-compulsiveness is relatively mild and controllable, they can have a very orderly and effective marriage. The more extreme the traits of either partner, the more difficulty they will have in living together and cooperating effectively.

The passive man and the dominant woman. Each feels a neurotic need for the other. He needs someone to lead and even dominate him in the relationship; she needs someone to control. Conflicts arise because he inwardly resents being dominated and she resents not having her own dependency needs met.

The paranoid man and the depressive woman. This is a relationship with sadomasochistic-like asymmetry. He is jealous and hostile and feels a need to hurt other people. She is depression-prone, has low self-esteem, and is quick to accept blame and shame. In short, she feels a need to be hurt. He projects his own shortcomings onto her (projection). She assumes blame for wrongs she did not commit (introjection). The woman in such relationships frequently grew up with critical, demanding parents, and she subconsciously finds a mate to match. Accepting false blame is the only life she knows. (We also frequently see the reverse of this scenario: *the paranoid wife and the depressive husband.*)

The obsessive-compulsive man and the asthenic woman. She is emotionally and physically sick and has a need for someone to take care of her totally. Her husband feels inadequate in the world and has a need to take care of someone who is weaker than he is. Conflicts arise when she begins to resent total dependence on someone else and when he begins to resent her drain on his life and his happiness.

The passive-aggressive man and the passive-aggressive woman. Both are manipulative, immature, and bent on receiving more than they give. They are unable to understand the needs of each other because they are so self-centered. Dr. Frank Minirth counseled one such couple. Each accused the other of being selfish and childish, and both were startled to learn that their Minnesota Multiphasic Personality Inventories showed them to be extremely similar in personality type, as well as extremely immature and self-centered. They could see it in each other but were blind to their own personalities.

Our personalities are much like our faces: it's hard for us to see them unless someone holds up a mirror to us. Sometimes we ourselves are the hardest people for us to get

■

People often use personality types as excuses for divorce. "Obviously," they say, "we're just incompatible. We each married the wrong person." At the Minirth Meier New Life Clinics, we always confront this kind of thinking. It is impossible to marry the "wrong" personality type, since any two types can get along if both people are committed to Christ and each other and are willing to work on their relationship. "Marital incompatibility" is an artificial term devised to provide an easy escape from a difficult situation.

■

THE COMPLETE LIFE ENCYCLOPEDIA

to know, yet other people—particularly trained and experienced counselors and doctors—can help us find insight into who we really are and how we really function. The professional therapist will observe and listen, noting communication patterns, pointing out games and evasions, penetrating defense mechanisms, educating us about the various personality types and how they interact, and formulating strategies for dealing with problems and resolving conflict.

While differences in personality can and do cause serious conflict in a marriage, those differences can be understood and overcome. Earlier, we compared certain personality types to oil and vinegar, because you see them together all the time but they don't naturally tend to mix well. Clearly, that does not mean that oil and vinegar are "not right for each other." Season well with salt and pepper and a touch of Dijon (or, in a relationship, add love and caring), then shake vigorously (add work and commitment), and you have a delightful vinaigrette dressing (or a happy relationship).

A healthy marriage depends on maturity, not personality. Instead of asking ourselves, "Is my mate right for me?" we should ask ourselves:

- Are we willing to be tolerant and flexible?
- Are we willing to settle disputes rationally and according to biblical principles?
- Are we willing to practice the principles of healthy communication?

Couples—and especially Christian couples—do not have to settle for marital unhappiness. They have the power to make it better. A first step involves learning to accept the other's personality as a given, without demanding any change from the mate. Each mate has an equal responsibility for making the marriage work.

It is especially important that spouses not displace negative emotions from their pasts onto their mates. One partner may be experiencing enormous anger that he or she takes out on the other partner, not realizing that the source of the anger is really an unresolved conflict dating from childhood. Such conflicts should be settled within the *shelter* of marriage but not at the expense of one's partner.

(For related subjects, see DYSFUNCTIONAL FAMILY; EMOTIONS; FAMILY; MARRIAGE.)

PERSONALITY DISORDERS

If you look at the list of major personality disorders, you will see that it looks like the list of personality types already discussed in this article. The reason the list of personality disorders matches the list of personality types is that any personality type can become a disorder when the traits of that personality become sufficiently entrenched, extreme, and destructive.

Briefly defined, a personality disorder is a deeply ingrained pattern of negative behavior that is defeating to oneself or destructive to others. Personality disorders are characterized by behavior patterns rather than by symptoms. In other words, an individual with a personality disorder does not just have symptoms, such as anxiety or depression. The individual also has behavior patterns that interfere with his or her own ability to function and with relationships with other people.

MAJOR PERSONALITY DISORDERS

DISORDER	CHARACTERISTICS
Avoidant	Hypersensitivity to rejection
Borderline	Instability in a variety of areas
Dependent	Failure to assume responsibility for one's own life
Histrionic	Overly emotional/expressive, egocentric, having poor sexual adjustment
Narcissistic	Grandiose sense of self-importance
Obsessive-compulsive	Preoccupation with rules, order, and details
Paranoid	Suspicion, mistrust of people, hypersensitivity
Passive-aggressive	Passive resistance to demands for adequate performance
Schizoid	Withdrawn, reserved, seclusive
Schizotypal	Oddity of thinking and behavior (sometimes called "simple schizophrenia")
Sociopathic (Antisocial)	Violation of the right of others

Disorders commonly begin during adolescence or even earlier. In a true personality disorder, these patterns become so firmly fixed that the affected individual is extremely resistant to treatment and personal growth, so that the personality disorder tends to be present throughout the individual's life. This last statement needs to be strongly underscored and restated so there is no mistake: *Personality disorders tend to be incurable,* apart from a miraculous intervention from God.

Sometimes, after a disordered individual has caused a great deal of turmoil in a family, an organization, or a church, that individual goes into counseling, appears to make progress, and is then restored to a position where he or she again does enormous harm. People who are unacquainted with personality disorders tend to be very naive about the entrenched nature of the disorder and the harm those disordered traits can cause. Some individuals with personality disorders are particularly adept at hiding their destructiveness and charming their way into situations in which they can do enormous harm. Some subtle and deceptive disorders must be approached with special wariness:

The Histrionic Personality Disorder. This is the Seductive Woman Syndrome, described in the book of Proverbs, the woman who manipulates and flatters, who is seductive and often involved in serial relationships (in or out of marriage), who feels but does not logically think, who is emotionally unstable, who is vain and self-centered, who is naive and overly dramatic (see Proverbs 2:16–19; 5:3, 6; 6:25; 7:10–21, 26; 9:13; 30:20).

In Proverbs 2:16 and 19, this disordered personality is called "the immoral woman" and "the seductress," and it is said, "None who go to her return, nor do they regain the paths of life." That is a recognition of the almost incurable nature of this disorder, from a human perspective.

But that qualifier "almost" is all-important. For in John 4, we find one of the most famous histrionic women in history, the woman who meets Jesus by the well of Sychar. She is a seductive woman who has been through five marriages, and at the time of the story she is living with a man she is not married to. As you read between the lines of that story, it is almost unmistakable that she is "coming on to" Jesus, behaving in a seductive way. Empty and starved for authentic love, she is attracted to the genuine compassion and unconditional acceptance of Jesus, and she responds to Him in the only way she knows how to interact with a man: she employs her seductive charm. But Jesus intervenes in her life in a way that shakes her disordered personality to the core. There is hope for the histrionic woman, and that hope lies in the supernatural intervention of God in her life. Though rare, we have seen cases of healing from the histrionic personality disorder in our clinical experience.

Pastors, counselors, and other church workers need to take special precautions when dealing with histrionic women. Histrionics sometimes behave seductively in order to prove that the pastor-counselor is just as bad as every other man. Whether or not he does anything wrong, she may report that he seduced her and may ruin his reputation. If possible, it would be best for a church to have a female counselor on staff who can counsel other women, particularly women who demonstrate histrionic traits. If a male pastor or counselor must counsel women, the office door should be left ajar with a secretary positioned at a desk nearby. He should never schedule counseling appointments after hours or Saturdays, or meet with women in his or her home or over lunch or dinner.

The Explosive Personality Disorder. This individual may be extraordinarily winsome and charming when building friendships or when dating and courting. The explosive nature of his personality emerges suddenly and unexpectedly when he is provoked, frustrated, or stressed. Some people don't discover that they have married mates with explosive personality disorders until a year or more into the marriage. After the first domestic violence erupts, the incidents of violence become increasingly more frequent and more severe.

A person with this personality disorder will frequently display extreme repentance and remorse following an episode of violence. He may resume and reintensify his charming and extra-attentive ways. But he remains just as unpredictable and potentially dangerous as ever, though the people around the explosive individual will want to believe the best and trust that he is "cured."

Explosive personalities are often highly control-addicted (see CONTROL ADDICTION). They may profess love, but their love is often of a possessive, self-seeking, manipulative kind. In the case of spouse-abusing explosive personalities, this possessiveness is one reason that it is often so difficult for abused spouses to leave the relationship. First, the possessive, control-addicted abuser won't let the abused spouse leave; in his mind, he cannot let this person out of his control, and he may threaten her with death or violence. Second, because the explosive personality professes such undying love in such charming, attentive ways, accompanied by sincere-sounding remorse for past episodes of abuse, the abuse victim (who is often dependent by nature) responds by returning to the arms of the abuser. Everything is fine—until the next time the explosive individual is triggered by frustration, conflict, or stress.

Explosively disordered personalities are also found to commit other unexpected acts of violence. The suave, charming young man who has wined and dined his female friend, then suddenly turns on her and attempts date rape is one example. Others make the headlines by shooting an offending motorist on the freeway or by shooting a building full of innocent people after being fired from a job. What is most perplexing about explosive individuals is the dual nature of their personalities. They may be quiet and unassuming, or even positively charming, until provoked. Then there is a frightening Jekyll-Hyde transformation. After a violent incident, his neighbors and acquaintances often look into the lens of the news cameras and say, "What a shock! He always was such a quiet, charming person. We all liked him."

The narcissistic personality disorder. Narcissistically disordered individuals are excessively self-centered. They lack empathy and are often unable to recognize the pain of others. They have an exaggerated sense of their own importance, they believe their difficulties are unique, and they tend to exploit people for their own ends. Narcissists spend a great deal of time fantasizing about their own power, success, brilliance, and idealized love. They are very concerned about their public images. Narcissists believe they deserve special favors but show no inclination to return them.

Regrettably, there are narcissistically disordered personalities holding positions as pastors or evangelists. Some use their positions of prestige and power to manipulate, exploit, and control people. Though such individuals are rare, there are some disordered persons who use people "in the name of the Lord" to accomplish their selfish goals and who have very little insight into their own disordered personalities. They have superficial relationships with their mates and children, not because they are absorbed with their work, but because they are serving their own interests.

We all have the seeds of narcissism within us: selfishness, arrogance, denial, preferring to blame others for our sins rather than truthfully examining ourselves and repenting. Indeed, in a sense, we are all supposed to become Godlike—not in the sense that narcissists see themselves as Godlike: seeking power, controlling others, demanding admiration (worship) from others. Rather, we are to become like God (and like His Son, Jesus) in our *character:* becoming unconditionally loving, accepting, forgiving, and humble in our service to others. True Godlikeness (which the Bible calls *godliness*) is the complete opposite of narcissism.

The sociopathic personality disorder. Sociopaths are selfish, uncaring, lacking in empathy or conscience, and quick to rationalize their own faults and to shift the blame onto others. They engage in repeated conflicts with other members of society and are unwilling to be loyal to individuals, groups, or social values. Their failure to follow rules, however, is not a result of ignorance or lack of intelligence; in fact, many are geniuses at what they do (unfortunately, what they do is evil).

Sociopaths are irresponsible, impulsive, untruthful, unpredictable, and insincere. They view themselves as brilliant and others around them as "chumps" and victims to be exploited or bullied. Not only do they feel no guilt, many actually derive an emotional high from abusing, exploiting, and "conning" other people. They are insensitive to guilt and rarely learn from experience (including the experience of punishment). They blame others for their problems and their behavior, often rationalizing their antisocial acts as the fault of their parents or their society. They have little or no plan for their lives and live for momentary pleasure and gain.

Sociopaths can be found in all walks of life and particularly in places where they can abuse and exploit people. Though they tend to have little ambition, some manage to "con" their way into responsible positions in businesses, organizations, and even in churches. However, the most severely disordered sociopathic individuals are usually found in prison or on parole. These are the repeat-offending career criminals. These extreme sociopaths are the most troubling and frightening individuals our society produces.

A sociopath is commonly defined as having had conflicts with society from an early age (prior to age fifteen). These acts may include truancy, vandalism, burglary, drug abuse, auto theft (or other vehicular crimes), assault, or abusive sexual behavior. It is a pattern of several different behaviors, not one criminal action, that marks the individual with a sociopathic personality disorder. If this pattern persists beyond age eighteen or so, then the diagnosis of this personality disorder is frequently made.

Perhaps the most prominent and troubling characteristic of the sociopath is the apparent absence of anxiety and guilt feelings. These are the feelings that lead to repentance and change, and the lack of these feelings gives human counselors and the Divine Counselor, the Holy Spirit, very little in the way of a handle with which to reach this person and turn his or her life around. The Bible speaks of people who harden their hearts until they can no longer feel guilt. God is always ready to receive sinners, and He continually seeks to convict people of sin and their need of salvation. When a person continually rejects God and closes the door to his or her conscience, God's Spirit eventually ceases to strive to convict that person of his or her need. Some theologians have described this spiritual "point of no return" as the unforgivable sin. God's judgment on the hardened, unrepentant sociopath (and on all who willfully give themselves over to sin and destructive behavior) can be found in Romans chapter 1.

Though the lack of conscience is a mark of the sociopath, some individuals with this disorder do come to know Christ as Savior. As they mature in Christ, they may become progressively less sociopathic. Apart from salvation, few sociopaths make significant improvement, even with prolonged psychotherapy. Those who do claim to have given their lives to Christ should be handled with great care: they should be encouraged to grow in Christ but should not be given too much trust and responsibility too quickly. Many sociopaths are masters of disguise and will use the guise of a new Christian in order to further exploit people they view as "religious chumps."

Sociopaths rarely go into psychological counseling or psychiatric treatment unless ordered to do so by a court or as a pretext to obtain drugs. Counselors must handle sociopaths with extreme care and must pursue a tough, confrontational approach. Many psychiatrists prefer not to waste time on people who are so severely disordered that they are considered incurable. "Diagnose them, then discharge them" is their motto.

As Christian therapists, however, we have more hope than that. We have seen some sociopaths become Christians. Intellectually, at least, sociopaths can understand the Gospel and can put their faith in Christ. We have also seen some sociopaths "mellow with age." They sometimes seem to expend much of their self-centered energy as they get older.

See also ABNORMAL PSYCHOLOGY; EMOTIONS; SELF-ESTEEM

PERSONALITY TYPES AND DISORDERS

Prayer

Prayer is the process whereby finite human beings become intimate with the infinite God of the universe. Prayer makes the realities of God's Word personal and tangible in our lives. More can be accomplished by prayer than we ever dreamt was possible.

This intimate communion with God through prayer is made possible by Christ's death for us and by His indwelling Holy Spirit. Effective prayer is only possible in a relationship with God through Christ. Once that relationship has been established through faith in Christ, God desires fellowship with us. The Bible tells us that God delights in our prayers (see Proverbs 15:8).

THE INGREDIENTS OF PRAYER

Prayer may consist of *praise* (see Psalm 9:11), *confession* (see 1 John 1:9), or *thanksgiving and supplication* (see Philippians 4:6). Confession is a form of emotional and spiritual respiration: we breathe *out* our guilt and sin, and we breathe *in* God's grace and forgiveness. Thankfulness is our acknowledgment of God's goodness in our lives. Supplication places God's unlimited resources at our disposal, giving God the opportunity either to answer our request or to teach us more of Himself through telling us to wait or to seek a deeper sense of His will.

Perhaps the most profound expression of prayer is the prayer of *praise*. In praise, we lose sight of ourselves and gain an expanded vision of God. Praise can take the form of speaking to God, but it can also take the form of singing to God or praying His words from the Scriptures back to Him.

One commonly overlooked aspect of prayer is *listening*. "Be still, and know that I am God," says Psalm 46:10. Many people make the mistake of only talking to God in prayer and never listening for His answers. But communion with God is a two-way dialogue. As you wait and listen to God in the stillness of your prayerful meditation, He has an opportunity to bring important thoughts and insights to your mind that can improve your daily life and enable you to walk closer to Him throughout the day.

> **Communion with God is a two-way dialogue.**

When we truly understand what takes place when we pray, we have to be amazed at the fact that the Creator of the universe has chosen to link His power to our prayers. Jesus has said, "If you ask . . . I will do" (see John 14:13–14). We could also take that promise to imply, "If you don't ask, I may not do it." God's assurance to us is that His strength is made available to us through prayer for our own needs and the needs of others. He will always answer prayer, though His answer may not always be exactly what we expect.

If we want to have an effective prayer life, we need to make sure that our hearts have been prepared to meet God on an intimate basis. Following are the conditions for a prepared and prayerful heart:

1. Confession of sins (see Psalm 66:18; 1 John 1:9). When we confess sin, we accept God's forgiveness, we cleanse ourselves of guilt, and we clear the way to forgiving ourselves.

2. Obedience to God's Word as we understand it (see Proverbs 28:9).

3. Purified motives and the elimination of selfishness from our hearts (see James 4:2–3).

4. An attitude of faith and trust in God for every need and problem in our lives (see John 15:5; Romans 8:28; Philippians 4:13).

5. Healed relationships and a clear conscience toward others (see Matthew 6:12; 1 Peter 3:7).

THE PRACTICALITIES OF PRAYER

From the Scriptures, we can derive several practical guidelines for prayer:

1. Remember that prayer gives us immediate, intimate access to God the Father. We pray to the Father in the name of the Son. We need no other mediator between ourselves and the Father, because Jesus is our mediator. Through His death on the cross, all sin barriers between ourselves and our Heavenly Father have been torn down.

2. There are no special words we need to pray. Some people, influenced by the Shakespearean-sounding language of the King James Bible, like to address God with words such as "Thee" and "Thou," and to use flowery turns of phrases. Those who feel more comfortable doing so (as a sign of reverence and respect) should do so. But there is no reason that we shouldn't address God very simply and conversationally. In prayer, God wants the sincerity of our hearts, not a performance.

3. There is no special posture needed for prayer. We can pray on our knees, sitting down, standing up, driving in our cars, standing in line at the checkout counter, anywhere and in any position.

4. When we pray, "In Jesus' name, Amen," we should be aware that this means more than just appending the Lord's name to our prayers. We are also acknowledging our desire that our prayers be conformed to the will of the Lord. When an ambassador goes to a foreign country and presents his credentials to a foreign government, he comes in the name of his country. He comes to express the will of his country. When we go to the Father in prayer, we come in the name of Jesus, seeking to conform our prayers to the will of Jesus. In this way, we will never be disappointed in prayer. If God chooses to give an answer to our prayers that is not as we expected, then we know that we need to change our expectations so that they align with His will.

5. Pray any place. Pray at any time. Pray for any reason. As we become more and more aware of God's continuing presence alongside us, our entire lives will become an offering of prayer to God.

MAKING A DAILY, HEALTHY HABIT OF PRAYER

One of the keys to a healthy faith and a healthy emotional life is a daily, healthy habit of meeting alone with the Lord. This spiritual discipline is called a *daily quiet time.* A quiet time involves Bible study, meditation, and prayer. Regular time spent in communion with God improves thinking, emotional well-being, behavior, and relationships. Here are some suggestions for an effective quiet time:

1. Make your quiet time a regular, daily habit. Choose a time when you can meet with God alone and undisturbed. Clear your schedule of all distractions and interruptions during that time.

2. Select a special place for your quiet time—your bedroom, your breakfast nook, your office, any place where you can spend about half an hour in undisturbed solitude.

3. Keep a notebook or journal of significant insights and observations that come to you during Bible study and prayer. Also, keep a record of prayer requests and answers to prayer.

As you follow this process, you will find you have more power in your life to break sinful habits, to rechannel unproductive or self-defeating thinking, to conquer depression and anxiety, to gain confidence, and to prepare yourself to be a witness for Jesus Christ. Don't neglect this special time of joy and growth. The Bible tells us that God desires to meet with us, and as we make our relationship with Him a number one priority, we will find that we truly enjoy intimacy with Him.

See also FAITH

Premenstrual Syndrome

Premenstrual syndrome (PMS) involves a cluster of debilitating physical and emotional symptoms that usually begin about seven to ten days before a woman's menstrual period. The symptoms usually cease once the menstrual flow begins. (If symptoms last the entire month, the problem is something other than PMS.) Major symptoms include:

- bloating (*edema* or water retention)
- loss of energy
- headaches
- muscle pain
- difficulty concentrating
- anxiety, depression, or other mood changes
- extreme irritability
- impulsiveness
- a tendency to ruminate on self-critical fault patterns
- extreme mood swings (tearfulness, anger, withdrawal, guilt, embarrassment)

One or all of these symptoms occur to some degree in about half of all women of childbearing age. A small number have symptoms so severe that they are virtually incapacitated. A requirement for a diagnosis of PMS is that there are no other major psychiatric factors that would account for these mood changes, such as panic disorder, major depressive disorder, manic-depressive disorder, or multiple-personality syndrome.

There continues to be much debate about what specifically causes PMS, but it most likely involves a combination of organic and psychological factors. Some medical experts believe it is linked to a change in noradrenaline, a brain chemical that controls moods. Others point to the periodic increase in prostaglandin hormones during the menstrual cycle. Recent research has been directed toward discovering the effect of diet upon the chemical changes that occur in cycles in a woman's body.

If your symptoms are severe, you should consult your physician for an evaluation. Many treatments for PMS are available, but no single treatment works for everyone. Your physician may have you try one or more of the following in order to determine which is the most effective in your case:

Vitamin B6. Some doctors prescribe 100 milligrams to be taken twice a day. Although a number of women report that their PMS symptoms are alleviated greatly on this regimen, it should be tried only under a doctor's supervision. Vitamin supplements can be dangerous if used incorrectly.

Progesterone suppositories. Many women claim to feel better after using these, but research results are contradictory regarding progesterone's value in treating PMS.

Antidepressants. This treatment is mainly used for patients with clinical (serious and long-lasting) depression. But a significant percentage of women say they experience relief from PMS by using the antidepressant Tofranil (generic equivalent: Imipramine).

Bromoscriptine. This drug helps minimize the breast discomfort that typically accompanies PMS.

Dietary changes. Decreasing the intake of salt, sugar, and caffeine helps decrease swelling, hypoglycemia symptoms, and the emotional agitation that often occurs before the menstrual period.

Diuretics. Some women use diuretics to alleviate bloating (edema).

Counseling. This often-neglected approach to controlling PMS focuses on resolving anger and other issues from the past, and on relieving current emotional pressures that can increase the severity of PMS symptoms.

An excellent book on premenstrual syndrome has been written by a Christian gynecologist and a nutritionist: *PMS: What It Is and What You Can Do About It* by Sharon M. Sneed and Joe S. McIlhaney, Jr. (Baker Book House, 1988).

Psychosis

A psychosis (plural *psychoses*) is the most severe of all mental disorders. It is a disorder that causes a person to exhibit a disordered sense of what is real and not real (losing touch with reality), along with signs of a disturbed personality. People who are in a

463

psychotic state are frequently unable to meet their own basic needs and are sometimes a danger to themselves and others. Hospitalization is usually required in such cases.

Examples of common psychoses include:

Schizophrenia, the most common form of psychosis, characterized by withdrawal from the outside world.

Paranoia, a form of psychosis characterized by a fanciful but consistent system of delusions (irrational beliefs), often involving being the target of a conspiracy.

Affective psychosis, an extreme mood disorder such as psychotic depression or psychotic manic-depression. Psychotic mood disorders differ from (and are far more rare than) common neurotic forms of depression and manic-depression. Psychotic forms of depression differ from neurotic forms in that (1) the depressed or manic-depressive individual loses touch with reality and (2) the individual does not see his depression as abnormal. (Compare with DEPRESSION and MANIC-DEPRESSION.)

Psychotic symptoms may also be observed in patients afflicted with Alzheimer's disease, head trauma, brain tumors, epilepsy, syphilis, withdrawal from severe alcohol addiction, and extreme manifestations of the schizotypal personality disorder. Counseling techniques have limited value in helping people with psychoses, since it is hard to help a client develop insight into his or her disorder when the individual's sense of reality and reason are impaired. A number of drug treatments are available to help manage psychotic symptoms.

Rape

Rape is a sexual act that one person forces on another. Rape may involve sexual penetration, oral sodomy, anal sodomy, or penetration with objects. The rape victim may be female or male. In rare cases, the rapist may not even touch the victim but may force the victim (through threats and intimidation) to perform a degrading sex act. The rapist may or may not use a weapon to intimidate the victim. Despite these variations in how the crime is perpetrated, it is still an act of rape, and it is a traumatic incident from which any person will require help in order to recover.

Rape interrupts and invades a person's life at the deepest level. Although rape involves sex, it is fundamentally an act of violence, not an act of passion. The most prevalent emotion a rape victim feels during the commission of the act is not a sexual emotion but the emotion of terror, of horror, of fear for her life and revulsion over the violent invasion of her body and innermost being. Rape victims overwhelmingly report believing they were going to be killed.

After being raped, an individual will feel that her life will never be the same again. And it is true that she will be changed by this experience. She will never be able to undo what has happened, nor erase the memory. She can expect to experience emotional pain, grief, fear, insecurity, humiliation, anger, and perhaps feelings of false guilt and self-blame. She may also experience hindrances in her ability to trust others, to give and receive love, to enjoy healthy sex, and to be fully functional at work. Nightmares, numbness, heart palpitations, pain, rapid breathing, and rapid heart rate are also common features of postrape trauma. These effects are temporary. Most rape victims recover and become functional again.

Most authorities on the subject divide rape into two categories, *stranger rape* and *acquaintance rape*. Stranger rape is what most of us think of as rape: being accosted in a parking lot or a dark alley or by a burglar-rapist in one's own home. The thought strikes terror into the heart of every woman. Statistics show that being raped by an acquaintance, however, is far more prevalent than stranger rape, accounting for around 60 percent of reported rapes and possibly a much higher percentage of unreported rapes. When a person chooses to be in the company of another person, who then turns sexually violent, this form of acquaintance rape is called *date rape*. One of the most problematic complications of date rape is that the victim concludes that "no one will believe me if I report it" or "they'll think I was asking for it." It is important to remember that rape is rape, whether the perpetrator is previously known to an individual or not. Accepting a date with someone does not constitute an invitation to be assaulted.

One issue that complicates the guilt problem for some rape victims is that they may experience orgasm in the course of the rape. This does not mean that the victim subconsciously enjoyed being raped. Sometimes, when a person experiences acute fear, the body's systems become agitated and hyper-responsive because of accelerated heart-beat and higher levels of adrenaline. Some people respond to extreme fear by blacking out or by involuntarily voiding their bowels or bladders or by experiencing involuntary climax. This does not suggest that the rape victim experienced sexual pleasure or desire. This only demonstrates the intensity of the fear of rape.

Rapists are not motivated to violence primarily by lust. There is undoubtedly an element of lust somewhere in the rapist's emotions, but the overwhelming motivation behind rape goes far beyond even basic animal passion. The three major motivations for rape are:

1. Power. Individuals who feel powerless or controlled in life sometimes commit crimes in order to feel they have power over someone else. The power-hungry rapist derives gratification from seeing his victim helpless and degraded. Humiliation, intimidation, and terrorizing behavior signal a power motive in the rapist. This is the most common motive for rape.

2. Anger/revenge. For the perpetrator, rape may be an act of revenge carried out in anger against some person in the rapist's past—an absent person who is symbolized by the actual victim. The revenge-motivated rapist is brutal and unpredictable and often attacks suddenly and ferociously, rather than luring a victim as the power rapist might do.

3. Sadism. Some individuals derive sexual pleasure from the pain of others. Power and revenge issues are sometimes involved in sadism. These individuals learned early in life (possibly by being sadistically abused themselves or by witnessing acts of sadistic sex) to associate sex with violence. To these individuals, sex *is* violence and violence is sexual. Thoughts and images of torture and killing, even if there is initially no sexual

■

No one asks to be raped. No one is responsible for rape but the rapist. Most rape victims feel some measure of guilt over their assault, but this is false guilt. Rapists are 100 percent to blame for their actions.

■

component to these thoughts and images, can cause the sadistic individual to become sexually aroused.

If you are the victim of rape, you will find that recovery takes place in several phases:

1. During the first few hours after the rape, you should get to a place of safety and get help. Your first impulse will be to wash yourself after a rape, but *don't wash yourself until the authorities have a chance to gather evidence against the perpetrator.* Do not shower or douche. You may change clothes, place the original clothes you were wearing during the attack in a bag, and take them with you when you go for help.

Locate a rape crisis center by calling your local YWCA or checking the front of your phone book for a rape hotline. The people who answer the phone can tell you how to go about reporting the rape to the police and how to obtain medical care. It is advisable to go to the hospital emergency room after a rape, even if you feel you have not been physically injured. A hospital can give you treatment to prevent sexually transmitted disease.

2. During the first week following the attack, get into counseling and a rape survivor's support group. You need to begin immediately to deal with the emotional aftermath of this traumatic event. It helps to ventilate your emotions in the presence of people who understand and who can express the same feelings you are feeling.

You should also be alert to signs of sexually transmitted disease—irritation of the genitals, soreness or itchiness, or vaginal infections (see SEXUALLY TRANSMITTED DISEASES). Also be on the alert to other medical problems—sleeplessness, lack of appetite, nausea, or other symptoms. These medical problems may have either a physical or emotional basis.

You will feel very insecure, and you will be easily startled for some time to come. You may even think you see the rapist when it is just a shadow or someone who physically resembles the rapist. You have to keep telling yourself that you are safe now. You may want to take a self-defense class in order to boost your confidence and sense of security.

Remind yourself that you are going to be okay. Recovery takes time and patience, but you will recover. Keep telling yourself that you are not to blame. If you experience feelings of self-hate or self-blame, offer these feelings to God for healing, and disclose these feelings and work through them in counseling and in your support group.

Restructure your surroundings and remove reminders of the rape. If you were attacked in your home or your car, consider moving or getting a different car. Even if you were raped elsewhere, make changes in your life so that you gain a sense of a new beginning. Rearrange your furniture or redecorate your house. Take a class that will help rebuild your self-esteem. Become involved in a ministry in your church.

If you are married or in a dating relationship, talk through your feelings with that person and involve that person in your counseling. If this person cannot be understand-

Assigning the Blame for Rape

The fact that rapists rape because of power issues, anger/revenge issues, or sadism should make one fact perfectly clear: rape is not sex, and rapists are not lured by their victims into committing crimes. Rape victims are not "bad people" because they have been raped. Rape victims do not provoke attacks or "ask for it." Rapists rape for their own reasons, and they alone are responsible for their crimes. Rape victims are not to blame for being raped.

ing and supportive, he must be confronted and educated to understand what has happened to you.

3. In the long term, maintain your counseling and support group relationships until you feel strong enough and secure enough to "go it alone." Stay involved with your closest, most supportive friendships, particularly your same-sex friendships. Give yourself time to feel ready to re-enter a sexual relationship. Don't worry if you are uncomfortable with sex for two months or more, but make sure you continue working on your emotional issues, including the wounds in your sexuality.

Many people find it helpful to their recovery to become activists against crime and violence, either by becoming politically active in organizations such as Women Against Rape or the National Organization for Victim Assistance or by becoming rape counselors or facilitators of rape survivor support groups in the community or in a church.

If you are a friend of a rape victim, here are some suggestions: Express your caring. Don't express anger or disbelief. Don't blame. Don't minimize the seriousness of the attack. Ask the victim if she wants to be held and physically supported (don't touch the victim without permission). Express your belief in her story and that you are proud of her for surviving the attack. Allow the rape victim to ventilate anger and grief. Listen to the rape victim talk. Be supportive, offer counsel, but allow the individual to make decisions so she will feel empowered and in control. Help the individual locate a rape hotline, drive her to the hospital, and volunteer to stay by your friend. One of the best resources for healing any rape victim can have is a good friend.

■

Many states have special victim-assistance funds that provide compensation to crime victims that can be used to defray medical and legal expenses that result from being raped. Rape counselors or local social agencies should be able to provide information on how to obtain victim assistance.

■

Relationship Addiction

Sarah could not remember a time when she truly felt loved. Her stepfather and stepbrother belittled her as "ugly" and "stupid." Her own mother sometimes joined in the verbal abuse. When Sarah was ten, her mother committed suicide by hanging. Sarah found her mother's body in the basement after school. To this day, that image is burned into Sarah's memory. Like any young child will do when something terrible happens in the family, she absorbed the guilt and shame of that experience. Sarah believed her mother's suicide was her fault. *If only I could have made my mommy love me,* she thought, *she wouldn't have had to die . . .*

After her mother's death, Sarah's stepfather put her in the car and drove her two hundred miles away to her aunt's house. Her aunt wasn't home, so he just left Sarah there. When the aunt arrived, she was furious to discover that she had been "stuck" with Sarah.

During those painful years, growing up unwanted and unloved, Sarah often thought about God. She was a behavior problem for her aunt, and her aunt took her to Sunday school in the hope that a dose of religion might "straighten Sarah out." Sarah become

467

convinced that God must truly hate her to make her so stupid and ugly, to make her mother die, to make her life so miserable. Her two overriding emotions were anger and shame.

When Sarah was fourteen, she was befriended by a new young man in the neighborhood, a boy of seventeen who had just moved in a few doors down from her aunt's house. He was friendly and attentive, and he didn't seem to think Sarah was stupid or ugly or bad at all. So it was only predictable that, one day when her aunt was gone and Sarah was alone in her bedroom with this older boy, she lost her virginity.

From that time on, Sarah had many boyfriends, and she let them use her body again and again. She hated sex, but she loved male attention. She loved to be touched and she loved to hear their empty words of flattery. Some even said, "I love you, Sarah," though they all abandoned her sooner or later. Sarah learned that she could hold on to some of these relationships a little longer if she behaved the right way and said the right things. She was willing to pay any price to keep a boy interested in her. She even let some of the boys do some terrible things to her: ridicule her, taunt her, hit her, hurt her sexually. As long as they didn't abandon her, she was "happy."

This pattern continued into adulthood. Sarah was married three times by age thirty, and she had undergone many live-in arrangements and affairs. Somehow, all the men in her life abused her or abandoned her or both.

By age forty, Sarah had attempted suicide twice, both times using sleeping pills. She came into the clinic for counseling after the second suicide attempt. As her counselor talked to her, it became clear that Sarah didn't really want to die, but she was in a great deal of emotional pain. Twice she had cried out for help by nearly killing herself. The rest of her life had been spent in a search for love in a series of unloving, abusive relationships.

Sarah had a *relationship addiction*.

RELATIONSHIP ADDICTION: A DISORDER OF ATTACHMENT

A relationship addiction is a codependent emotional attachment to another person. The relationship addict responds to other people who seem to offer attention and caring. "A relationship addiction," says Stephen Arterburn, "is a *disorder of attachment* to another person. It is this sense of attachment, of being needed, that is paramount in the heart and mind of the relationship addict. This individual doesn't necessarily want sex. In fact, he or she may actively dislike sex. But relationship addicts want to be wanted. They crave attention, even if it is destructive attention, such as abuse. For the relationship addict, the terror of being abandoned and alone is greater than the pain of being abused. That is why so many relationship addicts remain in destructive relationships. They are hooked on the attachment. The relationship is their drug. No matter how abusive and destructive the relationship becomes, no matter how degrading to their personal dignity, these individuals can't live without it."

One of the engines that drives relationship addiction is *wounded self-esteem*. Relationship-addicted individuals are convinced that no one can ever love them for who they are. They continually gravitate toward unhealthy relationships because (1) unhealthy relationships are familiar (it's all they ever knew during childhood); and (2) they cannot experience successful relationships with emotionally healthy people. Healthy individuals are strong enough to leave when the relationship addict's problems begin to manifest themselves. The addict knows that it is pointless to establish a relationship with a healthy person, because that will only lead to abandonment. So, unconsciously, the addict gravitates toward dysfunctional people.

Another engine that drives relationship addiction is *fear*. The individual fears rejection, abandonment, and failing to measure up. He or she is a quivering mass of insecurity. "I can't survive alone" is the addict's core belief. Yet it is this very fear that tends to destroy relationships and drive people away from the addict. This fear sets a cycle in motion and keeps it turning, propelling the addict from one unhealthy relationship to another.

Coupled with this fear is an intense sense of *guilt*. Relationship addicts continually apologize, even when they do nothing wrong. The pattern of guilt was laid down in their lives during childhood, when they took responsibility for their parents' problems, abusive behavior, alcoholism, divorce, or death. The addicts then transferred this guilt to their adult relationships. A strong sense of guilt is very appealing to sexual predators and exploitative personalities, since it makes relationship addicts extremely vulnerable—and that's another reason addicts are prone to unhealthy relationships. Relationship addicts are very self-obsessed—not in the sense that they are prideful and narcissistic but in that they are totally focused on their own mistakes, failures, pain, and problems. They set impossible standards for themselves, which only compounds their guilt when these standards are unmet.

Another engine that drives relationship addiction is *a distorted perception of other people*. The relationship addict tends to view each new acquaintance through a romantic glow. Any person who shows a bit of interest becomes Prince or Princess Charming. Addicts cannot be objective about people; all flaws, weaknesses, and even warning signs are mentally "airbrushed" away, replaced by a glamorized aura of perfection. The addict attaches to this new relationship like a barnacle to a boat's hull and soon announces to all friends the discovery of the latest Mr. or Ms. Right.

In time, the relationship inevitably sours. Prince or Princess Charming turns out to be an abuser, or gets bored, or gets fed up. As the relationship deteriorates, the addict retreats into *denial:*

"Yes, it hurts when he beats me, but it's only because he wants me so much that he hurts me. If he didn't love me, why is he still here?"

"She says she's going to leave me, but if I try harder, everything will be okay."

"I don't like it that he has affairs, but if I can just find a way to please him, he'll love only me."

Another engine that drives relationship addiction is *anger*. Ironically, relationship addicts are some of the angriest people alive, yet they frequently don't show it and aren't even aware of it. At first meeting, they seem amiable and pleasant, maybe even a bit shy, but always sweet and smiling. They want to be liked. Yet deep inside is a seething reservoir of rage—and when you look into their history, it is not hard to see where that rage comes from. They resent the abuse or neglect of childhood and the repeated abandonment of adulthood. They are resentful over the fact that they have to work so hard to please others, to avoid giving offense, to meet the needs of others, to deny their own needs just to be liked, yet no one cares about their needs.

Symbiotic Relationships

Symbiosis is a situation in which two dissimilar organisms attach to each other and use each other to sustain themselves. In the ocean, various species of fish allow so-called "cleaner shrimps" to crawl over their bodies, picking off parasites and other foreign matter. In the desert, the yucca plant is pollinated by the white pronuba moth and in turn allows the moth to lay eggs in its flowers, and the eggs hatch larvae that bore holes in the yucca and feed off its seeds. In the field of human relations, relationship addicts link up with sex addicts and form a symbiotic partnership in which each partner feeds on the other's disorder.

Relationship addicts are the perfect prey for sex addicts because their inbred guilt and shame sets them up to take the responsibility and blame for other people's actions. Sex addicts love shoving their responsibility and their guilt off onto other people, and relationship addicts eagerly receive it. In fact, this is the only stable emotional attachment a relationship addict can make—though we hasten to add that "stable" does not equal "healthy." The sex addict often finds exactly what he is looking for in a relationship addict: someone who will always be there, will accept the sex addict's multiple infidelities and other abuses, and will even take the blame!

In some cases, there may be some elements of genuine caring and concern in these relationships. But most of these relationships involve exploitation of vulnerabilities. Sex addicts are usually experienced seducers, and relationship addicts frequently mistake their practiced approach and polished line for romantic sincerity.

When the relationship addict discovers that the sex-addicted partner is unfaithful, the relationship addict does not respond with outrage. Whereas healthy people would consider infidelity an act of betrayal and abandonment, the relationship addict sees it as a problem to be repaired. Relationship addicts love to "fix" other people and their problems. They also believe that a bad relationship (which they think is all they deserve) is better than no relationship at all. *Besides,* they reason, *if he (or she) is going to other people for sexual fulfillment, it must be my fault.*

THE PROFILE OF A RELATIONSHIP ADDICT

Below are a number of characteristics that identify a person who is caught up in an addiction to people and relationships.

Childhood pain and deprivation. Most addicts were wounded, abused, rejected, or abandoned in childhood. As a result, they feel rejected and unloved by family, by the world, and by God.

Extreme insecurity. Addicts are afraid of the stresses and risks of life. They are indecisive. They attach themselves to other people in order to absorb strength and courage from another person, to be protected, and to escape the terror of being alone in the world.

An unhealthy view of love. Relationship addicts do not understand unconditional love. They believe love must be earned by being "good enough" to be loved.

Rare but inevitable outbursts of anger. Relationship addicts are unconsciously angry, and no one can keep his anger bottled up forever. Sooner or later, it inevitably explodes. These episodes are followed by excessive remorse and promises to do anything to make it up, anything to prevent abandonment.

Self-effacement and self-sacrifice. Relationship addicts cater to the needs of others—though in fact this is a way of meeting their own needs to be loved and accepted.

An eagerness to "fix" or "rescue" others. Relationship addicts are rescuers, committed to fixing people who, in general, do not want to be fixed. They seek out needy people, and the needier they are, the more attractive they are to the relationship addict.

Extreme caution around others. Relationship addicts walk on eggshells, terrified of doing or saying anything that might cause people to reject them.

An attraction to abusive or emotionally rejecting people. They seek romantic relationships with people who are symbolic equivalents of their abusive or emotionally rejecting parents. This is often part of an unconscious desire to carry on the no-win struggle for the love and attention that was denied them in childhood.

Sudden, desperate attachment or fixation. Relationship addicts move from attraction to attachment with incredible speed, hoping to bond the relationship before the other person can get away. This tends to scare off healthy, whole people who are sensitive to a relationship that "moves too fast."

A notable absence of whole, healthy friendships. Past and present relationships and acquaintances tend to be replete with needy people; by contrast to them, the addict can appear to be normal.

Indifference to, or disgust with, sex. Sexual intercourse is not a source of joy or pleasure to most relationship addicts, although they do enjoy the closeness and touching of foreplay (which they interpret as love and affection). The sex is only a means to an end, and it must be endured as the price of holding on to the relationship.

An inability to receive from others. Relationship addicts give but cannot receive from others. They have to earn love, they have to sacrifice self, they have to accept abuse. If someone helps them or gives to them, they feel guilty and inadequate.

Excessive endurance of destructive behavior. The addict's ability to endure abuse, infidelity, and rejection in a destructive relationship continually amazes the addict's friends and relationships.

Overblown expectations. Relationship addicts constantly tell themselves and others that *this* relationship is different from all the rest. Hope springs eternal, in spite of all past experience. The beginning of each new relationship is greeted with euphoria and a certainty that "I finally know what true love is!"

Defensiveness and denial. Those who attempt to "talk sense" to a relationship addict will be treated either to sweetly pleasant denials ("Thank you, but I know what I'm doing") or to hostility ("This is *my* life and you don't know what you're talking about!").

Poor self-image. Relationship addicts feel too fat (or too thin), too homely, too stupid, too flawed in one way or another. They feel alienated from themselves, from God, and from other people.

Hunger for attention. Relationship addicts may turn compliments aside ("Oh, you're just saying that," or "It's nice of you to say so, but I'm really no good at that"). Inside, however, they eat up such comments and compliments.

Frequent depression. Relationship addicts have few emotional resources to draw upon to carry them through tough emotional times. They are angry, guilt-ridden, and filled with self-loathing, which is a perfect setup for depression.

Compulsive and addictive. Relationship addicts are frequently polyaddicted, and subject to such compulsive behaviors as overeating, bulimia, overspending, gambling, alcoholism, and so forth. With time, these patterns tend to become increasingly intertwined.

Control addiction. Many relationship addicts are also control addicts (see CONTROL ADDICTION) and seek out people who can be manipulated. Though the relationship addict may appear, at first glance, to be the meek, subservient slave of a domineering partner, it is frequently the relationship addict who has the invisible upper hand in the relationship. Relationship addicts have learned, through years of trial and error, where the hidden marionette strings are and how to pull them. They know what to do and say in order to get attention and affection and how to keep their partner (who is often a sex addict) interested and attached.

THE STAGES OF RELATIONSHIP ADDICTION

A relationship addict's descent into an addictive relationship tends to follow a fairly predictable progression of stages:

1. *Obsession.* The individual is obsessed with self, with past hurts, with resentment, with the need to dissolve his or her pain by bonding with another person.

2. *The hunt.* The obsession magnifies, and the addict seeks a new relationship, using techniques and approaches that have been learned and developed from past experience.

3. *Recruitment.* There are many ways to approach a "target." If the addict senses the other person has a vulnerable ego, he or she may try flattery. A show of helplessness or submissiveness is more effective with domineering types. The addict knows how to adjust his or her "mating call" to fit the personality of the "target."

4. *Gratification.* If the "target" responds, the addict enjoys new energy and even euphoria. The normal emotions of the addict are lifted—fear, guilt, anger, depression. The addict now has something—and someone—to live for.

5. *Return to normal.* The addict is okay—for now. He or she feels complete, no longer alone, because of the relationship. But with time, the superficiality of the relationship begins to show.

6. *Justification.* Pain creeps in as the addict seeks to justify the dishonest, manipulative means used to seek out the "target." The addict also tries to justify being in a relationship with a person who is so dysfunctional.

472

7. *Blame.* The addict begins to blame others for problems, including being abused by the partner. Most likely objects for blame: the addict's parents, friends, past relationships, anyone and everyone who has ever disappointed the addict.

8. *Shame.* The addict realizes that he or she has become bound to yet another destructive relationship. Blame turns inward and becomes shame.

9. *Despair.* Past guilt and present shame collide to produce hopelessness. The addict feels trapped in yet another dead-end relationship. The "I-told-you-so's" of friends and family make a hollow ringing sound in the addict's soul.

10. *Promises.* The addict swears to never, ever do it again. "I'll get help," the addict says. "I'll get counseling. I'll stay away from the singles bar. I'll become a nun." That is guilt and shame talking, and these toxic emotional forces only serve to keep the addictive cycle in motion.

"None of this behavior makes sense, not to the addict's friends, and not even to the addict himself," says Stephen Arterburn. "The judgment and perception of relationship addicts become so distorted by pain and self-obsession that their ability to make decisions is impaired. They may take stupid risks and seek relationships in dangerous places. They may scratch and claw to hang on to destructive, abusive relationships. They will put up with unbelievable humiliation just to avoid being abandoned. They manipulate and control their partner with their obsessive love. They fling their half a soul at a potential partner, hoping that this other person will reciprocate and attach to them and make them whole. But when it's all over, they're more damaged and broken than when the relationship began.

"Finally, if they're lucky, they come to the end of themselves. They hit bottom. That's when God can work. Once they recognize that they can never fix themselves, once they reach the bottommost depths of their own broken hearts, the cycle is broken. The relationship addict is ready to begin the process of recovery."

The Twelve Steps of Sex and Love Addicts Anonymous

As adapted for use with relationship addiction, the Twelve Steps read:

1. Admitted we were powerless over sex and love addiction—that our lives had become unmanageable.
2. Came to believe that a Power greater than ourselves could restore us to sanity.
3. Made a decision to turn our will and our lives over to the care of God as we understood God.
4. Made a searching and fearless moral inventory of ourselves.
5. Admitted to God, to ourselves, and to another human being the exact nature of our wrongs.
6. Were entirely ready to have God remove all these defects of character.
7. Humbly asked God to remove our shortcomings.
8. Made a list of all persons we had harmed, and became willing to make amends to them all.
9. Made direct amends to such people wherever possible, except when to do so would injure them or others.
10. Continued to take personal inventory and when we were wrong, promptly admitted it.
11. Sought through prayer and meditation to improve our conscious contact with God as we understood God, praying only for knowledge of God's will for us and the power to carry that out.
12. Having had a spiritual awakening as a result of these steps, we tried to carry this message to sex and love addicts, and to practice these principles in all areas of our lives.

(Pages 67–68, reprinted from the Basic Test of Sex and Love Addicts Anonymous. Copyright 1986 with permission of The Augustine Fellowship, Sex and Love Addicts Anonymous.)

TREATMENT AND RECOVERY

Hitting bottom is the worst moment in any addict's life. For the relationship addict, it may mean that the man she has attached herself to has nearly beaten her to death. Or that the sex-addicted woman he married has given him genital herpes. Whatever the circumstances, the fact remains: the addict cannot take one more day of the addiction. The excuses, denials, and rationalizations no longer work. All the empty resolutions of the past have been exposed. All hope is gone—unless the addict puts an end to procrastination and decides to take action.

The first step is for the addict to go into treatment. But the idea of treatment scares many people. What goes on in a treatment center? What will happen to me? Will it even work? Part of the fear centers around the terror of being discovered. For decades, the addict has been building an elaborate network of emotional defenses. Now this individual will have to bare shameful secrets in order to purge the pain and the irrational impulses that have kept him or her enmeshed in destructive relationships. Even after hitting bottom, the fear of the healing process is great.

"Is treatment scary?" says Stephen Arterburn. "Sure it's scary. You have to be honest with other people, and honest with yourself. Honesty is scary. But it pays off. Recovery is doing the thing you fear the most—because the alternative is even worse."

Treatment for relationship addiction, as practiced at the Minirth Meier New Life Clinics, is simple and effective. It is a process of helping the relationship addict abandon self-defeating attachments, so that he or she can begin building genuine loving relationships. At last, the relationship addict can stop searching for "love" and finally discover *love*. It is a process that enables addicts to understand and deal with the hidden emotional forces that drive the addictive behavior. This recovery process is based on the Twelve Steps, a practical and spiritual recovery program first used by Alcoholics Anonymous and now used as a recovery approach for many different forms of addiction.

The Twelve Steps require that people take responsibility for their own recovery. (No one's going to fix you. *You* have to fix you.) The Twelve Steps help to open one's mind, heart, and will to God, the Source of all health and healing. Embodied in the Twelve Steps are five principles of emotional healing:

1. Acceptance. Recovery means accepting the truth about one's own addiction, shedding all evasions and denial, and surrendering to a Power greater than oneself—God.

2. Confession. Recovery requires that the person tear down the walls of silence and secrecy that have kept him or her isolated from friends, from family, from God, and even from himself or herself. Here the individual penetrates the secrets of his or her soul, for it is only what he or she hides that truly hurts him or her. The person confesses his or her faults to another human being, to God, and to himself or herself. And with confession come cleansing and renewal.

3. Forgiveness. The guilt, shame, anger, and bitterness that have collected in one's soul for all these years must be purged. The addict does that by learning to forgive others and to forgive himself or herself. Forgiveness resolves the past and clears a path into the future.

4. Accountability. Once a person attains recovery, he or she must learn how to *keep* it—and that means making himself or herself accountable to others for his or her progress and growth. Accountability keeps one from falling back into harmful patterns and guards one against complacency and self-deception.

5. Love. One of the identifying marks of addiction is self-absorption and self-obsession. One of the identifying marks of emotional health is outward-directed, Christlike love. Only when a person focuses on loving God, authentically loving others,

THE COMPLETE LIFE ENCYCLOPEDIA

and loving himself or herself in an appropriate way can he or she truly experience healing from addiction.

These principles form the basis of recovery. As a person moves deeper into the recovery process he or she:

- experiences genuine love
- discovers true intimacy
- fills up the emotional void within us
- confronts the true meaning of life
- encounters authentic union with God

With all of these wonderful benefits that are derived from courageously entering into the process of recovery, why do some people shrink from it? Why do some people choose to cling to their disorders rather than embrace the health, the wholeness, and the genuine love that are available to them? Here are some of the reasons:

- Dysfunctional behavior attracts attention—and relationship addicts crave attention.
- The pain isn't great enough yet; the individual hasn't hit bottom.
- Fear of the unknown.
- Fear of exposure. Guilt is private; shame is public.
- Pride.
- Physiological or psychological addiction to a substance.
- Fear of failure or change; retreating from reality.
- "Praying for a miracle." People want life to be easy, but life is difficult and requires work. The miracle God wants to work *in* us is the miracle He wants to work *through* us, through our commitment to our own healing. Seeking a quick fix is a sign of emotional and spiritual immaturity.

Once an individual sets foot on the path to recovery, life begins to change for the better. Emotional and spiritual growth leads to new and exciting insights about oneself and about life in general. The relationship addict learns how to receive love and grace from God, from other people, and from himself or herself. Not "love," not that false euphoria that accompanies the early stages of an unhealthy, destructive relationship, but genuine *love,* the unconditional Christlike love that was denied us in childhood, which eluded us in adulthood, and which has been the object of our searching and desiring all along.

Finally, we are able to experience healthy relationships with healthy people. We learn that the progression of a healthy relationship is:

1. attraction
2. mutual interest
3. enjoyment
4. giving of self
5. sacrifice
6. love
7. intimacy
8. discernment of God's will
9. commitment
10. marriage
11. sexual intimacy
12. deepening trust
13. ripening maturity

See also FAMILY and MARRIAGE

Relationships

Healthy people create healthy relationships, and healthy relationships help us to become healthy people. Through mutual commitment, unconditional love, acceptance, and forgiveness, relationships grow in depth and meaning and stability over time. This is true of all our relationships in all areas of our lives: our friendships, our family relationships, our marriage relationship, our relationships with fellow Christians in the church.

Our society does not do a good job of modeling healthy relationships. "Watching movies and TV," says Stephen Arterburn, "you get the idea that the goal of relationships is to take what you can get and get what you can. It's as if a human relationship were like a financial investment: you set your goals, pick your investment vehicle, put in the required amount, then sit back and wait for the return. If that return is not what you anticipated, just withdraw your investment and take your business someplace else."

That's not the way healthy relationships work. Relationships require commitment and patience. A healthy person doesn't ask, "What's in this relationship for me?" but "What can I give to you?"

THE INGREDIENTS OF A HEALTHY RELATIONSHIP

What are the ingredients of a healthy relationship? There are many, but we will focus on seven:

1. Realism. Healthy relationships are reality-based. Healthy individuals don't deny emotions, ignore problems, or tiptoe around "undiscussable" issues. Healthy relationships are honest, open, and realistic.

2. Honesty. A true relationship cannot exist on a foundation of dishonesty or secrets. The more lies, denials, and secrets there are in a relationship, the more dysfunctional that relationship is. Truth builds trust, and trust builds relationships. Lies break trust, and trust, once broken, is not easily mended. Broken trust creates cracks in the relationship. Truth creates relationships that endure and grow.

3. Friendship. Whether a relationship is between two marriage partners, a parent and a child, two friends, or two young lovers, the basis of the relationship should be *friendship*. Even a passionate romance should be a friendship. Passion comes and goes; friendship endures. When this base of friendship is missing, the relationship is shallow, and the two partners in the relationship run the risk of using each other for their own ends. This is not friendship; it is exploitation.

4. Forgiveness. Forgiveness resolves the past and clears a path into the future. It is a miraculous gift of love between two people, made possible by the forgiveness we have received from God through Jesus Christ. Every relationship has its problems, hurts, ups, and downs. It is forgiveness that enables a relationship to survive these painful passages and to continue growing and flourishing.

5. *Security.* Many of us have come from insecure childhoods. Or we feel insecure on the job, at school, or in some other aspect of our adult lives. A healthy relationship, however, is a secure harbor in an uncertain world. When so much of our lives are lived on the knife-edge of risk and turmoil, we all need at least one relationship, a true friendship, in which we will feel safe and secure. The key to true security in relationships is *love:* "There is no fear [or insecurity] in love," says 1 John 4:18, "but perfect love casts out fear."

6. *Vulnerability.* Guardedness and wariness kills relationships. The freedom to be vulnerable enables relationships to grow. It's a beautiful thing to go where, if we fall, we fall into the arms of a friend. The freedom to be vulnerable requires trust and a sense of confidentiality. We need to know that we can disclose our deepest selves, our most intimate secrets, our hurts, our dreams, our emotions—and every secret, every feeling will remain within the safe, secure enclosure of that relationship.

7. *Sacrifice.* Go to the newsstand and you'll find many magazines devoted to the self (there is even a magazine with the title *Self*). But you won't find any magazines devoted to sacrifice. Yet healthy relationships are impossible without it. Most people are used to making demands in relationships, but how many of us are willing to make sacrifices? Sacrifice means being willing to give up some of our rights during times of conflict. It means being attentive to the other person's needs and feelings. It's one thing to love when the going is easy, but true relationships are built when love requires the surrender of our wishes and our rights. Nothing strengthens a relationship like sacrifice.

HOW TO BUILD A CLOSE, HEALTHY RELATIONSHIP

When our triune God created the universe and the human race, He did so through the medium of a *relationship.* "Let Us make . . ." are His words in Genesis 1:26. Jesus affirms the relationship within the triune Godhead prior to creation in John 17:24— "for You loved Me before the foundation of the world."

Ever since creation, everything that lives exists in an elaborate network of relationships. Plants, for example, grow in relationship to their environment. They are rooted in the soil, they reach for the sunlight, they depend upon insects for their pollination, they spread their seeds by means of the wind. Pull them out of the soil or block the sunlight and they wither and die. Shield them from insects and the wind, and they cannot reproduce. To survive, plants must be connected to the rest of the created order.

Human beings must be connected through relationships as well. We draw our life from our connections to God and to other people. Through our relationships with others, our lives bear fruit and we evangelistically reproduce ourselves in the lives of others. We cannot grow in isolation. Those who try to live in isolation are attempting to violate the basic nature that was designed into us at creation. It is not good that men and women be alone.

One of the most fundamental and unique aspects of Christian relationships is the concept of *unity* in relationships. It is the concept Jesus described in John 17:23: "I in them, and You in Me; that they may be made perfect in one, and that the world may know that You have sent Me, and have loved them as You have loved Me."

"God is love," says 1 John 4:8. His very essence is a quality found in all healthy relationships: *love*. In order to be a whole person and a whole Christian, we must have loving relationships. "Beloved," says 1 John 4:7, "let us love one another, for love is of God; and everyone who loves is born of God and knows God." Clearly, then, relationships and love are at the very core of God's nature. We are creatures created in His likeness, and relationships are also our most fundamental need.

How, then, do we build the close, loving relationships God intended us to have?

First, we must let down our defenses, including the defense mechanism called *denial*. Denial says, "I'm doing okay. I don't need relationships." Honesty says, "It's not good for me to be alone. I need love and relationships."

Second, we must let go of our idealized fantasies about relationships. This is especially true of romantic relationships, where so many of us buy into the phony, unrealistic ideals of love that are sold in soap operas and romance novels. But it is also true of friendships. Sometimes we expect too much of a friend or spouse because of an idealized image of who that person should be and how he or she should behave. Instead of expecting the other person to meet our needs, always be available to us, and never engage in conflict with us, we should reexamine ourselves and ask, "What kind of friend am I? Do I listen to my friends and my spouse so I can hear their needs and so I can be a better friend to them?"

Third, we must learn to pry the lid off our hearts and open our hearts to others. We must learn to express the caring and love we feel—and also the hurt that we feel. Healthy relationships thrive on honesty. As Proverbs 27:5 says, "Open rebuke is better than love carefully concealed." When we open our lives to each other, living in the light of truth, our relationships grow closer, stronger, and healthier.

Fourth, we should periodically assess the health and strength of our most important relationships. These relationships include:

Relationships with family of origin. Your family of origin is the family you grew up in—your biological parents or your adoptive parents. Do you have happy memories? Or are you filled with rage or despair when you remember how you were treated? Are you comfortable with your present-day relationship with your family of origin? Is there pain or distance in that relationship? Is there anger? Is there unfinished business that needs to be done, such as forgiveness or making amends? Are there unhealthy dynamics in that relationship (enmeshment, codependency, controlling, manipulation, and so forth)? If there are unresolved issues in your family of origin, you may need counseling and/or a support group to help you build a more healthy relationship in that area of your life. In your relationship with your family of origin, is there realism, honesty, authentic friendship, forgiveness, security, vulnerability, and sacrifice?

Current family relationships. In your mind's eye, put your hand on the doorknob of your home. How do you feel about walking through that door? Are you walking into a warm, fun, safe place? Or does your stomach knot up?

If you are married, focus on your relationship with your spouse. When discussing with patients this aspect of their relationships, we often ask, "To whom are you married?" This always evokes a double take, especially if the spouse is sitting in the office. Yet this is a very important question. We are asking, "Where is the greatest intensity of your emotional commitment? Are you emotionally married to your spouse? Or to a child? To your job? To food, alcohol, or some other addiction? What is the source of your emotional warmth and comfort?" In your relationship with your spouse, is there realism, honesty, authentic friendship, forgiveness, security, vulnerability, and sacrifice?

And are those seven qualities present in your relationship with your children? With other people living under your roof?

Relationships with friends. It's also important to have healthy outside friendships. It's great to consider your spouse your best friend, but a wife also needs a good female friend she can share with, and a husband needs a male friend to enjoy activities with. In your relationship with your friends, is there realism, honesty, authentic friendship, forgiveness, security, vulnerability, and sacrifice?

Relationship with God. What were you taught about God as a child? How do you feel about Him now? Do you have a daily conversation with Him through prayer and reading the Bible? Do you see God as a source of unconditional love—or as a source of judgment and criticism?

CHOOSE YOUR FRIENDS WISELY

"He who walks with wise men will be wise," says Proverbs 13:20, "but the companion of fools will be destroyed." Clearly, we would do well to choose our friends wisely! "Whether we like it or not, whether we intend to or not," says Dr. Paul Meier, "we will tend to become more and more like our friends."

Does that mean we should avoid having non-Christian friends? "Absolutely not!" replies Dr. Meier. "We must be in the world while remaining unstained by it. We must be witnesses of Jesus Christ—and how do we witness to people if we are cut off from them, if we have no relationships with non-Christians? However—and this is a *big* however—as committed Christians, we should want our most intimate friends to be committed Christians. We should never overestimate our ability to withstand worldly influences. It is much easier for a non-Christian to pull a Christian down than for a Christian to pull a non-Christian up!"

Close Christian friendships serve several important functions in our lives. First, Christian relationships help us to grow and become better Christians and better people. "As iron sharpens iron," says Proverbs 27:17, "so a man sharpens the countenance of his friend."

Second, Christian relationships improve our emotional health. No human being is an island. There is no such thing as a happy hermit. Loneliness is painful and unhealthy. In Genesis 2:18, after the Lord God created the first man, He said, "It is not good that man should be alone." We were created to live in relationships and in fellowship with other human beings. We deeply desire to know other people and to be known by them, to have at least one other human being truly enter our lives, to understand our pain, and to share our joys.

Third, Christian relationships provide a line of defense against depression. One of the most basic sources of depression is emotional isolation. Depression may be said to consist of repressed feelings of sadness and anger. In counseling, we frequently find that depressed people are sad because they are alone and they are angry because they feel no one will love them. The fact that people have a capacity for depression is a powerful statement of the fact that relationships matter to people, and people deeply need relationships.

Whose fault is it when we are friendless?

Most of us would say, "It's somebody else's fault! Why won't anyone love me? Why won't anyone be my friend? Why won't anyone reach out to me?"

But think about it: somewhere, someone else is thinking the exact same thoughts. Why aren't *you* loving that person, reaching out to that person, being a friend to that person? If you will just take the step of reaching out to another lonely person, you will end not only that person's loneliness but your own as well! We must assume 100 percent of the responsibility for building friendships. "A man who has friends must himself be friendly," says Proverbs 18:24, "but there is a friend who sticks closer than a brother."

What keeps us from making friends and being friendly? For most of us, it is *fear*—the fear of rejection. But what most of us forget is that *everybody* fears rejection. It's a universal fear. Somebody has to make the first move—and when someone finally does reach out and demonstrate friendliness, the other person is grateful and appreciative of the attention.

■

Seek intimacy in friendships rather than quantity.

■

Remember, you don't need a great number of friends. Most of us should count ourselves fortunate if we only have four or five truly close friendships in an entire lifetime. Another translation of Proverbs 18:24 gives us a different perspective on that verse: "A man of many friends comes to ruin, but there is a friend who sticks closer than a brother." In other words, Solomon is counseling us to seek *intimacy* in friendships rather than quantity. A friend who sticks closer than a brother is better than a cast of thousands!

See also FAMILY; LONELINESS; MARRIAGE

Religious Addiction

Religious addiction is a dependency upon religious beliefs and religious practices as a way of avoiding having to deal with reality, with anxiety, with pain, or with sin. People use religious addiction as a substitute for genuine growth, for genuine faith, and for a genuine relationship with God. Religious addiction is often used as a means to avoid having to deal with one's real problems and issues.

"Rick is a prime example of someone who used religious addiction as a 'drug' to escape his real problems," recalls Stephen Arterburn. "He was in our sex addiction program at the clinic. He was an exhibitionist. He compulsively exposed himself on a frequent basis, at least once a week. In our clinic, he was making slow progress. His sexual compulsivity was very deep-rooted, and it was complicated by the fact that his pastor repeatedly undermined our efforts, telling Rick that he didn't need psychological treatment. One day, Rick announced he was leaving treatment because God had healed him. He had experienced 'deliverance' during prayer. We knew Rick wasn't ready, but we couldn't stop him.

"What Rick experienced—as do most religious addicts—was relief from feeling guilty and from feeling responsible for his sexually compulsive behavior. He had replaced his sex addiction with a religious addiction, which allowed him to avoid responsibility for working through his exhibitionistic behavior. He was substituting a religious 'fix' for a sexual 'fix'—replacing sexual exhibitionism with religious legalism and religious rituals."

You might think, "What's wrong with that? He's replacing a bad addiction (exposing himself) with a good addiction (being religious). Shouldn't he be encouraged to do so?"

"No," Arterburn replies. "First, religious addiction is not a 'good addiction.' It is as destructive in its own way as other addictions. Second, by retreating into religious addiction, Rick is avoiding the truth about himself (and only the truth can set us free). He is avoiding true healing and true wholeness. And he is avoiding an authentic relationship with God, which leads us to honesty, reality, and growth. The sources of Rick's exhibitionism were passive-aggressive anger toward women in general, and probably toward his mother in particular. His compulsive exhibitionism was an unconscious strategy to circumvent his anger and his feelings of low self-worth; now he was using compulsive religiosity to avoid the same issues.

"Rick placed all the responsibility for changing his life on God—'God delivered me'—and accepted no responsibility for changing himself. The next time Rick exposes himself (and there is always a next time until these issues are resolved), he will run back to his 'God,' pray to be 'delivered' again, then continue on with his life with his denial intact. He doesn't have to face reality or take responsibility, and so the process repeats itself again and again."

MIND-ALTERING, MOOD-ALTERING FAITH

"Oh, come now!" you might say. "I can accept the fact that substance abuse is addiction. I can even understand how people can become addicted to sex or gambling. And now people are even going to Twelve Step groups because they're powerless over a compulsion to overwork or overspend. But an addiction to *religion?* Now you've gone too far!"

This reaction is common—and understandable. At times it must seem that there is hardly any form of human behavior that *isn't* addictive. And it may seem that the recovery movement goes too far in identifying this or that issue as a reason to start another Twelve Step program. But the problem of religious addiction is a very real problem.

Let's start with a definition of addiction: when a person is excessively devoted to something, or when a person surrenders compulsively and habitually to something, that pathological devotion is an addiction. The presence of a psychological and physiological dependency on a substance, relationship, or behavior results in addiction. When a person is willing to sacrifice family, job, economic security, and sanity for the sake of a substance, relationship, or behavior, then that condition constitutes addiction. When a destructive relationship to something becomes the central part of the person's life, when all else is sacrificed for the sake of that sick relationship, that person is said to be addicted.

Addictions develop when people seek relief from pain, a quick fix, or an immediate altered mood. When a person develops a pathological relationship to this mood-altering experience or substance that has life-damaging consequences, addiction exists. The addict becomes devoted to the source of mood alteration and, by giving up everything for that change in feelings, comes to worship the addictive act with body, mind, and spirit.

In our clinical experience at the Minirth Meier New Life Clinics, we have observed all of these conditions to exist in people who are addicted to religion. Just as people use drugs and alcohol as mind-altering, mood-altering substances, we have seen people use religion in the same way. People become intoxicated to escape reality, to escape from guilt, to escape anxiety, to escape responsibility, and to retreat from having to deal with their problems and sins. Religious addicts use their religiosity in the same way and for the same reasons. Just as drugs and alcohol distort reality and warp the substance abuser's ability to think clearly, the religious addict's perception of God and his ability to perceive spiritual truth also become distorted and warped. Religious addiction is *not* just an extreme form of the Christian faith; it is a *false* faith, a *deceptive* faith. Religious addiction is a mind-altering, mood-altering system of beliefs and behaviors. And it is destructive to those who are hooked on it, and to their loved ones.

Some religiously addicted individuals have spent their whole lives in a world of religious fanaticism and fantasy, hiding in their compulsive behaviors and delusions. They believe they are honoring God, but they are only circumventing reality, easing their pain, and attempting to work their way to heaven. Some are in dangerous cults, some are in denominational churches, some are attending a local church on the corner in your neighborhood, and others are seeking God in isolation. Some learned their harmful faith from their parents, others encountered legalistic or cultic faiths upon entering adulthood, and still others invented their own private systems of harmful faith. But because these individuals can look around them and see so many others like them, they do not believe there is a problem. They think that they and others like them have discovered "the truth." They are unaware that they have completely missed God in their search for Him.

Most religious addicts have four common characteristics that have contributed to their compulsivity:

1. Rigid parents. Having grown up in rigid homes, rigidity of behavior and thought are the only way of living these people have known. So they frequently seek out rigid, legalistic belief systems when they become adults.

2. Experience of disappointment. A deep wound from a major disappointment is in the background of most religious addicts—the loss of a parent, a divorce, an abandonment in later life. Religious addicts are attracted to religious groups that promise acceptance without risk of disappointment.

3. Low self-esteem. People with low self-worth feel alienated and isolated. They long to belong and be accepted. Religious manipulators, such as cult leaders and abusive,

> ■
>
> *Religious addiction is not just an extreme form of the Christian faith; it is a false faith, a deceptive faith.*
>
> ■

THE COMPLETE LIFE ENCYCLOPEDIA

power-hungry pastors, know this and have an unerring "radar" for picking out wounded followers who want to feel important and accepted.

4. *Victims of abuse.* Childhood abuse often leads to further victimization in adulthood. Victims of childhood abuse often seek abusive religion, featuring an abusive religious leader or even an abusive God, to fill the void left by abusive parents.

THE TRAP OF CHURCHAHOLISM

A person with harmful faith is worshiping a false god just as surely as an alcoholic worships a bottle of booze. That person is just as likely to be willing to die for his false god as a drug addict is willing to die for his needle or his next hit of crack. The misled faithful cling to their addictive, destructive religion to dodge the emotional turmoil of facing the reality of their circumstances. Their lives focus on the religion and not on God. The religion engulfs them, and they lose themselves to it.

Others become trapped in an unhealthy involvement with a church. Conviction turns to addiction, and the pain is eased with excess activity. Most are not able to see for themselves that the involvement is unhealthy. If someone is not able to point out what they are doing, they continue in their compulsive behavior, convinced they are honoring God. The warmth of fellow followers (most of whom are also addicted) melts away the addict's ability to analyze the situation objectively. The addict becomes lost in an organization that looks good from the outside but that is actually a wall of separation between the follower and God.

This behavior, compulsive churchaholism, is a form of activity much like workaholism. A compulsive churchaholic is obsessed with the need to do more and more through church work. Church is his drug. Like the workaholic who invests everything in work, eluding the responsibilities that come with relationships, the religious addict creates an atmosphere that revolves around church work. Any interpersonal relationships the churchaholic has are an incidental by-product of his obsessive-compulsive service to the organization. At any sign of conflict or anxiety, the compulsive churchaholic retreats into church work. All genuine intimacy and self-appraising honesty can be avoided by throwing himself, body and soul, into so-called "dedicated service." In times of great pain and disappointment, the religious addict tends to increase his desperate involvement in church work, just as a drug addict would retreat even more desperately into his substance abuse.

Churchaholism is not a dependency on God nor is it honoring to God; it is a retreat from grace and from truth. Churchaholics have embraced a counterfeit religion. Work is the focus of everything. Rather than retreat to the loving arms of God, they drown their pain in compulsive religious activity. As they work harder and harder, they buy into the illusion that God applauds their efforts—even though they no longer have time

> When religious addicts are able to see their condition clearly and to understand that there are other people in the same condition—including many who have become liberated from their addiction—they begin to have hope that they can change and be healed. Once they view what they have done with their lives as an addictive process, they are often able to break through their denial and seek the help they need. With the power of God and the support of fellow strugglers, there is hope for recovery from addiction to harmful religion.

> Religious addicts do not know who God really is.

483

for family, and they are leaving a trail of wounded lives in their wake. They are compulsively working their way to heaven and paying their own price for their guilt. Grace is just a religious concept to them; they do not internalize God's grace or forgiveness.

ADDICTIVE COMPONENTS OF RELIGION

Anyone can become addicted to just about anything. One can become addicted to feelings of righteousness, to being "in the know" and religiously superior to others, to an obsession with repetitive prayer. It's important to note that Jesus criticized these obsessive traits in the Pharisees of His own day. One can also become addicted to emotional highs resulting from worship and praise, to the feeling of being a part of something exciting, to the feeling of belonging to something important. Being a part of a tight-knit fellowship of other believers produces wonderful feelings, and these feelings of relationship should be enjoyed in a healthy Christian church fellowship. These feelings only become addictive when they become the purpose of the endeavor rather than a wonderful by-product of worshiping God.

Many people retreat into a religious group in times of stress or disappointment. They seek the safety of church when their powers are exhausted and they feel lonely, abandoned, and scared. Security is found with other believers focused on God. Often the persons feel so welcomed and safe that they desire to continue in the faith because of the people. God is not the primary factor. The addictive emotions are feelings of acceptance and warmth. These believers think they are growing in faith, but they closely resemble the businessmen who go to church just to make contacts.

Worship provides an example of how an unbalanced practice of faith can lead to addiction. An intense worship experience involving song and praise can push an individual to emotional highs. These emotions trigger the release of brain chemicals called *endorphins*, natural secretions that are chemically similar to the narcotic called morphine. People can actually become "hooked" on the experience that produces this natural narcoticlike substance in the brain. This is not to say that emotions have no place in religious faith; they clearly do. But some people substitute the emotionalism of religion for authentic worship and faith. People who do so are practicing a form of religious addiction.

True addiction always results in separation from God. It starts as a substitution for God and eventually becomes a wedge between the person and God. The alcoholic feels unloved and rejected by God. The booze efficiently destroys the presence of God and blocks a person's knowledge of God. In a similar way, a religious addict replaces God with a caricature of God. The addict sees God with a score card writing down every wrong thing that has happened. To the addict, the only way to erase the sins from the score card is hard work. Eventually, religious work replaces God completely.

Adrian Van Kaam has called addiction in all its various forms "a perverted religious presence that has lost its true object." All addicts seek something spiritual when they begin to slide into addiction. They are looking for peace, and their addictive agent (drugs, alcohol, work, sex, or whatever) acts as an anesthetic for their emotional and spiritual pain, providing a false sense of peace. The interaction with the addictive agent actually becomes a religious experience with its own behavioral rituals and rules. After a while, the anesthetic begins to wear off, and the addict must "graduate to stronger stuff." This is true of religious addiction as well. The less relief the addiction provides, the more intricate the rituals become to heighten the experience. As the rituals and rules increase, God is pushed further and further to the side until God Himself—the true

484

object of spiritual longing—is out of the picture completely. The addiction has taken over the religious functioning of the individual.

This explains why the Twelve Steps are so effective in treating addictions. Since addiction is a substitute for true spirituality in the first place, the only hope of healing addiction is to restore the addicted individual to spiritual sanity, to put spirituality back where it belongs in that person's life, to replace the addiction with the true spirituality that the individual was seeking all along. All addicts, religious addicts and otherwise, crave something that will grant them the experience of wholeness, of being significant, of having meaning and purpose in life. Religious addicts seek these experiences in religious activity. Because religious commitment is generally applauded and admired, this addiction is more deceptive than most.

The true presence of God in one's life doesn't provide escape from reality and responsibility. A true relationship with God gives us a firmer grip on reality and the sturdy courage to face our sins and problems with maturity and honesty. True comfort doesn't come from immersing ourselves in compulsive behavior as an anesthetic to pain but from authentic healing from the Great Physician, who surgically removes our emotional and spiritual cancers and restores our souls to health.

THE PROGRESSION OF RELIGIOUS ADDICTION

Religious addiction tends to follow a three-stage progression. Recovery is most likely at either end of the progression. In the early stage of the addiction, the addict may be able to see enough of the truth to pull out before it is too late and he is hopelessly hooked. In the late stage of the addiction, the addict is so hopelessly mired in the addiction that he "hits bottom," sinks into despair, and recognizes his need for change.

There are three stages of religious addiction.

The Early Stage: First Experience

- Extreme stress. Increased stress impairs judgment and obscures warning signs of harmful faith.
- Repeated disappointments. Feelings that nothing works out right lead a potential addict to seek quick-fix solutions to lost expectations.
- Miserable existence. The addict has turned in many directions for hope and found none.

The Sources of Religious Addiction

- **Abusive parent, often the father. Abuse may be physical, emotional, or sexual.**
- **Child deprived of nurturing. Neither parent meets the basic emotional needs of the child.**
- **Feelings of alienation. Child feels detached from the family and what is perceived as a perfect world for others.**
- **Attitudes of perfectionism from imperfect parents. Demanding parents inflict the child with an irrational desire to be perfect and make no mistakes.**
- **High expectations. The parents are relentless in demanding the child be what they were not and attain what they did not.**
- **Low affirmation. Although the child exerts tremendous effort, the parents are never satisfied and rarely provide positive feedback to the child.**
- **Parents' addiction problems. Frequently, one or both parents will be alcoholics or sex addicts, or they will exhibit some other obvious compulsive behavior.**
- **Absent father. A child of divorce may have little male influence.**
- **Feelings of being dirty. Abuse and negative attention leave a child feeling guilty and dirty.**
- **Poor peer relationships. Afraid to share personal reality with others, the child feels cut off emotionally from friends and often seeks destructive relationships.**
- **Vivid fantasy world. Reality becomes so difficult that the child creates a fantasy world and retreats to it frequently.**
- **Feelings not shared. The home has provided little freedom to express emotions, and the child never learns how this is done or why it is helpful.**

- Feelings of insignificance. The addict starts to believe life does not matter and there is no productive part to be played in it.
- Spiritual search initiated. Out of despair the addict seeks spiritual answers as a last resort.
- Loneliness. Any attention from any source would be welcomed.
- Hoping for someone to solve misery. Solving the problems seems too difficult; there is a need to be rescued.
- Increasing doubts about God. Wondering if God cares or if God is real, he or she is more vulnerable to variations of traditional faith.
- Increasing dependency on others. Association with others allows for delusional thoughts and existence in an unreal world.
- Feelings of guilt. Nothing can be done to overcome powerful guilt feelings.
- Feelings of insecurity. A terrible disaster seems to be lurking, and everything seems to be a potential sign of doom.
- Geographic cures. In an attempt to solve problems, the addict believes a fresh start will make life better but discovers it has further complicated the problems.
- Loss of other interests. Family, friends, and other activities are replaced with the compulsive activities surrounding the practice of hurtful faith.
- Abandonment by friends and family. Associates become so irritated by obnoxious behavior that they no longer spend time with the religious addict.
- Unwillingness to discuss problems. The individual becomes unapproachable about increasing out-of-control behaviors.
- One-sided sermons. Edicts, Scriptures, and judgments so fill the dialogue with the person that all conversations cease.
- Faith attached to a person. A comforting person (such as a strong leader) becomes the link to harmful faith.
- Intoxicating affiliation. The first experience with a new faith group produces immediate mood alteration.
- Growing attraction. Every new meeting, person, and experience increases the attraction to the harmful faith group.
- Heavy church attendance. Attendance becomes a means of avoidance and a way to be part of the group with little relationship with God.
- Conformity with other addicts. The person starts to look, dress, and talk like others in the group.
- Lack of intimate relationships. Intimacy with friends and family is sacrificed for the sake of religion.
- Growing denial and self-justification. The person becomes blind to problems and justifies behavior.
- Scripture used as a weapon. Verses are quoted to judge others and justify self.

The initial stage of religious addiction is a difficult one to spot. Many who do the same things as religious addicts are actually involved in a real faith. Outwardly they may be indistinguishable from religious addicts, but inwardly their motives and foundations are different.

The Middle Stage: Complete Attachment

- Immersed in the system. The person becomes an active member, identifying completely with the group.
- Knows propaganda of the group. Many pieces from the leader's writings are readily quoted.
- Outspoken. Little regard is shown for offensive comments made in the name of faith.
- Giving unusual amounts of money. Basic needs of the family are sacrificed to have gifts noticed by the organization and win favor.
- Relates to few people outside the group. Relationships are limited to other misled believers.
- Recruitment of others. Motivated to recruit others to the harmful faith, the addict does not attempt to bring others closer to God.
- Self-medication. The religious experience becomes an intoxicating high that medicates the addict's pain. Each new day is a search for a new religious high.
- Disappointed if ecstasy does not occur. Longing for the emotional catharsis that brings relief, the addict searches for other forms of relief when the harmful faith does not produce it.
- Dual addictions. Other addictions develop, such as eating, drinking, and having illicit sexual encounters, as the pleasure from religious ecstasy wears off.
- Difficult to handle rejection. Those refusing to join the group are discounted to overcome the feelings of rejection.
- All-encompassing practice of faith. Every area of the addict's life is affected by the destructive faith.
- Always searching for ways to further the faith. Every activity is used as a means to talk about the group and its beliefs.
- Discovery and use of special gifts. Self-manufactured and authentic spiritual gifts are used to exploit and manipulate.
- Claims of special anointing. The addict believes God has provided a more unique mission and more unique gifts than the less faithful have.
- Increased pressure. The drive to perform and please does not stop.
- Involvement for survival. The addict becomes trapped in the system with no choice but to conform or risk mental upheaval. The addict is totally dependent on the system for survival.
- Deepening denial. Unable to see the price being paid for the magical thinking, the addict refuses to question the reality of the faith.

The Late Stage: Descent to the Bottom

- Despair. The addict begins to sense hopelessness because the harmful faith is not producing the desired results.
- Erratic behavior. Knowing something is wrong and refusing to change beliefs, the addict attempts to fix the problem by changing behavior rather than the heart.
- Resentment and anger. As the addict's world falls apart, everyone else is to blame, and everyone else is a source of rage.

- Obsession with beliefs. Continually wondering what is wrong with the faith, the addict questions, ponders, and thinks through each belief until the addict is completely unable to concentrate.
- Deep depression. Collapse of beliefs leads to the inability to function.
- Physical deterioration. Depression and stress take their toll on the body, resulting in fatigue, lack of appetite, and medical complications.
- Stagnation. Once faith is lost, all else seems lost, and the addict is unable to do anything but obsessively ponder past mistakes.
- Searching for another fix. Other addictions such as food, drugs, and sex intensify as the addict seeks relief from other sources.
- Fear. Experiencing major insecurity, the addict becomes afraid of everyone, seeing each person as a threat. The addict is afraid to continue in the hurtful faith system and afraid to get out.
- Financial collapse. Work-related problems and financial irresponsibility often result in financial collapse.
- Family deterioration. Stress and distrust destroy family relationships, resulting in affairs and divorce.
- Hitting bottom. Running out of self-will and manipulation, the addict must give up the addiction and turn to God.

TREATMENT AND RECOVERY

Few people come to our clinics and say, "Please help me, I'm a religious addict!" They come because they are depressed, alcoholic, anorexic, suicidal, or in some other way sensing extreme pain in their lives. They don't know why they hurt. They just hurt. It is always an exciting and profound moment for them when they discover that the root of all their other problems is a dependent relationship with a harmful belief system. Finally they have discovered why they feel bound up and alienated. Now they have a glimpse of the real source of their pain, and they can begin working on their healing. The steps of treatment and recovery from religious addiction are:

Step 1: Penetrate Denial

Our first objective in helping people recover from religious addiction is to break through their wall of denial. We try to help them identify their unhealthy relationship with religion as their primary issue. They must learn to see that religiosity is hurting their relationships with the people they care about. This process of breaking down denial usually begins with confrontation or intervention. People close to the addict must express how they feel so that he can finally see the hurt his addiction is causing others. With acceptance of this truth, there is a good chance for recovery.

Addicts are understandably reluctant to let go of their religious addiction. Alcohol is just a substance, workaholism is just an activity, but religion is a worldview, a way of perceiving reality. It is not easy to totally discard one's belief structure, even when convinced that it is causing harm to oneself and to others. Some addicts must see their belief system take everything away from them—their life savings, their emotional health,

It usually takes a major shock to shake a religious addict loose from his belief system. That shock may be a confrontation or intervention, or it may be an experience of "hitting bottom."

488

their physical health, their families—before they realize they have been pursuing an illusion.

Once denial is penetrated, however, recovery becomes possible. ∎

Step 2: *Surrender to God*

The addict is confronted or hits bottom and is no longer able to deny his addiction. He has no choice but to surrender to God. At this point, many religious addicts will go into counseling or join a Twelve Step recovery group for religious addicts. The Twelve Steps require that an addicted individual admit that his life is unmanageable, and that he turn his life over to a Power greater than himself. His addictive religious system is gradually being peeled away, and he is left alone with his absolute need to build an honest relationship with the living, true God. This relationship must replace the old religion. The addict must surrender to God.

Step 3: *Mental Recovery*

In counseling, we confront the hurtful thinking of religious addicts. Addictive thinking tends to be extreme, drawn in stark black-and-white terms of good and evil, right and wrong. Certainly there are moral absolutes that we must recognize, but to the addict, *everything* is extreme, *everything* is black and white. One mistake, and the addict feels like a failure—so addicts are frequently incapable of admitting mistakes to themselves or others.

The religious addict needs to learn that life is a learning process and we are always growing and changing. Sin is a part of our humanity and can be overcome through the power of God. Failure is not final; we can recover. Religious addicts are hard on themselves and others; our task is to help them discover grace, so that they will become merciful to themselves and others and so they can experience the true peace of forgiveness.

We try to help addicts correct their faulty filtering of reality. Draw a dot in the middle of a piece of paper, hold it up to the addict, and ask him what he sees, and he will say, "A black dot." In reality, he sees you, he sees a white piece of paper, and he sees a black dot

The Twelve Steps to Overcoming Religious Addiction

1. We admitted that we were powerless over our compulsive religious behaviors and harmful faith—that our lives had become unmanageable.
2. We came to believe that a Power greater than ourselves could restore us to sanity.
3. We made a decision to turn our will and our lives over to the care of God.
4. We made a searching and fearless moral inventory of ourselves.
5. We admitted to God, to ourselves, and to another human being the exact nature of our wrongs.
6. We were entirely ready to have God remove all these defects of character.
7. We humbly asked Him to remove our shortcomings.
8. We made a list of all persons we had harmed, and became willing to make amends to them all.
9. We made direct amends to such people whenever possible, except when to do so would injure them or others.
10. We continued to take personal inventory, and when we were wrong, promptly admitted it.
11. We sought through meditation and prayer to improve our conscious contact with God, praying only for knowledge of His will and the power to carry that out.
12. Having had a spiritual awakening as a result of these steps, we tried to carry this message to other religious addicts and to practice these principles in all our affairs.

(Adapted from the original Twelve Steps of Alcoholics Anonymous, and used without any implied endorsement by AA.)

which occupies a fraction of one percent of the surface area of that paper. He has filtered out everything but that tiny little dot. That is faulty filtering, and most addicts do this with their entire perception of reality. They focus on the negative, on the ugly, on the

489

dirty, on the impure. They are hypercritical and negative about everything, including themselves. Our task is to help them learn not to filter out the good and the pure, not to focus only on the little black dots in life.

Step 4: Emotional Recovery

We seek to help addicts separate their emotions from reality. Most addicts tend to base their perceptions on their emotions. "I feel bad," they think, "therefore, I must *be* bad." If they feel disappointed, they assume God must be disappointed in them. These responses are rooted in low self-worth. When they hate themselves, this self-hatred colors everything they think about. Recovery from addiction requires that the individual learn to sift reality from emotion, so that his or her perception of truth becomes clearer.

Step 5: Spiritual Recovery

By labeling this and the preceding steps "Step 3" through "Step 5," we do not mean that they are sequential. In fact, mental recovery, emotional recovery, and spiritual recovery must take place *simultaneously,* for all of these dimensions of ourselves—mind, emotions, and spirit—are intricately interwoven.

Spiritual recovery requires that the religious addict shed the decades of religious propaganda that have shaped his hurtful belief system. He must start fresh, recognizing that he really doesn't know what to believe about God, about Jesus, about faith, or about the Bible. He must begin reading the Bible as if he has never read it before, asking God to help him see it with new eyes, and to peel away the scales of religious prejudice from his eyes. The addict's entire faith should not be thrown away, since there is a kernel of truth embedded there. But what should he keep and what should he discard? The answer lies in learning to question his old belief system, item by item, rather than disqualifying the entire structure.

The recovering addict needs to be in a group with other recovering people who will provide accountability and insight and who will be alongside him as he acquires and sifts new information from his study of the Bible. There are Christian support groups available, many of them specifically designed to meet the needs of religious addicts. A counselor or church should be able to help one locate such a group. A healthy support group is comprised of people who unconditionally love and accept people and welcome strugglers; who give people the freedom to express emotions without having to live up to the expectations of others; who are nonautocratic and noncontrolling (groups with authoritarian leaders are essentially cultlike and should be completely avoided).

Step 6: Relational Recovery

Religious addiction frequently brings great pain and alienation from family relationships. Recovery requires that relationships be mended that can be. Effective treatment must involve the family. If not, the family will disintegrate.

Families of addicts tend to be very angry, both with themselves and with the addicts. Treatment focuses on allowing family members to express their feelings and move beyond them. Once this occurs, the family can re-form and re-bond into a unified system of support and love.

THE COMPLETE LIFE ENCYCLOPEDIA

HOPE FOR THE RELIGIOUS ADDICT

There is great hope for the recovering religious addict. This hope comes through the development of a new faith, pure and free from the poison of addiction. For more insight into the causes and cure for religious addiction, read *Faith That Hurts, Faith That Heals* by Stephen Arterburn and Jack Felton (Thomas Nelson, 1992).

Are You a Religious Addict?   *SELF-TEST*

If you believe you (or someone you love) may be religiously addicted, answer the following questions.

YES	NO	
____	____	Has your family complained that you are always going to a church meeting rather than spending time with them?
____	____	Do you feel extreme guilt for being out of church just one Sunday?
____	____	Do you sense that God is looking at what you do and if you don't do enough He might turn on you or not bless you?
____	____	Do you often tell your children what to do without explaining your reasons, because you know you are right?
____	____	Do you find yourself with little time for the pleasures of earlier years because you are so busy serving on committees and attending other church groups?
____	____	Have people complained that you use so much Scripture in your conversation that it is hard to communicate with you?
____	____	Are you giving money to a ministry because you believe God will make you wealthy if you give?
____	____	Have you ever been sexually involved with a minister?
____	____	Is it hard for you to make a decision without consulting your minister? Even over the small issues?
____	____	Do you see your minister as more powerful than other humans?
____	____	Has your faith led you to lead an isolated life, making it hard for you to relate to your family and friends?
____	____	Have you found yourself looking to your minister for a quick fix to a lifelong problem?
____	____	Do you feel extreme guilt over the slightest mistakes or identified inadequacies?

— — Is your most significant relationship deteriorating over your strong beliefs compared to those of a "weaker partner"?

— — Do you ever have thoughts of God wanting you to destroy yourself or others in order to go and live with Him?

— — Do you regularly believe God is communicating with you in an audible voice?

— — Do you feel God is angry with you?

— — Do you believe you are still being punished for something you did as a child?

— — Do you feel if you work a little harder, God will finally forgive you?

— — Has anyone ever told you a minister was manipulating your thoughts and feelings?

If you answered yes to at least three of the above questions, we encourage you to seek Christian counseling for a possible religious addiction. If you cannot find a counselor in your area, contact the Minirth Meier New Life Clinics (1-800-NEW-LIFE).

Schizophrenia

Schizophrenia is a psychotic disorder that causes individuals to be out of touch with reality to a severe degree. The four distinguishing features of schizophrenia are:

1. fat, dull, or inappropriate mood, indicated by a blank stare or by laughing or smiling inappropriately
2. confused thinking, as evidenced by a tendency to ramble from topic to topic without logical association, making it impossible for others to follow the person's train of thought
3. detachment, preoccupation, and absorption in a world of private fantasies (*autism*)
4. severely reduced motivation and reduced ability to make choices (*ambivalence*)

The confused thinking and impaired mental associations of the schizophrenic individual are the result of scrambled neural transmissions (thought transmission from brain cell to brain cell). The effective transmission of thought impulses is normally dependent on a chemical in the brain called *dopamine* (a neurotransmitter). Neurological research

492

indicates a genetic predisposition to schizophrenia in some individuals, involving a genetic tendency toward neurotransmitter imbalance. This tendency may never trigger schizophrenia in some individuals but does in other individuals when they are placed under acute emotional stress. There is also evidence that schizophrenia can be traced in some people to painful early childhood environments.

The underlying thought disorder can be discerned by such symptoms as irrational, vague, or repetitive verbal communication. The individual may obscure or distort facts or reach conclusions based on disconnected logic or inadequate facts. Schizophrenic individuals frequently display an inappropriate facial expression *(flat affect),* which seems to indicate the nonexistence or distortion of emotions. For example, the individual may laugh while describing a personal tragedy.

Subtypes of the schizophrenic disorder include:

1. Autistic schizophrenia. Individuals are caught up in their own private fantasy world. Autistic schizophrenia tends to worsen progressively, and as the fantasies and daydreams increase, such individuals tend to withdraw more and more from people and reality.

2. Paranoid schizophrenia is characterized by delusions of being persecuted or delusions of grandeur. Anger may be a major symptom.

3. Disorganized or *hebephrenic schizophrenia.* This type is characterized by a silly or giddy emotional mood.

4. Catatonic schizophrenia is characterized by psychosomatic disturbances, excitement, stupor, and rigid posturing. Autistic withdrawal is also commonly seen in this subtype.

5. Residual schizophrenia describes individuals who have had a previous episode of schizophrenic symptoms (a *schizophrenic break*), but who are not currently psychotic, yet still show mild signs of the disorder (such as flat affect, social withdrawal).

6. Undifferentiated schizophrenia is a term applied when symptoms do not fit any of the basic subtypes or when they fit more than one.

Schizophrenia results in a disturbance of the will so that individuals become immobilized in the face of decisions. Individuals also tend to lose motivation and goal-directed activity.

Schizophrenia may also be accompanied by delusions and hallucinations. A hallucination involves hearing, seeing, or feeling things that are not real or present. Delusions involve unreal beliefs, such as delusions of grandeur (the schizophrenic person thinks he is a great person, such as Christ or Napoleon) or delusions of persecution (the individual thinks he is being spied upon or conspired against). Some schizophrenics experience delusions that they are being controlled by outside forces or people, that thoughts are being broadcast into their minds, or that other people can read their minds. A diagnosis of schizophrenia is usually made only if the symptoms have been present for six months or more. Modern medication has brought helpful results to a good percentage of cases, although many individuals do not respond well to treatment. However, even if some symptoms remain, individuals can often return to near-normal functioning.

Schizophrenia is a pervasive disorder that usually begins in adolescence or early adulthood. A person should be medically evaluated for schizophrenia if he or she demonstrates such signs as poor personal hygiene, strange behavior, eccentric dress, impaired role functioning, and disturbed movements such as eccentric mannerisms, strange facial expressions and grimacing, rigid posture, and reduction of spontaneous movements.

Self-Esteem

Julie was raised in a house with very strict rules. All the furniture in her parent's home was covered with plastic, and Julie and her brother were not allowed in the living room, lest they break one of the many delicate knick-knacks on display there. Throughout her childhood, Julie was made to feel dirty. If she played outside or rode her bike for a few minutes, her mother marched her upstairs and made her take a bath. It was not unusual for Julie to take two or three baths in one day. Her mother continually carped about Julie's appearance, about near-invisible specks and spots on her dress. And whenever Julie misbehaved, Julie's mother would say, "You filthy little beast!" or "You dirty little brat!" It seemed that all of Julie's childhood revolved around staying clean but feeling dirty.

Today, Julie is in her mid-forties. She has an immaculate home with beautiful furniture, all covered in plastic. She has strict rules for her family. She keeps the Dustbuster handy to pick up any stray crumbs, lint, or flyspecks that may appear on the carpet or on her children. Julie's husband is a workaholic who spends as much time away from home—and away from Julie—as possible. Her nine-year-old son is bright but quiet and withdrawn. For no apparent reason, he is doing poorly in school. And Julie's fourteen-year-old daughter is sullen, angry, rebellious, and sexually active.

■ *Knowing how we became the way we are, understanding the sources of our damaged self-esteem, is a major step toward becoming emotionally whole and healthy. As we grow stronger and more secure in our self-esteem, we not only make ourselves happier, we also have a more positive influence on the people we love.*

■ Even in her forties, Julie still takes as many as two or three baths a day. Her adult life, like her childhood, still revolves around staying clean but feeling dirty. Worst of all, she is passing her feelings of inferiority and contamination on to the people around her—her husband, her son, and her daughter. She strives for immaculate perfection, but when she looks in the mirror, all she sees is flaws and filth. And the worst part of it all is that she doesn't even know what she is doing to herself and her family—and she has no idea how she got that way.

SELF-ESTEEM: THE KEY TO EMOTIONAL HEALTH

Self-esteem is the elusive but essential ingredient of every healthy personality. Our sense of self-worth determines how well we function in every area of our lives, from our feelings to our behavior to our careers to our relationships with others to our relationship with God. Our self-esteem shapes our attitude toward life and determines whether we face the challenges of life with a "yes I can" or a "no I can't" attitude. Our

494

self-esteem is either the launching pad of our successes or the trap that triggers our failures.

Unfortunately, good self-esteem has gained a bad reputation in some quarters. Many people mistakenly equate self-esteem with arrogance, pride, and self-centeredness. Nothing could be further from the truth. The fact is that the one common denominator of all arrogant, prideful, self-centered people is that they almost always have very low self-esteem. The arrogance and pride are actually their way of compensating for the self-hate and self-blame they feel deep inside.

Good self-esteem is a profoundly biblical concept. When we have a healthy sense of self-worth, we have an accurate, biblically-based understanding of who we are in the eyes of God. There are biblical truths upon which we are to base our self-image, and which will produce greater confidence, a more positive outlook, and healthier relationships the more we internalize these truths:

Truth #1: We are created in God's image. This is a profoundly inspiring and ennobling truth. God's image has been stamped upon us. Yes, that image has been marred by sin, but it has not been erased completely. In fact, as Romans 8:29 tells us, God's image is being restored in us as we become conformed to the image of Christ through a day-by-day process of growth and sanctification.

Truth #2: We are fallen, but we are not worthless. Some people interpret the fact that we are fallen, that we have all sinned, as meaning that we are completely without value. This is not a biblical concept at all! Despite our sin, God values us. He cares so much about us that He has sent His Son, Jesus, to die for us and redeem us from our fallen state.

Truth #3: We are loved by God. It is a message that is so pervasive in Christianity that we sometimes fail to recognize how profound a truth it really is. "Jesus loves me, this I know" is a song we sing from childhood. And the most famous verse in the Bible tells us, "For God so loved the world that He gave His only begotten Son, that whoever believes in Him should not perish but have everlasting life" (John 3:16). Truly, God's love for us is a wonderful basis for healthy self-esteem!

The Bible gives us a good foundation for healthy self-esteem. It gives us a basis for a balanced and accurate self-appraisal. In its pages we learn that we are not to think too highly of ourselves—nor are we to think too lowly. As Paul tells us in Romans 12:3, we are to think soberly of ourselves—that is, with sound judgment, realizing that God has made each one of us to be unique and different from the next person. Each of us has been given a special personality and special abilities, talents, and characteristics. The more comfortable we are and the more confident we are in who God has made us to be, the more secure we feel—and the less need we feel to compensate for poor self-esteem with selfishness and sinful pride. As Josh McDowell says in his book, *Building Your Self-Image* (Tyndale, 1986), "A healthy self-image is seeing yourself as God sees you—no more and no less."

THE SOURCES OF OUR SELF-IMAGE

At birth, our self-image is largely a blank slate. We have no reason to think we are inadequate or incapable. We have no awareness of anything but physical and emotional needs. But soon after birth, we begin to acquire experiences, and these experiences begin to mold and shape us, mentally and emotionally. We receive messages, subtle and overt, verbal and nonverbal, intentional and unintentional. These messages tell us who we are and how we are viewed by others, particularly by our parents—those towering, godlike beings upon whom we depend for our very existence. Many of these messages tell us that we are inferior.

In a healthy family, these messages of inferiority will tend to be minimal and will be counteracted by messages of love, affirmation, and grace. In less healthy families, the negative messages will tend to take root in the child's soul. And in both healthy and unhealthy families, children will have unavoidable experiences that tend to tear down self-esteem and self-confidence: a child will make mistakes, a parent may die, a child may experience abuse outside of the home or emotional hurts at school.

The more these experiences and messages chip away at a child's self-esteem, the more emotional pain the child experiences and the more hindered the child becomes in reaching the potential God has created within him or her. A damaged sense of self-worth hampers individuals in their ability to:

1. face the challenges of life with confidence and motivation;
2. develop social intimacy with other people; and
3. develop intimacy with God.

Because approximately 85 percent of a person's adult personality is formed by age six, childhood influences profoundly shape and mold our adult behavior in all three of these important personality areas.

One of the unavoidable factors that tends to break down self-esteem during childhood is the fact that, in many ways, a child really is "inferior" to an adult. Children are small. Their movements are uncoordinated. They are not as strong as adults and cannot do many things that other people can do. They are naive and ignorant of many facts and often make statements that are instantly refuted or laughed at. They are inferior in authority. They are bossed and derided by older siblings. These factors cannot be erased from a child's life because they are integral to it. Parents must continually seek ways to counter the inevitable negative messages and experiences of childhood with positive messages and experiences.

During these crucial formative years, fathers sometimes forget how important they are to the continuing emotional growth of their daughters. A father may become very involved in encouraging a son's participation in sports while neglecting a relationship with the daughter. Sometimes daughters observe the attention their brothers receive from Dad, so to gain Dad's acceptance they may go through a tomboy stage, unconsciously seeking to produce in themselves the qualities that Dad seems to prefer. If this inner conflict is sufficiently intense, it can be carried on into adulthood, resulting in adult difficulties with sexual relations in marriage.

At the same time, parents should be careful not to overshield their children. Some well-meaning parents, trying to prevent their children from being exposed to harmful experiences, actually inflict more damage on their children's self-esteem. Overprotective, indulgent parenting sends a message to the child that he or she is not competent to handle the challenges of the world.

Adolescence confronts a young person with a whole new array of threats to his or her self-esteem. In addition to the pressures of academic performance come the pressures of measuring up to one's peers athletically and physically. As a young person's sexual awareness grows, a child can experience intense inner conflicts that affect self-esteem.

496

During the adolescent years, young people experience intense inferiority feelings as a result of comparing their physical attributes and defects with those of their peers. This is a particular problem for young people who were excessively praised for their appearance during childhood. Though there is nothing wrong with *occasionally* praising a child for his or her appearance (particularly when it involves reinforcing good grooming habits), it is much more healthy to build a child's sense of security around godly character traits. When a child's self-esteem is based on the fragile support of personal appearance, that child's self-esteem can be quickly shattered by the inevitable problems and pressures of adolescence: the physical changes of puberty, acne, the vicious teasing and taunting of other children, and so forth. Parents create a brittle and flimsy basis for their children's self-esteem when they:

- praise their children for being "pretty" or "cute"
- brag about their child's good looks to others in the child's presence
- enter their children in "baby beauty contests" or otherwise "make a big deal" of physical appearance

> ## Appearance and Self-Esteem
>
> Many children who grow up basing their self-esteem on their appearance learn to measure their self-worth on the basis of physical attractiveness for the rest of their life. In adulthood, their overriding concern is sex appeal. During their teen years, young people can always find someone with a prettier face, a better figure, or less knobby knees. The young woman who feels inferior on the basis of looks is more likely to compromise personal values in order to gain and keep the attention and affection of men. She may begin to dress and act seductively and will be more likely to allow herself to be sexually used by men, thinking that this is what she has to do in order to be "loved."

One of the reasons it is better to affirm children's good character and good behavior than to affirm their good looks is obvious: character and behavior defects are correctable. Physical defects (for the most part) are not. A child whose parents affirm good character and behavior will strive to build upon and improve those areas, and he or she will feel secure, happy, and emotionally healthy. Parents who affirm physical attributes run the risk of having their children's self-esteem shattered in the stormy adolescent years.

Children whose self-esteem is based on physical attributes tend to have greater struggles in their faith than children who are grounded in the security of character strengths. Many young people experience enormous bitterness and anger toward God (much of it at an unconscious level), whom they blame for not designing them well. "Why did God put such an ugly, worthless person as me on this planet? Why does He let me suffer like this?" Children with a strong, well-grounded sense of self-worth have a much greater ability to receive and internalize God's love, knowing that He designed them to grow in Christlike character qualities and to experience a joyful, abundant life.

THE SIGNS OF LOW SELF-ESTEEM

The following are a number of traits frequently found in people with low self-esteem. As you read through these traits, you may recognize yourself or someone close to you:

Compensating behavior. People with low self-esteem frequently seek to anesthetize or compensate for their emotional pain through substance abuse, workaholism, people-pleasing, compulsive sexual behavior, or other mood-altering behavior.

497

Intolerant or judgmental comments about other people. People with low self-esteem frequently try to displace their self-hatred onto other people through critical or caustic remarks. They may tend to react with anger or annoyance to the very flaws in others that consciously or subconsciously remind them of themselves. For example, an individual who hates herself for an inability to lose weight may be exceptionally critical of other overweight people.

Demanding or perfectionistic attitude. People often compensate for their feelings of inferiority by demanding perfection from themselves or other people—especially a spouse or children. The individual accepts other people conditionally and only if the performance is good enough. Unfortunately, the performance is rarely good enough. (See PERFECTIONISM.)

Depression. Pent-up anger, guilt, and self-hate frequently lead to depression. Symptoms of clinical depression include anxiety, sadness, disturbed sleep, inability to concentrate, indecisiveness, apathy, immobility, increased or decreased appetite, withdrawal, painful thinking, and suicidal thoughts. (See DEPRESSION.)

False pride and arrogance. People with low self-esteem often feel that the way to pull themselves up is to put others down. Such a person will actively disparage people around him, exercising intimidation, controlling behavior, power plays, all in an attempt to keep others in a subservient position so that the individual himself will appear to be "on top." People with low self-esteem may overemphasize competitiveness, conquest, possessing the best, or being the best.

Hypersensitivity and self-consciousness. Many people with low self-esteem will "go ballistic" when they perceive themselves as being criticized by others. They may be excessively concerned about what others think of them, and they are easily embarrassed.

KEYS TO IMPROVING YOUR SELF-ESTEEM

Even though our self-esteem is largely formed (for better or worse) by childhood experiences, there are a number of significant steps we can take to rebuild and remold our self-esteem so that we can live our lives with a more positive and accurate assessment of ourselves. Below are some suggested keys to improving your self-esteem.

Give up the right to judge, blame, and condemn yourself and others. God alone has the right to judge. We do not have enough information or insight to judge others, or even to judge ourselves. Our estimate of ourselves tends to be emotional and partial, but God knows us through and through, and He accepts us by His grace, by reason of the sacrifice of Jesus upon the cross.

Get in touch with your feelings. Learn to recognize your feelings. When you feel guilty or depressed, ask yourself, "Where do these emotions come from?" If you are like most people with low self-esteem, those emotions may have come from some painful experience in childhood, or from adolescent experiences of inadequacy, or from a self-defeating message that plays and replays in the back of your mind. When you fail or sin, recognize the feelings that arise in you, repent of the failure or sin, and make a decision to learn from your mistakes and move on.

Learn to accept praise from others. People with low self-esteem tend to turn compliments aside or to make some self-deprecating remark when praised. Instead of discounting the praise of others, examine what others say to see if there might be some truth in it. Often, other people recognize qualities in ourselves that we can't see. As we learn to see ourselves as others see us, we begin to grow and find healing in our self-esteem.

Speak up for yourself. Be assertive about your needs, your feelings, and your convictions. Believe in yourself, and force yourself to operate on the assumption that your opinions, your beliefs, and your needs are valid. Tell yourself, "I matter." (See ASSERTIVENESS.)

Avoid putting yourself down. Mistakes are a part of being human, so accept your humanness, forgive yourself, and get on with your life.

Be proud of the unique, special person God has created you to be. When you hate yourself, you are really blaming God for making a mistake. God doesn't make mistakes. As you learn to accept yourself, you will find you will be able to experience a closer relationship with God.

Think, speak, and act positively. Replace such messages as "I can't . . ." or "I have to . . ." with messages that say, "I can . . ." and "I will . . ."

Avoid the envy trap. One of the ways we beat down our self-esteem is by envying another person's abilities, appearance, possessions, status, opportunities, or income. You don't have to be anybody other than who you are. Your goal should be to become satisfied with what God has given you and with the person He has made you to be, while always being committed to growth and increasing maturity. (See CONTENTMENT.)

Replace negative self-talk with positive self-talk. What is self-talk? It is the sum of the unconscious and conscious messages we repeat to ourselves. Some of these messages are negative: "I can't do it. I always foul up. I'm so dumb." As you learn to replace these negative assumptions with positive statements, these negative messages are gradually erased and your self-esteem grows. (For a list of positive self-talk messages and how to apply them to your life, see SELF-TALK.)

BUILDING YOUR CHILD'S SELF-ESTEEM

One of the most loving acts we can do for our children is to help them develop emotionally healthy, biblically accurate self-concepts. Without a positive sense of his or her own worth, a child will not be able to experience the joy, freedom, contentment, confidence, and healthy relationships God intended him or her to have. Here are some suggestions to enable you to encourage a healthy sense of self-worth in your child:

- *Say, "I love you."* Children need to hear these three words. Particularly in their early years, children derive a large portion of their self-worth from how their parents relate to them. If they know their parents love them, children feel they can love themselves in a healthy way.
- *Emphasize character as much as achievement.* When you praise your child, remember to focus the child's attention on the aspect of achievement that is most important: character. For example, instead of only praising a child's grades, stress the fact that those grades represent your child's effort, commitment, maturity, and perseverance. You might say, "These grades tell me that God is really building some important character qualities into your life."

- *Praise with sincerity.* Children can spot empty or meaningless praise. Focus on character qualities rather than outward appearances.
- *Praise in private.* When you let your child know you are proud of him or her on a one-to-one basis, the child knows you mean it. These moments build relationships and help the child to feel "special" in a healthy, biblically affirmed way.
- *Invite your child to share opinions, ideas, and feelings.* This helps the child to feel valued and significant. Children should grow up thinking, "My thoughts are valid. My feelings are worth expressing." A child who feels valued and significant grows into adulthood feeling confident and competent.
- *Avoid criticizing your child's opinions.* Let your child explore ideas and opinions without being criticized for being illogical or unrealistic. A child whose thoughts are criticized eventually becomes a teenager who is unwilling to open up about such issues as peer pressure, drugs, sex, and other important issues. If you want to boost your child's self-esteem, invite his ideas, don't criticize them.
- *Answer your child's questions.* Encourage your child's questions, because this helps your child to know that you value his or her interests and thought processes. The more your child asks questions and gets good answers, the more confidence your child will have in his or her own intellect and curiosity.
- *Pay attention to your child.* Parents tend to give their children vague, distracted "uh-huh" or "that's nice" messages that signal to the child: "You don't matter." Show your child he or she is important. Get down on your child's level and look your child in the eye when he or she talks to you. Take a break from your work or your newspaper and give your child the gift of your time. Nod, smile, repeat back what your child says so that he or she knows you have heard. Answer fully, then give your child a hug.
- *Be willing to say, "I'm sorry."* We all disappoint or hurt our children from time to time. We make mistakes in disciplining. We lose our tempers and say things we don't mean. Properly viewed, these are opportunities to teach valuable life lessons and build stronger relationships. Apologize and ask forgiveness. Your child will learn that you value his or her feelings enough to say, "I'm sorry." And your child will learn from your example that a person can apologize without losing self-respect and self-esteem.
- *Pray with your child.* Your child needs to know that he or she matters to you and to God. Praying with your child provides a powerful boost to his or her self-esteem.

WE ARE VALUED

Every human being is valuable to God. "Are not two sparrows sold for a copper coin?" says Jesus in Matthew 10:29–31. "And not one of them falls to the ground apart from your Father's will. But the very hairs of your head are all numbered. Do not fear therefore; you are of more value than many sparrows." What a sense of security these words bring! Our God knows us so well that the hairs on our head are numbered, and He loves us so much that He sent His Son, Jesus, to bring us abundant life on earth and eternal life in the world to come.

We sin. We make mistakes. We have a long way to go before we reach emotional and spiritual maturity. But God does not consider us inferior. He places great value on us, and He wants to have an intimate relationship with us. The words of the psalmist give us a magnificent and exciting foundation for a healthy, biblically-grounded sense of self-worth:

> O LORD, You have searched me and known me.
> You know my sitting down and my rising up;
> You understand my thought afar off.
> You comprehend my path and my lying down,
> And are acquainted with all my ways.
> For there is not a word on my tongue,
> But behold, O LORD, You know it altogether.
> You have hedged me behind and before,
> And laid Your hand upon me.
> Such knowledge is too wonderful for me;
> It is high, I cannot attain it. . . .
> For You formed my inward parts;
> You covered me in my mother's womb.
> I will praise You, for I am fearfully and wonderfully made;
> Marvelous are Your works,
> And that my soul knows very well.
> My frame was not hidden from You,
> When I was made in secret,
> And skillfully wrought in the lowest parts of the earth.
> Your eyes saw my substance, being yet unformed.
> And in Your book they all were written,
> The days fashioned for me,
> When as yet there were none of them. . . .
> Search me, O God, and know my heart;
> Try me, and know my anxieties;
> And see if there is any wicked way in me,
> And lead me in the way everlasting (Ps. 139:1–6, 13–16, 23–24).

Self-Talk

**"Man is disturbed not by things
but by the view he takes of them."**
Epictetus

We all talk to ourselves, whether we know it or not. Though people can speak with their mouths at a rate of 150 to 200 words per minute, we carry on an inner dialogue with ourselves at an astounding rate of about 1,300 words per minute! This inner dialogue is called *self-talk*.

But what are we saying to ourselves in this high-speed internal conversation we have with ourselves? Research and our own clinical experience suggest that all too often, the messages we repeat to ourselves in the self-talk process are negative and self-defeating. Most of our self-talk is unconscious and undirected and reflects a number of automatic, illogical, painful assumptions we have built up about ourselves and about life. Unconscious self-talk tends to overemphasize painful events and to place too much emphasis on what other people think and say about us (or what we *think* they think and say). These negative messages are rooted in a low sense of self-worth (see SELF-ESTEEM).

But our self-talk doesn't have to be negative and self-defeating. We *can* monitor and change our self-talk. And as our self-talk changes, our self-esteem improves.

The concept of self-talk was pioneered by cognitive theorist Dr. Albert Ellis, who identified a set of commonly held but irrational and self-defeating assumptions on which many people seem to operate. The negative self-talk assumptions that Ellis identified include:

- "I need to be loved by everyone."
- "It is terrible when things are not precisely the way I want them."
- "Painful things that happen to me are due to circumstances or other people outside of my control."
- "I need to get upset about threatening things and focus all my attention on them."
- "It is better to avoid my problems than to face them."
- "I must be totally competent in every situation."
- "If something at one time has affected my life, it will always affect me."
- "I must be completely self-controlled."
- "Doing little or nothing about a situation will make me happy."
- "I cannot control my emotions and need not assume responsibility for how I feel."
- "There is always a right and perfect solution; there will be a catastrophe if I cannot identify it."

These negative messages lead to low self-esteem, to obsessive-compulsive behavior, to depression and anxiety, to self-defeat and failure, to lack of confidence, to distortions in our relationships, and to distortions in our faith. In his book *The Lies We Believe* (Thomas Nelson, 1989), Dr. Chris Thurman of the Minirth Meier New Life Clinics likens the brain to a tape deck and he likens self-talk to the tapes we play on that tape deck:

Your brain . . . can both record and play back, and it has access to a personal library of thousands of tapes ready to play at a moment's notice. These are tapes which hold all the beliefs, attitudes, and expectations that you have "recorded" during your life.

Some of the tapes inside your brain are truthful, such as "You can't please everybody all the time" or "Life is rough." Some of these tapes are lies, such as "I'm only as good as what I do" or "Life should be fair" or "Things have to go my way for me to be happy."

Many of your lie tapes have been around a long time, some even since childhood. You've listened to these tapes for so long that they feel true even though they are really lies. The longer a tape has been played, the more rigidly you believe it to be true.

Many lie tapes play in your mind without your even knowing it. They play unconsciously when life presses the play button. Unconscious or not, these tapes dramatically affect your feelings and actions each day. Ignorance is not bliss when it comes to these tapes. Unless they are made conscious, you are at their mercy.

Your emotional life hangs in the balance. It directly reflects whether your mind is dominated by lies or truth. If your mind has more lies than truth playing through it, you'll tend to be more emotionally unhappy and troubled. If, on the other hand, your mind has more truth than lies taped and running, you'll feel more well-being than misery. And if your mind is an equal mixture of both lies and truth, you will experience more of an up-and-down emotional experience. Both lies and truth want to control your tape deck, and whichever gains that control dictates what your life will be like.

The primary challenge, then, is not to attempt changing the circumstances surrounding us, although there is nothing wrong with improving them when we can. The primary challenge is to make our mental tapes as truthful as we can so that we will be able to handle successfully whatever circumstances come our way.

Lies produce emotional misery.
Truth produces emotional health.
It's as simple as that.

The key to erasing our negative self-talk and recording positive, truthful self-talk in its place lies in our ability to *monitor our thinking*. Many of the negative self-talk messages that play and replay in our minds are actually unconscious thoughts. It's very hard for our conscious minds to monitor unconscious thoughts. But if we search our feelings—especially in times when we are under emotional stress or feeling depressed or when we have just suffered painful setbacks in life—we will discover that there are some massively negative assumptions buried within us:

- "I don't deserve to be happy."
- "I can't hope for more than a minimum wage job."
- "I'll never be able to change."
- "How could God have made a worthless person like me?"

At the moment you become aware of such a feeling, you have just captured negative self-talk in the act of tearing you down. At such moments, take time to meditate in Scripture and repeat to yourself a self-talk statement that counters the self-defeating lie that is attacking you at the level of your unconscious mind. Make a conscious decision to refocus your thinking onto the positive aspects of your character, your accomplishments, your growth and progress, and most of all, your position as a child of God.

You should also be involved in a daily process of meditating on God's affirming truth about you and in positive self-talk statements. Many successful, emotionally healthy people have made a point of combining positive self-talk statements with their daily devotions (see "Your Daily Quiet Time" under FAITH). Here are some suggested

…ments, derived from both positive experience and from Scripture, which … to yourself on a regular daily basis and as needed, whenever negative

… care of me and meeting my needs."
… and forgives me; I accept His forgiveness."
… an everlasting love" (Jeremiah 31:3).
… all my sins are washed away" (Ephesians 1:7).
… strength to enact my new decisions."
… score of the good things in my life."
… choose to forgive and get on with my life."
- "I face up to my feelings."
- "My feelings are okay, and I'm getting better."
- "Of course I am important, and my feelings matter."
- "I have abundant life" (John 10:10).
- "I am a lovable person."
- "I am a useful person."
- "I am free of shame and condemnation" (Romans 8:1).
- "I am being changed and conformed to the image of Christ" (Romans 8:28–29, Philippians 1:6).
- "I am a new creation" (2 Corinthians 5:17).
- "I can reach the top."
- "I can do all things through Christ" (Philippians 4:13).
- "I'm getting the job done, one task at a time."
- "I am moving toward my goals."
- "I deserve to succeed in my career."
- "I am victorious" (Revelation 21:7).
- "I enjoy taking good care of myself."
- "I deserve to live."
- "I can enjoy healthy relationships."
- "My spouse is my best friend."
- "I am God's workmanship" (Ephesians 2:10).
- "I deserve to be healthy."
- "I deserve to enjoy a healthy sex life in my marriage."
- "My body is a gift from God."
- "I am happy to be the gender God created me to be."
- "I am holy and without blame before God" (Ephesians 1:4).
- "The child within me is a precious being, and deserves love and nurturing" (see INNER CHILD).

If you find you have difficulty monitoring your thoughts and getting in touch with your feelings—and many people do—then consider seeking professional counseling in addition to a regular program of daily meditation and repeating positive self-talk statements. Self-talk is a powerful tool for improving emotional health, but many people need additional help and insight in order to get the most benefit from positive self-talk.

Sex Addiction

Everyone has seen the lurid headlines of famous ministers or politicians caught in a sex scandal, losing their families, careers, and reputations to a compulsive sexual habit they were unwilling or unable to break. Many people struggle with seemingly unbreakable sexual habits. Perhaps you are one of those people.

Christians are far from immune to this problem. For millions of people—Christians included—sex is like a drug: it temporarily anesthetizes emotional pain (rejection, guilt, loneliness, fear, anxiety, or memories of abuse or failure), but it ultimately demands more and more of a person until it becomes the central organizing factor of daily life. It takes over. It controls. It ruins relationships and shatters self-esteem. It humiliates and degrades. It enslaves the individual in chains of obsession, compulsion, and addiction. The sex addict can no more live without his prostitutes or his pornography or his masturbation or his affairs than a heroin addict can live without his needle.

HOOKED ON SEX

Sex without intimacy works just like a chemical "fix" and even has a clear chemical component. Sexual arousal stimulates the secretion of natural narcoticlike brain chemicals that provide a sense of well-being but that can also reinforce a dependency on the sexual behavior. Sex gratification provides a speedy alteration of one's feelings (like alcohol and other drugs, it is "mood-altering"), and it provides an anesthetic for emotional pain. Eventually, however, the addiction takes over and the sex addict becomes powerless to change his behavior. He may want to change, and he may know he needs to change, since he sees this behavior could destroy his family, his reputation, and even his physical life (as some aberrant sexual behavior can involve injury or death, and any sexual behavior outside of marriage entails the risk of disease).

Sex addiction parallels other, more familiar forms of addiction in several ways:

Sex addiction builds a tolerance like other addictions. The addict frequently must progress to "stronger stuff" (greater frequency or more extreme behavior) in order to attain stimulation and gratification.

A sex addict who swears off his addiction eventually experiences symptoms of withdrawal. After a short time without a sexual encounter, the sex addict begins to think he may go crazy without sex; he becomes obsessive about reconnecting with his addictive behavior.

Sex addiction causes shame. At first, the addict chooses behavior that is not too far out of line with his values (there is a strong element of denial in this). He may tell himself that oral sex with another man's wife is not really adultery since there is no vaginal intercourse involved. As he inevitably graduates to "stronger stuff" or increased frequency, he eventually becomes involved in behavior he can no longer rationalize. He experiences shame, and to escape from this crushing burden, he attempts to shift the blame for his behavior onto others: parents, spouse, lovers, prostitutes, pornography vendors, society, and even God.

As you read through this article, you may be thinking, "Is that me? I often have strong desires, and I'm tempted by lust. I have a powerful sex drive. Does that mean I'm a sex addict?" Not necessarily. The following are characteristics of sex addiction that should help you determine if your impulses are merely strong or if they are addictive. Addictive sex is:

Secretive. The typical addict is conscious, on some level, of leading a double life. He may be thought of by his friends and even his family as a "good Christian," but he secretly engages in one or more of the following behaviors:

- use of pornography
- masturbation
- soliciting prostitution
- serial or multiple affairs

His secret life fills him with shame, and his biggest fear is that he will be discovered.

Isolated. The addict may carry on his sexual behavior alone. Or, if he has a sexual partner, his sexual behavior is detached and impersonal. The other person is an object, not a soul mate. There is little or no intimacy. The sex addict is usually self-focused, taking rather than giving.

Predatory. Addictive sex is self-gratifying and blind to the harm it causes others. It victimizes without regard to the shame and destruction it brings. It is frequently blind even to its own predatory nature. Many sex addicts live in denial, telling themselves that their victims want this relationship, benefit from the relationship, or "have it coming."

Empty. Sex in marriage brings completion and fulfillment. Addictive sex produces guilt, shame, regret, despair, and emptiness.

THE PROGRESS OF SEX ADDICTION

With mind-numbing consistency, in personality after personality, sex addiction finds its roots in a muddle of family dysfunction, frequently including incidences of abuse and abandonment. Studies suggest that over three-fourths of all sex addicts may have been sexually abused in childhood. At the same time, it's important to recognize that not all sex addicts were abused, nor do all abused children grow up to be sex addicts.

Some individuals become sex addicts later in life, without any indications of addictive tendencies during adolescence. They may learn to use sex as a maladaptive coping mechanism for stress and pressure. Or they may be exposed to pornography later in life, introduced either by a friend or by experimental curiosity. Society and the media work overtime to condition us to believe that sexual excess and abnormality are the norm. Sex sells, sex is profitable. There is no marketing percentage in sexual purity.

Other factors that contribute to sexual addiction include low self-esteem, controlling parents, a legalistic upbringing, traumatic experiences with the opposite sex, conflicts with the opposite-sex parent, emotional distance from the same-sex parent, and an inability to handle emotions in a healthy way. These are influences, however, not excuses. Harmful circumstances may influence us and pressure us, but we still have the power to choose. "Choices," says Dr. Frank Minirth, "are the hinges of destiny. We always want to blame others for our addictions and our problems, but the fact remains that we always have the power to choose to do right or wrong, to behave in a healthy way or an unhealthy way."

Like all addictions, sex addiction tends to escalate. "In the beginning," says Stephen Arterburn, "a person has an addiction. In the end, the addiction has *him*." Here is how a sexual addiction usually progresses:

Level One: Fantasy, Pornography, Masturbation

People in the first level of sex addiction easily rationalize their behavior: *After all, who am I hurting? I'm not committing adultery or fornication, right? There's no other person involved. I'm not being unfaithful to my spouse, am I? I mean, "unfaithful thoughts" don't really count, do they? Hey, everyone fantasizes! Everyone looks. Everyone engages in a little "mental undressing" of the opposite sex, don't they? Everyone pictures fantasy scenarios with other people, don't they? Well, don't they?*

People who engage in such rationalizations don't realize that the addiction battle is really a battle for the mind—and they have already surrendered!

Just as many heroin addicts started on the road to addiction through "harmless" marijuana, many sex addicts enter the world of hard-core sex addiction through the "harmless" gateway of sexual fantasy. Next, they fortify their fantasies with pornography. Through pornography, the addict can vicariously "experience" a group-sex orgy or sadism or other forbidden forms of behavior. Eventually, however, vicarious sex loses its power to stimulate. The "real stuff," the "hard stuff" is next.

Let's face it: the purpose of pornography is to serve as an aid to masturbation. Hugh Hefner built the Playboy empire on the backs of a lot of pathetic men and teenage boys, having lonely sex with magazines. Some people defend the "literary" articles and stories published in that magazine, but any literary content found therein is like a creamy white rose floating in a sewer. *Playboy*'s primary reason for existing is to stimulate masturbatory fantasies, period.

Many addicts expect marriage to eliminate their compulsion to masturbate. But they soon find that a real sexual relationship demands intimacy, and intimacy takes work. Since the sex addict uses masturbation to avoid intimacy, he soon returns to his compulsion, even when marital sex is available to him.

The first level of sex addiction is fantasy, pornography, and masturbation. Society treats such behavior as normal and harmless. But the first level opens the door to deeper levels of behavior—and deeper levels of addiction.

Level Two: Live Pornography, Fetishes, and Affairs

The second level takes the addict into behavior that society does not condone but does not consider criminal. Level Two behavior takes the addict out of the realm of self-stimulation and into behavior involving other people. This level includes such behavior as:

- frequenting bars with live nude entertainment
- fetishes (using items of clothing or other belongings of a real person for erotic stimulation)
- phone sex
- sexual touching of strangers ("accidentally on purpose," as in a crowded elevator)
- perversion (bondage, masochism, sadism, multiple partners, soliciting prostitutes)
- having an affair or multiple affairs

What do all these behaviors have in common? They demonstrate the ever-diminishing satisfaction that comes from sex without intimacy. Sex addiction is like greed: the individual always wants a little more.

Level Three: Prostitution, Voyeurism, Exhibitionism, and Other Minor Sex Offenses

As it progresses, sex addiction frequently crosses the line and becomes criminal behavior. These are, from a legal viewpoint, "minor" offenses. From a moral and psychological viewpoint, they are anything but "minor." The legal consequences of such acts are minor, but the harm to victims and perpetrators alike is substantial.

In our clinical experience, we find that people in this level are capable of the most desperate denials and bizarre rationalizations. Pastor Smith is caught having affairs with women in his counseling room (a crime in many states). Pastor Jones is nabbed by police in a "john sweep" of the local red-light district. "Well," sniffs Pastor Smith, "at least I wasn't degrading myself by paying for it like Pastor Jones! I mean, that's sick!" "Well," retorts Pastor Jones, "at least I wasn't using my own parishioners! I had the decency to keep my indiscretions out of the church!" Who's more righteous in this situation, Smith or Jones? Who cares?

One sex addict looks down on the voyeur who hides behind bushes and peeks in windows—even though his main reason for jogging after dark is the chance of catching a bedroom glimpse. Another sex addict changes clothes with the window shade up, but says to himself, "At least I don't go around schoolyards in a trenchcoat and 'flash' little kids!" Denial is very strong in Level Three.

Level Four: Molestation, Incest, Rape, and Other Major Sex Offenses

These behaviors are felony offenses, punishable by a year or more in prison—and a life sentence of shame and guilt.

Dr. James Dobson once interviewed mass sex-murderer Ted Bundy as he awaited execution in a Florida prison. Looking back over a life that included the murder of at least twenty-eight women and children, Bundy reflected that his path to the electric chair could be traced back to his first experiences with fantasies and pornography. "You

THE COMPLETE LIFE ENCYCLOPEDIA

reach a point where pornography only goes so far," he said. "You reach a jumping-off point where you start to wonder if actually doing it will give you that which is beyond just reading about it or looking at it." Certainly, there were several influences in Bundy's life besides pornography that pointed him in the direction of murder-for-thrills—the most important one being his own ability to choose right or wrong, good or evil. But his criminal behavior didn't start suddenly or come out of nowhere. It was a progression—and it all started with a thought.

THE ADDICTION CYCLE

Like all addictions, sex addiction operates in a cycle—or more precisely a downward spiral. Each stage in the cycle sets up and leads to the next stage, and the addict progresses through each stage in the cycle, around and around, down and down, like a cat chasing its tail around the sides of a bottomless well. The stages of that cycle are:

Obsession. The addict is focused on self and becomes obsessed with thoughts of finding relief from the pain of past hurts. Anger and shame are the primary emotional components. A sex-related event may trigger the sexual aspect of the obsession—an encounter with pornography, a sexual scene in a movie, a sexually-charged incident. The cycle has been set in motion.

The hunt. Thinking about sex and obsessing about sex is just not enough. The addict decides to act. He may seek out pornography or a sexual partner. After years of addiction, the "hunt" phase of the addiction cycle may become highly ritualized by long experience and habit. In the early stages of the addiction, however, the cycle is just beginning to pick up speed, like a merry-go-round ride that is just beginning.

Recruitment. The addict selects a victim—and yes, *victim* is the appropriate term. Anyone who is the object of impersonal sex is a victim, even if a willing victim. The victim may be a nude dancer, a prostitute, a nude model in a magazine, a child, or a lonely housewife in the downstairs apartment. The addict seeks a sex object against which to vent his lust—and proceeds one more notch along the cycle of addiction.

Gratification. This means orgasm, from masturbation or intercourse. Many addicts, however, surround the orgasm with elaborate fantasy rituals to intensify the experience—just the right kind of behavior or pornography to produce the ultimate fulfillment. But what seems like "the ultimate" during sexual arousal seems a bit shabby and degrading once the red haze of excitation begins to subside.

Return to normal. The excitement is over, the obsession lifts. Back to reality—and to guilt.

Justification. The addict says to himself, "I've done it again. I can't escape this addiction—but maybe I don't need to. After all, nobody was hurt. Everyone does it. I should just accept it. Sure, that's it. What I did was really okay."

Blame. The addict eventually finds his rationalizations wearing thin. He can't accept the blame himself, so he looks for a scapegoat: parents, society, even God. He may blame others for causing his addiction—or he may blame others for making him feel bad for his "perfectly normal" behavior.

Shame. Like an acid, guilt and shame eat through the blanket of denial and blaming the addict has wrapped around himself. He begins to feel the enormity of his sin and his addiction—and he feels worthless. The cycle continues.

Despair. "I'll never change," the addict concludes. "I'm hopeless." Self-esteem hits rock bottom. The addict often augments his sex addiction with other addictions to relieve the pain. In extreme cases, suicide becomes an option.

Promise. The addict pledges, "Never, never, never-ever again!" This is the direct precursor to the next wave of obsession. The promise focuses the addict's attention on thoughts of sex, practically guaranteeing a relapse. Every waking thought is trained on the behavior he has denied himself. The addict has now come full circle. He is right back at the obsession stage—only he is one level lower in his descent into addiction.

TREATMENT AND RECOVERY

No one else can heal a sex addict. The sex addict must choose to change. "If a sex addict wants to be healed," says Stephen Arterburn, "he must go straight through the pain and shame of his addiction. He must make a lifelong commitment to recovery. That means he must become involved in a recovery group—a place where other recovering addicts will share their own experience, hold each other accountable, and encourage one another to live lives of honesty and authenticity."

> ■
>
> *Accountability is a key concept for recovery from sex addiction.*
>
> ■

Accountability is a key concept for recovery. Sex addiction is a secret activity. Accountability rips the cover off one's secrets, letting the fresh air of truth and honesty into one's life. Behavior that is observed changes. In a sex addiction recovery group, the addict will be held accountable by the group and will preferably also have a single "sponsor" who will hold him accountable on an individual basis. Accountability means the addict is asked about his growth and progress, about how he is spending his time.

The addict must also be protected from lustful influences and must be provided with healthy substitutes, such as recovery reading material and tapes, Bible study and prayer, and fellowship alternatives. Here again, the recovery group plays a vital role in supplying these protective influences.

Most sex addicts will find it difficult if not impossible to free themselves from their addiction without therapy that is focused on their personal issues. For treatment referrals, contact a Christian psychologist or pastor in your area, or contact one of the Minirth Meier New Life Clinics (1-800-NEW-LIFE). For more information on sex addiction as well as relationship and romance addiction, read *Addicted to "Love"* by Stephen Arterburn (Servant Publications, 1991). If you suspect you may have a sex addiction, the self-test at the end of this article may provide revealing insights.

"Sex addiction is a shame factory," concludes Stephen Arterburn. "But healing and forgiveness are available. Whether you believe it or not, whether you feel it or not, God loves you unconditionally, and He wants to be part of your recovery process. Whatever your addictive behavior, it's time to turn it over to Him."

Are You a Sex Addict?

This sexual addiction questionnaire was developed by sexual addicts as an aid in self-diagnosis.

YES **NO**

_____ _____ 1. Do you sense that your sexual thoughts and/or behaviors are causing problems in your life?

_____ _____ 2. Have sexual thoughts interfered with your ability to function at work or at school?

_____ _____ 3. Do you worry that your sexual thoughts and/or behaviors are more powerful than you are?

_____ _____ 4. Do you sometimes think that you are the only person who has certain sexual thoughts or who engages in certain sexual behaviors?

_____ _____ 5. Do you fail to meet commitments or fail to carry out responsibilities because of your sexual behaviors?

_____ _____ 6. Do you struggle to control or to stop completely your sexual thoughts and/or behaviors?

_____ _____ 7. Do you fantasize about sex, or masturbate, or engage in sexual activity with another person in order to escape, deny, or numb your feelings?

_____ _____ 8. Do you think about sex either more or less than you would like to?

_____ _____ 9. Do you think of yourself as a person who has no sexual thoughts or desires whatsoever?

_____ _____ 10. Do you think that there is something wrong or abnormal regarding the frequency of sexual activity that you have or wish to have?

_____ _____ 11. Do you spend more money than you can afford to spend on sexual activities?

_____ _____ 12. Does it seem as though there is another person or force inside you that drives you to be sexual?

_____ _____ 13. Do you have two standards of fidelity—one for yourself and one for your partner?

_____ _____ 14. Do you think you would be happy if only you had enough sex and/or just the right sex partner(s)?

_____ _____ 15. Do you feel empty or shameful after having sexual fantasies or engaging in sexual activity?

_____ _____ 16. Do you feel obligated to have sex?

_____ _____ 17. Have you ever promised yourself that you would never again have another sexual relationship?

18. Do you find it necessary to fantasize during sexual activity?

19. Do you set rules regulating the frequency of your sexual thoughts and activities?

20. Do you dress in such a way as to make your body appear undesirable?

21. Do you set rules regarding when, how, or with whom you can be sexual, then break those rules?

22. Do you use sexual thoughts and/or behaviors to deal with, deny, or avoid problems in your life?

23. Do you use threats or promises in order to have sexual activity with another person?

24. Do you sometimes find yourself being sexual or flirting with someone and wondering how it happened?

25. Do you risk legal problems in order to be sexual?

26. Have you stayed in a marriage or other relationship only because you thought that relationship somehow protected you from being promiscuous?

27. Do you think that your sexual abilities are the most important qualities you have to offer another person?

28. Are you fearful of seeking medical attention for injuries related to your sexual activities?

29. Do you anxiously anticipate or fear trips out of town because of what you think you might do sexually while you're away?

30. When you have childcare responsibilities, do you put a higher priority on masturbating or being sexual than you do on the welfare of the child(ren) in your care?

31. Do your sexual thoughts and/or behaviors interfere with your spiritual or religious life? Do your sexual thoughts and/or behaviors cause you to believe that you don't deserve to have a religious or spiritual life?

32. Are you afraid to be left alone with children for fear of being sexual with them?

33. Have your sexual thoughts and/or behaviors led you to consider suicide, castration, or self-mutilation?

34. When you are in a relationship with someone, do you try to make sure that another sex partner will be available to you in case anything goes wrong with the first relationship?

35. Do you stay in unsatisfying, painful, humiliating, or otherwise unhealthy relationships only so that you can continue to be sexual with someone?

36. Do you spend time with people you don't even like or respect, hoping that you will have an opportunity to be sexual with them?

512

_____ _____ 37. Do you have sex with your partner even when he or she is ill?

_____ _____ 38. Does your sexual partner complain about your need for sex or your sexual behaviors?

_____ _____ 39. Does your partner refuse to participate in certain sexual activities with you?

_____ _____ 40. Do you either minimize or exaggerate the facts when discussing your sexual life with others?

_____ _____ 41. Have you ever tried to stop your sexual activity in an effort to end a painful relationship or behavior pattern?

_____ _____ 42. Do you initiate sexual activity with a partner before he or she is awake?

_____ _____ 43. Do you have chronic medical problems with your sex organs?

_____ _____ 44. Do you put yourself in danger by not taking reasonable precautions or by going to unsafe places in order to have sex?

_____ _____ 45. Have you lost a job or risked losing a job because of your sexual behaviors?

_____ _____ 46. Do your sexual behaviors cause you to violate the ethical standards, principles, and/or oaths of your profession?

_____ _____ 47. Do you scan printed material (novels, newspapers, magazines) or change channels on the television set just to find something that will stimulate you sexually?

_____ _____ 48. Do you regularly engage in fantasies involving self-abuse or other kinds of physical abuse?

_____ _____ 49. Do you trade material things (dinner, drugs, money) for sex?

_____ _____ 50. Do your sexual behaviors lead you to risk injury, illness, or death?

_____ _____ 51. Have your sexual behaviors led to treatment or hospitalization?

_____ _____ 52. Do you masturbate after having sex?

_____ _____ 53. Have you injured yourself due to the frequency, intensity, or nature of your masturbation or other sexual activities?

_____ _____ 54. Would you rather masturbate than be sexual with a partner?

_____ _____ 55. Do you spend time looking through windows, hoping that you might see something that will stimulate you sexually?

_____ _____ 56. Do you follow people on the street, pick up hitchhikers, or drive around in your car, hoping that these activities will lead to sexual encounters?

_____ _____ 57. Do you undress, masturbate, or engage in sexual activities in places where strangers are likely to see you?

_____ _____ 58. Do you feel compelled to dress a certain way or to take part in certain rituals in order to masturbate or be sexual with another person?

___ ___ 59. Do you seek out crowds so that you can rub against people or other-wise be in close physical contact with strangers?

___ ___ 60. Do you make phone calls to strangers in order to talk about sex or masturbate?

___ ___ 61. Do you masturbate while driving?

___ ___ 62. Have you ever been sexual with animals?

___ ___ 63. Have you replaced a collection of pornographic material after destroy-ing one collection and vowing never to purchase pornography again?

___ ___ 64. Do you masturbate or engage in sexual activity with partners in public places?

___ ___ 65. Do you steal money in order to engage in sexual activities?

___ ___ 66. Has an important relationship in your life ended because of your inabil-ity to stop being sexual outside of that relationship?

(Reprinted from Hope & Recovery: A Twelve Step Guide for Healing from Compulsive Sexual Behavior [1989], available through Hazelden Educational Materials, Center City, MN, 800-328-9000. Used by permission.)

Sex and Sexuality

The book of Genesis tells us that when Adam was created, he was made to experience a perfect relationship with God. But God knew that Adam was incomplete if he had no one of his own kind to love. "It is not good," the Lord said in Genesis 2:18, "that man should be alone." Adam was created in God's own image with a built-in desire to love and to be loved. So a wife was given to Adam so that he and his wife could experience together that deepest of human experiences, the experience called love.

The love that God intended husbands and wives to experience together is three-dimensional: (1) *agape*-love, God's own unconditional love, rooted in the will, in our ability to make healthy, godly choices; (2) *phileo*-love, family love, affectionate love, the self-sacrificing love of strong family ties; and (3) *eros*-love, romantic love, the passionate love that bonds two people together in an experience of emotional and physical fusion. Another perspective on these three dimensions of love is to view them as the (1) *spiritual* plane of love *(agape)*; (2) the *emotional* plane of love *(phileo)*; and (3) the *physical* plane of love *(eros)*. All of these dimensions of love are God-given and beautiful, and each of them has a spiritual dimension. In a Christian marriage, all three of these forms of love are intended to work together in harmony to produce a healthy, joyful, satisfying relationship.

The spiritual dimension of marital love is suggested by 1 Peter 3:1–7, which tells wives and husbands to love and honor each other as "heirs together of the grace of life, that your prayers may not be hindered." When all three dimensions of love are fully functional in a marriage, both the wife and the husband are more open and receptive to the Spirit of God. From the time of Adam until today, God has designed marital love to be a channel of spiritual wholeness and health.

Genesis 2:23–24 tells us the sex act—the act of physical and emotional fusion between two individual human beings—seals a loving commitment between them:

And Adam said:
"This is now bone of my bones and flesh of my flesh; she shall be called Woman, because she was taken out of Man." Therefore a man shall leave his father and mother and be joined to his wife, and they shall become one flesh.

God designed the act of marital sex to be an intimate covenant between a husband and a wife, symbolizing the sacred, lifelong, committed relationship they share. It is the physical sealing of the contract between them, expressing the mutuality and exclusivity of their love for each other. A committed relationship of sexual fidelity affirms a couple's commitment, not only to each other but to God and His eternal plan for the human race. As expressed within the safe, secure enclosure of marriage, the sex act is a statement from one partner to another: "I honor you by giving you an aspect of my body, of my emotions, and of my personality that I share with no other human being."

THE MOST IMPORTANT, LEAST UNDERSTOOD SEX ORGAN

We have just described the biblical ideal and spiritual meaning of sex in marriage. For many Christians, however, the experience of sex in marriage falls far short of that ideal in many ways. Case in point: Ray and Sonja.

Here was a couple who seemed to have it all. Ray was successful, well-built, and handsome. With Sonja at his side, they were a matched set, a perfect picture of tanned, blond, athletic good looks in a two-story Tudor house in one of the best neighborhoods in town. But behind the closed doors of their bedroom, this picture did not look nearly so happy.

After five years of marriage, Ray and Sonja were engaging in sex only once or twice a month, and some months not even that. When they did have sex, it was usually over Sonja's objections or stall tactics, and the results were almost always frustrating. Sonja refused Ray's attempts to give her pleasure; her unspoken attitude was, "Take what you want, then leave me alone." Frequently, Sonja would stop Ray in midintercourse, saying that he was hurting her. But usually, their sex life just didn't get that far. When she

515

sensed that Ray was in an amorous mood, Sonja frequently went to bed early, claiming not to feel well. But Ray wasn't fooled—and he felt frustrated and rejected by his wife.

When he finally had enough, Ray suggested that they get professional counseling. Sonja reacted in panic, and absolutely refused. Ray dropped the subject—for a few weeks. But he returned to the subject again and again. Finally, he said, "Sonja, if you don't love me, then this marriage is over and I'm going to end it."

"What are you talking about?!" Sonja protested. "Of course I love you!"

"This problem between us is getting bigger and bigger, and it's affecting more and more aspects of our lives. I'm miserable, you're miserable. But you refuse to go for counseling. I know the idea of counseling scares you, but if you really love me, if you are really committed to this relationship, then you will do whatever it takes to save it, and to resolve these problems. If you won't do that, well—"

The truth is, Ray was half-bluffing. He loved Sonja too much to leave her—yet. But he saw that their relationship was steadily deteriorating, and that hidden sexual issues were at the heart of the problem. He also saw that the sexual problem was generating many other problems in their marriage. Even though Ray was not yet ready for divorce, he was committed to forcing the issue. His own pain and frustration aside, he loved Sonja enough to want to see her become emotionally healed of whatever was hindering her sexual enjoyment and whatever was causing her emotional pain.

As we shall see, Sonja was dealing with emotional issues that even she did not fully, consciously understand. She was living proof of a truth about sex that often surprises people: our most important (and least understood) sex organ is right between our ears. It is the *brain*. Personal problems, distractions, fears, misconceptions, past experiences, both conscious and unconscious, are factors that can powerfully affect one's ability to enjoy a satisfying, mutually pleasing sexual relationship in marriage.

THE ANATOMY OF SEXUAL INTIMACY

Men and women experience the sexual act in ways that are subtly but significantly different. Men and women are stimulated by different sensory and emotional input. Their thinking differs. The graph of their emotions differs in height and intensity.

A man is "turned on" by visual stimuli. He can experience complete sexual satisfaction in a shorter period of time than a woman. A woman is "turned on" by communication, by experiencing a sense of emotional closeness, intimacy, and security. The person who understands the difference between his or her own sexual experience and that of his or her partner will be able to make adjustments so that *both* partners can experience a more mutual and satisfying sexual union.

In our clinical experience, we have found that many adults experience problems in marital sex because of a lack of clear, detailed information about sex. Many individuals and couples feel embarrassed talking frankly about sex. But sex is an important aspect of our lives, and our sexuality affects many other dimensions of who we are, including our emotions, our relationships, and our spirituality.

In clear, candid terms, let us take a stage-by-stage look at the act of sex, how God designed our sexuality to function, and some of the reasons that our sexual relationships sometimes dysfunction. The act of sex can be viewed in five phases: desire, excitement, plateau, orgasm, and resolution. We will examine each phase in turn:

516

Phase 1: Desire

The first phase, *desire,* is an emotional phase. It begins with the thoughts and feelings of one or both marital partners. From the very first moments of the sexual experience, we find significant differences between men and women. The sights, the sounds, the fragrances, or a single kiss can be enough to excite the man. His arousal may be instantaneous and build swiftly. After just a glimpse of his wife in her negligee, he may go from having other plans (say, watching *Nightline* on TV) to being highly aroused.

A woman is aroused in a much different way. Words, actions, touch, and her relationship with her husband all encourage a woman's desire. Her arousal may emerge slowly, beginning as early as that morning, when her husband compliments her as he leaves for the office. It may continue building when he makes a thoughtful phone call that afternoon, suggesting they go out for dinner that night. It may intensify over dinner with a deep exchange of glances, some caring words, a touch, a smile. For a woman, the act of sex is an act of completion to relations that have been carried on throughout the day, not just in the preceding twenty minutes.

There are pleasures in these early stages of the sex experience—but there are also fears. His primary fear, now and later, is that his sexual performance might fall short, that he might fail to bring his wife to orgasm, that he might fail to complete a satisfactory episode for them both. His wife's fear is different from his, generally centering upon being unwanted sexually.

If problems appear during the desire phase, they are almost always the result of emotional or relational problems, not a physical dysfunction. (We will examine some of these problems later in this article.)

Phase 2: Excitement

The next phase, *excitement,* is a physical phase. In both sexes, the pulse quickens, the blood pressure rises, the skin flushes with a pink glow of excitement. In the man, this increased flow of blood causes the penis to rise and become erect. The woman experiences a corresponding erection of her clitoris, and also releases a slippery, wet lubricant from her vagina. He is physically ready to enter her, and she is physically ready to be entered—although the process of lovemaking need not progress immediately to vaginal intercourse. This is a time when both partners may explore each other, caress and hold each other, and enjoy each other—slowly, patiently, pleasantly building toward that moment when "they shall become one flesh."

Phase 3: Plateau

Here, at the *plateau* stage, the sexual experience levels out. The excitement of initial arousal is maintained, increased, and probed by both partners as they mutually give and receive pleasure. The man's sexual plateau is naturally fairly short—a few minutes or so. The woman's sexual plateau is longer, so in most mutually caring and healthy relationships, the man will learn to "pace" himself, to prolong his sexual plateau, so that he can better meet the sexual needs of his wife.

To reach orgasm, most women find it helpful if the husband manually strokes her clitoris for five to fifteen minutes as their desire intensifies. Rather than diminishing the man's ultimate pleasure, this lengthened plateau tends to increase it. His own sexual

517

excitement intensifies as he sees, hears, and feels his wife's mounting pleasure. Simultaneous orgasm is not necessary in sex; in fact, setting a "goal" of simultaneous orgasm can place pressure on the wife to "fake" orgasm at the same time her husband experiences orgasm, resulting in sexual frustration for her. This pressure can also be a distraction that reduces the husband's pleasure. Sex should be enjoyed in the moment; it should not be goal-oriented. However, as the husband learns to prolong his own sexual plateau while helping his wife to experience full excitement, simultaneous orgasm does become more possible and—whether simultaneous or not—the orgasm each experiences will be more intense and pleasurable.

If problems arise during the excitement or plateau stages of lovemaking, the source of the problems may be emotional or may be physical. Couples experiencing any sexual dysfunction during this phase—such as painful intercourse, loss of erection, or premature ejaculation—should consult a physician so that physical causes can be identified or ruled out. Sources of physical problems in this phase of lovemaking may include use of alcohol or drugs, certain blood pressure medications, fatigue, stress, obesity (either as a physical impediment or because the obese person feels unlovely and unsexy), hormonal problems, and certain diseases. About half of the sexual dysfunctions that occur during this phase of the sex experience can be resolved through counseling.

Phase 4: Orgasm

Orgasm is the top of the sex experience and the shortest of the five phases. For the husband, orgasm involves the ejaculation of semen in an explosive spasm of pleasure. For the wife, orgasm involves rolling waves of intense pleasure. Orgasm is accompanied by a further quickening of pulse and respiration, further rise in blood pressure, involuntary contractions of various muscles, and thrusting of the pelvis to propel the pleasure of orgasm to its peak.

Sexual dysfunction in this phase of the sexual experience commonly involves physical problems. The husband may have difficulty maintaining erection or attaining an erection at all *(impotence)*. Or he may be unable to control the timing of the orgasm, so that he experiences orgasm too early *(premature ejaculation)*. The wife may fail to achieve orgasm or may reach orgasm only occasionally. Her outer vaginal muscles may spasm, tightening down so intensely that he cannot enter at all. Many of these physiological problems may actually have a nonphysical cause. Sometimes men and women simply don't fully understand their bodies and how they function sexually. They may expect each other to respond as they do, and they may not fully understand how to give pleasure to each other. Sometimes, simply understanding the functioning of the penis or the clitoris—and how to stimulate these organs—can resolve sexual problems.

Here, communication is important. Partners should convey to each other what kinds of behavior give them pleasure and what techniques are helpful in producing arousal and stimulation to orgasm. Open, honest exchange is absolutely essential, both with regard to sexual activity they enjoy and to sexual activity that they are not comfortable with.

There are many popular myths that contribute to sexual dysfunction and sexual dissatisfaction, including:

518

- "Both partners must experience simultaneous orgasm."
- "Every sexual experience must lead to orgasm for both partners."
- "A good spouse never says no to sex."
- "Good girls are passive and never initiate sex."
- "Good girls don't enjoy sex."
- "It's my spouse's fault if I don't achieve orgasm." (More likely, you need to be more open about expressing your likes and dislikes.)
- "A woman is incapable of orgasm anyway, so why try?" (You'd be amazed how many men have bought this one!)
- "If the sexual performance isn't athletic, it's not erotic."
- "Sex should be dramatic and as graceful as a ballet, just like in the romance novels." (Romantic books and movies are not sources of accurate sex information; they are sources of fantasy. Your love life is real, and provides infinitely greater pleasure than a manufactured fantasy.)

Phase 5: Resolution

In the *resolution* phase, men and women again follow somewhat different paths. As the man's sexual organ returns to its nonexcited state, he experiences a rich sense of well-being. He toboggans rapidly from the mountaintop of orgasm to the flatland of resolution. For him, the focus of the sex act was orgasm, and the sex act ended with the last wave of orgasmic pleasure. The postorgasmic period for the man is called a *refractory* period (or *refraction*), meaning that his sexual energy has been largely spent, and he will not be able to achieve orgasm again until he regathers additional sexual energy (in young men, refraction may last as little as fifteen minutes; in older men, refraction may last a few days or longer).

The woman's resolution phase follows a very different path. She is capable of multiple orgasms, and her primary sex interest centers on the closeness and emotional union the sex act provides. She will descend the mountain at a much more leisurely pace as her primary and secondary sexual organs return to their nonexcited states. If restimulated during this phase, she may experience another orgasm.

At the Minirth Meier New Life Clinics, we often see clients who experience sexual dysfunction because of misplaced ideas about what the Bible has to say about sex. Sex is meant to be enjoyed, freely and exuberantly. In a Christian marriage, physical affection is beautiful in the eyes of our loving God, who created us to give and receive love in all its splendid dimensions. A healthy sexual union promotes good mental health in the couple, and that healthy sense of joy and satisfaction in life then radiates out to the entire family.

Marriage partners whose spouses are insensitive to their sexual needs or feelings about sex will be tempted to meet those needs in unscriptural and neurotic ways. Healthy marital love is patient. Healthy marital love is kind. Expressed with joy and freedom within the protective boundaries of marriage, the gift of sex is a beautiful and profound expression of our humanity and our spirituality.

The joyful expression of sexual love in marriage is a gift from God and is designed to be an exciting, satisfying, and meaningful statement of deep love between a husband and a wife. Marital sexuality is described in the Bible as clean and good, and thus should be free of inhibitions (see especially The Song of Solomon, in which the bride dresses seductively for her husband and is sexually playful and aggressive). The apostle Paul states that marital sex is an important component of Christian marriage and should not be avoided or interrupted except for brief periods by mutual agreement. Within a Christian marriage, there is room for great variety and experimentation as long as both partners are comfortable with that expression. Gentleness, erotic foreplay, and fun are essential to a meaningful and joyful sex life.

SEXUAL PROBLEMS AND SOLUTIONS

Both emotional and physical problems can lead to sexual dysfunction. Following are some of the most common problems and their solutions.

Sexual Taboos

Among the most common dysfunctions a new couple must deal with are sexual taboos learned in childhood. Those deep-seated precepts include such assumptions as, "Sex equals sin." One of the consequences of such false assumptions is that people who buy the idea that "sex equals sin" also begin to believe that the reverse is true: "Sinful equals sexy." That is why many taboo-ridden individuals have trouble being sexual unless there is a "dirty" aspect to their sexual behavior. This results in guilt over even normal sexual behavior and also produces low self-esteem.

Many taboo-plagued individuals, feeling that being sexy is the same as being illicit or immoral, will shut down their sexuality soon after the marriage. Problems with intercourse—painful intercourse, loss of erection, or lack of sexual feeling—are common problems that emerge in such relationships. Though the symptoms are physical, the causes are largely emotional and spiritual.

We frequently counsel couples whose premarital sex was far more satisfying than any they're experiencing in marriage. It's a function of that same old "sex-is-dirty" attitude. Before marriage, sex is illicit, sinful, exciting, a forbidden pleasure—and it's fun. After the wedding ceremony, sex is no longer dirty and illicit, no longer forbidden—and thus it's no longer fun. Couples need to learn a new and healthy attitude toward sex: "Sex is great, it's good, it's fun, and it's the most fun when it takes place in marriage. Let's enjoy each other, let's explore each other and experiment with new techniques. Let's give each other pleasure."

Another sexual taboo that harms marital sex is the *incest inhibition*. This taboo is based on an unconscious assumption that "It's wrong to have sex within the family." This taboo often arises when children never see their parents expressing affection or romantic feeling for each other, and particularly in family arrangements where the parents have separate bedrooms.

This taboo may have been a major influence on the "free love" movement of the 1960s and 1970s. Many young baby boomers, raised in the sexually restrained period of the 1950s and early 1960s, didn't have much opportunity to see their parents as romantic, sexual people. In many such homes, sex was not discussed; the "facts of life" were learned at school or from peers rather than the home. The result: many young people concluded their parents were "hung up" and inhibited about sex, and that sex had no place in the home. Unable to see the home as a place where sex was okay, they rushed to the other extreme, taking sex outside of the traditional family home. "Living together" replaced marriage, "significant others" replaced spouses, and the "sexual revolution" took off. If the young people of the 1950s and early 1960s had been able to see their parents behaving in an appropriately sexual way within the home—hugging, kissing, showing affection toward each other—perhaps they would have had less reason to practice their sexual behavior in nonhome settings.

Time-Release Attitudes

Many couples unconsciously absorb attitudes from their parents and even from prior generations. These attitudes are like "time-release capsules" that were a part of our grandparents' sexual attitudes and that continue to affect our sexual attitudes and behavior in the present.

Sexual Attitude Inventory

This self-test is designed to help you determine if your present sexual behavior has been affected by "time-release attitudes." The following statements are meant to be a guide in helping you analyze the attitudes of your own family of origin. Avoid thinking of these statements in terms of blaming or positive-versus-negative assessments. Simply answer as objectively as possible so that you can gain clearer insight into your own sexual attitudes and where they came from.

Check the statements which apply to you:

____ "In my family, sex was not discussed."
____ "My mother and father hugged and kissed in front of the children."
____ "My parents slept in separate beds."
____ "My parents believed that a marriage should be faithful and permanent."
____ "My family used affection as a reward for good behavior and withheld it for bad behavior."
____ "My mother thought intercourse was a wife's duty."
____ "I received excellent sexual information from my parents."
____ "I never felt free to ask my parents anything about sexual issues.'"

Look back at the statements you checked above. Are there any actions or attitudes in your childhood that might be influencing your married life today? Consider your own attitudes toward sexuality and check the following statements which apply to you:

____ "It is important to me that we greet each other affectionately after being apart all day."
____ "I like to be held and touched without always having intercourse."
____ "I am easily embarrassed when I am nude in the presence of my spouse."
____ "Sex is too embarrassing for me to talk about."
____ "I think that sex outside of marriage is okay."
____ "I believe sex should be honored within the marriage."

521

_____ "I think it's okay to use sex as a weapon or reward."
_____ "I think that the woman should do whatever the man wants."
_____ "I feel free to talk about my mate and our intimate sex life with my friends."
_____ "It is all right for the woman to initiate sexual activity."
_____ "I believe that a man should take the lead in sexual intercourse."

Do you see any patterns from your childhood reflected in your present life? Talk about these issues with your spouse. Then consider a sexual relationship covenant, like the one below:

1. I agree that we may differ on some things, and I agree to respect your opinion and feelings.
2. I agree to be open and honest about our sexual relationship.
3. I agree that the only way I can really please you is to let you guide me, and I am willing to do so.
4. I agree not to use sex as a weapon or reward.
5. I agree not to criticize or make fun of my mate's sexuality.
6. I believe that God's teaching and guidelines about sexual relationships are important and agree to make them a part of our marriage.

We've found that verbal or written covenants, such as these, can often serve as a foundation for an honest sexual relationship in a strong, healthy marriage.

(Adapted from _Getting Ready for Marriage_ by Jerry Hardin and Dianne Sloan [Thomas Nelson, 1991]. Used by permission.)

Past Sexual Abuse

In our clinical experience, we have never seen a woman who was sexually abused in childhood who didn't suffer some degree of sexual dysfunction in adulthood. The cause–effect correspondence of sexual abuse to sexual dysfunction appears to be 100 percent. Our sexuality is the most intimate and personal aspect of ourselves. When an adult or older child crosses a child's sexual boundaries, it is an invasion of the deepest, most sensitive, most vulnerable aspect of that child—and it occurs at a time when the most fundamental layers of the child's personality are being formed. Sexual abuse and other traumatic sexual experiences leave their mark deep in the psyche, the soul, of that individual, creating distorted and often painful attitudes toward sex, including marital sex. Healing is possible, even in extreme cases, but professional counseling is almost always necessary in cases involving memories of childhood sexual abuse.

For a thorough discussion of abuse issues, see ABUSE; we also recommend reading _The Wounded Heart,_ by Dr. Dan Allendar (NavPress, 1990).

Guilt

Back to the case of Ray and Sonja.

Ray finally convinced Sonja that, if she cared about him and about their marriage, she had to get professional help. In counseling, Sonja's worst fear came true: she was no longer able to hide the truth that she had kept buried for almost eight years. For all that time, Sonja had been guarding a secret that no one else knew. Ray didn't know.

Sonja's own parents didn't know. In the beginning, she met alone with the counselor, without Ray being present. There, piece by agonizing piece, she told the following story:

When she was nineteen years old and in college, Sonja had become romantically and sexually involved with one of her professors. In the course of that relationship, she became pregnant. The professor persuaded Sonja to have an abortion, and he paid for it. After he was sure that the pregnancy was indeed terminated, the professor then terminated the relationship.

Sonja was devastated—and she never told anyone about the affair, the pregnancy, or the abortion. Sonja and Ray had not been sexually active prior to their marriage. Sonja had never claimed to be a virgin, but Ray had never asked and she could never bring herself to tell him what she had done. In fact, she had actually managed to wall off that part of her life so that she hardly ever thought about it on a conscious level.

Unconsciously, of course, the guilt still simmered beneath the level of her awareness. Guilt over the affair. Guilt over the abortion. Guilt over concealing her past from her husband.

Once the counselor had helped Sonja face the truth of her past, it was time to call Ray in—but Sonja was terrified at the prospect of admitting her past to her husband. "He'll hate me," she cried. "I just know our marriage is over because of this, but I can't keep living this lie."

Ray sat down at Sonja's side, and she told her story. Ray listened and did not interrupt. Finally, emotionally spent, Sonja finished and waited for Ray's response. He responded with love and support. "I just wish you'd told me this years ago," he said, hugging her.

Sonja and Ray continued weekly therapy for a few months, and then cut back to a once-a-year "emotional checkup." Sonja has received Ray's forgiveness and God's, and she has made a great deal of progress in forgiving herself. She has grieved the loss of her unborn baby and the years of pain and anxiety the abortion has cost her. Today, Sonja is turning her pain into help for other women, volunteering as a lay counselor at a crisis pregnancy center.

Though healing has not been easy, Sonja and Ray now experience a healthy and satisfying sex life. Guilt has been replaced by grace. Sonja's view of sex has been transformed from one of sin and regret to one of joy and completion.

Guilt is often the culprit when sexual intimacy is disrupted. Guilt over past sexual sins. Guilt over abortion. These issues are directly related to sexuality, and the connection between sex-related guilt and sexual disfunction is a straight line. In our clinical experience, we have repeatedly observed that if married couples do not resolve the special problems generated by a past abortion, they tend to experience an emotional divorce. Trust is ruptured, and emotional issues such as depression and anxiety are extremely common. Husbands frequently feel threatened and angry, even when they (like Ray) do not know what the wife's secret issue is. The sin must be forgiven, and the loss must be grieved, in order for the woman to experience emotional liberation, and in order for the couple to experience sexual wholeness. (See also ABORTION; GUILT; SHAME.)

Many people, like Sonja, fear going into counseling because they think they will have to undergo a prolonged, intense, invasive analysis of their past and their personality. This, however, is rarely the case. Most cases of sexual dysfunction owing to marital

523

issues can be resolved in a relatively small number of counseling sessions. At the Minirth Meier New Life Clinics, our approach to counseling involves understanding, empathy, grace, forgiveness, and unconditional affirmation.

Sexual Problems Owing to Infertility

Many couples experience sexual problems when they are working on infertility issues and trying to "make a baby." Often, when a couple begins to focus on sex as a means of procreation rather than a means of emotional and relational union, sex becomes mechanical. The husband and wife experience anxiety and pressure. The man begins to feel he is being used as a sperm factory rather than a husband. The wife becomes so preoccupied with "baby-making" that she doesn't feel sexy—and she doesn't come across as sexy, either. Couples who experience sexual dysfunction because of infertility need to relax and rediscover the romance of their relationship. If they refocus on the excitement and the pleasure of exploring each other sexually, they will experience greater enjoyment in sex—and they will also be more likely to conceive.

Marital Conflict

Resentment and frustration are common sources of sexual dysfunction. How can we expect to drop our physical defenses and make our bodies vulnerable to our spouses when, emotionally and relationally, we are guarded, wary, and hostile? Often, in cases of sexual dysfunction, there are unconscious feelings of anger and bitterness that we are not even aware of. On this unconscious level, we want to get back at our mates for some perceived injury or history of offenses—and we see sex as a weapon we can use. So, without even consciously knowing why, we fail to perform sexually. Our mates are frustrated as a result, and we have (unconsciously) "won."

Through counseling, the reasons for this hostility can be brought out into the open and resolved, so that both partners can experience a more satisfying sex life—and a more healthy marriage. The health of a couple's sex life tends to mirror the health of the marriage. Sexual dysfunction may only be a symptom of a larger problem.

In our clinical experience, we often encounter couples with totally different views of their sexual problems. The husband may be focused only on the symptom of unsatisfying sex. "If things were better in bed," he says, "everything would be all right." But the wife views things differently. "If we weren't under so much financial stress," she says, "sex would be a lot better." It may well be that she is angry with her husband over his mismanagement of the family finances, or that she is simply feeling stressed by worries over unpaid bills. The husband in this case is being shortsighted in only wanting to view the sex issue in isolation. All marital problems are interrelated, and for one aspect of the marriage to be healed, we usually need to get a clear picture of the healthy and dysfunctional aspects of the marriage as a whole.

A common scenario involves a husband who has been sexually inadequate on one or two occasions (perhaps he failed to achieve or maintain erection because of fatigue or self-consciousness). As a result, he becomes embarrassed and anxious, seeing himself as a failure. This insecurity causes him to view the bedroom as a reminder of his failure and a place to be avoided. This is a vicious emotional cycle, where one or two minor failures serve to reinforce future failures, producing a pattern of defeat and discouragement.

Couples should also understand that there are cycles to their sexual relationship.

524

From time to time, sexual adjustments need to be made. Certainly, newlyweds (married two years or less) must make many such adjustments. But even older couples go through cyclical periods of drawing closer or shutting down sexually. Some couples may tire of a sex life that has become routine, and sexual activity may decrease for a while. Then they may return to a very active sex life, punctuated by new passions, new techniques, a new sense of exploration.

Impotence (Decreased Sexual Performance in Men)

Some decrease in sexual desire and activity is normal in men when they reach their fifties (and sometimes even in their forties). As men get older, it sometimes takes longer to achieve erection. However, impotence is often related to physical causes that are treatable, including diabetes (specifically diabetic vascular disease), prostate infections, vascular (circulatory) disease, and spinal cord disorders. Men who are demonstrated to have low testosterone levels may benefit from testosterone replacement therapy (hormone injections).

Nearly all men will experience difficulty in attaining an erection from time to time, usually due to fatigue, stress, illness, mental distraction, or alcohol use. These occasional problems are not true dysfunctions and should not be cause for concern. A healthy couple laughs off such temporary problems with a "better luck next time" attitude, and a caring husband accepts the situation and proceeds to give pleasure to his wife.

Premature Ejaculation (Early Orgasm in Men)

Premature ejaculation is ejaculation before or just after coitus (penetration) begins. Loss of erection usually follows. The sources of premature ejaculation are usually emotional, and counseling is recommended.

Retarded Ejaculation (Delayed Orgasm in Men)

Retarded ejaculation is a common problem. The man finds himself unable to achieve orgasm after a sufficient time. He becomes anxious and concerned about his performance. His wife's vagina may become uncomfortable. Both partners find the sex act increasingly pleasureless. The reasons for a single incident of retarded ejaculation are anxiety about sexual performance (trying too hard), fatigue, stress, illness, mental distraction, or alcohol use. If retarded ejaculation becomes a pattern, there could be either physical or emotional factors involved. A medical exam is recommended; if medical causes are ruled out, then counseling is indicated.

Frigidity (Decreased Sexual Desire or Performance in Women)

Frigidity is the most common sexual dysfunction in women and may be persistent or only temporary. It may involve sexual arousal with an inability to achieve orgasm, or it may involve complete inhibition of sexual desire and sexual functioning. Women who experience this problem almost always see themselves as sexual failures and wonder, "What's wrong with me?" Many find this condition very destructive to their self-esteem and tend to feel incomplete in their womanhood. This dysfunction, however, is frequently treatable, either medically or psychologically. Potential causes of frigidity include *dyspareunia* (painful intercourse; see page 526), anxiety, guilt, depression, life stresses and pressures, fear of genital injury, or fear of pregnancy.

Occasional periods of sexual dormancy do not necessarily signal a dysfunction. It just means that a couple is working out a sexual rhythm. When problems persist, however, and communication doesn't seem to be working, professional counseling is indicated.

525

Another common source of frigidity is a lack of knowledge by one or both partners of the importance of the female clitoris in guiding female sexual response. Increasing the understanding of both partners about sexual techniques and sexual response can be helpful in overcoming this problem.

Also, when a woman feels inhibited about expressing her sexual needs, she may also shut down sexually. Because women tend to become aroused more slowly than men, they may become unsatisfied and disappointed with sex when their husbands fail to meet their needs.

Frigidity can frequently be overcome when couples are willing to discuss their sexual issues openly and without blaming. An understanding, patient, and loving husband can often help to calm the fears and other emotions that contribute to this dysfunction. If communication between partners does not resolve the problem, a medical exam is recommended; if medical causes are ruled out, then counseling is indicated.

Dyspareunia (Painful Intercourse in Women)

Vaginal pain during intercourse sometimes makes sex impossible. This leads to embarrassment, anxiety, fear, and low self-esteem, which increase the likelihood of future dyspareunia and frigidity.

Possible physical causes of dyspareunia include pregnancy, obesity of either partner, hip joint problems, inflammation of the pelvic organs, prolapsed uterus, ovarian cysts, a thick hymen, inelastic vaginal walls, and vaginal scarring from past surgeries. Psychological causes include fear of pain or injury (because of past incidences of dyspareunia) and fear of pregnancy. These fears can cause the vaginal muscles to contract involuntarily (*vaginismus*) and prevent the penis from entering.

Husbands sometimes cause dyspareunia in their wives by entering too forcefully or engaging in intercourse too aggressively. Increased sensitivity and gentleness on the part of the husband is required in such cases. Also, the use of lubricants can be helpful.

Sex During Pregnancy

Sexual intercourse is normally possible until quite late in a pregnancy, unless the woman has suffered a previous miscarriage. Women who have miscarried should discuss the possibility of sex during pregnancy with their doctors. The first fourteen weeks of a pregnancy are especially crucial for women with a history of miscarriages, since sex may entail an increased risk of causing miscarriage or bleeding.

SEX AND INTIMACY

Some people use the terms *sex* and *intimacy* as if they are interchangeable. They are not. Sex is physical; intimacy is mental and emotional. You can have intimacy without sex and you can have sex without intimacy, but healthy couples learn to use sex to build intimacy and to use intimacy as an enhancement for sex.

Intimacy is emotional closeness and involves communicating thoughts and dreams, sharing feelings, mutually supporting and caring for each other, and demonstrating affection in nonsexual ways. Tragically, many people (especially men) substitute sex for intimacy. Men, by nature, are quickly aroused, and their sexual desire is grounded in

■

Approximately one-fifth of all women experience painful intercourse at some time in their lives.

■

526

the immediate senses. Women, however, are much more responsive to emotional intimacy and affection. Some men feel either threatened by—or indifferent to—affectionate behavior. They want to get right down to business, and once the sex act is concluded, they are satisfied. Men, who tend not to feel emotions as deeply as women, will sometimes use sex to fulfill all of their emotional needs—and as a result, they will ignore the emotional needs of their wives.

"We'll have a problem or an argument, and then we'll make up and he'll make love to me," women commonly complain in counseling. "Then he'll act like everything's okay. But I need more than sex. I need to be close to him. I need his affection. I need to be held and talked to. I'm tired of appeasing him with sex. I need *intimacy.*"

In emotionally healthy couples, lovemaking is more than a recreational object, more than just fun—although it should be fun as well! Lovemaking is a channel to deeper emotional intimacy, one of many such channels to emotional closeness. Sex is fun and exciting, but it is also intensely meaningful. It is a unique relationship we share with one other person in the world.

One of the keys to creating and maintaining emotional intimacy is to keep the romance alive. Romance is the art of nurturing love and intimacy. It involves all the little details (some planned, some spontaneous) of a romantic relationship: holding hands, an unexpected hug or kiss, a love note, a rose on the pillow, a surprise candlelight dinner, a gift for no reason at all. Romance is the art of listening to the silent expressions of each other's heart. Feelings drive our behavior, and behavior also drives our feelings, so romantic behavior produces romantic feelings, which in turn lead to deeper intimacy.

The paradox of sex is that it is the most pleasurable when pleasure is not the primary goal. Couples who focus only on physical pleasure in sex tend to become bored and disappointed once they reach a saturation point in their relationship. But couples who focus on intimacy find that the pleasures of sex do not grow old, and they continually find new pleasures as they penetrate to new and deeper levels of emotional intimacy. When we seek emotional intimacy and emotional intensity in sex, the result is that sexual pleasure is intensified. When climax is achieved, it is a climax not only of the body and of the brain, but of the soul.

Sex Education

In a 1939 magazine ad for feminine napkins, a fully grown young woman sits before a counselor's desk looking worried and frightened. A counselor old enough to have shaken hands with Moses sits behind the desk. The caption reads, "These girls must be told." The caption refers not to sex education itself but to information about menstruation.

That was 1939. These days, in our world-gone-haywire, the young lady in front of the desk is probably in grade school. For reasons not fully understood by medical science, girls today begin experiencing menstruation earlier than their mothers and grand-mothers did. In addition, children are exposed to sexual information, sex-oriented entertainment and advertising, sex-oriented dangers (such as rape and incest), and sexual temptations to a vastly greater degree than young people were a generation or two ago. For their own protection, children need to be told the facts of life—and the sooner the better.

In recent years, momentum has been growing to provide sex education in the schools. Though well-intentioned, such efforts are often counterproductive, since secular sex-ed instructors tend to dispense sexual information in a "values-free environment." The problem is that there is no such thing as a "values-free environment," since the absence of values in itself makes a values statement. The result is teaching that says to young people:

- "All sexual choices are morally equal."
- "We will show you the mechanics of sex, and what you do with this information is up to you."
- "Here is how to have sex without producing babies, and how to have sex with a reduced risk of catching or transmitting a disease."

Information of a sexual nature must be imparted carefully and must be suitable to the age level of the child. Children are surrounded by so much bad information or slanted information or destructive information that it is imperative that they get good information as early as possible. Unfortunately, most Christian parents wait too long to tell their children the facts of life—and thus they leave their children unprotected against the destructive moral forces that pervade our society.

The purpose of sex education in public schools and the purpose of sex education in the Christian home are not the same. Sex-ed classes in schools have only two purposes: (1) to prevent the birth of unwanted babies; and (2) to prevent the spread of sexually transmitted disease. Christian parents are concerned, of course, about these two issues, but they are concerned about so much more than that. Christian parents want their children to grow to be spiritually and emotionally healthy adults with happy, satisfying marriages. To achieve this goal, young people must be given appropriate, accurate information that is surrounded by Christian love and Christian values.

EDUCATING BY EXAMPLE

Like it or not, whether we say anything about sex or not, we parents are already instructing our children about sex and sexuality. We do this in three ways:

1. We model our own gender role by the things we do and say every day.
2. We model an attitude toward the opposite sex by the way we behave toward and speak about our spouses.
3. We teach directly by answering questions the children ask whenever the subject arises.

Our children receive messages about sex and sexuality throughout their relationships with us, in the form of vignettes that are imprinted as memories. This form of teaching is almost entirely subliminal, below the level of conscious awareness. Dad doesn't set out to teach sexuality when he makes a kind comment about his wife (or an unkind one). And the child doesn't actively think, "So *that's* how a man is supposed to behave." The child registers all of these impressions in the depths of the unconscious mind—which is the hidden-but-powerful level of our minds that tends to control the course of our lives much more than we ever realize.

The question that confronts you as a parent is: Are you going to consciously and thoughtfully teach them God's truth about sex and sexuality? Or are you going to unthinkingly pass on your worst habits and attitudes about relating to the opposite sex? Now is the time to get serious about educating your children about sex.

IMPARTING HEALTHY VALUES

God intended the parents and the home to be the primary means of transmitting sex information and sexual values—not the schools, not the media, but *parents*. Parents are the child's most important role models. Parents are the primary shapers of the child's image of God and moral awareness. And that means *both* parents.

This is not to say that parents should try to do it all. In fact, there are some issues that kids just won't discuss with their parents. Perhaps this is caused by the inborn taboo of incest, a sense that just *talking* about sexual matters with parents makes them uncomfortable. Whatever the source of it, there is an invisible barrier between children and their parents that keeps the children from bringing many of their feelings, questions, problems, and concerns to their parents. All kids—even those who have excellent relationships with their parents—will seek information from sources beyond the home. They want independent corroboration of what their parents tell them. And they want information to fill in any gaps left by their parents.

What are some of these outside sources your kids will consult? Street lore. R-rated movies on cable TV (if not at your house, then at a friend's). Pornography. You may think, "My kid? No way!" Don't be so sure. There is pornographic material of the most shocking nature within the reach of most kids today. It's a morally dangerous world out there, and your children are wading through it, trying to make sense of it, trying to sort through the conflicting messages they hear from their parents and from the influences of the surrounding culture. Studies and clinical experience show that a large percentage of what adolescent boys know about sex they have learned from pornography. Adolescent girls are not generally interested in porn, but they pick up a great deal of information (and misinformation) from romance novels, soap operas, and tabloid talk shows. Clearly, such sources leave huge gaps in our children's education about life (see TELEVISION AND OTHER ENTERTAINMENT MEDIA).

In their book *When Love Is Not Enough* (Focus on the Family, 1992), Stephen Arterburn and Jim Burns cite some shattering statistics about young people and sex:

- Twelve million American teens are sexually active; 81 percent of males and 67 percent of females have had intercourse while teenagers.
- Seventy-four percent of teenagers indicate that they would choose to be in a live-in relationship either before marriage or instead of marriage.
- More than 500,000 babies are born each year to unmarried American girls under eighteen.

> ■
>
> *If you, as a parent, are waiting for "just the right time" to tell your children about sex, you are already too late! You are already teaching them.*
>
> ■

- The average high school student watches an average of ten hours of MTV per week, much of which consists of sex-drenched and even sadomasochistic rock videos. Meanwhile, only about 10 percent of American young people receive a positive, healthy Christian sex education.

Clearly, we parents have our work cut out for us. And we can't do it alone. We need to be working in concert with teachers, pastors, and church youth leaders to provide education and role models our children can relate to. We need to be willing to talk with our kids about sex and values, both in planned "facts-of-life" talks and in those moments of opportunity when a question comes up. And we need to avail ourselves of the many excellent sex education resources that are available in Christian bookstores, written from a biblical perspective.

WHAT DO WE TELL THEM?

Some suggestions for helping your children to have a healthy attitude toward sex:

- Make sure your children are aware, from preschool age on, what parts of their body are private and should not be touched by other people. Make sure they have strong personal boundaries from an early age and that they know to tell people who touch them inappropriately, "Don't do that!" And make sure they know to tell you about any such incident, even if they have been told not to tell.
- Avoid acting shocked, secretive, or embarrassed by the subject. If some event (such as a TV news story about AIDS or abortion) provokes a question from your child, answer the question calmly and as fully as the child is ready to understand. Don't cloak the subject in mystery or make it seem shameful. Sex is natural, and children should know that it is a subject you feel comfortable talking about.
- When discussing sex with your child, use the correct terminology: *intercourse, sex, penis, vagina,* and so forth. Avoid euphemisms such as *sleeping together.* A child is likely to come away with the idea that simply sharing a bed with another person can result in pregnancy. Try to view this subject from the child's point of view, and make sure you don't create confusion for the child by prudish use of language.
- If questions arise regarding difficult subjects such as homosexuality, prostitution, oral sex, or anal sex, be as frank as possible, given the child's intellectual and emotional level. Make sure that curiosity is satisfied, but don't volunteer information the child is not prepared to handle.
- By the time your child is fourteen or so, you should have given that child clear, candid information on (1) how the physical act of love between a man and a woman actually takes place, including a clear understanding of what an erection is, what a vagina is, and so forth; how venereal disease is spread (including the connection between AIDS and anal sex; see SEXUALLY TRANSMITTED DISEASES); and (3) the purpose of sex, as ordained by God for marriage, the fact that sex bonds two people as nothing else can, and that it is a primary unifying factor in a lasting marriage (for a spiritual perspective on sex in marriage, see SEX AND SEXUALITY).

WHAT TO TEACH YOUR CHILD AND WHEN

This chart summarizes approximately what sexual knowledge a child is capable of assimilating and when. These summaries are general in nature, of course, and your child may be ready for a given level of information either sooner or later than this chart indicates. You should be aware, however, that the fact that your child uses certain sex-related terms or seems to understand sexually-oriented subjects on TV does not necessarily mean that the child has a good grasp of sex and sexuality. Young people can pick up a lot of salacious language and ideas on the school bus and still be totally ignorant.

CHILD'S AGE	CHILD'S DEVELOPMENTAL STAGE AND ACHIEVEMENTS	PARENTS' ROLE IN SEX
Birth to three	Establish an identity apart from the parents.	Model a healthy attitude toward one's own gender and toward the opposite sex.
Three to five	Oedipal stage (the child competes with the same-sex parent for the love of the opposite-sex parent); child observes the parents, clarifies sexual roles, and establishes gender identity.	Continue modeling healthy attitudes, plus refrain competing for affection.
Early grades	"Hates" opposite sex; completing grasp of maleness and femaleness.	Answer questions as simply as possible. Don't supply too much detail or volunteer too much information.
Late grades	Beginning to look around at opposite sex (but won't admit it); starting to pick up sexual innuendo in the media; starting to notice changes in body.	Time to be honest when confronted with pointed questions. Child should learn about disease, pregnancy.
Junior high	Aware of sex. Girls and boys sublimate sexual energy with grandiose daydreaming, athletic or rough activity.	Parents explain how sex works, about the dangers of sexual activity outside of God's plan for marriage. Parents should also share some of their own sexual feelings from this age and from their teen years so the children sense empathy and identification. Parents should answer questions fully.
High school	Girls intrigued by romantic thoughts and dreams. Boys feel physical desires. Sexes are mutually attracted with a desire to experiment.	Parents model love and fidelity. No prying, keep communication open. Demonstrate empathy.

531

- If you don't know the answer to one of your child's questions, say, "I'll get back to you with an answer about that"—then make sure that you do!
- Acknowledge and affirm that your young person's hormonal urges are normal. Draw upon your own experience and feelings from when you were his or her age. "When I was your age, I felt the same way," you might begin. "I remember the time when . . ." In this way, you verify to a child who is undergoing powerful urges and confusing changes that he or she is okay and that everything is going to be all right.
- Give your child practical suggestions and guidelines regarding dating. Young people of both sexes are scared to death of dating and of this whole new boy-girl thing. They intensely want to relate to the opposite sex, but even more intensely, they fear doing or saying the wrong thing. Adolescent insecurities are a part of one of the hardest passages of growing up. But you can ease your children through this passage by suggesting places to go, fun things to do, even things to talk about.
- Maintain an open relationship and good communication with your children of both sexes. Parents sometimes spend more time strengthening a daughter's moral fiber than a son's because the daughter is the one who can get pregnant. However, it is just as important for a Christian young man's moral and emotional development—and later marriage relationship—that he keep himself as sexually pure as a Christian young woman.

The thought of talking to their kids about sex turns many parents' blood to quivering lime Jell-O. Yet those who have done so will tell you that there are few greater satisfactions in life.

THE JOY OF SEX EDUCATION

Sex education is not just about giving our kids a list of warnings. It is a *positive, affirmative* experience in which we present the beauty and meaning of marital sex as it was designed by a loving God. It is the experience of helping to shape our children's understanding and appreciation of their own maleness and femaleness. Make sure you don't miss out on this experience. Next to the joy of explaining God's gift of salvation to our children, there are few greater privileges in Christian parenting than the joy of explaining to them God's gift of sex.

See also DATING AND COURTSHIP

Sexual Disorders

A sexual disorder is an emotional and behavioral maladjustment resulting in sexual activity that is unhealthy or abnormal and that is a result of psychological factors rather than medical factors. Following are some of the most common sexual disorders.

Gender Identity Disorder

Gender identity disorder involves feelings of dislike for one's own inborn maleness or femaleness. This disorder usually surfaces in childhood, prior to puberty, if a boy wishes to grow up to be a woman, hates his male genitalia, and desires the traits of a woman; girls with this disorder may insist they are boys and may desire or claim to have male genitalia.

Individuals with gender identity disorders are emotionally confused or experiencing conflict in their view of themselves. In young adulthood, individuals with this disorder may complain about having to wear the clothing of their own gender and may participate in activities usually associated with the opposite sex. Some are so repulsed by their own genitalia that they have their bodies cosmetically and surgically altered to resemble the opposite sex.

Some gender identity confusion is experienced during the emotionally turbulent years of adolescence, and the vast majority come through this time with their inborn gender identity intact. A certain percentage of young people, however, manifest homosexual preferences.

For a thorough discussion of gender identity disorder, male homosexuality, lesbianism (female homosexuality), causes of the disorder, and treatment options, see GENDER IDENTITY DISORDER.

Pedophilia

Pedophilia is sexual disorder in which an adult individual derives sexual excitation and gratification from relationships with children. Individuals with this disorder are called pedophiles and are unable to experience satisfying adult sexual relationships. They usually have extremely low self-esteem and see less threat of rejection from a child than from an adult. Pedophiles are typically men; female pedophiles are rare. Sexual contact between adult males and young boys is referred to as *pederasty*.

Pedophiles generally engage in fondling or genital exposure, though intercourse or sodomy is sometimes engaged in. Children may respond with fear (depending in large part on whether the pedophile uses threats or force), or the child may even engage willingly in the act. In either case, the child is almost certain to experience guilt, shame, and other severe emotional consequences, many of which are likely to persist into adulthood (especially in the absence of counseling). Parents who react to discovery of the abuse with alarm or anger frequently compound the child's emotional problems many times over. Adults who were sexually abused in childhood almost always experience some form of sexual dysfunction or disorder as a result of the earlier abuse.

Pedophilia is one of the most serious sexual offenses in our system of laws. Though the law takes crimes against children very seriously, the law is no more severe than the judgment of Jesus, who said, "It would be better for him if a millstone were hung around his neck, and he were thrown into the sea, than that he should offend one of these little ones" (Luke 17:2).

■

More than half of all cases of pedophiliac abuse involve relatives or acquaintances of the child or the child's family.

■

Paraphilia

Paraphilia is a general term used to describe a range of behavior patterns in which an individual achieves sexual excitation in response to objects or situations that are

533

outside of normal patterns of sexuality. Individuals with this disorder are usually impaired in their ability to experience satisfying sexual intimacy in marriage. Examples of paraphilia include:

- *Fetishism,* in which an individual uses objects such as hair, undergarments, or other items to produce sexual excitement. The object is usually associated with a person the individual knows or knew intimately during childhood.
- *Transvestism* (also called "cross-dressing"), dressing in the clothes of the opposite sex, practiced by heterosexual individuals in order to experience sexual arousal.
- *Exhibitionism,* habitual exposure of one's genitals to an unsuspecting stranger for the purpose of sexual excitement.
- *Frotteurism,* the act or fantasy of touching a nonconsenting partner (as in a crowd on the street, in an elevator, or on a bus) to achieve sexual excitement.
- *Voyeurism,* habitually seeking opportunities to witness unsuspecting people who are naked, disrobing, or engaging in sex.
- *Sexual masochism,* seeking sexual excitement by being hurt, bound, or humiliated.
- *Sexual sadism,* seeking sexual excitement by inflicting pain or humiliation on another person.

THE ORIGINS AND TREATMENT OF SEXUAL DISORDERS

Sexual disorders frequently have their origins in various forms of childhood abuse. Violent or hostile manifestations of sexual disorders are clearly driven by resentment that runs very deep in the personality of the individual. Hostility can be clearly seen in such acts as exhibitionism (with its intent to shock and degrade the opposite sex) and sadism (with its intent to inflict pain and humiliation). Past emotional conflicts sometimes produce erroneous concepts about sexuality that need to be examined and corrected. Sexual disorders are complex, and treating them is not a simple matter. However, most sexual disorders can be resolved with the guidance of a professional counselor and with the client's commitment to growth and change through a faith relationship with God.

Sexually Transmitted Diseases

Sexually transmitted diseases (or STDs, formerly known as venereal diseases) are infections that are acquired primarily or exclusively through sexual behavior. These infections are the result of bacteria, viruses, or fungi that tend to attack or thrive in the mouth or genital tract and that are unable to survive for long periods outside of a human host. Many STDs can be present for years without manifesting any symptoms. Transmission of STDs by neutral objects (towels, dishes, toilet seats, doorknobs, or clothing) is so unlikely as to be virtually impossible.

The best treatment for STDs is *prevention*. Any person who is sexually active runs the risk of contracting an STD—and the risk increases as the level of promiscuity increases. Despite talk of "safe sex" or "safer sex" involving condoms (protective latex sheaths worn over the penis), there is no such thing as "safe sex" except sex that is practiced between a husband and wife in a committed relationship of mutual fidelity, where neither partner is infected by an STD. No other method provides guaranteed protection. At best, condoms are only partially effective, because they sometimes break or leak.

One of the unfortunate by-products of the massive media attention given to AIDS is that other STDs have been almost completely ignored. Many people are largely ignorant of other STDs that are vastly more common than AIDS. For example, many people are completely unaware of the existence of the most common STD of all, chlamydia. Because of the often misleading media promotion of "safe" or "safer sex" with condoms, many people are unaware that condoms provide little or no protection against several very serious STDs, including herpes and genital warts. A condom only covers the penis, and some STDs can be spread through contact with other points in the genital region besides the penis.

The most serious STDs are AIDS (Acquired Immuno-Deficiency Syndrome) and syphilis, which spread from the reproductive tract and invade other systems of the body, producing wide-ranging and life-threatening effects. AIDS is the most dreaded plague of our times, since it is degenerative, debilitating, incurable, and fatal, and because AIDS opens the door for other dreaded diseases (such as pneumonia and cancer) to invade the body.

Following is a listing of the most common forms of sexually transmitted disease.

There is no such thing as "safe sex" except sex that is practiced between a husband and wife in a committed relationship of mutual fidelity.

CHLAMYDIA

Chlamydia is the single most common STD in America (an estimated four million new cases annually). It is not a life-threatening disease, but it can involve serious effects. It is similar to (and often accompanies) gonorrhea. It is caused by a parasitic bacteria that lives in the cells of the human body and spreads by contact with infected mucous membranes. Chlamydia is often present without any symptoms (particularly in women) and can become chronic if left untreated.

Symptoms of chlamydia may be mild, and may go away, only to return with later complications if left untreated. Symptoms may include:

- painful urination
- discharge from penis or vagina
- abdominal pain
- urethral itching

Complications of chlamydia may include:

- pelvic inflammatory disease (PID) in women
- ectopic pregnancy (pregnancy outside of the womb) due to PID
- sterility in both men and women
- urinary tract infection in men
- infants born to women with chlamydia may develop pneumonia or conjunctivitis (eye infection)

Detection and treatment: Chlamydia is easily detected by medical tests and is reliably treated with antibiotics.

GONORRHEA

Gonorrhea is another very common STD (an estimated two million new cases each year), caused by a bacterial infection. It is progressive and, if untreated, becomes chronic. Gonorrhea is spread through contact with infected mucous membranes in the genitals and mouth. Like chlamydia, gonorrhea may be present for a lengthy period of time without symptoms.

Symptoms of gonorrhea (if any) will usually appear in two to ten days after infection, and may include:

- painful urination
- discharge from penis or vagina
- sore throat (if contracted through oral sex)
- rectal pain or discharge (if contracted through anal sex)
- heavy menstrual bleeding or bleeding between periods

Complications of gonorrhea may include:

- pelvic inflammatory disease (PID) in women
- ectopic pregnancy (pregnancy outside of the womb) due to PID
- sterility in either men or women
- birth defects causing blindness
- arthritis, skin lesions, infection of the brain or heart

Detection and treatment: Gonorrhea is easily detected by smear or culture and is treated with antibiotics; strains of the bacteria that have become resistant to standard antibiotics may be effectively treated with newer medications.

SYPHILIS

Syphilis is caused by bacterial infection. If untreated, it becomes chronic and ultimately fatal.

536

Symptoms of syphilis may appear as late as twelve weeks after infection. Possible symptoms in the first twelve weeks include:

- painless sores (chancres) on the genitals, mouth, or elsewhere (chancres may appear in the vagina and go unnoticed)
- swollen lymph nodes

About six weeks after the first symptoms appear, the following symptoms may come and go in cycles:

- rash
- fever
- flu-like symptoms

Complications of early-stage syphilis involve childbirth, and may include:

- miscarriage
- birth defects
- infection of the fetus

If undetected and untreated, the disease may become chronic and the following complications may result years later:

- brain and spinal cord damage
- blindness
- mental deterioration
- death

Detection and treatment: Even if no symptoms are present, syphilis can be detected by a blood test. However, the blood test may give negative results for an infected individual as long as twelve weeks after exposure. Once a diagnosis is made, syphilis is reliably treated with antibiotics.

HERPES

Herpes is caused by a virus. There are two types of herpes virus. Type I commonly produces cold sores of the mouth. Type II generally produces outbreaks in the genital area. Both types, however, can infect either area. Herpes can be transmitted by kissing. The disease is chronic, incurable, and highly contagious by sexual transmission, but the symptoms can be controlled. Herpes is not fatal. The disease is spread by contact with a sore or with genital secretions containing the virus. The virus then permanently establishes itself in the nervous system, where it can stay dormant for many months. Long before the individual is aware of infection, he or she may infect other people. The virus often spreads to others even when no symptoms (such as open sores) are visible.

Symptoms of herpes may be so mild that they go unnoticed, or a severe outbreak may occur within ten days after infection. The first outbreak of herpes is usually severe. Some symptoms of the initial outbreak resemble flu symptoms. Symptoms may include:

- muscle aches, fever, swollen glands, leg pain, abdominal pain
- painful sores and blisters around genital area or mouth

The sores and blisters subside but usually return at repeated and unexpected intervals throughout the individual's lifetime.

The most serious complications involve childbirth. Infants can acquire the virus during passage through an infected mother's birth canal and may experience central nervous system damage or death. When an expectant mother is known to be infected, Caesarean delivery is recommended.

Detection and treatment: Herpes is detected by a culture sample. It does not respond to antibiotics. A drug called Acyclovir, taken orally or applied topically in ointment form, can help control the symptoms of this incurable disease.

A common problem surrounding herpes is the sense of discouragement and depression this chronic disease causes. Herpes support groups exist to help individuals work through the emotional issues that often accompany this diagnosis.

GENITAL WARTS

Genital warts are caused by a viral infection called HPV (human papilloma virus). The HPV virus is highly contagious during intimate body contact and is now known to be a cause of cancer in humans.

Symptoms of HPV infection may appear as late as eight months after infection. Symptoms may include:

- irritation and itching in genital area, followed by:
- soft, flat, wartlike growths that tend to increase in size. (Warts on the cervix or in the vagina may be detectable only by medical examination.)

Complications of HPV infection may include:

- infection of infants in pregnant mothers
- potential risk of cervical cancer in women
- potential risk of cancer of the penis in men

Detection and treatment: Detection usually involves visual observation of warts or detection during gynecological examination. Immediate treatment is important. Warts can be removed surgically or chemically, though the virus can remain dormant and may recur. Infected women should have an annual Pap smear because of cancer risk.

Genital warts are not to be confused with other varieties of warts. *Over-the-counter wart removal remedies are ineffective against genital warts and may even be harmful.*

AIDS (Acquired Immuno-Deficiency Syndrome)

AIDS is a disease caused by a virus carried in human body fluids, such as blood and semen. It is a sexually transmitted disease and is most frequently transmitted during anal intercourse, which is why the disease tends to be transmitted most frequently during male homosexual behavior rather than heterosexual behavior. AIDS can, however, be transmitted during heterosexual behavior, through anal sex, vaginal sex, and oral sex. Anal sex is the most common method of transmission because the lack of natural lubrication in that region leads to tearing, rectal bleeding, and an exchange of body fluids between the sexual partners. Because of vaginal lubrication, vaginal sex is less likely than anal sex to produce an exchange of body fluids that would allow the virus into the bloodstream of the uninfected partner; the rate of infection by this means appears to be low. Oral sex becomes a likely path to infection if the mouth or gums of the uninfected partner contains sores or lacerations that would allow the virus to pass into the bloodstream.

AIDS is also transmitted through contaminated hypodermic needles and syringes during abuse of narcotics such as heroin. An AIDS-infected pregnant mother can pass the virus on to her baby before or during childbirth. AIDS used to be more commonly transmitted by blood transfusions involving tainted donated blood, but measures have been taken by the medical community that have drastically reduced the possibility of receiving tainted blood.

The virus that causes AIDS is called HIV (Human Immuno-Deficiency Virus), and a person who is medically determined to have the HIV virus is said to be "HIV-positive" even if no symptoms of AIDS are yet present. A diagnosis of AIDS is made only after symptoms appear. AIDS is incurable and it is invariably fatal.

AIDS sometimes makes its presence known by a complex of mild symptoms called ARC (AIDS-related complex). ARC symptoms may include fever, weight loss, swollen glands, and diarrhea.

The AIDS virus is not easily or casually transmitted. It is not transmitted by air or through water, or through casual contact such as a handshake or a hug. There is *absolutely no risk* of contracting AIDS by donating blood. A misconception has arisen on this issue because of the fact that some people have been infected by *receiving* tainted donated blood transfusions during the time before the blood supply was being adequately monitored for AIDS. The time period during which a person was most likely to have received AIDS-tainted blood was from late 1978 (when AIDS was first identified in the United States) and mid-1985 (when blood-donor screening came into routine use). The blood supply is extremely safe today.

HIV itself does not produce death. Rather, it attacks the immune system, allowing other diseases (called *opportunistic infections*) to invade the body. These infections, which the body could ordinarily control with a healthy immune system, have free reign in the body. It is these infections (notably cancer and pneumonia) that usually produce death. Other complications of AIDS include blindness and brain and nervous system deterioration.

Detection of AIDS involves a blood test that is analyzed for human antibodies that are produced after the HIV enters the bloodstream. The virus itself cannot be directly detected, and it may take up to twelve weeks for the body to develop the antibodies after being infected. That means that there is a twelve-week "window" following infection during which a person could be tested, the test would not reveal any antibodies (and thus would not indicate any HIV infection), yet the virus could still be present in the bloodstream. Anyone who suspects that he or she has been exposed to AIDS infection should be tested at least twelve weeks after the suspected encounter with the virus. For AIDS testing, contact your physician, your local community health clinic, or an AIDS hotline listed in your phone book.

Though AIDS is not presently curable, the symptoms are managed with antiviral drugs such as zidovudine (AZT) and other new therapies which have been shown to slow the progression of the disease.

Because AIDS is so closely identified with homosexual behavior, many Christians have called AIDS "God's curse" upon the sin of homosexuality. Some understanding is needed. Homosexual behavior *is* sin, according to the Bible; but we believe it is presumptuous to call AIDS a curse from God. It would clearly be accurate to say that AIDS is a *consequence* of homosexual behavior, just as herpes and syphilis are consequences of heterosexual (and homosexual) behavior, and heart disease and cancer are consequences of gluttony. This doesn't mean that God actively and maliciously curses those who acquire any of these diseases. All behavior entails consequences. God's biblical warnings against sexual sins may, in one sense, be viewed as not only moral laws but rules of good health and hygiene. One truth we can glean from a clear understanding of STDs is that when we confine our sexual activity to the safe enclosure of marriage (as God intended), we virtually guarantee that we will not contract these diseases.

Shame

At a workshop on addictions, the participants compared notes and made a fascinating discovery: not one of the people attending the workshop had told friends or family what kind of workshop they were attending. The theme of the workshop was "Dealing with Shame"—and every single participant was ashamed to admit it! In fact, one woman participant could not even bring herself to say the word *shame*. She referred to it as "the S word." Others lowered their voices whenever they spoke of their (shhh!) shame.

Even though shame is a basic emotion that all human beings experience, it often is so personal and so secret that no one wants to discuss it. Yet shame is the issue that drives almost every compulsive, self-defeating behavior known to the human race. Shame is at the root of all addictions. It may be forgotten, hidden, or disguised, but the shame is there, it is real, and it drives behavior. When people take alcohol or immerse themselves in workaholic activity or become involved in addictive sex or obsessive-compulsive cleansing rituals, they are unconsciously trying to cover up their hidden core of shame.

In counseling, it is sometimes the shame that surfaces first. In other cases, the addiction surfaces first. Because shame and addiction always go together, whenever we encounter one, we always look for the other. The addiction may not be anything as overt as alcoholism or cocaine addiction. It may be an addiction to relationships or to spending or to religious legalism—but shame and addiction can always be found together.

SOURCES OF SHAME

Shame can arise from many sources. Following are some common circumstances that can create what is called a *shame base* in a human personality.

Carried Shame

Sometimes shame trickles down from generations far beyond your parents' generation. The source of shame might date back to your grandparents, great-grandparents, or even great-great-grandparents. A dramatic example of this is the self-help group that currently meets regularly in Germany in an effort to heal the wounds left by a past generation. The group's members? The adult relatives of Nazi officials. These people are still haunted by the horrible acts committed by their now-deceased family members.

Of course, the "sins" of your relatives may not be very sinful at all. To qualify as a source of shame they need not be serious or frowned-upon acts, such as a bankruptcy, an illegitimate birth, or a crime. Instead, they could be nothing more than nagging little feelings and doubts that whisper to you, for whatever reason, that your family isn't as good as other families.

In the popular Broadway classic *Showboat,* one of the main characters is a beautiful entertainer who is a favorite with everyone on board the showboat and with the audiences along the riverbank. However, her secret shame is that she has an African heritage. She tries to hide the truth, but when it is made public she is so disgraced that she leaves the showboat and retreats into the degrading life of an alcoholic.

Although the *Showboat* story is fictitious, a similar kind of shame was experienced by many immigrants who came to the United States from Europe in the first half of this century. Rather than being proud of their ethnic roots, they tried to bury them. They Americanized their names and style of dress, and they quickly forgot the traditions of their homeland. They adopted the language, standards, and trappings of their new country, but they often couldn't shake the feeling that they were not as good as persons born in the States. These doubts formed a quiet shame base that spilled down from generation to generation. The unspoken shame probably motivated many determined immigrants to prove their value by working incredible hours, amassing fortunes, building businesses, and becoming famous.

A well-known example of this is former Chrysler CEO Lee Iacocca, who recalled in his book *Iacocca* (Bantam, 1986) the prejudice he faced as one of the few Italians growing up in Allentown, Pennsylvania. When classmates mocked him and made fun of his name, he tried to follow his father's advice: "Use your head instead of your fists." He used his head so well that he generally was the second-best student in his class. The top scholar was another child of immigrant parents, a Jewish girl.

Shame of Addiction

Parents who suffer from an addiction are usually ashamed of their dependency. Even if they deny or defend the addiction, at some level they feel guilty about it. Dad may be addicted to extramarital affairs, and when confronted with his actions he rationalizes, "It's normal. Some men have to act out their sexuality, and I happen to be one of those men."

Or Mom may be a compulsive overeater who minimizes her addiction by saying, "Oh, I just love to cook, and I love to eat, so I don't mind being a little heavy." In reality, she is a lot like the man with the sex addiction. In spite of their protests, these people feel considerable shame about the lack of control in their lives. They offer excuses, but deep down they don't believe their own rationalizations. Neither do their children. The kids sense the shame, and they share it.

A Child's Feelings of Embarrassment

Sometimes children are tremendously ashamed of their parents, and for good reasons. We once counseled a woman whose father's rageaholism constantly embarrassed her in public. She recalled times when he would treat the family to dinner at a fancy restaurant, but by the end of the meal all of the children had fled to the restrooms or to the car in tears. Dad would argue with the manager about the quality of the food, or he would rant at the waiter and refuse to leave a tip because the service wasn't up to his standards.

It took many therapy sessions before our patient realized that her father was addicted to rage because of his own shame: his deep sense of inadequacy. Only by "pulling rank" and picking on a person in a subservient role did Dad bolster his sagging self-esteem and anesthetize his feeling of worthlessness. The actions that deadened his shame caused a tremendous build-up of shame for his children.

Jacqueline Kennedy Onassis is a good example of a well-known personality who suffered embarrassment because of a parent's dysfunction. Jackie's handsome father, called "Black Jack," was famous for his good looks and his well-publicized womanizing. Even after marriage to Jackie's mother, he made no attempt to curb his appetite for nonstop love affairs. He even bragged of being unfaithful on his honeymoon. Because of the family's social standing, the eventual divorce made headlines. Details of the scandal were the talk of the town.

Such a source of shame can make addiction predictable. Jackie's addiction of choice was shopaholism. Her shopping habit raised eyebrows when, during her first year in the White House, she engaged the famed and pricey designer Oleg Cassini to create over one hundred dresses for her. In 1961, a bill for $40,000 covered the cost of gloves and other incidentals. Her compulsion to splurge continued in her years of marriage to millionaire Aristotle Onassis: she was reputed, during the first month of their marriage, to have spent at a rate of $3,000 per minute.

Clearly, the emotion of shame can be costly in more ways than one!

Separation from God

All persons have an inner need for God. On some level we are all aware of this need, even though we may deny it to ourselves and others.

How does this become a source of shame? In two ways. First, children may be ashamed of their parents' lack of connection with God. They witness the presence of religion in their friends' homes, and they compare it with the absence of religion in their own family. Something is missing, and the absence of that "something" is a source of shame.

A second way that shame can spring from a separation from God is when victims of applauded addictions allow their addictions to take the place of God. One of the by-products of all addictions is that the compulsion—whatever it may be—becomes that individual's god. When this occurs, the person worships the compulsion and becomes even more detached and distant from God.

Examples of extreme rebellion against religion often mask a deep unmet hunger for God. The rebellion itself may be an upside-down expression of the profound yearnings for union with God, yearnings that are universal. Tragically, anger or rebellion against an overly rigid human parent can become confused with rebellion toward a Heavenly Father. The end product of such rebellion is alienation from God, and spiritual alienation only compounds the already existing shame base.

Emotionally Divided Marriages

Along the same lines, another source of shame is what we call fractured marriages. This occurs when the children in a family are ashamed of what they see as a weakness or division in their parents' relationship.

We once counseled a man who suffered a great deal of shame about his parents' platonic marriage. Simply put, they had stopped sleeping together years earlier and had even occupied separate bedrooms. Although nothing was ever said about the arrangement, the young man felt the deep split in the union. Long before he understood what a normal husband-wife sexual relationship entailed, he knew that something was missing in his parents' marriage. It wasn't the same as the marriages he had witnessed all around him, and the difference became a source of shame.

The Shame of Poverty

Poverty is one of the most common sources of shame we see in our clinical experience. Bess Myerson, the beauty queen who grew up in a Bronx housing project, was driven to succeed far beyond the standard of her impoverished Jewish family. She earned the title of Miss America, became a television personality, was a spokesperson for a huge corporation, ran for the United States Senate, and was a well-known consumer advocate. But her drivenness also had a negative side. She was a convicted shoplifter, had a track record of volatile relationships with married men, and has been the subject of at least two books that paint her as a neurotic, insecure woman who would stop at nothing to get what she wanted.

But poverty isn't the only source of shame that is related to money. Rigid control of a family's funds is another. If Mom is stingy or Dad is a Scrooge, a child can translate their message to mean, "You don't deserve to have money." We once treated a young executive whose spending sprees could easily be traced to the shame imposed by his father. Dad made a good living, but he would only buy items for his children if they begged him for them. Our patient remembered many times when he would cringe at the thought of having to ask Dad for schoolbooks, a baseball glove, or new clothes. The boy's requests usually were granted, but only after a long lecture about the value of money.

Another source of shame connected to money is grandiose spending. Children can sense whether their parents are overspending or spending for maladjusted emotional reasons. Shame and embarrassment result when Dad tries to "buy" friends for his son or daughter by lavishing money on expensive gifts, tickets to special events, or dinner at fancy restaurants.

One of our patients, in treatment for bulimia, said that her workaholic father never would give of his time or his affection, but he would slip cash into her wallet without telling her. Rather than pleasing her, his generosity made her ashamed. "I felt like a prostitute," she told us. "My dad was buying my emotional love."

Shame Caused by Family Secrets

At least three kinds of secrets can be powerful sources of shame for children:

1. Secrets that are kept from children by their parents. Perhaps Mom became pregnant before she and Dad were married, and they have lied about wedding and birth dates ever since. Or perhaps Dad was dishonorably discharged from the military. Or maybe Mom had an abortion when she was a teenager. The nature of the secret isn't important. What matters is that something dark and mysterious was withheld from the children. They know it, and they carry around a burden of shame because of it.

2. Secrets that the whole family keeps from the outside world. A classic example is alcoholism. All members of the family work together to cover up Mom's "little problem." They pass it off as an illness. They make excuses for her slurred speech by blaming her migraine headache medication. If she seems unsteady when she walks, her inner ear infection is the culprit. They hide her car keys, cancel her appointments, and live in fear that someone someday will find out the truth.

3. Secrets that children keep from their parents. For example, if Dad is a rageaholic, his daughter may decide not to show him her algebra examination with the failing grade on it. Withholding the test results seems more logical than enduring the horror of one of his tantrums.

Shame of Personal Addictions

Some people contribute to their own shame, building on a shame base they have already received from a dysfunctional family of origin. For example, a workaholic may be addicted to achievement and working as a way of compensating for the shame of having an alcoholic father. The workaholic's own addiction to perfectionism and achievement multiplies the shame that already existed. He cannot achieve the standards he has set for himself, and he recognizes that his compulsion causes his family to suffer, but he can't stop himself—and the result is guilt and shame.

HOW TO REDUCE YOUR LEVEL OF SHAME

Locating the source of shame is the first big step toward reducing your level of shame. The next big step is to attack the shame and rebuild your self-esteem. Here are some suggested exercises that can help you reduce your level of shame:

Inventory your false guilt and authentic guilt. Begin by making two lists. On the first list, write down all those areas of behavior, compulsion, and addiction that you feel guilty about and that you are responsible for. On the second list, write down areas of shame, guilt, and embarrassment for areas that are not your fault and that you should feel no responsibility for. This second list is the list of your sources of *false guilt*.

We all experience both authentic and false guilt. Authentic guilt is helpful in enabling us to stop sinful, self-destructive, and self-defeating behavior, so that we can make healthy changes in our lives. False guilt is based in a false sense of shame over factors that we cannot control. For example, if Arnold sexually abuses his stepdaughter, Jane, Arnold ought to feel guilty for his sin. In fact, what usually happens is that it is Jane who feels the guilt and shame for what Arnold did. What Jane feels is *false* guilt and *false* shame. The feelings of shame are real, but they are not based in reality.

Journaling your shame. Write a letter to your parents, to a past abuser, or to anyone else who might have been responsible for specific incidents of false guilt. In this letter, acknowledge what the false guilt was all about—then hand responsibility for the guilt over to its rightful owner. This letter need not ever be read by the person to whom it was addressed. The purpose is not to blame others but to give you the opportunity to step out from under the false responsibility you've been shouldering for so long.

This exercise not only reduces your shame base, it helps to give you a new sense of direction. For example, if you are living out your parents' career expectations for you because your father never achieved his career goals, you might write a letter to your father in which you give back to him the feelings of drivenness and ambition he imposed on you. Those feelings of drivenness are false shame feelings, and you should not have to own them. As soon as you hand that shame back to your father, you gain a new sense of your own direction in life. No longer does someone else set your course; you set your own course in life.

We often tell our clients, "If you don't hand your false shame back to those who gave it to you, you'll surely hand it down." You'll hand it down to your children as part of a generational cycle of dysfunction.

Build a network of friends. Another effective antidote to shame is encouragement from a group of friends. People who suffer from shame tend to isolate themselves. Just as a child buries his or her head or goes off to a corner after being publicly scolded, adults often retreat to the sidelines. They deprive themselves of that meaningful connection as a way of punishment. The more isolated they become, the more heavily the burden of shame weighs on them. They have too much solitary time, and they use it to agonize about their shame. People who are recovering from shame need to hear the voices of affirming, loving, supportive friends who will balance and counter the negative inner voices of false guilt and shame.

Say goodbye to the past. Most people who are addiction-prone are either overly connected with their families or have broken all ties, in which case they are overly connected to painful memories and toxic emotions associated with the past. The goal is to achieve some kind of healthy middle ground. We're not suggesting that communication be cut off or relationships severed. Rather, healthy boundaries must be established to prevent family ties from binding too tightly.

Turn shame over to God. This is the most important key to removing shame from our lives. One of the central messages of the Christian faith is that we do not have to carry the weight of guilt and shame by our own limited human power. Once we became united to God through faith in Jesus Christ, the price for our guilt and shame was paid at a cosmic level. We don't have to shoulder the weight of our own shame, the shame of our parents, or the shame of those who have abused and humiliated us. We do not have to become our own codependent saviors. We do not have to engage in the self-sacrifice of compulsive overachievement or compulsive self-atonement.

Shame has been settled forever. It has been nailed to the cross of Jesus Christ. (For more information on how to have a relationship with Jesus Christ so that shame can be forever removed from your life, see FAITH.)
See also GUILT; SELF-ESTEEM; SELF-TALK

> **The person who has been furiously running away from his past must stop, turn, walk back, and face the past squarely. Then and only then can he turn his back and walk away from his past with a clear sense that the shame of the past has been dealt with, grieved, and released.**

Singleness

Singleness is a struggle for many people—not only because of the feelings of loneliness that many single people experience, but even more so because of the attitudes and unspoken messages that confront many single people. Even many well-intentioned Christians convey, either subtly or overtly, that being single makes a person less than complete or less than fully adult. Many single people are tired of hearing the insensitive question, "When are you going to get serious about your life and start a family?"

People in the married world often have little conception of what it is like to be a single person in one's twenties or thirties or beyond. They also often assume (mistakenly) that singleness is a state of incompletion. The truth is that, for many people, it is a state in which God has placed them and in which God can use them in a special way.

In 1 Corinthians 7:7–8, the apostle Paul says, "For I wish that all men were even as I myself [that is, unmarried]. But each one has his own gift from God, one in this manner and another in that. But I say to the unmarried and to the widows: It is good for them if they remain even as I am." Whereas some Christians view single people as "second-class citizens" in the kingdom of God, Paul makes it clear that he views single people as having a special, honored place in the kingdom. Paul is not disparaging marriage, because he is quick to add, in verse 28, "But even if you do marry, you have not sinned."

> **For many people, singleness is a state in which God has placed them and in which God can use them in a special way.**

Paul does not say that *either* being married or being single is a superior state. Rather, in verses 25–40, he makes the case that single people are not as heavily weighed down with the cares and responsibilities of the world as married people are, so they are more free to devote themselves to ministry for God. "But I want you to be without care," he explains in verses 32 and 33. "He who is unmarried cares for the things of the Lord—how he may please the Lord. But he who is married cares about the things of the world—how he may please his wife."

Though singleness can be a gift from God, one should also consider the possibility that he or she may have contributed to or caused his or her own singleness in some way. There are many reasons people remain single.

Those who are single should not worry that they have missed the best God has to offer. They already have the best, in terms of their ability to use their time to serve God to the utmost. And if, in God's timing and in accordance with God's will, the single Christian finds someone to marry, then that will be God's best for his or her life at that time.

Advice for the Unhappily Single

If singleness is a painful struggle for you, there are steps you can take that, in God's timing, may lead you out of singleness and into a fulfilling relationship. Those steps are:

1. *Be honest with yourself about your feelings.* Admit to yourself that you feel lonely, insecure, and unloved. You may even feel angry and resentful toward God and others. Many single people wonder, "Why doesn't someone come along and love me?" Or "Why doesn't God bring someone special into my life?" In fact, that resentment could even be part of your problem. Bitterness is an unattractive feature, and if you project any bitterness or anger in social situations over your singleness, there's a possibility that you could be emotionally sabotaging potential relationships. Acknowledge your feelings, face them, work through them, and release them. You'll be happier, and your personality will be much more pleasing and attractive.

2. *Learn to accept yourself and to be content in your present state.* Accept yourself in your human imperfection. Accept your singleness. Learn to focus on the positive aspects of your life: your freedom, your health, your career, your relationship with God. (See CONTENTMENT.)

3. *Ask God to help you find your ministry so that you can focus on serving Him.* Learn to trust God and His plan for your life, and ask Him to use the skills, talents, and spiritual gifts He has given you for others and for His eternal purposes. If you feel friendless, let God be your Friend.

Some have a difficult time fitting in with others. They may need help in improving their social skills. Or they are shy and have a hard time reaching out to others and making friends. Or they have set such high standards for a marriageable mate that no one in their dating experience seems to measure up. Or they are simply lazy, drifting through life without really focusing on relationships, letting the years elapse until one day they say, "Hey, I'm turning thirty (or forty)! And I'm still all alone!" Or they have grown up with (or later acquired) unhealthy and negative attitudes toward dating and interaction with the opposite sex (this is sometimes the case with people who are hyperreligious and legalistic). Or they have gone through one or more disastrous relationships and were so discouraged and disturbed by the emotional pain that they are unwilling to make themselves vulnerable in relationships again. Or they have derived an unhealthy image of romantic relationships and marriage from the poor example of divorced parents (this is particularly common when the divorce was messy, acrimonious, and painful for the child).

Don't let bitterness, anger, and discontentment deprive you of the joy and fulfillment you can experience as a Christian single person. For now, God has blessed you with singleness. Tomorrow He may bless you with another person to share your life with. Whatever state you are in, be sure to enjoy the blessings of that state, and let God use your life to count for Him.

See also LONELINESS

Sleep and Sleeping Disorders

We spend about one-third of our lives asleep. Though the amount of sleep necessary for effective functioning and alertness varies from person to person, the average person requires about eight hours of sleep per night. Most adolescents need about nine hours a night, elementary school children about ten, preschoolers about twelve, and infants at least sixteen. Sleep is intended by God to help maintain and heal our bodies and minds.

Although it is possible to go for short periods on little or no sleep, long-term sleep deprivation can produce serious mental and emotional effects, ranging from irritability to irrational thinking to hallucinations. Healthy sleeping habits are sometimes ignored by zealous Christians who feel a need (probably rooted in obsessive-compulsive personality traits) to overwork themselves in "service" (so they think) to God. This inevitably leads to excessive stress, mental exhaustion, physical exhaustion, and burnout.

Sleep follows a definite and predictable pattern:

Stage 1: A brief stage in which the heart rate slows, muscles relax, and brain waves (as measured by an electroencephalogram) become irregular.

Stage 2: Sleep deepens, revealing characteristic tracings (called "sleep spindles") on the electroencephalogram.

Stage 3: Sleep is even deeper. The electroencephalogram shows correspondingly different wave patterns.

Stage 4: Sleep is at its deepest level, producing delta waves on the electroencephalogram. This level of sleep lasts about fifteen minutes, and the entire four-stage cycle repeats throughout the night, occupying about three-fourths of the total sleep period. Sleep researchers call this period NREM (or non-REM) sleep.

The remaining one-fourth of the sleep period is spent in REM sleep. REM stands for rapid eye movement, because this stage is identified with a rapid darting movement of the eyes under the eyelids. The eyes move in a coordinated fashion, suggesting that they appear to be "looking" at objects in a dream. REM sleep periods occur on the average of 90 minutes or so, and last from 5 to 25 minutes. REM sleep is associated with the strongest, most vivid, and easily recalled dreams of sleep.

Although the sleeper does experience some relaxation during REM sleep, there is also considerable activity during this period: pulse and respiration increase, blood pressure rises, and muscles twitch. Males often experience an erection of the penis during REM sleep, even though there is no sexual content in the dream. The cerebral cortex—the region of the brain that performs such higher brain functions as reasoning and analyzing—is highly active during REM sleep, suggesting that some very dynamic and complex mental activity takes place during this phase of sleep.

Dreaming appears to be an essential component of sleep. Some people claim never to dream, but research clearly shows that everyone dreams, even if some people rarely or never recall their dreams upon awakening. Dreaming, like sleep, appears to be essential to our mental well-being. Being deprived of sleep or of dreams leads to irritability and a disturbed ability to perceive reality.

What is the function of dreaming? Sigmund Freud believed that dreams reveal the deepest recesses of the personality, the unconscious mind, and that those hidden thoughts, emotions, and motives are revealed through the symbols of dreaming. According to this explanation, then, dreaming enables people to resolve and reduce emotional tensions by purging and expressing hidden emotional issues that the person cannot or will not examine in a conscious, waking state.

In the Bible, we see God speaking to human beings through dreams. Such occasions, however, are rare in Scripture, and why certain dreams were considered particularly important is not clear. In the present age, people should be extremely careful of attaching too much prophetic significance to their own dreams, or of acting rashly or unwisely in response to something they have heard or seen in a dream.

There are a number of sleep disorders that can alter our sleeping and dreaming patterns and that signal problems that need to be resolved. Typical sleep problems include:

- *Night terrors.* Experiences of night terrors *(pavor nocturnus)* are not unusual among children between the ages of five and seven. A child experiencing night terrors will scream at night and appear terrified. The child may not respond to adult efforts to wake and calm him for several minutes. Once awakened, the child will often describe a single, stark, frightening image (not a nightmare with a plot), and the child may insist that the image was real, not a dream. Night terrors occur most commonly during the first two hours of sleep, during the non-REM cycle.
- *Somnambulism (sleepwalking).* This sleep disorder involves such behavior as sitting up in bed, leaving the bed, and (rarely) running or screaming while still asleep. Sleepwalking usually occurs during NREM sleep, and sleepwalkers run the risk of injuring themselves because they are not aware of their surroundings. On waking, sleepwalkers have little or no memory of their behavior while asleep.
- *Narcolepsy.* This disorder, the inability to stay awake for more than a few hours at a time, tends to arise during adolescence as well as in adulthood. Narcoleptic individ-

■

An occasional episode of sleepwalking is not uncommon among children, though repeated episodes are rare. The cause of sleepwalking is unknown. Sleepwalking by adults is rare and usually occurs in individuals who sleepwalked as children. In persistent cases, sedatives may be needed to help the sleepwalker stay in bed.

■

549

uals must nap once or several times each day in order to function. They are also subject to bouts of extreme weakness (cataplexy), which may cause them to fall down under the influence of strong emotions (anger, laughter, and so forth). The tendency to narcolepsy is sometimes controlled with medically prescribed amphetamines.

- *Insomnia.* This common sleep disorder involves the inability to fall asleep. People often experience insomnia when they go to bed and begin mentally planning the next day's activities. Planning is a function of the prefrontal lobe, and it is thought that this mental activity in the prefrontal lobe causes the reticular activating system of the brain, which controls sleeping patterns, to become aroused so that sleep is prevented. Individuals with this problem should avoid thinking about plans and schedules after going to bed and should instead let their brains "wind down" with light entertainment (TV or reading), Scripture meditation, and prayer.

  The overuse of stimulants such as tea or coffee can cause insomnia. So can worry, tension, and anxiety. In fact the inability to get to sleep is a symptom that may contribute to a diagnosis of anxiety disorder in some individuals (see ANXIETY). The inability to *stay* asleep is one symptom of depression; the individual may have no trouble going to sleep but may awaken at three or four in the morning and not be able to return to sleep (see DEPRESSION).

- *Sleep apnea.* This condition is both a sleep disorder and a breathing disorder. As the individual falls asleep, breathing becomes shallow or stops. After fifteen to twenty seconds, the sleeping individual attempts to resume breathing, though the air passage may be obstructed by the tongue and throat tissues. Full breathing begins again when the individual is fully awake. In rare cases, hundreds of episodes take place in a single night, causing the individual to be extremely tired and sleepy the next day. Sleep apnea can be a frightening experience for many people, but it can be corrected by wearing a device that pressurizes the individual's air intake.

Sleeping pills are often used to induce sleep and reduce the likelihood of the individual awakening during the night. The benefits of drugs, however, tend to lessen with use, and prescription drugs may lead to dependency. Nonprescription sleeping pills usually contain antihistamines that produce a heavy, drugged feeling and are not advisable for use by all individuals. Since many sleep disorders have a psychological component, we believe it is advisable to seek the underlying reasons for the sleep disorder rather than to numb the symptoms with medications. In some cases, however, carefully monitored use of medications can be helpful for limited periods of time.

Here are some practical suggestions to help you enjoy a regular habit of healthy sleep:

- Don't worry if sleep doesn't come immediately. The average person takes about thirty minutes to fall asleep.
- Don't take daytime naps.
- Exercise early in the day.
- Avoid taking a stack of work or a head full of worries to bed.
- Watch a brief amount of relaxing television just before bed (comedy is healthier to go to bed on than a hard-hitting event-oriented show like *Nightline* or *Crossfire*).
- Read an escapist novel (*not* financial reports or a news magazine) before turning out the light.

- Avoid eating a heavy meal at bedtime.
- Avoid use of stimulants such as coffee, tea, colas, or tobacco within four hours of bedtime. Avoid alcohol, too (though it is not a stimulant, alcohol can distort sleep patterns).
- Eat a high protein dinner and drink warm milk at bedtime.
- Take a hot bath to relax your muscles.
- Never go to bed angry with your spouse.
- Combine music and deep breathing.
- Avoid over-the-counter sleeping medications.

Above all, *relax*. Usually, the harder you try to get to sleep, the more worried and anxious you will feel, and the more wide-awake you will be. The best way to get to sleep is to *stop trying* to get to sleep!

Soul

"Now may the God of peace Himself sanctify you completely," says 1 Thessalonians 5:23, "and may your whole spirit, soul, and body be preserved blameless at the coming of our Lord Jesus Christ." This passage, as we examine it in context with the rest of Scripture, gives us insight into the three-dimensional nature of our humanity. We consist of:

1. a *spirit;*
2. a *soul;* and
3. a *body.*

At the Minirth Meier New Life Clinics, we view this passage of Scripture as a reference to the fact that we all have a *spiritual nature,* a *psychological nature,* and a *physical nature.* Each aspect of our humanity may be considered separately and distinctly, and each has a unique function in our lives. Yet all of these aspects work together and complement the whole.

It is important to note that the Greek word Paul uses for *soul* in this passage (and which is frequently used throughout the New Testament) is *psuche,* from which we get the word *psychology.* As used and understood in the Bible, the soul *(psuche)* consists of the mind, emotions, and will—and these components are precisely what we study, explore, and treat in the fields of psychology and psychiatry.

We find the three-dimensional aspect of humanity first described to us in the earliest portions of Scripture. In Genesis 2:7, we read, "And the LORD God formed man of the dust of the ground, and breathed into his nostrils the breath of life; and man became a living being." The Hebrew word for "breath of life" is *neshamah,* which also refers to the human spirit. And the word for "a living being" is *nephesh,* which is also translated as "soul." Here, then, we see that God forms a *physical body* out of the dust of the ground, breathes a *spirit* into that physical body, and that body becomes a living *soul,* with intellect, emotions, and a will.

We have found that this three-dimensional model of our humanity is not only biblical but practical. It makes everyday sense. It explains why Christians have emotional problems. For while our spirits have been regenerated by faith in Jesus Christ, our souls still contain the residue of past wounds and past sins. That is why Paul, in Romans 12:2, urges us to be transformed on a continual basis by the daily renewing of our minds. The spirit is saved once and for all by the grace of God, but the soul must be gradually changed, transformed, and conformed to the image of Christ (see Romans 8:28–29) by a process of growth and regeneration.

In the New Testament, the word *soul* is most often used as a synonym for the person, for the *self.* In fact, Bible translators have often rendered the word soul as "self." That is why the parallel passages in Matthew 16:26 and Luke 9:25 have very similar wording, but one passage records the word *soul* and the other records the word *self.* Thus, the soul *is* the self. Each of us is composed of genetic potential, reposited in the body, plus spiritual capacities, plus a unique personality, reposited in the self or soul. With our bodies, we are in contact with physical reality. With our spirits, we are in contact with the inner world of the spirit and of God. Between the body and the spirit resides the soul, with its intellectual functions, its emotional functions, and its self-directing power of choice and will.

Psychiatry and psychology, in focusing on the soul or psyche of human beings, seek to help individuals who are confused, weakened, or distorted in some area of their mind, emotions, or will. The Bible also focuses on these aspects of the human soul—mind, emotions, and will. Psalm 139:14 describes the intellectual dimension of the soul, the mind and its ability to know: "Marvelous are Your works, and that my soul knows very well." Second Samuel 5:8 describes the emotional dimension of the soul when it speaks of those "who are hated by David's soul." Job 6:7 and 7:15 use phrases such as "my soul refuses" and "my soul chooses," speaking of the will and the ability of the soul to make choices.

Psychological problems may be manifested by any one or all three of these dimensions of the soul. Toxic emotions like anger and bitterness can poison the soul, clouding our thinking and distorting our ability to make healthy, rational choices. Problems with mental functioning can distort our perception of reality and cause us to experience disproportionate emotions and to make choices that are not reality based. Problems with the will—particularly problems involving sinful choices—can affect the mind, as it attempts to rationalize, deny, and suppress the knowledge of the harm our choices have caused; and problems with the will can cause emotional problems, leading us into sorrow, regret, guilt, anxiety, and depression.

These different aspects of the soul are often at war with one another. First Peter 2:11 warns us to "abstain from fleshly lusts which war against the soul." Fleshly lusts may include greed, the lust for power, or sexual lust. Clearly, sexual lust is a complex activity, involving our physical (hormonal and sexual) dimension and our soul (mind, emotions, and will) dimension. When we give in to lust, we set our mind, emotions, and will at war with each other, creating inner conflict, guilt, and anxiety. Peter, in this

■

Another word for soul is self.

■

passage, wants to spare us from that pain and psychological damage, as well as the spiritual damage, that sin brings.

Paul talks about the inner warfare of the soul when he says in Romans 7:15, "For what I am doing, I do not understand. For what I will to do, that I do not practice; but what I hate, that I do." All of us—particularly those of us who struggle with compulsions and addictions—can identify with those tormented words of Paul.

These inner conflicts are at the base of many of the mental and emotional problems we treat at the clinics. Our clients include both Christians and non-Christians, and it is clear to us, from the Scriptures and from clinical experience, that both Christians and non-Christians experience psychological problems. But we also find that Christians have resources at their disposal that non-Christians do not have: the insight of the Scriptures, the power of prayer, and the comfort of the Holy Spirit. As we work on the mental, emotional, and volitional (will-related) issues of our souls, we know that God, the Great Physician, is alongside us, leading our minds toward His truth, healing the wounds of our emotions, offering His infinite wisdom to guide our choices.

And restoring our souls.

Stress

Stress is a term we use to refer to any external influence that disturbs the natural functioning and internal equilibrium of the mind and body. Stress is produced by major changes in life or emotional disturbances (such as a relocation, a job change, grief and loss, or major financial changes), disease, physical injury, or prolonged demands on one's mental or physical endurance. Our minds and bodies are amazingly designed by God to withstand a great deal of stress. However, if the stress persists for too long, or if the nature of the stress is too extreme and intense, the stress-management systems of the body become overwhelmed and illness may result.

Illnesses produced by excessive stress are called *stress diseases* and include both physical and mental/emotional disorders. Physical stress diseases include ulcers, colitis, asthma, high blood pressure, and eczema (a skin condition). Mental/emotional consequences of stress include effects ranging from anxiety and depression to the psychotic disorder called schizophrenia, in which an individual can lose touch with, and withdraw from, reality.

A major dynamic of the mind's and the body's response to stress is the so-called *fight or flight response,* a built-in survival mechanism that physically prepares the body to protect itself against an external threat. Once this response is triggered by a stressful event, certain physical changes take place in the body. The adrenal glands, located atop the kidneys, begin secreting stress hormones called *adrenaline* and *noradrenaline.* These hormones are released quickly into the bloodstream, where they immediately begin

■

Just as a racing engine will eventually rattle apart if it is constantly revved up and never maintained or allowed to rest, the human body and mind will inevitably rattle apart if placed under constant, intense stress.

■

preparing the body for action. They stimulate the heart to beat faster. Blood vessels constrict and blood pressure rises. Energy-giving sugars are released from the liver's stores. The body revs up like a racing car's engine before the driver pops the clutch and roars down the speedway. The body's systems are tuned to top performance, ready either to face a threat or to flee from a threat at top speed.

All of these responses are taxing on the body. It is easy to see that if the body remains at this highly-tuned pitch for a long time, or returns to it often (as will happen when a person is under persistent, wearing stress), physical illness and mental disorders are bound to result.

Our goal, however, is not to eliminate stress but to manage stress—and to manage our own response to stress. A certain amount of stress in our lives—besides being inevitable—is healthy, positive, and motivating. Our bodies are wonderfully designed to operate under reasonable levels of stress. But we often magnify the harmful effects of stress in our lives by responding to it in an unhealthy way. One of the most common, self-defeating responses to stress is the practice of *negative self-talk*, particularly self-talk that emphasizes words such as *always* and *never*: "My life is *always* out of control; I'll *never* get my work finished!" Such thoughts instantly trigger the fight-or-flight response in most human beings. (See SELF-TALK.)

People who are involved in serving the needs of others are particularly prone to stress: pastors, missionaries, teachers, doctors, nurses, social workers, police officers, and business administrators. In such environments, schedules tend to be hectic and stressful, and there is frequently more negative feedback (complaints, conflict, lack of acknowledgment for service) than there is positive (appreciation and gratitude). Positive feedback tends to reduce stress levels and to fortify our physical-mental stress-management systems. Negative feedback tends to multiply and magnify the damaging effect of stress on our systems.

The end result of a stress overload is a condition called *burnout*. The physical and emotional warning signs of burnout include:

- decreasing ability to function or perform
- detachment or withdrawal from people
- excessive, chronic fatigue (lack of energy)
- depleted motivation ("I don't feel like doing anything")
- exhaustion
- boredom
- cynicism
- increased impatience and irritability
- feelings of being unappreciated
- negative changes in work habits and relationships
- increased paranoia (feeling suspicious, distrustful, apprehensive)
- disorientation and confusion
- inability to concentrate
- physical complaints (headaches, backaches, stomach problems)
- depression
- suicidal thoughts

THE HOLMES-RAHE SOCIAL
READJUSTMENT RATING SCALE

Stress factors impact our lives in different ways. This table, developed by psychological researchers in the mid-1960s, assigns point values to a list of stressful life changes that are common to us all. The researchers, T. Holmes and R. Rahe, concluded that an accumulation of 200 or more life change units in a single year tends to increase the risk of psychiatric disorders, including anxiety and depression. As you reflect on your life during the past year, read through this table and see how many life change units your life scores. The answer could yield a great deal of information regarding your own emotional issues.

EVENT	SCALE OF IMPACT
Death of a spouse	100
Divorce	73
Marital separation	65
Jail term	63
Death of close family member	63
Personal injury or illness	53
Marriage	50
Fired at work	47
Marital reconciliation	45
Retirement	45
Change in health of family member	44
Pregnancy	40
Sex difficulties	39
Gain of new family member	39
Business readjustment	39
Change in financial state	38
Death of close friend	37
Change to different line of work	36
Change in number of arguments with spouse	35
Mortgage over $10,000	31

EVENT	SCALE OF IMPACT
Foreclosure of mortgage or loan	30
Change in responsibilities at work	29
Son or daughter leaving home	29
Trouble with in-laws	29
Outstanding personal achievement	28
Wife begins or stops work	26
Begin or end school	26
Change in living conditions	25
Revision of personal habits	24
Trouble with boss	23
Change in work hours or conditions	20
Change in residence	20
Change in schools	20
Change in recreation	19
Change in church activities	19
Change in social activities	18
Mortgage or loan less than $10,000	17
Change in sleeping habits	16
Change in number of family get-togethers	15
Change in eating habits	15
Vacation	13
Christmas	12
Minor violations of the law	11

(We should note in passing that the mortgage amounts—greater than or less than $10,000, a substantial-sized mortgage in the 1960s—should be adjusted to reflect today's inflated property values.)

(For a thorough discussion of burnout, its causes, and its cure, see the article on BURNOUT.)

The key to managing and responding to the stress in your life is to commit yourself to a balanced priority system in every aspect of your lifestyle—your career, your church life, your family life, your inner being, and your relationship with God. Jesus exemplified this balanced approach to dealing with the stresses of His life by maintaining close, supportive friendships and by withdrawing into times of solitude and spiritual refreshment whenever the stressful opposition of the religious leaders or the pressures and demands of the crowds became too great. Here are some suggested ways of patterning your response to stress after His, so that you can have a balanced life and a well-managed stress-load:

1. *Take regular retreats.* This includes weekend outings, vacations, spiritual retreats, and time alone. These times of refreshment are important in helping you regain your perspective and in restoring your mind and body.

2. *Get plenty of physical rest and sleep.* Physical rest and sleep help your brain to replenish essential biochemicals, which help you cope with stress. Establish a regular sleeping and waking schedule. Avoid caffeine and nicotine. If you have trouble falling asleep, get up and do something relaxing: read, listen to music, watch a comedy on TV, or drink a glass of warm milk. Go back to bed when you feel sleepy. (See SLEEP AND SLEEPING DISORDERS.)

3. *Laugh.* Look for ways to enjoy life and to find the humor in life. Laughter is a potent weapon against stress. Whereas stress triggers the release of stress hormones that damage your body over the long run, laughter triggers the release of brain chemicals that lift your mood, clear your thinking, and balance your perspective.

4. *Monitor your self-talk.* Eliminate terms like "should," "must," "ought," "have to," "always," and "never" from your self-talk about your work and your circumstances. Learn how to give yourself positive messages (see SELF-TALK).

5. *Exercise.* Just twenty minutes or so three times a week spent exercising can bring enormous benefits by helping you release physical and emotional tension, enhancing your circulation, improving your mental alertness, and helping you feel better.

6. *Forgive.* One of the leading factors in poor stress management is the tendency most of us have to hold on to bitterness and to ruminate about injustices and hurts that have been done to us. Emotions such as anger and resentment have a damaging effect on our bodies' ability to manage stress. (See ANGER; FORGIVENESS.)

7. *Maintain a network of support.* Schedule times to be with close, supportive friends. Offer support to them and receive support from them in times of stress (you may even want to form a stress support group or Bible study group). Talk through your feelings and your circumstances, and ask them to pray for you. In general, you are not looking for advice so much as you are looking for people who will listen, who will be positive and supportive, who will help you gain a healthy and balanced perspective on your life. We are much better able to manage our stress level when we feel we are not alone.

8. *Meditate and pray daily.* Scripture meditation and contact with God help to reduce stress. Effective Scripture meditation should have an element of adventure, joy, and spontaneity. Choose a quiet, relaxed environment, sitting or kneeling in a comfortable place. Plan to spend twenty minutes or half an hour reading, listening for God's

The TV series M*A*S*H gives us an example of people who responded to prolonged and intense stress, and who staved off burnout, by means of injecting laughter into their grim circumstances.

thoughts, stopping whenever a passage seems especially meaningful. Tailor your reading by choosing passages that address the stress issues in your current life. Some examples:

Marital stress: Ephesians 5:22–23; Colossians 3:18–19; 1 Peter 3:1–7; 1 Corinthians 7:1–5.

The stress of parenting: Deuteronomy 6:4–9; Ephesians 6:1–4; Colossians 3:20–21; Proverbs 13:24; 29:15.

Anger: Ephesians 4:26–27; Leviticus 19:17–18; Romans 12:15–16; Proverbs 15:1; 19:11; Ecclesiastes 7:9; Colossians 3:8; Matthew 5:21–24.

Resentment: Hebrews 13:12; Ephesians 4:31; Acts 8:23; Proverbs 14:10.

The need to forgive: Ephesians 4:31; 2 Corinthians 2:7; Luke 6:37; Matthew 6:14; Mark 11:25.

The stress of life's trials: James 1:2–5; 1 Peter 1:6–7; 4:12–19; Job 23:10; Romans 5:1–5; Philippians 1:27.

The stress of suffering: 2 Corinthians 1:3–4; 4:7–18; 12:7–10; Hebrews 12:5–11; Romans 5:15; 8:28–29; John 9:1–3; Mark 5:21–42; 1 Peter 1:3–9.

Anxiety: John 14:27; Philippians 4:6–8; Matthew 6:25–34; Psalm 27:1, 14; 34:4; 56:3.

Burnout: Study the example of Elijah in 1 Kings 18 and 19.

Stress is inevitable, but the way we respond to stress is optional. In all but the most extreme and overwhelming situations, we have the power to choose how to respond to the stresses that are a daily part of our lives.

Suicide

Shannon was a mother of three, the wife of a prominent real estate broker and church elder. Like her husband, Shannon was very involved in church as a deaconess and as part of the evangelism visitation team. Her church friends viewed her as a "supermom" who had it all together. Only a few of her closest friends from church knew Shannon's secret: she struggled with deep bouts of depression and had unsuccessfully attempted suicide three times, using prescription drug overdoses.

One day, Shannon's husband, Lyle, came home early from the office—as he often did when Shannon was undergoing one of her "blue spells." Every time she had attempted suicide before, he had gotten a feeling that he should stop by the house and check on her. Each time, he had arrived in time to get help for her. The previous suicide attempts were "cries for help," he believed—dangerous, potentially fatal, but more focused on alleviating her emotional pain than on actually destroying herself.

This time, however, when Lyle arrived home, there was no cry for help. The house was eerily silent as he made his way from room to room, finally arriving at the bedroom, where he stopped, stunned and heartbroken. This time Shannon had chosen a different means of suicide, and this time she had indeed set out to destroy herself. She had hanged herself from one of the rafters of their vaulted bedroom ceiling.

No one likes to think about suicide. No one likes to discuss the possibility that even Christians become depressed and commit suicide. But it happens, and choosing not to talk about it will not make the truth go away. Suicide, it is said, is a lonely way out with no way back, a permanent solution to a temporary problem. It is the number ten cause of death among adults and the number two cause of death among teenagers. It is also a profoundly *selfish* act (though the suicidal person is probably not able to comprehend it as such), because suicide inflicts more emotional pain and guilt on the survivors than almost any other form of loss could possibly do.

THE SOURCES OF SUICIDE

Nobody wants to die. People in emotional pain invariably do everything they can, everything they know how to do, to end their pain before choosing to end their lives. People decide to die when they see absolutely no other alternative to ending their pain.

The pain that produces suicidal impulses can arise from a number of different sources, including:

- early environmental factors
- physical illness
- mental illness
- shame
- loneliness
- a lack of emotional coping skills
- heredity
- imbalances in brain chemistry

Add to these factors the stresses and painful events of daily life—school problems, family conflict or deterioration, an incident of violence, a broken romance, a major financial loss, a job loss, substance abuse—and the risk of suicide is dramatically magnified.

Marital status plays a large part in suicide risk. People who have never been married are twice as likely to take their lives as married people. People who are divorced or widowed have the highest suicide rate of all. Single white males over age 45 are also statistically at higher-than-normal risk. Economic status is also a factor: suicide is much more common among higher economic classes than low or middle classes.

Most of those who attempt or commit suicide have a history of emotional problems, and depression is the number one cause of suicide. If you or someone you know is experiencing severe depression, it is extremely important that you obtain immediate professional help. The pain of depression is intense, but that pain can be alleviated. Depression is curable. The warning signs of clinical depression fall into four broad categories:

1. *Moodiness:* A sad facial expression, frequent crying or moping, downcast features, and a look of exhaustion and discouragement, and unkempt appearance.

2. *Painful Thinking:* A depressed person will often be introspective in a self-defeating, self-blaming way. The individual will agonize over past mistakes, about "what ifs" and "if onlys" and will frequently wallow in guilt even when totally innocent. This individual will also take an exaggerated and pessimistic view of his problems and will bitterly condemn himself or others for those problems. In the vast majority of cases, this person feels completely helpless and boxed in by his problems, and his perception of those problems is usually out of proportion to reality.

3. *Anxiety:* The depressed individual often develops signs of anxious, irritable behavior. He may seem tense, nervous, and agitated.

4. *Physical Symptoms:* Negative mental and emotional activity in the brain stimulates the production of brain chemicals that affect body functions. Sleep is affected; in some cases, the individual has trouble getting to sleep, but more often the individual awakens in the middle of the night and can't get back to sleep. During waking hours, body movements usually decrease, and a stooped posture and signs of physical exhaustion may appear. Appetite and body weight are affected (both are usually diminished, though not always). Digestion is affected (diarrhea, constipation, or alternating bouts of both). Sexual interest disappears. Tension headaches, dry mouth, rapid or irregular heartbeat are frequently observed. In women, the menstrual cycle may stop *(amenorrhea)* or become irregular *(dysmenorrhea).*

About 75 percent of all people who attempt or commit suicide have seen a doctor within the preceding four months. Few of them actually said to their doctor, "I feel suicidal." It is as though they were hoping the doctor would help them make the pain go away—but the subject rarely comes up.

Over two-thirds of people with moderate-to-severe depression experience thoughts of suicide. Suicide risk tends to be greatest in the early stages of severe depression (before the individual has sought treatment), or paradoxically when the individual is recovering from depression. Depression paralyzes the will, and at the deepest point of depression, a person is often too severely immobilized to take self-destructive action. But as the individual gains emotional strength, he or she sometimes is able to summon the will to end the pain that still remains. Tragically, if these people could be helped, they would find that they were closer to emotional recovery than they realized. They got out of the race as the finish line was just coming into view.

SIXTEEN WARNING SIGNS OF SUICIDE

Most suicide threats are either a cry for help or an attempt to manipulate others. The problem is that there is no way to know for sure if the individual is truly determined to kill himself or not. In fact, he may not know for sure himself. Therefore, all people who threaten suicide should be taken seriously. One of the myths that many people believe about suicide is "People who threaten suicide never do it." Wrong. All too often, they do. In fact, more than 10 percent of those who make a suicide threat or an unsuccessful suidice attempt, are later successful. Most people who commit suicide have left some sort of warning, such as the statement, "My problems would be all over if I were dead," or "Everyone would be better off if I were dead."

Women attempt suicide about five times more frequently than men, but twice as many men as women are successful in the attempt. Men tend to use more violent means (such as a gun) to commit suicide. Women are more likely to use suicide as either a cry for help or an attempt to get attention. Every three minutes, someone makes a suicide attempt in America, and about one out of seven of those attempts succeeds.

We have identified sixteen factors or symptoms that are commonly found in suicide cases. Those warning signs are:

1. The individual manifests intense emotional pain, such as is seen in cases of depression, along with symptoms such as early morning sleep disturbance, loss of appetite, and loss of sex drive.
2. The individual expresses feelings of hopelessness.
3. The individual has a prior history of suicide attempts or has warned others of suicidal intentions.
4. The individual has severe health problems.
5. The individual has experienced a significant loss—the death of a spouse, the loss of a job, or something similar.
6. The individual has made a specific suicide plan.
7. The individual manifests chronic self-destructive behavior, such as drug abuse, alcoholism, risky sexual behavior, or something similar.
8. The individual has high or perfectionistic personal standards and an intense ambition to achieve.
9. The individual has experienced intense and disturbing events during the preceding six months.
10. The individual manifests disheveled and unkempt appearance.
11. The individual shows a lack of concentration, decreased work performance, or failing grades.
12. The individual withdraws from friends, family, and regular activities.
13. The individual gives away prized possessions, puts financial matters in order, draws up a will, writes "goodbye" letters (with either an obvious or a cryptic "suicide note" tone)—all part of a process of tying up loose ends and preparing to die.
14. The individual demonstrates a fascination or obsession with death.
15. The individual makes threats such as "I'll show them! They'll be sorry when I'm gone!"
16. The individual makes indirect statements of a death wish, such as, "I wish I'd never been born," or "Everyone would be better off without me."

IS SUICIDE A SIN?

Suicide is a tragedy beyond comprehension, primarily because it is so unnecessary. Depression is treatable. However painful life feels now, it can be made good again. People who commit suicide almost invariably do so when they are not thinking clearly and perceiving life realistically. If they were, they would know that their problems are temporary and solvable. In our experience at the Minirth Meier New Life Clinics, we treat many people who have been suicidal or who have attempted suicide. In most cases, it only takes about two months of therapy for people who were formerly suicidal to reach a point where they are absolutely amazed that they ever considered suicide.

■

Suicide is a sin. The injunction "Thou shalt not kill" is not invalidated simply because the murder victim is oneself. Suicide is never God's will.

■

561

People who commit suicide are intensely self-preoccupied. They are not thinking about the effect of their death on the surviving spouse, the surviving children, or other friends and relatives. Those effects on others are devastating and long-lasting. Children commonly blame themselves for the suicide of a parent, and statistics show that children of parents who committed suicide are many times more likely than the general population to choose suicide as a solution to their adult problems. Suicide is a horrible and destructive legacy to leave a child.

Suicide is a sin. The injunction "Thou shalt not kill" is not invalidated simply because the murder victim is oneself. Suicide is never God's will. The Bible records only seven cases of suicide: Abimelech (see Judges 9:54), Samson (see Judges 16:30), Saul (see 1 Samuel 31:4), Saul's armorbearer (see 1 Samuel 31:5), Ahithophel (see 2 Samuel 17:23), Zimri (see 1 Kings 16:18), and Judas Iscariot, whose suicide is recorded in all four Gospels. We believe it is significant that none of the individuals who committed suicide in these biblical accounts was acting in accordance with God's will at the time.

Does this mean that people who commit suicide have committed an unforgivable sin and that they cannot enter heaven? No. God alone knows the state of a person's heart. The person who has trusted Jesus Christ as Savior and Lord but who experiences emotional problems or severe stresses that lead to suicide does not abrogate his or her faith by abrogating his or her life. One sinful act—the sin of suicide, in this case—does not doom a person to an eternity without God. Only the act of rejecting Jesus Christ can accomplish that.

> *God knows our frame, and He remembers that we are dust. Being human, we are prone to poor judgment, rash acts, distorted emotions, selfishness, depression, and sin. That is why God has given us His grace and His Son, Jesus. Those who have attempted suicide need our understanding and compassion, not condemnation.*

HOW TO SAVE A LIFE

Most suicidal people, despite their pain, want to live—but they need to know that somebody else wants them to live. They generally think, "Nobody cares." If just one person would show them true caring, their lives might be saved. Here are some actions you can take to save a suicidal person:

- *Take suicide threats seriously.* Don't dare the individual to "go ahead and do it" or say, "You wouldn't really do that." Many people have taken that dare. Act on the premise that the intention is real.
- *Encourage the individual to express his or her feelings.* Be unshockable. Listen reflectively and nonjudgmentally. Restate in your own words what the person says so that he or she feels heard and understood. Avoid discounting or arguing with that person's feelings. The feelings are real, even if you don't think they are based on an accurate perception. Be warm, patient, accepting, and understanding.
- *Avoid judging or countering what the person says.* Statements like "Suicide is a sin," "Suicide is bad," or "People who kill themselves go to hell" will cause the person to shut down and avoid sharing feelings. Feeling isolated makes the person more likely to commit suicide.
- *Don't avoid "the S word."* Don't think that by mentioning suicide, you are putting the thought in that person's head. He or she is already contemplating suicide. By approaching the issue directly, frankly, and without embarrassment, you show

the person that this is not a shameful issue. It is simply an issue that must be talked through and resolved. Suicidal individuals are usually relieved when someone else brings up the question. Your willingness to discuss it in a matter-of-fact way demonstrates acceptance, caring, and the fact that you do not condemn the individual for such thoughts.

- *Never promise to keep the suicide gesture secret.* Say, "I can't promise I won't try to save your life. I can't promise I won't try to get help. I'm not willing to let you die. I love you too much to make such a promise, and I hope you love me too much to ever put me in that position."

- *Get the individual to promise not to hurt himself or herself.* It is amazing how often suicidal people will keep such a promise, particularly if you couple it with a specific time frame. For example, "Promise me you won't hurt yourself for the next week without talking to me or a counselor first." Then be sure to check in with that person and keep renewing the "contract" until he or she is out of danger.

- *Help the individual obtain professional treatment.* This is probably the single most important and beneficial thing you can do. Offer to contact or locate a professional counselor. Offer to accompany the individual on the first visit or two.

- *Remove the means of suicide.* This is especially important if the individual has made a suicide plan. Make sure there are no dangerous objects around, then call for help. In a dire emergency, call 911. If there is no immediate danger, call a counselor or suicide prevention hotline. Don't leave the person alone.

- *Pray* for *that person and* with *that person.* Depressed people often feel isolated from people and alienated from God. Your prayers link you and the other person in fellowship and help him or her to sense a connection with God. Prayer assures people that they are cared for, they are important, and they are not alone in their pain.

A final word about preventing suicide: If an individual succeeds in committing suicide, don't own that tragedy as your own personal failure. If a person is determined to take his or her own life, you don't have the power to stop that person. It is not your fault.

WHAT ABOUT YOU?

Have you ever considered making a fatal choice? Have you ever struggled with depression? Do you feel boxed in by life and by circumstances? Life is difficult, but life doesn't have to defeat us. God has given us many resources to enable us not only to survive, but also to experience true joy, peace, and happiness. Those resources include:

- *Relationships.* Your connection to the people you love is more important than your failures or your achievements. If you don't feel you can go on living for your own sake right now, then commit yourself to living for your children, your spouse, and your friends. There is no greater hurt you could inflict on them right now than your death.

- *Christian friendships.* Pick up the phone and call someone. Even if it's 3 o'clock in the morning, call someone. Even if you have to call collect, call someone. You'll be glad, and your friend will be glad. Be honest about what you are feeling and what you have been considering. Don't be afraid to say, "I feel terrible, and I've been thinking about suicide."
- *Emotions.* Your emotions are painful right now. Express them. Cry, yell, pound your fists into something soft, but *express your emotions.* Breathe deeply, again and again. Then pick up the phone and call a counselor or a suicide hotline and verbalize your emotions.
- *Prayer.* God is alongside you right now. Ask Him for a reason to live. Ask Him to help you sense the value and preciousness of your one and only irreplaceable life. As you pray, place your hand on your chest and feel the beating of your heart. Thank God for the life He has given you, and ask Him to help you to use your life to bless other people.
- *Pets.* If you have a pet, hold it gently but tightly. Stroke it and talk to it. Let your pet love you back.
- *Promises.* God has promised us that He will never leave or forsake us (see Hebrews 13:5). And Paul said, "I can do all things through Christ who strengthens me" (Phil. 4:13). The promises of God are sure, and they give us the hope to go on living, to keep on growing, to continue piecing together this puzzle called life.

You may think you have a reason to die, but you have many more reasons to live. We all have the power to choose, as Hamlet said, "to be or not to be." But the choice God calls us to is clear. He has given us the gift of life, and He asks each of us to say "yes" to that gift, day by precious day.

> People are most likely to have distorted thinking when their emotions are pent up and their pain is stuffed down inside them. Getting your emotions out into the open is a first step toward resolving them and purging the pain.

Television and Other Entertainment Media

"Ward, I'm worried about the Beaver."

Times have sure changed since the 1950s, when TV mom June Cleaver would say these words to her husband on the family sitcom *Leave It to Beaver.* She might have been worried that "the Beav" had locked himself in the bathroom because of a bad haircut, or that Beaver and his brother, Wally, were fighting, or that the Beaver was spending too much time around Wally's obnoxious friend, Eddie Haskell. But she wasn't worried that her boys were smoking crack or considering suicide or papering their walls with pinups from *Hustler.*

The entertainment media of the 1950s reflected a simpler, safer time for young people. Yet the entertainment media of our own age does far more than reflect a culture.

It has become so powerful and pervasive that it is actually shaping our culture. On a continuous, 24-hour-a-day basis, thousands of images of violence, brutality, horror, immorality, and satanism are piped into our homes over the airwaves and by cable or on rented videotapes. Some of this electronic sewage is even pumped into our homes through unexpected gateways, such as our telephone lines and home computers. As we look at the newspaper headlines or survey the scene at the mall or go "channel surfing" with the remote control, it becomes clear that the values that pour daily from our entertainment media are flooding our homes and washing over an entire generation, drenching them in ideas and behaviors that are completely at odds with Judeo-Christian values.

Television also has an *emotional* effect on our children. Psychological studies show that television violence tends to make children more fearful and influences them to act more aggressively. Violent scenes stir strong emotions in both adults and children, and this emotional impact magnifies the brain's memory storage and retrieval abilities, causing these violent images to become deeply embedded in the child's mind. (See MEMORY.)

The emotional effect of television on adults is also profound. Though many American adults use "the tube" as a way of relaxing and escaping from their problems, studies show that TV (specifically, *violent* TV) often has the opposite effect and actually increases anxiety levels. One study found that heavy television watchers are significantly more distrustful of other people, more fearful, and more anxious than the general population. This study found that not only do violent *entertainment* programs stir up negative emotions in their viewers, but local TV *news* shows, with their "film-at-eleven" approach to murders, robberies, and traffic accidents, tend to create the view in the minds of their viewers that they live in a dark, dangerous, hostile world.

Both programming and advertising contain messages that are subtly destructive of our Christian values. Some are messages of narcissistic self-obsession ("I'm worth it!") and materialistic self-gratification ("Who says I can't have it all?"). A continual stream of images of the lifestyles-of-the-rich-and-famous sort creates the impression that happiness comes through riches, that life should be easy, that if we just carry the right gold card or use the right deodorant, our happiness is assured. These are lies, but they are attractive lies. It is not surprising that some people are more attracted to the lie that "You can have it all" than the truth of Jesus, who said, "In the world you will have tribulation; but be of good cheer, I have overcome the world" (John 16:33).

Many young people today are growing up with a sense of entitlement, a sense that all the good things life has to offer should be handed to them: a free education, a good job, a fast car, an expensive stereo, all the "happiness" that unbridled materialism has to offer. This attitude can be traced in large part to an entertainment medium that depends for its existence on advertising dollars and a consumer-oriented consciousness. The television industry thrives on materialistic values and entitlement-minded viewers; Christian values of sacrifice and "moderation in all things" are bad for business.

Television technology is morally and psychologically neutral. There is nothing evil or immoral about an electron gun exciting the phosphors inside a cathode ray tube to create a flickering image on a TV screen. Television can be useful in teaching values and in contributing to a child's emotional, intellectual, and spiritual maturation. There are

TV programming and advertising contain messages that are subtly destructive of our Christian values. The industry thrives on materialistic values and entitlement-minded viewers; Christian values of sacrifice and "moderation in all things" are bad for business.

565

many Christian and secular companies producing quality video entertainment for children and adults. There are quality offerings on broadcast and cable sources, such as the Disney Channel, the Family Channel, and the Discovery Channel.

THE MTV GENERATION

Everyone has heard of MTV, but few parents have bothered to watch it for themselves. They should. "Again and again," says Stephen Arterburn, "I find that parents haven't a clue what kinds of influences their kids are being exposed to. They have no idea of the powerful impact the music industry has on the values and emotions of young people. Parents who are not aware of MTV are neglecting their responsibility as parents. I would even go so far as to say that they are passively allowing their children to be sexually abused by MTV. They are allowing their children to be seduced away from Christian truth and Christian values, and even away from their families, by the sex-drenched, often sadomasochistic and Satanic messages that play continuously on MTV."

MTV has stamped its logo on an entire generation of young people—the MTV Generation—and is now both the leading mirror and the leading shaper of the youth culture today. Over 55 million American homes are now wired for MTV, plus many more millions of homes in forty-plus countries around the world. With its fast-cut, hyperkinetic music video imagery, MTV has changed the way all of us watch TV. For example, one recent 30-second commercial for the McDonalds fast-food chain featured 37 separate images—*an average of more than one image per second.*

A generation ago, parents used to worry about "suggestive" lyrics in rock-and-roll music. Today, there is nothing suggestive about it. A great deal of rock music is *explicitly* obscene, violent, and anti-Christian. Combined with powerful video images, this music has the power to penetrate and saturate the souls of our young people with messages that are destructive beyond belief. On MTV, young people see pop icons such as Michael Jackson and Madonna, clad in leather or filmy lace, grabbing their crotches and simulating masturbation, or having their bodies stroked by dancers in scenes of simulated group-sex orgies, all as part of throbbing, rocking, rapping dance routines.

Parents should not hesitate to monitor what their children watch and listen to. If music or videos are found to be offensive, then it's time to call a family meeting and set down new rules. Objectionable CDs and videos should be confiscated. You may decide to pull the plug on MTV. This is a decision that should be discussed with your children so that they understand your loving concern for their spiritual, moral, and emotional welfare. A suggested approach: "As your parents, we were unaware of what you have been watching and listening to. We want to be fair, so we are going to reimburse you for the tapes and CDs we are taking away. But in the future, we will expect you to show good judgment regarding the materials you bring into this house and expose yourself to. You now know the rules that we are setting today. If you bring any unacceptable CD into this house, whether it belongs to you or to a friend, it will be destroyed, and the cost of it will be on you."

Be open and frank with your child, but avoid getting hysterical, authoritarian, or dictatorial. Encourage your child to make healthy entertainment choices on his own. Because of the sexual and Satanic nature of much that appears on MTV, discussion of these media influences may need to be coupled with discussion of issues such as drugs, the occult, AIDS, sexuality and sex addiction, pornography, and masturbation. If a few weeks or months of monitoring your children's music and videos reveal that there is a continuing and ongoing problem, you may want to consider pastoral or psychological counseling for your child (a youth pastor may be a good place to begin counseling, particularly if there is good rapport between your child and the youth pastor).

COMIC BOOKS, COMPUTER GAMES, AND MORE

When most adults think of comic books, they remember *Superman* and *Captain America* and *Archie* comics—cheaply printed magazines that used to sell for twelve cents a copy on the racks at the corner drugstore. Stop and browse at the comic book rack next time you're in the corner drugstore and you will probably be in for a shock. You'll see profanity, scenes of violence and torture, drugs, Satanism, strong sexual content, and the ridicule of Christian values. In the stores that specialize in selling only comic books (and similar collectibles, such as trading cards), you'll usually find much stronger stuff than the drugstore racks sell—including hardcore X-rated comics. Parents should be aware of what kinds of comic books their children are reading and where they are buying them.

Parents also underestimate the influence of personal computers over the values and morals of their children. Sexual jokes, digitized erotic images, Satanic messages, and sex-oriented computer games can now be downloaded at a rate of 14,400 bits per second from thousands of computer bulletin boards around the country. Photographic-quality images of raw sex are passed from computer to computer in GIF (Graphics Interchange Format) computer files on floppy disks or via modem. And the miracle of CD-ROM allows computer users to play hard-core pornographic movies on their computer monitors in high-resolution Super VGA color and stereophonic sound. Here is a typical ad for so-called "adult" material on CD-ROM, found in a major computer-oriented magazine:

SEXY SOFTWARE!

We're gonna make you sweat!
Hardcore SVGA GIFs, animated games for Straight/Bisexual/Gay!
Some of the nastiest XXX full-color pics and mini-movies you've ever seen!
Singles, couples, groups—joystick-grabbing excitement!
Shipped in generic "wife-proof" labels!
VISA, MasterCard, Discover Card only!
(Must state 21 or older when ordering.)

Computer porn isn't the only danger that computers pose. Many computer games and even video games (of the Nintendo and Sega Genesis variety) contain scenes of graphic violence, sexual violence, and occultism that are dangerous to young minds. If you don't know how your family computer is being used, you should look into it right now. If you are not computer literate, ask a computer-literate friend to examine your computer's hard-drive directories and CD-ROM libraries. Be sure you know what computer bulletin board services have been accessed by your computer. You may discover that a portion of your credit-card bill or your child's allowance is being spent on computer porn or Satanic computer games.

DIAL-A-PORN

Most people today are aware of 900 numbers that people can call for an advertised fee ranging from a dollar to over ten dollars per minute. These numbers offer services from consumer information to instant polling for radio talk shows. But the most famous and controversial use of 900 numbers is dial-a-porn. Callers listen to sexual fantasies, sounds and descriptions of sex acts (including rape, bestiality, group sex, and child sex), or have live "dirty" conversations with anonymous women as an aid to masturbation. These services are skilled in persuasion techniques for keeping callers on the line longer than they had planned, and it is not unusual for shocked phone-owners to receive phone bills containing hundreds or thousands of dollars in "phone sex" charges. You should be aware that the courts have held that parents are responsible for these charges, even if the parents were not aware their children were making these calls.

Some teenagers try dial-a-porn services out of curiosity and become hooked (phone sex is a form of sex addiction). Many young people are now in psychiatric treatment for this addiction (see SEX ADDICTION). The phone sex scandal received national media attention in 1987, after a twelve-year-old boy molested a four-year-old girl after spending two hours on a 900 sex line.

Phone companies now offer 900 blocking systems so that these numbers can't be dialed from a blocked phone (usually for an additional fee). However, many phone-sex purveyors have circumvented the 900 blocks by offering access through a toll-free 800 number system, which then switches the caller into a dial-a-porn service with the meter running. "The best defense against a phone sex intrusion into your home is not a phone block," says Dr. Paul Meier, "but raising responsible, informed children. If you haven't yet discussed this issue with your children, now is the time to do so. After about age ten, it becomes increasingly likely that your children will be introduced to dial-a-porn by a friend. They need to know the dangers of this medium—and they need to know that *you* know. Tell your children that a lot of kids have gotten hooked on this behavior, that thousands of dollars have been wasted, that the result in many lives is years of shame, sin, and emotional harm."

TEENS AND PORNOGRAPHY

Ron is a youth minister. He has a wife and a four-year-old son, and he is widely respected in his church. But Ron has a shameful secret: he is a sex addict, with an uncontrollable urge to engage in masturbation with pornographic material. In fact, he admits in counseling that he finds sex alone more enjoyable than sex with his wife. His addiction to pornography goes back to when Ron was twelve years old, when he discovered his father's hidden stash of *Playboy* and *Penthouse* magazines. This was especially confusing to the boy because his father was a pastor.

Our clinical experience at the Minirth Meier New Life Clinics tells us that such stories are all too common in Christian families. Pornography can be as addictive as any drug—and the shame it produces is often worse than the shame of drug addiction. Exposure to pornography in adolescence can destroy the innocence of childhood and turn a young person's steps toward a life of compulsive involvement with sordid, shameful sexual behavior.

Pornography is a ten-to-fifteen-billion-dollar-a-year business in America, resulting in the sale of some twenty million sexually explicit magazines every month. About 15 percent of all videos rented and sold in America are pornographic—and that does not count the vast amount of hard-R-rated material available on video or cable TV. The specific targets for much of this material are teenagers—boys and young men who are at the height of their sexual curiosity, emotional vulnerability, and hormonal activity.

How should you respond if you find pornography in your own home? First, don't ignore it or minimize it. What commonly happens is that a parent discovers one piece of evidence of a child's involvement in pornography: a magazine, a video, a phone bill. The child protests innocence or claims it only happened this once—"I just wanted to see what it was like, and it will never happen again." This is rarely the case. Most parents don't discover evidence like this until the child has been sneaking such material for a while. The evidence the parent finds is usually the tip of the iceberg. You are doing your child a disservice if you believe his protests of innocence. In fact, the child may have carelessly left the evidence where it could be found as an unconscious cry for help. This is a significant shame issue for young people, and they may not know how to ask for help.

Next, talk to your child about pornography, sex addiction, and masturbation. Teach him to respect his own body and the bodies of other people. Make sure your child receives an appropriate and spiritually based sex education (see SEX EDUCATION). Parents often take the position that "what a child doesn't know won't hurt him." Wrong. In matters of sex, ignorance is not bliss. And it's not safe. A great deal of sex addiction can be traced to the adolescent years, when young people were feeling highly charged sexual feelings and were being exposed to pornography and other sexual temptations but were receiving no responsible sex education information from their parents.

Upon discovering pornography in a child's closet or under a bed, many parents react with hysteria, screaming, tears, or shaming. Many refuse to get professional help for their children because they are ashamed or they fear that counseling will unearth family skeletons. These reactions only compound the problem. If your child has a problem with pornography, and if you really love him, you will seek immediate help. This problem is bigger than you or your child. You need help—all the help you can get—to resolve this issue and help your child back to a healthy view of his own sexuality.

■

Pornography is no longer confined to XXX-rated movie theaters in seamy downtown districts. Porn is in every suburb, in video stores in brightly lit shopping malls right around the corner from where you live. It's available from your cable TV company or through your phone. How do you counteract the onslaught of destructive material that is aimed at your family? With vigilance. With love. With instruction. With a clear Christian model of purity and integrity.

■

569

It is also crucial that parents set a good example for their children. Christian parents should never rent sexually explicit videos or allow pornographic material in their homes. Parents should make sure their marriage relationship (including their sexual relationship) is strong and healthy (see MARRIAGE; PARENTING; SEX AND SEXUALITY). Children should be taught that the human body is nothing to be ashamed of but that our bodies and our sexuality are special, a gift to be shared only with one's marriage partner within the safe boundaries of a committed Christian marriage relationship.

TEENS AND SATANISM

If there is one influence in our society that is even more frightening than pornography, it is Satanism. Occult and demonic influences are being disseminated through horror movies, rock music and videos, computer games, and fantasy role-playing games (such as *Dungeons and Dragons*)—and the targets of much of these materials are teenagers.

It is not unusual for children to examine occult material out of curiosity, but you should become very concerned and take immediate action if your child exhibits any of the warning signs of a morbid preoccupation or involvement with the occult or with Satanism. These warning signs include:

- obsession with rock music containing occultic themes
- any use of occult symbols, such as swastikas, daggers dripping blood, pentagrams, or inverted crosses
- keeping a diary or book containing secret writings, rituals, notes, drawings, symbols, or references to the devil
- strange drawings on the body or possessions; body or hand painting or tattoos (particularly in dark colors such as black or blood-red)

Additional indicators that a young person is susceptible to, or may be involved in, occultic activity may include:

- isolation and withdrawal from family and old friends
- dropping of favorite activities (sports, hobbies, and so forth)
- withdrawal from church and youth group activities
- low self-esteem
- decline in grades
- mood swings
- secretive behavior, "sneaking"
- disproportionate anger and rage
- major changes in eating or sleeping patterns

Parents should always take indications of Satanism seriously. A fascination with evil and death is not just a "phase" a child goes through. It is unhealthy and can be quite destructive. Under the influence of a satanic fascination, young people have committed suicide and homicide. Don't hesitate to seek counseling from professionals. Ask a pastor or counselor for the name of a Christian therapist who has a great deal of experience with cases involving the occult. Many teens become involved in the occult out of a natural adolescent hunger for power or knowledge or out of anger, which is a common component of the teen years. A counselor can help to uncover why the child rebels, why he or she is fascinated with magical powers and death. Once the reasons are uncovered, the healing and restoration can begin.

One of the most effective tools at your disposal is the power of prayer. Your connection with God is your armor—the armor with which you can shield not only yourself but your entire family. As a parent, you are engaged in a battle for your child's soul. On one level, it is a battle against the powerful forces of the media, the pornography industry, and the occult. But on an even more fundamental level, it is a battle against real but invisible spiritual forces. "For we do not wrestle against flesh and blood, but against principalities, against powers, against the rulers of the darkness of this age, against spiritual hosts of wickedness in the heavenly places" (Eph. 6:12).

Workaholism

Workaholism is a compulsive addiction to one's business or profession, the use of work as an anesthetic against emotional pain or as a barrier to keep others out and avoid having to deal honestly with relationships. Workaholism is driven by a low sense of self-worth; the individual compensates for feelings of worthlessness by striving for achievement and perfection. The workaholic's life is out of balance, and his or her priorities are disordered.

Work is honorable and is a means to an end—the end being that we are able to provide for the needs of our families. But the workaholic sees work as an end in itself, and ends up denying the emotional needs of his family by compulsively attending to business, meetings, traveling, and otherwise immersing himself or herself in career-related activities. For the workaholic, "meeting my family's material needs" is often a rationalization for his or her addiction. The workaholic may be successful and may provide many material blessings for his or her family—yet the family doesn't want those things. The family wants a relationship with the compulsive individual.

Many workaholics rationalize their behavior on spiritual grounds. This is especially true of pastors and missionaries who deny the needs of their families while claiming, "I'm doing the Lord's work." Symptoms of workaholism include:

- having been obsessed with grades in high school and college
- becoming preoccupied with a given thought and not being able to get it out of your mind
- being unable to rest or relax or enjoy a vacation
- continually thinking about work, even in bed or during outings

■

The tragic irony of workaholism is aptly described by Charles Swindoll, who said, "We worship our work, work at our play, and play at our worship."

■

- taking work-related materials (papers, reading, laptop computer) on vacation or to bed with you
- starting a job and being unable to feel at peace until it is finished
- having a sense that "I need to be doing something"
- having a frantic schedule and a too-long list of things to do
- having a long workday
- trying to do several things at once
- wanting to be in control of circumstances or of other people
- having high or perfectionistic expectations of yourself or others
- having few close friends with whom you can share feelings
- focusing on, and talking about, your accomplishments (particularly as a means of proving your worth to yourself or to others)
- an inability to say no, and a need for the approval of others

Workaholism is highly destructive to emotions and to relationships. This tendency creates frustration and blocks intimacy in marriage. The spouses and children of workaholics tend to become angry, frustrated, and depressed, because they feel rejected and unloved. Many children of workaholics use destructive or rebellious behaviors in an effort to get the attention of the workaholic parent. These behaviors may include eating disorders, drug abuse, sex, or even suicide.

The workaholic's perfectionistic and obsessive-compulsive personality traits can usually be traced to an overly critical and negative environment in childhood. Treatment and recovery involve both psychological and spiritual insight. If you are a workaholic, counseling can be helpful in enabling you to uncover the hidden emotional issues that drive you to overwork and overachieve. At the same time, if you have trusted Jesus Christ as your personal Savior (see FAITH), you may need to gain a deeper understanding of what God's grace really means in your life. In a very real sense, you are working to prove your own worth, which is a form of legalism, of trying to make your own atonement for sin through your own efforts.

Once you learn truly to accept God's grace, you will be able to experience rest, secure in the knowledge that whatever your personal sins and failures, whatever your feelings of guilt or shame, God accepts you, loves you, and forgives you just as you are. You can and you must learn to see yourself not as a flawed person in need of perfection, but as a growing person on the path toward wholeness. Mistakes and sins do not invalidate your worth; they are learning experiences to be repented of and profited from.

Learn to see your family as your first priority in ministry and achievement. You cannot do God's work adequately until you recognize that your family is God's work—and your responsibility. Learn to love your family, to relax with your family, and to attend to their *real* needs—their emotional and spiritual needs, not their "needs" for a bigger house or shinier car. Give your children the time, attention, love, fun, and discipline they deserve. Arrange a special time alone with each of your children on a regular basis (at least once a month—weekly, if possible).

Make time for your own needs—your need for time alone with God, for Christian fellowship, for reading, for exercising, for relaxation, for pleasure, for a satisfying sexual relationship with your mate. The Minirth Meier New Life prescription for the disease

A balanced approach to life will restore your life and your relationships to good health.

of workaholism could be compressed into two simple words: *balanced living.* Obsession with work is unbalanced and unhealthy.

Workaholism, even if it is practiced by pastors, missionaries, or other Christian leaders, is *not* of God. God's claim upon the life of the workaholic is that which is found in Matthew 11:28 and 30: "Come to Me, all you who labor and are heavy laden, and I will give you rest. . . . For My yoke is easy and My burden is light."

Bibliography

Alcoholics Anonymous World Services, Inc., ed. *Alcoholics Anonymous*. New York: AAWS, 1991.

Alcoholics Anonymous World Services, Inc., ed. *Alcoholics Anonymous Comes of Age: A Brief History of A.A.* New York: AAWS, 1957.

Alcoholics Anonymous World Services, Inc., ed. *Twelve Steps and Twelve Traditions*. New York: AAWS, 1953.

Allen, David. *In Search of the Heart*. Nashville, TN: Thomas Nelson Publishers, 1993.

Allendar, Dan. *The Wounded Heart*. Colorado Springs, CO: NavPress, 1990.

American Psychiatric Assn. *The Diagnostic and Statistical Manual of Mental Disorders DSM-III-R*. 3rd, rev. ed. Washington, DC: American Psychiatric Press, Inc., 1987.

Arterburn, Jerry. *How Will I Tell My Mother?: A True Story of One Man's Battle with Homosexuality and AIDS*. Nashville, TN: Thomas Nelson Publishers, 1990.

Arterburn, Stephen. *Addicted to Love*. Ann Arbor, MI: Servant Publications, 1991.

Arterburn, Stephen and Jim Burns. *Drug-Proof Your Kids*. Pomona, CA: Focus on the Family Publishing, 1989.

Arterburn, Stephen and Jim Burns. *When Love Is Not Enough: Parenting Through Tough Times*. Colorado Springs, CO: Focus on the Family Publishing, 1992.

Arterburn, Stephen, Mary Ehemann, and Vivian Lamphear. *Gentle Eating*. Nashville, TN: Thomas Nelson Publishers, 1993.

Arterburn, Stephen and Jack Felton. *Faith That Hurts, Faith That Heals*. Nashville, TN: Thomas Nelson Publishers, 1992.

Arterburn, Stephen and Tim Timmons. *Hooked on Life: How to Recover from Addictions and Codependency*. Nashville, TN: Thomas Nelson Publishers, 1989.

Augustine, Saint. *Confessions*. Ann Arbor, MI: J.W. Edwards, 1946.

Benson, Herbert. "Your Innate Asset for Combating Stress." *Harvard Business Review*, July–August 1974.

Boskind-White, Marlene and William C. White, Jr. *Bulimarexia*. New York: Norton, 1991.

Bradbury, Ray. *Dandelion Wine*. New York: Bantam, 1964.

Carter, Les. *Imperative People: Those Who Must Be in Control*. Nashville, TN: Thomas Nelson Publishers, 1991.

Carter, Les. *The Prodigal Spouse*. Nashville, TN: Thomas Nelson Publishers, 1990.

Carter, Les and Frank Minirth. *The Anger Workbook*. Nashville, TN: Thomas Nelson Publishers, 1993.

Case, Richard T., Paul D. Meier, and Frank Minirth. *The Money Diet*. Grand Rapids, MI: Baker Book House, 1985.

THE COMPLETE LIFE ENCYCLOPEDIA

Cloud, Henry. *When Your World Makes No Sense*. Nashville, TN: Thomas Nelson Publishers, 1990.

Decker, Bert. *You've Got to Be Believed to Be Heard*. New York: St. Martin's Press, 1993.

Dukakis, Kitty. *Now I Know*. New York: Simon & Schuster, 1990.

Ferguson, David, Teresa Ferguson, Chris Thurman, and Holly Thurman. *The Pursuit of Intimacy*. Nashville, TN: Thomas Nelson Publishers, 1993.

Fowler, Richard and Rita Schweitz. *Together on a Tightrope*. Nashville, TN: Thomas Nelson Publishers, 1991.

Half, Robert. "Resumania." *National Business Employment Weekly,* Sunday, October 2, 1988.

Hardin, Jerry and Dianne Sloan. *Getting Ready for Marriage*. Nashville, TN: Thomas Nelson Publishers, 1991.

Hemfelt, Robert, Frank Minirth, and Paul Meier. *Love Is a Choice*. Nashville, TN: Thomas Nelson Publishers, 1989.

Hemfelt, Robert, Richard Fowler, Frank Minirth, and Paul D. Meier. *The Path to Serenity*. Nashville, TN: Thomas Nelson Publishers, 1991.

Hensley, Dennis. *How to Manage Your Time*. Anderson, IN: Warner Press, 1989.

Hope & Recovery: A Twelve Step Guide for Healing from Compulsive Sexual Behavior. Center City, MN: Hazelden Educational Materials, 1989.

Iacocca, Lee. *Iacocca*. New York: Bantam, 1986.

Kübler-Ross, Elisabeth. *On Death and Dying*. New York: Macmillan, 1993.

Lewis, C. S. *Mere Christianity*. New York: Macmillan, 1960.

McDowell, Josh. *Building Your Self-Image*. Wheaton, IL: Tyndale, 1986.

Meier, Paul D. *Christian Child-Rearing and Personality Development*. Richardson, TX: Today Publishers, Inc., 1977.

Meier, Paul D. *Don't Let Jerks Get the Best of You*. Nashville, TN: Thomas Nelson Publishers, 1993.

Meier, Paul D. and Richard Meier. *Family Foundations: How to Have a Happy Home*. Grand Rapids, MI: Baker Book House, 1981.

Minirth, Frank. *The Headache Book*. Nashville, TN: Thomas Nelson Publishers, 1994.

Minirth, Frank and Walter Byrd. *Christian Psychiatry*. Old Tappan, NJ: Fleming H. Revell, 1977, 1990.

Minirth, Frank, Richard Fowler, Brian Newman, Dave Carder, and Sam Shoemaker. *Steps to a New Beginning*. Nashville, TN: Thomas Nelson Publishers, 1993.

Minirth, Frank and Paul D. Meier. *Happiness Is a Choice*. Grand Rapids, MI: Baker Book House, 1978.

Minirth, Frank, Paul D. Meier, Robert Hemfelt, and Sharon Sneed. *Love Hunger*. Nashville, TN: Thomas Nelson Publishers, 1990.

Minirth, Frank, Paul Meier, Robert Hemfelt, and Sharon Sneed. *The Love Hunger Weight-Loss Workbook*. Nashville, TN: Thomas Nelson Publishers, 1991.

Minirth, Frank, Paul D. Meier, Richard Meier, Brian Newman, David Congo, and Allen Doran. *What They Didn't Teach You in Seminary*. Nashville, TN: Thomas Nelson Publishers, 1993.

Minirth, Frank, Paul D. Meier, and Don Hawkins. *Worry-Free Living*. Nashville, TN: Thomas Nelson Publishers, 1989.

Minirth, Frank, Paul D. Meier, Richard Meier, and Don Hawkins. *The Healthy Christian Life*. Grand Rapids, MI: Baker Book House, 1988.

Minirth, Frank, Mary Alice Minirth, Brian Newman, Deborah Newman, Robert Hemfelt, and Susan Hemfelt. *Passages of Marriage*. Nashville, TN: Thomas Nelson Publishers, 1991.

Minirth, Frank, Brian Newman, and Paul Warren. *The Father Book*. Nashville, TN: Thomas Nelson Publishers, 1992.

Parker, Ken. *Reclaiming Your Inner Child: A Self-Discovery Workbook*. Nashville, TN: Thomas Nelson Publishers, 1993.

Parker, Kenneth F. and Van Jones. *Every Other Weekend*. Nashville, TN: Thomas Nelson Publishers, 1993.

Peck, M. Scott. *People of the Lie: The Hope for Healing Human Evil*. New York: Touchstone Books, 1985.

Peters, Tom. *Thriving on Chaos*. New York: Random, 1987.

Selby, Terry L. *The Mourning After: Help for the Postabortion Syndrome*. Grand Rapids, MI: Baker Book House, 1990.

Shakespeare, William. *Othello*. New York: Bantam Books, 1988.

Sneed, Sharon. *The Love Hunger Action Plan*. Nashville, TN: Thomas Nelson Publishers, 1993.

Sneed, Sharon M. and Joe S. McIlhaney, Jr. *PMS: What It Is and What You Can Do About It*. Grand Rapids, MI: Baker Book House Publishers, 1988.

Stephens, Larry. *Please Let Me Know You, God*. Nashville, TN: Thomas Nelson Publishers, 1993.

Stoop, David. *Hope for the Perfectionist*. Nashville, TN: Thomas Nelson Publishers, 1991.

Stoop, David and Stephen Arterburn. *The Angry Man*. Dallas, TX: Word Publishing, 1991.

Stoop, David and Jan Stoop, *The Intimacy Factor*. Nashville, TN: Thomas Nelson Publishers, 1993.

Tannen, Deborah. *You Just Don't Understand*. New York: Ballantine, 1990.

Thurman, Chris. *If Christ Were Your Counselor*. Nashville, TN: Thomas Nelson Publishers, 1993.

Thurman, Chris. *The Lies We Believe*. Nashville, TN: Thomas Nelson Publishers, 1989.

Thurman, Chris. *The Truths We Must Believe*. Nashville, TN: Thomas Nelson Publishers, 1991.

Tozer, A. W. *That Incredible Christian*. Harrisburg, PA: Christian Publications, Inc., 1964.

Vredevelt, Pam, Deborah Newman, Harry Beverly, and Frank Minirth. *The Thin Disguise*. Nashville, TN: Thomas Nelson Publishers, 1992.

Whitfield, Charles L. *Healing the Child Within*. Deerfield Beach, FL: Health Communications, Inc., 1987.

Wholey, Dennis. *Becoming Your Own Parent*. New York: Doubleday, 1988.

Willingham, Ron. *Integrity Selling*. New York: Doubleday, 1987.

Appendix

MINIRTH MEIER NEW LIFE CLINICS LOCATIONS

Arizona

Minirth Meier New Life Clinic
(Affiliate)
1550 S. Alma School Rd., Suite 240
Mesa, AZ 85210
Ph 602/730-1901
Fx 602/461-8205

Minirth Meier New Life Clinic
(Affiliate)
2535 E. Cactus Rd.
Phoenix, AZ 85032
Ph 602/730-1901
Fx 602/461-8205

Remuda Ranch
Jack Burden Road
Box 2481
Wickenburg, AZ 85358
Ph 602/684-3913
    800/445-1900
Fx 602/684-7903

Arkansas

Minirth Meier New Life Rice Clinic
10801 Executive Center Drive
Suite 508
Little Rock, AR 72211
Ph 501/225-0576
    800/488-4769
Fx 501/225-3412

California

Minirth Meier New Life Clinics West
Western Medical Center
1025 S. Anaheim Blvd.
Anaheim, CA 92805
Ph 714/772-4463
Fx 714/563-2863

Minirth Meier New Life Clinics West
CPC Rancho Lindo Hospital
7625 East Avenue
Fontana, CA 92336-2901
Ph 909/899-4866
Fx 909/899-4868

Minirth Meier New Life Clinics West
260 Newport Center Dr., Suite 430
Newport Beach, CA 92660
Ph 800/877-4673 (HOPE)
    714/760-3112
Fx 714/760-1839

Minirth Meier New Life Clinics West
Outpatient Services Locations
Ph 800/877-4673
Davis, CA
Fresno, CA
Laguna Hills, CA
Long Beach, CA
Los Angeles, CA
Los Altos, CA
Newport Beach, CA
Oakland, CA
Orange, CA
Pasadena, CA
Pleasant Hill, CA
Riverside, CA
Sacramento, CA
San Diego, CA
Van Nuys, CA
Ventura, CA

Colorado

Minirth Meier New Life Clinic
Rocky Mountain
7730 East Bellview Ave., Suite 304
Englewood, CO 80111
Ph 303/740-8002
Fx 303/740-6203

Georgia

Minirth Meier New Life Clinic
Ridgeview Institute
3995 South Cobb Drive
Smyrna, GA 30080
Ph 404/433-2200
Fx 404/434-6333

Illinois

Minirth Meier New Life Clinic
HCA Woodland Hospital
1650 Moon Lake Blvd.
Hoffman Estates, IL 60194
Ph 708/519-0988
Fx 708/519-1147

Minirth Meier New Life Clinic
2100 Manchester Road, Suite 1510
Wheaton, IL 60187
Ph 708/653-1717
     800/848-8872
Fx 708/653-7926

National Resources Division
Ph 800/266-5745
     (800-BOOKS-4-LIFE)

Kentucky

Minirth Meier New Life Clinic
(Affiliate)
Ohio Valley Counseling Center
7711 Buelah Church Rd.
Louisville, KY 40228
Ph 502/239-0780
Fx 502/239-3837

Maryland

Minirth Meier New Life Clinic
(Affiliate)
6707 Democracy Blvd., Suite 910
Bethesda, MD 20817

Minirth Meier New Life Clinic
(Affiliate)
1 Church Street, Suite 801
Rockville, MD 20850-4158
Ph 301/738-2396
Fx 301/738-9546

Michigan

Minirth Meier New Life Clinic
Margaret Montgomery Hospital
28303 Joy Road
Westland, MI 48185
Ph 313/525-6290
Fx 313/525-6446

Minirth Meier New Life Clinic
2060 43rd St.
Grand Rapids, MI 49508
Ph 616/281-8500
Fx 616/281-7008

Minirth Meier New Life Clinic
(Affiliate)
29260 Franklin Rd., Suite 118
Southfield, MI 48034
Ph 810/355-4300
Fx 810/355-4393

Minirth Meier New Life Clinic
(Affiliate)
Masterpeace Center for Counseling &
   Development
313 N. Evans St.
Tecumseh, MI 49286
Ph 517/423-6889

Missouri

Minirth Meier New Life Clinic
9717 Landmark Parkway Dr., Suite 208
St. Louis, MO 63127
Ph 314/849-2120
Fx 314/849-4844

Minirth Meier New Life Clinic
Alexian Brothers Hospital
3933 South Broadway
St. Louis, MO 63118
Ph 314/772-2921
Fx 314/772-6619

**Minirth Meier New Life
Skipper Clinic**
(Affiliate)
1411 E. Primrose
Springfield, MO 65804
Ph 417/887-3822
Fx 417/887-7773

Nevada

Minirth Meier New Life Clinics West
4220 S. Maryland Pkwy., Suite 308B
Las Vegas, NV 89119
Ph 800/877-4673

New Hampshire

Minirth Meier New Life Clinic
Hampstead Hospital
East Road
Hampstead, NH 03841
Ph 603/329-7260
Fx 603/329-7263

New Mexico

Minirth Meier New Life Clinic
6100 Seagull Lane NE, Suite 205
Albuquerque, NM 87109–2500
Ph 505/884-0200
Fx 505/884-5510

Minirth Meier New Life Clinic
Farmington, NM 87401
Ph 505/884-0200
Fx 505/884-5510

Oklahoma

Minirth Meier New Life Clinic
(Affiliate)
Brookhaven Hospital
201 S. Garnett Rd.
Tulsa, OK 74128
Ph 918/438-4257
Fx 918/438-8016

Oregon

Minirth Meier New Life Clinics West
Woodland Park Hospital
10300 NE Hancock Street
Portland, OR 97220
Ph 503/257-0769
Fx 503/257-5811

Pennsylvania

Minirth Meier New Life Clinic
Lakewood Psychiatric Hospital
342 Linden Creek Road
Canonsburg, PA 15317
Ph 412/873-2700
Fx 412/873-2727

Tennessee

Minirth Meier New Life Clinic
(Affiliate)
Tennessee Christian Medical Center
500 Hospital Drive
Madison, TN 37115
Ph 615/865-0300

Texas

Minirth Meier New Life Clinic
1701 River Run Road, Suite 901
Fort Worth, TX 76107
Ph 817/336-6633
Metro 817/429-1634
Fx 817/335-1755

Minirth Meier New Life Clinic
Green Oaks Hospital
7808 Clodus Field Dr.
Dallas, TX 75251
Ph 214/991-9504
Fx 214/934-8072

Minirth Meier New Life Clinic
14405 Walters Road, Suite 1000
Houston, TX 77014–1320
Ph 713/893-9294
    800/375-6689
Fx 713/893-9298

Minirth Meier New Life Clinic
911 Northwest Loop 281, Suite 312
Longview, TX 75605
Ph 903/759-2999
    800/281-8509
Fx 903/759-5273

Minirth Meier New Life Clinic
American Plaza
P.O. Box 21116
200 West Highway 6, Suite 410
Waco, TX 76702–1116
Ph 817/776-0660
Fx 817/776-7730

Minirth Meier New Life Clinic
BHC Richland Hospital
7501 Glenview Drive
N. Richland Hills, TX 76180
Ph 817/284-4751
Fx 817/284-0419

Minirth Meier New Life Clinic
Day Hospital
2071 N. Collins Blvd.
Richardson, TX 75080
Ph 214/437-4697
Fx 214/690-9309

Virginia

Minirth Meier New Life Clinic
(Affiliate)
11130 Main Street, Suite 301
Fairfax, VA 22030–5035
Ph 703/934-2900
    800/899-1994
Fx 703/359-7199

Minirth Meier New Life Clinic
(Affiliate)
4141 N. Henderson Rd., Plaza Suite 3
Arlington, VA 22203–2452
Ph 703/527-3200
Fx 703/527-2863

Minirth Meier New Life Clinic
Dominion Hospital
2960 Sleepy Hollow Road
Falls Church, VA 22044
Ph 703/237-9255
Fx 703/237-1912

Washington

Minirth Meier New Life Clinics West
Highline Community Hospital
16251 Sylvester Rd. S.W.
Burien, WA 98166
Ph 206/246-0789
     800/877-4673
     800/639-5466
Fx 206/243-4691

Minirth Meier New Life Clinics West
10564 5th Avenue NE
Seattle, WA 98125
Ph 800/877-4673
Fx 206/246-5862

Minirth Meier New Life Clinics West
2406 27th St. W, Suite 24
Tacoma, WA 98466
Ph 800/877-4673 (HOPE)

**The Dr. Fred Gross Christian
Therapy Program**

**The Dr. Fred Gross Christian
Therapy Program**
Orange County Community Hospital
6888 Lincoln Avenue, Suite K
Buena Park, CA 90620

Ph 714/236-7944 Admin
Ph 714/236-1150 Intake
     800/HELP-4-ME
Fx 714/236-1165

Canada

Minirth Meier New Life Clinic
(Affiliate)
Rose of Sharon Society
5755 Glover Rd., Suite 202
Langley, British Columbia
Canada V3A8H4
Ph 605/530-5500
Fx 604/530-5334

Corporate Offices

Minirth Meier New Life Clinics
2100 N. Collins Blvd.
Richardson, TX 75080
Ph 214/669-1733
     800/229-3000
Fx 800/778-5855

Minirth Meier New Life Clinics
570 Glenneyre, Suite 107
Laguna Beach, CA 92651
Ph 714/494-8383
Fx 714/494-1272

National Resources Division
1-800-BOOKS-4-LIFE
(800-266-5745)

National Radio Program
1-800-229-3000

THE
**MINIRTH MEIER
NEW LIFE**
1-800-NEW-LIFE **CLINICS**

1-800-NEW-LIFE
(800-639-5433)